INSIGHT GUIDES

ALASKA

Discovery
CHANNEL

APA PUBLICATIONS L
Part of the Langenscheidt Publishing Group

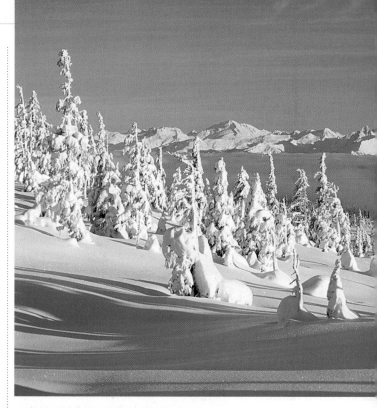

INSIGHT GUIDE
ALASKA

Editorial
Editor
Brian Bell
Updating Editor
Nancy Gates

Distribution
United States
Langenscheidt Publishers, Inc.
36–36 33rd Street, 4th Floor
Long Island City, New York 11106
Fax: (1) 718 784 0640

UK & Ireland
GeoCenter International Ltd
Meridian House, Churchill Way West
Basingstoke, Hampshire RG21 6YR
Fax: (44) 1256 817988

Australia
Universal Publishers
1 Waterloo Road
Macquarie Park, NSW 2113
Fax: (61) 2 9888 9074

New Zealand
Hema Maps New Zealand Ltd (HNZ)
Unit D, 24 Ra ORA Drive
East Tamaki, Auckland
Fax: (64) 9 273 6479

Worldwide
Apa Publications GmbH & Co.
Verlag KG (Singapore branch)
38 Joo Koon Road, Singapore 628990
Tel: (65) 6865 1600. Fax: (65) 6861 6438

Printing
Insight Print Services (Pte) Ltd
38 Joo Koon Road, Singapore 628990
Tel: (65) 6865 1600. Fax: (65) 6861 6438

©2008 Apa Publications GmbH & Co.
Verlag KG (Singapore branch)
All Rights Reserved
First Edition 1988
Seventh Edition 2008

CONTACTING THE EDITORS
We would appreciate it if readers
would alert us to errors or
outdated information by writing
to:
**Insight Guides, P.O. Box 7910,
London SE1 1WE, England.
Fax: (44) 20 7403 0290.
insight@apaguide.co.uk**

www.insightguides.com
In North America:
www.insighttravelguides.com

ABOUT THIS BOOK

The first Insight Guide pioneered
the use of creative full-color
photography in travel guides in 1970.
Since then, we have expanded our
range to cater for our readers' need
not only for reliable information about
their chosen destination but also for a
real understanding of the culture and
workings of that destination. Now,
when the internet can supply in-
exhaustible (but not always reliable)
facts, our books marry text and
pictures to provide those much more
elusive qualities: knowledge and
discernment. To achieve this, they
rely heavily on the authority and
experience of locally based writers
and photographers.

Like all Insight
Guides, this book
is the work of
many people.

Alaska is too vast and too diverse for
any one person to know every aspect
of it, but the team of expert writers
and photographers assembled here
bring to bear a formidable expertise.

How to use this book

The book is structured to convey an
understanding of Alaska's people
and culture, and guides readers
through its cities, national parks and
wildlife refuges:
◆ To understand Alaska today, you
need to know something about its
eventful past. Therefore,
the first section of the
guidebook covers the
state's history and cultures in
lively essays.
◆ The Places section
provides a complete run-
down of all the places worth

LEFT: cross-country skiers
at Spaulding Meadows,
near Juneau.

book builds on the earlier editions produced by **Janie Freeburg**, **Diana Ackland** and **Pam Barrett**.

Bill Sherwonit wrote the chapters on Chugach, Lake Clark and Wrangell-St Elias National Parks, McNeil River State Game Sanctuary, Southwest Alaska, The Arctic, Arctic National Wildlife Refuge, and several of the one-page background features. As author of a guidebook on Alaska's parks, the Anchorage-based Sherwonit has probably traveled through more of the state's national parks than most veteran rangers, and his advice here on surviving in Alaska's wilderness is based on experience.

Bill Bjork and **Debby Drong-Bjork** wrote the chapters on Fairbanks and the Interior. **Mike Miller** wrote on Juneau, Misty Fjords National Monument and the Panhandle communities; **Jeff Brady**, the editor and publisher of the *Skagway News,* wrote on Skagway. **Kris Capps** covered Alaska's Native villages and artifacts. **Douglas Ward**, author of the renowned *Berlitz Complete Guide to Cruising and Cruise Ships*, covered developments in Alaskan cruising, and **Heidi Sarna** compared the virtues of large and small cruise ships.

Among those who have written about Alaska's national parks are **Leslie Barber**, a member of the Citizens' Advisory Commission on Public Lands, **Rick McIntyre**, a naturalist and park ranger at Denali, and **Diane Brady**, a commercial pilot for an air taxi service. **Kaylene Johnson**, who married a pilot, wrote from experience about flightseeing.

Other contributors included **Chris Blackburn**, **Chris Carson**, **Kathy Hunter**, **Katy Korbel**, **Kyle Lochalsh**, and **Mark Skok**. The index was compiled by **Elizabeth Cook**.

seeing. Main sites of interest are coordinated by number with the maps. ♦ The Travel Tips listings section provides information on travel, outdoor activities, specialist tour operators, hotels, restaurants and festivals. Information may be located quickly by using the index printed on the back cover flap – and the flaps themselves serve as bookmarks.

The contributors

This latest edition of this long-time bestseller, updated by Anchorage-based **Nancy Gates**, has been restructured to reflect the changing face of Alaska. It was edited by **Brian Bell**, Insight Guides' editorial director, who made his first trip to Alaska in the 1970s to report from Prudhoe Bay on the construction of the trans-Alaska oil pipeline, and the

Map Legend

— ·· —	International Boundary
— — —	State Boundary
_·_·_	National Park/Reserve
— — —	Ferry Route
✈ ✈	Airport: International/Regional
🚌	Bus Station
❶	Tourist Information
✝ ✝ ✝	Church/Ruins
✝	Monastery
☾	Mosque
✡	Synagogue
🏰	Castle/Ruins
∴	Archaeological Site
∩	Cave
⚐	Statue/Monument
★	Place of Interest

The main places of interest in the Places section are coordinated by number (e.g. ❶) with a full-color map, and a symbol at the top of every right-hand page tells you where to find the map.

Contents

LEFT: A team competes in the Iditarod Trail Sled Dog Race.

Maps

Travel Tips

TRANSPORTATION

ACCOMMODATIONS

ACTIVITIES

CONTACTS

A–Z: PRACTICAL INFORMATION

THE BEST OF ALASKA: TOP ATTRACTIONS

Bears, birds, totems, train travel, skiing down glaciers, camping in the wilderness... Alaska can still astonish the most jaded of travelers

ABOVE: The **Iditarod Trail Sled Dog Race** – "the last great race on earth" – is run over 1,150 miles, involves more than 1,200 dogs, takes from 10 to 17 days to complete, and has prize money of $400,000. *Pages 308–9*

BELOW: Getting close to **brown bears** allows you to recognize their individuality – some are aggressive by nature but other are mild-mannered or even timid. Areas such as McNeil River State Game Sanctuary create safe conditions for bear watching. *Page 341*

ABOVE: Totem poles, tall and elaborately carved, are comparable to family crests and are used to tell a story or recall an event. The totemic symbols are often animals or birds – typically bears and eagles. *Page 301*

ABOVE: Trains such as the **McKinley Explorer**, with glass domes or open-air viewing platforms, penetrate deep into Alaska. *Page 354*

LEFT: Prime **fishing** in pristine waters offers anglers a sporting chance of reeling in massive king salmon, leaping trout, halibut, and northern pike. *Page 366*

ABOVE: With eight **national parks** and a **state parks** system of more than 3.2 million acres, Alaska has tremendous appeal to outdoor enthusiasts. *Page 187*

ABOVE: **Mount McKinley** is North America's highest peak, and is surrounded by one of the world's greatest wildlife sanctuaries, Denali National Park and Preserve. *Page 229*

ABOVE: The **northern lights** can be viewed most clearly in winter in the area around Fairbanks, which calls itself an "auroral zone." *Page 70*

LEFT: The **Trans-Alaska Pipeline** moves oil for 800 miles from the North Slope to Valdez, across three mountain ranges and 800 rivers and streams. *Page 53*

RIGHT: Alaska is the stronghold of **bald eagles**, which congregate in places where fish are plentiful. *Page 74*

THE BEST OF ALASKA: EDITOR'S CHOICE

Setting priorities, discovering secrets, the best wildlife viewing, the top sporting events, unique attractions... here, at a glance, are our recommendations plus some tips and tricks that even the locals won't always know

ONLY IN ALASKA

● **Denali National Park and Preserve**. A memorable trip to see North America's highest peak and one of the world's greatest wildlife sanctuaries. *Pages 229–39*.

● **Glacier Bay National Park and Preserve**. Sixteen massive tidewater glaciers flow down from snow-capped mountain peaks and plunge into ice-choked fjords—a dramatic backdrop for viewing wildlife, including bears, seals, humpback whales and eagles. *Pages 144–7*.

● **Aurora Borealis**. Displays (Northern Lights). Although these heavenly light shows can be viewed only in the darkened autumn or winter skies, in Anchorage, that begins in late August. *Page 70*.

● **Alaska's Thermal Resort** (Chena Hot Springs). Soak away your pre-conceived notions about a "frozen wasteland" in outdoor and indoor steaming-hot thermal pools, in summer or winter. *Page 265*.

● **Land of the Midnight Sun**. Cities, towns and villages throughout Alaska celebrate the summer solstice each year with parties and barbeques and, in Fairbanks, midnight tee time under natural light. *Page 248*.

ALASKA'S BEST-KEPT SECRETS

● **Exit Glacier**. This spectacular glacier, located in Seward is the only portion of the Kenai Fjords National Park accessible by road. A great place to take close-up glacier photographs, but watch out for falling ice! *Page 204*.

● **Lake Clark National Park and Preserve**. A short flight from Anchorage or the Kenai Peninsula, this offers boundless recreational opportunities for wildlife viewing, river running, kayaking, hunting and angling, yet it is among Alaska's least known, and least visited, national parks. *Pages 326–31*.

● **Richardson Highway**. This scenic road from Fairbanks to Valdez provides spectacular views of Worthington Glacier, the many waterfalls of Keystone Canyon, and Thompson Pass. *Page 259*.

● **Ship Creek**. This salmon-laden stream, within casting distance of downtown Anchorage hotels, is a favorite fishing hole for locals during lunch hour. *Page 366*.

● **Surf Yakutat**. Said by some to be one of the top, and certainly most unusual, surf beaches in the US. A great spot for surfing enthusiasts. *Page 161*.

LEFT: the bar at the Ice Museum, Chena Hot Springs.

BEST SPOTS FOR BEAR VIEWING

● **Brooks River and Camp** is located in Katmai National Park and Preserve. Safe viewing platforms allow you to watch bears feed on spawning salmon near the Brooks Falls. Visitors may stay at Brooks Lodge, or fly out on a day trip from Anchorage or the Kenai Peninsula. *Page 332.*

● **Denali National Park and Preserve** shuttle bus tours present visitors with excellent opportunities for spotting bears. *Pages 229–39.*

● **Kodiak Island** is famous for its healthy population of large brown bears. Bear-viewing tours will take you to see them in the Kodiak National Wildlife Refuge. *Page 322.*

● **McNeil River State Game Sanctuary** was created for the world's largest concentration of brown bears. Access is limited: visitors are selected by lottery. *Pages 337–41.*

● **Pack Creek** on Admiralty Island National Monument in Southeast also offers bear viewing from platforms, and is accessible by air from Juneau. *Pages 75, 111.*

ABOVE: a brown bear.

ABOVE: walruses are plentiful in the Bristol Bay area.

THINGS TO DO FREE AROUND ANCHORAGE

● **Drive to Hatcher Pass.** You can have a family picnic on the tundra, take a hike, or pick fresh berries on stunning alpine slopes. *Pages 214–5.*

● **Navigate the Coastal Trail.** Whether you travel by bike, in-line skates, (or skis, in winter) or your own two feet, the 11 miles of the Tony Knowles Coastal Trail, from downtown Anchorage to Kincaid Park, makes for a delightful after-noon. *Page 175.*

● **Eagle River Nature Center.** This center offers free nature programs, hiking trails, a viewing tele-scope, and natural history displays. Parking fee. *Page 177.*

● **Anchorage Coastal Wildlife Refuge.** A broad, open expanse just south of Anchorage, that is an excellent, wetland habitat for a variety of resident and migratory birds. Stroll along a wooden boardwalk for a chance to see salmon spawning. *Page 176.*

● **Windy Corner.** At Mile 107 on the Seward Highway, there are pull-outs that will allow you to safely park and look for Dall sheep, which are often and inexplicably standing on nearby craggy ledges, apparently watching the traffic go by. *Pages 177, 186.*

● **Beluga Point.** Just down the Seward Highway at Mile 110, telescopes are provided for spotting beluga whales. *Page 177.*

BEST FOR FAMILIES

● **Alaska Zoo.** A guaranteed, safe, close-up look at Alaska wildlife. *Page 174.*

● **Crow Creek Mine.** Try your hand at panning for gold at Southcentral's richest goldmine. A favorite with tourists and local miners, alike. *Page 179.*

● **Imaginarium.** This award-winning hands-on science discovery center features touch tanks, a planetarium and reptiles. *Page 173.*

● **H₂Oasis.** Alaska's indoor answer to the outdoor water parks in the lower 48 states. Enjoy a wave pool, lazy river, water-coaster ride and water slide. *Page 175.*

RIGHT: panning for gold.

UNIQUE SPORTING EVENTS

● **Iditarod Trail Sled Dog Race.** Known as "The Last Great Race," mushers and their dog teams dash 1,100 bone-jarring miles from Anchorage to Nome, crossing two mountain ranges, following the Yukon River for about 150 miles, then traversing the pack ice of Norton Sound. *Pages 308–9.*

● **World Eskimo Indian Olympics.** Hundreds of Native athletes from Alaska and the circumpolar nations gather each July in Fairbanks to compete in many exotic, and often painful athletic events. These competitions are patterned after the traditional Native hunting, fishing and gathering culture. Endurance, observation and a spirit of cooperation are all key ingredients in events like Ear Pull, Knuckle Hope and the Blanket Toss. *Pages 256–7.*

● **Great Alaska Shootout (Anchorage) and Top of the World Classic (Fairbanks).** Hosted yearly in November by the University of Alaska, these invitational college basketball tournaments have gained national prominence. *Pages 178, 367.*

● **Baseball Under the Midnight Sun.** During Fairbank's yearly summer solstice festivities, you can watch a baseball game (which has been played on June 21 for more than 100 years). It begins around 10:30pm and is played without any need of artificial light. *Page 248.*

ABOVE: more than 3,000 bald eagles gather in the fall.

BEST FOR BIRDWATCHING

● **Alaska Chilkat Bald Eagle Preserve (Haines).** This preserve is home to the world's largest gathering of bald eagles, and hosts a festival each November. *Page 151.*

● **Kachemak Bay (Homer).** Hundreds of thousands of shorebirds from as far away as Asia, Hawaii and South America visit the picturesque hamlet of Homer during spring migration. The city hosts the Katchemak Bay Shorebird Festival each May. *Page 209.*

● **Pribilof Islands.** These tiny islands 300 miles off the west coast are a nesting ground for nearly 200 species of seabirds. You can also spot "accidental" Asian migrants. *Page 345.*

● **Creamers Field (Fairbanks).** Originally a dairy farm, this migratory water-fowl refuge now plays host to sandhill cranes, Canadian honkers and ducks every spring and fall. *Page 251.*

● **Copper River Delta (Cordova).** The delta is a birder's paradise, home to the entire population of dusky Canada geese, and Cordova hosts a lively festival during May's migration. *Page 191.*

LEFT: a sled dog musher in the Yukon Quest race.

BEST RAIL TOURS

● **Aboard the Alaska Railroad** *Page 354.*
● The **Spencer Glacier & Grandview** tour from Anchorage aboard the Alaska Railroad is a chance to see gorgeous landscapes, close-up glaciers – even take a float trip – and be back in Anchorage for dinner.
● The **Hurricane Turn Train** is used by locals to reach remote cabins. Passengers may get off the train at any point along the 55-mile trip to fish, hike or enjoy a float trip, then flag it down on its return trip to Talkeetna.
● **The Anchorage to Seward** route also passes the Spencer Glacier and Grandview areas, but continues on to Seward, where you can take a day cruise into Kenai Fjords National Park.
● Traveling to **Denali National Park and Preserve** via train offers several good opportunities to view Mount McKinley, weather permitting.
● **Aboard the White Pass and Yukon Route Railroad.** You can retrace the steps of the historic Klondike Trail of '98, from Skagway to the White Pass Summit (elev. nearly 3,000 ft.) *Pages 153–4.*

ABOVE: the White Pass and Yukon Route Railroad.

ABOVE: some of the crafts produced by Native artisans.

MUST-SEE MUSEUMS

● **Alaska Native Heritage Center (Anchorage).** This is the place to learn about Alaska's Native culture, art and traditional customs and see Native artists at work. *Page 174.*
● **UAF Museum of the North (Fairbanks).** The University of Alaska museum has long been considered to be one of the top museums in the state. Exhibits include cultural artifacts, a huge mummified bison, a giant copper nugget, and more. *Page 250.*
● **Sitka National Historical Park.** Wind your way through a beautiful, old-growth coastal forest, view an excellent collection of totem poles, visit a museum and watch Native artisans at work. *Pages 134, 370.*
● **Alaska State Museum (Juneau).** It captures the entire state. The most notable exhibit is a model of a towering, two-story "eagle tree". *Page 139.*

FANTASTIC FESTIVALS

● **Talkeetna Moose Dropping Festival.** July. Score a bullseye with moose poops. www.talkeetnachamber.org
● **Polar Bear Jump-Off Festival**. Seward, January. Locals in bear costumes jump into Resurrection Bay. www.sewardak.org
● **Bering Sea Ice Golf Classic** Nome, March. Six-hole course on ice with bright orange golf balls. www.nomealaska.org
● **Fur Rendezvous** Anchorage, February. A week of varied contests to break up the winter. www.furrondy.net
● **World Ice Art Championships** Fairbanks, March. Carving masterpieces. www.fairbanks-alaska.com
● **Bear Paw Festival** Eagle River, July. Big parade, Teddy Bear Picnic, family fun. www.cer.org
● **Boardwalk Boogie** Pelican, May. Craft fair, filthy song contest, underwear race, etc. www.boardwalkboogie.com

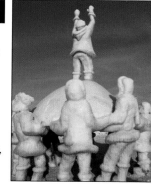

ABOVE: an ice art exhibit.

THE LAST FRONTIER

Some people say there are no more frontiers
to explore without leaving the planet.
But they're forgetting about Alaska

Alaska: the Great Land, the Last Frontier – more than 580,000 sq. miles (1½ million sq. km) that taunted early explorers and still challenges modern-day researchers. It also provokes a fascination that attracts more and more travelers looking for something that a conventional vacation cannot give them. The hint of urban sophistication in Anchorage and Juneau rapidly gives way to the frontier, where outdoor survival skills are among the most useful attributes a resident can possess.

America's 49th state is so broad, so unpeopled, and so roadless that small airplanes are more common than cabs in other states. There are more private pilots than truck drivers and cabbies combined. Men outnumber women (though women have coined the phrase "The odds are good, but the goods are odd"). The population numbers just over 670,000, almost half of whom live in one city, Anchorage. Nearly the entire state is raw, wondrous wilderness.

Alaska has lush rain-drenched forests and fragile windswept tundras. There are lofty mountains, still-active volcanoes, and spectacular glaciers, as well as 3 million lakes and endless swamps. Along with a handful of modern high-rise buildings, there are countless one-room log cabins. Within hours of dining sumptuously in a first-class restaurant it is possible to tread on ground that has never known a human footprint: ground belonging to the grizzly bear and the wolf and shared only reluctantly with human beings.

This varied land is best viewed from a small plane or surveyed from a canoe or kayak – or by foot; it cannot be seen properly from a car (though increasing numbers of people are exploring parts of the state by traveling the highways). And, although it would take forever to cover on foot, hiking is often the best way to touch the landscape, to appreciate its vastness, and discover its mysteries. Alaska is an outdoor world, a wilderness, a land of many faces, few of which can be explored by moving from hotel to hotel.

The Alaskan experience includes the sheer wonder of finding what hides

PRECEDING PAGES: viewing melting glaciers from a cruise ship; mountain house on the Ruth Glacier, south of Mount McKinley; after the photographer had retreated.
LEFT: many parts of Alaska are accessible only by air.
ABOVE: the mail arrives by floatplane; Native Alaskans.

beyond the horizon or over the next ridge. No one person has ever seen it all; no one person ever will. Therein lies the essence of Alaska. Its huge, untamed spaces, it has been said, are the great gift Alaska can give to a harrassed world.

When to go

Springtime (or "breakup") to an Alaskan is a hopeful time of dwindling snow berms, widening streets, emerging lawns and, most exciting of all, lengthening daylight hours. But to a visitor in the here-and-now of Alaska spring, it may look like dirty snow melting to reveal accumulated trash, huge puddles trapped by still-frozen drains on winter-ravaged roads and fickle weather conditions. March, April and early May are months of renewal for Alaskans, but visitors would be wise to allow sufficient time for the state to wake up, spruce up and set up for tourist season.

Just before the first cruise ship arrives, store merchants bring out lovely hanging flower baskets and the cities seem to "bloom" overnight. Gift shops, which may have been closed over the winter, are re-opened, swept out, shelves stocked and windows polished. The visitor season runs from mid-May to mid-September. During those months, all tours, parks, campgrounds, trains, buses, ferries, restaurants, hotels, B&Bs and other service-related facilities are running at full speed. Many offer bargain rates for the "shoulder seasons" of late May and early September. Summer in Alaska boasts mild temperatures and, in most areas, seemingly endless daylight.

If springtime is when Alaska showers and shaves, and summer is open house, fall feels like a time for getting together with a few close friends. Like spring, the timing of autumn in Alaska is a fickle business, and one can miss it altogether. Generally it begins to feel like fall in late August and

continues through mid-September. The trees and grasses turn golden, the spent fireweed magenta, and the mountains, below the "termination dust" of newly snow-capped peaks, a warm russet. Fall brings darkness back to the night sky of most of Alaska, and with it displays of the aurora borealis, or northern lights.

There are far fewer tourists in autumn – but fewer options, too. The favorite tourist destinations, lodgings, restaurants, transportations and other amenities taper off as suddenly as they gear up in late spring. The use of a private or rental car greatly increases sightseeing options. Careful research and planning is needed for a rewarding autumn visit to Alaska – but are well worth the effort.

If skiing, snowboarding, sled dog races and other winter sports appeal, a wintertime visit to Alaska is an excellent option. The Fur Rendezvous, held in Anchorage in February, is a yearly celebration that includes the World Champion Sled Dog Race, fireworks, art exhibits, fur auctions, a winter outdoor carnival (dress warmly), and much more. Fairbanks also celebrates winter with festivals, fireworks displays, sled dog races and the incredible sculptures of the World Ice Art Championship. ❑

ABOVE: canoes are versatile transportation; floatplane meets cruise ship in the Gulf.
RIGHT: the northern lights are best seen between late September and early April.

PRESERVING THE FRAGILE WILDERNESS

It's thrilling to visit pristine areas unchanged for a thousand years. But how can more people enjoy the experience without endangering that very wildness?

Y ou don't really know what wild means until you've been to Alaska. With one-fifth of the land area of the contiguous United States and more shoreline than all the other states combined, Alaska includes 150 million acres (60 million hectares) of national parks and forests, wildlife refuges and other designated preserves – ample territory for wilderness adventure. Its 38 mountain ranges, 3,000 rivers and 3 million lakes fall within climate ranges from temperate rainforest to arid arctic. Much of this territory is barely charted, let alone touched by the human foot.

Of Alaska's 15 national parks, preserves and monuments, only five can be accessed by road. Glacier Bay National Park (3.2 million acres/1.3 million hectares), for example, can be reached only by boat or floatplane. North America's premier mountain wilderness and its largest national park, Wrangell-St Elias National Park and Preserve (13.2 million acres/5.3 million hectares), is home to nine peaks of more than 14,000 ft (4,270 meters), including the 18,010-ft (5,490-meter) Mount St Elias, the continent's fourth highest peak (and the second tallest in the United States).

It also has the largest collection of glaciers in North America, the Bagley Icefield – which is the largest subpolar icefield on the continent – numerous wild rivers, and multitudes of wildlife. Yet only two unpaved roads, best negotiated by 4-wheel-drive vehicles, penetrate the park boundaries.

Exploring the arctic

Gates of the Arctic National Park, the northernmost of the state's parks, is a remote and unde-

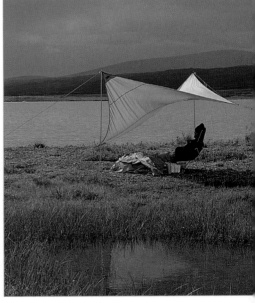

veloped 8.4 million acres (3.4 million hectares) of crags, fragile alpine meadows, crystal clear mountain streams, and sweeping arctic valleys. Without roads or trails, backpacking, mountaineering, river floating, and dog sled excursions are the best ways in which visitors can explore these arctic expanses.

Besides its federal parks and refuges, Alaska has state-managed parks and sanctuaries that are among the nation's finest, from 1.55-million-acre (630,000-hectare) Wood-Tikchik – the country's largest state park – to the Alaska Chilkat Bald Eagle Preserve and McNeil River State Game Sanctuary, where dozens of brown bears, some weighing 1,000 pounds (450 kg) or more, gather each summer to fish for salmon.

LEFT: watching a calving glacier in Tracy Arm Wilderness Area, Juneau.
RIGHT: camping with a low environmental impact.

Whether bears or birds, wildlife is abundant throughout much of the state's wilderness. Hundreds of thousands of caribou roam across sweeping tundra, Dall sheep graze in high alpine basins, seals sun themselves on ice floes, wolves howl from the tops of ridges, golden eagles spiral through blue skies and clouds, whales ply turquoise fjords.

When federal geographer Henry Gannett, a founder of the National Geographic Society, surveyed Alaska's expanse in 1904, he set the tone for today's ecotourism: "Its grandeur is more valuable than the gold or the fish or the timber, for it will never be exhausted." Alaska is a land where inhabitants and travelers sense that they can do no better.

Low-impact tourism

Unfortunately, the traditional tourist industry in the state often bypasses its great wilderness areas in favor of organized tours that take visitors by bus, train or airplane to cities, towns and developed parks. The majority of tourists see sights that are reached by road (such as Portage Glacier, Denali National Park and Preserve, and cities such as Anchorage, Juneau and Fairbanks) – but rarely step into untouched wilderness. Only one road goes into 6 million-acre (2.4 million-hectare)

GEOLOGICAL YOUTH

Alaska is a young country, geologically speaking. Composed of fragments of the earth's crust that rafted from the Pacific area on the backs of crustal plates and then "docked" together, the entire region is still in the process of coming together.

Its youth and place on the globe are responsible for much of Alaska's diversity. America's largest state has arctic tundra, 5,000 glaciers, icefields, six major mountain ranges, broad valleys, immense coastal rainforests and boreal woodlands, rugged coastal fjords, active volcanoes, 12 major river systems, 3 million lakes and countless islands. It covers more than twice the land area of its closest competitor, Texas, and it has 33,900 miles (54,500km) of sea coast – 50 percent more than the contiguous United States.

Denali National Park – a 90-mile (145-km) strip that bars most private vehicles. While this road channels more and more visitors into the park each year via bus tours – which cause minimum disturbance to the landscape and wildlife – only 31,000 of the park's 404,000 visitors in one recent year registered for backcountry permits.

Guides such as Bob Jacobs, owner of St Elias Alpine Guides in McCarthy, feel that visitors to Alaska should see a lot more, but, at the same time, the land should be protected. "Alaska is a wonderful classroom," Bob says. But, unlike school, "you don't need a schedule. In summer you can hike until 2am and sleep until noon."

On Jacobs' trips into the heart of the Wrangell-St Elias National Park you climb unnamed peaks, raft down swift, milky rivers and backpack for weeks at a time, enjoying the rich wilderness traditions that typify the Alaskan way of life. Alaska's a whole new experience once you've touched the 1,000-year-old ice of a massive glacier, rafted a raging river and heard wild creatures calling across unpeopled lands.

Jacobs helped pioneer a new industry now familiar as "ecotourism," which reveals to travelers the quintessential "wild" Alaska through environmentally-friendly outdoor adventures such as sea-kayaking, mountaineering and wildlife-watching.

Though the great majority of travelers continue to see Alaska by car, tour bus, or cruise ship, eco-

they did some wildlife viewing – although only an estimated 10 percent strike out away from traditional tourist areas into the pristine wilderness.

Protecting the land

Essentially, ecotourism means using the tourist industry as a tool to protect and enhance Alaska's natural beauty. "It's important to understand that we're a part of nature and a part of the plan," says Penney Hodges, who helped direct the Alaska Center for Coastal Studies in Homer. "We need to learn how to get back into balance with nature." By opening its doors to travelers in summer and to parties of schoolchildren in spring and fall, the

tourism – defined as low-impact vacations that allow people to learn about, enjoy, and help preserve the natural environment while disturbing local people as little as possible – has helped a steadily growing number of people to see wild and pristine areas of Alaska that are inaccessible to the masses. Traveling at nature's pace in a land that offers adventure and asks for respect, tourists gain an intimate awareness of life as it was 1,000 years ago.

The Alaska Travel Industry Association reports that in one recent summer around 1.6 million non-resident visitors spent nearly $1.5 billion, or about $930 a person. About half of these visitors said

center works to foster responsible human interaction with our natural surroundings and to generate knowledge of the marine and coastal ecosystems of Kachemak Bay through its environmental education and research programs.

Ultimately, ecotourism relies on pristine country and wildlife as its chief commodity, so there is great motivation to maintain the health of the land and the well-being of its wildlife. It is a clean industry, which could well take the place of some of its less-fastidious competitors.

Ecotourism in Alaska was initiated by a handful of small, independent operators and outfitters that led groups into the outback, while the mainstream industry concentrated on marketing developed resort areas. Now some large-scale

LEFT: a brown bear has right of way in Denali Park.
ABOVE: a humpback whale makes a splash.

organizations have developed policies and principles that depart significantly from traditional commercial concerns and lean toward low-impact tourism. Still, ecotourism still largely remains the domain of smaller, often family-operated, businesses that emphasize small groups and often do customized trips.

The guidelines of the American Society of Travel Agents spell out the ecotourism ethos: visitors should support local cultures; avoid littering; walk only on designated trails; support conservation-oriented programs; learn about local customs; avoid disturbing local habitat or buying products which utilise any part of endangered animals.

Eco-friendly options

Dozens of outfitters offer river rafting, tundra trekking, mountain climbing, bird-watching, whale cruising, wildlife photography safaris and sea-kayaking adventures, ranging from easy to strenuous. Some tour operators offer ecotours geared specifically toward senior citizens. Although some of these trips hark back to the days of the pioneers, they are usually made comfortable enough. Visitors can take advantage of experienced guides without having to acquire all the necessary skills themselves; and many of the backcountry meals approach gourmet quality.

Wildlife viewing is a major draw, especially for

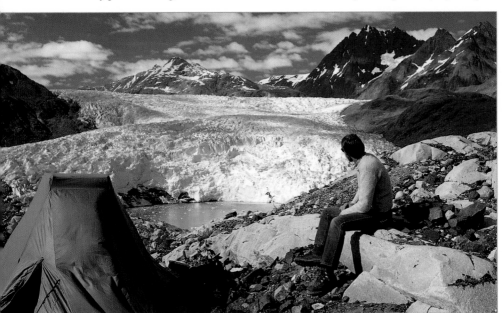

NATURAL WONDERS

When it comes to counting the most and the biggest, Alaska can amass some amazing statistics. It is one-fifth of the size of the contiguous United States, measuring 2,400 miles (3,860km) from east to west, and geographers have named more than 1,800 islands. Its mountains include 19 that are over 14,000ft (4,270 meters), and 17 of them are among the 20 highest peaks in the United States.

The state also has over 5,000 glaciers, and more than 3 million lakes. The largest of these, Lake Iliamna, just south of the Lake Clark National Park in Southwest Alaska, encompasses 1,100 sq. miles (2,850 sq. km). It is noted for its trout, salmon and grayling.

those hoping to see the monarchs of the land: the grizzly and its coastal cousin, the brown bear. One of the most notable areas is the McNeil River State Game Sanctuary, but visitors are strictly regulated by permit; only 10 people a day, accompanied by sanctuary staff, can visit the bear-viewing areas. This close supervision means that visitors have to apply in advance, and names are randomly drawn (by computer, nowadays). You have a better chance of getting to Brooks Camp, another top bear-viewing area, within Katmai National Park.

Other renowned bear-viewing areas include Denali National Park and Preserve, home to 200–300 bears; many can be seen grazing on plants or digging for ground squirrels near the Park Road. Kodiak National Wildlife Refuge, designated a refuge by President Franklin D. Roosevelt in 1941, is home to the largest bears on earth (they can reach 1,200 pounds/540kg). As much as 10 percent of Alaska's grizzlies live on Kodiak Island. "Big bears fill big hotels," said the controversial grizzly activist Timothy Treadwell, who was mauled to death by a bear in Katmai National Park in 2003. "People go to Alaska to see wilderness, to be part of what Earth used to be like. That's good for tourism. If you protect grizzly habitat, you protect your bread and butter."

Besides bears, people come from around the world to see other wildlife: Dall sheep, moose, caribou, wolves, bald and golden eagles, and all man-

"Do your homework. Look for organizations that go beyond making money. Talk to them. Get a feeling for their philosophy. Ask for references. That's the best policy."

Following some guidelines will help make your trip ecologically friendly. Check to see if an operator limits the number of people it takes into fragile areas. Does the company practice low-impact camping and hiking and vary the location of campsites from trip to trip in order to avoid scarring the ground in certain areas? Does it supply a reading list about the area and the type of activities you will be pursuing?

Top ecotourism companies are staffed by expe-

ner of songbirds, shorebirds, and seabirds, as well as the many marine mammals *(see pages 73–7).*

Ethical guidelines

Although ecotourism industry operators generally follow environmental ethics, they don't all abide equally by the unwritten code of minimal impact. Some people are now advocating a "green rating" system to distinguish between good and poor operators on an ecological impact scale.

Currently, no such system exists, but Bob Jacobs has some suggestions to enable would-be visitors to pick the right company to travel with.

rienced naturalists who always accompany their guests on journeys and offer extensive information along the way. Such specialists help minimize impact on wildlife by keeping groups at unobtrusive, safe distances. The companies should also be committed to energy conservation and recycling, as this helps preserve the environment that you have come here to enjoy.

Even if you're traveling on your own, you can do your part. Follow carefully the guidelines that come with backcountry permits from the park or forest service and write your own code for minimum-impact traveling, based on the points outlined above. It makes sense to preserve the grandeur of Alaska's wilderness and keep it wild for the benefit of future generations. ❏

LEFT: setting up camp in Glacier Bay.
ABOVE: flowers add color in the high tundra.

AN INDEPENDENT PEOPLE

Nearly a quarter of Alaska's population has moved to the state within the past few years. So how do you define a "typical" Alaskan?

efore Alyson Rigby Ronningen, who grew up in England, traveled to Alaska for the first time, she thought she had a pretty clear idea of what Alaskans were like: "They all wore flannel shirts, had big bushy beards, and they owned guns and big dogs," she recalled. Alyson eventually married an Alaskan and moved to the Far North. Once there, she looked around at her Fairbanks neighbors, confirmed her suspicions, and smugly told a friend, "I was right."

But Alyson was not a "typical" visitor, or even a run-of-the-mill new Alaskan. She spent her first winter living in a wall tent with her husband and new baby. While her husband worked as a carpenter nearby, she used a tiny wood stove for both warmth and cooking. Temperatures plummeted as low as $-30°$ or $-40°F$ ($-34°$ to $-40°C$) but Alyson stayed toasty by baking on her trusty wood stove.

Even some seasoned Alaskans would be horrified at spending a winter under those conditions, but Alyson conformed to what many believe to be an unspoken code of the north: be independent and self-sufficient.

In that way she was a "typical" Alaskan, yet it is difficult to generalize about what is typical, because it depends so much on where you choose to settle and under what circumstances you live. Alaska is so huge and the various parts of the state are so different from each other that the residents are bound to differ widely as well.

Anchored down in Anchorage

The hub of the state is its largest (although not its capital) city, Anchorage. Rural Alaskans often

LEFT: as part of an intensive ecology program, a radio-tagged eagle is being released into the wild.
RIGHT: Alaskans enjoy the phenomenal outdoor life.

joke that Anchorage is only 20 minutes from the real Alaska. That may well be true, but many urban Alaskans make the best possible use of those 20 minutes.

In a state where the median age is 34, Anchorage (with 42 percent of the population) is a city of young – but aging – professionals (here, as in much of the US, the population's average age in increasing). They include active outdoor-sports lovers, such as rock climbers, mountain bikers, whitewater kayakers and runners. Many people bring their outdoor toys to work with them, and at the end of the day, they head for the hills, the city's biking trails and parks, or nearby streams. In summer they don't have to worry about running out of daylight, either, because from late May through early August the sky never fully darkens.

People in Anchorage also spend a lot of time getting out of town. Lake Hood, a floatplane base in the city, is the largest and busiest such base in the world, with more than 1,000 take-offs and landings recorded on a peak summer day.

Where do they all go? Just peek out of a plane window as you fly into Anchorage and you will see hundreds of little getaway cabins tucked into the surrounding wilderness and the more remote areas. Those without their own cabins may fly to public-use cabins, developed campgrounds, or backcountry destinations where they set up their own campsites.

No water, no problem

John Power, a long-time Alaskan who became a "big city" resident in his early 40s, thought about getting one of those backcountry cabins when he first moved to Anchorage, but instead bought a 30-ft (9-meter) sailboat, which he keeps in Prince William Sound. Power, a geophysicist with the Alaska Volcano Observatory, moved to Anchorage from Fairbanks, where for many years he had lived on the town's outskirts in a little cabin with no running water and, like Alyson, just a wood stove for heating.

"I liked it," he says. "I liked living in a place where I didn't really have any neighbors. I liked not

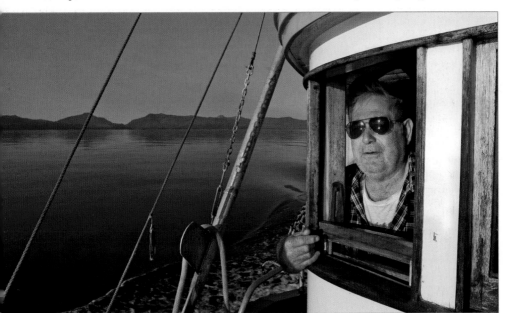

JACK LONDON AND THE YUKON

The prolific San Francisco-born novelist Jack London (1876–1916) joined the fortune hunters in 1897's Klondike Gold Rush and later created a romantically adventurous portrait of Alaska in such novels as *White Fang* and *The Call of the Wild*. In both books, sled dogs fight to survive in Alaska's unforgiving wilderness.

London shot dangerous rapids to get ahead of the other gold stampeders and, lacking fresh food in winter, developed scurvy. Having failed to strike it rich, he worked as a laborer back in San Francisco until a newspaper published his account of his trip down the Yukon. Today a log cabin in Dawson City is a Jack London Interpretive Center (tel: 867-993 5575).

having to worry about it when I left in winter, which I frequently did when I was traveling. It was inexpensive. I first got into that lifestyle when I was a student and I never really changed. I didn't have to worry about house-sitters, or about the plumbing freezing or the heat being on when I was gone." He misses his reliable little wood stove most of all. "I used to like getting up in the morning, building my fire and cooking pancakes in the kitchen with the wood stove roaring away," he says nostalgically.

There are several thousand Fairbanks-area residents who still embrace the wood-stove, no-running-water lifestyle with enthusiasm. These people usually fill 5-gallon (22-liter) water jugs at the laundromats in town, or at their places of employment. Showers are also available for public use at the laundromats of many communities.

When winter settles in and the mercury begins to drop, conversation generally revolves around the weather, particularly the frigid temperatures endured in the Interior and Arctic regions. Eventually, someone will complain about water pipes freezing and bursting, and those who have no running water try not to look too self-satisfied as they silently assure themselves that they have chosen the right lifestyle.

In communities along the Alaska coast, life revolves not only around the weather, but more importantly around the fishing season. Extra-Tuf rubber boots and heavy-duty raingear are the fash-

The Russian community

Some Alaskans came here long ago as visitors and stayed on, overcoming hardship and skepticism. Typical among them are the descendants of Russian immigrants in the Kenai Peninsula, Kodiak and Sitka. The first Russians came to Alaska in the late 18th century *(see page 24)* and established communities first in Kodiak, then in present-day Sitka, which became the headquarters of the fur trading Russian-American Company.

Both towns retain strong Russian influences, but it is on the Kenai Peninsula that a strict Russian Orthodox community survives, based around their "Island of Faith" near Anchor Point. Sur-

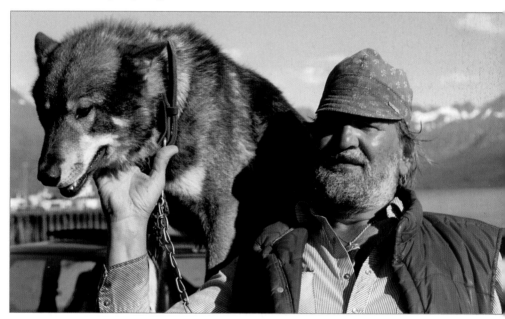

ion *du jour*. This is especially true in Kodiak, where fishing is not a summer activity, but a year-round economic necessity.

Since many students and some teachers fish, the school calendar is based on fishing openings and closures. When the fishing is poor, the whole town suffers. If people can't pay tradesmen's bills, businesses can't pay theirs either, and the economy of the whole community is in trouble. The population of Kodiak, like that of other fishing communities, swells in the summer when people arrive to fish, then contracts when they leave again at the end of the season.

LEFT: the Tlingit Indian owner of a fishing boat.
ABOVE: wolf and friend, Valdez.

vivors of persecution by the Orthodox Church, the government, and later the Stalinist purges, they call themselves "the Old Believers."

Today they work in local businesses, or operate companies of their own, and manage their own fishing fleet. But their lives revolve around their religious beliefs. The study of holy books is mandatory during periods of fasting before Christmas and Lent. They wear traditional clothes: the women and girls always cover their heads with scarves, and men dress conservatively, often sporting close-trimmed beards.

Yet they are no less Alaskan than the man who lives in the bush and calls the Lower 48 states "America," as if he inhabited a separate country; or the Anchorage college graduate, rushing from his downtown office to the mountain tops at weekends. In Alaska, everyone is free to be who they want to be, to start from scratch, to reinvent themselves, to become just another "typical" Alaskan.

Bush pilots

Life in Alaska can be tough, and it has always attracted people who are not easily daunted. Among the most intrepid of Alaskans are the bush pilots. Their history begins in the 1920s, when Alaska and the airplane became partners in a relationship best described as complicated bliss. Despite an obvious need, Alaska wasn't equipped for airplanes. There were lots of places to go, but

there was no place to land once you got there. This created a special breed of flyer: the bush pilot.

Alaska entered the aviation age courtesy of James V. Martin, who had contracted to fly an airplane over Fairbanks in honor of the 4th of July in 1913. He loaded his disassembled airplane on a steamship and sailed it to Skagway. There he transferred it to the White Pass and Yukon Railroad for the 125-mile (200-km) trip to Whitehorse, Yukon Territory, in Canada.

Finally, Martin loaded his plane on a stern-wheeler and steamed 800 miles (1,300km) down the Yukon River, then 100 miles (160km) up the Tanana and Chena rivers to Fairbanks. After the

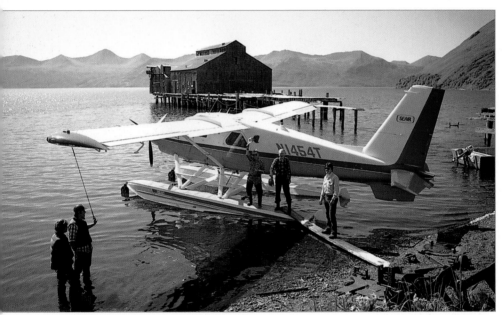

PAYBACK FOR THE PEOPLE

Because Alaska depends to such an extent on its natural resources, its citizens argued they should benefit directly from the exploitation of those riches rather than trust politicians to spend the money. In 1976, as the potential of the North Slope oilfield became apparent, voters passed a constitutional amendment creating the Alaska Permanent Fund. This trust fund invests a proportion of revenues from mineral sales and each October pays out a dividend to every qualified Alaskan resident. The sum has varied from $331.29 a person in 1984 to $1,963.86 in 2000. It is valued income, particularly for the poor, and it tends to lessen local opposition to further oil drilling in wilderness areas.

boxes arrived in Fairbanks, Martin reassembled the plane. It flew in exhibition for 11 minutes, was taken apart and carted out of the territory.

Conditions are easier today, but pilots must still turn out in all weathers and people still rely on them to turn up in emergencies, and to deliver the mail if not – they hope – the babies. And, although many people now take commuter planes between Alaska's larger communities, hundreds of flyers continue the bush pilot tradition, as they transport passengers and supplies to tiny villages and wilderness lodges and into remote backcountry, where they may land on glaciers, rivers, lakes, or tundra, just as pioneering pilots did a century ago. ❑

ABOVE: meeting the mail plane in Chefornak.

A Trapper's Life

L ife in the Alaskan bush can be exhilarating, but it is hard and often tedious. Trapping is one of the hardest, least profitable professions there is, and one that has changed little over the years, but there are those who love the life. One change, which has made life easier, is that many trappers now use snow-machines instead of the traditional dog sleds. This has its disadvantages: after all, dogs don't break down, as machines do, and a trapper now always needs to carry survival gear and showshoes for walking home when the engine inexplicably dies.

Twin sisters, Julie and Miki Collins, who live in the bush north of Denali and still work in traditional ways, are typical of some who have stuck to the dog sleds, and their story paints a picture of a hard but rewarding way of life.

A trapper must be able to control a sled drawn by a dozen huskies, capable of doing some 60 miles (100km) a day on a good trail, in temperatures dipping as low as –50°F (–45°C). Many things can go wrong on a trip: a sled could clump a sapling in its careening descent of a slope; there could be a dog fight, or a threat from runaway dogs; a last-minute repair job might be needed, or a sloppily loaded sled could buck burlap sacks of frozen fish from the canvas tarp. The towline can disconnect from the sled, sending the dogs flying in formation without their driver. And sometimes a 1,500-pound (700kg) bull moose can challenge the team's right to use the trail.

A trapper must remain constantly alert for unseen dangers: thin ice, deadly water hidden under deep snow, winter-stressed moose, open creeks, or a fresh tree blown down across the trail, all hazards which usually crop up suddenly and without warning.

There's always something to watch out for, and the trapper must work in close unison with the team. The dogs are guided verbally, with commands to tell a leader which trail to take, to order slack dogs to speed up, or to encourage the team as a whole when they begin to tire. By watching the dogs' ears, eyes and attitudes, an experienced trapper can determine whether the team scent a moose or an animal in a trap ahead, if they want to fight or balk, if they're happy, discouraged, or over-tired. Sensitive observation and interpretation of this subtle language enables a trapper to keep the dogs at peak performance.

The seasons are important in the remote Alaskan bush – for those working with machines as much as

for those still using dog teams. In the summer, many trappers concentrate on fishing and cultivating gardens for the rest of the year. Long hours may be spent picking berries for fresh fruit and jam. The fish nets must be run daily and the dogs fed with cooked whitefish or salmon and rice. Any extra fish are cut and dried for next winter.

In the summer months, too, trappers may take the opportunity to build dog houses and sleds, sew sled bags, dog booties and harnesses. Some trappers also tan and sew furs from the winter's catch, making hats and mitts which they can sell for extra cash. Summer is also the time when machines are serviced, so that there won't be too many engine prob-

lems when the trapping season starts again.

When the fall arrives, there are cranberries to be picked and root vegetables to be harvested and stored. And when the annual fish run begins, whitefish are netted and frozen whole for the dogs' food. With winter comes the trapping season, and the truly hard work: snowshoeing through deep snow; skiing miles to set trails; and cutting cord after cord of firewood. By late winter trappers are tired of constant work in bitter weather, and in need of a brief vacation.

So it goes. The yearly cycle of putting food up in summer and fall, and trapping and woodcutting in winter and spring. The weekly cycle, measured by the mail plane and the trapline rounds, and the daily cycle of mushing dogs, maintaining equipment and feeding fires. It's a hard life but, for many, a happy one. ❏

RIGHT: at the Anchorage Miners' and Trappers' Ball.

DECISIVE DATES

THE EARLY ALASKANS

30–10,000 BC

The migration of tribes from Asia occurs across a land bridge, which at the time linked Siberia and Alaska.

10,000 BC

The Aleuts settle in the Aleutian Islands. The name Alaska derived from their word "Alaxsxag" meaning "the object toward which the action of the sea is directed." Other tribes dis-

perse throughout North and South America but the Aleuts, the Eskimos (Inupiats and Yup'iks) and the Indians, which include the

Athabascans and the coastal Tlingits and Haidas, settle in Alaska.

THE RUSSIAN INVASION

1741

First Russian ships arrive. Vitus Bering turns back after his crew made one brief landing in what is now called Prince William Sound, and dies before he could reach home, while Alexei Chirikof lands on Prince of Wales Island, where some of his crew mysteriously vanish. The fur trade is established, and the Natives forced to hunt on the Russians' behalf.

1778

Captain James Cook visits the Aleutian Islands. His brief visit prompts English interest in the fur trade.

1784

Grigor Ivanovich Shelikof arrives on Kodiak Island. He enslaves and ill treats the Natives, then sets up the first permanent Russian settlement on Three Saints Bay where he builds a school

and introduces the Russian Orthodox religion.

1790

Alexander Baranof takes over the fur enterprise. He treats the Natives more humanely than his precessors, and moves the Russian colony to the site of the present city of Kodiak.

1799

The Russian-American Company is formed.

1802

The Tlingits raze to the ground the Russian town of Mikhailovsk, built near the site of present-day Sitka, on land they had sold to Baranof. Later, the Russians destroy the Tlingit village and establish New Archangel, capital of Russian America.

1812

Russia reaches a settlement with America over

PRECEDING PAGES: a train reaches the summit of White Pass, 1899.

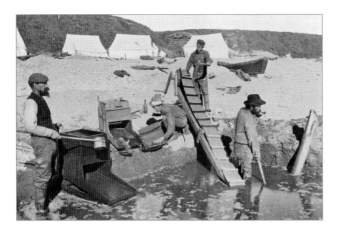

hunting rights in Alaska, but the agreement doesn't last.

1833

The British Hudson's Bay Company establishes a fur-trading outpost in Alaska.

Mid-19th century

Russian power diminishes. British and Americans undermine the fur monopoly and the Tlingits wage guerrilla war.

1866

A Western Union expedition under William H. Dall produces the first scientific studies of Alaska and the first map of the Yukon River.

AMERICA TAKES OVER

1867

US Congress, at the instigation of Secretary of State William Seward, buy Alaska from the Russians for $7.2 million.

1870s–80s

Fish canneries established around Nushagak Bay to exploit the huge runs of salmon. In the Aleutians, fur seals and otters are slaughtered ruthlessly. Whalers

pursue their quarries to the high Arctic.

THE GOLD RUSH

1880

Gold (above) is discovered at Silver Bow Basin, and the town of Juneau is founded.

1882

The Treadwell Mine, across the Gastineau Channel from Juneau, flourishes.

1896

Gold is discovered in the Klondike, a tributary of the Yukon, and the easiest route to it is by ship to Skagway. The White Pass and Chilkoot Trail to the gold fields are tackled by

thousands and Skagway becomes a thriving center.

1899

Gold is discovered at Nome in the far northwest. Many prospectors who had been unsuccessful in the Yukon move west to try again.

1902

Felix Pedro strikes gold in the Tanana Hills.

1903

The town of Fairbanks, near Pedro's strike, is founded on the site of a trading post set up by entrepreneur E.T. Barnette and named for a senator who had given him financial support.

Early 1900s

Prospectors flock to Alaska from all over North America and Europe.

1910

Kennicott, the richest copper mine in the world, starts operations in the Wrangell-St Elias mountains.

WORLD WAR II

1942

The Alaska Highway – the Alcan – is built (below) in

under nine months as both a means of defense and an overland supply route to America's Russian allies, after sea routes are cut off following the Japanese attack on Pearl Harbor. The Japanese land on the islands of Kiska and Attu. The villagers are interned in Japan for the remainder of the war. Aleuts living in the Pribilofs and Aleutian Islands' villages are evacuated.

1943

After a two-week battle the Americans re-take Attu in May. In July the Americans bomb Kiska and the Japanese retreat.

STATEHOOD AND OIL

1957

Oil is discovered at the Swanson River on the Kenai Peninsula.

1959

Alaska becomes the 49th US state in January, and is welcomed into the union by President Dwight D. Eisenhower *(below, on left)*.

1964

The Good Friday earthquake

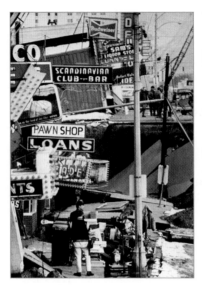

(above) hits Southcentral Alaska. Over 100 people are killed, mostly by tidal waves. Valdez, Seward, Cordova, Kodiak and several small villages suffer the worst effects.

1968

Oil is discovered at Prudhoe Bay.

1971

The Alaska Native Claims Settlement Act (ANCSA) gives Natives title to 44 million acres (18 million hectares) of land, and $963 million, distributed among specially formed Native corporations.

1971–77

The construction of the trans-Alaska pipeline to Valdez creates thousands of jobs and transforms Anchorage and Fairbanks into bright, modern cities.

1976

The Alaska Permanent Fund is created to ensure long-

term benefits from oil revenues.

1977

The trans-Alaska pipeline is completed. Oil begins to flow and the state economy booms.

1980

In one of the 20th century's landmark conservation successes, President Jimmy Carter signs into law the Alaska National Interest Lands Conservation Act (ANILCA), which adds 106 million acres (43 million hectares) of conservation lands, in national parks, wildlife refuges, and forests.

1989

The *Exxon Valdez* tanker hits Bligh Reef and spills 11 million gallons (42 million liters) of oil into Prince William Sound. A huge clean-up operation *(below)* is launched. Thousands of miles of coastline are inundated by oil and thousands of birds and mammals are killed. Litigation follows.

1990
A new decade sees logging and fishing in steady decline but the cruise industry *(right)* booming.

1992
The oil industry retrenches, causing big job losses

1995
Canadian fisherman protest about access to Southeast Alaska's troll king salmon fishery.

1996
A fierce debate begins over the question of whether rural residents – particularly Native peoples — should be granted a subsistence priority for the harvest of Alaska's fish and wildlife.

1998
The moose *(above)* is adopted as the state's official land mammal.

1999
The Alaska Native Heritage Center opens in Anchorage.

2000
A census puts the population at 626,932, a rise of 14 percent in 10 years.

2001
A fierce debate continues over the future of the Arctic National Wildlife Refuge's Coastal Plain; developers want it to be opened to oil and gas exploration and development; environmentalists fight to have it preserved as wilderness, while Alaska's Native peoples are split on the issue. There is talk of building a new pipeline, to ship Alaska's rich reserves of natural gas to the Lower 48 states.

2002
A fall of 28.6 inches (73 cm) of wet snow in March breaks all records.

2003
Bears maul to death author Timothy Treadwell, famous for approaching them up-close, in Katmai National Park.

2004
A record 708 fires burn more than 6.7 million acres (2.7 million hectares) in the interior.

2006
Sarah Palin *(below)*, a former mayor of an Anchorage suburb, is elected Alaska's first female governor.

2007
The House of Representatives votes to limit federal spending on road-building in Tongass National Forest. Ted Stevens, Alaska's senior senator, tries to reverse this. Many roads, runways, railroads and water and sewer systems in the state will wear out more quickly because of climate change, says a University of Alaska report. ❑

BEGINNINGS

Alaska was inhabited for thousands of years by various
Native groups, each with their own culture and language.
But the discovery that the territory was rich in furs
attracted the attention of Russian traders, and
changed the lives of the Native people for ever

W ho were the people who first thrived in such an unforgiving environment? Anthropologists believe the ancestors of the Alaska Natives migrated in several waves over a land bridge which joined Siberia and Alaska thousands of years ago.

When Europeans first encountered Alaska Natives in the early 18th century, there were dozens of tribes and language groups throughout the region, from the Inupiat Eskimos in the Arctic region to the Tlingits in the Southeast. Today, these first Alaskans are divided into several main groups: the southeastern Coastal Indians (the Tlingits and Haidas), the Athabascans (Interior Indians), the Aleuts, the Alutiiqs, the Eyak, and the two groups of Eskimos: Inupiat and Yup'ik. What follows is a look at their early, traditional subsistence lifestyles, before their (sometimes forced) transition into modern, western culture.

The Coastal Indians

These were probably in the first wave of immigrants to cross the land bridge, although many initially settled in Canada. The Tlingits were the most numerous; they claimed most of the coastal Panhandle, leaving only a small southern portion to the less populous Haidas. (In the late 1800s they were joined by the Tsimshian, Coastal Indians who emigrated from Canada to Annette Island off the southeastern coast. The Tsimshian live on the only federally recognized Indian reservation in Alaska.)

The Tlingits were excellent navigators, and were known to travel more than 1,000 miles (1,600km) south to trade with Native peoples in the Pacific Northwest. The standard of currency

was "blanket value," based on blankets made of cedar bark, dog and goat hair.

The Coastal Indians had great respect for the natural world, which provided them with all they needed. They believed that fish and animals gave themselves willingly to humans, and strove to acknowledge and honor that sacrifice. A bear killed for meat might be brought to the house, greeted with a welcome speech and placed in a seat of honor for a day or two. The bones of a consumed salmon were always returned to the river where it had been caught, to allow for reincarnation. Great care was taken to return all the bones, or else the fish would return deformed.

The Coastal Indians lived in a capitalist society that allowed private ownership. Each house-

---

LEFT: Native Alaskans have a long history.
RIGHT: a Tlingit woman in traditional dress.

hold owned economic goods, such as weapons, utensils and clothing – anything they had made themselves – while the clan owned religious titles and objects, for example, the right to perform a certain dance or practice a profession such as seal hunting.

In the social organization of the Tlingits and Haidas, status was determined by wealth. To maintain position, a person of power demonstrated wealth by giving a ceremonial potlatch when he would give away, destroy or invite guests to consume all his food and possessions. Those who received goods at one potlatch had to reciprocate and better their host in the future. Another impor-tant feature of the potlatch was the recitation of family histories and bloodlines.

The Athabascans

The Athabascan Indians of Alaska's harsh Interior were hunters and inland fishermen. Most lived in small nomadic bands along the region's rivers. If game was scarce, they might travel for days with-out food; in deepest winter they survived temper-atures of –50°F (–45°C) or less, sometimes without shelter or fire. Endurance and physical strength were prized; game was often run down on foot over difficult terrain.

Athabascans hunted salmon, hares, birds, cari-

COASTAL CULTURE

The mild climate and plentiful resources of the Pan-handle allowed the Coastal Indians to develop a rich culture over many years. They had leisure time to devote to social pastimes, travel and trade. They enjoyed ceremony and drama, and the traditional recitation of family histories and bloodlines kept an accurate account of the generations.

The painted designs developed by the Coastal tribes feature fish and animals, often in bold patterns of black and red. They decorated their crafted goods: domestic utensils, clothing, masks, canoes, ritual objects and the characteristic totems that marked family residences.

bou, moose and bear with the help of snares, clubs, and bows and arrows. But despite their inventive hunting methods periods of famine were not uncommon. Because they were semi-nomadic and hunted on foot, footwear was very important, and the Athabascans designed extremely efficient snowshoes made of birch.

Some Athabascan groups inhabited permanent winter villages and summer fishing camps. Most bands consisted of a few nuclear families, and had limited internal organization. Leadership was acquired by great warriors or hunters.

Athabascans also gave potlatches for a variety of reasons: to mark a death, to celebrate a child's first successful hunt, as a prelude to marriage. Those who aspired to leadership were expected to host especially memorable potlatches, at which the would-be leader would give away all his possessions then prove his prowess by providing for himself and his family for an entire year without outside help.

The Aleuts

This group settled the windswept islands of the Aleutian chain 10,000 years ago. Although their location allowed them to harvest the sea's bounty, they also had to contend with harsh and often unpredictable weather, as well as earthquakes and volcanic eruptions.

Aleut fishing technology included fish spears,

They made their skis by drying hair-seal skins over wooden frames. When the traveler went uphill the hair would dig into the snow and act as a brake; on the downhill journey the hair would lie flat to provide speed (much like modern synthetic ski "skins").

In winter Aleuts wore hoodless, knee-length parkas; in colder weather they added knee-length skin boots. Waterproof overgarments made from the intestines of sea lions were also worn, and this material was also fitted over the tops of their skin boats to keep the hunters dry.

Because of a ready supply of grass in the summer, Aleut women became skillful at basketry –

weirs, nets, hooks and lines. Various darts and nets were used to obtain sea lions and sea otters. Whales were usually killed with a poisoned, stone-bladed lance. The job of women and children was to gather shellfish at low tide.

Aleut society was divided into three categories: honorables (usually respected whalers), common people and slaves. At death the body of an honorable was mummified, and sometimes slaves were killed to honor the deceased.

Because of their dependence on the sea, Aleuts seldom journeyed far inland, but they did develop an ingenious method of transportation over snow.

LEFT: Natives from the Aleutian Islands.
ABOVE: young women show off their best furs.

their baskets were so closely woven that they could even hold water. Mats and some kinds of clothing were also made in this way.

The Alutiiqs

Close relatives of the Aleuts, Alutiiq peoples settled on the Alaska Peninsula, Kodiak Archipelago, and parts of the Kenai Peninsula and Prince William Sound. Sites dating back 7,000 years suggest the Alutiiqs were skilled maritime hunters and fishers. They paddled *bidarkas* while hunting sea lions, seals, sea otters and whales. They fished for halibut, cod, and salmon and harvested sea birds and their eggs. Occasionally, they hunted bears and caribou.

The people collected all manner of items to

make their clothes and build their homes and tools: animal skins, feathers, bones, sod, driftwood, grasses. Most houses were made of sod and dug partly into the ground; these semi-subterranean dwellings were often reinforced with whale bones or driftwood. Seal oil was used as a fuel to light their lamps.

The Eyak

The tribe's oral history suggests that the Eyak people traveled south through Alaska's Interior, then down the Copper River, to the Gulf of Alaska Coast, where they finally settled. Though their language has links to both Athabascan and Tlingit,

linguists believe it began to develop as a separate language some 3,500 years ago.

A relatively small group, the Eyak were sometimes raided by other coastal tribes, particularly the Alutiiq residents of Prince William Sound. They had friendlier relations with the Tlingit tribes of Southeast Alaska, who had similar social structures. The two groups regularly traded goods and even intermarried. Over time, much of the Eyak population was assimilated by the Tlingit's larger and more dominant society. (Today the Eyak tribe is Alaska's smallest Native group, with a little more than 100 survivors.) The Eyak, like other coastal tribes, depended heavily on the ocean's abundance.

The Eskimos

Eskimos, the Native group most familiar to non-Alaskans, were originally divided into two subgroups. The Inupiat Eskimos settled in Alaska's Arctic region, while the Yup'ik lived in the west. Life was a constant struggle against hunger and the cold. Seasonal food was stored against future shortage and for the long dark winter; and even though his own family might be wanting, a hunter always divided a fresh kill evenly throughout the community. Status within a village was determined by hunting ability.

Eskimo village sites were chosen for availability of food sources. The Arctic coast people depended on seal, walrus and whale, while the inland Eskimos – known as the Nunamiut – lived on a diet of caribou, birds and other small game animals. Eggs were gathered, and berries, roots and wild greens were eaten fresh, or preserved in skin containers.

The Eskimos used boats called *umiaks* to hunt larger sea animals. They also used smaller, one-man craft, called kayaks. Both were made of a frame of wood covered with skins or hides. Sleds and dog teams were used for winter travel, and in summer dogs were used as pack animals.

Women were skilled in basketry and sewing. They stitched and fitted waterproof garments made of animal intestine and fish skins. The Eskimos' everyday clothing of trousers, boots and coats were sewn from skins and fur, sometimes in complex geometric designs. The coats (parkas) featured an attached hood and ruff.

Eskimos are renowned for their fine carving, especially their small ivory pieces. In early times household utensils and weapons were beautifully ornamented. Using wood, bone, baleen (bony plates that line the mouths of baleen whales), walrus ivory and fossil mammoth tusks, Eskimos crafted dishes and knives, oil lamps, small sculptures and game pieces, and goggles to protect their eyes from the glare of snow and ice. The *ulu*, or woman's knife, is found in tourist shops today and is appreciated by contemporary cooks both for its beauty and its utility.

The Russian invasion

The story of Russia's invasion of the land long inhabited by Alaska Natives begins in 1741, when two tiny vessels, the *St Peter* and the *St Paul*, captained respectively by a Dane, Vitus Bering, and a Russian, Alexei Chirikof, set sail from Russia.

When Chirikof sighted land, it was probably the west side of Prince of Wales Island in Southeast Alaska. He sent a group of men ashore in a long boat. When the first group failed to return, he sent a second. Eerily, that group also vanished. Most likely, the men drowned or were killed by Indians. Chirikof pulled anchor and moved on.

In the meantime, Bering and the crew of the *St Peter* sighted a towering peak on the Alaska mainland – Mount St Elias, which at 18,000ft (5,500 meters) is second only to Mount McKinley among Alaska's highest mountains. Turning westward, Bering anchored his vessel off Kayak Island, in

Prince William Sound, while crew members went ashore to explore and find water.

Alerted by these explorers to the riches represented by the fur-bearing marine life and mammals, Russia threw itself wholeheartedly into setting up hunting and trading outposts.

For the Native populations, the coming of the Russians was an unprecedented disaster. Rather than hunting the marine life for themselves, the Russians forced the Aleut people to do the work for them. Hostages were taken, families split up, individuals forced to leave their villages and settle elsewhere. Eighty percent of the Aleut population was destroyed by violence and European diseases,

against which they had no defenses, during the first two generations of Russian contact.

Other Europeans

About this time, the British were continuing their search for the Northwest Passage, the fabled water route between the Atlantic and the Pacific. In 1778 Captain James Cook sailed north from Vancouver Island, through the Inside Passage and then along the Gulf Coast, to the Aleutians. Along the way, he explored a narrow embayment that would later be given his name: Cook Inlet. The Russians tried to impress him with the extent of their control over the region, but Cook saw how tenuous was the position of this ragtag group of hunters and traders stationed 3,000 miles (4,800km) from their homeland.

LEFT: traditional native headdresses.
RIGHT: Captain James Cook, who arrived in 1778.

Although Cook died in Hawaii after visiting Alaska, his crew continued on to Canton, China, where they sold their Alaskan sea otter pelts for outlandishly high prices. Britain became interested and increased its sailings along the northwest coast. Then came the Spanish, already well established on the coast of California.

Gaining a foothold

The Russians were determined to dig in and keep Alaska's fur wealth for themselves. One particularly ruthless individual, Grigor Ivanovich Shelikof, arrived in Three Saints Bay on Kodiak Island in 1784 with two ships, the *Three Saints* and the *St*

Simon. Fearing the foreigners, the island's Alutiiq residents tried to drive off the Russians, but failed. Shelikof responded by killing hundreds and taking hostages to enforce the obedience of the rest.

Having established his authority on Kodiak Island, Shelikof founded the first permanent Russian settlement in Alaska on the island's Three Saints Bay, built a school to teach the Natives to read and write Russian, and introduced the Russian Orthodox religion.

In 1790, Shelikof, back in Russia, hired Alexander Baranov to manage his Alaskan fur enterprise. Baranov moved the colony to the northeast end of Kodiak Island, where timber was available: the site is now the city of Kodiak. Russian members of the colony took Alutiiq wives and started families whose names survive today: Panamaroff, Petrikoff, Kvasnikoff, for instance. Baranov himself proved brilliant at managing the Russians who were the permanent hunting contingent on Kodiak Island. He also set up comparatively humane ground rules for interaction with the Koniag Natives.

Colonial powers

The Hudson's Bay Company, formed by the British in 1821, set up a post on the southern edge of Russian America in 1833. The British firm, more organized and better run than the Russian, began siphoning off trade.

Baranov began to depend heavily on American supply ships, since they came much more frequently than Russian ones. Also, Americans could sell furs in Canton (closed to the Russians).

The downside of the US presence was that American hunters and trappers encroached on territory the Russians considered theirs. In 1812 a

THE RISE AND FALL OF RUSSIA'S TRADE

In 1795, Alexander Baranof, concerned by the presence of non-Russian Europeans trading with Natives in southeast Alaska, established Mikhailovsk 6 miles (10km) north of present-day Sitka, on land he bought from the Tlingits. For a while, the Russians and Tlingits peacefully co-existed. But in 1802, while Baranof was away, Tlingits from a neighboring settlement, perhaps ruing their decision to allow the strangers onto their territory, attacked and destroyed Mikhailovsk. Intent on revenge, Baranof returned in 1804 with a Russian warship and razed the Tlingit village. He then built the settlement of New Archangel, which became the capital of Russian America.

Meanwhile, as Baranof secured the Russians' physical presence in Alaska, back in Russia the Shelikof family continued to seek control of Alaska's fur trade. In 1799, Shelikof's son-in-law, Nikolay Petrovich Rezanov, had acquired a monopoly on the American fur trade from Tsar Paul I. Rezanov then formed the Russian-American Company. As part of the deal, the Tsar expected the company first to establish new settlements in Alaska and then carry out an expanded colonization program.

By 1804, Alexander Baranof, now manager of the Russian-American Company, had consolidated the company's hold on fur trade activities in the Americas. But despite all these efforts, the Russians never fully colonized Alaska; for the most part they clung to the coast, shunning the rugged inland. By the 1830s their monopoly on trade in the region was weak enough to allow in the Hudson's Bay Company.

settlement was reached giving the Russians exclusive rights to the fur trade above 55°N latitude, the Americans to that below. The agreement didn't settle matters, however, and with Baranov's retirement in 1818 the Russian hold on Alaska was further weakened.

When the Russian-American Company's charter was renewed in 1821, it stipulated that the chief managers from then on be naval officers. Unfortunately, most naval officers did not have any experience in the fur trade, so the company suffered under a string of incompetent, albeit sometimes well-meaning, "governors."

The second charter also tried to cut off all con-

for the Russians in Alaska, for those coastal Alaska Natives who had survived contact – primarily the Aleuts, Alutiiqs and Tlingits – conditions improved, if only slightly.

The Tlingits were never conquered, and continued to wage guerrilla warfare on the Russians into the 1850s. The Aleuts, many of whom had been removed from their home islands and sent as far south as California to hunt sea otter for the Russians, continued to decline in population during the 1840s. For them, the naval officers of the Russian-American Company were a blessing: they established schools and hospitals for the Aleuts, and gave them jobs. Russian Orthodox clergy moved

tact with foreigners, especially the competitive Americans. But this strategy backfired, since the Russian colony had become used to relying on American supply ships, and the United States had become a valued customer for furs. Eventually the Russian-American Company entered into an agreement with the Hudson's Bay Company, which gave the British rights to sail through Russian territory. Pacts were also signed in the mid-1820s that allowed both British and US vessels to land at Russian ports.

Although the mid-1800s were not a good time

into the Aleutian Islands. Slowly, the Aleut population began to increase.

An American buy-out

By the 1860s the Russians were considering ridding themselves of Russian America. Overhunting had severely reduced the fur-bearing animal population, and competition from the British and Americans made things worse. This, combined with the difficulties of supplying and protecting such a distant colony, caused interest to wane.

A Russian emissary approached the US Secretary of State, William Henry Seward, about a possible sale, and in 1867 the US Congress, at Seward's urging, agreed to buy Russian America for $7.2 million – just under 2 cents an acre. ❏

LEFT: Grigor Ivanovich Shelikof, who founded the first permanent Russian settlement in Alaska.
ABOVE: William Seward (seated) buying for the US.

THE MAKING OF MODERN ALASKA

People regarded the new possession as a wild land, producing nothing but furs, until the discovery of gold in 1896 made the world sit up and take notice. In the 20th century the discovery of oil would change Alaska's fortunes yet again

America wasn't sure what, exactly, it had acquired when it bought Alaska. The interior had been little touched by the Russians, who had stayed in the coastal areas. US exploration, too, had been limited. In 1865, Western Union had decided to lay a telegraph line through Alaska across the Bering Strait to Siberia, where it would connect with an Asian line. Robert Kennicott, part of a Western Union surveying effort, had led his crew to Nulato on the banks of the Yukon River. He died the following year and William H. Dall took charge of scientific research. The Western Union expedition conducted the first scientific studies of the region and produced the first map of the entire Yukon River.

That same year (1866), workers finally succeeded in laying an Atlantic undersea telegraph cable, and the Alaskan overland project was abandoned. Dall returned to Alaska many times, recording many geographical features. A breed of sheep and a type of porpoise bear his name.

The Alaska Commercial Company also contributed to the growing exploration of Alaska in the last decades of the 1800s, building trading posts along the Interior's many rivers. Small parties of trappers and traders entered the Interior.

Exploring the Interior

Army officers sometimes undertook their own explorations. In a four-month journey, Lt Frederick Schwatka and his party rafted the Yukon from Lake Lindeman in Canada to Saint Michael near the river's mouth on the Bering Sea. Lt Henry T. Allen made an even more remarkable journey. In 1885 Allen and four others left the Gulf of Alaska, followed the Copper River to its headwaters, crossed the Alaska range and traveled down the Tanana River to the Yukon, portaged to the Kanuti and then the Koyukuk rivers. Allen went up the Koyukuk, then back down to the Yukon, crossed over to the coastal village of Unalakleet, and then made his way to Saint Michael. In all, his team explored about 1,500 miles (2,400km) of Interior Alaska.

Whether the United States knew what it had or not, the territory still needed to be governed. Unfortunately, back in Washington, DC, legislators had their hands full with post-Civil War reconstruction issues. As a result, a US Army officer, General Jefferson C. Davis, was put in charge.

The gold strike

It was the discovery of gold in the Yukon in 1896 that finally made the US (and the rest of the world) sit up and take notice of America's northern possession. A wave of fortune hunters clamored for passage to the Klondike.

The Klondike was in Canada's Yukon Territory, not in Alaska (as many would-be miners believed), but the easiest route was by ship to Skagway, in Southeast Alaska. Once in Skagway, miners had their choice of two brutal passes across the mountains to the Yukon gold fields: White Pass, also called Dead Horse Trail, because it was littered with corpses of pack animals, or the Chilkoot Trail, an old route used by Natives.

Alaska, in fact, had plenty of gold of its own, and many who didn't make their fortunes in the Klondike strike came back to look for it. An

nette, who had been forced to disembark from the steamer *Lavelle Young (see panel below)* with his entire load of supplies – some of which he was happy to sell to Pedro.

It was a match made in heaven: Pedro and his partner were delighted to be spared the long walk to Circle City, and Barnette was equally delighted to see his first customers walking out of the wilderness. Replenished with supplies, Pedro resumed prospecting and finally struck gold in July 1902. Shortly afterwards Barnette's outpost was transformed into a booming town. Named Fairbanks in honor of a US senator, the settlement grew as more miners and new businesses arrived. Public

earlier strike had established Juneau in Southeast Alaska, and gold was found in Nome in 1899. A combination of fortune and misfortune led to a gold strike and the birth of Fairbanks in the early 1900s. For several years a prospector called Felix Pedro had been searching the Tanana Hills of Alaska's Interior for a gold-rich creek he had stumbled upon years earlier but had been forced to abandon. As the summer of 1901 drew to a close, Pedro and his partner prepared to embark on a 165-mile (265-km) walk to Circle City for supplies. Plans changed when the men met E.T. Bar-

LEFT: troughs were constructed to separate gold from soil during the Klondike Gold Rush.
ABOVE: the Commerco Saloon in Nome.

BARNETTE'S GAMBLE

In 1901 E.T. Barnette had been trying to get thousands of dollars' worth of supplies up the Tanana River to Tanana Crossing, a point on the proposed Valdez-to-Eagle trade route. He convinced the captain of the steamer *Lavelle Young* to take him, his wife, his partner and the supplies to where the Chena River entered the Tanana.

The captain agreed to take Barnette farther if he could work the *Lavelle Young* through the shallow river channel, but if not the party would be put ashore. The channel proved impassable, and that was how Barnette ended up on a slough off the main Tanana River.

services, libraries and hospitals all eased the early days. Fairbanks had shanties on the fringes, but the center offered many of the conveniences to be found in more "civilized" settings. Traffic came and went on the river, and an overland route to Valdez cut days off a trip to the Lower 48.

Eventually the Tanana Mining District became a huge gold producer, and a powerful magnet for Americans and Europeans alike.

Of course, not everyone in Alaska was a gold miner. Many more found ways to profit from the gold rushes without actually panning for the metal themselves. At Ruby Creek, for example, gold strikes in 1907 and 1910 brought the predictable

THE WORLD'S RICHEST COPPER MINE

Precious and semi-precious metals to be mined in Alaska included copper. In 1910, the richest copper mine in the world started operation at Kennicott in the Wrangell-St Elias Mountains. The mine extracted more than 591,535 tons of copper ore from the earth, and in its heyday employed more than 800 workers.

Alaskans, particularly after canning was introduced. In 1878 businessmen built the first two canneries at Klawock and Sitka in southeast Alaska. In 1883 the Arctic Pack Company established a cannery at Nushagak Bay in Southwest

rush of miners to the area, giving birth to the town of Ruby. Newcomers arrived, some by small river-boats, others on large paddlewheelers. The steamers required large quantities of wood to keep them moving, and locals along the river bank were only too happy to sell them the wood.

Ruby grew from a tent city in 1911 to a bustling river port. With running water in summer, a theater, shops and cafés, it sought to provide all the amenities of its rival, Fairbanks. By 1917, at the height of the rush, creeks south of Ruby had yielded $875,000 worth of gold.

The coming of canneries

The more traditional ways of life – fishing, in particular – also provided a livelihood for many

Alaska, where they were able to exploit the immense runs of salmon.

Two years later the Alaska Packing Company opened a cannery across the bay, and by 1908, 10 canneries ringed Nushagak Bay. Kodiak's first canneries were built in the late 1800s, when word of phenomenal fish runs became widespread.

By the turn of the 20th century, commercial fishing had gained a foothold in the Aleutian Islands. Packing houses salted cod and herring, and salmon canneries were opened. But, before long, overhunting became a serious threat (see panel on opposite page).

ABOVE: the Newend & Glandon grocery store, Nome.
RIGHT: the Flying Tiger, used in Alaska in World War II.

World War II

On June 3, 1942, the Japanese launched an air attack on Dutch Harbor, a US naval base on Unalaska Island, in the Aleutians. US forces held off the planes, and the base survived this attack, and a second one, with minor damage. But on June 7 the Japanese landed on the islands of Kiska and Attu, overwhelming Attu villagers. The villagers were taken to Japan and interned for the rest of the war. Aleuts from the Pribilofs and Aleutian villages were forcibly evacuated by the United States to Southeast Alaska, where they too were interned.

In the fall of 1942, the US Navy began constructing a base on Adak, and on May 11, 1943, American troops landed on Attu, determined to retake the island. The bloody battle wore on for more than two weeks. The Japanese, who had no hope of rescue because their fleet of transport submarines had been turned back by US destroyers, fought to the last man.

The end finally came on May 29 when the Americans repelled a banzai charge. Some Japanese remained in hiding on the small island (only 35 miles long and 15 miles wide/ 56km by 24km) for up to three months after their defeat. When discovered, they killed themselves rather than surrender.

The taking of Attu was the second bloodiest battle of the Pacific theater; only Iwo Jima was more costly in terms of human lives.

The US then bombed the other occupied island, Kiska. But the Japanese, under cover of thick Aleutian fog, escaped via transport ships. After the war, the Native Attuans who had survived internment in Japan were resettled to Atka by the federal government, which considered their home villages too remote to defend.

World War II affected Alaska in unexpected ways. One was the construction of the Alaska–Canada Military Highway (Alcan), which was completed in 1942 at great speed (nine months) and great cost ($20 million) to form an overland supply route to America's "last frontier" – and northwesternmost line of defense. Running from Great Falls, Montana, to Fairbanks, the 1,420-mile (2,280-km) road – the work of 9,000 soldiers and 12,000 civilians – was the first stable link between Alaska and the rest of America.

New military bases also contributed to the growth of some cities. Anchorage almost doubled in size, from 4,200 people in 1940 to 8,000 in

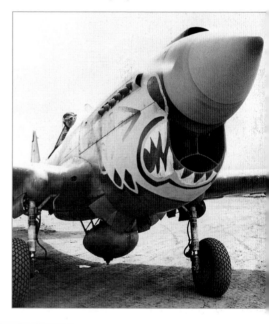

THE THREAT FROM OVERHUNTING

Whaling, a traditional marine occupation, continued well into the 20th century with no regard for overhunting. Bowhead whales, the awesome behemoths of northern seas, attracted a parade of whale hunters to the high Arctic. Following routes they had used since the end of the Pleistocene Age, the bowheads migrated twice yearly through the Bering Strait on their run from the southwestern Bering Sea to summer feeding areas in the Beaufort Sea. Weighing a ton per foot and reaching lengths of 60ft (18 meters), bowheads carry huge quantities of oil in their tissue.

Whalers seeking the oil pursued the bowhead to the edge of extinction, but their numbers have now recovered

to the point that Native whale hunters are able to harvest a limited number each year for subsistence purposes without affecting the population.

The American fishing, canning and whaling operations, as well as walrus hunting, were as unchecked as the Russians' hunting. The Aleuts soon suffered severe problems due to the depletion of the fur seals and sea otters which they needed for survival. As well as requiring the flesh for food, they also used seal skins to cover their boats, without which they couldn't hunt. The American newcomers also expanded into Interior and Arctic Alaska, exploiting the fur-bearers, fish and other game on which Natives depended.

1945. And two other catalysts were just around the corner: statehood and oil.

The push for statehood

After its purchase by the US in 1867 Alaska was variously governed by the US Army, the US Treasury Department and the US Navy. Finally, in 1884, the federal government declared the territory the District of Alaska, and a civil government was appointed by President Chester Arthur.

By the turn of the 20th century, a movement pushing for Alaska statehood had begun. But in the Lower 48, legislators were worried that Alaska's population was too sparse, its location too distant and isolated, and its economy too unstable for the territory to become a state.

World War II and the Japanese invasion of Attu and Kiska highlighted Alaska's strategic importance, and the issue of statehood was taken more seriously. Anticipating their home would eventually become a state, residents organized a constitutional convention in 1955. After 75 days, the participants drafted and approved a 14,400-word document that the National Municipal League called "one of the best, if not the best, state constitutions ever." That same year, a poll showed that 82 percent of Americans favored Alaska's becoming a state.

The discovery of oil at Swanson River on the Kenai Peninsula in 1957 helped the statehood movement, because it made Alaska less dependent on federal assistance. On January 3, 1959, President Dwight D. Eisenhower formally admitted Alaska to the union as the 49th state. William A. Egan was sworn in as the first governor, and Juneau continued to be the capital.

Disaster strikes

It was not long before the young state underwent its first trial. On March 27, 1964, the Good Friday earthquake struck Southcentral Alaska, churning the earth for four minutes. At an estimated 8.7 on the Richter scale – later revised upward to 9.2, under the current scale used to measure earthquake intensities – the Good Friday quake is the most powerful ever recorded in North America. The earthquake and its aftermath killed 131 people, including 115 Alaskans; most were drowned by the tidal waves (tsunamis) that tore apart the towns of Valdez and Chenega *(see panel below)*.

HOW THE 1964 EARTHQUAKE WREAKED HAVOC

Throughout the Prince William Sound region towns and ports were destroyed, land uplifted or shoved downward, islands tilted. The uplift destroyed salmon streams, as the fish could no longer negotiate waterfalls and other barriers to reach their spawning grounds. Ports at Valdez and Cordova were beyond repair – what land and mud slides didn't claim, ensuing fires did.

At Valdez, an Alaska Steamship Company ship was lifted by a huge wave over the docks and out to sea. Amazingly, most hands survived. Witnesses on shore swore that at one point they could see daylight all the way under the ship. There were very few witnesses, however, because most of those who had been waiting on the dockside to greet the ship were swept to their deaths.

Along Turnagain Arm, off Cook Inlet, the incoming water destroyed trees and caused cabins to sink into the mud. In Anchorage, huge chunks of road asphalt piled on top of each other like shingles and many buildings were destroyed. At Seldovia, near the junction of Kachemak Bay and Cook Inlet, fish processing facilities and an active fishing fleet were laid waste, along with Seldovia's harbor.

On Kodiak, a tidal wave wiped out the villages of Afognak, Old Harbor and Kaguyak, and damaged other communities. Seward, a thriving port town at the southern terminus of the Alaska Railroad, also lost its harbor.

Oil and land

Despite the extent of the catastrophe, Alaskans rebuilt many of the devastated communities. Four years later, the state experienced a different sort of upheaval. In the mid-1960s Alaska Natives had begun participating in state and local government and flexing their electoral muscles. More than 200 years after the arrival of the first Europeans, Natives from all ethnic groups united to claim title to the lands wrested from them. The government responded slowly until, in 1968, the Atlantic-Richfield Company discovered oil at Prudhoe Bay, and catapulted the ownership issue into the headlines.

Prudhoe Bay is on Alaska's Arctic coast, along

new urgency for an agreement, and in 1971 the Alaska Native Claims Settlement Act (ANCSA) was signed, under which the indigenous peoples relinquished aboriginal claims to their lands. In return they received title to 44 million acres (nearly 18 million hectares) of land and were paid $963 million. The land and money were divided among regional, urban and village corporations. Some have handled their funds wisely; others have not, leaving some Natives land-rich and cash-poor.

The settlement officially compensated Natives for the invasion of their lands. It also opened the way for all Alaskans to profit from the state's tremendous natural resource, oil.

the Beaufort Sea. Drilling at such a remote location would be difficult enough – but transporting the resulting crude to refineries in the Lower 48 seemed impossible. The answer seemed to be to build a pipeline to carry the oil hundreds of miles to the port of Valdez (rebuilt a few miles from the ruins of the previous town). At Valdez the oil would be loaded onto tanker ships and sent by water to the Lower 48. The plan was approved – but a permit to construct the pipeline, which would cross lands involved in the Native land claims dispute, depended on those claims being settled.

With major petro dollars on the line, there was

The pipeline

After ANCSA was signed, there remained the challenge of building a pipeline that would stretch from Arctic Alaska to Valdez. Between the two points were three mountain ranges, active fault lines, miles and miles of unstable *muskeg* (boggy ground underlain with permafrost) and the migration paths of wildlife, particularly caribou. The pipeline was designed with all these factors in mind. To counteract the unstable ground and allow animal crossings, half the 800-mile (1,280-km) pipeline is elevated on supports. The supports hold the pipe – and its cargo of hot oil – high enough to keep it from melting the permafrost and destroying the natural terrain. To help the pipeline survive an earthquake, it was laid out in a zigzag

LEFT: a Native Alaskan bark house.
ABOVE: Anchorage after the 1964 earthquake.

pattern, so that it would roll with the earth instead of breaking up. That construction was tested on November 3, 2002, when a magnitude 7.9 quake struck Alaska and the ground ruptured along a fault that ran beneath the pipeline. Many of the supports collapsed and the pipeline was temporarily shut down, but it withstood fierce shaking without any serious damage or leakage of oil.

The first oil arrived at Valdez in 1977. The total cost of the pipeline and related projects, including the tanker terminal at Valdez, 12 pumping stations and the Yukon River Bridge, was $8 billion.

During the years of pipeline construction, Anchorage and Fairbanks blossomed into bright,

of income to Alaska's state government. Since 1993, the fund has produced more revenue than the Prudhoe Bay oil fields, where production has halved from its peak in the late 1980s. Prudhoe Bay oil may dry up sometime during this century, but the fund should continue to benefit the state.

Tourism and the environment

In the second half of the 20th century, Alaska discovered another important source of revenue. Although visitors had been lured north by Alaska's natural wonders since at least the late 19th century, tourism got a big boost after World War II when men stationed in the region returned home

modern cities. As the oil bonanza took shape, per capita incomes rose throughout the state, with virtually every community benefitting. State leaders were determined that this boom would not end like the fur and gold booms – in an economic bust as soon as the resource had disappeared.

To this end, the Alaska Permanent Fund was created in 1976. Into the fund is deposited 25 percent of all mineral lease proceeds (including oil and gas). Income from the fund is divided in three ways: it pays annual dividends to all residents who apply and qualify; it adds money to the principal account to hedge against inflation; and it provides funds to the state legislature.

The fund, worth nearly $30 billion, is the largest pool of public money in the US, and a major source

praising its natural splendor. The Alcan Highway, built during the war, and the Alaska Marine Highway System, completed in 1963, made the state more accessible than before.

Tourism is now big business in Alaska: more than 1½ million people visit the state every year. Once there, they flock to the top attractions; Denali National Park, Katmai, Glacier Bay and other destinations within the Inside Passage, and the Kenai Peninsula. Wildlife-watching is a main attraction, although only a small proportion of visitors go deep into the wilderness.

ABOVE: pipeline technology in Alaska led the world.
RIGHT: tourists cruise into Misty Fiords.
FAR RIGHT: cleaning up the mess after an oil spill.

With tourism ever more vital to the economy, environmentalism has also risen in importance *(see page 59)*. Alaskans are working to balance the needs of their remarkable land with the needs of its residents. Much is already well protected – the Alaska National Interest Lands Conservation Act (ANILCA) of 1980 added 53.7 million acres (22 million hectares) to the national wildlife refuge system, parts of 25 rivers to the national wild and scenic rivers system, 3.3 million acres (1.3 million hectares) to national forest lands, and 43.6 million acres (17.5 million hectares) to national park land. As a result of the lands act, Alaska now contains two-thirds of all American national parklands.

The oil spill

Nothing better illustrates Alaska's struggle to protect the environment and to benefit from the state's natural resources, than the *Exxon Valdez* disaster. The tanker ran aground on March 24 1989, in Prince William Sound, releasing 11 million gallons (42 million liters) of crude oil into the water. The oil eventually spread along 1,100 miles (1,760km) of formerly pristine shoreline.

It was an ecological disaster of unprecedented proportions *(see panel below)*. At least 300,000 sea birds, 2,000 otters and countless other marine animals died as a result of the spill. Exxon spent $2 billion on cleaning up in the first year alone.

THE AFTERMATH OF THE OIL SPILL

During the summer of 1989, 12,000 workers descended on the soiled shores of the sound. They bulldozed blackened beaches, sucked up petroleum blobs with vacuum devices, blasted sand with hot water, polished rocks by hand, raked up oily seaweed, and sprayed fertilizer to aid the growth of oil-eating microbes.

For Alaska's tourism industry, the *Exxon Valdez* spill strained an already uneasy relationship with the state's petroleum interests. Not only did it generate horrendous international publicity but the influx of clean-up workers filled to capacity virtually every hotel and campsite in the Valdez area – which was bad news for the tourist industry, but very good for the Valdez economy.

Exxon continued its clean-up efforts into the early 1990s. In some areas, such as Smith Island, an oil-soaked wasteland after the spill, winter storms did more to wash the shore clean than any human efforts.

Government studies show the oil and the cleaning process itself caused long-term harm to the ecology of the Sound, interfering with the reproduction of birds and animals in ways that still aren't fully understood. Some fishermen, particularly those dependent on shellfish, worry about hard-to-measure impacts on their catch. Prince William Sound has largely bounced back, but some species still haven't recovered and scientists dispute the extent of the recovery

Today's issues

The past two decades have been marked by major changes in the state's economy, a push for Native sovereignty, increased friction between Alaska's urban and rural populations, declining oil revenues, and a search for new sources of revenue.

One of the biggest changes has been the economy's shift from one almost entirely dependent on resource extraction (and government employment) to a "new economy" that depends much more heavily on service industries, from tourism to shopping. Oil fields on Alaska's North Slope continue to be the primary fuel that drives Alaska's economy and state government programs, but even

oil production has slipped dramatically, to half of what it was during Prudhoe Bay's late 1980s peak. The timber and commercial fisheries industries have suffered even greater losses.

Centered in the Panhandle's Tongass National Forest, Alaska's timber industry has been on the skids since the 1980s; its two largest mills (one in Ketchikan, the other in Sitka) shut down in the 1990s due to changing Forest Service policies and decreased demand for wood pulp, causing hardships for many Southeast Alaska communities. Nowadays timber cutting and milling is done on a much smaller scale, but the widespread economic crisis predicted by many in the timber industry hasn't been realized, largely because there's been something of a tourism boom in the Panhandle.

Increased numbers of cruise ships travel the Inside Passage, bringing thousands of visitors to spend money in Southeast communities. In addition, smaller ecotour businesses are also thriving in some portions of the region.Much of the area's fishing industry, however, has been struggling.

Hard times for fishermen

Commercial fishing has been steadily declining – in some areas, precipitously – since the early 1990s. The fisheries most in trouble are those that harvest salmon. Declining numbers of fish, particularly western Alaska waters, have severely hurt rural residents who depend on commercial (and in some cases, subsistence) fishing for their livelihood. Several years in a row, the governor declared a state of emergency for parts of the state, because the salmon returns were so poor that people in many villages didn't earn enough money for necessities such as food and fuel.

THE BRIDGES THAT WENT NOWHERE

In Alaska, the saying goes, corruption flows like crude oil. Federal conspiracy, bribery, tax evasion, influence-peddling and self-dealing... all these charges and more have been leveled against Alaska's senators, congressmen and government officials, and the frequency of scandals encourage Senate committees in faraway Washington, DC, to regard it as one of the most ethically challenged states.

At the heart of many federal investigations has been the close ties between Alaska lawmakers and the powerful oil industry. Oil money doesn't talk, say cynics, it shouts. But the state's relatively small population and its remoteness from the rest of the nation can all too easily

tempt vote-hungry politicians into all manner of pork-barrel spending. One notorious example was the 2005 saga of the "bridge to nowhere," a proposed $230 million span higher than the Brooklyn Bridge intended to connect Ketchikan (population 8,900) with Gravina Island (population 50). The 15 to 30-minute wait for the ferry was inconvenient, argued local advocates, and it cost too much ($6 per car). A second, similarly priced proposal envisaged a bridge connecting Anchorage to the town of Knik (population 22).

Congress torpedoed both schemes, though it didn't reduce the amount of money allocated to Alaska in the particular appropriations bill.

Some areas, most notably Bristol Bay, have been hard hit by a double whammy: smaller numbers of fish and lower prices, brought on by a world-wide glut of salmon attributed to the rise of farmed salmon in countries like Chile, Canada, and Norway. Though Bristol Bay remains Alaska's biggest salmon fishery, its fishing fleet has had some disastrous seasons.

While salmon fishermen have struggled, commercial fishermen who ply the Gulf of Alaska and Bering Sea for bottomfish have so far continued to thrive. The North Pacific and Bering Sea bottomfish fleet continues to be the nation's richest. But many of the boat owners and fish

expanded role are national chains: huge "box stores" have been built in communities from the Panhandle to the Interior, from WalMart to Office Max, Barnes & Noble to Best Buy. New restaurants and hotel chains have been popping up, particularly in Alaska's urban centers. A high and steadily growing percentage of people now work in the service industry, where the jobs don't pay nearly as well as those in resource extraction.

Alaska's Native culture, too, has undergone some major changes. There's been a strong push for tribal sovereignty and both the federal and state governments have recognized a limited authority of tribal governments in Alaska's Native

processers are non-residents, who live in Washington and Oregon. To ensure that more of the fisheries' profits remain in Alaska, the federal agency that oversees the bottomfish industry has enacted a plan whereby Alaskan communities share a percentage of the earnings.

The retail chains arrive

Though slowed by the September 11, 2001 terrorist attacks on the US, Alaska's tourism industry continues to play an important and ever-enlarging role in the state's economy. Also playing an

LEFT: salmon fishermen have experienced hard times.
ABOVE: horse and buggy tours of Skagway indicate the growing importance of tourism in the state.

communities. Alaska's Native peoples continue to deal with the challenge of living "in two worlds" – their traditional culture, which stretches back generations, and the modern, western culture that has so greatly influenced Native communities throughout the state, in ways that have been both helpful and harmful. Few Native Alaskans would choose to return to a life without electricity, modern plumbing, snowmobiles, computers, and TV; but technological advances have also disrupted the family and community lives in many villages and Native leaders are fervently seeking a way to balance old and new.

A cultural revival begun in the late 20th century has continued to flourish as more and more people celebrate their roots and long-lived cultural values, celebrations and art, from dancing to mask making and story telling.

A cultural clash

One tradition that Native tribes continue to fight for is subsistence. Though it centers around the harvest of animals and plants, subsistence is about more than hunting, fishing, and gathering; it's a way of life that has spiritual and emotional importance to Native residents, particularly in rural areas beyond the road system. For more than 15 years, there's been a cultural clash over Native "subsistence rights." Some Alaskans – mostly white, urban sportsmen – insist that all residents must have equal access to fish and wildlife resources. However, most Alaskans – both Native and non-Native, urban and rural – agree that some sort of subsistence priority must be recognized, if the Native culture is to thrive.

There's been a strong push to change to the Alaska constitution, so that it guarantees a rural subsistence preference, but the Alaska Legislature has so far resisted enacting legislation that would allow a statewide vote. The federal government, meanwhile, has recognized a rural subsistence priority since the passage of ANILCA in 1980. Because the policies differ, the US government took over fish and wildlife management on

Alaska's federally managed lands and waters during the 1990s. This dual management system is unique to Alaska and complicates hunting and fishing regulations throughout the state.

Most Alaskans seek to heal urban vs. rural and Native vs. non-Native tensions. They also seek to find new sources of revenue to sustain and improve their lifestyles, while also protecting the magnificent wildness, abundant wildlife, and scenic splendor that makes Alaska such a unique place to live in – and to visit. ❑

ABOVE: Mina Weyliouanna hold a portrait of her grandparents by the family home collapsed by melting permafrost. Climate change has forced villagers to abandon Shishmaref, in the far north.

A YOUNG STATE

Alaska has a particular appeal for young people. Many of them have moved here from outside, probably because the state attracts those who both like and can cope with an active and not always easy life. According to the 2000 census, the average age of the population was 32.4.

Although the population is increasing rapidly, there are only about 664,000 permanent residents – very low compared with most other states in the union. Most of them live in urban areas, and more than half live in and around Anchorage.

According to the most recent estimates, Alaska Natives make up 12 percent of the population.

Economy and Ecology

Almost every dollar that flows through Alaska's economy originates from its land or water – or from government expenditures. The oil and mining industries extract vast wealth from under the ground, fishermen harvest much of the nation's seafood from the water, and loggers and tourism operators exploit the landscape itself. Other industries and the government pass those dollars from hand to hand, but natural resources are the primary fuels that drive the economy.

Oil is by far the largest industry; fishing is second and employs more people, but has suffered a downturn, largely because of competition from fish-farming operations in other parts of the world. Tourism also is a big employer. The logging industry has shrunk under the pressure of new environmental concerns. The government — federal, state, and local — employs more people than any other industry, and state government is largely funded by oil. The service industry has grown importance and employs a sizeable portion of Alaska's workers, but typically pays less than resource-extraction industries.

Oil and the environment

It's not surprising that most Alaskans support more resource development. Every new oil field discovered on the North Slope creates jobs and new government revenues that affect every citizen. When the salmon season is good, coastal towns thrive. And the flow of summer visitors employs thousands.

But many Alaskans also advocate environmental protection, and not only because they tend to be young and to spend time outdoors enjoying the beauty of the place. Fishermen know that oil spills damage the waters from which they draw their livelihood. Tourism operators know their clients aren't interested in visiting areas that have been clear-cut for logging (poor logging techniques can also threaten salmon-spawning streams).

When, in 1989, the tanker *Exxon Valdez* spilled 11 million gallons (42 million liters) of crude oil in Prince William Sound, both industries worked as hard to clean up the image of their products as Exxon did to scrape the oil off the shore *(see page 55)*. The fishing industry has largely recovered, but some species — herring and pink salmon, for instance – have not fully rebounded. Visitors to the Sound still see abundant wildlife, but again there's evidence

that some species, including orcas, have not yet recovered from the spill's toxic effects.

Large-scale logging has altered the environment in ways that affect other industries. Besides the ruined vistas, fishermen worry about logging near streams, which can harm or even destroy the habitat critical to spawning salmon and other fish.

Yet tourism and fishing, if unchecked, can harm the environment as well. In Glacier Bay National Park, environmental groups sued the National Park Service to stop it granting more permits for cruise ships to enter the bay, contending that they are scaring away the humpback whales. Cruise ship companies have also drawn criticism – and large fines – for pol-

luting the waters and air in southeast Alaska. There are questions, too, about noisy helicopter sightseeing in wilderness areas, a proposal for a new road in Denali National Park, and large-scale tourism.

As for fishing, environmentalists blame large-scale factory trawlers operating in the Bering Sea for reducing marine mammal populations by taking too many fish from the food chain. There are also concerns that bottom-fishing trawlers wreak havoc on the ocean bottom with their gear.

Only a fraction of 1 percent of Alaska's landmass is privately owned. The federal government controls more than half, and the state government about a third. It is therefore government's job to ensure that Alaska's lands, waters, and air are protected, even as companies exploit its natural resources. ❑

RIGHT: the Prudhoe Bay oil refinery.

VISITING ALASKA'S NATIVES

Tourists are a useful source of income as they experience
Alaskan Native cultures, but the people don't want
to be treated simply as a visitor attraction

Many Native Alaskans live a subsistence lifestyle that still depends upon collecting meat and fish during the abundant summer months and preparing it for storage to sustain them over the long winter. In the southern part of the state, Natives depend upon deer, salmon and other food from the sea. In the Interior, the Athabascans fish on the rivers and hunt caribou, moose, black bears, and waterfowl. Farther north, Eskimos hunt whales and seals, caribou and polar bears, geese and seabirds.

Most villages are located in remote areas without roads to connect them with cities and luxuries such as large well-stocked grocery stores. Until the early 1990s, about the only outsiders who spent any time in villages were friends, relatives, health care workers or teachers. Now the list is growing.

Villages welcome visitors

An international fascination with indigenous people has spread to Alaska, and village residents from Saxman Native Village in Southeast Alaska to Gambell on St Lawrence Island in the Bering Sea are cautiously opening their doors to visitors. Visiting an Alaska Native village can be a great adventure for people who are both flexible and open-minded. Organized tours are now offered to more than a dozen villages.

In these encounters, both the visitors and the visited learn from each other. Visitors learn how Natives live in various parts of the state and along the way they discard stereotypes about igloos, wardrobes of animal skins and rubbing noses.

PRECEDING PAGES: Yup'ik Natives ice fishing.
LEFT: an Inupiat walrus-skin blanket toss
to celebrate a good spring whaling season.
RIGHT: a Tlingit Indian girl.

"Visitors come with an expectation that they're going to go back in time," says the Alaska Native Tourism Council, an organization formed in 1992 to promote rural tourism and help Native groups who operate tours. "They find out that visually it's very familiar in terms of clothing – people wearing Nike tennis shoes – but the culture and life of the people haven't changed a lot. Value systems are still deeply rooted in the past and in their culture."

In recent years, as more and more young people leave villages for life in the cities, Natives have worked to keep their culture and their language alive. Tourism now provides an impetus for them to do so. Young Natives learn the dances and stories of old, passing them on to their own children and to the rest of the world.

Selling ancient rights

The 20th century brought numerous changes to the Native communities. Thirteen regional, four urban and 200 Native village corporations were formed to manage money and land received from the government as a result of the 1971 Alaska Native Claims Settlement Act. The measure approved the transfer of 44 million acres (nearly 18 million hectares) and $963 million to corporations in exchange for giving up their aboriginal rights to the land.

Some of these corporations have been phenomenally successful, parlaying the oil, mineral and other natural resource wealth of their lands into large annual dividends for members. Others made bad investments, and some were tainted by corruption. There has been increased debate as to whether the corporations serve the best interests of Alaska's Native peoples.

Although snow-machines have largely replaced sled dog teams as a means of winter travel and boats with motors are preferred to the skin boats that their ancestors used for fishing and hunting, Natives still follow traditional ways. Now, however, they must have money to buy gasoline for their snow-machines and bullets for their guns. Their subsistence way of life requires modern tools. It's a delicate balance. Natives struggle to

THE BEST WAY TO VIEW NATIVE VILLAGES

Contact the village council before you show up, to make sure that residents are happy to see visitors, or find a tour operator that includes Native villages on its itineraries. One company that arranges customized tours around the state is Explore Tours, 1415 East Tudor Road, Anchorage, AK 99507, tel: (907) 786-0192 or (800) 523-7405; www.exploretours.com. Tour Arctic highlights traditional Inupiat culture and village tours in northwest Alaska; 1001 E. Benson Road, Anchorage, AK 99508, tel: (907) 273-2457 or (800) 468-2248; www.tour-arctic.com. The Northern Alaska Tour Company does ecotours that emphasize both natural and Native cultural history; PO Box 82991-W, Fairbanks, AK, 99708, tel: (907) 474-8600 or (800) 474

1986; www.northernalaska.com. Another good resource is the book *Nae'da* (meaning "Our friends"), which includes contact information for all of the state's village tribal councils; for more information, go to www.thecirifoundation .org/publications.

Some residents worry about tourists walking into their houses unannounced, as if they were strolling into a Disneyland attraction, or indiscriminately snapping photographs. It is common courtesy to ask before taking pictures of people. Some villages, such as Gambell, prefer that you ask before taking any photographs at all. And the travel brochure publicizing Arctic Village specifically prohibits the use of video cameras.

keep their own culture intact as they embrace the conveniences of modern society.

The modern world, which lures away younger Natives, has also brought its share of ills to Native communities and many struggle to overcome high rates of alcoholism, suicide and domestic strife. A number of villages have voted to stay dry, with no alcohol allowed.

Yet modern conveniences have also made life a little easier. Under her fur parka, an Eskimo woman may be wearing a dress bought through a mail-order catalog. Her whaler husband and friends stay in touch with short-wave radio as they track movements of their prey through ocean

young people, the village decided to try tourism. It wasn't an easy decision: the 250 residents took seven years to achieve unanimous agreement. The first season, only a dozen people visited; the second, over 20 arrived. Instead of steady growth, the number of visitors has remained small at Huslia and many other small villages, which are remote and expensive to reach. In some ways that's a blessing: small communities would find it hard to handle large crowds of tourists. On the other hand, tourism hasn't brought the economic boom that many villagers anticipated. In some instances, as at Huslia, tourism programs have been temporarily put on hold, or even abandoned.   ❏

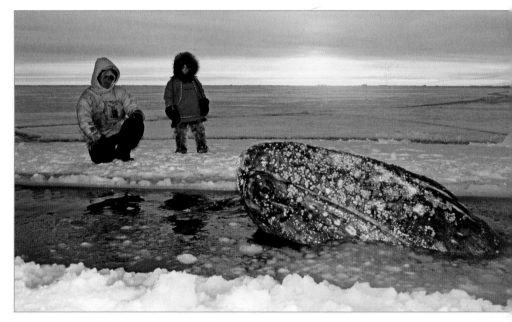

waters, and when the meat is consumed raw, as in the old days, they may supplement that meat with store-bought foods.

Tourism disappoints

For many remote communities, welcoming tourists is a step prompted by an increasingly gloomy economic outlook. In the Interior village of Huslia, for example, the Federal Bureau of Land Management had been hiring young villagers to fight summer forest fires, but a series of rainy seasons put a damper on that. To employ the

LEFT: sleds remain a practical means of transport.
ABOVE: an Inuit man and child contemplate a gray whale trapped in ice off Barrow.

LIFE IN WINTER

Sled dog racing, skiing, and aurora watching all help Alaskans get through the long, cold winters

Winter is Alaska's longest season, and its quietest – at least from a tourism perspective. Most visitors explore the state between the end of May and the beginning of September, when daylight hours are long and temperatures warm – though, in some parts, warm may mean only 50 or 60°F (10 or 15°C).

By mid-September, most tourists have gone south with the waterfowl and locals have begun preparing for the winter, which in most of the state will last seven or eight months. Yet Alaska is not a frozen wasteland, and unlike bears, its human residents do not go into hibernation.

The lowest temperature

As would be expected, Alaska's Interior and Arctic regions experience the most severe and prolonged winter conditions. The coldest temperature ever recorded in Alaska was –80°F (–62°C), at Prospect Creek Camp in January 1971. Barrow, the nation's northernmost outpost, averages sub-zero temperatures from December through March.

Temperatures bottom out in February, which has average daily lows of –25°F (–32°C) and highs of –12°F (–24°C). But Barrow isn't just frigid in winter – it's also very dark. The long winter night begins at noon on November 18 and lasts through January 24. That's 67 days from sunset until the next sunrise.

Winter in Anchorage

By comparison, Anchorage is downright bright and balmy. The city's shortest day (the winter solstice, December 21) has 5 hours and 28 minutes of daylight, plus a couple of hours of twilight. Its

LEFT: year-round cabins need to be well-insulated.
RIGHT: protection against the cold is essential.

coldest month, December, has average daily highs and lows of 20° and 6°F (–7° and –15°C). Even more moderate conditions are experienced in Southeast Alaska. Ketchikan, near the Panhandle's southern tip, has 7 hours, 6 minutes of daylight on the winter solstice and even its coldest month, January, averages above-freezing temperatures of 34°F (1°C).

For further evidence of Alaska's winter extremes, consider that the state's record snowfall for one season is 974.5 inches (2,475cm), at Thompson Pass (near Valdez) during the winter of 1952–53; nearly 300 inches (760cm) fell in a single month, February. The one-day record, also at Thompson Pass, is 62 inches (1.6 meters) in December 1955. Barrow holds the state record for the least snowfall in one season: 3 inches (7.5cm), in 1935–36.

The darkness and cold produce a variety of malaises, from cabin fever to seasonal affective disorder (SAD). To combat winter woes and help the longest season pass more quickly, residents around the state participate in a variety of activities and special events – some strenuous and skillful, others just plain fun.

Sled dog racing

Among the most popular cures for seasonal blues is sled dog racing, Alaska's official winter sport. And the best known of the mushing events is the Iditarod Trail Sled Dog Race, also known as "The Last Great Race" *(see pages 308–9)*.

The Iditarod is billed as a 1,049-mile (1,690-km) race but in reality mushers and dogs travel well over 1,100 miles (1,770km). The race celebrates the "mushers" who helped open up the state in the early 1900s and also commemorates a frantic dash in 1925 to get diphtheria vaccine to Nome, which was on the verge of an epidemic. The trail follows an historic freight-and-mail route established during the gold rush of the early 1900s. It crosses two mountain ranges, runs along the Yukon River for about 150 miles (240km) and crosses the pack ice of Norton Sound. From its

RIDING THE IRON DOGS

While some Alaskans choose to explore the winter landscape behind a team of sled dogs, many others prefer "iron dogs." Snowmobiles, also locally known as snowmachines and sno-gos, have replaced sled dogs as the primary means of winter transportation in most of rural Alaska, where roads are minimal. Though commonly used by bush residents for work, or simply "getting from here to there," snowmachines are also popular for recreation and racing in both urban and rural Alaska.

The most challenging snowmobile race by far is the Iron Dog Gold Rush Classic, a long-distance event along the Iditarod Trail between from Wasilla to Nome, then on to Fairbanks (a distance of nearly 2,000 miles/3,200km).

Another intriguing race is the Arctic Man Ski & Sno-Go Classic ("The Ultimate Adrenaline Rush"), which is staged in April in the Hoodoo Mountains near Paxson; on uphill stretches, a snowmobile pulls a skier at speeds of up to 86 miles an hour (138km/h).

It's relatively rare to see skiers and snow-machiners enjoying each other's company in the backcountry. Some recreational areas popular with both user groups – for instance, Chugach State Park in the mountains just east of Anchorage, Hatcher Pass in the Talkeetna Mountains and Turnagain Pass on the Kenai Peninsula – have designated snowmobile corridors, to minimize conflicts between these motorized and "quiet" human-powered activities.

ceremonial start in Anchorage – the first Saturday in March – until the final musher has reached the finish line in Nome, the Iditarod is given center stage throughout Alaska.

A contest in which men and women compete as equals – four titles were won by the late Susan Butcher, another by Libby Riddles – the Iditarod not only pits competitors against each other, but also against the wilderness and brutal winter weather. But most importantly, the Iditarod celebrates Alaska's frontier past. The first Iditarod took place in 1967, as a two-day event that covered 50 miles (80km). Six years later the inaugural race from Anchorage to Nome was staged.

February between Fairbanks and Whitehorse, in Canada's Yukon Territory.

At the other end of the mushing spectrum are the so-called "speed races," or sprints. People of all abilities and ages compete in limited-class races (most are divided into three-, five-, six- or eight-dog categories), while more serious speed mushers often "graduate" to the unlimited open-class events, which offer greater financial awards and prestige – and greater challenges.

The two most prestigious speed races are the North American Open, a three-day event staged each March in Fairbanks, and the Fur Rendezvous World Championship, another three-day affair

The mushers are the glamour figures in sled dog racing and the top contenders are household names. But many would agree that the dogs are the true heroes, the athletic stars, of this and other mushing events. They're specially bred, raised, trained and conditioned to race.

Speed and stamina

While the Iditarod is unquestionably Alaska's best-known sled dog race, dozens – perhaps hundreds – of other competitions are staged around the state. Another major long-distance event is the 1,000-mile (1,600-km) Yukon Quest, staged each

LEFT: high noon in Fairbanks in mid-winter.
ABOVE: a spectacular entry for an ice-carving contest.

IS SLED DOG RACING CRUEL?

Sled dog races, especially the Iditarod, have come under pressure in recent years from animal rights organizations who claim that, although most dogs are treated well, too many die or are injured in training or in a race. Figures are hard to come by, but causes of death include strangulation in towlines, internal hemorrhaging after being gougled by a sled, heart failure, and pneumonia.

Some sled mushers are alleged to abuse their dogs. In 1990 the iditarod's winner was given a lifetime ban for hitting a dog with a metal snow hook (although he was allowed back into the race 10 years later). Similar allegations against a musher in 2007 prompted the Iditarod's organizers to offer an independent investigation.

(teams run 25 miles/40km each day), and the main attraction of Anchorage's mid-February winter festival. While Iditarod champions such as Butcher, five-time champion Rick Swenson, and four-time winner Doug Swingley of Montana (the first "outsider" to win the Iditarod) have achieved far greater acclaim outside Alaska, several of the premier speed racers – George Attla, Charlie Champaine and Roxy Wright-Champaine among them – are every bit as famous within the state.

In addition to the well-known titles there is a range of middle-distance races, ranging from 100 to 300 miles (160 to 480km). A growing number of Alaskans also run dog teams purely for recre-

ation and several companies in the state's South-central, Interior and Arctic regions now offer sled dog rides and trips that range from a few hours in urban Alaska to a week or more in the state's remote wilderness.

Nordic and alpine skiing

Skiing is especially popular in and around the main towns. Anchorage has one of the nation's premier cross-country ski-trail systems: more than 100 miles (160km) of trails wind through a variety of terrain, with opportunities for both traditional diagonal striders and skate skiers.

The city's best-known Nordic center, at Kin-

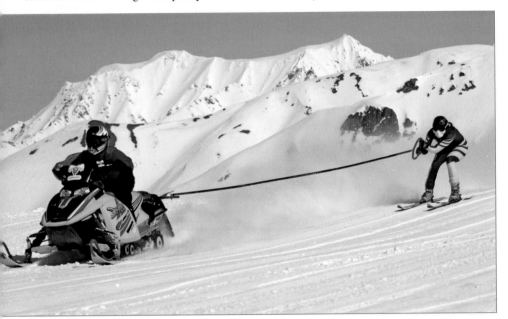

THE NORTHERN LIGHTS

Alaska is the best place in the USA to view the aurora borealis, or northern lights. Literally meaning "dawn of the north," this is a solar-powered light show that occurs in the earth's upper atmosphere when charged particles from the sun collide with gas molecules.

The northern lights occur most intensely in an oval band that stretches across Alaska (as well as Canada, Greenland, Iceland, Norway and Siberia). All the state, except parts of the southwest and the Aleutian Chain, are within the "auroral zone," with the best light shows visible north of the Alaska Range. One of the best views to be had is in Fairbanks, which calls itself an "auroral destination," in an attempt to lure winter visitors.

The aurora occurs throughout the year, but can be seen only on clear nights when the sky has darkened. In Alaska that means from fall through spring, with peak viewing in winter. Colors vary from pale yellowish green – the most common shade – to red, blue and purplish-red. Northern lights often begin as long, uniform bands, stretching along the horizon, but may develop vertical bars or rays, that give the appearance of waving curtains.

Some people claim they can not only see the aurora but can hear it as well. Scientists at the University of Alaska, Fairbanks, who have been studying the northern lights for years, are interested in such reports, but have yet to confirm them.

caid Park, has hosted several national championship races, as well as the Olympic Trials. For those who want backcountry solitude, Chugach State Park – Anchorage's "backyard wilderness" – has dozens of valleys and ridges to explore. Several well-used trailheads are within a half-hour's drive of downtown.

Other popular Nordic backcountry destinations within a half-day's drive of Anchorage include the Talkeetna Mountains, Chugach National Forest on the Kenai Peninsula, and the Peters Hills, the foothills of the Alaska Range.

While most of Alaska's lodges shut down for winter, a few cater to cross-country skiers. The

hill ski areas. They range from Alyeska's world-class facility in Girdwood, about 40 miles (65km) south of Anchorage, to the single-run volunteer operation at Salmonberry Hill outside Valdez.

The most unusual of Alaska's eight downhill sites (which include three in the Anchorage area, two near Fairbanks and one on Douglas Island, 12 miles/20km from Juneau) is the Eyak Ski Area, near the coastal community of Cordova. The tiny, single-seat Prince lift here used to operate at Sun Valley until it was replaced in 1969 by a triple-seat chair. Eventually the lift made its way north to Cordova, where it has been in operation every winter since 1974. ❏

three most popular Nordic retreats are Hatcher Pass Lodge, in the Talkeetna Mountains; Sheep Mountain Lodge along the Glenn Highway; and Denali View Chalet – also known as Sepp Weber's Cabin, after its builder and owner – in the Alaska Range foothills. Each of the lodges offers groomed trails, wood-fired saunas, heated rooms, home-cooked meals and other amenities. Both Hatcher Pass and Sheep Mountain are accessible by road, while Denali View is about 2 miles (3.2km) from the nearest road.

Though not known as a magnet for alpine skiers, Alaska nonetheless offers a wide variety of down-

LEFT: ski contestants in winter at Summit Lake.
ABOVE: traditional cross-country skiers near Nome.

WILDLIFE

Far from being a wasteland permanently covered with snow and ice, Alaska is a world teeming with wildlife, from birds to bears

More than 400 different species of birds have been officially documented in Alaska. With few exceptions, these species inhabit the state only during spring and summer and then migrate south. They come north to take advantage of the eruption of life which occurs on the tundra each spring, when a multi-colored explosion of flowers covers the ground and clouds of insects fill the air. The tundra offers an almost unlimited banquet of foodstuffs – plants, insects and small animals – for birds attempting to raise their hungry young.

Long-distance flyers

The Arctic tern is the world's record holder for migration distances. These gull-like birds breed and nest on the shores of Alaskan tundra ponds. In late summer, the terns and their young start a migration that will eventually take them all the way to the Antarctic. Summer is just beginning in the Southern Hemisphere as the terns arrive. The round-trip flight from Alaska to the Antarctic and back is approximately 25,000 miles (40,000km).

Other long-distance commuters include the American golden plover, the surfbird, the long-tailed jaeger and the Arctic warbler. Some plovers winter on the Hawaiian Islands while others migrate to Argentina. Tierra del Fuego, at the tip of South America, is the winter home of the surfbird; the jaeger spends its winters on the open ocean in the central Pacific or near Japan; the Arctic warbler resides in southern Asia in winter.

Alaska's state bird, the willow ptarmigan, was chosen by a vote of the state's schoolchildren. Along with its close relatives, the rock ptarmigan

and the white-tailed ptarmigan, the willow ptarmigan lives in Alaska year-round. A ptarmigan is brown in summer and white in winter, changing to blend with the surroundings. During extremely cold winter weather, ptarmigans keep warm by burrowing into snow drifts. The ptarmigan is usually found on high ground: look for them in willow thickets and on the open tundra.

While near tundra ponds, look for loons, grebes, geese, ducks, phalaropes, yellowlegs and sandpipers. On the tundra, watch for long-tailed jaegers, golden plovers, whimbrels, snow buntings, wheatears, sparrows and water pipits. Owls, woodpeckers, gray jays and chickadees are common in forested areas, as are goshawks, the large, handsome birds of prey which swoop down

LEFT: gray woves are watchful but keep out of sight.
RIGHT: the great gray owl.

through the trees and catch their prey completely unaware. Gulls, terns, murrelets, auklets, shearwaters (known for their highly developed powers of navigation), cormorants and puffins are found along the coastlines.

Mammals

The premier wildlife-viewing area in Alaska is Denali National Park *(see pages 229–39)*. Grizzlies, moose, Dall sheep, caribou, red foxes, snowshoe hares, beavers, Arctic ground squirrels, and hoary marmots are seen by almost everyone who visits Denali. The park's shuttle bus system is designed to maximize wildlife sightings. Because

the buses cause comparatively little disturbance, many animals, including grizzlies, can be photographed within 300 feet (90 meters) of the road.

If you are lucky, you may also spot wolves in Denali. Ranging from black to white, but more commonly gray in color, Alaska's wolves may be seen traveling alone, in pairs, or larger packs. Though they are usually not fond of human company and are more likely to be heard than seen, at Denali they have become habituated to the presence of vehicles and are sometimes spotted near the Park Road – or even trotting along it.

Denali and several other Alaskan national parks are textbook examples of what wilderness parks

WHERE EAGLES DARE

Alaska is the stronghold of the bald eagle, the national bird of the United States. More of them live in Alaska than in the other 49 states combined. White heads, white tails and 8-ft (2.4-meter) wing-spans make them easily identifiable, even at a great distance. They are most often seen where fish are common, especially along the coastal areas of southern Alaska, from the Aleutians to the southernmost Panhandle.

The best place to see large gatherings of bald eagles is near Haines, during October and November. A late run of chum salmon into the Chilkat River, just north of town, attracts thousands of bald eagles, which feed on the dead or spent salmon. A single tree may contain dozens of

roosting eagles – an extraordinary sight. Because fish are available throughout the winter in coastal areas, these bald eagles have no need to migrate from Alaska. You can visit the American Bald Eagle Foundation in Haines *(see page 151)* for attractive displays and useful information about the birds, which are no longer classified as an endangered species.

Golden eagles, the darker cousins of the bald eagle, are normally found in Alaska's Interior and Arctic regions, soaring above tundra and mountainous areas. They hunt rodents, such as the Arctic ground squirrel, rather than fish. The Polychrome Pass area of Denali National Park is an excellent place to see golden eagles.

were meant to be. A half-dozen or more protect entire ecosystems in a condition nearly identical to their original state. The population levels of wildlife such as Dall sheep, moose, caribou, hares, marmots, and ground squirrels are controlled not by human intervention, but by the area's natural predators: grizzly and black bears, lynx, wolver-

brown bears inhabit the coast. Partly because of the almost unlimited supply of salmon, adult male brown bears can grow to weights of more than 1,200 lbs (540 kg).

The best place to see them is at Brooks River and Camp, in Katmai, and the best time is in July, the peak of the sockeye salmon run. The McNeil River State Game Sanctuary, just outside the park, provides the ultimate bear-watching experience, but you literally have to enter a lottery to get in *(see page 340)*. A third option is to do guided day trips from Anchorage, Soldotna or Homer to view bears on the west side of Cook Inlet. Another excellent region to see brown bears is the Tongass

ines, foxes, and wolves, and raptors. If you are lucky enough to see a grizzly dig out a ground squirrel from its burrow or a wolf pack chase a caribou herd, you will be witnessing a scene which could have taken place during the last Ice Age.

Alaska's bears

Katmai National Park *(see pages 332–5)* is the most popular place to closely observe brown bears. At one time, grizzles and browns were classified as different species but they are now known to be the same animal (*Ursus arctos*). Grizzlies are residents of Alaska's inland regions, while

National Forest in Southeast Alaska, especially Admiralty Island where there's a bear-viewing program at Pack Creek. Admiralty's Native name is Kootsnoowoo, which translates to "fortress of the bears." Much of Kodiak Island *(see page 317)* is home to a particularly large variety of brown bear, which has long tantalized trophy hunters.

Black bears also inhabit much of Alaska. Smaller and more timid than grizzlies and brown bears, they prefer forested areas. Confusingly, black bears are sometimes brown in color; and brown bears can be so dark they may appear black. The best way to distinguish them is by looking for the hump which the brown/grizzly variety has at the back of its neck.

Polar bears live along the Arctic coastline. They

LEFT: a migrating herd of caribou.
ABOVE: polar bears can be fiercer than they look.

are among the largest land carnivores in the world, with some of the older males weighing over 1,500 lbs (680 kg). They spend most of their lives on the ice floes of the Arctic Ocean and can easily swim long distances in these frigid waters. True carnivores, they survive on a diet of seals and other marine mammals. Because they live in the remote Arctic, they are seldom seen by visitors.

Varieties of deer

It is sometimes said that a camel is a horse designed by a committee, and much the same could be said of the moose: its legs are too long and its nose is too big. But if you watch these lum-

bering creatures running or swimming you will realize that nature got it right after all. The best places to see them are in Denali Park and at the Kenai National Wildlife Refuge. The Athabascan Indians once relied on the moose for their survival, eating the meat and using the skins for clothing, blankets and boat making. The animals are still hunted extensively during the fall.

Denali is, again, the best – or at least the most accessible – place to see caribou, though its herd is among the state's smallest, with just a couple thousand animals. In all, more than half a million caribou migrate through the state, including two huge herds (the Porcupine and Western Arctic

STREAMS OF SALMON

The lives of brown bears and salmon are inextricably linked, since salmon are the bears' favorite food. The fish come in five varieties (sockeye, king, chum, coho, and humpback) and are as popular with fishermen as with bears – understandably so, since their flesh has so much more flavor than the farmed variety so often found in supermarkets. Witnessing a salmon run (from June to mid-September), when thousands of the fish cram the streams and leap the waterfalls, as they swim upstream to spawn, is a wonderful experience. Watching the bears who come to prey on them is unforgettable, though access to prime venues such as McNeil River State Game Sanctuary is limited *(see pages 337–41)*.

herds) each with more than 100,000 members. Like other varieties of deer, caribou are herbivores and will eat the available grasses and berries as they travel the very long distances between their calving grounds and their over-wintering areas.

Reindeer, the domesticated version of caribou, were introduced into northern Alaska in 1892 as a dependable source of food and clothing. Today, there are approximately 30,000 reindeer in Alaska. The largest herd lives near Nome on the Seward Peninsula. A small herd can be seen at the Reindeer Research Station in Cantwell, south of the entrance to Denali National Park.

Sitka black-tail deer are distributed throughout the Southeast and also on the Kodiak Archipelago, southwest of Anchorage: these small, rusty-brown animals (their coats turn gray in the winter) are most likely to be seen in Misty Fiords National Monument *(see page 118)*, Admiralty Island National Monument *(see page 114)*, and on Kodiak Island. Other island residents are the Roosevelt elk and mountain goats.

The musk ox

Nunivak Island, off Alaska's Southwest coast, is inhabited by a most extraordinary native animal: the musk ox, a stout, shaggy, creature which appears to be the result of an amorous encounter between a prehistoric ox and a mountain sheep. Musk oxen are few and far between, and shy in

of the city. Though their numbers have declined during the past decade, Cook Inlet's beluga population is believed to be stabilized.

A state-managed walrus-viewing program has been established at Round Island, in Bristol Bay, where thousands of bull walrus haul out every summer. Large numbers of walrus can also be seen in the Togiak National Wildlife Refuge and near Kotzebue and other northern communities. Harbor seals, sea otters, and sea lions are frequently sighted in the Gulf of Alaska and Prince William Sound. In fact, Alaska's coasts, like its inland areas, offer opportunities for wildlife watching which are difficult to match. ❏

the wild, but small herds roam the Arctic and some are held captive in research stations, particularly in the Large Animal Research Facility, part of the University of Alaska-Fairbanks.

Sea creatures

Alaska is rich in marine life: humpback, killer and minke whales can be seen in Glacier Bay and Kenai Fjords National Parks, as well as other coastal regions. Belugas – small, white whales – inhabit Cook Inlet and can sometimes be seen from Anchorage's coastal fringes, or the Seward Highway, as it winds along Turnagain Arm south

LEFT: brown bears go fishing; a caribou in the tundra.
ABOVE: harbor seal, Kenai Fiords National Park.

THE ALASKA SEALIFE CENTER

Accessible by highway from Anchorage, the Alaska SeaLife Center *(contact details, pages 203–4)* is a fascinating introduction to the plants and animals you might see on a guided boat trip in the waters of nearby Kenai Fjords National Park. The center re-creates habitats for harbor seals, Steller sea lions, and seabirds including tufted puffins, common murres and pigeon guillemots. Aquariums along one wall show the complete spectrum of local marine life.

Visitors can peer through scopes on the observation deck for a look at wild sea otters and harbor seals. In late spring, humpback whales sometimes enter the bay and can be seen from the center.

A WEALTH OF WILDFLOWERS

The flowering season in Alaska is relatively short, but it brings a profusion of brightly colored blossoms from the high tundra to the highway edge

When a tiny purple flower pokes out of the melting snow, Alaskans know spring has arrived. The pasque flower, or spring crocus, is the first of a colorful floral palate that will paint Alaska in the weeks that follow. The color cavalcade begins in late May, but some places won't see a blossom until mid-June or later. Then, as days lengthen, wildflowers reach for the sun from the most unlikely places – the crevice of a rock, the top of a ridge, alongside rushing streams, on top of coarse, dry gravel bars, or in the middle of the tundra.

The growing season is short, but critical, since flowering plants provide nutrients for the many animals that feed on them. Ground squirrels, marmots and other rodents start munching as soon as flowers bloom, and a bad year for flora is a bad one for dependent fauna, too. Plants of the same species may bloom as much as six weeks apart, depending on their location.

Fields of fireweed

Flowers on south-facing slopes receive more sunlight, so they are most likely to bloom before similar plants on cooler, north-facing slopes. And flowers in southern Alaska will blossom long before those in the state's northern reaches.

At mid-summer, whole fields and hillsides of bushy, bright pink fireweed saturate many parts of Alaska. Tall fireweed blooms from the bottom of the stem to the top, and Alaskans say that when the top flower finally blooms, it means that summer is almost over. It isn't unusual for dwarf fireweed, also known as river beauty, to completely cover gravel bars along glacial streams.

ABOVE: Pasque flowers
Purple pasque flowers, a species of anemone, are often the first wildflowers to emerge through melting snow. Their name is derived from "Pasch," which comes from both the Latin and Greek terms for Easter.

ABOVE: Bearberries
Bearberries grow close to the ground in rocky alpine areas and on the tundra, covering the ground like a carpet with coarse, leathery leaves and black berries. At lower elevations, berries are bright red. The fruits are juicy but have very little flavor and are not prized, although Eskimos will pick them in poor berry seasons and mix them with more tasty blueberries.

ABOVE: Cotton grass
Cotton grass grows along lakes, bogs and ditches, and in any wet, peaty soil. Like an exploded Q-Tip, the ball of cotton sits atop a stiff stem. The lower stems and roots of tall cotton grass are edible. Despite the name, this isn't a grass, but is related to the sedge.

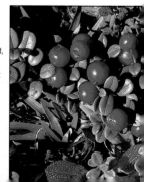

AN EXPLOSION OF COLOR

Above the treeline lies the tundra, a lumpy carpet of bushes, grasses, mosses, lichens, and flowers. Soil is scarce here and flowers cling to the edges of rocky slopes or windswept meadows. They hug the ground, offering brilliant bursts of color. Many have developed unusual adaptations that allow them to survive wind and often brutal temperatures.

The woolly lousewort, a delicate pink Arctic flower, has white hairs on its leaves to keep it warm when it blooms early in the season. The Arctic poppy has a flower shaped like a radar antenna, tracking the motion of the sun and reflecting its heat onto the seeds.

Many plants have pre-formed buds which take shape at the end of each growing season. When spring comes the following year, the buds are ready to open. The tundra's growing season is so short that plants need all these adaptations to increase their growing time.

The northern anemone *(above)* is one of the earliest wildflowers to bloom, often right after snow melts. The flowers measure a mere 1 inch (25 mm) in diameter.

Once temperatures drop, blueberries and cranberries ripen and the tundra is ready for harvest. Soapberries, scattered on gravel bars, in woods or on mountain slopes, are a favorite part of the bear's diet, because of their high fat content.

Above: Fireweed
Growing as high as 5 ft (1.5 meters), tall fireweed can turn a hillside into a blaze of bright pink or purple. This plant, probably the most commonly seen in Alaska, gets its name not from its color, but from its ability to renew itself rapidly after a fire, as its deep roots manage to escape the conflagration.

Above: Forget-me-not
The forget-me-not is the Alaska state flower. This lovely blue perennial blooms in late May to June. The leaves are slightly bristly and the flowers, which grow in coiled springs, are only about ¼-inch (7 mm) across. In many parts of Europe the forget-me-not has been seen as an emblem of love and remembrance since the Middle Ages — hence its evocative name.

Above: Arctic poppies
These delicate lemon-yellow colored flowers cover the tundra or grow in any sandy soil — sometimes right along the roadsides — from mid-June to late July. The inner temperature of this Arctic flower may be 18°F (10°C) warmer than the air outside.

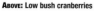

Above: Low bush cranberries
Look out for these glossy dark red berries after the first sharp frost of autumn. They nestle close to the ground, the warmest and least windy zone available to them, and remain on the plant throughout the winter.

SURVIVING IN THE WILDERNESS

The most successful explorers are those who take sensible precautions against threats, which can come from unexpected directions

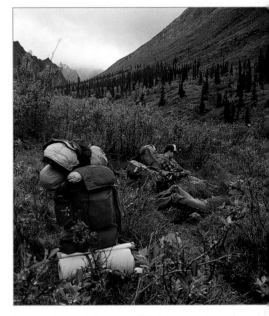

S ean Penn's 2007 movie *Into the Wild* captured Alaska's breathtaking beauty – and its deadliness. The film was based on the story of a 24-year-old Virginian, Christopher McCandless, who in 1992 starved to death near the Teklanika River, at the eastern edge of Denali National Park, after living in the wilderness for four months in an abandoned bus. Opinions vary about whether McCandless was mentally unstable or a victim of circumstances, but it is beyond argument that Alaska is an unforgiving environment unless proper precautions are taken.

Due to the latitude and varying weather conditions, travelers must have the appropriate equipment and be physically prepared for the activities they wish to pursue. Because there are so few roads and distances are so great, clear and precise communication is vital. This chapter isn't an exhaustive discourse on any one topic: its purpose is to cite several common problems and offer some simple solutions.

Variations in weather

Coastal and Southcentral Alaska: The word to remember when selecting equipment for coastal Alaska is rain. Some of this area receives up to 200 inches (508 cm) annually, so reliable rainwear is essential. If you plan to be outside for long periods, a waterproof suit (jacket, pants, and hat) and a synthetic pile or fleece jacket, will be used frequently. Rain is also the prime consideration when selecting a tent and sleeping bag. Tents must be able to withstand long wet spells. Sleeping bags filled with synthetic materials are better than down

---

LEFT: camping in the clouds usually requires the services of an experienced guide or outfitter.
RIGHT: taking a rest, Gates of the Arctic National Park.

because they retain more of their insulating qualities when wet.

The Interior: The Interior has dramatic seasonal contrasts. Summer temperatures are pleasantly warm while in winter the mercury can dip below –40°F (–40°C).

Even in summer, visitors should expect nighttime temperatures sometimes to dip below 40°F (4°C) – and perhaps even below freezing in the mountains. A hat and gloves and at least one heavy long-sleeved shirt, plus the usual jacket and rain gear will be useful, as will a mosquito headnet, which takes up little luggage space.

The extreme cold of winter demands the best quality equipment. A good down jacket, a hat, mittens and warm boots are essential. Camping in winter requires a sleeping bag that is comfortable at −40°F (−40°C) or colder.

Spring is the finest time, by far, to ski in the mountains. Temperatures may allow people to ski without shirts – although the sensible ones cover themselves in sunblock. But snow-blindness is a painful reality for unprotected eyes; mirrored sunglasses are best, but dark sunglasses will suffice. And there's always the chance of springtime blizzards and avalanches.

The North Slope: If the key word for coastal Alaska is rain, the equivalent for the North Slope is wind. The area is technically an arctic desert with less than 5 inches (13 cm) of annual precip-

agers of your destination and expected return date. Make firm arrangements to be picked up. Be certain that someone besides the pilot knows where you are going. In one case, a fisherman was dropped off in a remote location known only to the pilot. The latter had a fatal crash while returning to town, and it took several days of searching to locate the missing fisherman.

What happens if the plane crashes while you are in it? There is a legal requirement for all planes to carry emergency equipment. The required list includes food for each person for two weeks, an axe, first-aid kit, a knife, matches, mosquito headnets, gill net, fishing tackle and a pistol or rifle with

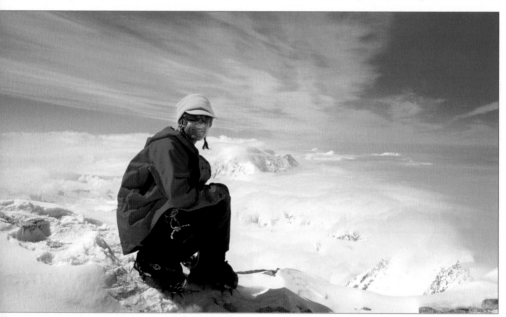

itation. But this meager amount should not be disregarded as it may fall as snow or freezing rain and be driven by gale force winds. Travelers to the North Slope need clothes that are windproof and warm and camping equipment that can withstand heavy winds.

Getting there

Charter flights: Check first to see if there is a regular air service – there is to some small villages and communities, and this will save you a lot of money. But if you are bound for the wilderness, a charter flight is necessary.

Before departure, be sure someone knows where you are going. If you have no alternative, inform the Alaska State Troopers and land man-

LEARNING THE RULES

Taking the trouble to learn a few basics could save your life if you were stranded in the wilderness. There is a record of one man in a desperate situation who spotted an Alaska State Troopers airplane flying over his campsite. He frantically waved both his arms over his head. When the plane flew over a second time, he waved again. The plane flew off.

It was only much later that the man realized his mistake; when he studied his hunting license, he saw that he had signaled, "Everything OK, don't wait." Sadly there was no happy ending: this information was recorded in a diary found when the man's body was discovered.

ammunition. A sleeping bag, snowshoes and a wool blanket are added to the list for winter travel.

Although most flights carry some survival gear, the requirements are sometimes ignored. Check the survival gear before taking off. If you decide to bring your own, keep as much of it on your person as possible. In winter fill your pockets; in summer, use a small waist pack. You may have to evacuate the downed craft quickly.

Every plane in Alaska is also required to carry a downed aircraft transmitting device (Emergency Location Transmitter, or ELT). Learn how to operate this device before you set off. If the pilot becomes incapacitated, you can activate the ELT

pants, sleeping bag, flare, candles, extra spark plugs, extra belts, shovel, chain, flashlight and high-energy food.

Automobile maintenance is vitally important. Even if you come to no real harm, it is expensive and time-consuming to break down on the road – towing charges can be very costly, especially in remote areas. Check the car carefully before leaving the city, and remember winter essentials: snow tires or studded tires, an operating engine heater and ample electrical cord to reach a power source.

When renting a car, inform the rental agency of your proposed route and confirm that maintenance is available along the way. Anticipating problems

and be rescued more quickly. Don't be deterred by these dire warnings: these precautions pertain only to the 0.5 percent of flights during which an inflight problem does occur.

Automobile travel: There is no Alaska law which governs what survival equipment should be kept in a vehicle, yet the average car is maintained less frequently than a plane, which means that far more cars break down while traveling.

In sub-freezing weather, a breakdown can be life-threatening as well as inconvenient. The Alaska State Troopers recommend the following survival kit: down coat, boots, mittens, hat, snow-

before traveling will avoid misunderstandings later. Most agencies have stringent rules about driving on gravel roads – and many road-accessible destinations require some driving on gravel.

Coping with mosquitoes

Alaska may have been spared snakes, skunks and termites but this has been more than compensated for by the mosquito. Billed sarcastically as the "Alaskan State Bird," these insects are a wilderness force to be reckoned with. Use the most powerful repellents available, such as the musk types or those with a high concentration of deet. Even in the face of these measures, the mosquito seems to thrive. Thick clothing will reduce the number of bites, but sometimes a headnet is the only means

LEFT: Well equipped hiker in Denali National Park.
ABOVE: it's prudent not to set too ambitious a pace.

of relief. Carry a mosquito net – there are some neat, lightweight ones available – and make sure that it is impregnated with repellent as well.

Encountering bears

For all the worries that people have about bears, humans are in fact a much greater danger to them than bears are to us. Many Alaskans have stories about encountering bears at close quarters, but there are a few tragic accounts. Most bears turn tail and run upon encountering people, but in some instances the bear will stand its ground. Or charge.

If you do meet a bear, stay as calm as possible. Talk to the bear, to identify yourself as a human,

but don't yell. And *don't run*. Running is usually the worst possible strategy, because it will likely trigger the bear's predatory instincts. Back away slowly and give the bear an escape route. Avoid getting between a female and her cubs. Some experts suggest that you raise your arms above your head and wave them slowly. If you're in a group, stand side by side, to increase your apparent size. In a forest you might consider climbing a tree, but remember that young grizzlies and adult black bears are good climbers.

Should a bear attack and make contact with you, it's usually best to fall to the ground and "play dead." Protect your head and neck and try to lie

THE THREAT FROM TIDES

There are large tidal variations in Southeastern Alaska, Prince William Sound, Cook Inlet and Bristol Bay. The extreme diurnal variation occurs in spring in Cook Inlet near Anchorage where high tide can be 38ft (11.5 meters) above low tide. Such tides present two dangers for those traveling through or near the water: swift incoming tides and strong currents, magnified in island areas.

Obtain a tide book from a fishing tackle shop, a hardware store, a bar or gas station. All too frequently, the fisherman standing on a rock working the incoming tide waits too long to retreat. This can be life-threatening. People traveling along beaches in vehicles must also be aware of the tides or they risk losing their transportation – or

worse. In the Anchorage area, people have got stuck and been drowned by the incoming tide.

Large tides create swift currents in constricted areas such as inlets, which can be a danger to those in small boats; avoid traveling in kayaks, skiffs, and other small watercraft at these times – it's perilous.

Given that Alaska's tidal shoreline, at 31,383 miles/ 50,506km, is greater than the shoreline of the Lower 48 states, it offers opportunities for surfers. The most popular beach is at Yakutat *(see pages 160–1)*, the northernmost community along the Inside Passage. More and more surfers have headed here since *Outdoor* magazine named Yakutat as one of America's top five surf towns.

on your stomach, but do not struggle. If you're wearing a pack, leave it on. Once a bear feels there's no longer a threat, it will likely end its attack. The exception to this rule is when a bear shows predatory behavior. Instead of charging in a rush, such a bear will show intense interest and may circle or stalk you. If you think a bear is treating you as prey, fight it off. Such behavior is extremely rare and most often involves black bears. Some bear researchers now recommend that any black bear attack should be fought off, because they are smaller, less aggressive animals than grizzlies and more easily intimidated. It would be almost impossible to fight off an adult grizzly.

tent site carefully and avoid trails, streams with spawning salmon, and berry patches. And don't attract bears with your food. Cook well away from your tents, store food far from your campsite, and don't eat odorous foods. Store garbage in air-tight containers or burn it, and pack out the remains.

Finally, carry a firearm only if you know how to use it. (Guns are forbidden in some wilderness areas.) One alternative is pepper spray, which comes in aerosol cans. Because the cans sometimes leak, it's best to store them in airtight containers. Notify pilots if you are carrying pepper spray; a leak inside the plane could disable the pilot and lead to a crash.

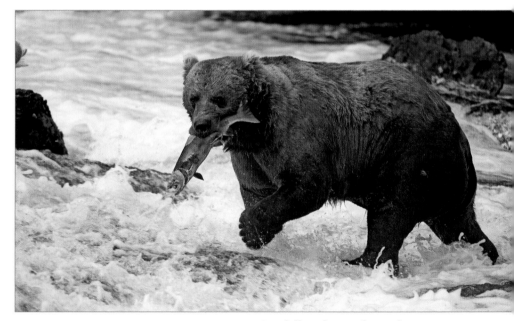

Some important strategies should be used to minimize chance meetings with bears. It's most important to avoid surprise encounters, which lead to the vast majority of bear attacks. Make plenty of noise while walking in the wilderness. Some people tie "bear bells" to their shoes or pack, but talking or singing is better. Human voices carry farther than tinkling bells. If bears hear your approach, there's less chance they'll be surprised and they're likely to leave.

Stay alert and look for signs of bear, such as tracks, scat, partially eaten salmon. Choose your

LEFT: various ways of repelling bears and insects.
ABOVE: remembering the bear's favorite food, it's best not to pitch a tent near a salmon stream.

Avoiding hypothermia

Beware of hypothermia, the sub-normal lowering of the body temperature. It is caused by exposure to cold, but aggravated by exhaustion, wind and wet clothing. Left untreated, a person suffering from hypothermia may become disoriented, incoherent, then unconscious, and may finally die. Never ignore shivering, it is the body's way of signaling for help. The time to prevent hypothermia is during the initial period of exposure.

The following suggestions may help prevent an emergency:
● *Try to stay dry*. Wet clothing loses most of its insulating value. Functional raingear is vitally important. Ponchos are almost useless.
● *Avoid the wind*. Wind carries body heat away

much faster than still air; it also refrigerates wet clothing by evaporation. If you feel yourself getting chilled, look for shelter from the wind.

● *Understand the cold*. Most people die of hypothermia when the temperature is between 30° and 50°F (−1° and 10°C). The majority of hikers underestimate the severity of being wet in Alaskan waters. Many rivers are fed by glaciers and their temperatures, even in mid-summer, aren't much above the freezing mark. Getting soaked can be fatal, and first-aid measures must be taken immediately *(see panel below)*.

● *End the exposure*. If someone shows any signs of hypothermia, or if it becomes impossible to keep dry with your existing clothing and conditions, make camp or end the trip.

● *Avoid over-tiredness*. Don't be too ambitious. Make camp before you get exhausted, and bring high-energy food to replenish your reserves.

Surviving avalanches

These pose a serious threat to winter mountain adventurers. Research has shown that most avalanches involving humans are triggered by people traveling through avalanche-prone terrain, whether by ski, snowshoe, or snowmobile.

A snow-covered slope is especially prone to sliding when its gradient ranges between 27° and

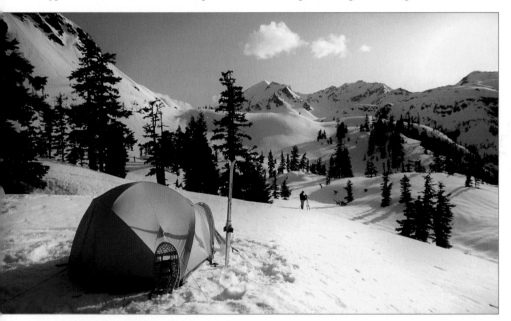

TREATING HYPOTHERMIA

If a member of your party develops hypothermia while in the wilderness – one of the first signs is violent and uncontrollable shivering – there are emergency measures you can take. Handle a victim gently, replace wet clothing with dry, and warm the core area of the body with hot liquids. Do not give a victim any alcohol as this could prove fatal; forget stories about a sip of brandy being restorative.

Avoid the mistake of rapidly warming the extremities, as it takes much-needed blood away from the core area and can result in unconsciousness. If the condition worsens, put a victim in a sleeping bag with another person, who will help warm the bag.

45°. On steeper slopes, the snow usually won't accumulate, and on shallower slopes, the angle is usually not sufficient to release snow. Avoid disaster by careful route selection and trip planning.

Don't ski through a likely avalanche zone – make sure you pass above or below it. Spend as little time as possible near the zone. Choose the route carefully to avoid steep mountain faces, especially after a fresh snowfall. And remember, spring is an especially dangerous season for avalanches, as the snow melts and the weight of the snowpack increases. If possible, take an avalanche-awareness class to learn more about safe winter travel in the mountains. ❏

ABOVE: pitching camp in Tongass National Forest.

Public-use Cabins

Somewhere between the extremes of posh wilderness lodges and down-to-the-basics tent camping, there's a third way that travelers can spend their nights in Alaska's backcountry: public-use cabins.

Given Alaska's often cool and wet weather — particularly in coastal areas — it can make all the difference to return to a roomy, dry, and heated shelter at the end of a day's explorations. And cabins provide an economical way of doing that. For as little as $15 a night, you can spread out your soaked clothing, pull up a chair, and read a book beside an oil- or wood-burning stove while your hiking or paddling partner grabs fresh greens from the cooler and prepares a gourmet meal on your camp stove (a limited number of cabins even have their own hot plates).

You don't have to worry about crowding, leaky tents, or a wild critter getting into your food supplies, which can be safely stored inside the cabin. All public-use cabins include heating stove, bunks or other platforms for sleeping, table, chairs, counter tops or shelves, and outhouse. Some also include propane-fueled lights, burner plates, stainless steel sinks, picnic tables with benches, wash area, and more. Visitors are generally responsible for bringing their own food, heating and cooking fuel, cooking utensils, food, water, cook stove, and bedding.

Frontier etiquette demands that, where possible, you attempt to leave cabins in better condition than you found them. You are encouraged to chop firewood, clean up the place and leave canned goods for the next occupants.

Where to find them

Balancing these "comforts of home" is the wildness and solitude to be found outside your shelter. Many public-use cabins are located in remote wilderness areas that can be reached only by boat or plane. Others can be easily reached from the road system. Many, particularly more modern cabins constructed in recent years, have been built so that they blend with their surroundings, so they have a minimal impact on the environment or wilderness aesthetics.

More than 250 such cabins are available for rent throughout much of the state, in state and national parks, wildlife refuges, Bureau of Land Manage-

RIGHT: the path leads to a public-use cabin in Kenai Fjords National Park.

ment lands, and Alaska's two national forests. Some are along trails, others are on lakes, or rivers, or forested coastlines, and still others are in alpine meadows.

Their nightly costs range from around $15 to $65 – a bargain for those seeking dependable protection from Alaska's unpredictable weather as well as some degree of comfort. (If necessary, they can also serve as emergency shelters.) Some can be rented only in summer, while others can be used year-round.

How to reserve them

Most cabins are available on a first-come, first-served reservation system and can be reserved up to six

months in advance. In nearly all cases, the length of stay is limited. It's best to check for specifics, because details vary from agency to agency. These include the National Park Service, Alaska State Parks, the US Fish and Wildlife Service, the US Forest Service, and the Bureau of Land Management (BLM).

Information on public-use cabins throughout Alaska and details on how to apply and pay for cabin rentals are available from Alaska Public Lands Information Centers in four locations: Anchorage (tel: 271-2737); Fairbanks (tel: 456-0527), Tok 883-5667) and Ketchikan (228-6220). Information is also accessible from the website www.nps.gov/aplic. Another good reference is *How to Rent a Public Cabin in Southcentral Alaska* (Wilderness Press, 1999), by Andromeda Romano-Lax. ❏

CRUISING'S IRRESISTIBLE GROWTH

Douglas Ward, the world's foremost authority on cruising, reveals the best ways of getting an up-close but comfortable view of Alaska's ice fields and glaciers

laska's cruise season is short, from May to September, and it can be misty, wet, and chilly in early and late summer. But the lure of the state's dramatic wilderness scenery, invigorating clean air, wildlife, and fascinating shore excursions have led to a phenomenal growth in cruise traffic. Indeed, about 59 percent of Alaska's visitors are now cruise passengers, served by more than 40 vessels. Ships have become larger, with more balcony cabins and more dining options, while fares have fallen. Wharves, docks, and quayside facilities have been renovated and expanded to cope with the growth.

Protecting the environment

To cruise in Glacier Bay (which is inaccessible by road), a cruise line needs an entry permit from the Glacier Bay National Park and Preserve. A limited number of permits are issued for the "prime season" (June 1–August 31), in order to protect the environment. These are spread around the cruise industry, although Holland America Line and Princess Cruises receive the greatest number because they pioneered cruises in Alaska.

Only two cruise ships (over 100 gross tons) are allowed into Glacier Bay each day, plus three cruise ships of under 100 gross tons (such as the ships of Majestic America Line, Cruise West, Lindblad Expeditions, American Safari Cruises – all of which are registered in the USA). About 210 cruise ship visits are made to Glacier Bay each year. In a typical summer season, the National Park Service issues more than 220 cruise ship entry permits. and has increased the seasonal use-day quota to a total of 153 days.

LEFT: approaching Hubbard Glacier in Glacier Bay.
RIGHT: a buffet lunch during a shore excursion.

THE MOST POPULAR CRUISE ROUTES

● The Inside Passage Route from Vancouver to Skagway, which usually includes visits to tidewater glaciers, such as those found in Glacier Bay's Hubbard Glacier or Tracey Arm (just two of the 15 active glaciers along the 60-mile/100-km Glacier Bay coastline). Typical ports of call might include Juneau, Ketchikan, Skagway and/or Haines.
● The Glacier Route, which usually includes the Gulf of Alaska during a one-way cruise between Vancouver and Seward or Whittier (the ports for Anchorage). Typical ports of call might include Haines, Sitka, and Valdez. Of special interest is the marine life of Hubbard Glacier and Prince William Sound.

It was the Cunard Line which, in the second half of the 1970s, had the idea of extending the standard cruise. Instead of sailing back to Vancouver, the company introduced one-way voyages from Vancouver to Whittier, the port for Anchorage, and included several up-close and personal visits to glaciers such as Tracey Arm and Hubbard. At Whittier, a train would take passengers to Anchorage, for a stopover, with a bus connection to the airport for their flights home. This was followed by even more extensive "Cruise 'n' Stay" vacations, which included a 7-day cruise, a hotel stay in Anchorage, from where passengers could head out to the surrounding areas and wildlife

lodges. Today, Anchorage serves as a point from which to take flights further north (to Fairbanks or Nome, for example), or to take a train with specially constructed domed railcars to Denali National Park and Mount McKinley.

The early days

The first organized cruises to Alaska took place when a young Chuck West, originally a bush pilot, formed a travel company called Westours. In 1954, he pioneered Alaska cruising using two small ships, the 1,835-ton *Yukon Star* and sister ship, the 1,833-ton *Glacier Queen*. Both ships carried 148 passengers in a one-class arrangement.

Larger ships were acquired in 1968 and 1971, and in the 1970s the company itself was acquired by Holland America Line. In 1973 Chuck West started a company dedicated to *small* ship travel: Alaska Sightseeing, which later changed its name to Cruise West.

The majors arrive

Soon major cruise brand names such as Cunard Line, Holland America Line, and Princess Cruises became interested in the region. But most of their vessels operated in the Caribbean and, to reach Alaska, had to go through the Panama Canal and northward along the American west coast to get to Vancouver – the Canadian port became the base of cruise operations because of restrictive US legislation *(see panel below)*. Alaskan cruising thus did not develop significantly until the 1970s, when the majors dedicated ships exclusively to the state.

The early itineraries were very basic, featuring just two or three port calls in a 7-day cruise. The first port of call was Ketchikan. This was typi-

WHY SO MANY CRUISES LEAVE FROM CANADA

The US Passenger Services Act of 1886 requires that only US flag and US-built vessels can be used to carry passengers between two US ports, but it allows foreign-flag vessel to pick up or drop off passengers while calling at a single US port. Since most large cruise ships are registered not in the United States but with a foreign-flag nation (such as the Bahamas, Bermuda, Liberia, Panama, and the United Kingdom), most cruises to Alaska start and end in Vancouver, British Columbia.

This meets the Act's requirements, but it does have the effect of keeping business away from ports in the Pacific Northwest, such as Seattle.

Any non-US flag ship leaving from and returning to Seattle (or Los Angeles or San Francisco) would also have to call at a Canadian port. While this may not sound a problem in theory, it is in reality for reasons of time, particularly in a 7-day cruise (the most popular vacation length). Canada has clearly been the major beneficiary of the US Passenger Services Act, and has built several contemporary cruise terminals specifically for the Alaska cruise market.

The Act is commonly known as the Jones Act – although, to be accurate, the Jones Act is a parallel piece of legislation drawn up in the early 20th century with the aim of providing protection for the US cargo fleet operating between two US domestic ports.

cally followed by a visit up a dramatic fjord, per-haps Endicott or Tracey Arm. The next port would be Juneau, and shore excursions focused on the vast, nearby Mendenhall Glacier. The third port was a visit to Skagway, (a former port and supply base for the gold digging community) or adjacent Haines, and then it was time to head back to Van-couver. As more coastal cities opened up, the rev-enue, taxes and number of visitors provided the economic incentive for greater development.

How the economy benefits

Alaska cruising has evolved into a big money maker for the cruise companies, and provides

emergency services and tourism infrastructure. Then there are the sums spent by passengers: $74 million in Juneau, for example, and $54 million in Ketchikan. Many jewelry and souvenir shops exist almost solely for cruise ship visitors.

The cruise industry also donates money to local communities, the most consistent givers being Hol-land America Line, and Princess Cruises (both owned by Carnival Corporation). For example, Holland America Line recently donated $200,000 in educational grants to the University of Alaska state-wide system, including a grant to fund a new writer-in-residence program. Holland America Line also hires an artist in residence for each of its

income and work for local, indigenous Alaskans who operate the land-based tourism infrastructure and cruise-related services. Alaska's government is also very happy, as it collects taxes, not only from visiting cruise ships, but also from every passenger carried, as well as sales taxes when vis-itors buy goods and services ashore.

The impact the cruise industry has had on the local economy is immense. For each passenger car-ried, the cruise lines pay between $65 and $80 in fees and taxes to cover state and local governments' cruise-related expenses, from port maintenance to

LEFT: souvenir hunting on a shore excursion.
ABOVE: smaller vessels make it possible to view seal colonies at close range.

Alaska cruise ships, a program that included a $250,000 gift to the Alaska Native Heritage Center.

Cooperation between cruise lines and the local utilities is close. In 2001 Princess Cruises spent $4.5 million to convert its ships to run off surplus power supplied by the Alaska Electric Light & Power from a special transformer installed shore-side in Juneau. When surplus power is available, the ships' diesel engines power down, and Princess Cruises pays for the electricity used, thus saving its own fuel and contributing to the local economy.

The one downside occurs in some ports when several large ships may be docked together, and there is congestion on shore excursions and in the crowded streets, restaurants and taverns.

Cruise-tours

Cruise-tours (a cruise plus a land extension) have become an increasingly popular way to see more of Alaska, particularly by those who have time and may only visit it once. This usually involves a cruise plus land stay in a hotel, or a cruise plus a train ride and hotel stay, all neatly packaged by the cruise lines.

Although the most popular cruises to Alaska last for seven days, extending a vacation by taking a cruise plus an escorted land tour can stretch to 18 days. *For contact details, see page 353.*

● **Alaska Cruise Trains**

Specially constructed domed railcars are featured in the cruise-tour programs of the major cruise companies: Holland America Line, Princess Cruises, and Royal Caribbean International/ Celebrity Cruises. The special domed cars (some of which are fitted with seats that can turn to allow passengers to face forwards or backwards) are part of the trains operated by the Alaska Railroad, which is owned by the State of Alaska. The railway extends northwards, from Seward through Anchorage to Fairbanks, a distance of 470 miles (756 km).

● **McKinley Explorer**

Holland America Line has original 1950s domed railcars, formerly operated on the Sante Fe Rail-

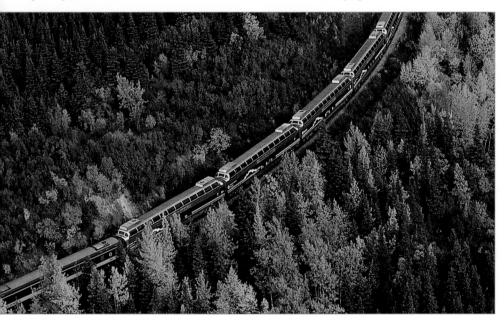

WHEN CROWDS ARE A NUISANCE

With almost 1 million cruise passengers a year visiting Alaska and several large resort ships likely to be in port on any given day, there's so much congestion in many small ports that avoiding crowded streets can be difficult. More of the same shops are the same places you'd find in the Caribbean. And, with more people around, wildlife is harder to spot. The more adventurous might consider one of the more unusual Alaska cruises to the far north, around the Pribilof Islands (superb for bird watching) and into the Bering Sea.

It's wise to remember that Alaska isn't always good weather cruising – it can be very wet and windy, and excursions may be cancelled or changed.

way, aboard the McKinley Explorer. The railcars, each named after an Alaska river, are extremely smooth, and run on six-wheel units ("trucks") instead of the usual four. The train has a full service dining car. The newer, two-level railcars have open-air viewing platforms.

● **Midnight Sun Express**

Princess Cruises has operated this train since 1984 between Anchorage and Fairbanks. The upper level of the cars is completely glass-enclosed (known as Ultra Domes). The train has a full-service dining car.

ABOVE: the specially constructed domed railcars of cruise trains offer fine paroramic views.
RIGHT: a Celebrity ship gets up close to the ice.

● Wilderness Express

The domed railcars on the Wilderness Express were specially constructed for Royal Caribbean International and Celebrity Cruises (owned by RCI) and have full-length vista-domes. The train has a full-service dining car.

Pre- and Post-Cruise Stays

The cruise lines have many combinations of pre- and post-cruise stays ashore to extend Alaska vacations. Two of the major lines, Holland America Line, and Princess Cruises (both companies are now owned by Carnival Corporation), have such comprehensive facilities ashore (hotels, tour buses, glass-domed railcars) that they are committed to Alaska for many years. Indeed, Holland America Line is among the state's largest private employers. Other cruise lines depend on what's left of the local transportation for their land tours.

For the more adventurous (and those with plenty of time), there are Alaska cruises to the far north, around the Pribilof Islands (superb for bird watching) and into the Bering Sea. These are infrequently operated by the smaller, specialist expedition cruise companies. ❑

Douglas Ward is author of the annual Berlitz Complete Guide to Cruising and Cruise Ships.

THE BEST SHORE EXCURSIONS

Shore excursions have increased in number (and cost) over the years; Holland America Line alone offers more than 100 optional excursions. These include flightseeing (by floatplane or helicopter), salmon fishing, hiking, glacial ice treks, mountain biking, train rides, jeep safaris, and whale watching. Here are some of the best:

● On cruises to Skagway, a trip on the White Pass & Yukon Route Railroad is recommended. This narrow-gauge track, built in 1898, now provides Alaska's most popular shore excursion. The railroad operates 19 diesel locomotives and one steam locomotive.

● Flightseeing excursions depart from Juneau and land on Mendenhall Glacier, which has signed trails and inter-pretive panels. Most floatplanes fly at around 2,000 ft, and all passengers have window seats.

● Tours to Denali National Park and Preserve can be made by helicopter, tour bus or self-drive Jeep. Wildlife includes moose, caribou, brown bears, Dall sheep and golden eagles.

● Prudhoe Bay provides close-ups of the TransAlaska oil pipeline and sightseeing along the Dalton Highway.

● A ride on the Mount Roberts tramway above Juneau, with great views across Gastineau Channel.

● Top-class salmon fishing expeditions to the Ninilchik River and Deep Creek, plus deep-sea charters for halibut.

● A walking tour of historic Ketchikan, with a trip to nearby Saxman Totem Park for fans of intricately carved poles.

Big ships vs small ships

Choosing a ship is a lot like buying a car. Should it be big or small? Classic or modern? Luxurious or functional? You must assess what you really want.

The difference between so-called "big ships" and "small ships" could hardly be more stark, and it isn't simply a matter of tonnage or floor space, but what they have to offer. These days, large mainstream ships tend to be very big indeed, carrying 3,000 passengers or more, soaring 14 stories above the water, and stretching to lengths of nearly 1,000 ft (300 meters). These are the so-called mega-ships, a term that came into fashion when "mega" meant ships of 75,000 gross tons or above.

By contrast, small ships in Alaska tend to be very small, measuring in the neighborhood of 100 ft (30 meters) in length and carrying between 12 and 140 passengers. Some are closer to yachts in size and appearance, others have the utilitarian feel of expedition ships, and still others look like the miniaturized cruise ships that they are.

A choice of entertainment

In examining whether a big or small ship would best suit your needs, you need to consider three main variables: the onboard experience you should expect during the course of your cruise, the kinds of itineraries and ports of call offered by each, and the cost.

By design, most big ships are busy places, with activities, entertainment, and meals programmed so that, if you cared to, you could be occupied during every waking moment you were on board. As such, they're ideal for families, allowing parents and children to pursue their own interests and stay out of each other's hair. They're also the better choice for people who, although they want to see the natural wonders of the 49th state, don't expect that glaciers, whales, and mountains will be able to hold their interest every minute of the day.

These people want a show in the evening, multiple restaurants for dinner, sports options (of both the active and couch-potato varieties), maybe a casino, and they might even like to take a dip in the ship's pool – if only for the kick of doing so within sight of an iceberg. For these people, Royal Caribbean, NCL, and Carnival are the top choices.

Those looking for a slightly more refined version of this same experience should check out tradition-minded Holland America or stylish Celebrity line, while those with the money to go with their refinement should opt for the luxury lines Crystal and Radisson, which feature much enhanced service, cuisine, and accommodations.

Accommodations and eating

Among the mainstream lines, accommodations run the gamut from smallish inside cabins to the ever-more-prevalent outside ones with private balconies, to absolutely palatial suites with personal butler service. Balcony cabins offer the pleasant option of landscape- and wildlife-viewing in the privacy of your own room, but if you're just as happy watching from pub-

lic areas you can save quite a bit on your fare by opting for an inside cabin (if you're not claustrophobic) or a low-end exterior one with a small window.

Eating at sea

Dining is another area of great choice on the big ships. Whereas a decade ago the most you could expect to find would have been a main restaurant with two seatings and a buffet option at breakfast and lunch, today's mega-ships are being built with multiple main dining rooms, casual options for every meal, specialty coffee-and-pastry cafés, and multiple, reservations-only restaurants serving Asian, Italian, French, steakhouse, and other menus, at an extra cost of around $5 to $25 per person per meal.

And if you want to work off the calories you are

likely to pack away at those restaurants, the mega-ships all have sprawling gym complexes, jogging tracks, and varying sports amenities, from the almost ubiquitous golf-driving nets and basketball/volleyball courts to Royal Caribbean's rock-climbing walls. In essence, sailing aboard a mega-ship in Alaskan waters is like checking into a smart, big-city hotel and then taking that hotel with you to the wilderness.

Small ships for watching wildlife

Across the board, small ships offer exactly the opposite kind of experience, with onboard dining, activities, and entertainment taking a backseat to the natural world outside. All meals are served in a single, simple dining

type of cruise. Typically, the range of accommodations on these vessels is limited, tending toward cozy outside cabins with few amenities.

Ports of call

Itinerary-wise, ships both large and small tend to visit the popular Alaska ports of Juneau, Ketchikan, and Skagway, where all passengers get exactly the same experience, although big ships tend to offer a wider range of shore-excursion options. One advantage small ships do have here is that, with fewer passengers, it takes less time to get on and off the ship, so you have more time in port and less frustrating waiting time. Small ships also have the advantage when it

room (with a small buffet also set out in a lounge at lunch and dinner times), while the only entertainment you might expect is, perhaps, a crew talent show or an informal lecture by the ship's onboard naturalist.

Instead of such inside-oriented activities, passengers spend their time out on deck with binoculars scanning for whales, bears, sea otters, and other wildlife – which they're much more likely to see from these ships than from the big ones, since small vessels are less obtrusive, can therefore sail closer to shore, and have passenger decks that begin only a few yards above the waterline. These same factors also mean you get a more intimate experience of Alaska, which is the main reason people choose this

comes to visiting smaller port towns like Petersburg and Metlakatla and sailing narrow wilderness passages like Misty Fiords National Monument – places from which the big ships are barred by their sheer bulk.

Counting the cost

Small ships, which cost more to operate, are far more expensive than the big mainstream lines. Consider your priorities and your budget. For the same amount of money, you could sail with a mainstream line and take all the best optional shore excursions (helicopter glacier treks, sport fishing, dog sledding); sail with a luxury line and find your own way around ports of call; or sail with a small-ship adventure line, where most off-ship wilderness activities are included in the cost. In the end, it's all a matter of taste. ❑

ABOVE: smaller ships get closer to the glaciers.

ALASKA FROM THE AIR

Even long-time Alaskans are awestruck by the view from the air. Flightseeing, a growing industry, provides two guarantees: the view will be incomparable, and there's not a bad seat in the house

ern tundra, much of Alaska is accessible only by air. And it may never look more spectacular than it does from above.

Travel by airplane

A plane trip in Alaska is almost always a breathtaking journey, but it's also a crucial mode of transportation. Beyond the major cities and towns, many communities can't be reached by road. Most bush villages appear on the map like disconnected specks without the usual web of asphalt connecting them to the outside world. Just about everything that goes in or comes out – people, mail, groceries, medicine – travels by air.

Given the importance of air travel, Alaska has been dubbed the "flyingest" state in the Union. One out of 58 Alaskans is a registered pilot, and one out of 59 owns an airplane. Lake Hood in Anchorage is the largest and busiest seaplane base in the world, averaging 234 landings and takeoffs a day; 800 per day are not uncommon in summer. Merrill Field, also in Anchorage, is also home to hundreds of small aircraft.

How to arrange a flight

This is a fairly straightforward matter. Air taxi and bush operators are listed in the Yellow Pages of any Alaskan telephone directory. Some companies offer a regular schedule of flights and destinations. Others operate on a charter basis and will take you just about anywhere you want to go. Still others specialize in flightseeing tours of the region's most scenic places. Want to spend a day

Flying through the Knik Valley in Southcentral Alaska, a Cessna 185 descends into the Gorge, a canyon with a glacier on one side and a sheer rock face on the other. The landscape dwarfs the buzzing aircraft, giving passengers the sense that they're riding inside the hull of a fragile flying insect. They drink in the astonishing view. Pastel-blue cracks on the face of the glacier are deep enough to swallow a 17-story building. No one speaks. It's a wondrous sight.

Even long-time Alaskans are awestruck by the view from the air. Who wouldn't be? Wild places stretch from horizon to horizon, untouched by human hands. From the lush rain forest of the southeastern panhandle to the delta wetlands of the western coast and the tapestry of the far north-

LEFT: pilot Rebecca Fisher by her K2 ski plane at Mount McKinley base camp.
RIGHT: a Cessna floatplane negotiates the Neacola Mountains above Lake Clark National Park.

or two fishing in complete solitude at a remote mountain lake, or perhaps a few hours trekking across an otherwise inaccessible glacier? If so, these are the people you need to see.

Bush planes range in size from a two-person Piper Super Cub to a 20-passenger DeHavilland Twin Otter. They are remarkably versatile aircraft designed to operate in the most rugged settings. Depending on season and terrain, they may be equipped with pontoons, skis, or tundra tires. Pontoons on an aircraft make convenient landing strips of coves, lakes, and streams; skis are used on ice and snow; and tundra tires, like big rubber donuts, cushion landings on gravel bars or soft, spongy

tundra. Helicopters are also an option for back-country travel, especially for close-up views of the terrain and extremely tight landings.

Legendary pilots

Bush pilots are an equally rugged and colorful bunch. Their courageous, comic, and sometimes tragic stories are the stuff of legend. Take Paul Claus, one of Alaska's most celebrated bush pilots. He's been known to land on a glacier so steep that he had to anchor the plane with an ice screw to keep it from sliding off the edge. To take off, he leaned out the window, cut the tether with a knife, and throttled off the slope. ❏

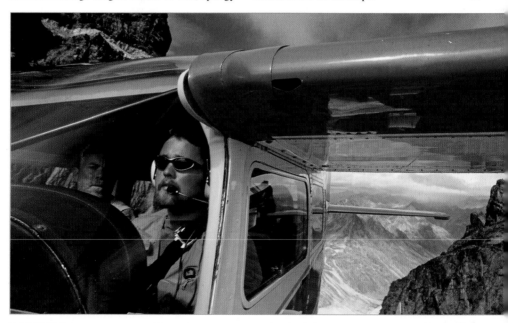

A CHECKLIST FOR PASSENGERS

Before you plan to fly into the wilderness, there are a few things you should keep in mind. First, air taxis aren't cheap. Cost varies widely depending on the destination, amount of gear, and the number of passengers, and is usually based on flight hours. Even a relatively short hop in the outback can cost as much as a flight from the lower 48 states to Alaska.

Second, patience is a virtue. Bad weather and mechanical problems often delays flights for hours or days, so bring extra provisions, a deck of cards, and a sense of humor. Impatience, know by some pilots as "get-home-itis," is a leading factor in small aircraft accidents.

Finally, put safety first. Don't hesitate to ask your pilot

if he or she has insurance and a commercial license, which requires a higher standard of training and aircraft maintenance than a private license. And be sure the plane has life vests, an emergency locator transmitter (ELT), and other essential safety equipment.

Never challenge a pilot's decision to cancel a flight; the sun may be shining where you are, but the weather at your destination could be dramatically different – and unsafe. Nor should you pressure a pilot to carry more people or gear than the aircraft can handle. Weight and balance are critical for safe flying.

Taking to the air in Alaska should be enjoyable. The experience is routine here, but it is very seldom boring.

PLACES

A detailed guide to the entire state, arranged
by region and with main sites clearly
cross-referenced by number to the maps

G iven that its landmass amount to one-fifth the size of the combined
Lower 48 states, it's not surprising that Alaska has six distinct geographic areas.
● **Southeast Alaska** (also known as the Panhandle) is a narrow, 400-mile (640-km) strip of land sandwiched between the
Pacific Ocean and Canada, and cut off from the rest of Alaska by
the towering St Elias range. It is covered by huge temperate rainforests nurtured by a mild climate: readings of 60° or 70°F (15°
or 21°C) are not uncommon in the summer, and winter temperatures don't often dip much below freezing.
● **Southcentral Alaska** lies along the Gulf of Alaska. A region of
mountains, fjords, tidewater glaciers, and forested lowlands, it includes Prince
William Sound, the Kenai Peninsula, Cook Inlet and Kodiak Island, as well as
the fertile Matanuska Valley. Temperatures vary from –20°F (–29°C) in winter
to 60°–70°F (15°–21°C) in summer.
● **Alaska's Interior** is a broad lowland cradled between the Brooks and
Alaska mountain ranges. It encompasses the mighty Yukon, Tanana and
Kuskokwim rivers. In some areas, birch and spruce thrive; others support
only vast reaches of tundra. Temperatures can fall to below –50°F (–45°C) in
winter and climb to 70–80°F (21–26°C) or higher in the summer.
● **Arctic Alaska** stretches north from the southern edge of the Brooks Range
to the Arctic Ocean. It contains huge stretches of tundra that flower spec-
tacularly in the night-less summer. Mid-summer temperatures
may exceed 80°F (26°C), while mid-winter temperatures can
sink to –40°F (–40°C) or below. The minimal rainfall of 5
inches (13cm) a year qualifies it as a desert.
● **Southwest Alaska** is the home of the Alaska Peninsula and
Aleutian Islands, which stretch 200 miles (320km) west into
the Bering Sea. A warm current from Japan meets the icy northern air over
the Aleutians, creating the rain and fog that enshroud them. Temperatures
range: 0°F (–17°C) to 50–60°F (10–15°C).
● **Western Alaska** and the Bering Sea coast stretch from the Arctic Circle
down to Bristol Bay. Much of the land is treeless tundra underlain with permafrost; the Yukon and Kuskokwim rivers flow through this harsh land on the
final leg of their journey to the sea. Temperature range: 0°F (–17°C) (with
frigid wind-chill factors) to 60°F (15°C). ❑

PRECEDING PAGES: kayaking in Lake Clark National Park; a traditional winter
sled dog train; a more mechanized train near Denali.
LEFT: an Alaskan pilot. **ABOVE:** glacier in Prince William Sound; Kenai Lake.

Alpha

Alaska

CHUKCHI SEA

RUSSIA

Anadyr Range

Arctic Circle

Gulf of Anadyr

Chukotsk Peninsula

Providenija

Cape Chukotskiy

Gambell

Savoonga

Saint Lawrence Island

Cape Singikpa

Southeast Cape

Northeast Cape

Point Franklin

Peard Bay

Point Barrow

Barrow

Smith Bay

Cape Halkett

Harrison Bay

Wainwright

Icy Point

Point Lay

Teshekpuk Lake

Prudhoe Bay

Umiat

Colville

Cape Lisburne

North Slope

Point Hope

Alaska Maritime NWR

De Long Mts

Mishteguk Mt 4230

Noatak National Preserve

Brooks

Anaktuvuk Pass

Anaktuvuk

Mt Doonera 8800

Kivalina

Cape Krusenstern National Monument

Noatak

Baird Mts

Gates of the Arctic National Park & Preserve

Wiseum

Kobuk Valley National Park

Endicott Mts

Coldfoot

Naukan

Cape Dezhnev

Shishmaref

Kotzebue

Noorvik

Selawik National Wildlife Refuge

Ambler

Kobuk

Bettles

Dalton Hwy

USA

Big Diomede I.

Little Diomede I.

Wales

Bering Land Bridge National Preserve

Kotzebue Sound

Deering

Alaska

Kanuti NWR

Koyukuk

Port Clarence

Taylor

Seward Peninsula

Granite Mt 2844

Koyukuk National Wildlife Refuge

Wolf Mt 4978

Tanana

Yukon

Livengood

Min

King I.

Teller

Cape Rodney

Nome

Council

Koyuk

Haycock

Koyukuk

Nulato

Galena

Mahley Hot Springs

Nenana

Cape Darby

Norton Sound

Kaltag

Innoko NWR

Ruby

Totson Mt 2714

Poorman

3

Unalakleet

Pastol Bay

Saint Michael

Nowitna

Kantishna

Cantw

Emmonak

Mountain Village

Marshall

Holy Cross

Yukon

Innoko

Idatrod

Ophir

Innoko National Wildlife Refuge

McGrath

Sterling Landing

Mt McKinley 20320

Denali National Park & Preserve

Petersville

Sovere

88

Scammon Bay

Hooper Bay

Kashunuk

Kuskokwim Mountains

Aniak

Sleetmute

Hoholitna

Stony

Mt Torbert 11413

Talkeetna

Skwentna

Palm

Hazen Bay

Toksook Bay

Mekoryuk

Baird Inlet

Dall Lake

Bethel

Yukon Delta National Wildlife Refuge

Kuskokwim

Kilbuck Mts

Aniak

Wood-Tikchik State Park

Mulchatna

Lake Clark National Park & Preserve

Chugiak

Krik

Anchorage

Nunivak Island

Cape Mendenhall

Kipnuk

Kwigillingok

Eek

Tikchik Lakes

Iliamna

Redoubt Volcano 10197

Hope

Kenai

BERING SEA

Quinhagak

Goodnews Bay

Platinum

Kuskokwim Bay

Ahklun Mts

Togiak National Wildlife Refuge

Togiak

Iliamna Lake

Aleutian Range

Seldovia

Homer

Kenai Peninsula

Kenai Fjo National

Sew

Cape Newenham

Hagemeister Island

Dillingham

Naknek

Katmai National Park & Preserve

Mt Douglas 7063

Kennedy Entrance

St Paul

Pribilof Islands

St George

Cape Constantine

Egegik

Naknek Lake

Mt Denison 7606

Shelikof Strait

Shuyak Island

Afognak Island

Bristol Bay

Becharof Lake

Karluk

Kodiak Island

Ugak Bay

Kodiak

Ugashik Lake

Nanatak

Kodiak NWR

Sitkalidak Island

Port Heiden

Alaska Peninsula NWR

Aniakchak National Monument & Preserve

Sitkinak Strait

Cape Rozhnof

Port Moller

Chignik

Castle Cape

Sutwik Island

Tugidak

Trinity Islands

Pavlov Volcano 8905

Alaska Peninsula

Alaska Peninsula National Wildlife Refuge

Perryville

Kupreanof Point

Chirikof Island

Attu

Cold Bay

False Pass

Unimak Island

Shishaldin Volcano 9372

Sanak Island

Deer Island

Unga

Nagai

Shumagin Islands

Agattu

Near Islands

Unalaska Island

Akutan

Akun

Tigalda

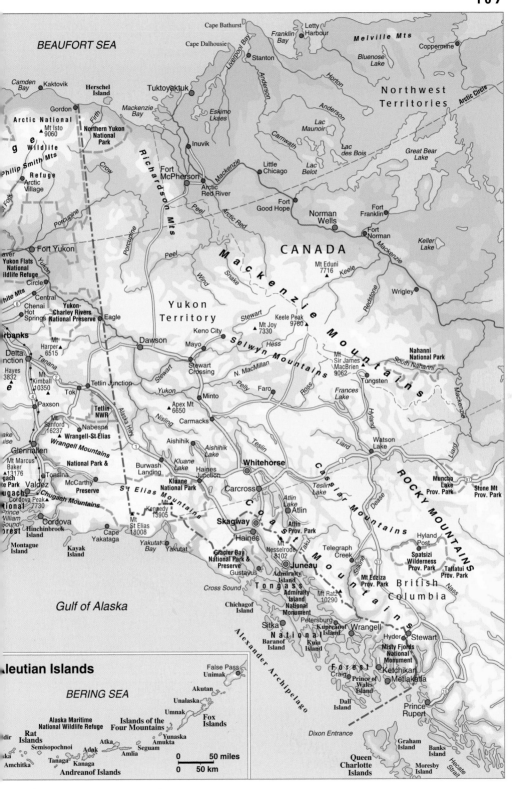

BEAUFORT SEA

Cape Bathurst
Letty
Harbour
Cape Dalhousie
Franklin
Bay
Melville Mts
Coppermine

Camden
Bay
Kaktovik
Herschel
Island
Tuktoyaktuk
Stanton
Liverpool Bay
Bluenose
Lake
Northwest
Territories
Arctic Circle

Gordon
Mackenzie
Bay
Eskimo
Lkaes
Anderson
Anderson
Horton

Arctic National
Mt Isto
9060
Inuvik
Carnwath
Lac
Maunoir
Lac
des Bois
Great Bear
Lake

Philip Smith Mts
g
Wildlife
Northern Yukon
National Park
Fort
McPherson
Little
Chicago
Lac
Belot

Refuge
Arctic
Village
Crow
Richardson Mts
Arctic
Red River
Mackenzie
Fort
Good Hope
Norman
Wells
Fort
Franklin

Porcupine
Peel
Arctic Red
Fort
Norman
Keller
Lake

Fort Yukon
Porcupine
Peel
CANADA
Mackenzie

aver
Yukon Flats
National
ildlife Refuge
Circle
Peel
Wind
Snake
Mt Eduni
7716
Keele
Wrigley

hite Mts
6
Central
Chenai
Hot
Springs
Yukon-
Charley Rivers
National Preserve
Eagle
Yukon
Territory
Stewart
Keele Peak
9780
Mackenzie Mountains
Redstone

rbanks
Mt
Harper
6515
Dawson
Keno City
Mayo
Mt Joy
7330
Hess
Sir James
MacBrien
9062
Nahanni
National Park
South Nahanni

Delta
nction
Tanana
Tetlin Junction
Stewart
Crossing
N. MacMillan
Selwyn Mountains
Tungsten
Liard

Hayes
3832
e
Mt
Kimball
10350
Tok
Yukon
Minto
Pelly
Faro
Ross
Frances
Lake

Paxson
Tetlin
NWR
Nisling
Apex Mt
6650
Carmacks
Teslin
Watson
Lake

Mt
Sanford
16237
Nabesna
Wrangell-St Elias
Aishihik
Aishihik
Lake
Liard

Glennallen
Mt Marcus
Baker
13176
gach
Tonsina
Wrangell Mountains
National Park &
Burwash
Landing
Kluane
Lake
Haines
Junction
Whitehorse
Teslin Lake
Cassiar Mountains
Dease
Muncho
Lake
Prov. Park
Stone Mt
Prov. Park

Valdez
McCarthy
Preserve
St Elias Mountains
Kluane
National Park
Carcross
Atlin
Lake
Liard
ROCKY MOUNTAINS

ugach
Cordova Peak
7730
Kennedy
Mt
13905
Skagway
Atlin
Atlin
Prov. Park
Telegraph
Creek
Hyland
Post
Spatsizi
Wilderness
Prov. Park

ional
orest
Cordova
Hinchinbrook
Island
Mt
St Elias
18008
Yakutat
Bay
Haines
Mt
Nesselrode
8102
Juneau
Stikine
Mt Ediza
Prov. Park
Nass
Taflatui
Prov. Park

Montague
Island
Kayak
Island
Cape
Yakataga
Yakutat
Glacier Bay
National Park &
Preserve
Gustavus
Admiralty
Island
Coast Mountains
Mt Ratz
10290
British
Columbia

Prince
illiam
ound
Cross Sound
Chichagof
Island
Tongass
Admiralty
Island
National
Monument
Petersburg
Hyder
Stewart

Gulf of Alaska
Alexander Archipelago
Sitka
Baranof
Island
Kuiu
Island
National
Kupreanof
Island
Wrangell
Misty Fjords
National
Monument

Aleutian Islands
BERING SEA
False Pass
Unimak
Akutan
Unalaska
Fox
Islands
Forest
Craig
Prince of
Wales
Island
Ketchikan
Metlakatla
16

dir
Rat
Islands
Semisopochnoi
Adak
Atka
Amukta
Yunaska
Umnak
Dall
Island
Prince
Rupert

ska
Amchitka
Tanaga
Kanaga
Amlia
Seguam
Andreanof Islands
0   50 miles
0   50 km
Dixon Entrance
Queen
Charlotte
Islands
Graham
Island
Banks
Island
Moresby
Island

Southeast Alaska: The Panhandle

Mt St Elias 18008

Wrangell-St Elias NP & R

Malaspina Glacier

Hubbard Glacier

St Elias Mountains

Mt Vancouver 15700

Mt Kennedy 13905

Kluane National Park

Mt Aylesworth 9310

Teslin

Canyon Creek

Haines Junction

Champagne

Alaska Hwy

Takhini

Lake Laberge

Big Salmon Range

Whitehorse

Yukon Territory

Johnsons Crossing

Wolf Lake

Klukshu

Dezadeash Lake

Kusawa Lake

Haines Hwy

Squaw Creek

Mt Hay 8870

Chilkat Pass 7300

Carcross

Marsh Lake

Tagish

Nisutlin

Wolf

Alaska Hwy

Teslin

Teslin Lake

Swift River

Dry Bay

Mt Fairweather 15300

Cape Fairweather

Lituya Bay

Russell Fjord

Alsek

Fairweather Range

Muir Glacier

Glacier Bay National Park and Preserve **8**

Klukwan

Porcupine

Alaska Chilkat Bald Eagle Preserve **9**

Haines

Port Chilkoot

Chilkat

Klondike Gold Rush National Historic Park **11**

Dyea

White Pass 2890

Glacier

Skagway 10

Bennett

Atlin Lake

Ben-My-Chree

Pike

Atlin Provincial Park

Mt Nesselrode 8102

Atlin

Galbraith

Nakina

Surprise

Lemieux

Klondike Hwy

Tak Inlet

Tak Arm

Lynn Canal

Chilkat Range

Inklin

Inklin

Taku

Nahlin

CANADA

British Columbia

Yakutat Bay

Ocean Cape

Yakutat **12**

Cordova, Valdez

Icy Point

Cape Spencer

Cross Sound

Elfin Cove

Cape Spencer

Pelican

Portage

Point Theodore

Gustavus

Glacier Bay

Excursion Inlet

Funter

Auke Bay

Mendenhall Glacier

Juneau 7

Douglas

Hawk Inlet

Hoonah

Chichagof Island

Tenakee Springs

Chatham

Cobol

Todd

Tongass

Admiralty Island National Monument

Pack Creek

Angoon

Admiralty Island

Sumdum

Windham

Mt Ogden 7482

Tulsequah

Taku

Stephens Passage

Seymour Canal

Coast Mountains

Sheslay

Tahltan

Telegraph Creek

Glenora

Mt Ediza Provincial Park

Kruzof Island

6 Sitka

Baranof

Mount Edgecumbe

Goddard

Baranof

Tyee

Island

ALASKA USA

Cape Fanshaw

Frederick Sound

Maury Peak 5575

Mt Ratz 10290

Whale Bay

Port Alexander

Chatham Strait

Kake

Kuiu Island

Tebenkof Bay Wilderness

Point Baker

Sumner Strait

Kupreanof Island 4

Petersburg

Zarembo Island

Mitkof Island

3 Wrangell

Wrangell Island

LeConte Glacier **5**

Baird Glacier

Stikine

Mt Whipple 3745

Iskut

Stikine

Unuk

Coronation Island

Cape Pole

Tokeen

Edna Bay

Warren Island

Etolin Island

Gulf of Alaska

Alexander Archipelago

National

Forest

Thorne Bay

Bell Island

Stewart

Hyder

Kincolith

Arrandale

Noyes Island

Klawock

Craig

Hollis

Meyers Chuck

Salt Chuck

Kasan

Loring

Prince of Wales Island

Baker Island

Waterfall

Wadley Cove

Revillagigedo Island **1**

Rudyerd Bay Punchbowl Cove

Ketchikan

Graviña Island

Saxman

Misty Fjords National Monument **2**

Hydaburg

Annette Island

Metlakatla

Dall Island

Kaigani

Cape Muzon

Cordova Bay

Cape Chacon

Clarence Strait

Duke Island

Behm Canal

Cape Fox

Portland Inlet

Dundas Island

Port Simpson

Dixon Entrance

Queen Charlotte Islands

Stephens Island

Porcher Island

Prince Rupert

Port Edward

N

0   100 miles

0   100 km

TOURING THE SOUTHEAST PANHANDLE

A cruise or ferry tour of the Panhandle is a good introduction to Alaska, giving the visitor a taste of the scenery and the culture

Ever since it emerged from the melting of the last great Ice Age 15,000 years ago, the great island-studded, 1,000-mile (1,600-km) passage of water that stretches from present-day lower British Columbia to the top of the Southeast Alaska Panhandle has been one of earth's treasures. The first Europeans to visit a portion of what is now called the Inside Passage did not get a friendly reception from the locals, however. In 1741 Alexei Chirikof, captain of *St Paul*, set sail from Russia. With his commander, Vitus Bering (who also was captain of the vessel *St Peter*), he left the Kamchatkan Peninsula in Siberia and headed east on a voyage of exploration and discovery.

The two captains were separated in a storm which struck soon after leaving port, and never saw each other again. Bering died after being shipwrecked on his voyage home. Chirikof and his crew sighted the high wooded mountains of what we now call Prince of Wales Island in Southeast Alaska on July 15, 1741. Two days later they dropped anchor near the present-day city of Sitka. It was there that tragedy struck, when two boatloads of sailors put ashore to reconnoiter disappeared without trace (see page 45).

These days, it is not often that visitors to the Panhandle fail to return to ship. When it does happen, it is probably because they lose track of time while hiking to the top of Deer Mountain in Ketchikan, get carried away in the pursuit of pleasure at the Red Dog Saloon in Juneau, or simply decide the fishing is too good to be hurried.

Lifestyles along the Inside Passage

The sights along the Inside Passage are surprisingly varied and seldom boring. There are two capital cities along the length of the passage, one Canadian (Victoria) and one American (Juneau), where life and lifestyle revolve largely around politics and bureaucracy. And there are tiny Native villages where the food on most residents' tables still depends on the skills of the hunters and fishermen.

There are homes and condos and high-rise hotels as modern as those in any of the world's communities, and there are tiny, hand-built cabins and camps which may be spotted – briefly, on a cruise or during a fly-by – in

ABOVE: a contemporary gold panner; fishing boats in Wrangell harbor.

isolated wilderness settings far from roads, stores, television stations or daily newspapers.

The geography and the geology of the Inside Passage varies greatly as well. At its southernmost end, the passage is protected by Vancouver Island, a large, elongated landmass that begins near the northern border of the continental United States and stretches almost 300 miles (480km) northwest, nearly half the distance up the British Columbia coast to Southeast Alaska.

Then comes the seaward protection of the Queen Charlotte Islands, not as large as Vancouver Island but a number of them – especially Graham and Moresby islands – quite sizeable nonetheless.

And finally, about where US jurisdiction resumes and Southeast Alaska begins, there's the Alexander Archipelago, a 400-mile (645-km) long maze of 1,000 massive and minuscule isles which, along with a 30-mile (48-km) wide sliver of mainland, make up the Southeast Alaska Panhandle. In this book, only destinations that fall within Alaska's state boundary are covered.

If the size and national colors of the islands of the Inside Passage vary, there is this commonality all along the way: lush green forests of spruce, hemlock, cedar, fir and other conifers cover whole islands and mountains except for snow-capped peaks, ice fields feeding glaciers and gravel beaches. Generous bays and exquisite little coves rival one another for attention, and major rivers course through great glacier-carved valleys, while waterfalls plunge from mountainside cliffs to the sea.

The islands' allure

Everywhere along the way are watercraft: seine boats with crews of half a dozen or more; small trollers and gillnet fishing craft with a skipper and,

maybe, a single helper; tugs pulling rafts of logs or barges of commercial goods; exotic yachts and simple open boats; cruise-ships; state ferries; freighters; even sailboats and kayaks. The reason for this concentration of watercraft, of course, is protection. The same islands which provide near-continuous evergreen beauty to visitors along the way provide buffers from North Pacific winds and weather that could otherwise threaten all but the toughest vessels.

The islands also protect and nurture a wide variety of wild creatures. Ashore, and beyond the gaze of spectators, numerous animals make their homes within the forests and even atop the mountains of the Southeast Alaska Panhandle. Charter a light aircraft at Yakutat, near the very top of the Panhandle, and you are likely to see moose and perhaps brown bear as well. Near Juneau or Ketchikan or any of the other cities in the region, there is a good opportunity to spot groups of white mountain goats.

Take one of the kayak excursions in **Glacier Bay National Park** in the northern Panhandle *(see pages 144–7)*, and as you paddle alongside forest or beach you just might see the rare "Glacier Blue" – a subspecies of black

ABOVE: Chilkat dancer in Haines; Skagway excursion. **RIGHT:** abundant sealife.

bear. Cruise or fly to Pack Creek on **Admiralty Island** *(see pages 114 and 123)* during the salmon spawning season and you can easily view and photograph dozens of huge, lumbering brown bears.

Spotting wildlife

Throughout the Panhandle, and down the coast of British Columbia as well, Sitka black-tail deer are numerous. This is one species of land animal you may be able to spot along the beaches from a cruise ship.

Sea mammals are easier to see from a boat, of course. Humpback and killer whales, cavorting porpoises in twos and fours, and sea lions, seals and sea otters by the dozen are frequent sights, much appreciated by vessel-borne visitors along the Inside Passage.

Eagles are everywhere – the white-headed, white-tailed bald eagle, symbol of the United States. You see them diving and swooping from the heights to grab unwary fish swimming near the water's surface, you witness the strength of their powerful talons as they rip salmon carcasses to shreds alongside spawning streams, and you see them high in the spruce trees, standing guard over heavy nests that are lodged in the forks of great branches.

Besides the eagles, there are huge black ravens, tiny gray wrens and black-capped Arctic terns (which come here from as far south as Antarctica), plus hundreds of different waterfowl, shorebirds, sea birds and upland species.

The fishing here is world-class. Perhaps your goal is to haul in a lunker king salmon of 50lbs (23kg) or more. Or maybe you want to test your skill against diving, dancing and frothing steelhead trout. Whatever your heart's desire, the fishing in this region is simply unbeaten anywhere else. In addition to kings and steelheads, there are coho (silver) salmon – considered by many to be, pound for pound, the gamest fish in salt water – plus sockeye salmon, halibut, rainbow trout, Dolly Varden and eastern brook trout (these latter two are actually chars).

With this concentration of fish, wildlife and scenic beauty, it's easy to see why increasing numbers of people choose to settle in this region.   ❏

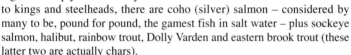

Getting There

Only three of the many Southeast Alaska communities are located on any road system; therefore travel to and within the area is generally by air or water. In fact, nearly 60 percent of all visitors to Alaska arrive by cruise ship.

The second most common mode of arrival is by air. Alaska Airlines offers, by far, the most comprehensive coverage of the state, with regularly scheduled jet service to every major community (and some incredibly minor ones – *see Yakutat, page 160*).

Regional airlines, air taxis and charter services (using small planes on wheels, skis or floats) provide transportation to any and all locations within the state, including Southeast. For information on local air carriers, check the visitor information web site of the community nearest your destination *(see Travel Tips, page 355)*.

The Alaska Marine Highway System ferries are the most common (and economical) option for travel between Southeast communities *(see page 117)*. Cross-sound ferry service, connecting Southeast routes with those in Southcentral and Southwest, is available twice monthly in summer. For schedules and rates, contact the AMHS directly (tel: 800/ 642-0066; www.dot.state.ak.us/amhs).

KETCHIKAN

Creek Street's brothels have turned into restaurants
and boutiques, but the area's frontier past is
commemorated in shows and exhibitions
highlighting totems, eagles and lumberjack skills

The city of **Ketchikan** ❶ tumbles down the densely-forested, mountainous, southwestern side of Revillagigedo Island until it reaches its distinctive angle of repose: stacks of steep-roofed houses cling to the wooded slope, while the business district, apparently unable to halt the momentum, surges forward onto pilings in the Tongass Narrows. Located near the southernmost boundary of Alaska, Ketchikan is a major port of entry for Southeast Alaska and is generally the first stop for Alaska-bound cruise ships and Alaska Marine Highway System ferries.

Salmon Capital

The "First City", or the "Salmon Capitol of the World" as it is referred to by locals, is an industrious community; one that has adapted through several economic "boom and bust" cycles. Many of the 7,600 residents (14,000, counting the surrounding areas) work in commercial fishing, fish processing, tourism, or logging.

The earliest inhabitants of the area were Tongass and Cape Fox Tlingit Indians, who established a fish camp by Ketchikan Creek and called it "kitschk-hin", or "thundering wings of an eagle". The region's mild, maritime climate and rich natural resources, primarily timber and fish, eventually drew non-Native adventurers. As more settlers moved into the area, the majority of the Tlingit population relocated to nearby Saxman.

In 1885, a founder of Ketchikan, Mike Martin, bought 160 acres of land from Tlingit Chief Kyan – a parcel that later became the town site. The first cannery was soon built along the creek and, by 1936, a total of seven canneries were operating in the area.

Following the discovery of gold and copper in the region, the City of Ketchikan (incorporated in 1900) became an important mining supply center. As the city grew, so did the demand for lumber. Ketchikan Spruce Mills opened its doors in 1903, and the city became the hub for logging activities and supplies. In 1954, the Ward Cove pulp

Main attractions
CREEK STREET
DOLLY'S HOUSE
SOUTHEAST DISCOVERY CENTER
DEER MOUNTAIN TRIBAL HATCHERY
 & EAGLE CENTER
TONGASS HISTORICAL MUSEUM
POTLATCH PARK
SAXMAN
TOTEM HERITAGE CENTER

LEFT: Totem Heritage Center.
BELOW: Ketchikan.

A guide at Dolly's House.

BELOW: Creek Street, Ketchikan.

mill was constructed nearby, and the operation provided many years of economic growth and stability for Ketchikan residents. The U.S. Forest Service eventually canceled its 50-year contract with the company, however, and the pulp mill closed in March 1997.

There were other reasons for fishermen, miners and loggers to flock to Ketchikan in the early 1900s. The town's infamous **Creek Street** ⓐ enjoyed a booming alcohol trade at the time of the territory's Bone Dry Law of 1917, the National Prohibition Act of 1920 and for many years to follow. Rowdy crowds gathered for the music, dancing and "social opportunities" of the notorious Star dance hall and the several houses of prostitution nearby. In 1953, this bawdy era of Creek Street ended as city officials permanently closed the doors of the brothels.

From brothel to museum

Today the wooden walkway of a chastened Creek Street leads tourists through a colorful array of gift shops, galleries, restaurants, coffee shops (featuring a delicious, locally roasted brew) and

Dolly's House, a popular brothel-turned-museum. While in the Creek Street area, you should take a ride on the **funicular tram** (entrance charge), which travels up the steep mountainside to the lobby of the beautiful Cape Fox Lodge Hotel. The brief ride will afford a good view of the city and a chance to enjoy fine dining at the hotel restaurant.

A stop at the **Ketchikan Visitors Bureau** ⓑ (131 Front Street; open daily summers 6am–7pm; year round, Mon–Fri 8am–5pm; tel: 800-770-3300; 225-6166; www.visit-ketchikan.com), located on the cruise ship dock, will help you plan your visit. The staff will answer questions and hand you a walking tour map as well as the *Ketchikan Art Guide*.

The Bureau's **tour center**, located in the same building, provides public restrooms, pay phones, an ATM (cash machine), a phone card dispenser and bicycle or scooter rentals. You may also purchase tickets at the center for local attractions (like the popular **Great Alaskan Lumberjack Show**) or to tour Ketchikan and surrounding areas via horse-drawn trolley, Hummer, motorcycle, ATV, tour boat, kayak, semi-sub-

---

Remote Adventuring in the Southeast

In addition to the major communities along the Inside Passage, there are countless other settlements worth a day's or a week's visit. Near Ketchikan, on Prince of Wales Island, a colorful old cannery has been converted into **Waterfall Resort** (www.waterfallresort.com), what the owners call "the most civilized resort in Alaska." It's within easy reach of some of Southeast Alaska's hottest salmon angling.

Angoon is the only settlement in **Admiralty Island National Monument**, a largely wilderness preserve that can be reached by air or sea from Sitka or Juneau, and that is famous for its salmon and large numbers of brown bears. **Kake**, which has the tallest totem pole in the state, is the jumping-off point for trips to **Tebenkof Bay Wilderness**, where experienced kayakers can spend days paddling the waters around the bays and coves of many tiny islands. **Hoonah**, the largest Tlingit village in Southeast Alaska, has some good hiking trails and a Cultural Center and Museum, which exhibits Tlingit art.

Small commercial fishing centers, like **Elfin Cove**, **Tenakee Springs**, with its hot thermal baths, and **Pelican**, though never touted as tourist towns, provide visitors with indelible memories of a very contented part of Alaska. Pelican can be visited on a day trip from Juneau through the **Icy Strait**, where you may well see humpback whales.

mersible or amphibious craft, aerial zip-line, or floatplane (to name a few).

The tour center can also help you arrange for a fishing charter from one of many local operators. Public transportation and taxi stands are close by for those who prefer to strike out on their own.

Be sure to visit the **Southeast Discovery Center** ❻ (50 Main Street; open daily 8am–5pm May 6–Sept. 27, Tues–Sat 10am–4:30pm Sept 28–May 5; tel: 228-6220; www.fs.fed.us/r10/tongass/districts/discoverycenter; entrance charge in summer only). This excellent interpretive facility, operated by the US Forest Service, will give you an overview of the Tongass National Forest, its history, wildlife, and various recreational opportunities including hiking, boating, kayaking, fishing, camping and remote cabin rentals. The center also features authentic totems, Native artists in residence, Tlingit, Haida and Tsimshian cultural exhibits, and a gift shop.

In addition to the Discovery Center and the Creek Street shops, the **Deer Mountain Tribal Hatchery and Eagle Center** ❼ (1158 Salmon Road; open daily 8am–4:30pm May–Sept; tel: 228-5530; 800-252-5158; www.kictribe.org/Hatchery; entrance charge) is an easy stroll from the downtown area, and offers a chance to see an active salmon and steelhead hatchery, visit a fish ladder, and watch live bird of prey demonstrations.

The small, but interesting **Tongass Historical Museum** ❺ is also nearby (629 Dock Street, open daily 8am–5pm May–Sept; tel: 225-5600; www.city.ketchikan.ak.us/departments/museums/tongass; entrance charge). Its photographic collection is a particular strength.

Potlatch Park

Among the Native peoples of North America's northwest coastal communities, a potlatch is a ceremony that includes not only a sumptuous feast of traditional Native dishes, but also the giving of gifts (often lavish) by the potlatch host. Ketchikan's newest totem site, **Potlatch Park** ❻ (9805 Totem Bight Road, open daily 7:30am– approximately 6pm; www.potlatchpark.com) was dedicated in August 2006 as a tribute to the major tribal ancestors of the Native villages of the Ketchikan area (including Metlakatla, Hydaburg, Craig and Kla-

TIP

The best way to see Ketchikan is on foot, as part of an organized tour or an independent ramble. But be prepared for rain. The town "enjoys" a yearly average of 13.5 ft (4 meters) of precipitation, so the chances of getting wet are excellent. Fortunately, most of the attractions are within a short walk.

Ketchikan

0 _____ 200 yds
0 _____ 200 m

Traditional totems captured a family's heritage in their design, and the pole's height was often an indication of wealth and power.

RIGHT: eating out in Ketchikan.

wock). The 5-acre (2-hectare) park, located 10 miles north of downtown, is situated in a wooded area facing the Tongass Narrows – the site of ancient Tlingit fishing grounds. It features 12 full-sized totems (the tallest measuring 42 ft/12.8 meters in height), five intricately carved tribal houses, a busy carving center, an antique car museum, an antique Alaskan firearm museum and an expansive gift shop offering a wide variety of local souvenirs, interesting Native art displays and free coffee.

The main tribal house is an exact recreation of an 18th-century dwelling, which would have housed up to 50 people, and is held together by gravity, as opposed to nails, fasteners and bolts.

Inside the nearby carving center, Brita Alander (a master carver of the Eagle Frog Clan of the Haida Nation of Ketchikan) and her staff are busy chiseling family stories into elaborate totems made from 36-ft (11-meter) cedar logs. Potlatch Park, owned by Kanoe Zantua (also of the Eagle Frog Clan) is well worth visiting by those interested in Native culture, as it "…stands in tribute to the souls of Alaska coastal communities."

Saxman

Just 2 miles (3km) south of Ketchikan is the Native village of **Saxman** ⑥ (actually an incorporated city, with a population of about 400 – primarily Tlingit – residents). The Cape Fox Corporation (www.capefoxtours.com) offers an interesting tour of the **Saxman Totem Park**, which includes a tribal house, carving center (where you can watch Native artisans at work), a cultural hall featuring Tlingit dance exhibitions, and a gift shop.

Other Cape Fox offerings include a trip to the historic George Inlet Cannery site, or an opportunity for fly-fishing in a remote river valley.

More totems are on show at the **Totem Heritage Center** ⑦ (601 Deermount St; open daily 8am–5pm Ma–Sept; tel: 225-5900; www.city.ketchikan.ak.us/departments/museums/totem; entrance charge), at the much-visited **Totem Bight State Historical Park** (10 miles/16km north of town on North Tongass Highway).

Ketchikan is also the jumping-off point for **Misty Fiords National Monument** *(page 118)*. The monument, 40 miles/64km south of Ketchikan, is accessible by boat or floatplane. ❑

RESTAURANTS

Annabelle's Keg and Chowder House
326 Front Street (Gilmore Hotel)
tel: 225-6009
www.gilmorehotel.com
A convenient downtown restaurant. Open daily for lunch and dinner. Fresh Alaska seafood and good desserts. Full bar. $–$$$$

Heen Kahidi Dining Room (Cape Fox Lodge)
800 Venetia Avenue
tel: 225-8001
www.capefoxlodge.com
Take a scenic tram ride up from the downtown shops to enjoy breakfast, lunch or dinner while enjoying the view. Extensive menu, full bar. $–$$$$.

Oceanview Restaurant
1831 Tongass Avenue
tel: 225-7566
www.oceanviewmex.com
Eclectic menu features many delicious Mexican or Italian dishes. Beer and wine. $–$$$

Burger Queen
518 Water Street
tel: 225-6060
Burgers, breaded halibut, grilled chicken, salads and more served up in generous portions. Tiny seating area, consider take-out or the free delivery. $

● ● ● ● ● ● ● ● ● ● ● ● ● ● ● ● ●

Price is for dinner excluding tax, tip and beverages: **$$$$** *$30 and up,* **$$$** *$20–30,* **$$** *$15–20,* **$** *under $15.*

Getting Around by Ferry

Alaska Marine Highway System ferries are the main means of travel around this region, but you need to plan ahead in the busy summer months.

For independent travelers with the luxury of time, cruising the Inside Passage aboard one of the 11 state-run Alaska Marine Highway System (AMHS) ferries is a relaxing, comfortable and reasonably convenient option for seeing the coastal communities of Southeast, Southcentral and Southwest Alaska. Since driving between these communities is, generally speaking, not an option, locals rely heavily on ferry travel as a primary mode of transportation.

If you're traveling in spring or fall, you'll likely see school athletes, debate teams or spelling bee contestants bound for competitions in neighboring (or far-flung) coastal communities. Residents of more remote towns travel to larger communities for doctor visits, shopping, business and countless other reasons.

US Forest Service interpreters are onboard the ferries during the summer months to give informative lectures and to point out the interesting sights along the way. Additionally, visitors generally have no problem getting Alaskans onboard to talk about their state.

The AMHS ferries offer clean, comfortable staterooms (for most ships; advance reservations are important), tasty, reasonably priced cafeteria-style food service, a bar, clean restrooms, hot showers (towel rental available) and various lounges (some with recliners) featuring large windows for easy viewing of the passing landscape. Should the captain see a whale (or other notable wildlife) en route, he'll usually make a public announcement and try to maneuver the ship to allow for a good view.

Traveling aboard the Alaska ferries is also a great option for families with children. There's plenty of wiggle room, and most ferries have a play area for toddlers, a video game room, a movie room and, if you pay extra for a stateroom, a good place to nap. Those without staterooms spread out sleeping bags onto the carpeted floors at night, stretch out in one of the many recliners, or pitch a tent up on the top deck near the solarium.

The downside of ferry travel is that if you bring a vehicle aboard the cost jumps considerably. You must make reservations early because the car decks fill up quickly for the summer months. The price for traveling non-stop from one end of Southeast to the other is not hugely different from that of breaking up your trip with stopovers at various communities along the way. But it may be a day or two (much more in some instances) before another ferry traveling in the desired direction comes along.

Information, routes, ship descriptions, fares and scheduling information are all available online at www.dot.state.ak.us/amhs, or telephone: 800-642-0066; 465-3941). ❏

ABOVE: backpackers use a ferry as a dormitory.
RIGHT: a ferry docks at Ketchikan.

MISTY FIORDS NATIONAL MONUMENT

The southernmost of Alaska's national monuments is a magical place, carved out by the steady progress of gigantic glaciers

BELOW: New
Eddystone Rock.

Misty Fiords was designated by the US Congress as a national wilderness as well as a national monument, and within the 3,570 sq. miles (9,240 sq. km) of its largely untouched coast and backcountry lie three major rivers, hundreds of small streams and creeks, icefields, glaciers, old-growth rain forest, snowcapped mountains and mountain-top lakes.

Glacial scenery

Eons ago, great glaciers thousands of feet deep filled what are now Southeast Alaska bays and valleys. Slowly but relentlessly they ground their way seaward from mountain-top heights. In the process they carved and scoured great steep-walled cliffs that now plunge from mountain summits to considerable depths below sea level. The effect of this carving and scouring has never been more beautifully evident than it is in **Misty Fiords National Monument ❷**.

It is the southernmost of Alaska's four national monuments and one of two in the Tongass National Forest (the other is Admiralty Island). Visitors to this 2.2-million-acre (890,000-hectare) wilderness experience every major ecosystem of Southeast Alaska, from the ocean swells on the outer coast to the high alpine lakes and icefields. There are tiny coves, great bays, and forest groves so thick you can barely see daylight through them.

Misty Fiords wildlife includes brown and black bears, Sitka black-tail deer, wolves, mountain goats, beavers, mink, marten, foxes and river otters. But it is not only a place of scenery and wildlife on a grand scale: it also has tremendous commercial value. Some of Alaska's most productive fish-rearing streams are located here.

There are very few marks of human activity inside Misty Fiords. The area's first human inhabitants, the Native Tlingits and Haidas, are believed to have settled here many thousands of years ago, after crossing the land bridge from Siberia, but there is little evidence of their passing.

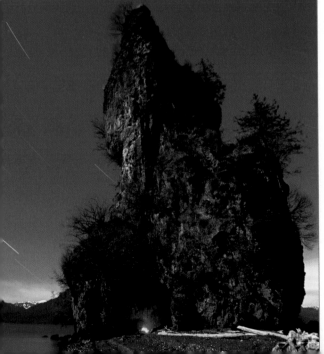

Touring Misty Fiords

No roads lead to Misty Fiords, and visitors can reach the monument only by water or by air. Some travelers opt for a combination cruise/fly tour – going in by water and out by air, or vice versa. Some cruise-ships visit the monument as part of an Inside Passage experience *(see page 89)*. You can fly there with one of several Ketchikan air charter companies; you can cruise there by charter boat; or (probably most convenient of all) you can sign on with an outfit called Alaska Cruises (tel: 225-6044 or 800-228-1905; www.goldbelttours.com), and take one of the yacht tours which the company schedules daily in the summer time.

These excursions, aboard one of the company's 90-passenger vessels, can either be a round-trip or one-way, with one part of the journey – either coming or going – done by air. Round-trip cruises last about 6½ hours, while combination cruise-flightseeing trips are 4½ hours long

On a typical cruise/fly tour, the boat will depart from near downtown Ketchikan in early to mid-morning, but coffee is always ready on the galley stove and donuts are on the serving table for passengers who arrive on the ship early. These boats are wide, beamy, comfortable cruisers with plenty of walking-around room, big view windows, and table seating for 32. When the weather is good, passengers can go onto an open-air deck above the cabin.

Salmon route

The sightseeing begins as soon as the boat's lines are cast off and the vessel begins its southeasterly path toward the lower end of Revillagigedo Island (the locals abbreviate it to Revilla Island), on which Ketchikan is located. Passing dockside fish processors, supply houses and the town's main business district, the vessel soon cruises past the entrance to **Ketchikan Creek**. Late in the summer, thousands of salmon assemble here before ascending the creek – and formidable waterfalls – to spawn in the upstream shallows and then die.

Shortly after Creek Street (Ketchikan's former red-light district), the boat goes past **Saxman** *(see page 116)*, a Native village containing one of the largest collections of totems in the state.

Next is **Bold Island**, where passengers line the port (left-hand) rails and windows of the vessel in the hope of seeing bald eagles perched in the island spruce trees. For Southeast Alaskans, such sightings are commonplace, though they never become dull. For visitors, the sight of America's national bird is a highlight of the trip.

At one point or another during the morning's cruise, most passengers will crowd into the yacht's little wheelhouse

No permit is needed for camping or in Misty Fiords, but visitors are advised to discuss plans with rangers before arriving. For details, contact the US Forest Service, tel: 907-225-2148.

BELOW: Punchbowl Lake, Misty Fiords National Monument.

Orca whales hunting for porpoises.

RIGHT:
a Sitka Black Tail deer crosses a hiking trail.

and talk to the skipper. Sometimes that's Dale Pihlman, former owner of the Alaska Cruises excursion firm. He generally welcomes the intrusion, as he is never reluctant to talk about the monument.

Pihlman, a former commercial fisherman, was one of the committed people who traveled to Washington in the late 1970s to lobby for the bill that created Misty Fiords National Monument in the first place. The provisions of the bill do protect most of the monument – and all of the wilderness – from any destructive exploitation.

Porpoise companions

As the boat cruises toward the fjords, the on-board guide and naturalist may announce that there are porpoises both fore and aft of the vessel, and the passengers – half going in each direction in order to keep an even kilter – scramble for a view of the small marine mammals. The porpoises swimming behind the yacht are too far away for a close look – they are visible only as leaping, playing creatures 300 feet or more astern. But the ones in front are only a few feet away, clearly visible, and just as clearly having

a wonderful time pacing the boat. For brief moments their dorsal fins break the surface of the water; at other times they dive. It's obvious they could easily outdistance the vessel, but they prefer to stay and play, and they will do so for 15 minutes or so.

By noon the vessel is in the monument and the skipper guides it through a narrow channel into an exquisite little tree-shrouded cove on **Rudyerd Island**. The naturalist points out the steep granite rock formations on the shore and the occasional jet black vertical streaks, a few inches to a couple of feet or more wide, that appear among the brown granite walls. These were formed 60 million years ago when earthquakes in the region cracked the granite, and hot molten magma came up from below the earth's surface to fill the cracks. The black streaks that you see are the magma.

Shapely rock

A little later, **New Eddystone Rock** *(see photograph on page 118)* comes into view. Depending upon the time of day when you see it and the angle from which you approach it, the rock can

Dressing sensibly for the Southeast

The temperate rainforest of Southeast Alaska features a mild, wet, maritime climate. Average winter temperatures range from 29° to 39°F (–2° to 4°C)in Ketchikan (southernmost city) to 18° to 31° (–8° to –1°C) in Yakutat (northernmost community). Summers average 51° to 65°F (11° to 18°C) and 47° to 60°F (8° to 16°C) respectively.

The entire Panhandle experiences heavy precipitation (13½ feet (4.1 meters) per year average in Ketchikan; 11 feet (3.3 meters) in Yakutat), which creates the ideal environment for the unique flora and fauna of the area.

These conditions also create the need for summertime visitors to bring along excellent protection from wind and rain. Plan to dress in layers (to allow for warmth and comfort in a variable climate), and make sure the outer-most layer is waterproof. A quality-constructed, hooded rain jacket (with a drawstring to pull the hood close to your face), a light-weight, knitted hat, gloves, waterproof pants, and comfortable, waterproof footwear are ideal. Umbrellas, on the other hand, are difficult to manage, block your view and turn inside out in a sudden gust of wind... but this provides amusement for the locals.

Wintertime travelers should add winter-weight hooded coats, warm knit hats, mittens and insulated boots to their clothing list.

resemble several things: sometimes it looks like a man-made building, at others, a ship under sail, or it can look exactly what it is – a high-rising volcano "plug" from millennia past. It was called Eddystone Rock by the British navigator Captain George Vancouver (1758–98), after whom the Canadian city is named, because he thought it looked very much like Eddystone Lighthouse off the shore of his native Plymouth, in England.

Overnight campers and kayakers who want to go into the fjords often travel along with the day visitors on Alaska Cruises trips, and this is the time they leave the ship in their smaller craft to paddle the waters off Winstanley Island. There's a US Forest Service cabin there, one of relatively few located on saltwater sites in Southeast Alaska.

The comfortable, weather-tight shelter is popular with campers who paddle around **Rudyerd Bay** during the day. The cruiser enters the bay and often meets a welcoming committee of at least 20 seals, which lie basking on the rocks of an island to port.

Minutes later, within the bay, the boat approaches the towering vertical walls of **Punchbowl Cove**. And it is here that you really begin to feel the magical, mystical effect of the place.

Punchbowl Cove

It can be truly eerie hereabouts, especially when – as the monument's name suggests – there is mist or cloud or fog in the air. Steep, stark granite walls descend from heights hidden in clouds. Waterfalls, which range from torrents to trickles, plunge from unseen sources just as high. Trees cling tenaciously to many of the cliff-sides, on surfaces that don't seem to have enough soil to support a house plant.

The waters around and beneath the boat are a cold, slate gray, and they descend to depths of 750ft (230 meters) or more. There have, as yet, been no sightings of sea monster reported in these waters – but it's exactly the right kind of place for them.

On board, thoughts turn to more practical matters: it is time for a lunch of seafood chowder, rolls and tossed green salad. After lunch, the vessel leaves Punchbowl Cove and cruises toward the head of Rudyerd Bay. Along the shore-

TIP

Pronouncing certain placenames in the Southeast can be tricky. Here's a guide:

Tlingit: *KLINK–it*

Haida: *HY–duh*

Tsimshian: *SIM–shee–an*

Revillagigedo: *ruh–vee–uh–ga–GAY–doh*

Metlakatla: *met–la–KAT–la*

Klawock: *kla–WOCK*

Gustavus: *gus–TA–vus*

Dyea: *die-ee*

Yakutat: *YAK–a–tat*

BELOW:
Walker Cove
seen from a skiff.

Humpback whales are one of the area's great sights.

for yet another memorable experience. On some trips the skipper will edge his boat right up to the bottom of a large plummeting waterfall, and passengers are given paper cups which they can fill with the icy water. By mid-afternoon, it is time for those who fly back to Ketchikan to disembark and board the floatplane which taxis gently up to the boarding platform.

From the air

Fifteen minutes later, goodbyes are yelled to those remaining and the pilot drifts his plane away from the vessel. He then gives the aircraft full throttle, and within a minute it is airborne. Within three or four minutes more the airborne passengers may well be spotting white, furry mountain goats, usually nannies and their youngsters, negotiating seemingly impossible cliff faces to the right of the plane. It is a dramatic flight back through the fjords, and the wildlife is only part of the excitement as the dark granite walls seem to be just inches away from the plane's wing tips – a bit too close for comfort, some may think, but passengers are in very safe hands. ❑

line that now replaces the steep cliffs, you may look out for bears, wolves or other wild creatures.

Creeks and waterfalls

The boat stops again an hour later, this time at **Nooya Creek** where, in season, 1,000 or more pink salmon descend to salt water each year from Nooya Lake in the high country. Here a trail leads to the uplands – although it is not as steep as the one which takes off, and up, from the Punchbowl Cove area visited earlier. Camping and trout-fishing opportunities at the ends of the trails are outstanding. Then, if you are lucky, it might be time

BELOW: up-close view of a waterfall in Rudyerd Bay.

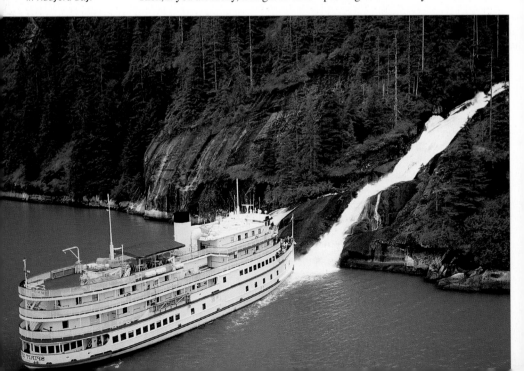

National Forests

Alaska is home to the nation's two largest national forests, the Tongass and the Chugach, located in the Southeast and Southcentral regions.

At nearly 17 million acres (6.9 million hectares, the **Tongass National Forest** (tel: 225-3101; www.fs.fed.us/r10/tongass) is by far America's biggest. Stretching the entire length of Alaska's Inside Passage, it encompasses three-fourths of the Panhandle. The Tongass was created in 1907 by President Theodore Roosevelt to protect the region's timber resources, wildlife, and fisheries; its name is taken from the Tlingit Indian tribe's Tongass clan.

Within the Tongass boundaries are huge expanses of old-growth coastal rain forest – about 32 percent of the total acreage. Over the years, a little more than 6 percent of this old-growth forest area has been harvested, mostly by clearcut methods. The remaining expanse, approximately 97 percent of the total old-growth area, remains today as it was 100 years ago, providing critical habitat for all sorts of animals, from brown and black bears to Sitka black-tailed deer, moose, mink, river otters, beavers, and five species of Pacific salmon. Birds range from eagles and owls to loons and songbirds.

One of the forest's prime wildlife areas is Admiralty Island, near Juneau, with one of the world's densest populations of brown bears; some 1,500 to 1,700 inhabit Admiralty, or about one per square mile. It is also has one of the world's largest concentrations of nesting bald eagles; biologists have identified more than 800 nests along Admiralty's 700 miles (1,100 km) of coastline. To protect its wildlife habitat, more than 90 percent of the island is protected as wilderness within Admiralty Island National Monument.

A second national monument is Misty Fiords, with more than 2 million acres (800,000 hectares) of coastal fjords, old-growth forest, mountains, rivers, lakes, and glaciers.

Besides its famed coastal forest, the Tongass includes a wide range of habitat, from coastal waters to high alpine tundra and huge icefields that feed hundreds of glaciers. Forest lands and waters are used for all sorts of recreation, from fishing to wildlife viewing.

Alaska's second national forest, the **Chugach**, includes nearly 6 million acres (2.4 million hectares) within its borders. Centered around Southcentral Alaska's coastal area, the forest reaches across three geographic regions: the northeastern Kenai Peninsula; Prince William Sound; and the Copper River Delta. Within its borders are Kayak Island, where Europeans first stepped foot on Alaskan soil; Columbia Glacier, one of the world's largest tidewater glaciers; and the Copper River Delta's rich wetlands, which serve as a critical staging and breeding area for North American waterfowl and shorebirds during their yearly migrations.

The Chugach encompasses many types of habitat, from lush forests and rugged coastline to high mountains, jagged ridges, ice fields and glaciers. It is a playground for all types of outdoor enthusiasts. One of the Chugach's most popular destinations is the Begich-Boggs Center (tel: 783-2326) near Portage Glacier, less than an hour's drive south of Anchorage. Additional information on Chugach National Forest is available from the US Forest Service in Anchorage (tel: 743-9500; www.fs.fed.us/r10/chugach). ❏

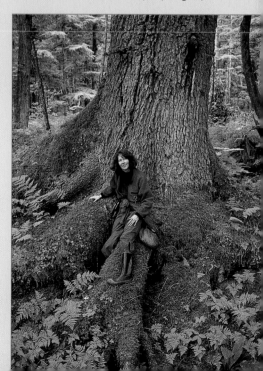

RIGHT: Tongass is an old-growth forest.

WRANGELL

Alaska
Anchorage
Wrangell

This was the only town in Alaska to fly the Russian, British and American flags. Today it is known for sports fishing and petroglyph spotting

Main attractions
GARNET LEDGE
JAMES AND ELSIE NOLAN
  CENTER
CHIEF SHAKES ISLAND
PETROGLYPH BEACH
MUSKEG MEADOWS
STIKINE RIVER
ANAN BEAR AND WILDLIFE
  OBSERVATORY

BELOW: Wrangell.

W hen you visit the heavily forested island community of Wrangell ❸, located 89 miles (143km) north of Ketchikan on Wrangell Island, what you see is pretty much what you get. There won't be any semi-submersible or zip-line tours like in Ketchikan; no streets lined with restored (or, as in Skagway, re-created), gold rush-styled false-front saloons or dance halls to amaze and amuse.

What you can look forward to is an authentic, working town of about 2,000 people, many of whom, for generations, have fed their families by logging in the Tongass, working in local sawmills or commercial fishing. National forest management policies, responding to environmental concerns, have curtailed much of the Tongass logging, and Wrangell's lumberjacks have done what their grandfathers and great-grandfathers before them did: adapt. Their city is in the process of transitioning to a broader-based economy that includes seafood processing, value-added timber products and tourism.

Wrangell is one of the oldest settlements in Alaska. It has the distinction of having been ruled by four nations: Tlingit, Russia, England and the USA.

Tlingit heritage

Ancient Tlingit stories tell of a migration to the area through "the hole in the ice", a possible reference to a river (flowing beneath the glacier ice) that led from interior Canada through the Stikine River corridor to the lush, coastal forests. The milder climate, protected coastal waterway and rich resources of the Stikine River delta must have seemed like paradise to the Tlingits, and they fiercely defended their newfound home against the Haida and Tsimshian who arrived later. These same Tlingit warriors were also skilled traders, and their area of commerce extended into interior Canada, up the Copper River and beyond.

Russian fur trade with the Stikine Tlingit began as early as 1811. Wrangell Island was named in honor of the manager of the Russian American Company,

Ferdinand von Wrangel, around 1830. In 1834, the Russians built a stockade, Redoubt St Dionysius, in the same general location as today's community of Wrangell. Recognizing the benefit of Russian protection and trade, Chief Shakes decided to relocate the nearby Tlingit village to a small island in the harbor near the stockade. In 1840, the British Hudson's Bay Company leased the stockade from the Russians, and the name was changed to Fort Stikine.

The Tlingit, while protesting the Hudson's Bay Company's use of their traditional trade routes, were already facing a new, more deadly battle. Two outbreaks of smallpox, in 1836 and 1840, resulted in the deaths of half of their population. By 1849, the over-zealous fur trade had dwindled, and both Russian and British interest in the area began to wane. One year following the US purchase of Alaska in 1867, a military post, Fort Wrangell, was built.

In 1861, an employee of the Hudson's Bay Company, Buck Choquette, found gold on the Stikine River and started the first of three gold rushes that shaped much of Wrangell's (and the rest of Southeast's) history. The second rush was in 1872, when two prospectors, Thibert and McCullough, found gold at Dease Lake (in Canada's Cassiar country). When the Klondike gold was discovered in 1897, Wrangell's population surged again as thousands of prospectors – and the attendant dance halls, gambling establishments, and mining suppliers – flooded the small town. Miners gathered provisions and then journeyed up the Stikine River into the gold fields.

The noted naturalist John Muir frequented the area in the 1880s. It is also told that the infamous Soapy Smith (*see page 153*) would occasionally hide out in Wrangell when the situation in Skagway became too dicey.

Cannery city

Wrangell incorporated as a city in 1903. Not long afterward, the flourishing fishing industry built several canneries within Southeast Alaska. By the late 1920s, four canneries (for salmon, shrimp and crab) were operating in Wrangell. Chinese workers, who were willing to work long hours for low wages, were brought to Southeast Alaska

Wrangell's harbor.

BELOW:
Chief Shakes
Tribal House.

Wrangell

The legendary Wyatt Earp served as Wrangell's marshal for 10 days in 1897 as he and his wife were en route to the Klondike. During these gold rush days, false-front shops lined both sides of Front Street, which was then built on pilings over the water. Two tragic fires, in 1906 and in 1952, destroyed most of these historic buildings.

BELOW:
children chisel the rocks at Garnet Ledge and sell the rocks to tourists.

to man the canneries. **Deadman's Island**, next to the Wrangell airport, is said to be where the Chinese preserved their dead in salt-brine barrels until they could be sent home for burial.

While somewhat off the beaten path of large cruise ships, small cruise ships often make regular stops in Wrangell. The community also welcomes the repeat business of many sport fishers, birders, and water enthusiasts headed for the Stikine River. Perhaps because the city has not experienced waves of passengers from multiple large cruise ships docking just offshore on the same day, Wrangell seems less altered by tourism than many other Southeast towns.

There are many sights unique to this delightful, laid-back town, so grab your quality rain gear and explore. On your way past the **city dock** area, you will likely see young merchants selling garnets dug from **Wrangell's Garnet Ledge ⓐ** *(see box below)*.

A good place to gather Wrangell information is the **James and Elsie Nolan Center ⓑ** (296 Campbell Drive; tel: 874-3699; www.wrangell.com). The center houses both the city's **visitor center** and

the **Wrangell Museum** (open Mon–Fri 10am–5pm May–Sept; weekend hours variable; entrance charge). The museum has a Tlingit spruce canoe and exhibts on gold, timber, fishing and trapping.

The visitor center's staff will connect you with the tour operators who will take you around by foot, helicopter, kayak, boat, bus or plane.

Chief Shakes Tribal House

Take a stroll out to **Chief Shakes Island**, accessible year-round by a walkway into Wrangell harbor. The island has intricately carved Tlingit totems and **Chief Shakes Tribal House ⓒ** (open for cruise ship arrivals or by appointment), listed on the National Register as an historic monument.

Also worth a visit is **Petroglyph Beach ⓓ** (1 mile from the ferry terminal), a State Historic Park which has the Southeast's largest concentration of ancient rock carvings. The origin of the petroglyphs remains a mystery. Visitors are encouraged to search the beach, where more than 40 known carvings are located. Visitors are free to take photographs, but rubbings should be made of

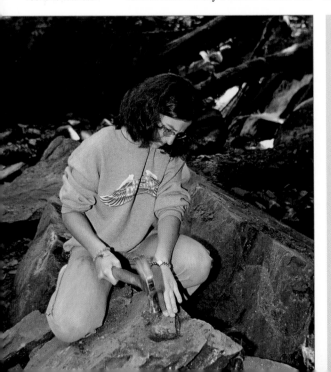

Garnet Ledge

The ledge, a few miles from town at the mouth of the Stikine River, was well known to prospectors during the 1860 gold rush. It was also the setting of a unique, all-women mining company, the Alaska Garnet Mining and Manufacturing Company, in the early 1900s. Ownership eventually transferred to Mr. Fred G. Hanford, the former mayor of Wrangell. The site was given to the Southeastern Alaska Area Council of Boy Scouts of America (in 1962) for scouting purposes and to allow the children of Wrangell to continue collecting and selling the stones. Today, many Wrangell families make the 9-mile (14-km) boat trip to the ledge each spring, allowing their entrepreneurial children to continue the tradition of chiseling, shoveling, and prying garnets from the rock ledge, and then returning home to sell them to summer visitors.

replicas only, which are located on the observation deck overlooking the beach.

Wrangell also owns the distinction of having a USGA-rated, 9-hole golf course, **Muskeg Meadows** **E** (tel: 874-4653; www.wrangellalaskagolf.com). The course's Raven Rule provides that "a ball stolen by a raven may be replaced, with no penalty, provided there is a witness." Club rental and transportation to the course is available at local stores.

The nearby **Stikine River** delta is a fabulous area for birders. The area hosts over 120 species of migrating birds in spring and fall. In April, as many as 1,600 eagles swoop down to feast on the local hooligan run, and thousands of snow geese stop over on their northerly trek. Other wildlife includes sea lions, otters, bears and moose.

A jet boat tour on the Stikine, said to be the fastest navigable river in North America, is a breathtaking opportunity for a rare glimpse of wild Alaska, or you could choose to soar over the area in a floatplane for a bird's-eye view. For a quieter and perhaps less adrenaline-soaked experience, canoes, kayaks and rafts are locally available.

Bear viewing

A trip by boat or floatplane to the **Anan Bear & Wildlife Observatory** (located 30 miles/48km southeast of Wrangell, near the mouth of the Bradfield Canal) provides an opportunity to see brown and black bears (plus bald eagles and sea lions) feasting on one of the largest pink salmon runs in the Southeast. Bears are viewed from a covered platform overlooking a waterfall. The US Forest Service has developed the Observatory (Wrangell Ranger District, 525 Bennett Street; tel: (907) 874-2323; www.fs.fed.us /r10/ro/naturewatch/southeast/anan/anan.htm). Guides escort you to the platform.   ❏

Picknicking in the Stikine River delta.

LEFT: ancient rock carvings on Petroglyph Beach.

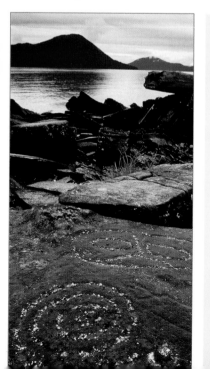

RESTAURANTS

Diamond C Café
223 Front Street
tel: (907) 874-3677
The third-generation owners of this clean, diner-style restaurant serve up breakfasts (early, during summer) and lunches only. A favorite gathering spot for locals, who heartily recommend the shrimp salad and the razor clams. $

Garnet Room (Stikine Inn)
107 Front Street
tel: (888) 874-3388; (907) 874-3388
www.stikine.com
Family-style restaurant affording beautiful views of the water and mountains, is open

daily for breakfast, lunch and dinner. The menu features fresh Alaska seafood, including a highly-touted seafood chowder. Beer and wine served. $–$$$

Zak's Café
316 Front Street
tel: (907) 874-3355
Considered by many to be the best spot in town for lunch (salads, home-made soups, wraps, sandwiches and burgers) or dinner (steak, seafood, chicken, and pasta). $–$$$
● ● ● ● ● ● ● ● ● ● ● ● ● ● ● ● ●
Price is for dinner excluding tax, tip and beverages: **$$$$** *$30 and up,* **$$$** *$20–30,* **$$** *$15–20,* **$** *under $15.*

PETERSBURG

The large cruise ships can't navigate the Wrangell Narrows to get here, which has helped Petersburg retain its small-town charm and the atmosphere of a bustling fishing village

Alaska has always been home to a diverse population, and the communities within the state reflect that diversity. The picturesque fishing hamlet of **Petersburg ❹**, on the northwest end of Mitkof Island, serves to illustrate that point. "Little Norway," as it is often called, is home to 3,100 residents. They offer warm, Scandinavian-styled Alaska hospitality to visitors of their charming city, which, like Wrangell, is not a port of call for large cruise ship traffic. Transportation to the city is provided by daily Alaska Airlines flights, air taxis, and the Alaska Marine Highway System ferries.

Humpback whales

Petersburg claims to be "blessed by geography," and so it is. This spic-and-span island community nestled in the heart of the Tongass, perches at the intersecting waterways of Wrangell Narrows and **Frederick Sound** – the latter being one of the best places in the world to observe the feeding behavior of humpback whales *(see margin note, page 130)*. The area waters are also home to Steller sea lions, harbor seals, Dall's porpoise, and orcas (killer whales).

Other wildlife common to Petersburg includes wolves, black bears, deer, moose, eagles, Canada geese, trumpeter swans and Marbled Murrelets. Just across the Frederick Sound are the towering peaks and glaciers of the Coast Mountains.

The mighty **LeConte Glacier ❺**, the

southernmost active tidewater glacier in the northern hemisphere, is a mere 20-minute boat ride away and is a good spot for seal-watching *(see box, page 130)*.

As is the case throughout most of the Southeast Alaska communities, the Tlingits were the first ones on the scene, using the north end of Mitkof Island as a summer fish camp. In the late 1890s, Peter Buschmann, a Norwegian immigrant, established a cannery, a sawmill, and by 1900, a dock on the island. The Buschmann family's homesteads eventually grew into a community known for

Main attractions
FREDERICK SOUND
LECONTE GLACIER
HAMMER SLOUGH
SONS OF NORWAY HALL
CLAUSEN MEMORIAL MUSEUM
EAGLE ROOST PARK
SANDY BEACH RECREATION AREA
OUTLOOK PARK

LEFT: local transportation.
BELOW: Fourth of July parade, Petersburg.

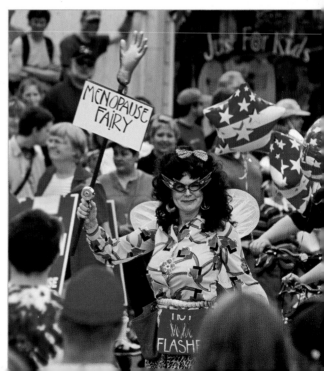

Humpback Whales
The waters of Frederick Sound and Stephen's Passage are uniquely rich in plankton, fish and marine mammals. The area is also the prime summer feeding grounds for hundreds of humpback whales each year. These endangered giants come to feed and play in Alaska waters prior to their fall return to Hawaii to give birth to their young. Whale watching tours are popular activities for many visitors to the Petersburg area.

BELOW: houses on stilts, Petersburg.

its strong Scandinavian influence. Today's Petersburg successfully maintains both its Tlingit and its Scandinavian flavors. Primarily a fishing town, the city also serves as a supply center for area logging camps.

The Chamber of Commerce and the US Forest service jointly operate the Petersburg **Visitor Information Center** Ⓐ (1st and Fram Streets; open in summer Mon–Sat 9am–5pm, Sun noon–4pm; winter hours Mon–Fri 10am–2pm; tel: 772-4636; www.petersburg.org). The center has information on lodging and a myriad of guided boat, floatplane, helicopter, kayak, glacier viewing, whale watching and fishing tours lasting from a few hours to a week or more. For those preferring unguided tours, boat, kayak and equipment rentals are locally available, as are remote drop-off and pick-up flights. The center also has natural history information and trail guides.

Expert information

The **Petersburg Ranger District Office** Ⓑ (12 North Nordic Drive; tel: 772-3871; www.fs.fed.us/r10/tongass/districts/petersburg/index.shtml) offers maps, as well as information on current conditions, area trails, and remote US Forest Service cabin rentals (advance reservations are essential for summer rentals).

The city of Petersburg centers on its harbor area, and nearly all the city's attractions are within easy walking distance. Take a stroll around the town and be sure to bring a camera. Petersburg is known for its natural beauty and unique public art displays, including interesting concrete stamps along the sidewalks and the colorful Rosemaling (Norwegian tole painting) on the homes and storefronts. You'll enjoy a variety of murals, totems and sculptures by local artisans displayed throughout the downtown and harbor areas, as well as in the local gift shops and galleries.

The boardwalk streets of **Hammer Slough** Ⓒ, the tidal area of a creek emptying into the waterfront, lead to an opportunity to photograph old, beautifully weathered boathouses reflecting in the slough's still water. The nearby **Sons of Norway Hall** Ⓓ, recognizable by the Viking ship "docked" in front, offers summer visitors a delicious buffet that includes Norwegian pastries, fish cakes,

Seals of LeConte Glacier

The glacier, part of the Stikine Ice Field 20 miles/32km east of Petersburg, is the southernmost, active, tidewater glacier in the northern hemisphere. Not only do giant hunks of ice crack off the head of the glacier and crash into the sea, but because of the deep (810-ft/247-meter) waters of LeConte Bay, the glacier also calves from underwater. Huge slabs of icy missiles shoot up past the water surface and into the air, and then splash back into the sea. These "shooters" can reach out hundreds of yards from the face of the glacier, seriously endangering boats that come too close. The sparkling, often deep-blue icebergs clog a spectacular 10-mile (16-km) long fjord. Seals nonchalantly lounge on, or swim around the floating bergs. In June, visitors to the glacier from Wrangell or Petersburg tours are often treated to the sight of new seal pups on the ice floes.

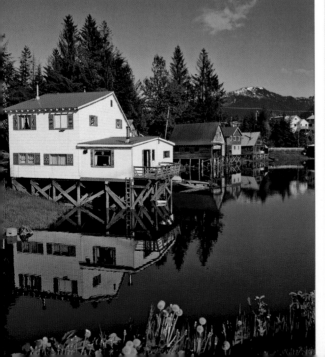

and pickled herring (times coincide with cruise ship arrivals).

You may also be treated to local storytelling and a performance of the **Leikerring Dance Group** (Petersburg children dressed in colorful Norwegian bunad costumes). It's worth stopping at the **Bojer Wikan Fisherman's Memorial** (next door), a memorial to those who lost their lives at sea.

History of fishing

The small but tasteful **Clausen Memorial Museum** ❸ (2nd and Fram streets; open in summer Mon–Sat 10am–5pm; winter Tues–Sat 10am–2pm; tel: 772-3598; www.clausenmuseum.net; entrance charge) offers an insight into the history and art of fishing, life in Petersburg and Tlingit culture. Video shows on history and culture complement the artifacts.

Eagle Roost Park ❻, on North Nordic Drive, close to the town's edge, provides a platform for viewing eagles roosting in trees. It also has picnic tables, and a pathway to the beach to explore tidal pools. As in Wrangell, there are ancient petroglyphs (rock carvings) that can be seen at low tide 3 miles (5km)

down Sandy Beach Road at the **Sandy Beach Recreation Area** ❼. Along with the petroglyphs are 2,000-year-old Tlingit stone or wooden fish traps, supposedly found only in the 40-mile (64-km) area around Petersburg.

On the way to Sandy Beach, the small **Outlook Park** contains a covered timber-framed shelter built by a local shipwright in the style of a Norwegian stave church. You can use the binoculars provided to scan Frederick Sound for marine life. ❑

Viking costumes are donned for the Little Norway Festival, held every May in Petersburg since 1958 to celebrate its Norwegian heritage.

Petersburg

0   200 yds
0   200 m

EAGLE'S ROOST PARK ❻

Hungry Point

Wrangell Narrows

Balder St

Charles West Street

Dolphin   Street

Petersburg Fisheries Cannery

North Boat Harbor

Excel   Street

Harbormaster

Visitor Information Center ❶ⓘ

Clausen Memorial Museum ❸

Fram   Street

Gjoa   Street

Petersburg Ranger District Office ❷

Haugen   Drive

Middle Boat Harbor

Bojer Wikan Fisherman's Memorial

Sons of Norway Hall ❹

Library

Ira Street

Sandy Beach Recreation Area ❼

SITKA

Although Alaska's fourth city in terms of population, Sitka is the biggest in the United States in terms of the area that falls within this borough by the Pacific

Main attractions
HARRIGAN CENTENNIAL HALL
ISABEL MILLER MUSEUM
NEW ARCHANGEL DANCERS
ALASKA RAPTOR CENTER
SHELDON JACKSON MUSEUM
RUSSIAN BISHOP'S HOUSE
ST MICHAEL'S CATHEDRAL
TRIBAL COMMUNITY HOUSE

BELOW: a cruise ship visits Sitka.

The historic city of **Sitka ❻**, population 8,900, sits on the western coast of Baranof Island in Southeast Alaska, backed by the Tongass National Forest and facing Sitka Sound and the open water of the Gulf of Alaska. Tlingit Indians lived in the area for many centuries before the island was discovered by Russian explorer, Vitus Bering, in 1741.

In 1799, Russian fur traders arrived. Alexander Baranov, of the Russian-American Company, built a fort and trading post, St Michael's Redoubt, a few miles to the north of Sitka's present-day location. Local Tlingits, fearing Russian domination and fur-trade enslavement, attacked the fort in 1802 killing most of the settlers. Baranov retaliated two years later by bringing a Russian warship into the harbor and bombarding the village.

The Tlingits fought bravely but after six days were driven from the area in what became known as the Battle of Sitka. The Russians then re-established the settlement and renamed it "New Archangel."

In 1808, Sitka became the capital of Russian America, and by the mid-1800s, the major port of the north Pacific Coast. Fur shipments to Europe and Asia were the primary commodity, though salmon, lumber and ice were also shipped to various locations along the western coasts of North and Central America.

America takes over

Eventually, as the lucrative fur trade declined, Russian interest in Alaska followed suit and, in 1867, Alaska was sold to the United States. The transfer ceremony was held in Sitka on October 18 (now a state holiday, "Alaska Day") and is re-enacted each year at the city's Castle Hill. Sitka remained the territorial capital of Alaska until 1906, when the seat of government was transferred to Juneau. Throughout the early 1900s, gold mines were an engine of growth.

During World War II, the US Navy built an air base on nearby Japonski Island, which housed an astonishing

30,000 military personnel plus more than 7,000 civilians. Following the end of the war, the Bureau of Indian Affairs converted some of the former military buildings into a boarding school for Alaska Natives, Mount Edgecumbe High School, which is still operational today, educating more than 400 students from over 100 Alaska communities. The island is also the location for a US Coast Guard Air Station and Boat Station, the Sitka campus of the University of Alaska Southeast, the Mount Edgecumbe Hospital and Sitka's Rocky Gutierrez Airport. The O'Connell Bridge, built in 1972, connects Japonski Island to Sitka.

Cruising port of call

Sitka's broad-based economy is fueled by various industries including fishing, fish processing, retail and healthcare services, government, transportation and tourism. Alaska Airlines offers daily flights to the community (as do various, local air taxi services), and the Alaska Marine Highway System provides both regular and high-speed ferry options. The city is a popular port for the cruise ship industry, and for good reason. There are many

interesting things to see and do within easy walking distance of the harbor (remember to bring adequate rain gear).

A convenient and profitable first stop is in the waterfront district at the **Harrigan Centennial Hall** Ⓐ (330 Harbor Drive; tel: 747-3225; www.cityofsitka.com/dept/cent/index), which houses both the **Visitor's Center** and the **Isabel Miller Museum** ("most days" 8am–5pm May 7–Sept 22, Tues–Sat in winter 10am–4pm; tel: 747-6455; www.sitkahistory.org; entrance charge). Check the schedule for performances of Russian folk songs and dances by the **New Archangel Dancers** (tel: 747-5516; www.newarchangeldancers .com; entrance charge).

The New Archangel Dancers were formed in 1969 to keep alive Sitka's Russian heritage through dance. Although the members of the troupe are not professional dancers and are not descended from Russians, they have performed throughout the US and in Russia.

Festival time

Held for three weeks each June, this renowned concert series features outstanding chamber musicians from around the world. A giant, panoramic window creates a stunning backdrop for the local concert hall stage, beckoning the audience's gaze beyond the musicians and out to the picturesque Sitka Sound. (www.sitkamusicfestival.org; tel: 277-4852; 747-6774 during June)

BELOW: the Russian Bishop's House.

The Convention and Visitors Bureau ⓑ (303 Lincoln Street, Suite 4, located downtown above Radio Shack; tel: 747-5940; www.sitka.org), while a bit tricky to find, is another helpful resource for visitors. Either location will provide you with the contacts for various tour operators wanting to show you the sights in and around Sitka via semi-submersible vessel, all-terrain vehicle (ATV), bike, bus or on foot.

Additional exploration options include wildlife cruises, diving and snorkeling, flightseeing, and kayaking.

If a self-guided walking tour is what you have in mind, you can make an east-to-west sweep of the city by heading, first of all, to the **Alaska Raptor Center** ⓒ (1000 Raptor Way; open Sun–Fri 8am–4pm May–Sept; tel: 800/643-9425; www.alaskaraptor.org; entrance charge). This small but fascinating facility's mission is to educate the public concerning raptors and their environment, to provide medical treatment for injured bald eagles (and other birds), and to conduct bald eagle research. Visitors have an opportunity for close-up raptor observation.

When leaving the Raptor Center, take a delightful stroll across Indian River and through an old-growth rainforest as you head downhill (toward the Sound) to the **Sitka National Historical Park Visitors Center** ⓓ (located at the east end of Lincoln Street; open daily 8am–5pm mid-May–Sept, Mon–Sat 8am–5pm Oct–mid-May, closed on Federal holidays during winter; tel: 747-0110; www.nps.gov/sitka; entrance charge). Within the 100-acre (40-hectare) park are beautiful Tlingit totem poles, the remains of historic Tlingit and Russian structures, and the 1804 battleground. Inside the cultural center is a museum featuring Indian history, art and Native artist demonstrations.

When leaving the Park, head west and stop at the **Sheldon Jackson Museum** ⓔ (104 College Drive; open daily mid-May–mid-Sept 9am–5pm, winter hours Tues–Sat 10am–4pm, closed holidays; tel: 747-8981; www.museums.state.ak.us/sjhome; entrance charge). It is the oldest museum in Alaska and features one of largest collections, gathered between 1888 and 1898, of Native cultural artifacts.

Russian Bishop's House

Continuing your westerly ramble, stop by the **Russian Bishop's House** ⓕ (103 Monastery Street; open daily mid-May–Sept 9am–5pm, Oct–mid-May by appointment; tel: 747-0110; www.nps.gov/sitk; entrance charge). A National Historic Landmark, this 1842 example of restored Russian colonial architecture, complete with original furniture, appliances and articles of clothing, gives you a glimpse of Sitka life during the Russian-America period.

Leaving the Bishop's House, head west again and visit the **St Michael's Cathedral** ⓖ (240 Lincoln Street; open in summer Mon–Fri 9am–4pm, call for weekend and winter hours; tel: 747-8120; donation requested). The reconstructed Orthodox cathedral replaces what was Alaska's oldest church structure from the Russian era. The earlier building was destroyed by fire in 1966, but nearly all the icons were rescued. The church was later rebuilt, strictly following the original plans.

You'll probably regret it if you don't have a look at the **Russian Block House ⓗ**, located behind the Pioneers' Home. It is a replica of one of the three original structures that once separated the Russian and Tlingit segments of town following the Natives' return to Sitka around 1824.

Close by is the **Tribal Community House ❶** (200 Katlian Street; call for performance times; tel: 888-270-8687, 747-7290; www.sitkatribe.org; entrance charge), which offers colorful Native dance performances, storytelling and other cultural events. A small gift shop features Native artwork. The building contains Southeast Alaska's largest hand-carved wooden house screen.

Castle Hill is just south, across Lincoln Street. In addition to being the site of the 1867 Russian/US transfer ceremony, it is the former location of Baranof's Castle, built in 1837 and destroyed by fire in 1898. Included in the National List of Historic Places, Castle Hill is managed by the Alaska State Parks System.

If you're fortunate enough to arrive at Sitka in June, and enjoy world-class chamber music, don't miss the **Sitka Summer Music Festival** (www.sitkamusic festival.org). To take in the sights outside of Sitka, consider a wildlife cruise to see humpback whales, sea otters, sea lions, and eagles. Birders would enjoy a trip to **St Lazaria National Wildlife Refuge** at the mouth of Sitka Sound, where you'll see thousands of seabirds, including tufted puffins, murres and auklets.

Outdoor activities

You could also take to the skies in a floatplane, scanning the forested landscape as you go for brown bears or Sitka black-tailed deer. A flight to peer into the volcanic crater of nearby, dormant Mt Edgecumbe or to view frigid expanse of the Baranof Icefields would both be excellent choices.

Sport fishers are not likely to be disappointed with local charter options. Kayak enthusiasts (of all abilities) have a variety of paddling opportunities in area water, some locations calm and serene, others more challenging. For tours involving any of these activities (and many more), contact Sitka's Convention and Visitors Bureau (*see page 134*). ❏

St Michael's Cathedral.

RESTAURANTS

Bayview Restaurant
407 Lincoln Street
tel: 747-5440
This busy, popular restaurant overlooking Crescent Harbor is open breakfast, lunch and dinner. Specializes in fresh-caught Alaska seafood, gourmet burgers, deli sandwiches, steak, pasta, soups and homemade desserts. Serves beer and wine. $–$$$$

Ludvig's Bistro
256 Katlian Drive
tel: 966-3663
www.ludvigsbistro.com
Mediterranean fine dining in Sitka! This cozy, upscale restaurant is open for dinner year round, offering fresh, locally caught Alaska seafood, steaks, tapas, fresh Bistro bread, soups, salads and desserts. Serves coffee, tea, beer and wine. $$$–$$$$

Nugget Restaurant & Bakery
600 Airport Drive (located inside the airport)
tel: 966-2480
Famous among frequent flyers along the Southeast Alaska route for their delicious pies, this full service restaurant also offers breakfast (throughout the day) lunch and dinner. Varied menu includes sandwiches, soups, fresh Alaska seafood and prime rib. Full bar. Their savory pies are famous throughout Southeast Alaska, especially to local travelers. Poor weather means that flights are often re-routed to (and delayed at) the Sitka airport, giving passengers a chance to stock up. The banana cream pie is a favorite. $–$$

Pizza Express
1321 Sawmill Creek
tel: 966-2428
Open daily for lunch and dinner, this is the place to go in Sitka for Mexican dishes and pizza. Consistently good food and reasonably priced. $–$$$

• • • • • • • • • • • • • • • • • • • •
Price is for dinner excluding tax, tip and beverages: **$$$$** *$30 and up,* **$$$** *$20–30,* **$$** *$15–20,* **$** *under $15.*

JUNEAU

Juneau is a small but busy capital, with narrow streets
and alleys leading to museums, galleries, and bars
downtown, and a variety of hiking trails
to nearby glaciers and icefields

The delightful city of **Juneau ❼** today is a far cry from the wilderness site where gold was discovered by Joe Juneau and Richard Harris in 1880. About 31,000 Alaskans – whites, Native Tlingits, and other ethnic groups – call the community home. Most work for the government (state, federal or local) or provide services for those that do, or are employed in the tourism industry.

The town is as modern as the state-of-the-art computer center in the State Office Building and as old-fashioned as the plantation-style Governor's Mansion a couple of blocks up the street. It's as sophisticated as its symphony orchestra and as earthy as the notorious Red Dog Saloon or the equally frontierish Alaskan Hotel bar nearby; as urban as its high-rise office buildings and high-comfort hotels, and as rugged as the northern wilderness of thick, lush forests, glacial ice and salt water which surrounds it. The wilderness begins literally where the houses stop.

Gold fever

The town was first named Harrisburg – some say because Harris, unlike his partner Juneau, was able to write and recorded it that way. But the name didn't stick: after news of the gold strike spread to Sitka and elsewhere, nearly 300 prospectors swarmed to the scene, and decided to rename the place Rockwell. Shortly thereafter it became Juneau. By whatever name, the camp was bustling with gold fever and, soon, gold produc-

tion. It didn't take long for simple gold pans, pickaxes and human labor to be replaced by miles-long flumes and ditches, carrying water to massive hydraulic earth-moving and sluicing operations. Within a decade of the Juneau/Harris discovery, wagon roads penetrated the valleys behind the camp-turned-town – roads you can still hike on.

Juneau is, of course, on the North American mainland. Across Gastineau Channel, on **Douglas Island**, even more furiously paced development took place. By 1882 the world-famous Treadwell

Main attractions
ALASKA STATE MUSEUM
MARINE PARK
RED DOG SALOON
ST NICHOLAS RUSSIAN
 ORTHODOX CHURCH
STATE CAPITOL
JUNEAU-DOUGLAS MUSEUM
GOVERNOR'S MANSION
MENDENHALL GLACIER

LEFT: the Red
Dog Saloon.
BELOW:
Juneau seen from
Mount Roberts.

ABOVE: the State Capitol in Juneau.

but somehow set apart from, the rest of the United States.

Early on, politics assumed considerable importance in Juneau. The future state's first political convention was held here in the summer of 1881. The camp became a first-class municipality under the law in 1900, and in 1906 the district government of Alaska transferred there from Sitka.

Frontier law

In 1913, Alaska's first territorial legislature convened, in what is now the Elks Hall on Seward Street. Nearly life-size photo murals of that distinguished group can be seen today on the first floor of the State Capitol Building. The all-male representatives and senators in the pictures look exactly what they were: rugged frontier types, most looking uncomfortable in stiff collars and ties.

As the city grew and prospered, enterprises such as fishing, saw-milling and trading became important. But gold powered Juneau. Miners labored daily in miles and miles of tunnels that honeycombed the mountains both on the mainland and on Douglas Island. For

Mine was operational and expanding. Near it, the proud community of **Douglas** grew up, and indeed rivaled Juneau in population, industry and miners' baseball for a good number of years. Eventually, more than 50 years later, the two towns would merge, but the Douglas community remains distinct to this day, much in the way that Alaska is part of, recreation on days off they scoured the wild country beyond the urban centers, digging, panning, hoping against hope that they, too, might strike it rich like Juneau and Harris. Yet these two early prospectors never realized much from their discoveries. Juneau died penniless in the Canadian Yukon and a collection had to be taken up to send his body home for burial in the city he co-founded.

Wartime boom

As the years passed there were ups and downs (definitely down when, in 1917, major portions of the Treadwell tunnels beneath the waters of Gastineau Channel caved in and flooded), but gold remained Juneau's, and Alaska's, mainstay, until relatively recent times. During World War II, the government ended an era when it closed down the massive Alaska-Juneau gold mine and milling operation for reasons of manpower and conservation.

But even with the mine closure, things didn't go too badly. By the time the 1944 shutdown came about, the city was experiencing something of a war boom, and with war's end there came a gradual but continuous rise in territorial government activity and employment.

By 1959, when Alaska became state number 49, government had all but filled the economic void left by mining's demise. And Juneau has since grown from a waterfront community hovering beneath the skeletal remains of the old Alaska-Juneau millsites, to a gregarious, upreaching, outreaching city spreading for miles to the north and south.

The city's size was established in the mid-1960s when Juneau and Douglas and the Greater Juneau Borough were unified by a democratic vote into the City and Borough of Juneau.

Juneau is a small town in terms of population, but in square miles it is the biggest town in North America and second biggest in the world. Its 3,108 sq. miles (8,050 sq. km) are exceeded only by the city of Kiruna in Sweden, which has 5,458 sq. miles (14,136 sq. km) within its borders.

Touring the capital

It's a good idea to start your tour of Juneau with a visit to the **Centennial Hall Visitor Information Center A** (101 Egan Drive; tel: 888/581-2201; www.traveljuneau.com), Year-round visitor information is also available at the Juneau International Airport and the Alaska Marine Highway System Ferry Terminal. Summertime information sources also include the cruise ship terminal and the visitor information kiosk located at Marine Park. You can get a city map at any of these locations, plus information about Juneau's many points of interest and tour operators.

One of its biggest attractions, the **Alaska State Museum B** (open daily in summer, 8:30am–5:30pm; in winter, Tues–Sat 10am–4pm; tel: 465-2901; www.museums.state.ak.us, entrance charge) on Whittier Street, within walking distance of downtown hotels and shopping. To visit the museum is to visit the whole of Alaska. Inuit culture is represented here in the form of small, intricate ivory carvings and a huge 40-ft (12-meter) *umiak*, or skin boat, of the type that were used for whale- and walrus-hunting

An isolated capital Juneau is the only state capital in the USA that is not accessible by road. Some locals feel this keeps tourism in check. Others say it is an argument for moving the seat of government to Anchorage.

BELOW: Juneau's winter temperature seldom falls below 20°F (–6°C) and it is seldom hotter than 65°F (18°C) in summer.

Juneau's Trails

Few capital cities in the world can offer such a variety of hiking trails, suitable for the fit and the not so fit, right on its doorstep.

The most memorable thing about Juneau for many people is the rich variety of hiking trails that can be reached easily from the dockside and city center. All of the starting points are clearly marked and you can get information about routes and the degree of skill and stamina needed from the US Forest Service volunteers at 8465 Old Dairy Road in the valley (open office hours Mon–Fri; tel: 586-8800; www.fs.fed.us/r10/tongass).

Among the best-known trails are Mount Roberts, Perseverance, and Mount Juneau. **Mount Roberts** takes off from a trailhead at the north end of Sixth Street. It's a steep climb, but a good one, with alpine ground cover above the treeline, and splendid views. You can cheat by hopping on the Mount Roberts Tram, which takes you from South Franklin Street, near the dockside, up to the treeline, where you can begin your hike, browse in the visitor center or watch a documentary in the theater.

The starting point for the more gentle and most popular trail, the **Perseverance Mine Trail**, is only a few blocks further north, on Basin Road. Before setting off, pop into the Last Chance Mining Museum, near the trailhead (open daily in summer; tel: 586-5338; entrance charge; tel: 586-5338) to get an idea of what life used to be like when the mines were functioning. On the Perseverance Mine Trail you have the chance to see and explore the ruins of some of the early mining sites, including the Silver Bowl Basin Mine and the Glory Hole. Or you can continue along the Granite Creek Trail, and hike as far as the creek basin.

The experienced and thoroughly fit hiker can link up with the steep **Mount Juneau Trail**, which provides the best view that can be had with two feet on the ground. Mainland Juneau and Douglas Island are laid out 3,500ft (1,100 meters) below the mountain summit, and the twisting, glistening Gastineau Channel seems to go on and on forever. This trail will bring you back full circle to join Perseverance near Ebner Falls. The less fit, or those with less time, can miss this loop, by retracing their steps from the Granite Creek Basin.

The **Sheep Creek Trail**, which starts in the southeast of the city, at Thane Road, takes you through the beautiful valley south of Mount Roberts, then up to Sheep Mountain and back on the Mount Roberts Trail.

Trails starting from Douglas

Several interesting trails start from Douglas, on the other side of the Gastineau Channel. The **Treadwell Ditch Trail**, which begins at D Street, is a 12-mile (20-km) hike to Eagle Crest, but it can become a much easier walk by going only as far as the Dan Moller Trail, then returning on the road. Only the really experienced should try the **Mount Bradley Trail**, which sets off from Fifth Street in Douglas. Mount Bradley is 3,400ft (1,040 meters) high and the going can be tough, although the scenic rewards are great. An easier walk is 2-mile (3.5-km) **Cropley Lake Trail**, which starts at Fish Creek Road.

There are hikes to suit all abilities and ages, but if you are a novice and feel nervous about setting out alone, contact the Juneau Parks and Recreation division, tel: 586-5226; www.juneau.org/parksrec. Park volunteers organize hikes for groups and families. ❑

ABOVE: the Last Chance Mining Museum.
LEFT: the glistening Gastineau Channel.

along the ice floes of the Arctic Ocean.

Southeast Alaska's ancient Native way of life is reflected in the re-creation of a community house, complete with priceless totemic carvings, and the Athabascan Natives, from the Interior, are represented with displays of a birch bark canoe, weapons and bead-decorated moosehide garments.

There is also gold-rush memorabilia, and natural history displays. Nor is the pre-gold rush Russian heritage ignored: orthodox religious exhibits include precious coins, priests' raiments, and the first American flag to be flown at Sitka when Russian America became American territory on October 18, 1867.

Most notable of all the museum's exhibits is the "eagle tree," just inside the front entrance. There, in the middle of a spiral staircase, a model of a towering spruce tree rises from ground level almost to the ceiling of the second floor. In a fork of the branches is a nest holding a very authentic-looking young bald eagle, with its magnificent 5-ft (1.2-meter) spread of wings outstretched.

Marine Park

Most of Juneau's other visitor attractions can be encountered in a walking tour along the community's docks and among its meandering, frequently narrow, streets and alleys. Go left along Egan Drive to **Marine Park C** overlooking the city's dock and wharf area. It's a small, but pleasurable place of benches and shady trees situated near the ramp where cruise-ship passengers land after being lightered from ships at anchor offshore. This is where half of Juneau seem to eat lunch, especially on sunny summer days. Street vendors in the vicinity offer food ranging from fried halibut to hot dogs, from tacos to Vietnamese spring rolls.

The Red Dog Saloon

Cross Ferry Way to South Franklin Street, where you will find art galleries and stores that entice you with displays of Alaskan ivory, jade, totemic wood carvings and leatherwork. Also on South Franklin (turn right from Ferry Way) is

the best-known bar in the city, the fun but touristy **Red Dog Saloon**.

Further up the street is the **Alaskan Hotel Bar**, which retains its gold-rush era decor and is well worth a visit. There are several seafood and other restaurants here, too, plus the standard assortment of merchants and professional offices.

Juneau's visitor information office – a re-creation of the town's first log school, later a brewery – is on Seward Street, parallel with South Franklin, and on the way to the tiny **St Nicholas Russian Orthodox Church D**, is one of the most picturesque houses of worship in Alaska. The onion-domed, octagon-shaped church, located on Fifth Street, was constructed in 1894 at the specific request of Ishkhanalykh, the then principal chief of the Tlingits of Juneau. It is the oldest original Orthodox church in Southeast Alaska and one of the senior parishes of the entire state. The building is open to the public, and a donation is requested.

Downhill on Fourth Street is the **State Capitol Building E** where tours are conducted daily in the summer. The capitol was built in the 1930s and many of its halls and offices have recently been refur-

Patsy Ann
A statue of a bull terrier, Patsy Ann (1929–42) sits on the wharf to greet disembarking cruise ship passengers. In 1934 she was dubbed "Official Greeter of Juneau, Alaska" by the mayor in recognition of her uncanny ability (especially as she was stone deaf) to anticipate the arrival of every ship.

BELOW: South Franklin Street.

Eating out by the harbor in summer.

BELOW: tourists visit Mendenhall Glacier by helicopter.

bished to reflect that era. You can see where the Alaska House and Senate meet during sessions; it's well worth a stop.

On the corner of Fourth and Main streets is the **Juneau-Douglas City Museum F** (open 9am–5pm weekdays,10am–5pm weekends in summer; Tues–Sat noon–4pm in winter; tel: 586-3572; www.juneau.org/parks/rec/museum; open daily in summer; in winter open Tues–Sat; summer entrance charge, free in winter). It has interesting displays on the town's gold-mining history.

Across the road is the **State Office Building G** on Fourth Street, where you can stroll through the skylighted great

hall. And on Friday, at noon, visitors to the sob can enjoy a special treat: a giant old Kimball theater organ – a magnificent relic of Juneau's silent movie days – has been relocated in the atrium of the building; visiting organists and local musicians celebrate the coming weekend by playing its pipes from noon to 1pm.

Two blocks beyond, on Calhoun Avenue, is the **Governor's Mansion H**, which cost $2 million to restore to the glory of its 1913 opening. You can photograph the exterior, but you can't go in.

Beyond the Governor's Mansion and across **Gold Creek** – where Joe Juneau and Dick Harris panned their first gold in the area – you come to the **Evergreen Cemetery I** where the two prospectors are buried. The two founders' burial monuments are not overly impressive, but the partially wooded cemetery is a popular place for visitors to stroll around and residents to walk their dogs. And after visiting the town, it's good to see where the two old prospectors ended up.

Mendenhall Glacier

From Juneau, a number of impressive glaciers can be reached by car or by trail, or viewed from the air. The best known is the **Mendenhall Glacier**, which can be seen from a US Forest Service information center about 13 miles (21km) north of town. The center sits on the edge of a frigid lake into which Mendenhall Glacier calves icebergs large and small. The face of the glacier is about 1 mile (2km) from the visitor center, while its 1,500 sq. miles (3,885 sq. km) of ice and snow is called the **Juneau Icefield**.

Perhaps the most exciting way to savor the glacier and its originating icefield is to take one of the flightseeing trips organized by one of several Juneau-based air charter companies, or to try one of the four helicopter carriers that offer 45 minutes or so flying over the great white deserts of snow, and a landing on the surface of the icefield. Some companies supply a guide and all the necessary equipment – boots, crampons, ice axes and so forth – for a two-hour trek and even a little ice climbing. ❑

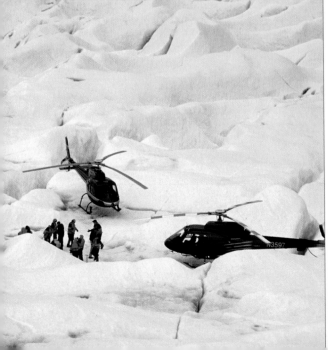

RESTAURANTS & BARS

Restaurants

Prices for a three-course dinner per person with a half-bottle of house wine:
$ = under $15
$$ = $15–$20
$$$ = $20–$30
$$$$ = over $30

The Goldroom
in the Baranof Hotel
127 N. Franklin Street
tel: 586-2660
Fine downtown dining featuring contemporary Northwest cuisine. Full bar. $–$$$$

Thane Ore House Salmon Bake
4400 Thane Road
tel: 586-3442
www.thaneorehouse.com
Located 4 miles south of downtown Juneau at the site of the historic Alaska Gastineau mine, this casual, rustic eatery offers indoor and outdoor seating daily (in summer) for lunch and dinner. Offers "all you can eat" helpings of delicious local wild salmon, halibut, barbequed beef ribs, burgers and all the trimmings. $–$$$

Breakwater Restaurant & Lounge
1711 Glacier Avenue
tel: 586-6303
www.breakwaterinn.com/restaurant/index.htm
A fine-dining establishment offering a lovely, waterfront view, fresh Alaskan seafood, steaks and prime rib. Also serves breakfast and lunch. Lounge has wines, spirits, microbrew beers. $–$$$

Douglas Café
916 Third Street
tel: (907) 364-3307
A favorite spot for locals. Hearty breakfasts (weekends only), delicious lunches (the burgers are legendary), and more sophisticated dinners. Fresh Alaska seafood. Locally brewed beer on tap. $–$$$

Twisted Fish Co. Alaskan Grill
550 S. Franklin Street
tel; (907) 463-5033
Open late-March–Sept 1, this busy seafood hot spot is on the waterfront near the cruise ship dock. Features fresh Alaska seafood, pizza, burgers and desserts. Serves beer and wine. $–$$$$

The Island Pub
1102 Second Street, Douglas
tel: 364-1595
www.TheIslandPub.com
Across the bridge from Juneau on Douglas Island, this fairly new restaurant features delicious, hand-pressed dough for its gourmet pizzas, baked in a fire-brick oven. Also serves sandwiches, salads and an outstanding steak wrap. Enjoy a wonderful view of water and of downtown Juneau. Open for lunch and dinner. The full bar offers a wide selection of beer and "malternatives." $–$$

Chan's Thai Kitchen
11820 Glacier Highway
tel 789-9777
This busy, small restaurant, located 20 minutes from downtown at the Auke Bay boat harbor, is popular with locals. Open for lunch and dinner Tuesday through Friday; Saturday dinner only. Menu favorites include cashew chicken, spring rolls, pad Thai, and other delicious Thai dishes. $

Kenny's Wok & Teriyaki
Sushi Bar
124 Front Street
586-3575
Enjoy consistently tasty Chinese and Japanese dishes in a casual, trendy setting. Extensive sushi bar. $

El Sombrero
157 S. Franklin Street
tel: 586-6770
Mexican cuisine includes menu items with Alaskan flair: halibut and salmon fajitas. Open for dinner only, casual. Serves beer and wine. $–$$

Olivia's de Mexico
222 Seward Street
586-6870
This locally owned Mexican restaurant has been operated by the same family, in the same spot for 30 years. Open for lunch and dinner, the menu includes favorites like halibut enchiladas and tacos, reasonably priced. Beer and wine served. $–$$

Red Dog Saloon
278 South Franklin Street
tel: 463-3658
Located near the waterfront, this raucous bar, complete with swinging doors, sawdust floors and loads of frontier memorabilia is a much-hyped tourist favorite.

The Alaskan Bar
167 S. Franklin Street
tel: 586-1000
This two-story Victorian barroom, built in the early 1900s, is loaded with frontier atmosphere, historic memorabilia and local patrons.

Triangle Club Bar
251 Front Street
tel: 586-3140
Where the locals head for a hot dog (and other light snacks) and beer, wine or spirits.

GLACIER BAY NATIONAL PARK

Alaska
Anchorage●

The glaciers of the bay have retreated dramatically
during the past two hundred years – a process which the
visitors on large cruise ships can see is continuing today

Main attractions
GUSTAVUS
FAIRWEATHER RANGE
BARTLETT COVE
SANDY COVE

BELOW: a
sparkling ice cave.

Glacier Bay National Park and
Preserve ❽ encompasses 3.3 million acres (1.3 million hectares).
Located at the northern end of Alaska's
southeastern Panhandle, the park's center
lies approximately 90 miles (145km)
northwest of Juneau and 600 miles
(965km) southeast of Anchorage.

Most visitors arrive at Glacier Bay on
large cruise ships or package tours, but
you can reach **Gustavus** by air and boat
charters from Juneau. This village of 500
year-round residents has an attractive
beach and the 9-hole **Mount Fair-**

weather Golf Course (tel: 907-697-
3080), which golfers in early summer
share with flocks of Canada geese.

In a land comprising three climatic
zones – marine to arctic – seven different
ecosystems support a wide variety of
plant and animal life. From the endangered humpback whale and Arctic peregrine falcon to the common harbor seal,
black and brown bears, mountain goats,
marmots, eagles and ptarmigans, Glacier Bay provides a rich overview of
Alaska's wildlife.

Glacier Bay's physical environment is
as diverse as any found in Alaska. Sixteen massive tidewater glaciers flowing
from the snow-capped mountain peaks
of the **Fairweather Range** (reaching
15,300ft/4,663 meters) plunge into the
icy waters of the fjords. Besides the
jagged icebergs, the ice-scoured walls of
rock lining the waterways, the salt-water
beaches and protected coves, numerous
fresh-water lakes and thick forests of
western hemlock and Sitka spruce are
also found in the area.

History and exploration

Evidence of human habitation in the
Glacier Bay region dates back 10,000
years. Researchers have outlined seasonal
patterns of hunting, fishing and gathering from semi-permanent villages. Native
Tlingit folklore includes tales of periodic
village destruction from earthquakes,
tsunamis, and other natural forces.

European exploration of the area
began in July 1741, when Russian ships

sailed the outer coast. French explorer Jean François de la Perouse arrived 45 years later, and in 1797 he published his detailed observations and map of Lituya Bay, with its five surrounding glaciers.

Other explorers followed, such as Captain George Vancouver, who charted the waters of the Inside Passage in the 1790s. But it was the widespread publicity soon after naturalist John Muir's first reconnaissance of the area in 1879 that stimulated extensive scientific investigations and early tourism. Where early explorers had found only a massive wall of ice, Muir paddled in waters newly released from glacial ice, which had begun to retreat up the fjords it had carved.

Today's visitors today see views very different from those which were observed in Muir's day, as glaciers – and their steady retreat – have further changed the landscape in the past century. In Muir's time, the network of fjords had not yet been established; a huge glacier extended into areas which are now open water. Early steamship excursions during the 1880s carried up to 230 passengers. But the flock of curious scientists and tourists halted abruptly when, in 1899, a violent earthquake struck, causing huge amounts of ice from the Muir Glacier to calve, falling into the sea. An unbroken jam of floating ice choked the waterway and extended more than 10 miles (16km) from the glacier's terminus.

When ships could no longer sail closer than about 6 miles (10km) to the Muir Glacier, excursions to the area ceased. Touring slowly developed again after 1925, when the Glacier Bay National Monument was established.

The glaciers retreat

These glaciers have, over time, retreated and advanced due to severe climatic fluctuations. De la Perouse and Vancouver both observed glacier ice at the mouth of the bay in 1786 and 1794. During Muir's trip to Glacier Bay in 1879, however, the ice had retreated 32 miles (51km) to a point near what is now the mouth of Muir Inlet. Ninety years later, the Muir Glacier had receded another 24 miles (39km). Today the bay is more than 65 miles (105km) long.

Glacier Bay visitors can often watch entire sections of glacier ice calve from 150-ft (46-meter) walls. The cracking ice

Whales at risk
Commercial whaling in the 20th century reduced the world population of humpback whales from an estimated 125,000 to just 5,000. Today the population is something like 20,000. Princess Cruise Lines paid a $200,000 fine and $550,000 to the National Park Foundation after one of its ships hit and killed a humpback whale in Glacier Bay.

BELOW:
examining a glacier at close quarters.

Getting close to a humpback whale.

BELOW: a good vantage point for spotting Glacier Bay's abundant marine life.

Plant and animal life

Two hundred years ago, when a glacier filled what is now a network of inlets in Glacier Bay, only a small number of plant and animal species inhabited the region. Since the retreat of the ice, life has flourished. Today, the nutrient-rich waters of the fjords are important feeding grounds for large marine mammals, and even the windswept, insect-free upper slopes of the glaciers provide welcome refuge for mountain goats and other animals.

The four land and three marine ecosystems in Glacier Bay support life forms adapted to the environment. Near Gustavus, an ecosystem of sandy grassland, thick coniferous forests and damp marshes provides habitat for sandhill cranes, river otters, wolves, bears, coyotes and moose. **Bartlett Cove**, the park's only area of development, lies within a region dominated by coastal western hemlock and Sitka spruce; watch for bald eagles flying overhead.

In the magnificent backcountry, you may climb to elevations of 2,500ft (762 meters), or much higher if you're an experienced mountaineer. Here, in the

produces a thundering roar, easily heard by those on the water. Huge bergs are set adrift, and waves sweep across sandbars outward from the glacier's tidewater base.

Kayakers are warned to keep a safe distance from the glacier faces. Those on the water, close to ice chunks slowly melting in the salty bay, may hear a crackling sound similar to breakfast cereal or champagne, which comes from the release of thousands of air bubbles that became trapped in the ice from high pressure during its formation. From the air, the sound cannot be heard above the drone of an aircraft engine, but the perspective of shimmering ice flowing from mountain top to sea is a dramatic one.

alpine tundra ecosystem, the thick vegetation of lower elevations is replaced by shrubby plants – alpine grasses and dwarf blueberry; the terrain is rocky, and snow patches remain in early summer. Delicate flowering plants and lichens should be respected, for regeneration in this environment is extremely slow; glacial history can be computed by studying the steady rate of lichen growth.

Although few visitors venture onto the higher snowfields and glaciers, life in this seemingly barren, mountainous environment does exist. The ice worm, which is the only earthworm known to live on snow and ice, feeds on a red-pigmented green algae and organic debris swept onto the frozen surface. Slightly less than an inch (2.5 cm) long, these tiny black creatures hatch their eggs in sub-freezing temperatures and are extremely sensitive to heat. The glacier flea, a vegetarian insect, also lives above the treeline.

Possibly the most threatened species here is the humpback whale. A migratory marine mammal that winters near Hawaii or Mexico, humpbacks feed in the icy waters of southeastern Alaska and Glacier Bay in the summer. Killer and minke whales are sometimes spotted in the bay as well. Environmentalists fear that excessive numbers of cruise ships may drive out the whales. Besides small intertidal creatures, Glacier Bay is also home to many fish and shorebirds. Sea lions and otters, harbor seals and porpoises are frequently sighted.

Park attractions

A small, free campground in Bartlett Cove fills to capacity only two or three times a season. **Sandy Cove**, approximately 20 miles (32km) north, offers a good anchorage and attractive scenery for those traveling by boat.

The National Park Service (tel: 907-697-2230; www.nps.gov/glba) provides interpretive programs and various activities. Guided nature and walking tours on two well-maintained trails start from Bartlett Cove, and slide-lecture shows are given in the lodge and on concessionaire vessels.

A floating ranger station in **Blue Mouse Cove** is open during the summer. The Park Service also staffs all cruise ships entering the park with naturalists to inform people about the landscape. ❑

Well equipped in the Fairweather Range.

BELOW: Dwarf Fireweed and Indian Paintbrush in front of the Brabazon Range, St Elias Mountains.

HAINES

Alaska
Anchorage
Haines

This quirky seaside town is hemmed in by glacier-laden mountains and is under the watchful eyes of thousands of bald eagles

Main attractions
FORT WILLIAM H. SEWARD
ALASKA INDIAN ARTS CENTER
TOTEM VILLAGE TRIBAL
    HOUSE
SHELDON MUSEUM AND
    CULTURAL CENTER
HAMMER MUSEUM
AMERICAN BALD EAGLE
    FOUNDATION
CHILKAT BALD EAGLE
    PRESERVE

BELOW: Haines has a population of around 1,800.

Most motorists traveling through **Haines ❾** are anxiously looking forward to only one of two things. If southbound, the main focus is *not missing the ferry*. They're intent on getting in line at the Alaska Marine Highway terminal, driving their car onboard, grabbing a bite to eat at the ship's cafeteria and then finally making their way to a recliner (or, better yet, a comfortable stateroom) to recover from an all-day, or all-night marathon drive.

If they're headed north, they're consumed with making it forty miles beyond

Haines to the Canadian border (appropriate paperwork in hand) *during the hours of operation*, then getting on with their all-day or all-night drive to Interior Alaska or Canada. Haines is a town most Alaskans have traveled *through*, but seldom *to*. And that's a shame, because this little city, in many ways, exemplifies the very best Alaska has to offer.

Like Wrangell and Petersburg, most major cruise lines bypass Haines, choosing to dock at Skagway, instead. The townspeople are somewhat divided over whether this fact constitutes a slight or a blessing. It certainly makes for less summertime congestion as the 1,800 local residents go about earning their living, primarily through commercial fishing, government, tourism and transportation. There is no major, commercial airline service to Haines.

The road connection

The city is one of only three Southeast cities (Haines, Skagway and Hyder) connected to the state's (or Canada's) road system. Air taxi service from Anchorage and various Southeast cities is available, and the Alaska Marine Highway Service provides regular ferry transports throughout the year.

For visitors clever enough to actually plan a trip *to* Haines, the opportunity to experience a genuine, small, quirky seaside Alaska town, hemmed in by glacier-laden mountains and under the constant, watchful eyes of literally thousands of bald eagles, is its own great reward.

Ancient trade route

Like most of Southeast Alaska, the first inhabitants of the Haines area were two tribes of Tlingit Indians, the Chilkat and the Chilkoot. The Natives called their home "Dei-Shu" or "End of the Trail." The ancient Tlingit trade route, up the Chilkat Valley into interior Canada later became the Dalton Trail used by prospectors to access distant gold fields. Today, parts of this long-used trail have become the Haines Highway, connecting Haines to the Canadian and Alaska road systems.

The noted naturalist John Muir visited Haines in 1879. Muir's traveling companion and friend, S. Hall Young, was the first missionary to arrive in the area. Muir and Young successfully petitioned the Chilkat for permission, and the Presbyterian Women's Executive Society of Home Missions for funds to build the Willard Mission and School.

The name of the mission was later changed to Haines in honor of the Society's secretary, Mrs. F.E. Haines, who raised the necessary building funds for the project. As the gold rush frenzy accelerated in the late 1890s, the area became a mining supply center. The fishing industry was also booming at that time, and by the turn of the century, four canneries were in full operation.

In 1904, responding to border issues with Canada, the first US government military post in Alaska (and the only one prior to WWII) was built just south of Haines and named **Fort William H. Seward** Ⓐ. The fort, in rather stark contrast to Haines' rustic frontier motif, was collection of stately, white clapboard buildings surrounding the central parade grounds. Understandable postal confusion concerning mail bound for Fort Seward, as opposed to the City of Seward (on the Kenai Peninsula in Southcentral) led to the renaming of the post to Chilkoot Barracks in 1922.

The fort was decommissioned in 1947, and its original name restored when it became listed as a Historic Landmark in 1972. Today, these same white buildings serve as private homes, accommodation establishments, art galleries and restaurants. Additionally, locals decided to construct a Tlingit clan house in the center of the Parade Field, making Haines' housing juxtaposition complete.

Threatened tribe
Having been denied any claim to land in the 1971 Alaska Native Claims Settlement Act, the Chilkoot Tlingit were in danger of seeing their culture die out. In 1990 the tribe, half of whose 480 members live in Haines, formed the Chilkoot Indian Association, which has rebuilt the tribal identity and plays a full role in the town's affairs and culture.

BELOW:
open year-round
for breakfast,
lunch and dinner.

Onion wine

For a souvenir of Haines that's different, try a bottle of local onion wine. To supplement income from an uncertain construction industry, David and Jeannie Menaker set up Great Land Wines (1817 Small Tract Road, tel: 907-766-2698) in 2000. Given Alaska's lack of grapes, they used locally grown cherries, carrots, rhubarb, dandelions, fireweed – and onions.

RIGHT:
a totem carver at work in the Alaska Indian Arts Center.

A walking tour brochure for Fort Seward is available at the **Haines Convention and Visitors Bureau Visitor Information Center** ❸ (122 Second Avenue; open Mon–Fri 8am–7pm, Sat–Sun 9am–6pm in summer; Mon–Fri 8am–5pm in winter; tel: 800-458-3579, 766-2234; www.haines.ak.us).

The staff will also connect you with local tour operators eager to show you the sites (in and around Haines) in a number of creative ways: kayak or bike rentals, rafting trips, day cruises, flightseeing, landings on glaciers (and dogsledding), Native cultural tours, fishing charters and birding or photography treks. The center also offers a bear-viewing guide, a birding checklist, area tide books, a list of ten nearby totem pole locations, plus maps and lots of helpful advice.

Regardless of whether you opt for a tour or take off on your own, you'll want to stroll over to Fort Seward and check out the **Alaska Indian Arts Center** ❸ (located in the old fort hospital building on the south side of parade grounds; open Mon–Fri 9am–5pm; tel: 766-2160; www.alaskaindianarts.com), where you can watch local carvers, silversmiths and other artisans at work. The **Totem Village Tribal House** ❹, (the one located in the middle of the parade grounds) offers performances of the **Chilkat Dancers Storytelling Theater** every weekday afternoon in summer (tel: 766-2540, entrance charge).

Pioneer museums

In the Small Boat Harbor area, visit the **Sheldon Museum and Cultural Center** ❸ (11 Main Street; open Mon–Fri 10am–5pm, Sat–Sun 1–4pm in summer; Mon–Fri 1–4pm in winter; tel: 766-2366; www.sheldonmuseum.org; entrance charge). The museum has Haines' pioneer history exhibits as well as those of early Native Tlingit culture.

For an even more unique collection, check out the one-of-a-kind **Hammer Museum** ❻ (108 Main Street; open Mon–Fri 10am–5pm summer only; tel: 766-2374; www.hammermuseum.org; entrance charge). In this interesting, though admittedly oddball museum you'll find exhibits of over 1,500 historic (and new) hammers used throughout the world for a dizzying array of purposes.

Continuing along Main Street, another

Alaska Bald Eagle Festival

Haines is famous for hosting the world's largest concentrated gathering of bald eagles (over 3,000). In celebration of this distinction, the town holds the Bald Eagle Festival in mid-November. Despite the winter rain/snow, winds, and cold, birders, photographers, artists and nature lovers of all ages and stages have been congregating here each year since 1994, prudently kitted out in polypropylene long underwear. They are powerfully drawn by eagles and perversely undaunted by weather, don their and channel their enthusiasm into guided eagle-viewing treks, photography workshops, and expert lectures. A highlight is the releasing of a rehabilitated eagle back into the wild and participants can even bid for the privilege of personally releasing the bird. For further details, visit the festival web site: www.baldeaglefestival.org.

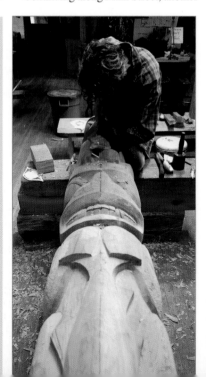

interesting museum is the **Tsirku Canning Co.** ⓖ (located at 5th and Main Streets; open mid-May–mid-Sept, hours vary, call for schedule; tel: 766-3474; www.cannerytour.com; entrance charge). This perfectly restored, working line of 1920s-era cannery equipment gives visitors an opportunity to watch the entire canning process while learning about the history of canneries in Alaska.

Eagle enterprises

To view interesting wildlife display, visit the **American Bald Eagle Foundation** ⓗ (located at 2nd Avenue and Haines Highway; open Mon–Fri 9am–6pm, Sat–Sun 1–4pm in summer only; tel: 766-3094; www.baldeagles.org). This natural history museum features more than 180 dioramas of mounted bald eagles and other wildlife common to the area. The center is a non-profit educational foundation dedicated to the protection and preservation of bald eagle habitat.

If you travel 18 miles (29km) out the Haines Highway, you will find roadside pullouts for eagle viewing in the **Chilkat Bald Eagle Preserve** ⓘ, created in 1982 by the State of Alaska, and probably the best spot in the world to view bald eagles. This is especially true from early October until January each year, when over 3,000 eagles congregate in the Chilkat Valley in order to feed on the late run of salmon spawning in the Chilkat River. The preserve also provides interpretive displays, trails and shelters. The prime viewing areas are from mile 18 to 21, but the eagles often disregard those boundaries and can be seen, sometimes a dozen or more to a single cottonwood tree, maintaining a constant, watchful eye on salmon swimming upstream. ❏

Chilkat dancers perform in Haines. The highly stylized blankets, depicting clan symbols and animals in abstract geometric patterns, could take a year to weave and were very valuable, selling for $30 (a huge sum) in the mid-19th century. A few weavers keep the tradition alive.

RESTAURANTS

Chilkat Restaurant and Bakery
5th Avenue & Dalton Street
tel: 766-3653
The bakery side of this establishment is where neighbors congregate for coffee, doughnuts and gossip. The restaurant side offers daily breakfast and lunch. Open for dinner, weekends only, featuring Thai dishes. $–$$

Commander's Room
in Hotel Halsingland, 13 Fort Seward Drive.
tel: 766-2000
Excellent seafood but creative meat dishes too. The chef has his own herb garden. Open for breakfast and dinner. $$$

Fogcutter Bar
Main Street, between 1st and 2nd Avenues
tel: 766-2555
Convenient to harbor, open year round. Light snacks, pool tables, big-screen TV and a dance floor. $

Lighthouse Restaurant (& Harbor Bar)
101 Front Street
tel: 766-2442
Breakfast, lunch and dinner. Casual but good dining, with a view of the waterfront. $$–$$$

Mountain Market
3rd Avenue & Haines Highway
tel: 766-3340
The place to go for wholesome foods, organic produce, soups, sandwiches, wraps, baked goods and fresh-roasted coffee. Open for breakfast, lunch and dinner, year round. $

33-Mile Road House
Mile 33 Haines Highway
tel: 767-5510
Locals head out the road for a change-of-pace restaurant, or to take relatives when they visit. Authentic roadhouse decor, historic memorabilia, consistently good food. Open year round. Beer and wine served. $–$$

• •

Price is for dinner excluding tax, tip and beverages: $$$$ $30 and up, $$$ $20–30, $$ $15–20, $ under $15.

SKAGWAY

The town was founded on gold and dreams, and its brief period of glory is re-created – in a suitably sanitized way, of course – for the enjoyment of today's cruise-ship tourists

BELOW: Skagway's architecture recalls the gold rush era.

Most he old familiar sounds are everywhere. You will hear them all the time in **Skagway** ❿ where the rollicking past has been preserved. On a calm midsummer night when the sun has just skipped behind the last peak, you can't help but hear them coming from behind those false fronts as you walk up the boardwalk on Broadway. They are the sounds of a not-too-distant era: ragtime pianos, whooping cancan girls, ringing cash registers, songs and raucous laughter; the happy sounds of gold fever run rampant at the start of the trail. They are re-created for the tourist market, to give visitors a taste of the past, and to boost the local economy.

There's no town in Alaska quite like Skagway when it comes to blending history with natural beauty. Situated at the northern end of Southeast Alaska's Inside Passage, Skagway is the natural jumping-off point for anyone taking the short-cut over the coastal mountains into Canada's Yukon. In 1897–98, stampeders took to the trail, and a town of 10,000 to 20,000 people sprouted. Today, many of the old buildings still stand and the town's 800 or so residents cater to the crowds of tourists.

Finding the pass

When you approach Skagway from the south – by Alaska Ferry, cruise-ship or air taxi – you see a tiny town at the base of a river valley surrounded by mountains ranging from 5,000 to 7,000ft (1,500 to 2,100 meters) above sea level, rising almost straight out of the salt-water fjord. You would not expect to find a pass to the closed-in valley, but there is one – the White Pass.

The first white man to discover it was Captain William Moore, a member of an 1887 Canadian survey party, a 65-year-old dreamer who had captained steamboats on rivers all over the Western Hemisphere. The big strike in the Yukon did not occur until August 1896, and by October 1897 Skagway's first newspaper reported 15 general stores, 19 restaurants, four meat markets, three wharves, 11 saloons, six lumber yards, eight pack trains, and nine hotels. Three other newspapers were established within a year.

Skagway was not alone in its quest to become the "Metropolis of the North." **Dyea**, a city on the bay 10 miles (16km) to the west, sprang up as well. It sat at the foot of the Chilkoot Trail, an established Native route that was shorter but steeper than the White Pass Trail.

The White Pass Trail, nicknamed "Dead Horse Trail" because of the 3,000 pack animals that perished in the canyon, was used by fewer prospectors, but Skagway won the battle for survival. The White Pass & Yukon Route Railroad laid its first tracks up the middle of Broadway in May 1898, and by 1900 the narrow-gauge line was completed, 100 miles (160km) to Whitehorse, future capital of the Yukon Territory. An easy route to the gold fields was established, and Dyea became a ghost town. Its sparse remains can be seen at the start of the Chilkoot Trail *(see margin note, page 156).*

The Klondike Rush had subsided by 1900, but Skagway was set up for life as the port for the Yukon. Its population has fluctuated between 400 and 3,000 in the years since, due to a continuous boom-and-bust cycle. Food, fuel, war supplies, minerals and tourists have all been hauled by the railroad in various volumes and numbers. In the early 1980s the railroad went through a bad patch and closed down, but was re-opened in 1988.

Riding the railroad

Riding the narrow-gauge train over the White Pass is the best way to get a feel of what the gold rush was like. You travel in turn-of-the-20th-century parlor cars, pulled by steam or diesel engines, which seem to cling to the small cut in the mountainside. Hundreds of feet below are the still visible remains of the old trails. Excursions are available to White Pass Summit (2,890ft/880 meters) or passengers may book a one-way ticket from Skagway to Fraser, British Columbia, where they continue to Whitehorse by bus. Visitors can also drive the Klondike Highway, completed in 1978, which climbs the opposite side of the canyon from the railroad. It is paved from Skagway to the junction with the Alaska Highway near Whitehorse.

The 3-hour drive gives you much the

"Soapy" Smith

Jefferson Randolph "Soapy" Smith, who had been chased out of Colorado, set up his gang in Skagway in 1897. For nine months, under the guise of a civic leader, he won the allegiance not only of prostitutes, gamblers and saloon keepers, but also of bankers, editors and church builders. But when one of his men robbed a miner (a common enough occurrence), Soapy refused to bow to vigilantes and return the gold. He died in a shootout while trying to break up the lynch mob.

BELOW: many of the old Victorian buildings were originally brothels.

same splendid scenery as is seen from the railroad: Skagway River Gorge, Pitchfork Falls, White Pass Summit, and the beautiful lake country of British Columbia and the Yukon.

The gold rush recalled

The center of activity in Skagway is along Broadway, which starts at the dock and ferry terminal, where more than 60 gold-rush era buildings still stand. The **Klondike Gold Rush National Historic Park** ⑪, created in 1977, took over ownership of many of these buildings and has since spent millions of dollars on their restoration. Private restoration has also taken place. Occupying the old buildings are curio shops, restaurants, saloons, hotels, art galleries, ice-cream parlors, and other businesses, many of them staffed by people in period dress, evoking a gold-rush setting.

Start a tour of the town with a visit to the **Klondike Gold Rush National Historic Park Visitor Center** ⓐ (open daily 8am–6pm in summer; tel: 983-2921; www.nps.gov/klgo) on the corner of Second Avenue and Broadway. The center contains a small museum, offers informative talks, shows an atmospheric movie about the gold rush days, and conducts free walking tours of the historic district three or four times a day.

Nearby, on the corner of Third Avenue and Broadway, and also under the egis of the National Historic Park, is the **Mascot Saloon** ⓑ. Built in 1898, when it was one of many bar-rooms designed to slake the miners' thirst, it has some well-displayed exhibits which conjure up the rough, tough atmosphere of the saloon's heyday.

The **Arctic Brotherhood Hall** ⓒ is just across the street. The exterior of the building is covered with thousands of pieces of driftwood. Inside, it has become the home of Skagway's **Convention and Visitors Bureau** (tel: 983-2854 or 888-762-1898; www.skagway.com).

Walk up Broadway and turn right on Fifth Avenue to **Moore's Cabin** ⓓ, built by the city's neglected founder and his son in 1887 and transferred to this spot when stampeders trampled over their land. This, too, has been renovated by the National Historic Park Service.

On the corner of Broadway and Sixth is **Eagle's Hall** ⓔ, where the "Skagway in the Days of '98" show re-creates the

Cruise congestion
As many as five or six cruise ships can dock at Skagway in a single day, disgorging more than 10,000 people. An average year will produce more than 800,000 cruise ship passengers, compared with 125,000 independent travelers. A full cruise ship calendar can be found at www.skagway.com

BELOW: the White Pass & Yukon Route Railway.

Skagway

0   200 yds
0   200 m

Soapy Smith story nightly. This one-hour melodrama follows an hour of live ragtime music and gambling. The dealers are cast members, the money is phoney, and some of the tables date back to the gold rush. The show's popularity has kept it going since 1925.

At the end of Seventh Avenue (turn right off Broadway just past the post office) is the **City Hall** ⑦, a century-old building that has been both a place of learning (the McCabe College, which is why it is often known locally as the "McCabe Building") and a courthouse. Outside, you will find a display of historic rail cars.

Gold Rush Cemetery

Running parallel with Broadway is State Street; follow this northeast for just over 2 miles (3km) and you will come to the **Gold Rush Cemetery**, where Soapy Smith and Frank Reid were laid to rest after reaching their violent mutual end.

In addition to the walking tours organized by the National Historic Park Center, there are tours arranged by several companies which will take you around the historic district and up to the Gold Rush Cemetery. Some use pony-carts, others old street cars or mini-buses.

Fun and festivities

Skagway has the reputation for being a party town, especially in summer: ask any Yukoner who bolts for the coast on weekends. There are two saloons which are usually hopping, especially on days when the larger cruise ships are in town.

Jazz musicians working on the cruise vessels sometimes jump ship in Skagway for a few hours to attend jamming sessions, because, they say, it's the only day of the cruise that they don't have to play "old folks' music." If business is good, the bars will stay open right through until 5am, the official closing time.

Visitors are welcome to join locals in the town-wide parties. The Summer Solstice Party, held on June 21 – the longest day of the year – is an all-night event, with bands performing in city parks.

A traditional gold-rush style Independence Day is celebrated on July 4, complete with parades, races and contests of all kinds. Four days later, on July 8, is Soapy Smith's Wake, a party and a champagne toast to Skagway's notorious con-

A one-armed bandit carries on the town's gambling traditions.

BELOW:
a local mural celebrates the railway tradition.

TIP

Dyea ghost town

Old Dyea, which was killed off by the coming of the railroad in 1900, can be reached by driving 9 miles (14km) along the twisting Dyea Road. There's little left of the town, apart from a few ruined cabins, but on the way the **Skagway Overlook** viewing platform provides a great view of Skagway and its surrounding peaks.

BELOW:
pioneer families tramped over the Chilkoot Pass.

man, which is held at the Eagle's Hall.

The Klondike Trail of '98 Road Relay is held on the second weekend of September. About 100 10-person teams run a distance of 110 miles (176km) from Skagway to Whitehorse, ending, naturally enough, with a party. In 1998, the centenary of the Klondike Gold Rush was celebrated in great style.

The construction of the White Pass and Yukon Route Railroad began on May 28, 1898. It was Alaska's first railroad and still has an international reputation as a first-class feat of engineering. The railway is still something to marvel at.

The last two weeks of June every year see the Dyea to Dawson race, in which competitors re-create the 19th-century gold-rush trek over the Chilkoot Trail to Lake Bennett, then take to canoes for the final leg: Dawson City in the Yukon.

Hiking around Skagway

Around Skagway, there is much to be seen. If you're reasonably fit and own a backpack, hiking the **Chilkoot Trail**, also part of the Klondike Gold Rush National Historic Park, is the most adventurous option for tracing the route of the gold

seekers. Managed by the park services of the United States and Canada, the trail extends nearly 35 miles (53km) from old Dyea to Lake Bennett, British Columbia.

Most hikers allow three to five days to fully capture the scenery and explore the thousands of gold-rush relics left behind during the stampede. A limited number of permits (about 50; fee charged) are available daily to cross the pass.

Contact the National Park Service (tel: 907-983-2921; www.nps.gov/klgo) or Parks Canada (tel: 800-661-0486; www.pc.gc.ca/lhn-nhs/yt/chilkoot).

As you approach the base of the Chilkoot Pass and look up at the steps carved in the snow by the day's hikers, you can't help but visualize the scenes of more than a century ago, when men went out, full of high hopes, to seek their fortunes, and so many returned empty-handed. Fortunately for us, it was captured in photographs and in print.

Edwin Tappan Adney recorded the scene for *Harper's Weekly* in September 1897: "Look more closely. The eye catches movement. There is a continuous moving train; they are perceptible only by their movement, just as ants are. The moving train is zigzagging across the towering face of the precipice, up, up into the sky, even at the very top. See! they are going against the sky! They are human beings, but never did men look so small."

There are several other trails, most of them described in a booklet obtainable from the National Park Service Visitor Center on the corner of Broadway and 2nd Avenue (open daily). The center will also advise you about camp-sites and United States Forest Service (USFS) cabins.

The **Dewey Lake Trail System** comprises various trails, the shortest (about half an hour each way) being to Lower Dewey Lake, where pink and silver salmon run in August and September, and which has picnic spots and camp spaces.

From here you can continue up to the Upper Dewey Lake and the Devil's Punchbowl. For a tougher hike, try the **Skyline Trail**, officially called the AB Mountain Trail, which starts on Dyea Road, just over 1 mile (2km) out of town, and takes a whole day from start to finish. The **Denver Glacier Trail** is another option. It takes you up the Skagway River to the Denver Glacier, but it's tough going and not for the faint-hearted.

The best weather for outdoor pursuits is in springtime. Skies are clear, the sun is hot, and the snow is still deep on White Pass until mid-May. Cross-country skiers and snow-mobilers drive to the top of the highway, and go all day. Later in the summer, after the snow has melted, hundreds of small ponds form on the moon-like terrain.

The White Pass and Yukon Route Railroad is still admired as a first-class feat of engineering.

Heading for the Interior

Since the opening of the **Klondike Highway** out of Skagway, more and more travelers have opted to drive the 360-mile (580-km) "Golden Circle" route to include both Skagway and Haines on their way to or from the Interior.

Driving up the Alaska Highway from the south, you can cut off to Skagway on the Klondike, put your car on the ferry for the short ride to Haines, and then proceed north along the Chilkoot River on the Haines Cut-Off till you meet the Alaska Highway again at Haines Junction. This is the most direct road route to Alaska's interior from the Panhandle. ❑

RESTAURANTS AND BARS

Alaska Gourmet
361 5th Avenue
tel: 983-2448
Open for breakfast, lunch and dinner. Offers pastries, soups, sandwiches, salads, local seafood, vegan dishes and desserts. Box lunches available to take along. $

Olivia's Restaurant at the Skagway Inn
Seventh Avenue and Broadway
tel: (907) 983-2289
www.skagwayinn.com
Fine dining featuring fresh Alaska seafood and local fresh produce from an organic garden next to the inn. Full bar and select wines available. Reservations required. Closed in winter. $$$$

Red Onion Saloon
Second Avenue and Broadway
tel: 983-2222
Decked out as a gold rush saloon with life-size replicas of 19th-century prostitutes. Occasional live music adds to the atmosphere. $

Sabrosa's
6th and Broadway
tel: 983-2469
This small café is a favorite with locals, offering indoor and outdoor casual dining in a peaceful setting. Deli-style sandwiches (on freshly baked bread), pasta, vegetarian meals and Mexican specials are on the menu. Open daily in summer for breakfast and lunch. Beer and wine is served. $

The Stowaway Café
Congress Way (near the small boat harbor)
tel: 983-3463
Grilled salmon and halibut are the specialty at this charming little house located a short distance from the historic sites. Open only during summer, this waterfront restaurant also offers a variety of beef and pasta dishes, and more. Small dining room (reservations recommended) and a walk-up window for lunchtime carryout meals. Beer and wine. $$–$$$

● ● ● ● ● ● ● ● ● ● ● ● ● ● ● ● ● ● ● ●

Price is for dinner excluding tax, tip and beverages: **$$$$** *$30 and up,* **$$$** *$20–30,* **$$** *$15–20,* **$** *under $15.*

THE GREAT KLONDIKE GOLD RUSH

Gold was discovered in the Klondike in a period of economic depression, attracting the penniless, the adventurous and the unscrupulous

During 1897–98, 100,000 people poured into Dawson in the Klondike in search of gold. Although Dawson is in Canada, the best way to reach it was by ship, 600 miles (960km) from Seattle to Skagway, then overland, across one of two treacherous passes – the White Pass from Skagway or the Chilkoot from Dyea. The former was believed to be slightly easier, but it was controlled by "Soapy" Smith – a villain who virtually ran Skagway during the gold boom *(see margin note, page 153)* – and stories of men being robbed and murdered were rife.

On the Chilkoot Pass it was the elements that were the killers, particularly avalanches and winter's extreme cold. The journey was made more difficult by the fact that, after some of the early prospectors died of starvation, the Canadian government insisted that each man should take a year's supplies – which weighed roughly a ton.

Dreams and desolation

Once the winter and the hazards of the trail were over, prospectors had to face the rapids and whirlpools of lakes and rivers, which they tackled in hand-made boats – denuding the forests to build them. Dreams of gold kept them going but by the time most of them reached Dawson, the productive claims were already allocated.

While some people became rich, and others found just enough to give them security, many of the so-called stampeders, having sunk everything they owned in to the enterprise, were ruined. It's estimated that fewer than 100 of the gold rushers retained or built on their wealth in the long term.

BELOW: Weighing up the wealth
Prospectors eye the scales and weigh the gold that has been gleaned during a long winter's work. By 1900, more than $250 million of gold had been found.

ABOVE: Disaster in the sun
Prospectors crossing the Chilkoot and White passes to Dawson, during the coldest winter in living memory, set up makeshift encampments en route. On Palm Sunday, 1898 spring sunshine began to melt the snow and an avalanche engulfed a Chilkoot Trail camp, killing 70 people.

DISHING THE DIRT IN DAWSON

Mining was a laborious business and those who went to the gold fields thinking the precious metal was there for the taking were soon disillusioned. The early prospectors had been lucky, striking gold near the surface, but by the time the great influx of hopefuls reached Dawson they were digging for gold which could be some 50ft (15 meters) beneath the surface. To reach it, they had to force their way through permafrost, burning fires to soften the land, then sinking shafts which might, or might not, hit the right spot.

Once the "paydirt" – the mixture of earth and gold – had been extracted it had to be separated and cleaned, and this was done in a primitive sluice. When the streams began to thaw in spring, water channeled through the sluice separated the precious dust from the dirt. The more sophisticated hydraulic sluicing methods introduced in Silver Bow could not be used in Dawson because of the difficulty of getting equipment across the passes.

The sluice pictured above is "Long Tom" in Nome, where gold was discovered in late 1899. Many prospectors, still gripped by gold fever, made their way there, empty-handed but hopeful, after the Klondike gold was exhausted.

LEFT: Cleaning up
Services sprang up in the towns and along the route. This laundry, set up in Dawson, was a welcome sight to people who had spent months on the trail.

TOP: Hard on the horses
Those who could afford it loaded their provisions and equipment on to pack horses, but many of the animals failed to survive the trip, hence the nickname given to the White Pass – Dead Horse Trail.

ABOVE: Juneau's beginnings
Gold was discovered in Silver Bow Basin almost two decades before the Klondike strike, and was a lot easier to reach. Gold pans and pick axes were soon replaced by hydraulic earth-moving and sluicing operations, and the camp eventually became the town of Juneau.

RIGHT: Somewhere to spend it
Mary's Hotel in Bonanza Creek was one of many roadhouses which sprang up along the Klondike creeks. These hostelries provided a few home comforts, and gave the lucky ones somewhere to spend their money, distributing the rewards of the gold fields.

YAKUTAT

Alaska
Anchorage
Yakutat

The tiny, superlative-laden community of Yakutat is far off the beaten path of, well, just about everybody. It is the northernmost town of Southeast Alaska, located on Monti Bay, the only sheltered, deep-water port in the Gulf of Alaska

Main attractions
MALASPINA GLACIER
HUBBARD GLACIER

BELOW:
fireweed brightens
Harlequin Lake, to
the southeast of
Yakutat.

The majestic 18,008-ft (5,489-meter) spire of Mount St Elias, the second-tallest mountain in North America, dominates the town's northwestern skyline of **Yakutat ⑫** (about 620 residents). Providing a formidable backup is the rest of the St Elias Mountain Range, the highest coastal range in the world (exceeding the Himalayas in vertical relief). The area also boasts the greatest number of glaciers in North America – giant ones – surrounding the town on three sides. In fact, the 45-mile-wide **Malaspina Glacier**, a few miles west of Yakutat, is North America's largest piedmont glacier and covers more area than the state of Rhode Island. The **Hubbard Glacier**, 30 air miles to the north, is the longest tidewater glacier in Alaska and features an open calving face over 6 miles (10km) wide.

Twice in recent history (in 1986 and again in 2002), this galloping glacier has built suspense among the world's glaciologists (and among *everyone* in Yakutat) by surging forward, damming the mouth of Russell Fjord, and creating an ominous, rapidly rising freshwater lake. In both instances the ice dam eventually gave way, allowing the water to flow into Yakutat Bay, the trapped marine mammals to escape to the sea, and the residents of Yakutat to breathe a sigh of relief.

Commercial fishing, fish processing and government form the primary economic base for the community. Most residents live a subsistence lifestyle, hunting and fishing to provide for their families, as they have for many generations.

The first settlers

Eyak-speaking people, driven from the Copper River area by Tlingit warriors, were probably the first settlers of Yakutat (the name meaning "the place where the canoes rest"). Throughout the 18th and 19th centuries, explorers from Russia, Spain, France and England made their way to the area's protected harbor. In 1805, the Russian-American Company built a fort in Yakutat to advance the sea otter trade. Tlingit warriors, having been denied access to their traditional fishing grounds by the Russians, eventually attacked and destroyed the fort. Gold was mined from the black-sand beaches of the area in 1886. The Swedish Free Mission Church built a sawmill and school in Yakutat in 1889, and by the early 1900s a railroad, store and cannery were constructed nearby. Like much of Alaska, Yakutat gained a sudden surge of military population during World War II, and a paved runway that is still in use today.

In fact, another local superlative involves that very runway: Yakutat is one of the smallest communities in the country to enjoy daily jet service (from Seattle and from Anchorage). Other options for travel include air taxis and floatplane services. In summer, the Alaska Marine Highway provides a scheduled ferry service, but only 2 or 3 times a month.

Big waves have attracted surfers in recent years. Other activities include beachcombing, birding and kayaking.

But Yakutat is probably best known for its world-class sport fishing. The Situk River, 11 miles (17km) from town, boasts the largest run of steelheads in the state. All five species of Pacific salmon may be found in the area (both in fresh and salt water). Other species include halibut, rainbow and cutthroat trout, Dolly Varden, and Northern Pike. Several lodges in the Yakutat area offer fishing packages that include transportation from the airport to the lodge, guided or unguided fishing trips, remote tent camps, preparing your fish for shipping, and providing all meals and supplies.

Outdoor activities

Most of these lodges also offer glacier and wildlife viewing (or flightseeing), hunting trips, photography treks, kayak or river-running support, boat rentals and a host of other services. The office of the **Yakutat Ranger District** (712 Ocean Cape Road; tel: 784-3359; www.fs.fed. us/r10/tongass/districts/yakutat/index) is a good source of information on a myriad of recreational options, including hiking, camping, kayaking and remote Forest Service cabin rentals.

For more details on the superlatives of this little community, contact the **Greater Yakutat Chamber of Commerce** (tel: 784-3933; www. yakutatalaska .com) or the **City and Borough of Yakutat** (tel: 784-3323; www.yakutatak.govoffice2.com). ❑

TIP

If you're planning a trip to Yakutat, bring your quality rain gear and dress in layers. Normal summer temperatures range from 42° to 60°F. This area receives some of the heaviest precipitation in the state, averaging 132 inches per year (including 219 inches of snow). You may also want to bring your wet suit and surfboard. Yakutat, in recent years, has become an exotic location for expedition-minded surfers.

LEFT: surfing is popular enough to justify a specialist surf shop in town.

RESTAURANTS & BARS

Glass Door Bar and Liquor Store
550 Mallott Ave. Tel: 784-3331
Full service bar and liquor store; bar snacks. $

Glacier Bear Lodge Restaurant
On Glacier Bear Highway, about halfway between airport and town. Tel: 784-3202
Continental breakfasts, and full lunch and dinner service. Burgers, salads, seafood, beef and pasta. $–$$$$

Yakutat Lodge
Aat the Yakutat airport, adjacent to Alaska Airlines. Tel: 784-3232
Full-service restaurant within the lodge offers a wide variety of dishes including steaks, seafood and Italian fare. Full bar and liquor store. $–$$$$

Leonards Landing Lodge
tel: 784-3245; 877/925-3474
www.leonardslanding.com
This secluded lodge (and its full service restaurant) is on the waterfront, at the end of the road (about 1½ miles from the center of town). Menu selections range from burgers to prime rib. Beer, wine and some liquor served. $–$$$$

• • • • • • • • • • • • • • • • •
Price is for dinner excluding tax, tip and beverages: **$$$$** *$30 and up,* **$$$** *$20–30,* **$$** *$15–20,* **$** *under $15.*

Gates of the Arctic National Park and Preserve
Prudhoe Bay
Old Crow
Arctic National Wildlife Refuge
Wiseman
Chandalar
Old Rampart
Porcupine
Coldfoot
E. Fork Chandalar
Venetie
Bettles
Evansville
Chandalar
Yukon Flats
Arctic Circle
Allakaket
Kanuti NWR
Stevens Village
Beaver
Birch Creek
Fort Yukon
Yukon Flats National Wildlife Refuge
CANADA
Yukon Territory
Wolverine Mt 4580
Rampart
Livengood
Circle
Central
Circle Hot Springs
Yukon-Charley Rivers National Preserve
Nation
Tatonduk
Tanana
Eureka
Elliott Hwy
Chatanika
Pinnell Mt 4935
Steese Hwy
Chena Hot Springs
Eagle
Eagle Village
Whitehorse
Manley Hot Springs
Fox
Ester
College
Fairbanks
North Pole
Chena River SRA
Chena
Salcha
Boundary
Dawson
Sulphur
Nenana
Anderson
Richardson
Big Delta
Mt Harper 6515
Chicken
CANADA
Diamond
Healy
Kantishna
Denali National Park & Preserve
Cantwell
Ferry
Suntrana
Delta Junction
Healy Lake
Dot Lake
Tok
Tetlin Junction
Ladue
Yukon Territory
Mt Russell 11670
Mt McKinley 20320
Denali State Park
Chulitna
Denali
Paxson
Mt Kimball 10350
Tanacross
Tetlin
Northway Junction
Northway
Tetlin NWR
Beaver Creek
Snag
Koidern
Petersville
Curry
Talkeetna
Sourdough
Mentasta Lake
Slana
Mentasta Mountains
Nabesna
Nutzotin Mountains
Chisana
Trapper Creek
Sovereign Mt 8846
Lake Louise
Gulkana
Glennallen
Chistochina
Gakona
Mt Sanford 16237
Tanada Pk 9358
Mt Wrangell 14163
Wrangell Mountains
Mt Bona 16421
Mt Logan 19850
Skwentna
Willow
Houston
Wasilla
Palmer
Tazlina Lake
Copper Center
Lower Tonsina
Mt Blackburn 16390
McCarthy
Kennicott
Chitina
St Elias Mts
Kluane National Park
Independence Mine SHP
Chickaloon
Glenn Hwy
Mt Marcus Baker 13176
Columbia Glacier
Klutina Lake
Thompson Pass 2771
Tonsina
Chitina
Mt St Elias 18008
Anchorage
Girdwood
Portage
Valdez
Patitlek
Bridal Veil Falls
Cordova Peak 7730
Cordova
Wrangell-St Elias National Park & Preserve
Bagley Icefield
Mt Tom White 11210
Malaspina Glacier
Captain Cook SRA
Nikiski
Kenai
Soldotna
Sterling
Hope
Whittier
Prince William Sound
Chugach National Forest
Bering Glacier
Kustatan
Kasilof
Cooper Landing
Moose Pass
Chenega
Hinchinbrook Island
Katalla
Cape Yakataga
Ice Bay
Clam Gulch
Ninilchik
Seward
Sargent Icefield
Latouche
Hinchinbrook Entrance
Controller Bay
Kayak Island
Cape Saint Elias
Anchor Point
Homer
Kachemak
Tustumena Lake
Kenai Fjords National Park
Blying Sound
Montague Island
English Bay
Seldovia
Kachemak Bay SWP
Pye Islands
Resurrection Bay
Portlock
Chugach Islands
Gulf of Alaska
Kennedy Entrance
Stevenson Entrance
Shuyak Island State Park
Dutch Harbor
Juneau

Southcentral and Interior Alaska

0 — 100 miles
0 — 100 km

SOUTHCENTRAL ALASKA

This vast expanse of awe-inspiring countryside includes Anchorage, Matanuska-Susitna Valley, Prince William Sound, Copper River Valley, and the Kenai Peninsula

Southcentral Alaska extends from the coastal fjords, glaciers and forests of the Kenai Peninsula and Prince William Sound areas, northeast through the remote Copper River Valley, or northwest through Anchorage (Alaska's largest city, in terms of population), then past the picturesque farmlands and sobering mountain ranges of the Matanuska-Susitna Valley, and finally to the wild, southern boundary of the alluring Denali National Park and Preserve.

The history of the various communities of Southcentral is as diverse as the land, itself. Athabascans were the first inhabitants of much of the area, though Alutiiq and Eyak peoples populated the area now called Cordova. Intrepid explorers from Russia traveled to the mainland of Alaska beginning in 1741, and were soon followed by other adventurers from Britain, Spain and America.

The discovery of valuable minerals, primarily copper and gold, drew boatloads of prospectors to the area, prompted the construction of two railroad systems in the early 1900s, and spawned many of the communities of both the Copper River Valley and Prince William Sound, as well as Seward, Anchorage, Palmer/Wasilla, and Talkeetna. From 1939 to 1957, US military construction created new roads, airports and harbors – plus employment opportunities – throughout the region.

Accessible adventures

Because of the mind-boggling size and scope of the state, today's visitors to Alaska are faced with a difficult choice: Which area should one explore during the typical two-week vacation? In many ways, it could be argued that Southcentral Alaska, because of the climate, location, availability of goods and services, road system and transportation options, may well provide most visitors with the greatest number (and variety) of accessible adventure options.

Anchorage is not Alaska's capital, but it has many of the attributes of a capital city. Approximately 42 percent of Alaska's total population resides here. Most visitors to Southcentral arrive in via commercial airlines into

PRECEDING PAGES: a hiker surveys Anchorage's skyline from the Chugach Mountains.
ABOVE: camping at Kenai Peninsula; Native art in Anchorage Museum.

Anchorage, by cruise ship (through Whittier or Seward), or by Alaska Marine Highway System ferry (through Whittier). Southcentral is largely connected by road and easily accessible by car (private or rental), RV or bus.

Flightseeing opportunities

Every town in Alaska, regardless of size, has some sort of airport, ranging from the modern Ted Stevens Anchorage International Airport, to unpaved strips in the bush. Pilots also land on beaches, gravel bars, and lakes where no constructed facilities exist. Air taxis can be chartered in most communities to take you to outlying villages, on day trips for dramatic flightseeing opportunities, or they will drop you off in remote areas for a backcountry experience, and return to pick you up at a pre-arranged time and location.

In addition to traveling to and within Southcentral by air, sea or road, there is also the delightful and scenic option of "riding the rails." While no US nor Canadian rail system provides rail service to Alaska, the Alaska Railroad (www.akrr.com) provides excellent (though not inexpensive) opportunities to see Southcentral Alaska during the summer months, from Kenai Peninsula city of Seward, north through Anchorage, Wasilla, Talkeetna and on into the interior city of Fairbanks *(see page 243).*

The climate

Summer temperatures in Southcentral Alaska are generally pleasant. Anchorage's July temperatures average from 51° to 65°F (10°–18°C), and average yearly precipitation is 15 inches (38cm) – compared to 162 inches (411cm) in Ketchikan, and 5 inches (13cm) in Barrow. While some summers in Southcentral may well be cool and rainy, the rain comes mostly in a con-

stant sort of drizzle; you may yearn for sunshine, but your vacation plans will likely be unaffected. And when the sun does shine, it hardly knows when to stop. Anchorage enjoys more than 19 hours of daylight at the summer solstice (June 20 or 21).

Plan to dress in layers for a visit to Southcentral Alaska. Long pants (although the locals, especially the younger ones, will likely be wearing shorts and "flip-flop" sandals), short-sleeved tee shirts, a light, rain and wind resistant, hooded jacket, and comfortable, casual walking shoes would be perfect for a summer visit. Add a fleece jacket, a warm, knit hat and gloves if you plan to go out on the water for a day cruise. If it's overcast or rainy, with even a slight wind, you'll be glad for the extra warmth.

Don't forget to bring sunscreen along, and mosquito repellant can be your best friend if you plan to camp or hike anywhere in Alaska. For wintertime visits, add a warm, winter-weight jacket, heavier hat and gloves, snow pants and warm, insulated boots to your ensemble. You may feel a bit bulky, but rest assured, you'll fit right in. ❑

Above: a fisherman and his floatplane; a well-equipped fisherwoman.
Right: unusually strong fall colors on the Seward Highway.

ANCHORAGE

Anchorage is a good jumping-off point for many parts of the state, but it has a lot more to offer, from interesting museums to lively nightlife, and ski slopes right on the doorstep

Alaska

Anchorage

Imagine you're a passenger aboard one of the many domestic and international air carriers serving **Anchorage ❶** daily. About three hours out of Seattle, the pilot announces you'll be landing in Anchorage in a few minutes – but, as you peer out of the window, you can see few signs of civilization.

Just as you're beginning to wonder if the pilot has lost his way, you spot Anchorage. Plopped down on a roughly triangular piece of land that sticks out into Cook Inlet, with Turnagain Arm bordering the southwest shore and Knik Arm the northwest one, the city sprawls out over a 10-mile (16-km) length, seeming to spread over most of the available land between the inlet and the Chugach Mountains to the east.

Commercial center

With over a quarter of a million residents and 42 percent of Alaska's population, Anchorage is the state's largest metropolis and its commercial center. This port city didn't get a good purchase on life until 1915, but in the decades since has developed from a railroad tent camp to a city of high-rise offices, ethnic restaurants, and world-class trail systems for biking, hiking, and skiing.

Captain James Cook, the British explorer, sailed into Cook Inlet in 1778, while looking for a Northwest Passage to the Atlantic. Trading furs and fish with

the Dena'ina Natives, he noticed that they carried iron and copper weapons, the first evidence of trade with the Russians who had set up trading posts in lower Cook Inlet and at Kodiak.

Russian influences can still be seen today at Eklutna, a Dena'ina village inside the northern boundary of the municipality of Anchorage.

When Cook found no way out of the arm of Cook Inlet to the south of Anchorage, he ordered his ships, the *Resolution* and the *Discovery*, to turn around, hence the name "Turnagain." Knik Arm gets its

Main attractions
SHIP CREEK
ANCHORAGE MUSEUM OF HISTORY AND ART
ALASKA CENTER FOR THE PERFORMING ARTS
IMAGINARIUM
OSCAR ANDERSON HOUSE MUSEUM
ALASKA NATIVE HERITAGE CENTER
EARTHQUAKE PARK
ALASKA ZOO
H2OASIS INDOOR WATERPARK
ANCHORAGE COASTAL WILDLIFE REFUGE
ALYESKA RESORT & SKI AREA
GIRDWOOD
EAGLE RIVER NATURE CENTER
EKLUTNA VILLAGE HISTORICAL PARK

LEFT: downtown Anchorage by night.
RIGHT: statue to Captain James Cook.

Snow sculpture in Anchorage.

name from the Eskimo word for fire, knik, which was used in reference to the Dena'ina people and their villages.

The gold rush

After Alaska was purchased from the Russians in 1867, gold seekers worked the land along Turnagain Arm and at Crow Creek and Girdwood, which is now the southern boundary of the municipality. The gold rush rapidly spread north and across Knik Arm. The old mining supply center of Knik is located across the inlet from downtown Anchorage.

During its short history, Anchorage has reverberated with the sounds of several major construction booms: laying track for the Alaska Railroad, building two adjacent military bases during World War II, the discovery and development of the Cook Inlet and Kenai Peninsula oil fields, and, in the 1970s, the construction of the 800-mile (1,285-km) trans-Alaska oil pipeline from Prudhoe Bay to Valdez. The most recent boom has been of the retail variety: several national chains have opened stores in Anchorage in the past 15 years.

Rugged individualism

The Good Friday earthquake of 1964, originally estimated at 8.7 on the Richter scale but now believed to have measured 9.2, was the most powerful earthquake ever recorded in North America, and it brought Alaskans together to work for a common cause. While the quake devastated many homes and businesses in Anchorage and in other communities, the reconstruction generated a mini-boom and Anchorage emerged a new city. Quakes still shake Anchorage and Southcentral Alaska occasionally, including a 7.9 tremblor in 2002.

During the past decade Anchorage has striven to overcome the consequences of its boom-and-bust economy – unemployment, out-migration, poverty, to name a few. During the boom times, Alaska's population was a transient one. The majority of people were lured by the promise of high-paying jobs.

In the 1970s, when the trans-Alaska pipeline was being built, the salaries for construction workers were in six-digit figures. Average salaries in Alaska are still slightly higher than those in most Lower 48 states, but services and goods tend to cost more here as well – on a par, perhaps, with New York or Los Angeles.

Backyard wilderness

Some people move to Anchorage from other parts of the USA because they are attracted by the adventure of living at the "last frontier." This is a city where one needs only to walk out of the back door to see – and, in some cases, step into – the wilderness.

Although some residents take off at weekends to pursue various outdoor activities, many others find no need to get away. Not surprising, perhaps, when it is quite common to see a moose outside the living room window, or a bald eagle flying overhead, and when you can share city parks with lynx, owls, and bears. Even wolf packs sometimes prowl the city's edges. Wildlife is so ubiquitous that no one who lives here blinks when they see a moose along the Glenn Highway. An estimated 2,000 moose, 200 black bears and 60 brown bears live in the metropolitan Anchorage area and nearby foothills.

Fishing enthusiasts have to go no further than **Ship Creek Ⓐ**, on the north side of downtown, to have the chance of catching a 40-lb (18-kg) salmon. The king salmon run lasts from early June to mid-July, and the silver salmon run from late July until later October. For regulations, check www.adfg.state.ak.us/.

Discovering the city

Anchorage is an air crossroads, with several major airlines offering direct flights, primarily from Seattle, but also from other US cities, Tokyo and the Russian Far East. It is as close to London or Tokyo as it is to Houston. More than 200 flights arrive daily at the Anchorage International Airport.

If you are staying downtown, you can easily explore this section of the city on foot. Laid out on a grid system, it is a very easy place to find your way around. Start at the **Visitor Information Center Log Cabin Ⓑ** (open daily) on the corner of 4th Avenue and F Street. Built in 1954, the log cabin is surrounded by flowering foliage in the summer. Note the 5,145-lb (2,333-kg) block of solid jade, the state's official gemstone, outside the cabin. Here you can pick up maps and brochures, including a booklet outlining a suggested

TIP

Getting Around

Local tour companies offer half-day and full-day tours of the city and surrounding area. The Anchorage Convention and Visitors' Bureau (tel: 276-4118; www.anchorage.net) has details of reliable organizations. There is a bus system, the People Mover, although its routes cater to the local residents rather than visitors. The transit center is located on 6th Avenue between G and H streets.

BELOW:
Ship Creek, famous for urban combat fishing downtown.

*The Visitor
Information Center
Log Cabin.*

RIGHT:
the Anchorage
Museum of
History and Art.

walking tour; or you could walk a block down the street and take one of the local trolley tours.

From here, you can cross the road diagonally to reach the **Alaska Public Lands Information Center ●** (open daily all year 9am–5pm; tel: 271-2737; www.nps.gov/aplic/). If you are planning on visiting national parks or taking part in any outdoor activities you will find it invaluable. You can see wildlife exhibits, watch videos on the various regions and activities available, and generally pick up all the information you'll need.

Armed with this information, you can then continue your urban tour. First go back to the **Old City Hall ●**, a classic 1930s construction next door to the Log Cabin, where the lobby holds a display of photographs and other exhibits that trace the city's history.

Continue your walking tour by heading east along 4th Avenue. You will pass many T-shirt shops and stores offering Native Art, including carved walrus ivory, soapstone and baskets. Genuine Native crafts are identified by a tag, either showing a silver hand or stating "Authentic Native Handicraft."

Three blocks past the mall (and the main post office), turn right down A Street to the **Anchorage Museum of History and Art** at Rasmuson Center ● (daily in summer 9am–6pm, Thurs only until 9pm; Wed–Sat 10am–6pm and Sun noon–5pm in winter; tel: 343-4326; www.anchorage museum.org; entrance charge). Among the museum's permanent collections are the Alaska Gallery, with historical exhibits, and a fine selection of Native art and works by travelers, explorers and early residents, displayed in skylit galleries.

Arts center

A few blocks west is the **Alaska Center for the Performing Arts ●** (tel: 263-2787; www.alaskapac.org). Some view this building (locally referred to as "the PAC") as a monstrosity, while others consider it to be architecturally innovative, but its lush flower garden beds certainly add to the beauty of the downtown area.

Alaskan artists have designed much of the interior, including the carpets and upholstery, and the center is decorated with numerous Native masks. Try to join one of the tours that are organized on Monday, Wednesday and Friday in sum-

What to do after dark

The Crow's Nest at the top of the Captain Cook Hotel (on the corner of 5th Avenue and K Street) has gourmet cuisine and a formal atmosphere, together with great views. But if you fancy a taste of nightlife in the last frontier, complete with sawdust on the floor, you won't do much better than Chilkoot Charlie's on Spenard Road. Don't bother with a coat and tie; this is where Alaskans go in their boots and jeans to dance, drink and be entertained.

If you want to mix food and entertainment, the Bear Tooth Theater-pub and Grill, just off Spenard Road, offers second-run movies on a big-screen, tasty food and draft beer or wine. Humpy's, across from the PAC, serves good beers, food and hosts live music performances. Anchorage also has a number of cinemas and theaters, as well as the events which take place at the PAC. See the local press for listings.

One popular and multiple-award-winning theater in the downtown area is Cyrano's (413 D St., variable hours, performances 7pm Thurs–Sat, 3pm Sun; tel: 274-2599; www.cyranos.org; entrance charge). This theater/coffeehouse/book store entertains locals and visitors alike with live theater (including classics, Alaska originals and contemporary works), comedy improv, poetry readings and more. Customers may enjoy beer and wine along with a selection of appetizers and desserts.

mer, at 1pm. There is no set charge, but a donation is appreciated.

Also, while you're there, those who long to see a display of the Aurora Borealis may do so, virtually speaking, via a 40-minute digital show set to music. Twenty-five years worth of nature's light shows may be seen within the PAC, at the Wilda Marston Theater (May 24–Sept 1; hourly shows from 9am–9pm daily; tel: 263-2993; www.thealaskacollection.com; entrance charge).

The PAC is a hub of activities for the arts. Performances by the Anchorage Symphony Orchestra and the Anchorage Concert Association begin in the fall. The Concert Association presents world-class performers in music and dance performances. Check local newspapers, especially the Anchorage Daily News, and visitors' guides for events.

One block further west, on the corner of 6th Avenue and H Street, you will find the **Oomingmak Musk Ox Producers' Co-op G** (tel: 272-9225; www.qiviut.com) where you can buy, or just admire, distinctive garments made of musk ox wool, called qiviut (pronounced *kee-vee-ute*). These are made in Inuit villages.

From the Co-op, turn up H Street again to 5th Avenue, where you will find the **Imaginarium H** (open Mon–Sat 10am–6pm, Sun noon–5pm; entrance charge; tel: 276-3179; www.imaginarium.org). While aimed primarily at children, this award-winning science museum has a wealth of exhibits and hands-on experiences that are also popular with adults. If you want to know more about marine life, wetlands and the solar system, this is a good place to find out.

Continue west a few blocks along 5th Avenue to M Street, to the **Oscar Anderson House Museum I** (open in summer Mon–Fri noon–5pm; closed in winter; entrance charge; tel: 274-2336), set in the attractive little Elderberry Park. Listed on the National Register of Historic Places, this is Anchorage's first wood-frame house, built by Swedish immigrant Anderson in 1915.

Leaving downtown behind

Outside the downtown area, but worth seeing, is the **Alaska Heritage Library and Museum J** (open in summer Mon–Fri noon–5pm; in winter Mon–Fri noon–4pm; admission free; tel: 265-

The Oscar Anderson House Museum.

BELOW: memories of yesteryear's transportation.

2834), in the lobby of the Wells Fargo Building on Northern Lights Boulevard and C Street. There is a large selection of Native art and artifacts and a number of works by Sydney Laurence (1865–1940), known as "the painter of the north."

Continue as far west as you can go along Northern Lights and you'll reach **Earthquake Park**, founded on the spot where, during the 1964 earthquake, 130 acres (52 hectares) of land fell into the inlet and 75 houses were destroyed. A walking trail and museum-quality interpretive signs

make it worth the stop, and there are good views of the city and Mount McKinley.

To the east, travel the Glenn Highway to the Muldoon Road Exit to reach the **Alaska Native Heritage Center Ⓚ** (open daily 9am–5pm in summer, Sat 10am–5pm in winter; entrance charge; tel: 330-8000; www.alaskanative.net), a gathering place for all of Alaska's Native cultures where you can learn about traditional customs and see master Native artists at work.

Alaska Zoo

Visitors unable to see a bear in the wild can see several (polar, brown and black) at the **Alaska Zoo Ⓛ** (4731 O'Malley Road,

Musk oxen can be seen at Alaska Zoo.

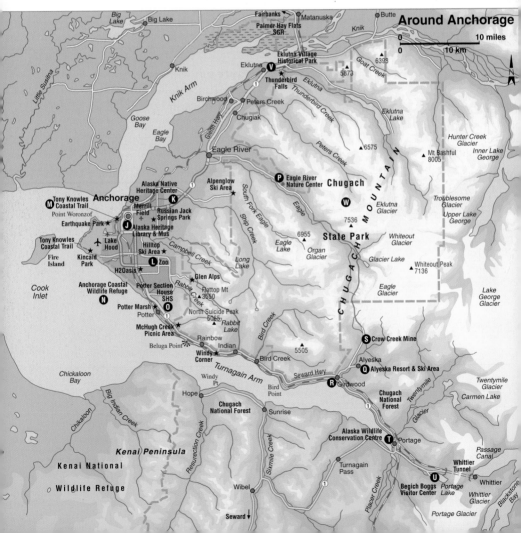

tel: 346 2133; open 9am–6pm daily and until 9pm on Tues and Fri in summer; admission fee). It's a 20-minute drive to the southeast of the city, and a shuttle bus operates from the Hilton, Captain Cook and Sheraton hotels. There's a two-hour naturalist tour in early afternoon.

The 25-acre (62-hectare) zoo houses just under 100 birds and mammals, including natives such as moose, musk oxen, and caribou, seals and otters, but also such non-natives as alpacas, Amur tigers and a Bactrian camel. Its most famous resident, Maggie, a Zimbabwean elephant who has been trained to play the harmonica, caught the attention of international animal rights activists, who argued that a lone tropical elephant could not be happy in a climate which confined her indoors most of the year. The zoo responded in 2006 by installing a $100,000 treadmill for Maggie's exclusive use, but in 2007 agreed that she should transfer to a zoo in the Lower 48.

The zoo had its genesis in 1966 when a local grocer, Jack Snyder, won a contest offering as a prize $3,000 or a baby Asian elephant, Annabelle. He chose the elephant and the idea of a zoo took shape.

Also in this area is **H2Oasis Indoor Waterpark** (1520 O'Malley Road, tel: 522 4420). It has wave pools, body slides, hot tubs, a children's pirate ship play area, and a Master Blaster water coaster that propels the brave in an inner tube in the same gut-wrenching manner as a roller coaster. It's a warm sanctuary for locals in winter.

Getting about by bike

Anchorage is a great place for cyclists, with more than 120 miles (190km) of paved paths, and plenty of bikes for rent (ask at the Visitor Information Center log cabin, which has maps of all trails).

The best-known and most scenic route is the **Tony Knowles Coastal Trail Ⓜ**, which starts near Elderberry Park on 2nd Avenue. The trail – which bicyclists share with walkers, joggers, rollerbladers, and stroller-pushing parents and the occasional moose – is 11 miles (19km) long and parallels Cook Inlet, continuing past Westchester Lagoon and Point Woronzof, and ending at Kincaid Park. In winter, the path becomes a

The Tony Knowles Coastal Trail.

BELOW: café society.

Dall sheep can be seen in spring and summer from the Seward Highway.

cross-country ski trail. There are other bike routes in town: trail maps are also available from the Parks and Recreation department, as well as at the Visitor Information Center. Bicycling is an ideal way to get around, and offers great views of the city and the waters of the inlet, where migrating beluga whales are sometimes seen on the surface.

Around Anchorage

If you want to experience the Alaska outdoor life, try a flightseeing trip. Excursions can easily be arranged by flight operators at Lake Hood or at Merrill Field. Not far from downtown near the international airport is **Lake Hood Air Harbor**, the busiest seaplane base in the world. On summer days when the skies are clear, there are 600 or more take-offs and landings. Channels on Lake Hood and Lake Spenard provide the runways for these seaplanes. Merrill Field (800 Merrill Field Dr.), located one mile east

of downtown Anchorage just off the Glenn Highway, was the first real airport in Anchorage and still today serves as a commercial service airport for the general aviation community. Alaskans fly into the bush for fishing, hunting, hiking and myriad other activities. If you want to experience the Alaska outdoor life, try a flightseeing trip. Flight operators at Lake Hood or at Merrill Field can easily arrange excursions.

On the southern edge of town, visitors can view a variety of waterfowl at **Potter Marsh**, part of the **Anchorage Coastal Wildlife Refuge** ❶. This 2,300-acre (920-hectare) wetland area is the nesting ground for migratory birds during the summer. Bald eagles, Arctic terns, trumpeter swans, sandhill cranes, shorebirds and many species of geese and ducks are commonly spotted; Canada geese and mallards raise their young here. From the boardwalk that borders Potter Marsh's western edge, salmon are visible from mid-July to September as they return to spawn in nearby Rabbit Creek.

Not far from Potter Marsh, along the Seward Highway, visitors have a chance to see larger wildlife. During spring and

Fur Rondy

Fur Rendezvous ("Fur Rondy") is a 10-day celebration featuring more than 150 events, ranging from the famous World Championship Sled Dog Race to the annual snowshoe softball tournament downtown between 9th and 10th avenues on the Delaney Park Strip. Competitions are held for the best snow sculpture (which draws competitors from as far away as Japan) and the fastest canoe in the Downhill Canoe Race. Other events include the traditional

Eskimo blanket toss and the largest outdoor public fur auction in the United States. The highlight of the carnival is the World Championship Sled Dog Race. For three days competitors run heats totaling 75 miles (120km). Participants start on 4th Avenue and continue on the city streets to the outskirts of town where

they circle back. Dog mushing is the official state sport.

At the beginning of Fur Rondy, the Miners' and Trappers' Ball is held. This is not a black-tie affair and everyone in the city is invited, although tickets must be purchased in advance. It is held in a huge warehouse and people arrive in every conceivable attire, some hoping to win the contest for the most unusual costume. Fur Rondy is a great time to experience what life is really like in Alaska. It is a time of camaraderie among the local people and they welcome visitors.

As the event is becoming more popular, it is best to book well in advance. Greater Anchorage Inc can be contacted for the exact dates of the festival and travel deals (tel: 274-1177; www.furrondy.net).

summer it is common to see Dall sheep peering over the rocks of the adjacent cliffs at passing motorists; the best viewing is at **Windy Corner**, about Mile 107. Several spots on this road allow visitors to watch the waters for belugas, the small white whales that chase salmon up the Turnagain Arm. Stop at Beluga Point Interpretive Site in spring and fall, where you will find spotting 'scopes, benches and information about the area.

If you just want to contemplate the beauty and mammoth size of Alaska, you can grab a take-out lunch in town and picnic at nearby **McHugh Creek Picnic Area**, just a few miles down the road from Potter Marsh. Here you can see miles down the inlet, look at the majestic mountains on the other shore, and take a short hike along the 9½-mile (15-km) long Turnagain Arm Trail.

At Anchorage's back door to the east is **Chugach State Park**; *(see page 184)* the park headquarters are located across from Potter Marsh in the **Potter Section House State Historic Site** (open Mon–Fri 8am–4pm; tel: 345-5014; www.alaskastateparks.org). Here you will find a railroad museum and an old rotary snow plow on the track behind the house. Chugach State Park covers 495,000 acres (200,500 hectares) and offers visitors a wide variety of opportunities to experience the Alaska outdoors without being too far away from civilization. Between June and September, various local groups organize nature walks to various parts of the park.

Eagle River Nature Center

The **Eagle River Nature Center** is north on the Glenn Highway from Anchorage. Only a 20-minute drive (14 miles/23km) from downtown Anchorage, Eagle River is a pleasant area. The nature center is another 15 to 20 minutes from downtown Eagle River, at the end of 12-mile-long (19-km) Eagle River Road. The drive through the lake-dotted valley is worth the trip in itself, and once at the center there are displays, nature videos, and several hiking trails, from easy to rigorous. During August the berries are plentiful, and cross-country skiing is a popular winter activity. The center offers daily naturalist programs (tel: 694-2108; www.ernc.org) in summer and weekend activities year-around.

TIP

Some local businesses operate sled dog tours that allow visitors to experience the excitement of riding in a dog sled; some travel the Iditarod Trail and another is based in Girdwood, south of Anchorage. The Girdwood run passes scores of ancient, hanging glaciers and stops in the wilderness for a homemade lunch. Visitors have a chance to mush the dogs and snowshoe during the lunch break.

BELOW:
cross-country skiing is popular in winter.

*Taking a rest
on the slopes.*

Winter activities

Winters are long in Alaska, but this is a special time of the year for visitors. During Thanksgiving week, the University of Alaska Anchorage, located on several acres of wooded land in the city, hosts the **Great Alaska Shoot-Out**, an invitational college basketball tournament. Seven Division I college basketball teams from across the United States come to Anchorage to compete in a tournament, which has gained national prominence and is televised via satellite.

After the Christmas holiday season, Anchorage residents prepare for their own 10-day carnival in February – **Fur Rendezvous** *(see panel on page 176).*

The best skiing

Downhill and cross-country skiing in Anchorage can be found in **Russian Jack Springs Park** with gentle slopes and rope tow for beginners. It also has 4 miles (7km) of lighted trails. The **Hilltop Ski Area** has a chairlift and is an excellent facility for novice skiers. It also has night skiing and is accessible by public bus. For advanced skiers, **Alpenglow at Arctic Valley Ski Area** offers slightly more challenging slopes. Two chair lifts, a T-bar and three rope tows service the area, which has a 1,000-ft (300-meter) drop. Runs can be very steep and maintenance is sometimes questionable.

Alaska's largest and most popular ski area – **Alyeska Resort & Ski Area** ⓠ is 40 miles (64km) southeast of Anchorage in Girdwood. With a vertical drop of 2,500ft (760 meters), it caters to all levels of skiers and is a full-service resort with both day and night skiing. The area has six lifts, including a quad chair lift and four doubles, and a high-speed gondola, which operates in the summer months, taking visitors to a restaurant on the mountain top.

The seven-story **Alyeska Prince Hotel** has more than 300 rooms, formal and informal dining, an indoor pool, a health club and meeting facilities.

For the cross-country skier, Anchorage offers more than 140 miles (225km) of trails. **Kincaid Park** on Raspberry Road has 34 miles (55km) of Nordic ski trails, nine of them illuminated. Near Service High School and Hilltop Ski Area, another trail is lit for skiers. In Chugach State Park, just east of the city, there are dozens of hiking trails, which in winter are frequently used by cross-country skiers. The **Glen Alps** area at the top of Upper Huffman Road offers breathtaking views of the city and is manageable for skiers of any level. To get to it, take the Seward Highway to the O'Malley turn-off going east, continue toward the mountains, turning on to Hillside Drive, and making a left on Upper Huffman, then follow signs to the trailhead.

An hour's drive north of Anchorage is an excellent cross-country ski area with a historical flavor. **Hatcher Pass** is at the heart of the majestic Talkeetna Mountains off the Glenn Highway on Fishhook Road. At the turn of the 20th century Independence Mine was a hub of goldmining activity. Today it is a state historic park and its abandoned buildings and old mining machinery have become landmarks of the past.

The area has miles of groomed ski trails that pass through treeless alpine bowls and on a clear day you can see all the way down the valley to the city of **Palmer** (20 miles/32km). Accommodations are available at a lodge that has individual cabins for guests (Hatcher Pass Lodge, tel: 745-5897; www.hatcher passlodge.com).

Heading south

With only two roads leading in and out of Anchorage, selecting a day trip is easy: you go north or south. Heading south on Seward Highway, visit Girdwood, Crow Creek Mine and Portage Glacier. The drive parallels the Turnagain Arm, an extension of Cook Inlet. Numerous spots along the 40-mile (65-km) drive to Girdwood offer spectacular views of scenery and wildlife: look out for Dall sheep, moose and beluga whales.

Girdwood R is a quaint community that sees an influx of tourists in the summer and skiers in the winter. A ride on the Alyeska Ski Resort tram *(see previous page)* on a clear day provides an incredible view of the surrounding mountains and the inlet. The town has a variety of shops worth wandering around, which offer traditional Alaskan souvenirs.

Outside Girdwood, 3 miles (5km) up Crow Creek Road, is **Crow Creek Mine S**. The placer mine and its eight original buildings are listed on the National

Girdwood's origins
Originally knows as Glacier City, Girdwood began life as a supply camp for miners working the local creeks. It was renamed in recognition of Colonel James Girdwood, a Belfast-born entrepreneur and linen merchant who staked the first gold claims along Crow Creek in 1896.

BELOW:
Crow Creek Mine.

Viewing Portage Glacier, which has been in retreat since the early 1800s but is now melting more rapidly than ever.

Register of Historic Sites. They represent the first non-Native settlement in the area. Visitors can pan for gold in this scenic setting, and for the robust, nearby **Crow Pass Trail** climbs through beautiful mountain valleys.

Continuing down the Seward Highway, at **Twentymile River**, visitors may often see Arctic terns, bald eagles, mew gulls and moose from the observation platform. Plaques on the platform have information on the various species.

Just beyond the Twentymile River is the **Alaska Wildlife Conservation Center** ❶ (Mile 79, Seward Hwy., tel: 783-2025; www.alaskawildlife.org; entrance charge), a 140-acre/57-hectare, drive-through animal park that is dedicated to the rehabilitation of orphaned and injured animals. Get a up-close look at Alaska's wildlife, and starting in May, their young.

Mile 78.9 is the turn-off for **Portage Glacier**. Following your turn, look on the right-hand side of the road is to see Explorer Glacier (there's an excellent photography vantage point). Stop at the bridge over Williwaw Creek to see salmon spawning from late July to mid-September. Sadly, Portage Glacier is rapidly retreating, and with it the once dramatic view of Portage Lake with its huge blue icebergs.

At the end of the road is the **Begich Boggs Visitor Center** ❶ (open daily 9am–6pm in summer; Sat–Sun 10am–5pm in winter; tel: 783-3242; www.fs.fed.us/r10/ chugach). The center's state-of-the-art displays cover the natural history of Chugach National Forest. Don't miss an award-winning documentary film, *Voices from the Ice*, shown hourly during the summer (entrance charge).

Black bear territory

There are several glaciers in Portage Valley with a number of trails where visitors can view glacial features, including a profusion of wildflowers and plant life. Take the short walk to **Byron Glacier**. Signs near Portage Glacier Lodge mark the road to the trailhead. Black bears, smaller cousins of the grizzly, are commonly seen in this area. Portage Glacier is the turn-around point for this trip to the south. From the visitor center there is a new road that will take you to the toll road and tunnel leading to the Prince William Sound community of Whittier *(see page 188)*. Call 1-877-611-2586 for road and tunnel opening information.

Heading north

Traveling on the Glenn Highway north of Anchorage on a day trip, visitors have an opportunity to observe the cultural remnants of Alaska's past and to enjoy several scenic areas in the fertile Matanuska-Susitna Valley.

In Eagle River, stop at the **Eagle River Nature Center**, 14 miles (20km) out of town in Chugach State Park. Continuing on the Glenn Highway, you will see beautiful **Mirror Lake** wayside area on the right. Here, if you're brave, you can swim in the icy water on a warm day or ice fish in the winter. A mile further takes you to the entrance **of Thunderbird Falls Trailhead**, also in Chugach State Park. This is a pleasant 1-mile (2-km) walk to the rushing falls.

Eklutna Lake is Anchorage's largest. There is a state park campground and a wide, multi-use trail to **Eklutna Glacier**, whose waters feed the lake, and good wildlife-viewing and berry-picking.

The Anchorage area's oldest building may well be the **St Nicholas Russian Orthodox Church**, which is part of **Eklutna Village Historical Park** , on the Eklutna turn-off, off the Glenn Highway. It was constructed with hand-hewn logs, and the surrounding spirit houses represent the interaction between the Natives and the Russians.

This was the site of the first Dena'ina Indian settlement east of the Knik Arm, in around 1650. The "spirit" houses show how Native beliefs were mixed with Russian orthodoxy. Spirit houses were placed over traditional graves and contained personal items thought to help the spirit in the afterlife. A three-bar orthodox cross was placed at the foot of the grave.

Small spirit houses indicate the resting place of a child and a large house with a smaller one inside means a mother and child were buried together. A picket fence around a spirit house means the deceased was not a Dena'ina. ❑

TIP

Weather warning
When exploring areas such as Crow pass Trail, be sure to have some basic hiking gear, including water and extra food and clothing, before attempting any hike into the mountains. Weather in Alaska can change quickly and dramatically, and hikers should always be prepared.

BELOW:
sleigh ride in Matanuska Valley.

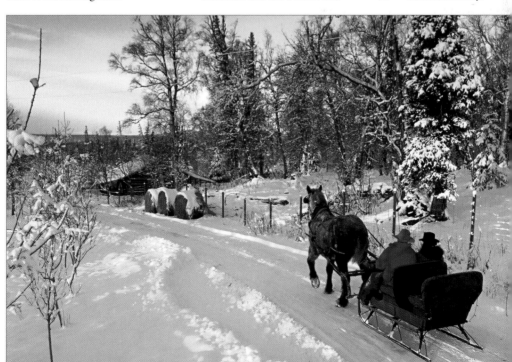

RESTAURANTS, CAFÉS & BARS

Prices for a three-course dinner per person with a half-bottle of house wine:
$ = under $20
$$ = $20–$45
$$$ = $45–$60
$$$$ = over $60

Aladdin's
4240 Old Seward Highway
tel: 561-2327
www.aladdinsak.com
Open Wednesday through Saturdays for dinner only. This family-owned and operated restaurant has attracted a sizeable and loyal clientele by consistently serving up excellent Mediterranean menu items, including falafel and mousaka.

Be sure to try the homemade lemon ice-cream. Beer, wine. $

The Bake Shop
Alyeska Resort
Olympic Circle
Girdwood
tel: 783-2831
www.thebakeshop.com
(40 miles/60km south of Anchorage on the Seward Highway, turn left onto Alyeska Highway and follow signs to ski resort)
This small bakery and sandwich shop is a year-round favorite with skiers and non-skiers alike. Famous for its delicious, daily (bottomless) homemade soups, fresh-baked breads, potato plates, sourdough pancakes, sandwiches, pizzas and especially its giant, warm sweet rolls. The dining is casual, the food simply terrific and the staff capable and kind. $

City Diner
3000 Minnesota Drive
tel: 277-2489
Reflecting a retro-diner style, this upscale, shiny chrome and glass eatery is one of the newer Anchorage dining options. Popular with the business lunch crowd; serves delicious, classic American comfort food. $

Club Paris
417 W. 5th Avenue
tel: (907) 277-6332
www.clubparis
restaurant.com
The bar up front is dark, smoky and full of character – a favorite haunt of long-time Alaskans; the steaks and prime rib served in the back are big, tender and flavorful. Full bar.
$$$–$$$$

Crow's Nest
939 West Fifth Avenue
tel: (907) 276-6000
www.captaincook.com/
restaurants.php
Located atop tower 3 of the Hotel Captain Cook, this multiple-award-winning restaurant offers fine dining and the best view in town of Anchorage, Cook Inlet and the Chugach mountains. Full bar. $$$$

Double Musky
Crow Creek Road
Girdwood
tel: 783-2822
This award-winning restaurant excels in Cajun-style Alaska seafood and steak cuisine. No reservations accepted. Busy, crowded, noisy, and delicious. $$$$

Glacier Brewhouse
737 West Fifth Avenue, Suite 110
tel: (907) 274-2739
www.glacierbrewhouse
.com
Popular downtown restaurant known for fresh Alaska seafood, rotisserie-grilled meats, wood-fired pizzas and hand-crafted ales. Open daily for lunch and dinner. $$–$$$

Gwennies Old Alaska Restaurant
4333 Spenard Road
tel: (907) 243-2090
An Alaska-themed (look for the totems) family-friendly restaurant

LEFT: Alaskan smoked salmon.

known for large portions for breakfast, lunch and dinner. $$–$$$

Kinley's Restaurant and Bar
3230 Seward Highway
tel: 644-8953
One of Anchorage's newer restaurants located in mid-town. Enjoy fine dining, excellent service, reasonable prices and delicious menu selections, including fresh Alaska seafood, steaks, lamb, chicken, pasta and more. Beer and wine. $$–$$$$

Lucky Wishbone
1033 E. 5th Avenue
tel: (907) 272-3454
This is a great chicken and burger joint that is popular with all sorts of people from local lawyers and oil executives to cabbies and mechanics. The homemade shakes are rich and creamy. $

Marx Brothers' Café
627 W. 3rd Avenue
tel: (907) 278-2133
Innovative fine dining and an extensive wine list can be found at this little frame house on a downtown bluff. Built in 1916, it has been renovated by the restaurant's owners. The 12-table cafe was opened in 1979 and has earned a reputation as one of Anchorage's finest restaurants, wor-

thy of a special occasion. $$$$

Moose's Tooth Pub and Pizzeria
3300 Old Seward Highway
tel: (907) 258-2537
www.moosestooth.net
This brewpub and pizzeria offers handcrafted ales and gourmet pizzas with a great range of toppings, such as artichoke hearts, feta cheese and spinach. $–$$$

Orso Ristorante
737 W. 5th Avenue
tel: (907) 222-3232
www.orsoalaska.com
Creative Italian cuisine assembled with fresh-made pastas and Alaskan seafoods, served in a bustling, cozy restaurant. Extensive wine list. Modern art on the walls adds to the Mediterranean ambiance. $$–$$$

Sack's Café
328 G Street
tel: (907) 274-4022
www.sackscafe.com
This popular urban café offers interesting combinations of ingredients all carefully prepared on main dishes such as chicken and scallops, free-range chicken and salmon or halibut. Especially popular at lunchtime and also for dinner before the theater or for a long and lazy Saturday or Sunday brunch. $$$–$$$$

Seven Glaciers

Restaurant
Alyeska Resort, Arlberg Road (40 miles/60km south of Anchorage on the Seward Highway, turn left onto Alyeska Highway and follow signs to the ski resort at Girdwood. Ride the Alyeska Ski Resort aerial tram up to this mountaintop restaurant (elevation 2,300 ft) for fine dining and extraordinary views of Turnagain Arm, the Chugach Mountain Range and seven "hanging" glaciers. Specializes in fresh Alaska seafood, beef and free-range chicken entrées. Full bar. $$$$

Simon and Seafort's
420 L Street
tel: 907-274-3502
www.r-u-i.com/sim
Fine dining and bar with an outstanding view of

Cook Inlet. Open for lunch and dinner with broad menu selections. Full bar. $$$–$$$$

Snow City Café
1034 W. Fourth Avenue
tel: 272-2489
Famous for delicious breakfasts, served all day in this popular restaurant. Sandwiches and vegetarian choices also available. $

Snow Goose Restaurant and Brewery
717 W. Third Avenue
tel: 277-7727
One of the original brewpubs in Anchorage, this restaurant features sunny, outdoor decks overlooking Ship Creek and Cook Inlet. Great local beers, pizza, burgers, beer-battered halibut, and ribs. $

RIGHT: fresh produce at Anchorage's Saturday market.

CHUGACH STATE PARK

Alaska

Anchorage

Established in 1970, Anchorage's "backyard wilderness" offers all sorts of recreational opportunities for residents and visitors within a short distance of Alaska's urban center

Main attractions

MOUNT BASHFUL
FLATTOP MOUNTAIN
EAGLE RIVER NATURE
CENTER
WINDY CORNER
TURNAGAIN ARM

BELOW: climbing in the Chugach Mountains.

Just to the east of Anchorage is a large and rugged chain of peaks, the **Chugach Mountains**. Stretching 300 miles (480km) across Alaska's Southcentral region, the range arcs from Cook Inlet almost to the Canadian border. The westernmost portion, touching the edges of Alaska's largest city, is encompassed by **Chugach State Park** Ⓦ, a 495,000-acre (200,000-hectare) piece of land that many locals have long considered their "backyard wilderness."

Among the oldest and largest of Alaska's state parks, Chugach was estab-lished in 1970, thanks to the determined efforts of a few Anchorage residents who wanted to protect the neighboring alpine wilderness. Their passion ignited a grass-roots movement of the sort rarely seen in Alaska, before or since.

Various recreational groups – hunters, horseback riders, skiers, hikers – had tried to get the western Chugach Range preserved as parkland since the 1950s, to no avail. Then, in 1969, the state announced it would open two of the range's forested valleys to commercial logging. One of those valleys, known as Indian, was especially popular with com-munity groups, ranging from the Boy Scouts and Girl Scouts to hikers and mountaineers. Appalled by the plans, four Anchorage residents – Sharon Cissna, Art Davidson, Ted Schultz, and Skip Matthews – filed a lawsuit and forced the state to cancel the sale.

Creating a jewel

Though satisfying, the court victory left the foursome wanting more. In August 1969, a group of about 20 activists began a campaign to establish a wilderness park, nearly a half-million acres (200,000 hectares) in size. Within a few months, they gained the support of nearly all of Anchorage's recreational organizations. They also garnered the backing of local politicians, who pushed a bill in the Alaska Legislature to establish a new park. Legislation to create Chugach State Park passed both the state senate and house in May 1970 and Gov. Keith Miller signed it into law in August of that year. Cissna, now a state representative herself and known in some quarters as the "mother of Chugach State Park," still marvels at the speed and ease of the effort, more than 30 years later. "I think it was meant to happen," she says. "It was a moment in time when the right people and the right idea came together at exactly the right time. And so we created a jewel."

The lure of Flattop

Though it is little known outside Alaska, Chugach is a wild and pristine wilderness on a par with many of America's national parklands. Within its boundaries are more than 150 peaks, dozens of glaciers, beautiful alpine valleys that in summer are brightened by dozens of wildflower species, and crystalline mountain streams. The mountains within Chugach park are modest by Alaska standards; the highest, **Mount Bashful**, rises only to 8,005 ft (2,440 meters). Yet many are steep, jagged peaks with substantial vertical relief, as they rise thousands of feet from sea level.

Still, the most popular of the Chugach's mountains is Flattop, a humble hill that looks as if its top has been sliced off. Standing only 3,550 ft (1,082 meters) above Cook Inlet at its summit, **Flattop Mountain** has a special pull on locals. Less than 15 miles (24km) from downtown Anchorage, Flattop is visible throughout the city. And city roads approach to within a mile or so of its base. Easy to find and easy to reach, Flattop is also easy to climb: from the main trailhead, the mountain's summit is only half a mile and 1,350 vertical feet away (412 meters).

When winter's snows have melted away, the ascent is more of a strenuous hike than a climb, though some rock scrambling is necessary near the top. (That's not to say the mountain can't pose dangers: over the years, a handful of people of people have died on its slopes.) Most people can be up and back to the trailhead within two or three hours. All sorts of people take the trail to Flattop's summit, from preschoolers to senior citizens, and hill runners to curious tourists.

Enough people do it each year – the great majority in summer – that Flattop is easily the most climbed peak in all of Alaska. Shuttle service to Flattop is available from downtown Anchorage at

What Visitors to Chugach Need to Know

The park is easy to reach from Anchorage. Several of its most popular trailheads can be reached from city streets, while other trails and park facilities are accessible from either the Seward or Glenn Highways.

Maps showing trailhead locations, campgrounds, and trail routes are available from Chugach State Park headquarters, located at Mile 115 of the Seward Highway in the **Potter Section House** (HC52, Box 8999, Indian, AK 99540; tel: 345-5014; www.alaskastateparks.org) or the Alaska Public Lands Information Center in downtown Anchorage (tel: 271-2737, www.nps.gov/aplic). Some three dozen trails crisscross the park, totaling nearly 200 miles (320km). Many have parking lots, information displays, and latrines at their trailheads.

One of the park's most popular facilities is the Eagle River Nature Center, at the end of Eagle River Road (30–45 minutes' drive from downtown Anchorage; tel: 694-2108; www.ernc.org). Among its attractions are natural history displays, Dall sheep spotting scopes, nearby trails, and year-round naturalist activities for adults and children; they range from guided hikes to bear-awareness talks, a winter astronomy program, plant and mushroom identification, and butterfly identification.

The prime visitor season is Jun–Sept, but locals frequent the park year-round. Summers tend to be cool, with overcast skies and frequent rain, often as drizzle. Summer daytime temperatures normally range from the 50s into the 60s Fahrenheit (12°–18°C), though temperatures occasionally rise above 70°F (21°C) or sink below freezing at night. Snowstorms may occur throughout the year at higher elevations.

*Biking near
Flattop Mountain.*

the Downtown Bicycle Rental shop (tel: 279-5293; www.alaska-bike-rentals.com).

For those who are more experienced and ambitious, there are dozens of peaks within a few hours of Chugach park's many trailheads. There are also remote ridges and valleys rarely traveled by humans. Hikers headed to Flattop may share the trail with dozens, or even hundreds of other people; but go a few miles beyond, and you can have an entire mountain or alpine basin to yourself.

The million or so people who enter the park each year are mostly locals. An economist once estimated that three-fifths of Alaska's population lives within 40 miles (64km) of Chugach Park. And they recreate here in myriad ways: camping, picnicking, berry picking, fishing, backpacking, hiking, skiing, snowmachining, mushing – the list goes on and on.

Abundant wildlife

Though it's on the perimeter of Alaska's urban center, Chugach is rich in wildlife. The park's alpine tundra, forested valley bottoms, and coastal waters are inhabited by nearly 50 species of mammals – from orca and beluga whales to little brown bats

and porcupines – 100 species of birds, 9 species of fish, and 1 amphibian, the wood frog. An estimated 2,000 Dall sheep live here, as well as some 500 mountain goats, 400 black bears, two- dozen grizzlies, and at least two wolf packs.

Some of the best Dall sheep viewing in Alaska occurs along Chugach's southern edge, at a place called **Windy Corner**. From April through August, ewes and lambs and young rams inhabit steep cliffs and grassy meadows above the Seward Highway and **Turnagain Arm** (a 40-mile/64-km saltwater channel that borders the mountains), between mileposts 106 and 107.

Peak viewing occurs in June and July, after the ewes have given birth. Only rarely are the older, full-curl rams seen; they prefer backcountry solitude, away from the highway crowds.

Moose are also seen along the park's fringes, though they prefer wooded habitat to alpine terrain. Black bears, too, are encountered in forested areas, along with squirrels and porcupines and more rarely, lynx. Eagles may be seen soaring above Turnagain Arm or alpine valleys, and there are many songbirds. ❑

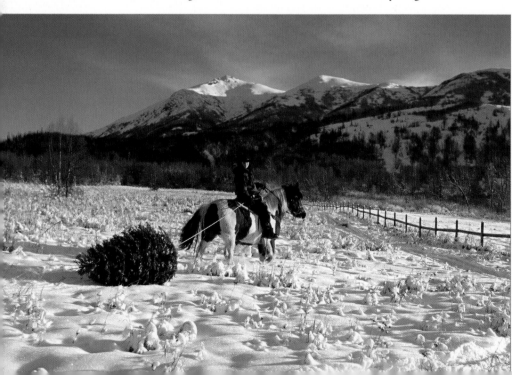

State Parks

Alaska is famous for its national parks. But most non-residents know little about the wild gems protected by the state's Division of Parks and Outdoor Recreation

Established in 1970 by the Alaska Legislature, the Alaska State Parks system has become the nation's largest and grandest; its 130 or so units encompass 3.2 million acres (1.3 million hectares), while stretching more than 1,100 miles (1,770km) across Alaska. Their numbers include recreation sites and areas, historic sites and parks, marine parks, wilderness parks, state trails, and a world-famous preserve: the Alaska Chilkat Bald Eagle Preserve, which each winter attracts between 1,000 and 4,000 eagles.

While many of those units are small and located along the road system, a handful rank among America's premier wilderness parks: Chugach, Kachemak Bay, Wood-Tikchik, Shuyak Island, and Denali.

Unspoiled wilderness

Three of those parklands – Denali, Kachemak Bay, and Wood-Tikchik – include lands and waters once proposed for national park status. Within their boundaries are rugged mountains, glaciers fed by large icefields, centuries-old coastal forests, high alpine meadows that grow bright with wildflowers in summer. Here too there are salmon-rich streams, enormous river-and-lake systems, and all manner of northern wildlife, from grizzlies and wolves, to Dall sheep, wolverines, little brown bats, whales, bald and golden eagles, loons and owls, and scores of songbird, shorebird, and seabird species.

Though these parks protect large expanses of unspoiled wilderness, they are, by Alaska standards, surprisingly easy to reach – and in most cases, easy to explore. Even the wildest, remotest state parks are within 325 miles (520km) of Anchorage. Chugach and Denali state parks are connected to Alaska's road system, while Kachemak Bay is a short boat ride from Homer, an end-of-the-road tourist town 220 highway miles (350km) south of Anchorage. None of the three requires air service to reach the backcountry. While Wood-Tikchik's wilderness is most easily reached by plane, the park's lowermost lake is only 20 road miles (32km) from Dillingham, the largest city in the Bristol Bay region. The remotest wilderness park, Shuyak, is less than 100 air miles (160km) from Homer.

By contrast, wilderness within Alaska's national parks in many cases is remote and expensive to reach. Two-thirds of the national units are more than 300 miles (480km) from Anchorage, and a third are within the state's Arctic region. Backcountry trips in most national parks require the use of air taxis.

Most parks are user-friendly, with campgrounds, public-use cabins, and trail systems. They also permit many activities, from hiking to sport hunting, skiing to snowmobiling, paddling to power-boating.

For more details, contact Alaska's Department of Natural Resources Public Information Center, 550 W. 7th Ave., Suite 1260, Anchorage, AK 99501-3557 (tel: 907-269-8400; www.alaskastateparks.org. ❑

ABOVE: wildlife is abundant in many parks.
RIGHT: Eagle River, Chugach State Park.

PRINCE WILLIAM SOUND

Glaciers, birds and marine life are the highlights of this wild country southeast of Anchorage, yet its towns – Whittier, Valdez and Cordova – are reminders that nature has its harsher side

Main attractions
WHITTIER
COLUMBIA GLACIER
MONTAGUE ISLAND
VALDEZ
CORDOVA
COPPER RIVER DELTA

BELOW: gazing over the Sound.

Few slide shows or promotional videos present pictures of rain in **Prince William Sound ❷**. Usually, it's sunshine flickering on water cascading from the flukes of a breaching humpback whale. Or perhaps kayakers wearing T-shirts are silhouetted in front of a brilliant blue-white glacier. Or sea otters float atop glossy reflections and munch on Dungeness crab plucked from the ocean floor. All such images are taken on the Sound's few clear days.

Each year those photographs, along with the stories told by the travelers who took them, draw more people to see the Sound's wonderful natural displays of flora and fauna, ice, forests and mountains. Few are disappointed, yet it is wise to remember that, as in much of coastal Alaska, it rains a lot here. Often it pours.

Getting there

You can savor the atmosphere of Prince William Sound simply by crossing it on a ferry or tour boat (*see page 353* for details of the Alaska Marine Highway ferry). **Whittier ❸** (population 117) is where many people begin a tour of the Sound. It is easily reached by road from Anchorage through tunnels in the Chugach Mountains. A new road connecting Whittier to the Seward Highway opened in 2000. Historically, the site where Whittier stands was a resting place for Native and Russian traders carrying their wares between the Sound and Cook Inlet. Later, gold miners and mail carriers crossed Portage Pass to reach the Iditarod Trail, which led to Alaska's far-northwest gold fields (now better known for Alaska's biggest sled dog race). But Whittier didn't really develop until World War II, when the army used its ice-free harbor for a strategic fuel dump and the town became an important military port. Troops blasted two tunnels through the Chugach Mountains to connect Whittier with the Alaska Railroad depot at Portage.

In the 1964 earthquake (*see page 52*), Whittier was hit by three successive tidal waves, one of which crested at 104ft (32 meters), and a huge amount of damage was done to the town and its harbor. There's not a lot to see in Whittier, a town of two tall concrete apartment blocks built by the military, in which all the residents live, but if you have some time to spare, the helpful **Visitor Center** staff near the Small Boat Harbor will give you information about the hiking trails around town. It's also a great place for sea kayaking, but it's best to organize this in Anchorage in advance.

Columbia Glacier

Passengers traveling by boat between Whittier and Valdez sometimes see bears and, occasionally, goats balanced on cliffs above them. Humpback and killer whales frequent the route, and Dall porpoises surf the bow wake. Sea lions haul out on rocks, and harbor seals rest on chunks of ice that drift with the wind and tide away from the glaciers. There are dozens of glaciers in the Sound, and some calve huge chunks of ice into the ocean in spectacular explosions of spray. **Columbia Glacier ❹** is the largest among the many that drop down from the Chugach Mountains into the north-

erly fjords of Prince William Sound.

Fed each year by enough snow to bury a five-story building, Columbia Glacier covers an area the size of Los Angeles. It flows more than 40 miles (64km) from the mountains to Columbia Bay, where its 4-mile (7-km) wide face daily drops hundreds of thousands of tons of pristine ice into the sound.

The glacier's output of ice increased in 1983, when it began a rapid retreat. Now, glaciologists estimate that 50 cubic miles (210 cubic km) of icebergs could possibly be released during the next half century. So much ice has filled the bay in recent years that boats can't approach the glacier as closely as they could in the past, when passengers were provided with a close-up view of massive flakes peeling from the 300-ft (90-meter) wall. When the flakes come down, the harbor seals resting on bergs in the bay are rocked by the resulting swells. They don't even look up.

Meanwhile, gulls and other birds swarm around the glacier face; the plunging ice stirs the seafood-rich water, bringing shrimp and other delicacies to the surface for their consumption. Thus,

BELOW:
a cruise ship
calls at Whittier.

Keystone Canyon, near Valdez, provides some of Alaska's best whitewater rafting.

BELOW: harbor seals at the Columbia Glacier.

the glaciers are an intrinsic part of the life cycle of Prince William Sound.

Quakes and tidal waves

Forces other than slow-moving glaciers also shape the land. Earthquakes cause sudden, dramatic changes in the lay of the country. On March 27, 1964 – Good Friday – bedrock shifted just west of Columbia Glacier. The shock waves, believed to have registered 9.2 on the Richter scale, were the most intense ever recorded in North America. In just a few minutes, extensive new beach lines emerged as the land rose in some areas;

in other places the ground sank, killing large stands of trees. The most dramatic geological adjustment occurred at the southern end of **Montague Island**, which tilted upward 38ft (11.5 meters).

But tsunamis did the most damage. Whittier suffered badly, but among the worst human disasters was that at **Chenega**, a village of 82 on an island south of Whittier near the western edge of the sound. A wave enveloped all the buildings but the school and one house, and swept away 23 residents. The village was rebuilt on another site 25 years later.

Many hard rock and placer claims lie under rockslides and fast-growing alder and hemlock. In a few places, like the Beatson Mine on **La Touche Island**, piles of tailings stand out, along with a few unstable old buildings, rust-red lengths of steel pipe and pumps, and stripped trucks whose tires have been eaten by porcupines.

Valdez

Valdez ❺, the next port of call for ferry and tour boats after Whittier and situated to the east of the earthquake epicenter, was completely destroyed, and had to be rebuilt on a different site. The tsunami that wiped out the waterfront also killed 32 people. Consequently there are no buildings of historic interest in Valdez, but it's a lively town of 3,700 residents, which grew to prosperity as the terminus of the trans-Alaska pipeline. Its setting, between the Sound and the Chugach Mountains, is splendid.

Drop in at the **Valdez Convention and Visitors Bureau** on Fairbanks Drive (open Mon–Sat in winter, daily in summer 8am–8pm; tel: 800-770-5954 or 835-4636; www.valdezalaska.org) for information, and to see their film about the 1964 earthquake.

The **Valdez Museum and Historical Archive** (daily in summer 9am–6pm; entrance charge; tel: 835-2764; www.valdezmuseum.org) on Egan Drive is worth a visit to see a variety of exhibits, including one on the *Exxon Valdez* oil spill.

Valdez can also be reached by air from Anchorage (there are numerous daily flights) or by the Alaska Marine Highway System's fast ferry out of Whittier (www.dot.state.ak.us/amhswww.akferry.com). You can also rent a car here and drive along the **Richardson Highway** through the scenic Copper River Valley toward **Glennallen** and the Wrangell-St Elias National Park *(see page 194)*. It's a beautiful stretch of road. Leaving Valdez, you pass the site of the original, pre-1964 town, although there's not much to see except a commemorative plaque.

Some 12 miles (20km) further on, you come to the **Keystone Canyon** and the lovely **Bridal Veil Falls**. Drive on for another 7 miles (11km) or so and the trans-Alaska pipeline comes into view. Nearby is an attractive camping spot with good trout fishing.

Carry on up to **Thompson Pass**, perhaps Alaska's most spectacular mountain road. Passing the Edgerton Highway junction (82 miles/132km from Valdez), you will reach **Copper Center**, a village that was an early mining camp and is well worth a stop (accommodation available) before visiting the national park.

Cordova

Cordova ❻ became a transportation center in the early 20th century. The important mineral was copper, and the deposit, the richest in the world, was at **Kennicott**, 200 miles (320km) up the Copper

TIP

The Copper River Delta Shorebird Festival

Every May, bird lovers flock to the tidal flats of the Prince William Sound community of Cordova for the Copper River Delta Shorebird Festival. Itl provides exciting opportunities to observe millions of migrating shorebirds as they rest and feed in the rich Delta area. The festival includes workshops, community events and other related activities. For more details, contact the Cordova Chamber of Commerce (tel: 424-7260; www.cordova chamber.com)

Cordova, a pretty community of wood-framed houses.

RIGHT:
Cordova's harbor.

and Chitina rivers *(see page 194)*. Cordova, still an attractive community of wood-framed houses, was born a railroad town with the arrival of a shipload of men and equipment on April 1, 1906. The railroad was the brainchild of Michael J. Heney, an engineer who had also pushed the White Pass & Yukon Route Railroad through the White Pass from Skagway to Whitehorse in Southeast Alaska in 1900.

Engineering achievement

For the next five years, Cordova was the operations center for the Copper River & Northwestern Railroad construction project. Along with the oil pipeline, this ranks among history's greatest engineering achievements. Heney had to contend with temperatures of –60°F (–50°C), a ferocious wind that knocked boxcars off the tracks, and drifting snow that buried his locomotives.

The ore transported was almost pure copper, and it added to the fortunes of the railroad backers, a syndicate led by J.P. Morgan. But by the mid-1930s the price of copper had fallen and all the high-grade ores had been mined; in 1938 the railroad was abandoned.

Cordova today is a pretty little fishing town where not much happens. You can't reach it by road. Whittier–Valdez ferries stop here, and a new dock has brought some of the cruise ship operators to town. Otherwise, it is reached by a short flight from Anchorage, and airport buses run you into town. The **Chamber of Commerce** on 1st Street will fill you in on current activities.

The **Small Boat Harbor** is a lively spot and there's the **Cordova Historical Museum** (open Mon–Sat 10am–6pm and Sun 2–4pm; $1 donation recommended; tel: 424-6665; www.cordova museum.org) with historical and marine exhibits including many evocative old photographs; and there's a marvelous view of the town and the Sound from the **Mount Eyak Ski** area.

But the main attractions of the area are out on the 50-mile (80-km) Copper River Highway, which traces the railroad line across the biologically rich **Copper River Delta** to Child's Glacier. The delta is a birdwatcher's paradise, home to the world's entire nesting population of dusky Canada geese and swarms of migrating waterfowl.

How to see the sights of Prince William Sound

Various tour companies, large and small, offer day trips into the many fjords surrounding Whittier. Tidewater glaciers thrill visitors and seasoned boat captains alike with their sudden, percussive, cracking sounds followed by thunderous roars as massive chunks of ice break loose and crash down into the sea. Larger companies, like Prince William Sound Cruises and Tours (tel: 800-992-1297; 277-2131; www.princewilliamsound.com), will arrange transportation from Anchorage via motorcoach or train, and a day cruise into western Prince William Sound.

Exciting glacier tours operate out of Valdez as well. Stan Stevens Cruises (tel: 866-867-1297, 835-4731; www.stanstephenscruises.com), for example, offers comfortable 6½ and 9½-hour tours to visit the magnificent Columbia Glacier (the largest tidewater glacier in Southcentral Alaska), or a 9½-hour cruise to witness the active calving of Meares Glacier in the eastern area of the Sound.

The surrounding coastal areas provide rich habitat for whales, seal lions, puffins, seals, sea otters, bears, goats and eagles (and much more), and multiple sightings are common. For a complete listing of tour options for both Whittier and Valdez, contact the Whittier Visitor Center (tel: 472-2327; www.ci.whittier.ak.us) or the Valdez Convention and Visitors Bureau (tel: 800-770-5954, or 835-2984; www.valdezalaska.org).

Industries in flux

The Sound is still rich in copper and gold, molybdenum, tungsten and silver. However, low mineral prices mean those resources will be left in the ground for the immediate future. The timber industry has also been doing poorly, and fur harvesting has long been abandoned.

The Sound continues to heal, and though wildlife officials have reported seeing returning animals, the long-term consequences for the ecosystem are unknown. But commercial fishing remains a major source of income for the 7,500 people who live along the Sound. In the mid-1990s, a record 14 million pink salmon returned to the port of Valdez, but runs have been erratic in recent years and the commercial fishing industry is suffering from increased competition in other parts of the world plus lower prices.

Some of the most promising resources in the Sound are its wilderness and its wildlife. After author Rex Beach documented the construction of the Copper River & Northwestern Railroad in his 1913 bestseller *The Iron Trail: An Alaskan Romance*, Cordova and its nearby glaciers became one of the state's greatest attractions. Some visitors moor their boats in Prince William Sound's coves and sleep on board; kayakers and others often pitch tents on beaches. The increase in requests for cabin-use permits is one sign of a growing number of visitors to the Sound.❑

Ecotourists dig for clams in Prince William Sound.

RESTAURANTS

Cordova

Cordova Ambrosia Restaurant
410 First Street
tel: (907) 424-7185
Open for dinner in summer only, seafood and pizza, along with other Italian dishes are served in a family-friendly atmosphere. Beer and wine are available. $–$$$

Killer Whale Café
507 First Street
tel" (907) 424-7733
Café is open for breakfast, lunch and dinner, offering soups, sandwiches made with freshly baked breads, and daily specials. $

Valdez

Alaska's Bistro
102 N. Harbor Drive
tel: (907) 835-4447
Mediterranean cuisine featuring local seafood and pizza. Large windows overlook the harbor. Full bar. $$–$$$

Mike's Palace Ristorante
201 North Harbor Drive
tel: (907) 835-2365
Across the street from the boat harbor, Mike's offers a varied menu that includes Italian, Mexican and American dishes. Beer, wine. $–$$$

The Pipeline Club
112 Egan Drive
tel: (907) 835-4332
This establishment offers fine dining, evenings only, from a menu that specializes in steak and fresh Alaskan seafood. You can also play a round of pool or indoor golf. Bar. $$$–$$$$

Whittier

Swiftwater Seafood Café
Located "on the triangle"
tel: (907) 472-2550
When possible, dishes are made from local rockfish, shrimp or halibut. Menu includes fish and chips (or shrimp and chips), homemade chowders and rhubarb crisp. Satur-

day night favorite is smoked prime rib. Beautiful view. Beer and wine. $

Café Orca and Gallery
Located "on the triangle"
tel (907) 472-2549
Specializes in grilled meats and fish (and even steak fries)—no deep frying. Fresh Alaska seafood dishes including halibut, red salmon and homemade crabcakes. Organic burgers, chowders, gourmet sandwiches (some vegetarian) and salads, all beautifully prepared. Espressos. Dining area looks out on Prince William Sound. $–$$

Lazy Otter Café
Located next to east boat ramp
tel: (907) 472-OTTR (6887)
Cozy café offers delicious chowders, bagels, sandwiches, soft-serve ice cream, and espressos. $

● ● ● ● ● ● ● ● ● ● ● ● ● ● ● ● ● ● ●

Price is for dinner excluding tax, tip and beverages: **$$$$** *$30 and up,* **$$$** *$20–30,* **$$** *$15–20,* **$** *under $15.*

WRANGELL-ST ELIAS NATIONAL PARK

America's largest national park has emerged from obscurity to become a magnet for those seeking backcountry adventure

BELOW: a glacial rock in the park.

Until the mid-1980s, **Wrangell-St Elias National Park and Preserve ❼** was an overlooked and undervalued mountain wilderness. Created in 1980, America's largest park – at 13.2 million acres (5.3 million hectares), the size of six Yellowstones – was also one of its least known and least visited. But some time in the late 1980s, Wrangell-St Elias was "discovered." And, though it hasn't yet become "the next Denali" as some in the tourism industry had predicted, the park's use has grown significantly in the past 10 to 15 years. Before visiting the park, stop off at the headquarters and visitor center at **Copper Center ❽** on the Richardson Highway 6, some 200 road miles (320km) east of Anchorage, for video programs, maps, publications, and advice.

A potted history

At the turn of the 20th century, a couple of prospectors named Jack Smith and Clarence Warner spotted a large green spot in the Wrangell Mountains, on the ridge between the Kennicott Glacier and McCarthy Creek which proved to be mineral staining from a fantastically rich copper deposit.

Mining engineer Stephen Birch bought the copper claims and won the backing of the Guggenheimer brothers and J.P. Morgan. Known collectively as the Alaska Syndicate, the investors formed the (misspelled) Kennecott Mines Co., which later became the Kennecott Copper Corp.

The copper discovery sparked the construction of the 200-mile (320-km) Copper River & Northwestern Railroad, connecting the mining camp to the coastal town of Cordova. When the mine closed in 1938 it had produced over 4½ million tons of ore, worth $200 million. At its peak, 600 people lived at **Kennicott ❾**. The main settlement included all the operations needed to mill the ore, as well as houses, offices and stores, a school, hospital, post office, dairy and recreation hall. Just down the road, a second community, eventually named McCarthy, sprang up around 1908.

In a perfect complement to staid, regimented Kennicott, **McCarthy** ⑩ played the role of sin city. Among its most successful businesses were several saloons, pool halls, gambling rooms and back-alley brothels. In its heyday, 100 to 150 people lived in McCarthy. But after the mine shut down, only a few people stayed on.

For decades after the mine's closure, McCarthy–Kennicott served as the quintessential haven for Alaska recluses. But more recently the region has become a major tourist draw, complete with lodges, a hotel, bed-and-breakfast inns, ice-cream parlor, air-taxi operators, wilderness guide operations, museum, and even an espresso bar – impressive for a community whose year-round "hard core" population numbers a couple of dozen people.

Access to the park

The northern entry to the park is the 45-mile (72-km) Nabesna Road, which connects the state's highway system with the tiny mining community of **Nabesna** ⑪ (population about 25). The road's first 5 miles (8km) are paved; the remainder is gravel. Four-wheel drive vehicles are recommended for the final 5 miles, which cross several creeks and are not regularly maintained by the state.

Motorists should check for updated road conditions before making the drive, as sections of it are occasionally washed out during summer rainstorms; call ahead to park headquarters and check in at the ranger station, at mile 0.2. Planned improvements include more passing places and wayside natural history exhibits.

Although some gold, silver, copper, iron and molybdenum were discovered in the Nabesna area early in the 20th century, a much bigger attraction now is the wildlife. Caribou, moose and even grizzlies may be spotted in the open countryside bordering Nabesna Road, and large populations of Dall sheep are found in the hills surrounding the 9,358-ft (2,850-meter) Tanada Peak, about 15 miles (24km) southwest of the road's end. (Trophy hunting for sheep and other species is allowed in the preserve, which encompasses about 37 percent of the unit's total area.)

The principal avenue into Wrangell-St Elias is **McCarthy Road**; 60 miles

Map on page 164

When to visit
The park is open year-round, but peak visits occur in August. Wildflowers and mosquitoes peak in June and July. The prime mountaineering season is from mid-March to early June. Snow is possible at any season in the high country.

BELOW: the abandoned Kennicott Mine.

Robert Kennicott

The town and the glacier are named after an American naturalist, Robert Kennicott (1835–66), who worked at the Smithsonian Institution. He identified Alaskan natural history specimens during an 1859 expedition and in 1865 joined a mission to determine a route for a telegraph line between the USA and Russia via the Bering Sea. He died of heart failure the following year while traveling up the Yukon River.

BELOW: the interior of McCarthy Lodge.

(95km) long and unpaved, it stretches from Chitina, at the park's western boundary (where it connects with the Edgerton Highway) to the "gateway" community of **McCarthy**, located deep within one of America's most spectacular wildlands. At its doorstep are rugged peaks that rise above raging rivers, fed by massive glaciers.

The number of people funneled down McCarthy Road has grown dramatically, from about 5,000 in 1988 to more than 20,000 currently. Overall park visitation has increased at a slower pace, but still jumped nearly fourfold in 25 years (from 14,000 to 50,000 visits).

Only a small percentage of those who drive the McCarthy Road actually visit the park's awesome backcountry. Most are content to hang out in McCarthy, take hikes to the nearby **Kennicott Glacier** and **Root Glacier**, or travel some 4 miles (7km) to the abandoned Kennecott copper mining camp (the original company misspelt the name). Until 1997 visitors could reach McCarthy-Kennicott only by crossing the glacially fed Kennicott River on hand-pulled trams. These historic trams have been replaced by a foot

bridge that makes the crossing considerably easier. Local residents remain opposed to any sort of vehicular bridge, however, fearing it might open up their community to large-scale "industrial" tourism, so visitors still have to leave their cars, trucks and RVs behind.

Treasures beyond the road

The park's real treasures lie in a wild and magnificent alpine world that wilderness guides call "North America's mountain kingdom." It's a kingdom that includes four major mountain ranges – the St Elias, Chugach, Alaska and Wrangells – and six of the continent's 10 highest peaks, including 18,008-ft (5,490-meter) **Mount St Elias**, fourth-highest in North America.

Here, too, is North America's largest subpolar icefield, the **Bagley**, which feeds a system of gigantic glaciers; one of those, the Malaspina Glacier, covers an area of more than 1,500 sq. miles (4,075 sq. km) – larger than Rhode Island. Hubbard Glacier, which flows out of the St Elias Mountains into Disenchantment Bay, is one of the continent's most active glaciers; in 1986, Hubbard was nicknamed the "Galloping Glacier" when it surged more than a mile and sealed off Russell Fjord. The ice dam later broke and the glacier retreated, but it advanced again in 2002 to create yet another temporary ice dam and scientists say it's only a matter of time before the Hubbard closes off the fjord permanently.

The glaciers have carved dozens of canyons; some, like the Chitistone and Nizina, are bordered by rock walls thousands of feet high. Rugged, remote coastline is bounded by tidewater glaciers and jagged peaks. The park's alpine superlatives, along with those of neighboring Kluane National Park in Canada, have prompted their combined designation as a World Heritage Site.

Much of what's been "discovered" in Wrangell-St Elias by modern-day explorers was known to local residents centuries ago. This is especially true of the **Skolai Creek-Chitistone River** area, the most popular of the park's backcountry destinations.

More recently, both the Chitistone and Skolai Pass routes were used by stampeders traveling from McCarthy to **Chisana** ⑫, the site of Alaska's last major gold rush. Chisana's boom times lasted only a few years, from 1913 to 1915. But during that short period, as many as 10,000 people may have traveled through the mountains. Fewer than 10 people now live year-round in Chisana, located within the northeast corner of Wrangell-St Elias.

Modern explorers

Nine decades later, people attracted by wilderness values rather than gold are retracing the footsteps of the Chisana stampeders. This newest rush into the Wrangell-St Elias backcountry is, so far, much smaller and more benign. Most modern explorers lured into this vast mountain landscape bring a minimum-impact ethic and leave little or no trace of their visit. Still, there's no question that they are having a cumulative effect.

In the first four years that he explored the Skolai–Chitistone area, wilderness guide Bob Jacobs saw only one set of footprints not made by his own parties. A quarter-century later, it's difficult to go more than a day or two without seeing signs of other backpackers, or at least hearing aircraft traffic. The increased use

TIP

River crossing
The park authorities warn that most backcountry routes require numerous creek and river crossings. Bridges and log crossings are virtually nonexistent. Many rivers and streams are impassable, even for experts. Others can change quickly from trickling creeks to raging torrents. It is best to cross early in the day when possible. The widest or most braided portion of the channel is usually the most shallow.

BELOW: an ice cave on Root Glacier.

Sunset in the Chitina River Valley.

BELOW: lichen-covered rock, Wrangell–St Elias National Park.

sense of the word. The scale of things is immense. In every direction are stark, jagged, ice-carved peaks, most of them unnamed and unclimbed. Here, too, are massive, near-vertical rock faces thousands of feet high, hanging glaciers and waterfalls by the dozen.

Yet for all the rock and snow and ice, this is not a barren or alien world. In the valley bottoms are alder groves and tundra meadows brightened with legions of rainbow-hued flowers: blue forget-me-nots, lupin and Jacob's ladder, purple monkshood, yellow paint brush, white mountain avens, tall pink fireweed and wintergreen. Ptarmigan hide in the alder, clucking in the early morning like roosters. Bands of Dall sheep inhabit high rocky places, while occasional moose, wolves and brown bears prowl valleys and hillsides. The valleys are also home to pikas, ground squirrels, shorebirds and robins. And overhead, eagles soar.

has taken a toll; there's been some trampling of vegetation, littering, crowding, and a growing potential problem with bears that have learned to associate humans with food. "It's a much more fragile environment than a lot of people realize and in places you can find evidence of degradation," says Jacobs.

It was only natural that the Skolai–Chitistone area became Wrangell-St Elias' heaviest-used backcountry area. It is one of the park's premier wilderness spots, ruggedly spectacular country in the heart of the mountains. Yet despite its vast, primeval richness, the area is easily accessible by plane, located less than 30 miles (48km) from McCarthy – a short hop by Alaska bush pilot standards.

This is "big country" in the truest

Preserving the wilderness

All these variables have dramatically boosted recreational visits to Skolai and Chitistone valleys, and park officials are keen to protect them. Their biggest con-

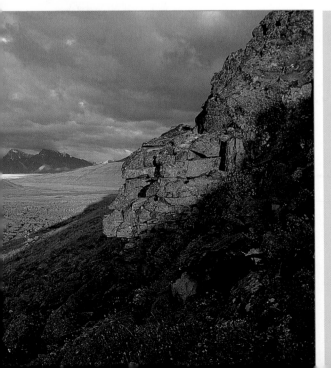

Coping with mosquitoes

Jokingly referred to as the "Alaska State Bird," mosquitoes fare extraordinarily well in Alaska's climate and are especially prevalent between mid-June and the end of July. While there are reported to be from 25 to 40 different species common to the state, there have been no reported cases of West Nile Virus and the two mosquito species that transmit it in the Lower 48 don't live in Alaska.

Visitors are encouraged at wear long sleeves and long pants made of tightly-woven, light material – mosquitoes are supposedly attracted to darker colors – while hiking in the backcountry. Mosquito repellant is helpful and can be bought in almost any store. In remote areas the use of mosquito headnets is advised. And – not that it's any consolation – the caribou are attacked just as much as humans.

cern isn't the traditional wilderness traveler, but the novice explorer. Visitor education is one solution. Another has been to spread the use to other beautiful but neglected areas – for instance, to **Tebay Lakes**, which are similar to the high sierras, with beautiful granite peaks, excellent fishing and hiking.

Other areas that haven't been used as heavily include **Goat Creek**, which offers good hiking, and the wide-open, wildlife-rich upper Chitina Valley. There's also the remote and stark coastline of the park's southeastern edge, where sea-kayakers can paddle among seals, sea lions, sea otters and orca whales in Icy, Yakutat and Disenchantment bays, or roam among icebergs loosed from tidewater glaciers.

Commercial facilities

Many of Wrangell-St Elias' natural wonders are inaccessible to those who remain along the road system. Only in recent years have a small number of trails been established, giving access to parts of the backcountry.

From Nabesna Road, the **Skookum Volcanic Trail** leads to a tundra area with interesting volcanic dikes and basalt flows and is ideal for day hikers.

Two other trails begin along the McCarthy Road; one leads to the Crystalline Hills, which offer superb views of the surrounding mountains and the Chitina River valley. A longer, more challenging backcountry route, the **Dixie Pass Trail**, follows a path used by prospectors and miners.

Aside from those limited access points, air-taxi services provide transportation into the park and several guide outfits offer river-rafting, climbing and trekking opportunities. Increasingly popular are "flightseeing tours," out of McCarthy, Chitina, Gulkana and Nabesna. Overnight lodging is available at McCarthy and Kennicott and a "wilderness lodge" is located in the backcountry, but park facilities are intentionally minimal.

There's a primitive campground along the McCarthy Road and several public-use cabins (built by miners, hunters or trappers) in the backcountry, available on a first-come first-served basis. A list of facilities and services is available from park HQ (P.O. Box 439, Copper Center, AK 99573, or visit www.nps.gov/wrst/). ❑

TIP

Essential Precautions
In the backcountry, assistance may be miles or days away, so travelers must be self-sufficient and schooled in wilderness survival skills. Even in summer the weather can change suddenly and storm systems may delay pick-ups by several days, so bring extra provisions, rain gear and warm clothing.

BELOW:
trees provide shelter for Wrangell's wildlife.

KENAI PENINSULA

This is Alaska in a nutshell: glaciers, salmon fishing, hiking trails, stunning scenery and friendly towns, all within easy reach of Anchorage

Alaska
Anchorage

I t's often said that Alaska is too big to see in a single lifetime, let alone a single vacation. But there is one place where tourists can sample most of the best of Alaska, and do so within a few weeks: the Kenai Peninsula.

The entire peninsula is within easy driving distance of Anchorage, and people in the city like to refer to the Kenai as their backyard. But please, don't use that line on the peninsula. On a map of the state, the Kenai Peninsula looks deceptively small. It's worth remembering that the peninsula covers 9,050 sq. miles (23,000 sq. km), making it larger than the combined areas of Rhode Island, Connecticut and Delaware. It is bordered by Prince William Sound and the Gulf of Alaska on the east and Cook Inlet on the west, and attached to the mainland of Southcentral Alaska by a narrow mountainous neck of land at the north.

Artistic center

The peninsula is home to one of Alaska's more artistically inclined cities, Homer. The population is also very socially aware, and for every development-minded resident, you'll find another who belongs to an environmental group. Some apparently belong to both camps, which is partly what makes Homer such a lively place.

Touring the peninsula

Driving from Anchorage, you will cross into the peninsula just south of **Portage**, a town that formerly sat at the eastern

end of Turnagain Arm, the thin finger of Cook Inlet that separates the peninsula from the Anchorage Bowl. Portage was completely destroyed by the 1964 earthquake, and only a few ruins remain. About 5 miles (8km) after passing the wreckage of Portage, you begin to climb through the Kenai Mountains, with a maximum elevation of about 3,500ft (1,050 meters).

Mileage along the Seward and Sterling highways is measured from Seward. At about Mile 70 is the summit of **Turnagain Pass**, elevation 988ft (296 meters).

Main attractions

HOPE
MOOSE PASS
SEWARD
COOPER LANDING
STERLING
SOLDOTNA
KENAI
NINILCHIK
HOMER
SELDOVIA

LEFT: camping by Kenai Lake.
BELOW: an inviting Seward eatery.

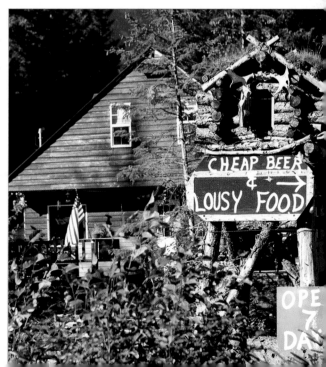

CHEAP BEER

LOUSY FOOD

OPE 7 DA

It's popular in winter for cross-country skiing and snow-machining.

The pass and much of the area along the highway are part of the **Chugach National Forest** (tel: 743-9500; www.fs. fed.us/r10/chugach). Creeks, lakes and campgrounds are scattered through this area. The camps' opening dates can vary with the weather, but generally they are open from Memorial Day through Labor Day (the last Monday in May to the first Monday in September).

Fees are charged for camp use. Facilities often include tables, fire grates, tent pads and some type of water and sanitary facilities. While fires are usually allowed in these sites, it's a good idea to carry a small camp stove with you. If you do decide to light a fire, you must take care to extinguish it properly, and try to restore the area before moving on.

Resurrection Bay, outside Seward.

Hope

The first town you encounter on the peninsula is **Hope ⑬,** a mining community of about 150, founded in the late 1890s. A trip to Hope requires a 16-mile (25-km) detour onto the Hope Cutoff, Mile 56 of the Seward Highway, but it's

BELOW RIGHT: participants in Seward's 4th of July race.

worth it. The town is the site of the oldest schoolhouse in Alaska – a red, one-room school still in use. Other attractions include the one-room Hope–Sunrise Historical & Mining Museum on Old Hope Road (open Memorial Day–Labor Day Fri–Mon noon–4pm; tel: 782-3740; free), a store, a couple of cafés, a bar and a lodge.

An ideal site for pink salmon fishing, moose, caribou and black bear hunting, Hope also is the head of the **Resurrection Pass Trail**, one of the most popular hiking areas on the peninsula. The trailhead is located at Mile 3.5 of the Resurrection Creek Road. The entire trail is 38 miles (60km) long, and hikers emerge at **Schooner Bend**, Mile 52 on the Sterling Highway.

One option is to turn off the Resurrection Trail at Mile 20 and take the 10-mile (16-km) **Devil's Pass Trail**, which emerges at Mile 39 of the Seward Highway. The Resurrection Pass Trail connects with the Resurrection River Trail to form the 72-mile (116-km) Resurrection Trail from Hope to Seward.

The Forest Service operates some cabins along the Resurrection Trail; most

Athabascans, Alutliqs and Russians

The peninsula was originally home to Dena'ina Indians, a branch of the Athabascan family, and to Alutiiqs. Their descendants still live here, mostly in small, remote villages, but they now account for something less than 10 percent of the population. Modern ways have long since replaced those of the Natives; they speak and dress very much like their white neighbors, and have a lifestyle which melds traditional and mainstream American ways.

The Russians were the first whites to establish permanent communities on the peninsula. From their base on Kodiak Island, they sent out missionaries to found churches all along the eastern shore of Cook Inlet. The town of Kenai began when a Russian settlement was established in the center of a Dena'ina village in 1791.

Other Russian-founded communities include Seldovia, which also dates to the 18th century, and Ninilchik, founded in the early 1800s. Seward didn't then exist as a town, but the area around Resurrection Bay was used as a shipbuilding site for the Russian-American Company. Early Russian influence is still to be seen in the onion-domed churches, and heard in the names of places and people in some peninsula communities.

have bunk space for six, and wood stoves. If a cabin is on a lake, it usually has a row boat and oars. Campers must bring their own food, utensils and sleeping bags. Because of the route's popularity, it is wise to make cabin reservations well ahead; they can be made up to six months in advance (tel: 877-444-6777; www.reserveusa.com).

The Resurrection Pass Trail can take between two and six days to cover, while the entire route may take a week or more. Trout fishing is possible in several lakes. The trail also provides spectacular scenery for the photographer. If you don't want to hike the entire route you can take a wonderful day hike, starting at either end.

The Seward Highway

On leaving Hope and rejoining the Seward Highway, the first decision is whether to go west or head south at the Seward Junction at Mile 40. To the south lie Moose Pass and Seward; to the west lie Cooper Landing, Kenai, Soldotna, Anchor Point, Ninilchik, Homer and Seldovia, which can be reached only by taking a ferry. There are several smaller towns as well, including Clam Gulch and Kasilof.

Heading south, the first community is **Moose Pass** ⓮. This is a quiet town of less than 200 people. Residents enjoy hiking, fishing and biking – the town has one of Alaska's relatively few bike trails. One of the highlights of the year is the annual Summer Festival, held to celebrate the solstice. The exact date of the festival changes from year to year, but is always held on the June weekend with the most total hours of sunlight. Activities include a barbecue, carnival, softball games and an auction.

Continuing south on the highway you come to **Seward** ⓯, an attractive city of about 2,600 residents. Founded in 1903, it was for years the leading port city of Alaska. It was eventually eclipsed in that role by Anchorage, and the 1964 earthquake devastated the economy. Twenty years later, it began to regain its financial legs and now is once again a thriving

port. A visitor center is located at the entrance to town, on the highway, and another one can be found at the Chamber of Commerce railroad car, located at 3rd Avenue and Jefferson Street (open daily in summer).

Almost diagonally opposite is the **Seward Historical Museum** (open daily in summer 9am–5pm; winter hours vary; tel: 224-3902; entrance charge). The town library, on 5th Avenue, features a summer book sale, photographs and a film on the effects of the 1964 earthquake on Seward.

One of the main attractions of the area is **Resurrection Bay**. Charter boats for sailing or power excursions on the bay are available at the city harbor, as are kayak rentals. Boats can also be hired for sightseeing or fishing trips. The state ferry system also has a dock in Seward, offering trips to Kodiak and the Prince William Sound areas.

Seward is the northern terminus for a number of cruise ships crossing the Gulf of Alaska. These ships bring thousands of visitors through Seward on their way to or from Southcentral Alaska.

Another major attraction is the **Alaska**

Drivers brave snowy conditions on the Seward Highway.

BELOW: Kasilof's Tustemena Lodge displays 24,000 hats – and a painting of Elvis.

TIP

Celebrations

Highlight of the year in Seward is the **4th of July** celebration, which includes an all-town barbecue, a parade, acrobats, fireworks and the Mount Marathon foot race: racers make a mad scramble up a mountain behind the town, and then take a wild slide down. Another special event is the annual **Silver Salmon Derby**, a week-long fishing contest with good prize money. It begins on the second Saturday of August.

BELOW: cycliing by Kenai Lake.

SeaLife Center, built on a 7-acre (3-hectare) site next to the Marine Education Center on the shores of Resurrection Bay (301 Railway Ave; open in summer daily, 8am–7pm; in winter daily, 10am–5pm; tel: 224-6300 or 800-224-2525; www.alaskasealife.org; entrance charge). This marine science enterprise, which opened to the public in 1998, combines research on saving marine species and aiding recovery from industrial damage, with the rehabilitation of maimed or stranded birds and mammals. It also aims to provide education and entertainment for the thousands of visitors who visit the center each year.

Kenai Fjords National Park

Seward is also the gateway to **Kenai Fjords National Park** ⓖ (tel: 224-7500; www.nps.gov/kefj), declared a national monument in 1978 and designated a national park two years later. As well as the rugged coastal fjords for which it is named, and the glaciers which, for many, are its chief attraction, the park is home to porpoises, sea otters, sea lions, humpback and orca whales, puffins, bald eagles and other animals.

Several local tour operators offer frequent wildlife cruises into the park, starting from Seward's Small Boat Harbor.

Most of the park is only accessible by boat: the only vehicle access is to the northwest of Seward, at Exit Glacier Road. Exit Glacier is the most easily accessible point of the **Harding Icefield**, a remnant of the Ice Age that caps a section of the Kenai Mountains 50 miles (80km) long and 30 miles (48km) wide. The glacier itself lies less than a mile (1km) past the car parking area at the end of the road; you simply head up the trail, passing a visitor cabin along the way.

It's an easy walk to the face – but visitors are warned to not get too close, because of the danger of falling ice. There are ranger-led hikes but you can go it alone, taking care not to go beyond the warning signs. A challenging hike rises along the side of the glacier to the icefield above. For further information on this and all aspects of the park, contact the Visitor Center on 4th Avenue by the Small Boat Harbor in Seward (tel: 224-7500).

After leaving the park and initially driving north, it's time to head west on the

Sterling Highway. Turn left at the junction; the road is marked as Alaska Route 1. Out toward **Cooper Landing** ⓱, you enter an area that's been closed to Dall sheep hunting. As a result, it's often a good area to spot them. But looking for sheep while driving can be dangerous, so pull off at one of many designated stops before peering up to look for the white specks high on the peaks.

Cooper Landing is a community of about 350 people, spread out along the headwaters of the Kenai River. Here the river is a beautiful turquoise color, and in winter the open stretches of water are a prime feeding ground for majestic bald eagles. Sport fishing (particularly for salmon and rainbow trout), hunting and tourism, are the area's main industries, although the town began as a mining area.

At nearby **Kenai Lake**, you can fish for Dolly Varden, lake trout, rainbow trout and whitefish. The Kenai River has trout and four species of salmon. Trophy rainbow trout, some weighing as much as 20 lbs (9 kg), are caught here by spin- and fly-fishing enthusiasts, and catch-and-release fishing is widely practiced. Rafting is another popular activity on the river, and several local businesses offer fishing and float trips. Hunting and fishing regulations vary: game regulation booklets are available free from the Department of Fish and Game. Many sporting goods shops also offer copies of the regulation manuals.

Continuing west, just outside of the Cooper Landing area at the confluence of the Kenai and Russian rivers, is the turn-off to the **Russian River Campground**. The site is easy to spot in the summer, as it's usually busy. The 20-mile (32-km) **Russian Lakes Trail** is a delightful and not over-demanding hike, with cabins en route. Reservations are needed (tel: 877-444-6777; www. reserveusa.com). The Russian River is the largest freshwater fishery in Alaska, and draws more than 30,000 fishermen each year, all hoping to catch a red salmon.

Kenai National Wildlife Refuge

Heading west on the Sterling Highway, you leave the Chugach National Forest and enter the **Kenai National Wildlife Refuge** ⓲. Refuge regulations, as well as trail maps and information about

Puffins inhabit the Kenai Fjords National Park.

BELOW: the small boat harbor at Seward.

Peninsula Paddles

For those interested in seeing the Kenai by canoe, kayak or river raft, various companies offer water adventures lasting from a few hours to several days. The adrenaline levels of the trips vary as well, from serene floats along quiet streams to Class V white-water thrillers. The convention and visitors bureau nearest your destination (see page 377) will have the best information on self-guided paddling routes or professionally-guided kayaking or river rafting opportunities.

things to do in the refuge, are available from the unit's Soldotna headquarters (tel: 262-7021; www.r7.fws.gov), up Ski Hill Road from the Sterling –Highway south of the Kenai River Bridge. The refuge, which was established by President Franklin D. Roosevelt as a wildlife range to preserve the moose population, then later expanded and given refuge status, is also the habitat of coyotes, grizzlies, caribou, and wolves. It comprises the western slopes of the Kenai Mountains, and spruce and birch forested lowlands bordering Cook Inlet.

Among the major recreational areas in the refuge is the 20-mile (32-km) **Skilak Lake Loop**, which intersects the Sterling Highway near the Visitor Center. This road takes you to **Skilak Lake**, and also provides access to several other smaller lakes, streams and some 200 miles (320km) of trails in the area. The most arduous trail is the Skilak Lookout Trail, which takes you up some 1,450ft (440 meters) and provides stunning views. The Visitor Center provides details on the Swanson River Canoe Trail.

Skilak Lake itself has a surface area of some 24,000 acres (57,600 hectares).

It is prone to sudden and violent storms – warning signs should be taken very seriously. The lake offers fishing for salmon, trout and Dolly Varden.

Sterling

To the west from Cooper Landing along the highway you come to **Sterling** ⑲, a community of about 5,000, based at the confluence of the Kenai and Moose rivers. It's a very popular salmon-fishing area, and is the main access point to the Swanson River oil field and an endless string of lakes that are excellent for canoeing. Another attraction of the area is the **Izaak Walton Recreation Site**. It is believed the area was an Eskimo village more than 2,000 years ago and several depressions mark the sites of ancient houses.

Sterling is also the site of the popular Moose River Raft Race, an annual event that is held on the weekend after the 4th of July. Area businesses construct rafts in a variety of categories, then race down the Moose River to the Kenai River.

Soldotna

Heading on past Sterling, you come to the city of **Soldotna** ⑳, seat of the bor-

Fishing Fever

The name "Kenai" is synonymous with the term "fishing," especially during salmon season—and on the Kenai River, that's pretty much all summer long. When word spreads that the salmon are "in," (meaning tremendous numbers of salmon have suddenly decided to fight their way upstream to spawn) fishers from throughout Southcentral impatiently wait until the workday is over, then jump into cars and drive three hours (or more) south to the Kenai River. There they stand, shoulder-to-shoulder along the banks of the river, casting their fishing lines in a mostly-friendly synchrony called "combat fishing."

When someone actually hooks a fish and yells out "fish on," a time-honored code of conduct demands that all other fishers reel in their empty lines to give that angler the best chance of landing his prize. Then it all starts over again. As everyone "limits out" or becomes

exhausted with the effort (usually in the wee morning hours), they load themselves and their fish into their cars for the long drive back home. Often there's just enough time for a quick shower and to head back to work. There's no known cure for this type of "fishing fever." It has to run its normal course, usually lingering from early June through mid-September.

Should you feel yourself susceptible to this particular recurrent "malady," Alaska State law requires both resident and non-resident anglers, 16 years of age or older, to have a valid sportfishing license in their possession while fishing.

Nearly every grocery, sporting goods, or general merchandise store sells sportfishing licenses, or you can purchase them by mail or online.

To do so, and to learn about current state fishing regulations, contact the Alaska Department of Fish and Game, P.O. Box 115525, Juneau 99811-5525; tel: 465-2376; or www.admin.adfg.state.ak.us/license.

ough government and home of about 3,900 people. With its central location at the intersection of the roads to Kenai and Homer, Soldotna has become the hub of the central peninsula. It is a popular spot to meet up with professional fishing guides, most of whom specialize in helping their clients find king salmon.

The amount of traffic on the Kenai River has become the subject of state-wide controversy. Twenty-five years ago, only a handful of locals fished for king, sockeye and silver salmon on the river. Now the Kenai River system is the most popular sport fishing area in the state, and has been designated a Special Management Area to protect its natural resources and manage the recreational use of the river.

Consult state park officials, or local officials from the Department of Fish and Game, for the most up-to-date information on river use. Information is also available from the **Visitor Center**, at the corner of the Sterling Highway and Kalifornsky Beach Road, which also houses the offices for the local Chamber of Commerce (tel: 262-9814; www.soldotna chamber.com).

Soldotna's festivals include Progress Days, held on the last weekend in July, a winter sports festival and the sled dog racing championships, which take place in late February. Because of its location near the coast, Soldotna often doesn't receive enough snow to cover the sled dog course. For that reason, the city usually stockpiles snow scraped off the city streets, to spread over the course a few days before the races.

Located on the southwest edge of Soldotna is the Kenai Peninsula College. Among its major programs is petroleum technology, reflecting the area's tie to the oil industry.

Kenai

Heading west from Soldotna on either the Kenai Spur Highway or Kalifornsky Beach Road, you come to **Kenai ㉑**, the largest city on the peninsula with a population of about 6,900, and also the oldest permanent settlement, founded (in the center of a Dena'ina village) by Russian fur traders and Orthodox priests in the late 18th century.

Kenai is home port to a good share of the peninsula's drift-net fishing fleet. In

Sunset over the Kenai Mountains.

LEFT:
Wood carving shop in Soldotna.
BELOW: fishing on the Kenai River.

In the saddle at Kachemak Bay.

BELOW: aurora over Ninilchik's Russian Orthodox Church.

summer a parade of boats can be seen coming in and out of the mouth of the river in a quest for red salmon. During the spring, the flats along the mouth of the river are temporary nesting ground for thousands of snow geese. They stay in the area for about two weeks and are a popular subject for early-season photographers.

Kenai is also home to the peninsula's largest airport and has the most regularly scheduled flights. Airlines also fly in and out of Anchorage, Soldotna, Seward and Homer, and charter flights can take you almost anywhere else.

Diverse culture

One of Kenai's main attractions is the **Kenai Visitors' and Cultural Center** on the corner of Main Street and Kenai Spur Highway (open daily in summer; tel: 283-1991; www.visitkenai.com; free). The center features exhibits and displays of Kenai's rich and diverse culture, from its Native and Russian history through the industries that currently fuel the area: oil and commercial fishing.

Head down Overland Avenue, where you will find Fort Kenay, although the present one is only a replica of the original 19th-century fortification. On the other side of Mission Street is the **Holy Assumption Russian Orthodox Church**, the oldest Orthodox place of worship in Alaska.

If you follow Mission Street to Riverview Avenue you will come to the **Beluga Whale Lookout** where, in early summer, you can watch for white whales feeding on salmon in the river.

Special events include the 4th of July parade and the "Christmas Comes to Kenai" celebration on the weekend following Thanksgiving; the fête includes a fireworks display at about 4pm. Since the peninsula has very long days during the summer, the people of Kenai hold off on fireworks until November, when they can easily be seen against the dark late-afternoon sky.

Continuing north of Kenai on the Spur Highway, you come to the Nikiski industrial area, with a large chemical plant, two oil refineries and a natural gas liquification plant. The plants aren't open to the public.

The area north of Kenai has several names. Some call it simply "North Kenai," while others say "Nikishka," "Nikiska," or "**Nikiski.**" The latter name won a popularity vote in the area, but stick to what the locals say when talking to them.

North of the refineries is the **Captain Cook State Recreation Area ㉒**, a popular spot for hiking, camping, fishing, and snow-machining. There are a couple of good campsites and great views across the Cook Inlet. Much of what you see across the inlet is part of the **Lake Clark National Park** (tel: 781-2218; www.nps.gov/lacl; *see pages 326–31 for a detailed description*). Charter flights to the park can be arranged in Kenai – ask at the Visitor Center there for details.

From the recreation area, drive along the Bridge Access Road and connect with Kalifornsky Beach Road to return to the Sterling Highway. Farther south, the highway begins to parallel Cook Inlet and runs past some fine clamming areas in the appropriately named Clam Gulch. Digging for clams requires patience, practice, a shovel and pail, a fishing license and a current tide book. But for those who like to eat the mollusks – particularly the razor clams, said to be the best of all – a day in Clam Gulch could well be one of the highlights of their visit. You could stay at the local lodge, which serves very good clam chowder in its restaurant.

At Mile 135 on the highway is **Ninilchik ㉓**, a fishing village founded by the Russians more than 100 years ago. Fishing is still popular here today, with many visitors coming in search of halibut or salmon. The town's 800 residents mostly live in recently constructed homes along the highway. The original village, which can be visited, is an attractive spot, sitting on the inlet at the mouth of the Ninilchik River.

On a hill above the old village is the town's Russian Orthodox Church, not open for tours but still used by the parish. The modern community of Ninilchik hosts the Kenai Peninsula State Fair on the third weekend in August. Ninilchik is another good spot for clam digging.

Continuing south, you come to **Anchor Point ㉔**, the most westerly point in North America that is accessible by continuous road system. The 1,800-member community hosts a king salmon derby from Memorial Day weekend through the third weekend in June. In addition to kings, the area is a popular fishing spot for silvers, steelhead, halibut and trout.

Homer

Still farther south is **Homer ㉕**, the southern terminus of the Sterling Highway. Homer sits on the shore of **Kachemak Bay**, which is known for the variety of its marine life. Homer itself, a pleasant little town in a picturesque setting between mountains and sea, is best known for the Homer Spit, which extends 5 miles (8km) out into the bay.

Major attractions include boat tours and halibut-fishing trips, but call into the **Homer Visitor and Information Center** at 201 Sterling Highway (open daily in summer; tel: 235-7740; www.homer alaska.org) to find out what else is offered.

Be sure to stop at the **Alaska Islands and Ocean Visitor Center** (95 Sterling Hwy, open daily in summer, 9am–6pm; tel:235-6961; www.islandsandocean.org; free). Operated as a partnership between

The graveyard at Ninilchik's Russian Orthodox Church.

BELOW: carved figures at Kachemak Bay.

Map on
page 164

Which road?

*Most Alaskans do not
know the numerical
designation of the
state's highways. Per-
haps because there are
so few roads, they are
always referred to by
name. Most any
Alaskan knows the
Seward Highways
heads south from
Anchorage to the
Kenai Peninsula, and
that the Glenn High-
way heads north
through Palmer to Tok.
Few would be able to
tell you that portions
of both roads are des-
ignated as Highway 1.*

BELOW:
a good day's
catch in Homer.

the Alaska Maritime National Wildlife
Refuge and the Kachemak Bay Research
Reserve, the center offers guided walks
that include exploration of the slough,
tide pools and the marine discovery lab.

You will also discover the **Pratt
Museum** on Bartlett Street (open daily
in summer; tel: 235-8635; www.pratt
museum.org; entrance charge), a natural
history museum that focuses on marine
life in Kachemak Bay. It also has an
award-winning exhibit on the effects of
the Exxon Valdez oil spill.

Homer has quite a reputation as a local
arts center. On Pioneer Avenue, which
joins the highway, art galleries display
pottery and jewelry as well as paintings.
In downtown Homer there are also several good restaurants and souvenir shops,
and there are productions year-round by
an amateur theater company.

The town is also the jumping-off point
for trips to the other side of the bay,
which is dominated by **Kachemak Bay
State Park** ㉖ (tel: 235-7024 or 262-
5581; www.alaskastateparks.org), with the
Grewingk Glacier, rugged mountains,
coastal rain forest, steep-walled fjords,
and alpine tundra. Also across the bay

are **Halibut Cove** – where there are more
artists and galleries – and the pleasing
little town of Seldovia. The state ferry
service links Homer to Seldovia, Kodiak
and Whittier during the summer.

Seldovia

Seldovia ㉗ (tel. 234-7612; www.seldovia
.com) is accessible only by air and water.
You can bring a vehicle on the state ferry,
but it isn't necessary; the town is within
easy walking distance. It is home to yet
another of the peninsula's still active
Russian Orthodox churches. Seldovia's
Russian history predates the church,
however. It was the site of one of the earliest coal mines, first worked in the late
18th century. By the 1890s, the mine had
been exhausted and Seldovia had
become a fishing and shipping center.

Much of the town's boardwalk area
was destroyed during the 1964 earthquake. Seldovia also has a winter carnival, which brightens up the peaceful,
quiet months. With the bulk of visitors
gone and with plenty of nearby trails for
hiking and cross-country skiing, winter is
one of the nicest times to venture over to
the southern shore of Kachemak Bay. ❑

RESTAURANTS

Prices for a three-course dinner per person with a half-bottle of house wine:
$ = under $20
$$ = $20–$45
$$$ = $45–$60
$$$$ = over $60

Seward

Apollo Restaurant
229 Fourth Avenue
tel: (907) 224-3092
Stroll two block north of the Alaska Sealife Center and have lunch or dinner. Serves Greek and Italian cuisine, steaks, pizza and Alaskan seafood, Mediterranean style. Beer and wine. $$–$$$

Peking Restaurant
338 Fourth Avenue
tel: 224-5444
Consistently well-prepared Chinese fare, pleasantly served. $–$$

Ray's Waterfront
1316 Airport Way
tel: (907) 224-3816
Large windows overlook Seward's small boat harbor in this popular local restaurant. Lunch and dinner offered daily. Deliciously prepared seafood and chowder. Box lunches can be made up to take along on your fishing charter. Full bar. $$–$$$$

Resurrection Roadhouse
Mile 0.5 Exit Glacier Road
tel: 224-7116
Located on the Seward Windsong Lodge property in the beautiful Resurrection River Valley. Open seasonally. Fresh Alaska seafood and steak entrées. Full bar. $$–$$$$

Soldotna

Mykel's
4287 Kenai Spurr Highway
tel: (907) 262-4305
Located in the Soldotna Inn. Serves breakfast, lunch and dinner. Menu includes fresh Alaskan seafood, steaks, poultry and pasta dishes. Bar. $$–$$$$

Sal's Klondike Diner
44619 Sterling Highway
tel: (907) 262-2220
Where the locals head when they want burgers, sandwiches, halibut fish and chips and more served in an efficient, friendly manner. Children's menu. $

Homer

Café Cups
162 W. Pioneer Avenue
tel: (907) 235-8330
Locals and visitors alike crowd into this cozy dining room for lunches and dinners that feature fresh pasta, local seafood and an eclectic, but reasonably priced, wine selection. $$$

Fat Olive's
276 Ohlson Lane
tel: (907) 235-8488
Mediterranean food prepared on a wood-fired oven. Serves lunch and dinner daily. Beer and wine. $$–$$$

Homestead Restaurant
Mile 8.2, East End Road
tel: (907) 235-8723 or (907) 235-3447
This former log roadhouse 8 miles (13km) from downtown Homer specializes in steak, prime rib and seasonal seafood creatively prepared with garlic, citrus fruits, macadamia nuts or spicy ethnic sauces. Closed in winter. Beer and wine. $$$–$$$$

Saltry in Halibut Cove
tel: (907) 296-2223 or (800) 478-0400 (Central Charters) for reservations
Across Kachemak Bay in Halibut Cove. Serves local seafood as sushi or in curries and pastas. A wide selection of imported beers. Take the Danny J ferry from the Homer Spit boardwalk through Central Charters. Reservations necessary. Closed mid-Sept–late May. $$–$$$$

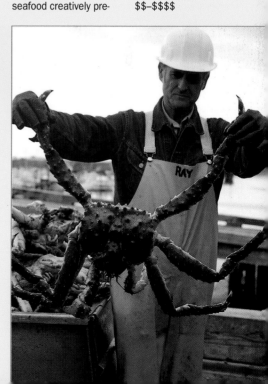

RIGHT: king crab caught at Homer.

MATANUSKA-SUSITNA VALLEY

Alaska

Anchorage

"Yahoo! Mat-Su!" is the slogan for this area, referred to locally as "the Mat-Su," or simply "the Valley." The phrase captures the spirit of cowboy enthusiasm common to those who live, farm, hike, fish, hunt, dog mush, mud bog, and snowmachine here

Main attractions
PALMER
WASILLA
TALKEETNA

BELOW:
a caribou bull
crosses the river.

The stunningly beautiful and diverse Mat-Su area encompasses the Matanuska-Susitna River Drainages, over 23,000 sq miles (6 million hectares), beginning 35 miles north of Anchorage on the Glenn Highway, north along the Parks Highway to the southern border of Denali National Park and Preserve, and east along the Denali Highway as far as Lake Louise, near Glennallen.

Wildlife sightings in the area likely include moose, bear (brown and black), birds (bald eagles, hawks, owls, swans, and loons), and on the far northern and eastern edges of the Mat-Su, impressive caribou herds. Historically the agricultural breadbasket of Alaska, today the Mat-Su is one of the state's fastest growing residential and commercial regions.

A host of new housing developments, springing up on former farmland, are filled with people who commute daily to Anchorage, at least an hour's drive (under ideal weather and traffic conditions) south along the Glenn Highway.

The making of the Mat-Su

The Mat-Su Valley has an interesting history, beginning in 1935 when President Franklin D. Roosevelt – in response to the crushing economic depression and widespread drought of the times – invited 203 families from the hardest-hit states of Minnesota, Wisconsin and Michigan to journey to Alaska for a new start with the Matanuska Colony Project. The name of each family was drawn from a box, and 40 acres (16 hectares) of farmland per family were parceled out.

The community of **Palmer**, established in 1916 as a stop along the Alaska Railroad's track to the Chickaloon coalmines, was selected to be the base of operations for this "New Deal" project. Housing options for the colonists were few, and barns were non-existent. Following plans drawn up by a government architect, the colonists began constructing homes and the area's distinctive 32-ft square, gambrel-roofed barns, many of which are still standing today.

The members of Matanuska Colony

faced many of the same problems common to the Valley's current-day farmers: short growing season, high freight and labor costs, and great distances to relatively small markets. Within five years, more than half of the original 203 families had given up and left the area; by 1965, fewer than 20 of the original colonists were still farming.

Driving north from Anchorage along the Glenn Highway, just before reaching the city of Palmer you'll come upon a broad expanse of flat, marshy grasslands of the **Palmer Hay Flats State Game Refuge A**. The 45 sq miles (116 sq km) of the refuge provides nesting and feeding grounds for tens of thousands of various duck and geese species en route to and from northern breeding grounds. Trumpeter and tundra swans also frequent the marshlands during spring and fall. Sandhill cranes may be found in the drier, more isolated regions. The area is a major calving and wintering ground for the Matanuska Valley moose population. The streams, wetlands, tidal sloughs, lakes and tide flats of the refuge are also popular recreation areas for local salmon fishers and waterfowl hunters.

An excellent place to begin your exploration of the Mat-Su is at the **Visitor Information Headquarters B** (Parks Hwy. to Trunk Rd. Exit, 7744 E. Visitors View Court, next to Mat-Su Regional Medical Center; open daily 8:30am–6:30pm, mid-May–mid-Sept; tel: 746-5000; www.AlaskaVisit.com). The friendly folks inside the log cabin structure can give you information on tours, attractions and lodging options in the area, and also have a pay phone, free wi-fi internet access and a gift shop.

Palmer

After leaving the Mat-Su Visitor Information Headquarters, head a few miles farther north along the Glenn Highway to **Palmer C**, a small farming town of 5,500 residents happily situated in a majestic rural setting, and conforming to the image many visitors expect of Alaska. The city offers a variety of modest lodging and restaurant options, as well as an 18-hole golf course with distracting views of the surrounding mountain and glacier grandeur.

Stop in at the **Palmer Visitor Information Center and Museum D** (723 S.

Pick your own
Although most produce sold in Alaska comes from outside the state, Mat-Su Valley vegetables – such as carrots, peas, cabbage and potatoes – are sold in the field (where, for a price, you can pick your own produce), in local markets, and at roadside farm stands.

BELOW: fly fishing on Rabbit Creek, Palmer Hay Flats State Game Refuge.

Valley Way; open daily May–mid-Sept 9am–6pm, winter Mon–Fri 10am–4pm; museum hours 9am–3pm Mon–Fri; tel: 745-2880; www.palmerchamber.org; donations welcome) to chat with those who know the town best. The museum displays colony-era household relics, farm implements and woodworking tools. Many local artists have their works displayed here as well, and just outside the building you can stroll through an interesting garden area featuring various local flowers and legendary vegetables.

A short walk from the visitor's center is the **Colony House Museum** **E** (316 E. Elmwood Ave.; open Tues–Sat 10am–4pm, May 1–Aug. 31; tel: 745-1935; entrance charge), a restored Colony home (circa 1935), where you'll likely hear a direct descendant of an original pioneer family describe what life was like during the Matanuska Colony Project.

Palmer is best known for being the site (in late August) of the **Alaska State Fair**

A rider takes a tumble at the Alaska State Fair.

F (tel: 745-4827; www.alaskastatefair.org), which features the famous valley produce. Grown to gigantic proportions due to proper seed selection, careful tending and 19 hours of sunlight during the growing season, the largest cabbage wins the blue ribbon – and it must weigh at least 75 lbs (34 kg) before it is even eligible to enter the competition. Displays also include farm animals and hand-made local items. There is a colorful carnival and a host of food stalls. The 11-day event, which ends on Labor Day, attracts more than 250,000 people a year and shouldn't be missed.

Independence Mine

One of the highlights of any trip to the Mat-Su is a visit to Hatcher Pass and the **Independence Mine State Historical Park** **G**. Accessed just north of Palmer at Mile 49.5 Glenn Highway, turn left onto Palmer-Fishhook Road (which becomes Hatcher Pass Road), and make the scenic drive on the well-maintained, paved roadway through pleasant woodlands. The Little Susitna River runs alongside the road as you begin to climb and gradually wind your way to an elevation of 3,886 ft (1,184 meters) at Hatcher Pass.

The **Hatcher Pass Lodge** is located 17 miles (27km) from the Glenn Highway turnoff. This rustic establishment, open year round, offers good food, reasonable prices, cabin rentals, and spectacular views of the Talkeetna Mountains and alpine foothills that will have you looking around for Heidi and her grandfather. The area is a popular year-round recreational destination for hiking, picnicking, berry picking, camping, and, in winter, skiing, snowboarding and snowmachining.

A mile or so beyond the lodge is the gravel parking area for Independence Mine State Historical Park (open in summer, exact dates weather-dependent; tel: 745-2827; fees charged for guided tours). You can ramble on your own (or take a guided tour) through abandoned buildings of this 1930s gold mine operation, at that time one of the largest producers in Alaska, employing more than 200.

Willow

Beyond the mine area, Hatcher Pass Road continues along, now as an old-time, un-maintained, real Alaska gravel road. During the summer (that brief interlude when the snow is gone) you can complete the 49-drive (from the Glenn Highway turnoff) to **Willow** Ⓗ (located on the Parks Highway), a community of nearly 2,000 residents. The scenery of this stretch is nothing short of spectacular, but the road is steep, narrow, often rough, and switch-backed. It is not a good option for large RVs.

Also just north of Palmer is the **Palmer Musk Ox Farm** Ⓘ (Mile 50, Glenn Hwy; open daily in summer 10am–6pm; in winter by appointment; tel: 745-4151; entrance charge), with the world's only domesticated musk oxen. In

The Northern Lights illuminate a barn near Palmer.

BELOW: giant cabbages at the Alaska State Fair.

Local girl makes good
Wasilla may be a small
town, but a former
mayor, Sarah Palin
(pictured on page 39),
fought her way in 2006
to become Alaska's
first female governor. A
former beauty queen,
she was nicknamed
Sarah Barracuda in
tribute to her aggres-
sive play as a member
of her high school
basketball team.

the summer, visitors can watch the newborn creatures romping with their parents in the pasture. The coats of these shaggy animals produce a rare type of wool known as qiviut. The material is used by the Alaska Natives to create hand-knitted hats, mittens, gloves and scarves in traditional patterns.

The Oomingmak Musk Ox Producers' Co-op in downtown Anchorage *(see page 173)* also sells a range of these products. It is believed that the lightweight wool is the warmest material in the world, and articles made from it make unusual gifts or mementos.

The **Williams Reindeer Farm** 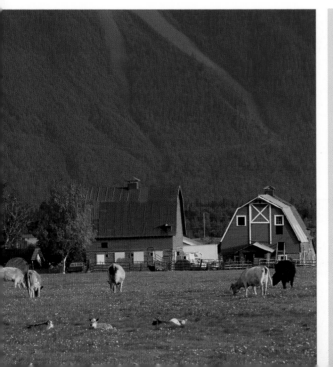 (5561 Bodenburg Loop Rd., in the Butte area off the Old Glenn Highway; open daily in summer 10am–6pm; tel: 745-4500; entrance charge) offers a rare chance to get a close look at the smallish creatures that are Santa's seemingly unlikely choice for worldwide air cargo transport.

Lake Louise

Continue your road trip farther east along the Glenn Highway, past the small communities of Sutton, Chickaloon and Eureka; at Mile 159.9, turn left and drive the 19 miles (30km) to **Lake Louise** 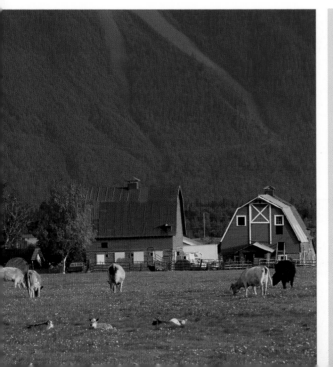. This 37 sq-mile (96-sq km) lake is a popular locale for trout fishing. The surrounding areas afford views of Tazlina Glacier, private lodges, campgrounds and, in winter, adventurous (though frigid) snowmachining and cross-country skiing opportunities. The Nelchina caribou herd can been seen passing through this region during spring and fall migrations.

Other wildlife sightings common to the area include cormorants, trumpeter swans, and ptarmigans, as well as wolves, bears, wolverine, foxes and moose. If you drive 27 miles (43km) farther east, you will arrive at the Copper River Valley community of Glennallen *(see page 191)*.

Wasilla

Once your exploration of Palmer is complete, drive north along the (George) Parks Highway to visit **Wasilla** 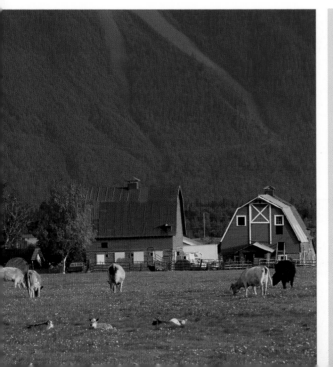 (*wa sill uh*), the "Home of the Iditarod", the land "among the lakes", and mile after mile of strip-mall-styled commercial development with the attendant traffic, especially during the early morning and late afternoon hours of heaviest commuter travel. Wasilla (population 6,775) is the site of

BELOW: farmers in the area have to cope with a short growing season.

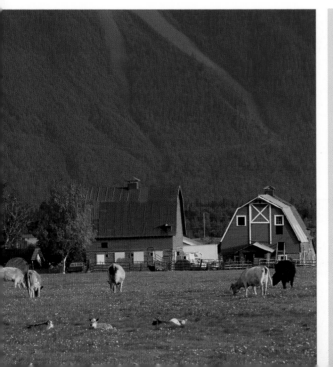

Versatile transportation

Take a look around at the vehicles in Wasilla: an interesting array of RVs (some commercially built, others creatively scabbed together from eclectic materials), and large, powerful pickup trucks with mud-encrusted ATVs loaded onto the back, and pulling fishing boats or campers along behind. In winter, these same trucks are still here, but pulling snowmachine-laden trailers, or with a team of sled dogs peering out from their custom-built, mobile kennel cubbies. The stores and other businesses that line both sides of the Parks Highway in Wasilla provide almost anything local residents or visitors could need or want. It's a great place to stock up on supplies before driving, flying, snowmachining or boating to more remote locales.

many of the large, new residential developments in the Valley. Housing and land prices are generally more reasonable here than in Anchorage; the trade-off is that most residents must then make the daily one hour (plus) commute each way – in all kinds of weather – to their Anchorage jobs. That's OK, though. In Wasilla, the folks tend to be hard drivers, hard workers and hard players.

Like many of the other cities and towns in Southcentral, the community of Wasilla arrived by rail. The original Dena'ina Indian residents called this area Benteh, or "among the lakes," sandwiched as it is between Lake Lucille and Wasilla Lake. The name "Wasilla" came from the highly-respected local Dena'ina Indian, Chief Wasilla. Depending on whom you ask, the name means either "breath of air," or else it's simply a derivative of the Russian name, "William."

The first non-Native settlers of the region lived in the nearby town of Knik, a "boom town" of about 500 people in 1915, providing supplies and services to the gold miners at Cache Creek and Willow Creek. In 1917, Wasilla was founded following the construction of the Alaska Railroad. The residents of Knik, realizing the advantages of living near a rail service, simply packed up and moved there. Some actually dragged their houses along behind them (perhaps the ancestors of today's Wasilla pickup drivers waiting at the traffic lights), leaving Knik to become a ghost town. The construction of the Parks Highway in early 1970 opened up road access to the area, and made it possible for families to live in Wasilla and commute to jobs in Anchorage. The city was incorporated in 1974.

The Iditarod Trail Sled Dog Race is run from Wasilla.

The Iditarod's HQ

Wasilla's main claim to fame today is as the home to the world famous Iditarod Trail Sled Dog Race *(see pages 308–9)*. The **Iditarod Trail Headquarters and Museum** Ⓜ (Mile 2.2 Knik Road; open year round, summer daily 8am–7pm, winter Mon–Fri 8am–5pm; tel: 376-5155) is well worth a visit. Aside from the very interesting exhibits depicting the

BELOW: campfire at dusk by the Matanuska River.

Plans, trucks and tractors at the Museum of Alaska Transportation and Industry.

history of the Iditarod, there's a unique gift shop and, during the summer, you can go for a dog sled ride (daily 9am–5pm).

There are two other museum options in Wasilla. The **Dorothy Page Museum** (323 N. Main Street; open tel: 373-5973; www. cityofwasilla.com/museum), was named in honor of Dorothy G. Page, who joined with Joe Reddington, Sr. in 1967 to organize the first Iditarod Trail Race, a 50-mile race (run in two 25-mile heats) to commemorate the 100th anniversary of US purchase of Alaska from Russia. The museum, housed in a 1931 structure that has previously served as a community hall for social, political and even sporting events, offers exhibits, programs and lectures on the history of gold mining and dog mushing (among other things) in Wasilla. You can also visit the historic buildings of the **Old Wasilla Townsite Park** while you're there.

BELOW: sharing the news in Talkeetna.

The **Museum of Alaska Transportation and Industry** (3800 W. Museum Dr., off Mile 47 Parks Hwy.; open summers only; tel: 376-1211; www.museum ofalaska.org) displays interesting examples of old planes, trains, tools, vehicles and farm equipment. But what people living in or traveling through Wasilla really enjoy most is not inside any building, but rather in campgrounds, on mountain trails or at salmon streams, all within easy driving distance from the traffic lights.

For a complete list off Wasilla's recreational options, check with the Mat-Su Visitor Information Headquarters (*see page 377*).

Talkeetna

If you're driving north of Wasilla on the Parks Highway towards the Interior, don't pass up the opportunity to spend a few hours in **Talkeetna** ㉘ (pronounced *tal **keet** nuh*; turn north at Mile 98.7, then travel 14 miles (22km) along the Talkeetna Spur Rd.), the staging area for climbers from around the world planning to summit Mount McKinley.

The Talkeetna Lodge (on the right, about a mile before Talkeetna), owned by the Cook Inlet Region, Inc. (CIRI) Native corporation, is a clean, modern, beautifully "rustic" post-and-beam style hotel nestled in a quiet, wooded area of Talkeetna. On clear days, a fine view of Mt. McKinley awaits you on the observation deck in front of the hotel.

In Talkeetna's "downtown" area, renovated, rustic miners cabins have been spruced up and converted into gift shops, lodgings and restaurants. The town is famous for its annual Moose Dropping Festival (held in July), which includes a parade, vendors, booths, and fun, quirky events like the Mountain Mother Contest (where mothers compete in diaper changing, wood chopping, water hauling and pie making for the coveted "Crown of the Mountain Mama") or the Moose Drop Dropping (where shellacked and numbered moose nuggets are dropped from the air onto a target).

There's generally music and dancing in the evening, some of which is likely not suitable for families.

Talkeetna also offers fishing charters, river rafting adventures and flightseeing tours to Mt. McKinley. Contact the Talkeetna Chamber for more details (P.O. Box 334, Talkeetna 99676; tel: 733-2330; www.talkeetnachamber.org).

Denali State Park

An often-overlooked option for those wanting to see Mt. McKinley during their Alaska vacation is to visit **Denali State Park** ㉙, where outstanding views of the mountain are possible from a less-crowded vantage point. One of the best roadside views, weather permitting, may be enjoyed from the southern viewpoint (Mile 135.2).

You can also take a day hike to **Kesugi Ridge**, or if you're interested in backpacking adventures, a trek into the **Peters Hills** (in the western end of the park). Both options offer stunning, panoramic views of Mt McKinley – if the weather cooperates.

Other recreation opportunities include camping, and kayaking or canoeing (rentals available) at the **Byers Lake Campground**. Wildlife common to the park includes (but are not limited to) moose, grizzly and black bears, wolves, lynx, coyotes, red fox, snowshoe hares, and land otters.

The area is also rich in birding opportunities, as more than 130 species use the park for breeding or during migration. Additional information is available at the

TIP

Safety in Denali
Because the state park is essentially a wilderness, hiking trails are not always clearly marked and good USGS topographic maps are essential since whiteout conditions can occur in any season. These can be found at the Visitor Contact Station at the Alaska Veterans Memorial, Mile 147.1, Parks Highway.

BELOW:
trains offer an effortless trip through the wilderness.

From Talkeetna by Train

The Alaska Railroad offers flag-stop service for a 55-mile (88-km) wilderness run from Talkeetna to Hurricane and back. The train leaves Talkeetna, usually Thursday through Sunday only, at 11:45am and returns in time for dinner. It threads its way along the Susitna River and through the Indian River Canyon.

Passengers can get off the Hurricane Turn train for a fishing or river rafting adventure along the way, and then board the train again on its return trip (or else camp overnight and flag down the next day's train). Since 1923 locals have been using this route, one of the last flag-stop services in the country, for accessing remote cabins in the area.

Tickets may be purchased on board (cash only), or make advance reservations by calling 800-544-0552 or 265-2494.

Hatcher Pass.

staffed visitor contact station, Mile 147.1, and at bulletin boards in the park, or contact the Denali Ranger (Alaska State Parks, Mat-Su/CB Area, HC 32, Box 6706, Wasilla 99654-9719; tel: 745-3974; www.dnr.state.ak.us/arks/ units/denali1.htm).

For full coverage of Denali National Park (not to be confused with the state park, see pages 229–39.

Mat-Su Backcountry

Conveniently accessible from Anchorage, the backcountry opportunities of the Mat-Su are plentiful and varied. The area has the largest trail system in the Alaska State Parks network, offering more than 2,000 miles (3,200km) of trails for all abilities. Prime examples include a nature walk through Denali State Park, where you can – when the weather conditions smile upon you – catch rare and glorious glimpses of Mount McKinley and the Tokositna Glacier.

BELOW: fall colors in the tundra.

Or you can travel to the **Hatcher Pass** area and take a leisurely stroll through historic mining buildings from the 1930s, or spend a pleasant afternoon picking blueberries or cranberries (if you're lucky enough to be there from mid-August through September – or until the snow returns).

Another excellent option is to explore some of the many trails in the **Talkeetna Mountains** – leading to alpine valleys, tundra vistas and mountain streams – on foot, ATV or, in winter, snowmobile. If your preferred sightseeing vantage point is the seat of a canoe or kayak, you've been blessed.

The **Nancy Lake Recreation Area** (Mile 67.2 Parks Highway, near Willow) offers water enthusiasts a total of 130 interconnected lakes for their paddling pleasure – also canoe and kayak rentals, remote cabin rentals, campgrounds and superb fishing for rainbow trout, arctic char and northern pike.

Guided rafting adventures (whitewater or leisure floats) are available on the **Matanuska or Knik Rivers**. For details on these (and other) adventures in the Mat-Su, go to www.AlaskaVisit.com. ❏

RESTAURANTS

Prices for a three-course dinner per person with a half-bottle of house wine:
$ = under $15
$$ = $15–$20
$$$ = $20–$30
$$$$ = over $30

Palmer

Hatcher Pass Lodge Restaurant

17 miles from the Glenn Hwy intersection on the Hatcher Pass Rd
P.O. Box 763
tel: 745-5897

This lodge-style restaurant, which is located in an unpretentious A-frame building at Hatcher Pass, offers an amazingly varied menu of simple-but-tasty beef, chicken, and seafood dishes, as well as salads and a choice of delicious sandwiches. The service is surprisingly fast, the portions generous, the company of fellow-diners eclectic and the view spectacular. Bar. $–$$

Vagabond Blues

642 S. Alaska Street
tel: 745-2233

Located in the center of downtown Palmer, this trendy café offers delicious vegetarian soups, salads, sandwiches and wraps and locally roasted coffee. Casual

environment, patrons generally bus their own tables before leaving. Frequent live performances by local musicians. $

The Valley Hotel Restaurant

606 S. Alaska St.
tel: 745-3330

The place local residents congregate for basic small-town restaurant fare. Nothing fancy, but you can count on generous portions, friendly staff, clean dining area, large and varied menu, consistently good food. Bar. $–$$

Wasilla

Alpine Garden Grille

Mile 45.2 Parks Hwy, 259 South McCallister Drive
tel: 357-6313

This restaurant's stated goal of fine dining in a setting of casual elegance is being well received by local Wasilla diners. The menu is described as international with Italian and French influence. Specialties include a baked brie with roasted garlic appetizer, oven-roasted leg of lamb and hazelnut-stuffed chicken roulade. Desserts made fresh daily. More than 100

wines are available. $$$–$$$$

The Cadillac Café

Sylvan and Mile 49 Parks Hwy
tel: 357-5533

This small, upscale café, offers a wide variety of delicious dishes. Favorites include halibut tacos, burritos, specialty burgers and gourmet pizzas. Beer and wine. $–$$$

Shoreline Restaurant

(Best Western Lake Lucille Inn), 1300 W. Lake Lucille Dr.
tel: 800-780-7234

Within one of the area's better hotels, this restaurant offers a quiet, pleasant place to go for that special night out in Wasilla. Windows afford lovely view of the lake and mountains beyond. Open breakfast, lunch and dinner. Dinner menu primarily features beef, chicken and seafood entrées. Bar. $$–$$$$

Talkeetna

Foraker Restaurant

Mile 12.5 Talkeetna Spur Rd
tel: (907) 733-9500 or (888) 959-9590
www.talkeetnalodge.com

Located in the Talkeetna Alaskan Lodge, this elegant restaurant offers breakfast, lunch and dinner, but only during the summer tourist season. Features Alaska specialties and fresh seafood. Full bar. $$$–$$$$

Talkeetna Roadhouse

Main and C Street
tel: (907) 733-1351

Originally built in 1917 as a staging house for gold miners' supplies, today the establishment is a roadhouse that offers lodging as well as a bakery and café. Hearty breakfasts and lunches served daily in summer, limited hours in winter. A popular spot for Mt. McKinley climbers. $$

RIGHT: eating out at Talkeetna.

THE INTERIOR

You can follow in the footsteps of the 19th-century gold prospectors and discover the beauties, and the hardships, of Alaska's Interior. The area includes Denali National Park and Preserve, Fairbanks, Outlying areas, and the Alcan highway

The cry of "Gold!" has lured men and women to the Interior for more than a century. That initial, passionate hunger for a handful of valuable nuggets – spawning the first of Alaska's many "rushes" – is history now, but the spirit of the Interior still summons the adventurer.

The extraordinary wildlife-viewing, photography, and backcountry opportunities of Denali National Park and Preserve *(see pags 228–39)*, the many historic sights and sounds of the heartland city of Fairbanks (the second-largest population base of Alaska; *see pages 242–55)*, and the scattered, outlying communities, hunkered down in the wilderness along mighty rivers, still sing out their siren call. And those who answer that call board planes, catch trains (from Southcentral Alaska), or simply pack up their cars (or RVs) and head north *(see The Alcan, pages 240–1).*

There *is* gold in the Interior, gilding every aspen leaf in the autumn explosion of color, glancing off the wingtips of geese, shimmering in the river current as it flows into a blazing sunset. It splashes across the midnight sky as the aurora and dances as moonlight over the hulking white shoulders of mountain peaks. And for a few days each spring, this gold lies strewn like nuggets, captured for a moment in a carpet of wildflowers. Many who visit the Interior also find that the people have what can only be called hearts of gold. There is a longstanding tradition of caring, generosity and warm-heartedness that welcomes the traveler back again and again to the edge of the frontier.

Stark contrasts

The Interior of Alaska, that one-third of the state north of the Alaska Range, south of the Brooks Range and east of Alaska's western coastal areas, is an area of stark contrasts. Mount McKinley, 20,320ft (6,195 meters) and snow-capped year-round, towers above the temperate Tanana and Yukon valleys. The Alaska Range is girdled with miles and miles of glaciers, while in the valleys, forests of white spruce, birch and aspen fold into straggly stands of black spruce, tangles of willow, and muskeg.

If you are visiting the Interior in summer, as most people do, try conjur-

PRECEDING PAGES: Alaskan brown bear (Ursus arctos) mother and cub.
LEFT: Mount McKinley. **ABOVE:** playing a sealskin drum; panning for gold.

ing up an image of what it would be like in winter, with low light reflecting blue off the snow-covered riverbed, and temperatures plummeting to –40°F (–40°C) or below. Summer weather is glorious, with nearly around-the-clock daylight and temperatures as high as 96°F (36°C). Travelers often find it hard to sleep because of all the light. The most practical advice is: don't even try to sleep until you're really tired, but enjoy the late evening light – this is the season that makes the cold dark winter worth enduring.

You will also find that the later evening is a fine time for photography. Light of this quality is experienced at lower latitudes for only a few moments around sunrise and sunset. In Alaska's Interior, the special glow hovers for hours, casting gigantic shadows and ethereal reflections.

Exploring the rivers and woods

Outdoor adventure is the glue that binds people to the land in the Interior. The mountains, rivers and valleys offer unparalleled opportunities for hiking, canoeing, hunting and fishing. The best source of outdoors information is the **Alaska Public Lands Information Center** at 250 Cushman Street, Fairbanks (tel: 456-0527; www.nps.gov/aplic). This multi-agency information center and museum sells maps and answers questions about all categories of land.

The usually blue skies of summer coupled with hundreds of miles of wild and scenic rivers make water travel a natural pastime. Canoeing offers an idyllic opportunity to observe game animals undisturbed as the boat slips silently past. In Fairbanks, you can find many businesses that rent canoes.

With the entire Interior river system at your paddle tip, deciding where to explore depends on ability and time. The Chena and Chatanika rivers offer a multitude of easily accessible possibilities for day trips or longer expeditions. For experienced wilderness canoeists, the more challenging clear waters of the

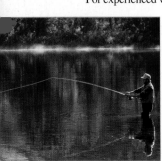

Birch Creek can be accessed at Mile 94 Steese Highway, or consider a 5-day sojourn on the broad sweep of the **Tanana River** from Delta to Fairbanks. These rivers are all conveniently accessible by road. If you own a collapsible kayak, numerous remote rivers can be reached by plane.

Legendary fishing

The Interior is a fisherman's promised land, and the Arctic grayling is its manna. The flash of the strike and the fight of the silver streak on light tackle is a treasured memory for many. The Clearwater, Salcha, Chatanika and Chena rivers are superior grayling producers and are accessible by road. In fact, all clear-flowing creeks and rivers in the Interior are well-stocked with grayling. Northern pike, burbot, and lake trout abound in the clear, cold waters throughout the Interior.

A visit to the Interior presents a rare opportunity to savor the very heartland of Alaska, to observe wildlife doing what they've done for thousands of years, to paddle quietly along picturesque, wild rivers, to hike rugged mountain trails to glorious panoramic vistas, to pan for gold, or to visit the area's many historic mining camps and museums to learn more about Alaska's colorful history. ❏

Top: train at El Dorado mine, Fairbanks; **Left:** fishermen are lured to the Interior.
Right: getting close to the clouds on Mount McKinley, Denali National Park.

DENALI NATIONAL PARK AND PRESERVE

Dominated by the magnificent Mount McKinley, Denali,
one of the world's greatest wildlife sanctuaries,
is the most visited of all Alaska's national parks

laska's Athabascan Indians called the mountain by several names, but they all meant essentially the same thing: "The High One." Denali was the most common of those names and it's the one preferred by many Alaskans today, though the peak's official name remains **Mount McKinley**. Whether Denali or McKinley, North America's highest peak (20,320ft or 6,195 meters) is also among the continent's most spectacular. In one sense it is among the highest mountains in the world: the north face of Denali rises almost 18,000ft (5,500 meters) above its base, an elevation gain which surpasses even Mount Everest.

The mountain is surrounded by one of the world's greatest wildlife sanctuaries, **Denali National Park and Preserve ⑳**. A one-day trip through the park will almost certainly allow you to see grizzly bears, caribou, Dall sheep, moose and perhaps a wolf. Denali Park is, for many, the ultimate Alaskan adventure.

Geology and history

Denali is part of the **Alaska Range**, a 600-mile (960-km) arc of mountains stretching across the state from the Alaska Peninsula almost to the Canadian border. The oldest parts of the range are made up of slate, shale, marble and other sedimentary deposits formed under an ancient ocean. Approximately 60 million years ago, the collision and subsequent overlapping of two tectonic plates produced such intense heat that sections of the earth's crust began to melt. A gigan-

tic mass of molten rock deposited beneath the current location of Denali eventually solidified into granite.

The overlapping of the plates caused the whole region to rise. Granite and sedimentary rock were forced upward to form the mountain range. As the uplift petered out, the process of erosion slowly wore down the range. As Denali is chiefly composed of erosion-resistant granite, it wore down at a slower rate than surrounding sedimentary rock. A later period of tectonic plate collision and uplift began two million years ago and continues to

LEFT: the Alaska Railroad provides access to the park.
BELOW: Mount McKinley.

An Arctic ground squirrel in Denali.

this day. This ongoing uplift is responsible for the towering height of Denali.

The first humans came on seasonal hunting trips to what is now Denali Park about 12,000 years ago. Later, the Athabascans followed suit, but built their permanent villages in lower, warmer, sheltered locations, next to lakes or rivers that offered dependable fishing. However, the lack of large salmon runs limited Native habitation.

The Athabascans of the Yukon and Tanana rivers gave Denali its name. They said the mountain was created during a battle between two magical warriors. The raven war chief, Totson, pursued his enemy Yako across a sea. Totson threw a magical spear at his adversary but Yako turned a gigantic wave into stone and deflected the weapon. The solidified wave became the mountain they called Denali. In another Athabascan story, Denali is called "the home of the sun." During the longest days of summer, the sun makes an almost complete circle in the local sky and drops below the horizon for only a few hours. From certain angles, it appears that the sun rises and sets from behind Denali.

The first recorded sighting of Denali by a white man occurred in 1794. While sailing in Cook Inlet, the English Captain George Vancouver sighted "distant stupendous mountains covered with snow." Undoubtedly this was the Alaska Range. Other explorers, surveyors and adventurers in later decades commented on the mountain's great size and estimated its height.

The naming process

Denali became known as Mount McKinley through a strange set of circumstances in 1896 when William Dickey went on a gold-prospecting expedition in the area just south of Denali. While camped within sight of the mountain, he met other miners and they argued at length whether gold or silver should back US currency. (The miners were against the gold standard while Dickey was for it.) When Dickey later returned to the Lower 48, he wrote an article about his Alaskan adventures, and proposed that the highest mountain in the Alaskan Range be named after the Republican presidential candidate William McKinley, the champion of the gold standard.

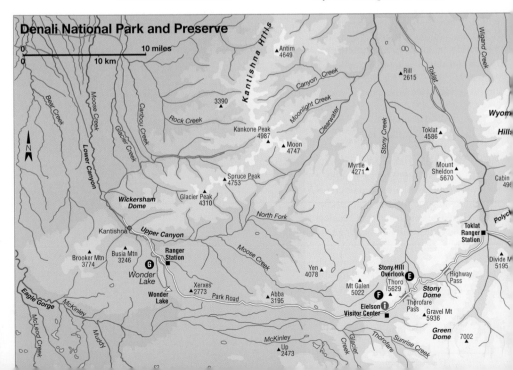

Denali National Park and Preserve

0 _____ 10 miles
0 _____ 10 km

N

Kantishna Hills

Antim 4649
Canyon Creek
Rill 2615
Toklat
Wigand Creek
Wyom
Hills

3390
Rock Creek
Moonlight Creek
Clearwater
Toklat 4586
Cabin 496

Kankone Peak 4987
Moon 4747
Stony Creek
Mount Sheldon 5670

Beag Creek
Moose Creek
Caribou Creek
Glacier Creek
Lower Canyon

Spruce Peak 4753
Myrtle 4271
Polyc

Wickersham Dome
Glacier Peak 4310

Kantishna
Upper Canyon
North Fork
Toklat Ranger Station

Brooker Mtn 3774
Busia Mtn 3246
Ranger Station **G**
Moose Creek
Yen 4078
Stony Hill Overlook **E**
Highway Pass
Divide M 5195

Wonder Lake
Xerxes 2773
Park Road
Abba 3195
Mt Galen 5022
Thoro 5629 **F**
Stony Dome
Eielson Visitor Center **i**
Thorofare Pass
Gravel Mt 5936

Eagle Gorge
McKinley
McLeod Creek
Muddy
Wonder Lake

McKinley
Up 2473
Glacier Creek
Thorofare
Sunrise Creek
Green Dome 7002

McKinley won the 1896 election and the name stuck.

One of the first white men to explore the Denali region was a naturalist and hunter, Charles Sheldon, who proposed that it be set aside as a national park and wildlife preserve. Sheldon made two extensive trips through the area in 1906 and 1907–8, and thought that the opportunity to see and study wildlife was the most impressive feature of the region.

After leaving Denali, he used his influence as a member of the powerful Boone and Crockett Club to gather support for his proposed Denali National Park. Largely due to Sheldon's efforts, the park became a reality in 1917. To his disappointment, Congress chose to call it Mount McKinley National Park.

The Sourdough Expedition

While Sheldon was campaigning for the park, others were endeavoring to make the first ascent of Denali. In late 1909, four miners (Billy Taylor, Pete Anderson, Charley McGonagall and Tom Lloyd), not intimidated by the fact that they had never climbed a mountain before, decided to scale Denali. They figured if they had survived the Alaskan winters they could do anything.

The so-called Sourdough Expedition set off from Fairbanks. ("Sourdough" was the nickname given to prospectors because of the yeasty mixture they brought with them to make bread) in December 1909 and spent much of the next few months establishing a series of camps. The group reached Denali's Muldrow Glacier in March. And on the morning of April 3, 1910, McGonagall, Taylor and Anderson set out for the summit from their camp at 11,000ft (3,300 meters), carrying a spruce pole that they hoped would be visible from mining

Spring comes to Wonder Lake, near Mount McKinley.

camps at Kantishna, and evidence of their ascent. McGonagall stopped part way up, but by mid-afternoon Taylor and Anderson stood atop Denali's North Peak: they had achieved their goal despite their total lack of experience. Unfortunately for them, the North Peak is 850ft (260 meters) lower than the South Peak, Denali's true summit. Taylor and Anderson were never credited with being first to the continent's top.

In 1913 Hudson Stuck and a party of three climbers mounted the first Denali expedition to actually reach the mountain's summit. Using route descriptions made by earlier parties, they ascended the Muldrow Glacier, which flows down the northeast side of Denali.

After a difficult climb, they reached Denali Pass, the saddle between the North and South Peaks, only 2,100ft (640 meters) below the summit. The high elevation, low oxygen and extreme cold made those last few hundred feet the hardest part of their climb. Walter Harper, a young Athabascan employed by Stuck and the strongest member of the team, was the first to stand on the summit of Mount Denali.

TIP

Camping permits

A backcountry use permit, required for overnight camping, must be obtained in person at the Backcountry Information Center (adjacent to the Wilderness Access Center) in summer and at park headquarters in winter. A quota system is enforced.

BELOW:
relaxing at a camp in Kantishna.

Recent changes

From 1917 to the early 1970s, few people visited Mount McKinley National Park. The park's remoteness and lack of direct access by vehicle combined to limit tourism. In the five years prior to 1972, the average annual number of visitors was about 15,000. In 1972, the Anchorage–Fairbanks Highway was completed and it suddenly became much easier for tourists and Alaskan residents to get here. In a short time, the numbers jumped to more than 140,000 a year, almost a ten-fold increase over the previous figures.

National Park Service rangers were concerned about the effect this dramatic rise would have on the park and the quality of visitors' experiences. One major problem was that the single dirt road that bisects the park was too narrow to handle the increased traffic. Another concern was the park's wildlife, which in the past had always been readily visible from the road. The extra traffic and noise created by a ten-fold increase in numbers was likely to drive the animals out of sight; and huge influxes of people could result in more encounters with the park's dangerous animals, grizzly bears and moose.

The creative solution to these problems was the initiation of a shuttle and tour bus system: private vehicles must be parked in the entrance area and visitors board buses that run throughout the day, causing little disturbance to wildlife. However, visitors are allowed to drive their own vehicles as far as the Savage River bridge, about 15 miles (24km) from the park entrance. That first stretch of road is paved, while the 75 miles (120km) or so beyond are gravel. The park road is closed beyond Mile 3 in winter, but a campground loop is plowed for campers.

In the 1970s, Congress debated how to establish new national parks in Alaska. Most of the proposals also called for an expansion of Mount McKinley National Park to include scenic areas and critical wildlife –habitats not within the original boundaries. The Alaska National Interest Lands Conservation Act (ANILCA), passed in 1980, partially resolved an old controversy: recognizing the longstanding Alaskan use of the name Denali, Congress renamed the area Denali National Park and Preserve, although the mountain is still officially McKinley.

Arriving in the park

The entrance to Denali Park is along the **George Parks Highway**, 240 miles (385km) north of Anchorage and 120 miles (193km) south of Fairbanks. Access to the park is also provided by the Alaska Railroad, which has a daily summer service from Anchorage and Fairbanks. The train depot, the **Visitor Center** Ⓐ (tel: 683-2294, summer only), a bookstore and grill, the Wilderness Access Center, the Murie Science and Learning Center, the Riley Creek Campground, a Post Office and a general store are all within walking distance of each other. Shuttle buses provide a free service between them every half hour.

Campground and backcountry camping registration also takes place at the **Wilderness Access Center**. Denali Park has seven public roadside campgrounds containing a total of 215 sites. A couple of them, Igloo Creek and Sanctuary River,

are very small and have no water. One is for backpackers only. Some advance reservations are accepted campgrounds by phone or fax (tel: 800-622-7275, fax 907-264-4684; reservation forms can also be downloaded from www.nps.gov/dena) and the rest are available on a first-come, first-served basis.

During the peak summer season (late May–early Sept), all sites are quite often occupied by mid-morning. Should you arrive to find all campgrounds within the park full, you might check with the private campgrounds (located outside the boundary) that cater, primarily, to RV campers.

Dogsled demonstrations

While in the park entrance area visit the sled dog kennel, located behind the park headquarters building at Mile 3 of the Park Road. Since the 1920s, park rangers have used sled dogs as a means of patrolling the park, as they are the most practical means of getting around Denali in the winter months. The dogs have become so popular with visitors that rangers put on several dogsledding demonstrations every day during the summer season.

A guard on the McKinley Explorer.

BELOW: shops on the George Parks Highway.

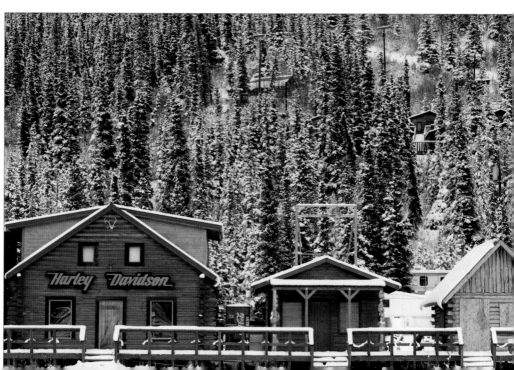

The shuttle bus system

The adventure of experiencing Denali National Park by road really begins when you step on a shuttle bus for an all-day trip into the park. There are several different bus trips, which all start at the **Wilderness Access Center**. The rangers can give you a bus schedule, and will explain how the system works.

The green shuttle bus trips, which go the whole 85 miles (136km) to Wonder Lake, do not provide a formal guided-tour program, although drivers will answer questions and help spot wildlife. Passengers can get on and off anywhere along the road, space permitting. The buses get very full in summer and should be booked well in advance (tel: 800-622-7275 or 272-7275), or at the Wilderness Access Center two days ahead.

The Denali History Tour bus goes to Primrose Ridge, about 17 road miles (27km) into the park, and the Tundra Wildlife Tour to the Toklat River (mile 53) or, if Denali is "out", to the Stony Hill Overlook (Mile 62). Snacks are included in the tour bus ticket price and there are periodic rest stops, but passengers must re-board the same bus (tel:

800-276-7234 for reservations). Further information about the two bus systems can be obtained on the park's website, www.nps.gov/dena.

Your chances of seeing wildlife, as well as Denali itself, are increased by taking as early a bus as possible. The first few depart at 6am. During the rest of the morning they leave every half-hour. The early buses are often in high demand. No food or drinks are available along the bus route, so be sure to take with you what you'll need for the day. Always be prepared for cool temperatures and rain regardless of what the early morning weather might be like.

The first leg of the bus route is the 14-mile (22-km) stretch between the entrance and the **Savage River**. The first glimpses of Denali hove into view in this area. This section of the Park Road goes through prime moose habitat; any time a moose or other animal is spotted, the bus will stop to allow passengers to watch and photograph the wildlife.

Moose are the biggest animals in the park – mature bulls can weigh as much as 1,500lbs (680kg). During the spring, watch for calves in this area. Cow moose

TIP

Alaska from the air
Flightseeing tours of Mount McKinley, plus landings on Ruth Glacier, are offered by Talkeetna Air Taxi (tel: 800-533 2219 or 907-733 2218).

BELOW: skiing at Ruth Glacier.

National parks from the air

If you're visiting Alaska as your dream vacation and trying to spread limited financial resources across a very large state, here's a sound piece of free advice: Go ahead and splurge by taking a flightseeing trip. You'll be glad you did, because no other mode of exploration will give as good an overview of all that makes this land so extraordinary. Soar over mountain peaks, swoop low over glacier-laden fjords, land on a glacier, peer down into deep, icy crevasses and get a panoramic, bird's-eye-view of wildlife, rivers, forests and scenic alpine meadows you'll otherwise only see in travel brochures. Air taxis and flightseeing companies are located in cities and towns throughout Alaska. For specific information on the flightseeing opportunities of your dreams, check with the Convention and Visitors Bureau in the city nearest your Alaska destination.

usually have one or two calves each year. At birth, a calf weighs about 30lbs (14kg). Moose calves are one of the fastest-growing animals in the world. By their first birthday, they often weigh over 600lbs (270kg).

Each September and October this section of Denali Park becomes a rutting ground for moose. The huge bulls challenge each other over harems of cows, and they are deadly serious. A bull can kill his opponent with his sharp antler points. Rutting bulls and cow moose with calves should always be considered extremely dangerous and given a wide berth. If they are approached too closely, both cows and bulls will charge a human. If you should surprise a moose, run from the animal immediately; unlike bears, they will not chase you down once you leave their "personal space."

Primrose Ridge

As your bus continues beyond the Savage River, you will pass a mountain to the north known as **Primrose Ridge ⑧**. Dall sheep are often seen on the higher slopes of Primrose. They have pure white wool – perfect winter camouflage – but

in summer, they readily stand out against the green tundra or dark rock formations. Like all wild sheep, Dall are generally found on or near steep cliffs, which are their security, as no predator can match their climbing speed or agility. Wolves and grizzlies can usually only catch weak or injured sheep, or those that have wandered too far from the crags.

The Dall ewes utilize the steepest cliffs in this area as lambing grounds. With luck, you may be able to spot young lambs on the higher slopes. Within a few days of birth, the lambs can match their mother's climbing ability. The lambs spend hours each day playing games of tag, king of the mountain and head-butting, which helps them develop their strength, agility and coordination.

Bands of rams may also be seen in the Primrose Ridge region. Rams are very concerned with the issue of dominance. A band will establish a pecking order based on the size of their horns, which are their most important status symbol. The older

Dall lambs seem to be born with the ability to climb.

BELOW:
two moose
exchange views.

rams have horns of such size that they can easily intimidate the younger ones. Head-butting contests determine which of the mature animals will be dominant. The reward comes during the fall rutting season when the top rams are the ones who get to do most of the mating.

The grizzlies of Sable Pass

By the time you reach **Sable Pass ⓒ** at Mile 39 you are surrounded by tundra, which is any area of plant growth above the treeline. Sable Pass has an elevation of 3,900ft (1,188 meters), well above the average local treeline of 2,400ft (730 meters). The cool temperatures and strong winds at these altitudes are too severe for trees. The low-growing tundra vegetation survives by taking advantage of the slightly warmer and less windy micro-environment at ground level.

Sable Pass is prime grizzly country. So many bears use this area that the Park Service has prohibited all off-road hiking here. Denali Park's total grizzly population is estimated at 200–300 bears. Grizzlies are omnivores: like humans, they eat both meat and vegetation. They would prefer to eat large animals such as moose, caribou and Dall sheep but they are not often successful as hunters. Tundra plants make up at least 90 percent of their diet. The tundra vegetation in places like Sable Pass offers a dependable, easily obtainable source of nutrition.

Grizzly cubs are born in January or February in the mother's hibernation den. The sow gives birth to between one and four cubs – the average is two – weighing about 1lb (200gm) each. Sable Pass is one of the best places in the world for viewing grizzly families. You may see the cubs being nursed, or racing across the tundra, play-fighting with each other. The sow usually drives off her young when they are 2½ years old, when they may weigh 100–150lbs (45–67kg). She then breeds again and gives birth to another litter the following winter.

When it feels threatened, the grizzly is among the most dangerous animals in North America. No visitors have been killed by a grizzly since the park's creation in 1917, and only a few people have been injured in bear attacks here, but these are large, powerful animals that can threaten your life if they are agitated or alarmed by your behavior. Visitors should

TIP

Hiking hint

Hiking on the tundra in Denali guarantees unstable and soggy footing. Many hikers wear knee-high rubber boots to keep their feet dry. A walking stick can be helpful.

BELOW: hiker above the Toklat River, Polychrome Pass.

do everything possible to avoid provoking a bear. Most will steer clear of humans if given the opportunity. The few attacks by bears on people in Denali have almost always been provoked, for instance mothers protecting their cubs from people who approached too closely. Park rangers can give you information on avoiding problems with grizzlies.

Your bus will stop for a rest break at **Polychrome Pass ⓓ** at Mile 45. The visually stunning, brightly colored Polychrome cliffs are volcanic rocks formed around 50 million years ago. The spectacular view to the south includes part of the Alaska Range, as well as a vast area of tundra.

Wolf observation

Polychrome Pass is a good place to watch for wolves. A local pack sometimes uses these flats as its hunting grounds, especially in spring when caribou are in migration. The Denali wolves range from white to black but most are gray. They may be traveling alone or in small groups. If a pack is sighted, look for a wolf with its tail in the air. This will be the alpha wolf, the leader of the pack,

although he may well be bringing up the rear. The alpha male often delegates the lead position to the beta wolf, his second in command.

In a wolf pack, the only members who normally breed are the alpha male and the alpha female. Their litter is born in the spring and all other members of the pack help to feed the young pups. Feeding a litter of five to 10 pups is a difficult job, even for the entire pack. If all its members tried to breed, the territory could not support the offspring. The pack is better served by limiting breeding to the dominant pair, who have proved themselves to be the fittest animals.

Much of what is now known about wolves was discovered by Adolph Murie, a biologist who was assigned to the park in the 1930s: he was the first scientist to extensively study wolf behavior in the field. Much of his observation took place in the Polychrome area. In 1944, Murie published *The Wolves of Mt McKinley*, one of the great classics of animal behavior. He concluded that wolves, which were preying primarily on the sick and weak Dall sheep, caribou and moose, were a necessary part of the

Tundra flowers.

BELOW:
observing a gray wolf in Denali Natiional Park.

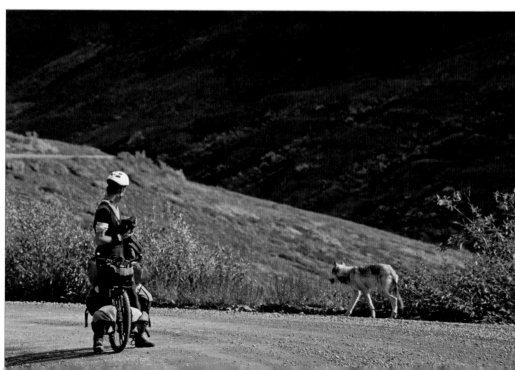

Denali ecosystem because they ultimately helped to keep their prey species in a strong and healthy state.

Caribou country

Caribou, the most social of the large Denali animals, are commonly seen in the Highway Pass area at Mile 58. In the spring, herds of several hundred pass through this area, heading toward their calving grounds to the east. Later in the season, they migrate back, moving toward their wintering grounds in the western and northern sections of the park. The herds are constantly on the move. Even as they feed, they rarely browse for more than a few moments. If they spent too long in one area, they would kill off the fragile tundra vegetation.

Caribou, like moose, have antlers rather than horns. Antlers are formed of bone and are shed every year, while sheep horns consist of keratin, the same material as our fingernails, and are never shed. The caribou bulls' antlers are fully developed by September and are used to fight for harems. These matches usually occur between Highway Pass and Wonder Lake. After their rutting season is over, the antlers drop off; without their massive weight the caribou have a better chance of surviving the winter, a stressful time.

Denali Park is a paradise for watching and photographing wildlife. Binoculars and a telephoto lens will allow you to enjoy the animals from a safe distance and in a way that won't disturb them. Grizzlies, bull moose and cows with calves should never be approached. Dall sheep and caribou bulls are fairly tolerant of people if you allow them to spot you when you are still a long way off, so they know you are not a predator.

As your bus approaches **Stony Hill Overlook E**, Mile 61, be prepared for a spectacular view of Denali. From the overlook, it is 37 miles (60km) to the summit. On a cloudless day, the crystal-clear Alaskan air makes the mountain appear much closer. After a stop at Stony Hill, the bus will continue 4 miles (6km) to **Eielson Visitor Center F** (extensively remodeled in 2007–8). Park rangers here can answer your questions and suggest good hiking routes in the local area. Restrooms, drinking water, maps and books are available here.

If you are on a shuttle bus that continues on to **Wonder Lake** , an additional 20 miles (32km) beyond Eielson, this will add about two hours to your day. If the weather is clear, it's well worth the time, particularly in the fall when the color is brightened by reds, oranges, and yellows, and caribou frequent the area. Denali remains in full view along the entire route. On the way, many species of waterfowl are seen in tundra ponds. In the evening, beavers can be seen swimming across these small ponds.

Walks and hikes

Most of Denali National Park is a true wilderness, and the best way to experience the park is by getting off the road, even if you go only a quarter mile or so. There are few official trails and these are mainly in the entrance area. Elsewhere, you are on your own. Despite the vast size of the Denali wilderness, route-making is not difficult for those who are experienced with maps. Since most of the park is open tundra, it is easy to choose a destination visually and hike straight to it, though often the distance is farther than you might expect and the terrain more rugged. You may leave the

shuttle bus wherever you choose, hike for a few hours and then catch a later bus anywhere along the road.

Good areas for day hikes include the Savage River, Primrose Ridge, Polychrome and Highway Passes, the Eielson area and Wonder Lake. Before you begin a day-hike, talk to a ranger at one of the visitor centers about safety tips. Maps of the area are available at both centers. Permits are required for overnight trips into the park's backcountry.

National park rangers offer a wide variety of interpretive programs to help you appreciate the area. Schedules of activities are posted at the Denali Visitor Center and at other locations throughout the park. The award-winning, high-definition film *Heartbeats of Denali* is shown throughout the day in the Denali Visitor Center's Karstens Theater. Evening programs are offered on a regular basis in most campgrounds. Guided walks and half-day hikes are given each day in different sections of the park. ❏

Moose antlers on display in Denali National Park.

BELOW:
outdorr cooking in Denali.

THE ALCAN

They said it couldn't be built. But the Alaska–Canada Highway, conceived as a military route in World War II, now runs all the way from Seattle to Delta Junction

Main attractions
PALMER
WASILLA
TALKEETNA

BELOW: more than 18,000 men helped build the highway.

In 1942, while the world was at war, thousands of American soldiers drove bulldozers instead of tanks, as they spent eight months building a 1,500-mile (2,400-km) highway from Dawson Creek, British Columbia, to Delta Junction, Alaska, just south of Fairbanks.

Construction of the Alaska–Canada Military Highway (the Alcan) was approved by President Franklin D. Roosevelt after the bombing of Pearl Harbor in 1941. The road linked the contiguous United States to Alaska, then still a territory, and a part of the US that many feared would be the next target. (In a propaganda broadcast, the Japanese forces thanked workers for opening a way for their own troops.)

Some said it couldn't be done, but construction, which began in March 1942, was completed in October. Soldiers battled the untracked wilderness of western Canada and eastern Alaska, along with spring mud, mosquitoes and, in fall, subfreezing temperatures. Rather than following the most direct route, the road linked existing airfields at Canada's Fort St John, Fort Nelson, Watson Lake and Whitehorse. At the project's peak, more than 11,000 military troops and 7,000 civilians were at work on the highway.

Wildlife viewing

Today, the former military road provides a leisurely and scenic way for visitors to reach Alaska year-round. The Alaska Highway still more or less follows its original path, wiggling its way northwest through British Columbia and the Yukon into Alaska's Interior. But what was once a wilderness adventure road is now a paved highway. The scenery is still breathtaking and the chances of seeing wildlife are good, but continual road improvements have eased many of the dangers that once made driving north to Alaska an ordeal.

Which is not to say the road is a Sunday drive. It's only two lanes wide, often without a center line, and although the entire length is asphalt-surfaced, sections have to be repaved continually. Drivers should watch for wildlife and construction workers on the road as well as potholes, gravel breaks and deteriorating shoulders. On the northern section of the highway, frost heaves – the result of the freezing and thawing of the ground – cause the pavement to ripple.

It's a long drive. Numerous towns dot the map along the highway, but stretches of wilderness threaten drivers with tiredness or boredom. And the "towns" are often no more than a collection of houses clustered around a store/gas station/hotel. When accidents occur, particularly in winter, it can be a long time before someone happens along to rescue a stranded or injured driver.

"I survived"

Despite the rigors of the road, more than 100,000 people make the trip every year. In Alaska, you'll often see cars sporting bumper stickers that proclaim "I survived the Alcan Highway." Most travelers make the journey during the summer months – June, July and August, when the days are long and the weather poses fewer hazards. From Seattle it's about 2,300 miles (3,700 km) (including the route along Interstate 5 to Trans-Canada Highway 1 and BC Highway 97 to Dawson Creek) and it takes most people about a week. An excellent guide is the Alaska *Milepost*, a 770-page map book (updated yearly) that documents the Alcan, plus almost every mile of every major highway in the state. ❑

It's a long way to London....

BELOW:
bull moose are
a traffic hazard.

FAIRBANKS

Beneath its workaday exterior, Fairbanks is a lively place with a friendly population. It offers the clearest view of the northern lights, and the museum at the University of Alaska Fairbanks is one of the best anywhere in the state

On August 26 1901, E.T. Barnette had just been dropped on a high wooded bank along the Chena River, along with 130 tons of equipment. How did this riverboat captain, dog musher and aspiring entrepreneur become marooned deep in the Alaska wilderness? The answer has all the ingredients of a true Alaskan adventure tale.

The birth of Fairbanks

Barnette journeyed to the Klondike in 1897, taking what was considered the rich man's route. He sailed from Seattle to St Michael (a coastal community, located on an island at the mouth of the Yukon River), where he was supposed to catch a sternwheeler to Dawson.

But when he arrived in St Michael, the boat had already departed. Undaunted, Barnette and several others bought a dilapidated sternwheeler, and set off for Dawson. Barnette piloted the craft to Circle and finally arrived in Dawson via dog sled, after freeze-up. He prospered that winter selling much-needed supplies to men in the gold fields, but the Klondike was too tame for the likes of this man.

During the winter of 1901, Barnette returned south to Seattle, and arranged a deal that, he speculated, would make him a rich man. He and a partner purchased $20,000 worth of equipment to outfit a trading post, not in the Klondike but at the half-way point of the trail connecting Valdez, on the coast, with Eagle, on the Yukon River. Barnette considered this

to be a strategically sound location to build what he hoped would become the "Chicago of the North," the industrial hub of the territory. It was at this point that the Valdez-to-Eagle Trail crossed the Tanana River, and he planned to accommodate both overland and river traffic.

Barnette shipped the equipment to St Michael and departed for Circle to purchase a sternwheeler. He arrived in St Michael without incident, but there the sternwheeler struck a submerged rock, and the bottom was torn from the boat. At this point, Barnette was more than

Main attractions

IMMACULATE CONCEPTION CHURCH
EAGLE RIVER
EKLUTNA
GIRDWOOD
OLD FEDERAL COURTHOUSE
EMPRESS THEATER
PIONEER PARK
STERNWHEELER NENANA
MUSEUM OF THE NORTH
CREAMERS FIELD
ESTER

LEFT: prepared for winter.
BELOW: a global outlook.

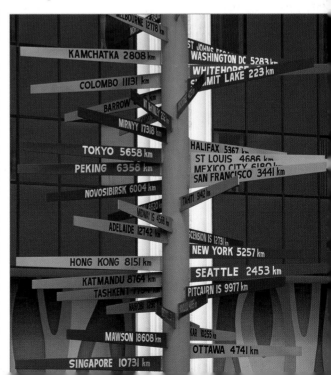

1,000 miles (1,600km) from his destination with 260,000lbs (120,000kg) of equipment, including a horse, a quantity of food, no ready cash and a worthless sternwheeler. It was time for another partner. He convinced the customs agent in St Michael to co-sign notes and made him a full partner.

Barnette struck a deal with the captain of the sternwheeler *Lavelle Young* to take him to Tanacross (Tanana Crossing). The fine print on the contract stated that if the *Lavelle Young* went beyond the point where the Chena joined the Tanana River and could go no farther, Captain E.T. Barnette would disembark with his entire load of supplies, no matter where they were.

As destiny would have it, the *Lavelle Young* could not float through the Tanana shallows, called Bates Rapids, so the captain steamed up the Chena River, convinced by the increasingly desperate Barnette that it would join up again with the Tanana River. It did not. Captain Barnette had no choice but to offload his massive pile of gear on a high bank with a good stand of trees. It seemed that his string of bad luck could get no worse.

The bridge across the Chena.

The new gold rush

Two down-and-out prospectors watched the sternwheeler's progress up the Chena from a hillside, now called Pedro Dome, about 20 miles (32 km) north of where Fairbanks is now located. The miners had found some "color" but no major strike, and were faced with the frustration of a 330-mile (530-km) round-trip hike back to Circle City to replenish much-needed supplies. The prospectors, Felix Pedro, an Italian immigrant, and Tom Gilmore, eagerly set off for the stranded boat, hoping to purchase necessities.

Barnette was surprised to see the prospectors but pleased to sell them anything they needed. Still possessed by his wild scheme to establish a trading post at Tanacross, Barnette sent to Montana for Frank Cleary, his brother-in-law. Cleary would guard the cache of supplies while Barnette and his wife returned to Seattle to obtain a boat capable of traveling the remaining 200 miles (320km) up the Tanana River to Tanacross. Braving the –40°F (–40°C) temperature, the Barnettes departed for Valdez and points south in March 1903.

In their absence Cleary decided to outfit Felix Pedro again, on credit this time because Pedro had no collateral. Although this broke Barnette's rule, Cleary's decision proved wise and shaped the future of the Interior. Just three months later, in July 1902, Pedro quietly announced to Cleary that he had struck paydirt.

Learning of the strike upon their return to the Chena camp later that summer, the Barnettes immediately abandoned all thoughts of moving to Tanacross. They had two shiploads of supplies in hand and were on the brink of the next gold rush. Clearly, there was money to be made.

Hundreds of gold-hungry prospectors swarmed out of Circle City, Dawson and Nome, and stampeded to the newest – and, supposedly, the richest – gold fields in the north. By the time they arrived, much of the promising land was already staked, most of it by "pencil miners" like Barnette who secured the claims only for the purpose of selling them later.

These clever businessmen staked as many as 100 claims of 20 acres (8 hectares) each, thus controlling vast amounts of potentially rich ground. And still the stampede continued.

On the return trip from Seattle, Barnette had spoken with Judge Wickersham about naming his little settlement. The judge offered his support to Barnette if he would use the name "Fairbanks," for Senator Charles Fairbanks of Indiana, who later became Vice President under Teddy Roosevelt; Fairbanks it was.

The community of Fairbanks in 1903 consisted of Barnette's trading post, numerous tents, a few log houses, and wooden sidewalks where the mud was particularly deep. What a fine tribute to the senator from Indiana.

Fairbanks today

Unless you have driven up the Alaska and Richardson or Parks Highways, you'll arrive in **Fairbanks ③** at the Fairbanks International Airport. You have to handle your own luggage as there are no porter services. Many hotels offer guests free transport and will send a vehicle if called. Taxis are usually plentiful, and there is also a limousine service (although it is more likely to be a van).

While 31,000 people call Fairbanks home, few people visit the town in winter, unless they absolutely have to; the

Long and short days
The maximum daylight on June 21 (summer solstice) in Fairbanks is 21 hours, 49 minutes. The sun rises at 1:59am, and sets at 11:48pm. On December 21, the sun rises at 10:59am and sets – just 3 hours and 42 minutes later – at 2:41pm.

BELOW: panning for gold in Fairbanks, tourist-style.

The Immaculate Conception Church.

BELOW:
temperatures can
fall to –40°F for
days at a time.

city's short days and frigid temperatures are hardly a draw; on the winter solstice, Fairbanks gets just three hours and 42 minutes of sunlight. Temperatures plummet to –40°F (–40°C) or even lower for days or weeks at a time, with the average December temperature registering –14°F (–26°C) in the city. A rather unpleasant side effect of temperatures below –20°F (–29°C) is ice fog, which hangs in the still air. The fog results from a temperature inversion trapping ice crystals, smoke and exhaust fumes in a blanket of cold air which stays close to the ground.

Orientation

The best source of information is the **Fairbanks Convention and Visitor Bureau and Information Center ❹** at 550 First Avenue (open daily in summer 8am–8pm; daily 10am–5pm in winter; tel: 456-5774 or 800-327-5774; www. explorefairbanks.com). This finely constructed log building offers hundreds of brochures on Alaskan attractions, and there is a visitor information telephone number, 456-INFO. The recorded message is available at any hour, is updated daily, and may include information on events as diverse as an evening opera performance or the starting time of a dog race. The bureau also provides a free, comprehensive visitor's guide to the Interior and a brochure for a self-guided tour of the town.

Here you will notice the monument to E.T. Barnette, marking the place where the town was born, which also makes it a good starting place for modern-day explorers. Here, too, is the obelisk that marks **Milepost 1,523** of the Alaska Highway. The milepost is hidden behind posing tourists most of the summer. Even with the completion of the Dalton Highway to Prudhoe Bay, Fairbanks has, since World War II, been touted as the end of the highway. Residents like to say that this is where the road ends and the wilderness begins.

A stroll through town

Several commercial sightseeing tours of Fairbanks' downtown area are available, but one good way to see the town is to turn right across the Cushman Street Bridge pausing for a look at the Chena River. The **Immaculate Conception Church ❸** stands directly across the

Ice sculpting

Competitors in the World Ice Art Championships, held in Fairbanks in March, carve their masterpieces from mammoth blocks of ice cut from ponds. Freezing together blocks, lifted into position by fork-lift trucks, can enable sculptures up to 24 ft high (7 meters) high. These can survive for three or four weeks in a park by the Chena River, depending on the weather. *See also page 257.*

From May to September, you can view ice carvings at **Fairbanks Ice Museum** (500 Second Avenue, tel: 907-451-8222, www.icemuseum .com, entrance fee). A film chronicles the championships, you can have your picture taken sitting in an ice chair, and a 20-ft (6-meter) ice slide provides a brief thrill.

river from the Information Center. The church originally stood on the opposite side of the river at the corner of First and Dunkle. In 1911, Father Francis Monroe decided it should be closer to the hospital on the north side of the Chena. Many Catholics pitched in to move the building across the frozen river. Visitors are welcome to come inside and enjoy the stained-glass windows and the pressed-tin ceiling paneling.

Half a block north on the opposite side of the street is the *Fairbanks Daily News Miner* building at 200 N. Cushman Street. The *News Miner* publishes seven days a week, carrying on a long tradition. Judge Wickersham published the first paper, the *Fairbanks Miner*, on May 9, 1903. All seven copies sold for $5 each, making the first edition one of the most expensive in the world. He used the money to help finance his 1903 expedition to climb Denali (Mount McKinley) – the first group to ever make such an attempt. Wickersham's pioneering group reached an elevation of about 11,000 ft (3,350 meters) before being turned back by near-vertical walls and tremendous avalanches.

Recross the Chena River to **St Matthew's Episcopal Church** **C** at 1029 First Avenue. The altar of St Matthew's was carved from a single piece of wood, but no one is quite sure of the origin of the huge chunk. The stained-glass windows are of special interest; they portray images of Jesus, Mary and Joseph with Alaskan Native features.

Near the church, at the corner of First and Cushman, is the **Key Bank** **D**, which was started as a First National Bank on that very site in June 1905. "Square Sam" Bonnifield and his brother John founded the bank, now the oldest national bank in Alaska. "Square Sam" was given his nickname because he had been an honest gambler in Circle City, and miners could turn their backs while he was weighing a poke of gold.

Downtown

Head south down Cushman Street, the heart of downtown Fairbanks – although not exactly a fast-throbbing one. The **Old Federal Courthouse** stands near the intersection of Second Avenue and Cushman. When Judge Wickersham (the man who originally suggested to Barnette that

Winter and summer
An increasing winter draw is the aurora borealis; Japanese tourists, in particular, have been coming to Fairbanks to watch the spectacular northern lights ripple and wave in winter skies. But then there's summer, with the sun lingering for up to 22 hours each day. In July, the average temperature in Fairbanks can be more than 61°F (16°C)

BELOW:
winter, when
Fairbanks is left
to the Alaskans.

the town should be called Fairbanks) officially moved the Federal Court here in 1903, he built the courthouse on this piece of real estate, donated by Barnette, securing the future of the young settlement. The original wooden structure burned down, and the present building was completed in 1934. It included the first elevator in the Interior. Federal offices soon required more space and were relocated, leaving the building open for tasteful remodeling into office space and shops.

The next stop is **Co-op Plaza** at 535 Second Avenue. Of 1927 vintage, this building was Captain Lathrop's gift to the people of Fairbanks. Before then, the buildings in Fairbanks were constructed of wood because, it was believed, no other material could withstand the test of a –60°F (–51°C) winter. This concrete affair was originally the **Empress Theater**, outfitted by Captain Lathrop with 670 seats and the first pipe organ in the Interior. Fairbanks' locals tend to use "the Co-op" as a meeting place, so be sure to take a look. People visiting Fairbanks from the villages often eat at the diner and visit the specialty shops.

During the mid-1970s, while the trans-Alaska oil pipeline was under construction, Second Avenue was the scene of incessant activity, with bars packed at all hours. Workers flew to town during rest periods from remote construction camps, only to spend most of their time (and money) along Second Avenue.

If you carry on down Cushman, you will come to the area known as **The Line**, the block of Fourth Avenue to your right, as far as Barnette Street. To ensure that no one unwittingly wandered into this sinful area, the booming city of Fairbanks erected tall, Victorian wooden gates at both ends of the avenue. Both sides of the boulevard were lined with small log cabins housing prostitutes. The Line is gone now, replaced by the less colorful downtown businesses and parking lots.

The Ice Palace

Cross Cushman Street again and continue on Fourth Avenue past Lacey Street. These names also originated from Judge Wickersham, always alert for an opportunity to win political friends, who requested that the streets be named for Congressmen Francis Cushman of Tacoma and John F. Lacey of Iowa.

TIP

Seeing the lights
Fairbanks is one of the best places to see the aurora borealis (or northern lights). In Fairbanks, auroral displays are visible an average of 243 days per year.

RIGHT: a tribute to the pioneers, *The Unknown First Family.*

Midnight Baseball

Fairbanks residents do not allow the summer solstice to slip by uncelebrated. On June 21, the semi-pro Alaska Goldpanners baseball team plays the Midnight Sun game at Growden Field with the first pitch crossing the plate at 10:30pm –and the entire played under natural light. Also known as the "high noon at midnight classic" the annual event celebrated its 100-year anniversary during the 2005 summer solstice. There is also an arts and crafts fair, a midnight fun run (attracting 3,000+ runners), and speedboat racing, when sleek racing boats propelled by twin 50-horsepower outboard motors zoom down the Chena, Tanana and Yukon rivers to Galena, returning at breakneck speed to Fairbanks and the finish line at Pike's Landing.

On the next block, bounded by Lacey and Noble streets and Third and Fourth avenues, towers the "**Ice Palace**." Officially the **Northward Building** Ⓔ, it was the first steel-girded skyscraper built in the Interior, and became the inspiration for Edna Ferber's 1958 novel *Ice Palace*. The "palace" in the novel is a modern skyscraper built by a ruthless millionaire named Czar Kennedy. Fairbanks' locals recognized in Czar Kennedy the reflection of a prominent businessman, developer and politician, Captain Austin E. Lathrop.

That's about all there is to downtown Fairbanks, except for the attractive park known as **Golden Heart Plaza**, next to the **Visitor Center**, between Wendell Street and the Chena River (go south up Lacey Avenue from the Ice Palace), where you'll find the bronze statue entitled *The Unknown First Family*.

City shopping

Fairbanks offers a cornucopia of gifts for the traveler. Gold-nugget jewelry, always a favorite, is priced by the pennyweight (dwt) with 20 dwt equal to one troy ounce (1 dwt = 1.555 grams). Remember that nuggets used in jewelry command a premium price, which is higher than that for raw gold.

Native handicrafts from the Interior are also treasured souvenirs. The Authentic Native Handicraft Symbol assures visitors that they are buying the genuine article. Be careful, as counterfeits abound. Favorite items include beaded slippers, beaded mittens and gloves, birch bark baskets, porcupine quill jewelry and dolls made with fur.

Pioneer Park

Pioneer Park Ⓕ, a 44-acre (18-hectare) city park at the corner of Airport Way and Peger Road, to the south of the downtown area, is a snapshot of life in the Golden Heart of Alaska (open daily in summer 11am–9pm; admission free; tel: 459-1087; www.co.fairbanks.ak.us. parks&rec/pioneerpark/; or write to PO Box 71267, Fairbanks, AK 99707). You can get a shuttle bus to the park from the Visitors' Bureau and from many of the main hotels in town.

The **"Mining Valley"** on the west end of the park exhibits many machines used to extract gold. Sluice boxes, dredge

TIP

The fur trade
The Alaskan Interior produces some of the finest lynx, marten, wolverine, fox and wolf fur in the world. Many people disapprove of buying furs; if you want them, Fairbanks is the place to purchase raw or tanned furs and fur coats, jackets and hats – although you should be aware of customs regulations if you are taking such items out of the United States.

BELOW:
barbecue at
Pioneer Park.

TIP

Bird's-eye view

A memorable way of seeing those parts of Interior Alaska close to Fairbanks is by taking a flightseeing trip in an air taxi, helicopter or hot-air balloon. Operators change, but the Fairbanks Convention and Visitor Bureau has up-to-date details of reputable firms (www. explorefairbanks.com).

BELOW:
Pioneer Park.

buckets, a stamp mill and other equipment lend an air of authenticity to the display.

Take a stroll through the **Mining Town** section of the complex, which includes an assortment of original structures rescued from the boom-town period. Every building is a piece of history, including Judge Wickersham's home, the first frame house in Fairbanks, which was built by the judge in 1904 as a surprise for his wife. It is a rather melancholy reminder of life in early Fairbanks: the bedridden Mrs Wickersham spent most of that summer sleeping in a tent as fresh air was thought to help cure tuberculosis.

In Nenana *(see page 261)*, even the building now housing the **Park Office** had a spicy past as a brothel, and the **Gold Rush Town** is packed with small shops containing an interesting array of crafts.

The **Sternwheeler Nenana** is listed in the National Register of Historic Places because so few of these vessels remain. It was a classic paddlewheeler with a colorful history on the waterways of the Interior. Imagine leaning back in the captain's chair, the stack belching sparks, and the crew scurrying about the deck as

you maneuver the craft through the Yukon River.

Within the park you'll also find the **Alaska Native Village**, with artifacts and demonstrations of crafts still carried out in remote parts of the Interior.

If you get hungry, follow your nose to the **Alaska Salmon Bake** (open daily in summer 5–9pm) – great value for a tasty Alaskan meal; king salmon, halibut and ribs are grilled over an open alder fire to give them a very special flavor. After dinner, you could saunter over to the **Palace Saloon** and enjoy a drink while cancan girls entertain you.

University pursuits

The **University of Alaska Fairbanks** ⓖ (UAF) is located on a bluff overlooking Fairbanks and the Tanana Valley (take a Red or Blue Line bus from the town center). Established in 1917 as the Alaska Agricultural College and School of Mines, UAF is the main campus for a system that operates four-year satellites in Anchorage and Juneau. An emphasis on high latitude and Alaska research has earned UAF an excellent reputation.

The 2,500-acre (1,000-hectare) campus is a town unto itself, with its own post office, radio and TV stations, a fire department and the traditional college facilities. A trip to the UAF campus is well worthwhile, and it's also a good opportunity to relax en route at the turnout on Yukon Drive and absorb the view of the Alaska Range. The large marker, with mountain silhouettes and elevations, helps you identify the splendid peaks fringing the southern horizon. It's the best Fairbanks view you'll get of Mount McKinley. Free guided walking tours of the university are offered most days during the summer (tel: 474-7211; www.uaf.edu).

The **University of Alaska Museum of the North** ⓗ on the UAF campus is a great idea for visitors to the Interior (907 Yukon Drive, tel: 474-7505; www.uaf. edu/museum; open daily in summer 9am–7pm; in winter, weekdays 9am–5pm and weekends noon–5pm; entrance charge). The museum is one of the best in the state, dividing Alaska's regions with an interdisciplinary approach to each, including cultural artifacts and scientific equipment. Displays include prehistoric objects extricated during mining operations from the permanently frozen ground. A huge, 36,000-year-old bison carcass found near Fairbanks, preserved in the permafrost, is displayed, complete with skin and flesh.

The Native Cultures displays are an educational introduction to the Athabascan, Eskimo, Aleut and Tlingit cultures. The collections date back to 1926, when the president of the school assigned Otto William Geist the task of amassing Eskimo artifacts. In the summer, there are daily shows on the aurora and Native culture.

Tours are also provided at the **Geophysical Institute** (tel: 474-7558 for tour information or check www.gi.alaska.edu), a world center for arctic and aurora research, during which a spectacular film of the aurora borealis is shown. A free UAF off-campus tour is offered on Yankovich Road about 1 mile (2km) from Ballaine Road at the **Large Animal Research Station** (tel: 474-7207),

formerly known as the Musk Ox Farm. These woolly prehistoric creatures graze in research pastures together with moose, reindeer and caribou.

A wildlife trail

Save a little shoe leather for a very special wildlife trail situated within the city limits of Fairbanks. **Creamers Field** ❶ (tel: 459-7307; www.creamersfield.org) at 1300 College Road was originally Charles Creamers' dairy farm, started in 1920. The 250 acres (100 hectares) remained in active production until the land was purchased by the state and was set aside as a waterfowl refuge in 1967.

While hiking the nature trails you can see many species of animals, including diving ducks, shorebirds, cranes, foxes or even a moose. The real show, however, takes place in late April to early May and again in August and September when the sandhill cranes, Canadian honkers and ducks congregate in the field – it really is something to see. Take a Red Line bus to the trailhead, where the Department of Fish and Game office will provide you with a trail guide.

It's safe to approach this grizzly, on display at the University of Alaska Museum.

BELOW:
the University of Alaska Fairbanks.

Wheel into the past

Riverboats have never been far removed from the history of Fairbanks, since E.T. Barnette's load of supplies was put ashore. Jim and Mary Binkley continue the tradition with river tours aboard the 700-passenger *Discovery III*. The four-hour, twice-daily excursions cover 20 miles (32km) on the Chena and Tanana rivers. The Binkleys' narration brings history to life along the river banks.

To reach the sternwheeler's port of departure at the landing off Dale Road, take Airport Way toward the airport, turn onto Dale Road, and watch for the signs. Reservations are recommended (tel: 479-6673 or 866-479-6673; www.riverboatdiscovery.com).

As you float along, take note of the **Pump House Restaurant**, where you might like to eat later *(see page 255)*.

Special events in Fairbanks

The winter festival spirit has been revived in Fairbanks and is now called the **Winter Carnival**, celebrated during the second and third weeks of March. Fairbanks has traditionally hosted the **North American Open Sled Dog Championship** at this time. The North American, as locals refer to it, was first run in 1946 and is not to be missed. The sprint race is run on three consecutive days (20 miles/32km the first two days and a tough 30 miles/48km the third day), with the start and finish line in downtown Fairbanks on Second Avenue. It attracts the finest sprint dog mushers, racing teams of up to 20 dogs.

Another sled dog race, not a sprint, is the **Yukon-Quest**, a grueling 1,000-mile (1,600-km) race between Whitehorse, Yukon Territory, Canada, and Fairbanks, following the old Gold Rush and mail delivery routes. Held in February, the race, first run in 1984, ends in Fairbanks in odd-numbered years and runs in the opposite direction in even-numbered years. The fastest recorded time, in 2007, was 10 days, 2 hours and 37 minutes. The Quest challenges the sturdiest of long-distance mushers.

A full slate of events continues throughout the festival including ice carving. The **Festival of Native Arts** takes place in February at the university's main campus, along with Native-style potlatches.

Moose matters

Moose, like caribou, have antlers instead on horns. They shed their "racks" following the fall mating season, and begin to re-grow them in the spring. During the month of June, the points on moose antlers grow over one centimeter – and gain as much as one pound in weight (450gm) – per day.

BELOW:
Discovery III
on the Chena.

The Olympics

For those in Fairbanks during July, the **World Eskimo-Indian Olympics** is recommended. The list of games includes some surprises as well as the expected: the blanket toss competition is fun to watch, as is the Native Baby Contest; the Knuckle Hop, Ear Pulling and Ear Weight competitions are exactly what they say, and seem excruciatingly painful; and the muktuk-eating contest (muktuk is whale blubber), fish-cutting and seal-skinning competitions are opportunities to learn more about the Native cultures. It is also a rare opportunity for travelers to buy arts and crafts directly from Native artisans – beadwork, baskets, skin garments, masks and carvings. *(For more, see pages 256–7).*

Although officially called the **Alaska State Fair** on even years and the **Tanana Valley Fair** on odd years, almost everyone uses the latter name every year. The fair, held at the College Road fairgrounds during the second or third week of August, has grown to be the most popular event in the Interior, with attendances of more than 100,000 people. The prime attraction for travelers is the Harvest Hall filled with colossal vegetables. Here you will see what the long hours of summer daylight can produce in the Interior, including huge radishes and 70-lb (32-kg) cabbages.

Then there is nature's own special event, the northern lights *(aurora borealis)*, which are seen frequently and vividly in and around Fairbanks from late August through early April (when skies are darkest). In winter this extraordinary show can last for hours; in mid-summer the sky is too light for it to be visible.

The fringe

To enjoy a trip back in time, head for the settlement of **Ester**, 7 miles (11km) from Fairbanks off the Parks Highway. To the outsider, Ester is just another faded mining community, but during the summer, the **Malemute Saloon** swings open its doors to vaudeville shows and evening readings of Robert Service. The latter usually silences even those lively *cheechakos* (newcomers to the north) who hang around near the door. The sawdust floor and sourdough bartenders pushing beer across the bar mingle in a frozen moment,

TIP

Take to the river
You can get a relaxed view of Fairbanks by hiring a canoe and spending the day paddling around the Chena River. Canoes can be hired for $35–40 a day from Alaska Outdoor Rentals & Guides (Pioneer Park, tel: 457-2453) or 7 Bridges Boats & Bikes (4312 Birch Lane, tel: 479-0751).

Spot the difference in Golden Days

Felix Pedro, the prospector who hit gold back in 1903, sported a beard, and so does most of the male population during the third week of July when Fairbanks celebrates Golden Days. One event is a Felix Pedro look-alike contest *(pictured right)*, and there is a re-enactment of Pedro's ride into town after he discovered gold in 1902.

His ride is part of the festival's biggest attraction, a parade through downtown Fairbanks complete with antique cars, clowns, and marching bands. Innocents need to be aware of the roving jail, because those not wearing a fund-raising button are liable to be incarcerated for as long as it takes them to bribe the jailkeeper.

Other party events include an E.T. Barnette Look-Alike Contest and a Hairy Legs, Chest, Beard and Mustache Contest. A Rubber Duckie Race offers prizes worth more than $20,000. Spectators buy numbered

tickets, after which the Golden Days executive committee drops about 6,000 yellow ducks, each carrying a number, from the Wendell Street Bridge into the Chena River. The numbered ducks float downstream to the finish line at the Golden Heart Plaza.

Golden Days has been described as a politically incorrect blend of Mardi Gras, Halloween and Founders' Day – with a decidedly Alaskan twist.

*Hard hats for sale
on Steese Highway.*

BELOW:
gold dredge on
Steese Highway.

and past and present become one as the deep-voiced rendition of Service's *The Shooting of Dan McGrew* rings out. Locals hang around the **Red Garter**, and everyone enjoys the **Ester Gold Camp Restaurant**. The rest of the year, the 1,800 residents of Ester sink into the solitude of small-town Alaska.

The gold dredges in the vicinity of Fairbanks, mute since 1966, stand like aging, silent dinosaurs, with necks outstretched, waiting. The dredges, like so many pieces of local history, are strewn about the hills waiting for some new purpose.

The easiest of the dredges to visit from town is **Gold Dredge No. 8**, rusting at Mile 9 Old Steese Highway. The five-deck ship, over 250ft (76 meters) long, displaced 1,065 tons as it plied the gold pay dirt of Goldstream and Engineer creeks. Tours of the dredge are available daily during the summer (tel: 457-6058; www.golddredgeno8.com). At time of writing, the admission fee was $25, which includes a chance to try your hand at gold panning; you keep what you pan as a memento. The dredge is only 600 feet from the best view of the **Trans-Alaska oil pipeline** (at Mile 8.4), which parallels the highway above the permafrost-rich ground.

The big ditch

Large-scale mining demands lots of water. J.M. Davidson proposed building an 80-mile (130-km) water system to bring water from the Chatanika River to the diggings on Fox, Cleary and Goldstream creeks. A 5,000-kilowatt power plant was erected, as well as six or seven dredges, and shops and camps to maintain the equipment and house the crews.

During construction of the **Davidson Ditch**, sections of the Steese Highway were built to facilitate access. The Ditch was completed in 1930 and was capable of carrying 56,000 gallons (254,500 liters) of water a minute. After the dredges were put to rest, this system continued to generate electricity until the flood of 1967 destroyed it. Remnants of the Ditch are visible in several places along the Steese Highway. ❑

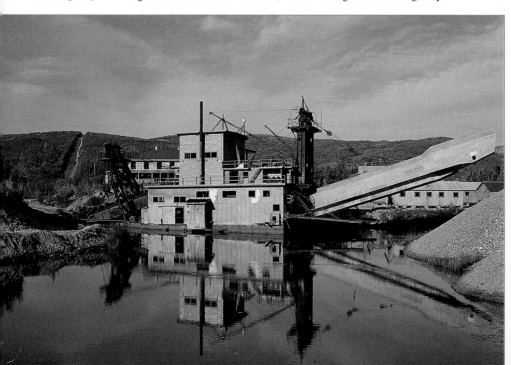

RESTAURANTS & BARS

Prices for a three-course dinner per person with a half-bottle of house wine:
$ = $15 or less
$$ = $15–$20
$$$ = $20–$30
$$$$ = over $30

Bakery Restaurant
69 College Road
tel: (907)456-8600
Home-style meals and freshly baked deserts in a family-friendly restaurant. Open for breakfast, lunch and dinner. $–$$

Gambardella's Pasta Bella
706 Second Avenue
tel: (907) 457-4992
www.gambardellas.com
Southern Italian cuisine, including its famous lasagne, is served indoors on white tablecloths or, in summer, outside on a garden terrace. Beer and wine. $–$$$

Pike's Landing
4438 Airport Way
tel: (907) 479-6500.
www.pikeslodge.com
A favorite local restaurant and bar located on the banks of the Chena River. Dine inside on linen-draped tables or out on the deck in the sunshine. Lunch and dinner. $–$$$$

RIGHT: Fairbanks eateries provide great variety.

The Pump House Restaurant and Saloon
796 Chena Pump Road
tel: (907) 479-8452
www.pumphouse.com
Steak and seafood served in large dining rooms in an historic gold-mining building on the banks of the Chena River. Tables on a deck over the water are available, weather permitting. Beer and wine. $$$–$$$$

Soapy Smith's
543 Second Avenue
tel: (907) 451-8380
Reliable burgers served in family-run café dressed up as pioneer saloon-bar. $$

Thai House
526 Fifth Avenue
tel:(907) 452-6123
A Thai family, dressed in beautiful national costumes, serves excellently prepared (spicy) Thai cuisine in a simple storefront restaurant. $

The Turtle Club
Mile 10 Old Steese Highway,
tel: (907) 457-3883
www.alaskanturtle.com
Known for delicious, generous servings of prime rib and seafood, fine wine and friendly service. This busy, casual restaurant, a favorite with locals and visitors, is located ten miles out of Fairbanks. Bar. $$–$$$$

Two Rivers Lodge/ Tuscan Gardens
Mile 16 Chena Hot Springs Road
tel: (907) 488-6815
www.tworiverslodge.com
Located inside a rustic log roadhouse, this outstanding restaurant's menu includes excellent steak and seafood served in a relatively formal setting. Outside, on the deck over the duck pond, inexpensive, casual meals are cooked in a Tuscan brick oven. Bar. $$–$$$$

THE WORLD ESKIMO-INDIAN OLYMPICS

The annual games in Fairbanks may seem pretty whacky, but there's a good reason why the participants are proud of their skills

To those unfamiliar with Alaska Native tradition and lifestyle, the athletic feats performed during the annual World Eskimo-Indian Olympics in Fairbanks each July may seem bizarre. What are those people doing hopping around on their toes and knuckles? And why are they playing tug-o-war with their ears? You won't see conventional events here, such as the pole vault or the 100-meter dash. Instead, be prepared for games of raw strength, endurance, agility and concentration.

Games of survival

Survival has been the name of the game for Alaska's Native people for thousands of years. It was essential to be disciplined both mentally and physically, to be ready for the unexpected. It was also important to work together for the common good.

The four-man carry, for example, represents the strength needed to haul firewood or moose or caribou carcasses back home. During this game four men hang from a fifth, who walks as far as he can before collapsing. The one- and two-foot high kicks require contestants to jump off the floor and kick a suspended object before landing on the kicking foot. The kicks are said to have originated as a means of signaling to a village, while the messenger was still some way off, that a whale had been taken and the villagers should help haul the massive animal to shore. Other events include the blanket toss, fish-cutting competition, and seal-skinning contest.

The games, first held in 1961, bring to life a time when Native people would gather in villages for friendly competitions, story-telling, dancing and games. The host village provided food and lodging and visitors brought news from the surrounding areas. The six interwoven rings of the WEIO represent Alaska's six major tribes: Aleut and Alutiiq, Athabascan, Eskimo (Inupiat and Yup'ik), Haida, Tlinglit, and Tsimshian.

RIGHT: The high jump
A woman competes in the one foot high-kick. Native women began participating in the annual games in the 1970s and in 1983 were allowed to enter the punishing "knuckle hop," in which competitors, adopting a push-up position, have to hop forward on their knuckles and toes.

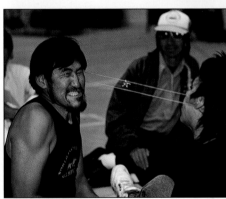

TOP: Team spirit
Traditional dancing has always been an important aspect of the Eskimo-Indian Olympics, and contestants are lured onto the floor to join spectators during any breaks in the competition. There are also performances by various dance groups.

ABOVE: A not so playful tug
The ear pull, among the most painful of the games' events, is strictly a game of endurance. Elders say the ability to withstand great pain was necessary for survival. Contestants sit on the floor facing each other with a piece of twine looped over one of their ears. A tug of war begins. If the twine slips from a participant's ear, the other contestant wins the round. The winner is the one who wins two out of three rounds. Then there's the toe kick, the Eskimo stick pull, the arm pull, the ear weight…

SNOW SCULPTING: AN EPHEMERAL ART

Anchorage is a long way from Fairbanks and the Eskimo-Indian Olympics, but it has its own crowd-pulling event, the annual Fur Rendezvous. Snow sculpting is among its most popular attractions, and holds its own against zany games of snowshoe softball and sled-dog races. Dancing salmon and skating penguins are among the figures sculpted out of snow. The finished creations draw hundreds to the display site north of downtown.

Sculptors, working alone, in pairs, or as a team, create their whimsical masterpieces from giant blocks of soft, clean, hard-packed snow. Each block stands 10ft (3 meters) tall and stretches 8ft (2.5 meters) across. Towering lights allow participants to work round the clock during the week preceding the festival. The rules are pretty straightforward: no power tools, props or extra snow; other than that, almost anything goes.

Unlike ice sculpting, which is more precise and requires greater skill, snow sculpting attracts a wide variety of participants, from scout troops and high-school students to corporate executives – anyone crazy enough to want to spend hours in the cold turning a block of show into a gold rush-era saloon, a trapper's cabin or a replica of The Three Bears.

LEFT: Old-fashioned beat
A village elder drums and sings during the games. The drums are made in the traditional style, using animal skin stretched tightly across a wooden frame.

BELOW: Balancing act
A young competitor concentrates hard as he tries to maintain his balance on the greasy pole, one of the events most popular with the games' onlookers.

BELOW RIGHT: Break dance
A Native woman dances to the infectious beat of the drums during a pause between competitive events.

ABOVE: Dance costumes
Spectators often wear elaborate dance costumes, whose material depends on which part of the state the wearer comes from. Many have intricate bead work.

BEYOND FAIRBANKS

Mining trails, dogsled tracks, and rivers provided early
transportation links connecting Fairbanks to the
surrounding communities, and with the rest of Alaska

Trails, like the threads of a spider's web, spun into Fairbanks from every direction in the early 1900s. The more popular routes were eventually transformed from dog-sled tracks to the paved and gravel roadways that now link the rest of Alaska to Fairbanks, the commercial hub of the Interior.

The first trail-cum-highway in all of Alaska, the **Richardson**, was originally a pack trail between the then-bustling mining settlements of Eagle and Valdez. Following the gold rush, the trail was extended to Fairbanks, linking the Interior to an ice-free port. Today, the Richardson – named after Wilds P. Richardson, the US Army general who managed the road's upgrade in 1910 – joins with the Alaska Highway for the 98 miles (157km) between Fairbanks and Delta Junction.

North Pole

If you take the Richardson Highway, your first stop may well be 14 miles (22km) southeast of Fairbanks at **North Pole** ㉜, the home, children are delighted to learn, of Santa Claus. Urban renewal forced Santa to move closer to the highway, where he's situated today. He poses year-round for pictures at **Santaland** (tel: 907-488-9123; www.santalandrv.com), a thriving RV park on the Richardson Highway, and one that gives visitors an idea of the enterprising types who homesteaded this area during the 1930s and 1940s.

They were a new wave of pioneers who found Fairbanks too crowded and

who didn't mind living in this low-lying basin where winter temperatures are severe enough for the nickname "North Pole" to stick and become official.

Today, North Pole is home to more than 1,700 people and a surrounding population of 13,000. It has its own utilities, brand-new shopping malls and a large Williams petroleum refinery taking crude from the nearby trans-Alaska pipeline. It is best known as the town where it's Christmas all year round, where the **Santa Claus House** (101 St Nicholas Drive) sells every kind of fes-

Main attractions
NORTH POLE
EAGLE
NENANA
CENTRAL
CIRCLE
CHENA HOT SPRINGS
LEVENGOOD
MINTO
MANLEY

LEFT: the northern lights. **BELOW:** Santa checks his mailbox at North Pole.

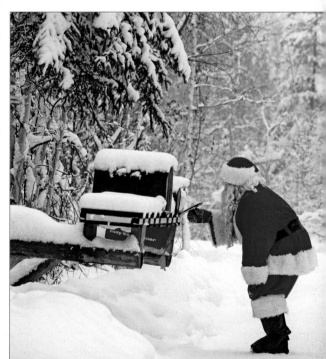

tive item you could dream of, and the post office is swamped with children's letters in December and it will mail letters "from Santa" for $7.50 or $10.

As surely as there is gold in the hills, there are buffalo and barley in **Delta Junction** ③. The **Tanana Valley** is one of the state's largest agricultural areas, with most of the farming centered in the Delta area. Despite the typical Interior winter climate, the valley supports the Delta Barley Project, a state-sponsored attempt to introduce large-scale grain production to the Interior. Although beset by troubles, at 90,000 acres (36,500 hectares), this farming venture, begun in 1978, keeps alive the pioneering spirit.

But what about the buffalo? Although they could be the spirit watchers of the shaggy bison who ranged the Interior millennia ago, this herd was actually imported from Montana and introduced to the area specifically as a game animal. The original 23-member herd now numbers a few hundred. They have even been granted their own large farm but this in no way discourages them from haunting the barley patch. Although the buffalo are rarely seen from the road in summer,

Beware of collisions.

RIGHT:
panning for gold
in the Yukon River.

pull over at Mile 241 on the Richardson Highway and scan the country across the Delta River for a possible glimpse.

Landing up at Eagle

After Delta Junction the Richardson becomes the Alaska Highway. Follow this some 110 miles (175km) to Tetlin Junction and take the rough gravel Taylor Highway for a further 160 miles (255km) and you will come to **Eagle** ③, where the road ends (the road closes in winter and snow isolates the community). This is a jumping-off place for Yukon River paddlers, as well as an official stop for river explorers floating from Dawson City. The first city on the American side of the Yukon, Eagle has a post office where river travelers check in with US customs.

Present-day Eagle had its beginnings in 1874 when the far-reaching and powerful Northern Commercial Company (NC) stretched its commercial fingers along the Yukon River and established a trading post near here. With the arrival of prospectors overflowing from the 1898 Klondike gold rush at Dawson City, just upriver over the border in Canada, this quiet riverbank was transformed into a

A Town Called Chicken

The Interior town of Chicken, Alaska is located about 100 road miles southwest of Eagle, at mile 66 of the Taylor Highway. The original inhabitants of the area were Han Kutchin Indians. Following the discovery of gold on (what is now) Upper Chicken Creek in 1886, a settlement was soon established as a hub for miners of the Fortymile Mining District. The residents wanted to name their new town "Ptarmigan," after the plump, ground-dwelling, game bird (now the state bird of Alaska) but were unsure of the spelling. They eventually settled on the more easily spelled "Chicken."

The author Robert Specht brought considerable notoriety to the area with the publication of *Tisha*, in 1984. Based on a true story, the book told of a 19-year-old schoolteacher, Anne Purdy, who traveled to Chicken in 1927, taught the children, married a local Indian man and remained in the community throughout much of her life. The dozen or so buildings of the original town site are listed on the National Register of Historic Place.

Today, the town's 22 residents enjoy lives of quiet isolation, home schooling their children and fur trapping during winters, and panning for gold or working in tourism in summer.

brazen mining town of 1,700 people. Seized by gold fever, thousands more, digging in every tributary of the Yukon, swept through the territory.

Judge James Wickersham built a federal courthouse here in 1900, a major army fort was established, and the Valdez-to-Eagle telegraph line spun out an historic message in 1905 when Roald Amundsen, passing through after his successful expedition into the Northwest Passage, made his announcement to the world from Eagle. By 1910 the gold muckers had vanished, trekking after even richer dreams near Fairbanks. They left behind 178 people, about the same population as today. But the buildings still stand and Eagle has undertaken a program to restore many of its fine older structures.

The Eagle Historical Society (tel: 547-2325; www.eagleak.org) conducts a free walking tour that includes **Judge Wickersham's Courthouse**, built by fines he imposed on gamblers and prostitutes in the rowdy mining town. Inside are the judge's desk and an early map of the country constructed of papier-mâché and moose blood. Also open for inspection is US Army **Fort Egbert**, abandoned in

1911, and the only remaining frontier fort of its type left in the state.

Summer visitors will find the basic necessities – laundry, restaurant, lodging, groceries, gas station, airstrip and mechanic shop. For those who want to go further "upriver," a daily commercial cruise motors between Eagle and Dawson City. Make reservations in advance with Gray Line of Alaska (tel: 277-5581; www.graylineofalaska.com), which also offers a package tour of the area. For information on paddling through the Yukon-Charley Rivers National Preserve, contact the National Park Service Visitor Center, just off 1st Avenue across the airstrip from town (tel: 547-2233; www.nps.gov/yuch).

Railway town

Take State Highway 3, the **George Parks Highway**, 64 miles (103km) south of Fairbanks and while still in the rolling hills of the Tanana Valley you will reach the town of **Nenana** ㉟. Taken from the Athabascan word Nenashna, Nenana loosely translates as "a good place to camp between two rivers," and it's appropriately situated at the confluence of the Tanana and Nenana rivers. Always one of

TIP

Getting Around
Chartered airplane operators can be contacted in Fairbanks, North Pole, Delta and Tok. Fly-in fishing is an expensive proposition, but the spectacular scenery and bountiful catches make it good value.

BELOW: historic boiler in Eagle.

the main river-freighting centers in Alaska, the town changed when the Alaska Railroad was completed in 1923. Older residents of Nenana still remember the stifling hot July day in 1923 when President Warren Harding drove in the golden spike signifying completion of the federally owned railroad.

Built in part with excess equipment from the Panama Canal Project, the railroad made headlines in 1985 when it was purchased from the US government by the state of Alaska. Shortly thereafter the station was listed on the National Register of Historic Sites, and now incorporates the **Alaska State Railroad Museum** (open daily in summer, 9am–6pm; admission free; tel: 832-5556 year-round and 832-5500 in summer). The train still chugs along at about 50mph (80km/h) but it doesn't make scheduled trips.

Nenana is also the terminus port for tug and barge fleets that still service the villages along the Tanana and Yukon rivers, loaded with supplies, fuel and tons of freight. For a closer inspection of an old tug, visit the refurbished *Taku Chief* behind the **Visitor Information Center** on the corner of A Street and Parks Highway.

Nenana is home to the **Nenana Ice Classic**, Alaska's coolest lottery. In an event that could only be held in the land of ice and cabin fever, cash prizes totaling $300,000 are awarded to those who guess the exact time – to the minute – of spring break-up on the Tanana. Break-up is that moment when suddenly there's more water than ice on the river, when massive blocks of ice surge and grind against one another in a spectacular release of winter energy. A tripod frozen into the river and attached by wire to a clock tips over when break-up occurs.

The Tanana River again becomes the focal point a month or so later with **River Daze**, celebrated during the first weekend in June. One event is the raft race down the Tanana from Fairbanks to Nenana, when participants create a variety of floating contraptions and enter them as rafts. Anything goes in this race, providing it floats and utilizes only "natural" power.

Off to the gold fields

To drive the **Steese Highway** northeast of Fairbanks is to travel with the spirits of the old gold prospectors. The road angles to the northeast for 162 miles

Gold prospector Felix Pedro (left) and partner

BELOW:
the Alaska State Railroad Museum.

(260km) before ending at the Yukon River. Go past the Gold Dredge No. 8 and the viewing point for the Trans-Alaska pipeline *(see page 254)*, and you will come first to the community of **Fox** at Mile 11, an early mining encampment which took its name from a nearby creek. The community is best known now for its excellent spring water. The symmetrical piles of gravel surrounding Fox are the dregs of the mighty earth-eating dredges. The piles lie like great loaves of bread, browned on top and awaiting the next course.

Next stop is the **Monument to Felix Pedro** at Mile 17 (27km), a modest reminder of the Italian immigrant who was the first to strike it rich in these valleys in 1902 – a find that provoked a stampede. Gravel in the creek on the opposite side of the road has shown some "color," so you could practice panning here.

The subsequent 3 miles (5km) of road gradually ascend to **Cleary Summit**, which offers a magnificent panoramic view of the Tanana Valley, the White Mountains and the Alaska Range. Back in 1905, the notorious "Blue Parka Bandit" found this encompassing lookout quite handy for his trade: Charles Hendrickson, engineer-turned-robber and terror of the trails, haunted these granite crags, pinching the pokes of unsuspecting gold miners *(see margin note)*.

Pioneer camps

Anyone interested in Alaskan gold-rush lore will not want to miss **Fairbanks Creek Road**. Leave the Steese Highway and Cleary Summit and travel south along the ridgeline for 8 miles (13km) to Alder Creek Camp. Beyond this, there's a 1-mile (1.5-km) walk to **Meehan**, an abandoned machine-shop area where maintenance was done on mining equipment, and rusted equipment can still be found strewn along the trail.

Fairbanks Creek Camp is an additional 2 miles (3km) below Meehan. Dredge No. 2 met an untimely end in 1959 along this creek when a deck hand decided to use dynamite to open an ice-blocked hole, and the dredge quickly sank. Fairbanks Creek relinquished many tusks, teeth and bones of Pleistocene mammals during stripping operations. One famous fossil is a well-preserved baby woolly mammoth found in 1949.

Gamblers gained notoriety in the saloons of the boom and bust towns. One who went on to national fame was Tex Richard, 24 years old when he trekked into Circle City in 1895. He later built Madison Square Garden in New York City.

BELOW: the Trans-Alaska Pipeline.

Central's summer influx

The old Circle District is not yet devoid of gold or the miners who search for it. Some of them live in **Central** ㊱, a small mining community strung out along the Steese Highway and described by locals as "three miles long and one block wide." An active winter population of less than 100 swells to nearly 1,000 during the summer months when miners and vacationers return. Since the addition of a permanent school in 1981, more and more "summer people" have stayed on late into fall. Overnight accommodations, camping facilities and general "pit-stop" services are available in the town.

A worthwhile stop is at the **Circle District Historical Society Museum**, located on the highway (open daily in summer noon–5pm; entrance charge; tel: 520-1893). The museum displays authentic pieces of mining equipment alongside gold nuggets, dog sleds, a period cabin containing genuine artifacts, and examples of some of the hardy alpine wildflowers that are found on Eagle Summit.

Gold nuggets weren't the only pleasures that warmed the miners' souls during the rush. In 1893 William Greats crept into a small valley for a closer look at the steaming witches' cauldron he had spotted. He must have been a popular fellow for a time, leading colleagues to the mineral springs he'd discovered.

Circle City

All roads end some place. For the Steese, it's all over at **Circle City** ㊲, a tiny community 50 miles (80km) south of the Arctic Circle, poised along a bend in the Yukon River. In gold-rush days Circle had a population of 1,000; today that has dwindled down to about 100.

Once the largest gold-mining town on the Yukon, Circle was nearly abandoned after the gold strikes in the Klondike and Fairbanks areas and little now remains to be seen by visitors. Gone are Jack McQuesten's two-story log store, two dozen saloons, eight dance halls, theaters and the music hall that earned Circle City the somewhat exaggerated title of the "Paris of the North." In their places reign a modern-day trading post with a motel, a café, a general store, a bar and a gas station. Rudimentary tourist facilities are geared for summer visitors. Chartered flightseeing trips and boat tours are available, but it's wise to call ahead.

There's usually plenty of waterfront activity in this popular stopping-off place for canoeists and rafters traveling the Yukon River. One popular river trip begins in either Eagle or Circle and terminates at Fort Yukon or farther downstream under the Dalton Highway bridge.

Circle, so named because early miners thought they were camped at the Arctic Circle (although they actually had about another 50 miles/80km to go), still offers some activity. Fishwheels smack the water as they turn in the current, flat-bottomed boats zoom up and down the river and barges still make their way to points upriver. River travelers could easily miss all of this; the "land" in front of Circle is actually an island concealing another channel of the mighty Yukon.

To get a real feel for the town, wander upriver to the Pioneer Cemetery and look at some of the weathered gravestones of the early settlers.

Chena River State Recreation Area shelters one of the state's most visible moose populations. Other wildlife includes bears, caribou, wolves, wolverines, lynx and river otters. Hikes of varying length, from one hour to three days, are possible on the park's trails.

BELOW: a cabin at Chena Hot Springs.

Chena Hot Springs Resort

Take a right turn at Mile 3 on the Steese Highway and you will go rollercoasting through some stunning countryside on Chena Hot Springs Road. This paved beauty, which is only 56 miles (90km) long, passes through the middle of the 254,000-acre (103,000-hectare) **Chena River State Recreation Area** (*see margin note, opposite*), and terminates at the gates to the **Chena Hot Springs Resort** ❸ (tel: 451-8104 or 800-478 4681; www.chenahotsprings.com).

The closest thermal resort to Fairbanks and the best developed with regard to the comfort of guests, the resort is commercially equipped with all the necessities for extended, year-round visits, and has winter ski trails and the **Aurora Ice Museum**, sculpted from 1,000 tons of ice and snow, has rooms with sleeping bags on ice beds covered with reindeer hide; the temperature averages 28°F (−2°C). Most alluring are the steaming hot-water pools of **Monument Creek Valley**, and the indoor swimming and indoor and outdoor soaking facilities.

Those interested in a cool chance to witness the spectacular northern lights may do so during a winter visit to the resort, while soaking in the 110°F (43°C) water of Rock Lake. Or you can hop on one of the resort's large track vehicles and rumble to the top of a nearby ridge for unobstructed views. There's even a yurt for your comfort, complete with tea, cider and hot chocolate.

Blueberries and black gold

The last of the four major highways in the Interior extending out of Fairbanks (five if you count Chena Hot Springs Road) is the **Elliott Highway**, running northwest, and continuing on to the Dalton Highway. The Elliott branches off the Steese 11 miles (18km) north of Fairbanks and winds through 152 miles (245km) of gold-mining country trimmed with broad valleys, bubbling creeks, blueberries and poppies, homesteads and mining camps.

The Dalton Highway

Livengood ❸, near the junction of the Elliott and Dalton highways, once held the "end-of-the-road" position, but the isolated little community was transformed into a pipeline construction camp. Five months of intensive labor,

An invigorating dip in the outdoor hot springs at Chena Hot Springs Resort.

BELOW: the Aurora Ice Bar serves up martinis in sculpted ice glasses.

Easy riding.

BELOW: the Dalton Highway will take you beyond the Arctic Circle.

and millions of tons of gravel created a 414-mile (666-km) service road paralleling one of the most ambitious projects ever undertaken in the North American Arctic – the Trans-Alaska pipeline.

This service road-cum-state highway, officially called the **Dalton Highway** but often known as the "Haul Road," opened up thousands of acres of wilderness territory that can be explored from the comfort of a vehicle. The road is maintained from Livengood to Prudhoe Bay, and although privately owned vehicles used to be allowed only as far as **Disaster Creek** near Dietrich Camp, about 280 miles (450km) north of Fairbanks and 200 miles (322km) south of the Arctic Ocean, the whole length of the roadway is now open to the public.

A journey north on the Dalton Highway *(see page 285)*, above the Arctic Circle, through the land of sheep, bears, wolves and foxes is a challenge. Several tour companies offer excursions to the Arctic Circle and Prudhoe Bay. But if you choose to do it alone, beware. Conditions are hazardous; the roadway is rough and dusty in summer and slippery in winter. Because this is primarily a service road,

heavily loaded 18-wheelers rule the route. Automobile towing charges on the highway are expensive, and rental agencies do not allow their cars to be driven on it.

Service station facilities and emergency communications are available at only two locations, the Yukon River Crossing at Mile 56, where you will also find the Yukon Crossing Visitor Center; and Coldfoot at Mile 173.6, shortly before you get to Wiseman. For road conditions, tel: 451-6511 or check http://511.alaska.gov.

Manley Hot Springs

If you feel you can do without the challenge of driving the Dalton Highway, continue to the left on the Elliott Highway when you get to Livengood. This will take you to the Athabascan village of **Minto** on the Tolovana River, and to **Manley Hot Springs**, a good spot if you feel like pampering yourself.

The resort has closed, but the hot springs are still open for use, a short walk from a public campground that the local community maintains. Beyond the resort is the little mining center of **Manley**, where the road runs out. ❑

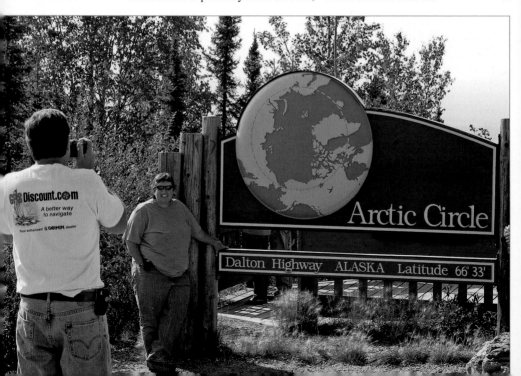

Yukon Villages

Labor-saving devices and the other benefits of modern technology could transform life in the remote Interior. Yet their impact has been slight.

What lies beyond Pedro Dome, Cleary Summit and the White Mountains? What is it that the Chena, the Chatanika and the Tanana rivers are all drawn toward? It is, of course, the Yukon River, flowing north of Fairbanks, and seemingly possessing a magnetic force of its own.

If Fairbanks is the heart of the Interior, the Yukon is a life-supporting artery. Not unlike the pioneers, today's visitors to Fairbanks often feel the urge to soar over the mountain peaks or float with the river current right to its mouth.

Centuries before European explorers spread out over the land, the Yukon River and its many tributaries were a common link in the survival of the nomadic Athabascan tribes living in the Interior. Ironically, the Yukon then provided access to intruders who came up-river in their sternwheelers from St Michael on the Bering Sea to reap the benefits of the fur country and the gold fields.

An unmerciful land

When explorers, missionaries and fortune hunters penetrated this wilderness in the 19th century, the Athabascans were living as they had for generations, subsisting on salmon, moose or caribou, berries and water birds. They were survivors in a harsh and unmerciful land, still living a semi-nomadic life, but with the arrival of outsiders, they congregated into small communities for better protection against whatever dangers might present themselves.

Scattered along the Yukon are the Athabascan river villages. Dozens of tiny settlements still exist in this inhospitable northern land. The historical perspective of each community varies, but, remarkably, they are part of 21st-century Alaska, while paying silent tributes to the Athabascans of the past.

It would be naive to believe that the villages are untouched by the modern world. Conversely, it would be presumptuous to assume that they continue to provide a viable existence due only to space-age technology. Generally, villagers maintain a traditional subsistence lifestyle, hunting, fishing, trapping, gardening and gathering berries. Daily life embraces the rhythm of the seasons, and survival demands adjusting to weather conditions and unpredictable wildlife cycles, just as it has always done.

Elementary schools, many containing modern equipment and built in the 1980s when oil dollars began financing the state, are a part of every village, and many villages also offer high school education to their young people. Typical village teenagers, carrying the dreams of their ancestors, often find themselves at a crossroads, both personally and culturally.

The village elders, those keepers of the culture, go on dispensing wisdom. And, while many of the benefits of 21st-century life are enjoyed, village pride seems to have deepened in recent years, as outside influences have pressed into the core of Athabascan strongholds. Almost forgotten dialects now roll easily from the lips of youngsters. Ancient drumbeats and dances are as popular as rock music. The village is a microcosm of contrast, evoking a strong sense of the past as it surges toward the future. ❑

RIGHT: having fun in a Yukon village.

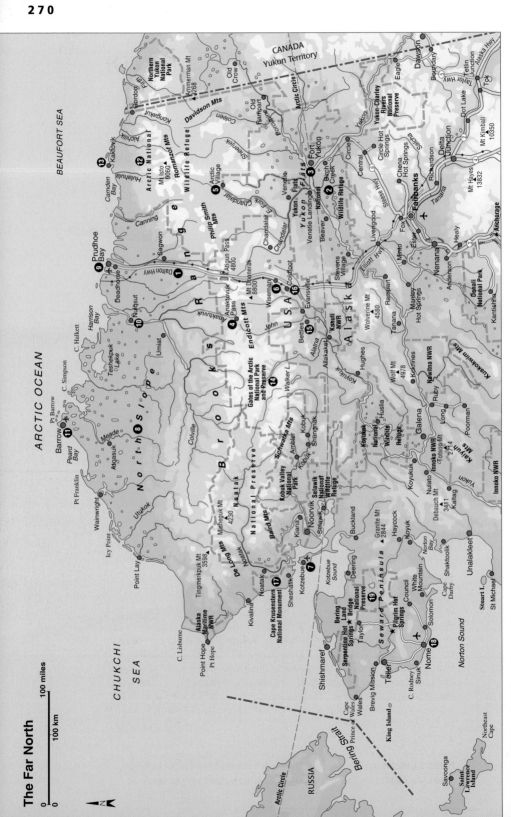

The Far North

100 miles

100 km

ARCTIC OCEAN

CHUKCHI SEA

BEAUFORT SEA

CANADA
Yukon Territory

Arctic Circle

Ammerman Mt
2268

Old Crow

Davidson Mts

Dawson

Eagle

Boundary

Tetlin Junction

Alaska Hwy

Tok

Taylor Hwy

Mt Kimball
10350

Northern Yukon National Park

Kongakut

Gordon

Kaktovik

Camden Bay

Old Rampart

Coleen

Fort Yukon

Rampart

Dot Lake

Circle Hot Springs

Chena Hot Springs

Delta Junction

Richardson

Mt Hayes
13832

Ivishak

Nichilik

Romanzof Mts

Mt Isto
9060

Hulahula

Canning

Sheenjek

Arctic Village

Chandalar

Venetie

Circle

Central

Steese Hwy

Tanana

Arctic National Wildlife Refuge

Philip Smith Mts

E Fork Chandalar

Yukon Flats

Beaver

Livengood

Mmo

Esto

Fox

Fairbanks

Anchorage

Healy

B r o o k s   R a n g e

Atigun Pass 4800

Mt Doonerak 8000

Wiseman

Coldfoot

Stevens Village

Elliott Hwy

Manley Hot Springs

Nenana

Anderson

Denali National Park

Kantishna

Prudhoe Bay

Deadhorse

Sagwon

Dalton Hwy

Anaktuvuk Pass

Evansville

Bettles

Alatna

Wolverine Mt 4580

Rampart

Tanana

Rutqsut

Harrison Bay

Umiat

John

Walker L.

Allakaket

Hughes

Kanuti NWR

Koyukuk

Wolf Mt 4978

Kokrines

Ruby

Poorman

Kuskokwim Mts

ARCTIC OCEAN

Barrow
Pt Barrow

C. Simpson

Teshekpuk Lake

North Slope

Colville

Gates of the Arctic National Park and Preserve

Endicott Mts

Noatak

National Preserve

Schwatka Mts

Kobuk

Ambler

Shungnak

Hughes

Huslia

Galena

Nulato

Koyukuk

Koyukuk

Galena

Kalyuk Mts

Totson Mt 2844

Debauch Mt 3411

Nowitna NWR

Innoko NWR

Yukon

Innoko NWR

Peard Bay

Atqasuk

Meade

Ikpikpuk

Pt Franklin

Wainwright

Icy Point

Point Lay

Tingmerkpuk Mt 3598

De Long Mts

Misheguk Mt 4230

Baird Mts

Kobuk Valley National Park

Kobuk

Selawik National Wildlife Refuge

Kiana

Noorvik

Selawik

Buckland

Granite Mt 2844

Haycock

Koyuk

Norton Bay

Shaktoolik

Unalakleet

C. Lisburne

Point Hope
Pt Hope

Alaska Maritime NWR

Kivalina

Noatak

Cape Krusenstern National Monument

Kotzebue

Kotzebue Sound

Sheshalik

Deering

Seward Peninsula

White Mountain

Council

Cape Darby

Norton Sound

CHUKCHI SEA

Shishmaref

Cape Prince of Wales

Wales

Brevig Mission

King Island

C. Rodney

Sinuk

Teller

Bering Land Bridge National Preserve

Serpentine Hot Springs

Pilgrim Hot Springs

Taylor

Solomon

Nome

St Michael

Stuart I.

Arctic Circle

Bering Strait

RUSSIA

Saint Lawrence Island

Savoonga

Gambell

Northeast Cape

THE FAR NORTH

This vast land of caribou migrations, oil fields and protected wilderness consists of The Arctic, Gates of the Arctic, Arctic National Wildlife Refuge, Cape Krusenstern and the Seward Peninsula

When people think of Alaska, they're usually not picturing the moss-laden, towering Sitka spruce of Southeast, nor picturesque fishing communities like Cordova or Dillingham, and certainly not the modern high-rise apartment buildings, satellite dishes or trendy shopping malls of Anchorage; they're envisioning vast, desolate stretches of windswept, treeless tundra, pack ice dotted with prowling polar bears, Eskimos venturing out on whale hunts in walrus-skin boats, or perhaps wooden racks perched on the banks of a remote river fish camp – loaded with colorful, dangling strips of drying salmon. They're thinking "land of the midnight sun" or perhaps of endless, dark frigid winters – all of which are accurate descriptions of Alaska's Far North.

But that's by no means a complete list. This northernmost part of the state is, indeed, a place of extremes. It's a land that evokes many strident opinions, yet few visitations. It's a wilderness where self-sufficiency will save your life, while carelessness will surely claim it. It's a treasure trove of scarce and invaluable natural resources for an increasingly needy world, located beneath an incredibly fragile arctic ecosystem that could easily and forever be destroyed.

Diverse regions

Alaska's Far North includes many diverse regions, each with distinct climates, peoples, wildlife and other distinguishing characteristics, and the resultant lures and liabilities for travelers. The remote **Yukon Flats** area, for example, extends eastward from the Dalton Highway to the Canadian border. The Flats are situated in a marshy area near the Yukon River and its Porcupine and Chandalar River tributaries. The region, not surprisingly, is prime breeding grounds for more than 150 species of birds and important spawning grounds for fish, including three species of salmon. This area is also extremely isolated, expensive to visit, difficult to traverse and, in summer, swarming with thick clouds of mosquitoes.

PRECEDING PAGES: planes bring food, parcels and visitors to remote Arctic villages.
ABOVE AND RIGHT: a helicopter hovers over a glacier; watching the ice break up.

The glorious and remote mountains of the Brooks Range extend east-west across the wide expanse of northern Alaska. And nestled right in the "heart" of the Range is the stunning **Gates of the Arctic National Park and Preserve**. It's important to note that this Preserve has no roads, no grocery stores, no amenities or services whatsoever – not even medical help.

Yet it is a wilderness historically inhabited by Native Inupiaq Eskimos and Athabascan Indians, and also by trappers and homesteaders, who together add up to a whopping 1 person per every 5,000 acres (2,000 hectares). The Preserve does offer 8 million acres (3.2 million hectares) of pristine wilderness for those who are adequately prepared, self-sufficient and in need of a prolonged ramble, river-run or climb within a wild, unpeopled land.

Arctic National Wildlife Refuge

East of Gates of the Arctic, between the Dalton Highway and Canada, and north from the Brooks Range to the coastal tundra is much-discussed **Arctic National Wildlife Refuge** (ANWR). The Refuge encompasses traditional subsistence areas and homelands of both the coastal Inupiaq Eskimos and the interior Athabascan Indians. Its arctic and subarctic ecosystems support the greatest variety of plant and animal life in any Park or Refuge in the circumpolar region. Probably the most noted mammals in ANWR are the nearly 200,000 caribou that make up the Porcupine and Central Arctic Herds. These herds make yearly migrations from the boreal forests of Interior Alaska and Canada to summer calving grounds in ANWR's coastal plains—the same area thought by many to contain significant quantities of oil and gas. Of ANWR's 19 million total acres (7.7 million hectares), it is these 1½ million acres of

coastal plains that have spawned national and even international debate on whether to allow oil and gas development in the Refuge, or to preserve it as a wilderness area for future generations.

Farther west along the northern coast of Alaska's Far North is the **North Slope** and the industrial oil facility called **Prudhoe Bay**. Transient oil workers regularly cycle in and out from their homes and families in the more populated areas of Fairbanks, Anchorage, the Kenai Peninsula, or even Texas to their two- or three-week stints on the North Slope. They eat, work and sleep in the surreal environment of large indoor work stations and housing buildings, which may include a library, gymnasium, cafeteria and satellite TV.

But the North Slope is considerably more than just Prudhoe Bay. Continued westerly travel along the coastline of the Arctic Ocean leads to the tiny Inupiat community of **Nuiqsut** (population 400) and then the lethally cold **Barrow** (population 4,000), the largest Eskimo settlement in the world and the northernmost community in North America.

ABOVE: whale bones at Barrow; checking out the Trans-Alaska Pipeline.
OPPOSITE PAGE: a brown bear catches his lunch.

In the western coastal area of the Far North, located just above the Arctic Circle on Kotzebue Sound is the City of **Kotzebue**. A major transportation and services hub for northwestern Alaska, this predominantly Eskimo community of 3,000 residents also serves as the jumping-off point for treks into **Noatak National Preserve**, **Kobuk Valley National Park**, **Bering Land Bridge National Preserve** and **Cape Krusenstern National Monument**.

And finally, southwest of Kotzebue is the Seward Peninsula and, on the southwest corner of the Peninsula, the City of **Nome**. A resilient town that's endured countless boom and bust cycles, the 3,500 residents of Nome seem to just keep coming back for more. It's a frontier community with a colorful history of miners frantically panning the streams and turning over the beaches in search of gold. Visitors still today, in fact, are welcomed to try their hand at panning for gold on the sandy beaches of Nome.

Nome is also a blessed sight for the mushers and dog teams of the grueling 1,150-mile Iditarod Trail Sled Dog Race *(see pages 308–9)*, as the suddenly re-energized teams dash toward the finish line located under Nome's famous burl arch. The race commemorates a far more sober "race for life," when desperately-needed diphtheria serum was delivered to Nome by dogsled in 1925.

Wild and bewildering

Travelers considering a trip to Alaska's Far North – particularly to the most remote Refuges, Monuments and Preserves – should give the idea the most careful consideration. While regularly scheduled airline service is available in the larger communities of Barrow, Kozebue and Nome, far-flung destinations are generally accessible by floatplane or bush plane alone.

It's a place where all possible contingencies must be carefully planned out in advance. It is a wild, even bewildering locale, unlike any other, featuring polarized extremes of weather, temperatures, daylight, resources, geography, peoples and even politics. It's the sort of place adventurers often dream of, but are only rarely gifted with the opportunity, skills and tenacity to experience. ❑

Public Lands in the Far North

The following list includes some of the major public lands within the Far North. For more complete information on all public lands within Alaska, contact the Alaska Public Lands Information Centers at www.nps.gov/aplic.

Alaska Maritime National Wildlife Refuge (http://alaskamaritime.fws.gov).
Arctic National Wildlife Refuge (http://arctic.fws.gov)
Bering Land Bridge National Preserve (www.nps.gov/bela)
Cape Krusenstern National Monument (www.nps.gov/cakr)
Gates of the Arctic National Park and Preserve (www.nps.gov/gaar)
Kanuti National Wildlife Refuge (http://kanuti.fws.gov)
Kobuk Valley National Park (www.nps.gov/kova)
Koyukuk National Wildlife Refuge (http://koyukuk.fws.gov)
Noatak National Preserve (www.nps.gov/noat)
Selawik National Wildlife Refuge (http://selawik.fws.gov)
Yukon Flats National Wildlife Refuge (http://yukonflats.fws.gov)

THE ARCTIC

The lands north of the Arctic Circle can be grouped into four main areas: the Yukon Flats lowlands just south of the Brooks Range in eastern Alaska; the northwest coast; the Brooks Range; and the North Slope

S tretching east-west from the Canadian border to the Bering Sea and north-south from the Arctic Ocean to the Arctic Circle, (66° 33' north latitude), Alaska's vast Arctic region comprises about a quarter of the state's mainland. It's a region characterized by extremes of light and temperature; rural communities of mostly Native inhabitants; vast stretches of wilderness; several of Alaska's wildest parklands and refuges; America's largest oil field – and its largest caribou herds.

Only a small percentage of travelers come this far north; but those who do will find wilderness on a scale unmatched anywhere else in Alaska or the other 49 states. Here too they will find a thriving Inupiat Eskimo culture that balances its centuries old subsistence lifestyle – including the annual hunt for whales – with modern technology and western culture.

The majority of visitors to this region get here by plane, but each year a few thousand also drive the **Dalton Highway ❶**, or Haul Road, the only road into the Arctic that connects with Alaska's statewide highway system *(see page 285)*.

The Yukon Flats

Extending from the Canadian border to foothills just east of the Dalton Highway, this is a flat, marshy, lake-dotted area dominated by the northernmost segment of the **Yukon River** and several large tributaries, including the Porcupine and Chandalar Rivers. Few visitors come here, both because it is remote and expensive to reach, and because it is difficult to get around. Another negative: it is also a major mosquito-breeding ground in summer.

The primary recreational activities are boating and fishing, within the **Yukon Flats National Wildlife Refuge ❷** (tel: 456-0440; http://yukonflats.fws.gov), the third largest member of the nation's wildlife refuge system. Encompassing 8.6 million acres (3.5 million hectares) of lowland lakes, streams, and wetlands, the aptly named **Yukon Flats** is best known for its avian breeding habitat; the

Main attractions
DALTON HIGHWAY
YUKON FLATS NATIONAL
  WILDLIFE REFUGE
FORT YUKON
ANAKTUVUK PASS
ARCTIC VILLAGE
WISEMAN
KOTZEBUE
NORTH SLOPE
PRUDHOE BAY
NUIQSUT
BARROW

LEFT: polar bears prey on seals.
LEFT: ice fishing in Kotzebue.

refuge is one of North America's premier waterfowl nesting grounds.

Ducks and geese come here from such varied wintering grounds as Costa Rica, Mexico, and Russia. By summer's end, some 2 million ducks and geese – including one-fifth of the continent's canvasback ducks and large numbers of Canada and white-fronted geese – will prepare to leave the refuge's 40,000 lakes and ponds on southbound migrations. Large numbers of common, Pacific, and red-throated loons are among the 150 species of birds to breed here each year.

Nearly all those birds leave in fall, though 13 species live here year-round, from boreal chickadees to great gray owls, spruce grouse, and ravens.

As might be expected the flats' many rivers are important spawning grounds for fish, including three species of salmon – chinook (or king), chum, and coho – that travel more than a thousand river miles to reach these waters.

The Yukon Flats has some of the continent's greatest annual temperature extremes. In deepest winter, temperatures may drop to –50°F (–45°C) or even lower for weeks at a time. In such extreme cold, trees may crack and ice shatter, while sounds are carried for miles in the dense, dry air. In summer, by contract, temperatures of up to 100°F (38°C) have been recorded here – the highest temperatures ever noted north of the Arctic Circle.

The region is home to Athabascan Indians, but few communities are located here. The largest, **Fort Yukon ❸**, is located near the confluence of the Yukon and Porcupine Rivers. Home to 600 people, mostly Athabascans, Fort Yukon is used as a jumping-off spot by visitors to the Yukon Flats and Arctic National wildlife refuges. Contact the headquarters of those refuges for information on air-taxi services and other local businesses that operate in the refuges.

The Brooks Range

Extending east-west across the width of Alaska, the **Brooks Range** is Alaska's northernmost chain of mountains, the farthest-north extension of the Rocky Mountains. More than 700 miles long and up to 200 miles across (1,000 by 320km), the Brooks Range is considered by many to be Alaska's premier alpine

*Athabascan crafts
for sale.*

BELOW: a remote lodge in the Brooks Range, reached most easily by floatplane.

wilderness. Within the chain are several distinct groups of peaks, from the Baird and De Long Mountains in the west, to the Endicott and Schwatka Mountains in the central Brooks and the Philip Smith, Romanzof, and Davidson Mountains in the east. Here too are several of Alaska's premier conservation units, protecting much of the range's wild lands and wildlife.

Remote and expensive to reach – and therefore visited by relatively few people – this range is relatively subdued by Alaskan standards; its tallest peak, **Mount Isto**, is only 9,060 ft (2,761 meters) high and few others reach higher than 6,000 ft (1,820 meters). But that is one of its beauties. Wave after wave of mountain ridges can be ascended by adventurers with little or no mountaineering experience. And once upon a ridgeline or mountain top, you can look across a mountain wilderness that seems to go on forever.

That's not to say these mountains are easy to climb; ascents of tundra and bare rock require stamina and good conditioning. And while many of the mountains are rounded domes or sedimentary rocks, several groups within the chain rise precipitously into the sky. The most notable of those are the **Arrigetch Peaks**, in the central Brooks Range. Taken from the Nunamiut Eskimo people, the name for this group of granite spires means "fingers of the hand, extended."

For a mountain chain, the Brooks Range gives a sense of wide-open spaces. In part this is because much of the range is north of the tree line, and ground-hugging tundra plants populate valley bottoms as well as high alpine meadows. But the openness is also accentuated by the broad glacially carved river valleys that cut through the mountains north and south.

Like other portions of the Arctic, the Brooks Range is a place of extremes. Winters are long, cold, and dark. The sun disappears for days to weeks at a time (the farther north you go, the longer the winter night lasts) and temperatures drop to –40°F (–40°C) or even colder for long stretches. Winter's first snows may arrive in August and the landscape doesn't thaw and begin to "green up" until May or even sometimes June. Summer's short season is marked by weeks of light, low rainfall – much of the Brooks Range qualifies as a desert climate because of its low precipitation – and bursting life.

Summer wildlife

A surprising diversity of wildlife can be found here in summer. Dozens of birds species nest in lowlands and alpine meadows; most avoid the long, harsh winter by migrating long distances each spring and fall but a few – for instance, chickadees and ravens and ptarmigan – somehow survive year-round. Mammals include the grizzly and black bear, moose, Dall sheep, wolves, foxes, wolverines, porcupines and caribou. The caribou, as much as grizzlies and wolves, symbolize this northern mountain chain. Hundreds of thousands migrate through the Brooks Range each year on yearly migrations; after wintering on the range's southern fringes, they head north in late winter toward calving grounds on the North Slope, then return south at summer's end.

Yukon River
The Yukon is Alaska's longest river, flowing about 2,000 miles (3,200km) from its headwaters near Atlin Lake in northern British Columbia to the Bering Sea. Its entire length was floated in 1883 by Lt. Frederick Schwatka, mostly on a log raft, the "Resolute."

BELOW:
arctic fox cubs.

Canoeing on the Yukon River.

BELOW: a gray wolf in the Noatak National Preserve.

Only a handful of human settlements are located here; most of those are along the mountain's fringes and number a few dozen people or less. Most of them are Native communities, of Athabascan or Eskimo origin. One village, **Anaktuvuk Pass ❹**, is deep within the Central Brooks range, at 2,300 ft (700 meters) along the Arctic Divide. This is the only remaining settlement of Alaska's Nunamiut people, a tribe of inland Eskimos whose nomadic ancestors followed migratory herds of caribou across the western Arctic. The Nunamiut maintained a semi-nomadic lifestyle deep into the 20th century, following caribou and other game across the landscape in small groups. Not until 1949 did they permanently settle at Anaktuvuk Pass.

About 300 people now live in Anaktuvuk; all but a few are Nunamuit. Nearly everyone depends on subsistence harvesting – hunting, fishing, trapping, berry picking – to some degree, with caribou at the center of it all. No longer do residents need caribou for tools and shelter, but the animals remain a chief source of food. Some people still use caribou parts for clothing: boots, parkas, gloves, and hats.

Arctic Village

Much farther to the east is **Arctic Village ❺**, a community of about 150 people, mostly Athabascan Gwich'in. Like the Nunamiut, the Gwich'in were once a semi-nomadic people. They remain dependent on the Porcupine Caribou Herd, which numbers more than 130,000 animals and ranges through northeastern Alaska and northwestern Canada.

Both Arctic Village and Anaktuvuk Pass are located within preservation units (the Arctic National Wildlife Refuge and Gates of the Arctic National Park, respectively) and are sometimes visited by Brooks Range adventurers; however, both communities have limited visitor facilities.

The small town of **Wiseman ❻** represents a third culture: white gold miners. Prospectors were drawn to the area in the early 1900s, but that boom has long passed. Today the town's 20 or so residents are a mix of miners, trappers, and homesteaders who've found a niche along the Middle Fork of the Koyukuk, not far from the Dalton Highway. Also known as the Haul Road *(see page 285)*, the Dalton Highway is the only road to cross the Brooks Range, as it connects Interior Alaska with the Prudhoe Bay oilfields.

Much of the Brooks Range wilderness is protected within a series of seldom-visited parks, preserves and refuges that have few or no traveler facilities: from west to east, these include the **Noatak National Preserve** (tel: 442-3890; www. nps.gov/noat), **Kobuk Valley National Park** (tel: 442-3890; www.nps.gov/kova), **Gates of the Arctic National Park** (tel: 694-5494; www.nps.gov/gaar; *see pages 292–5 for a more detailed discussion)*, and the **Arctic National Wildlife Refuge** (tel: 456-0250; http://arctic.fws.gov; *see pages 286–91 for more details*).

Northwest Alaska

At the Arctic's far western end, from lowland flats south of the Brooks Range then north along the mountain chain's western fringes, is an area inhabited by several Inupiat Eskimo communities, the majority of whom still depend on traditional subsistence lifestyles. Several small Inupiat villages are located along the **Kobuk River** just south of the Brooks Range: **Kobuk**, **Shungnak**, **Ambler**, and **Kiana**, to name a few. Other communities are along the coast, from Selawik in the south up through Kivalina and Point Hope.

The landscape ranges from the tundra-topped hills and mountains of the Brooks Range to lowland forests and wetlands south of the mountains and coastal marshes and beaches where marine mammals such as walruses and seals haul out. Polar bears roam the offshore sea ice, occasionally coming onto land and whales migrate past the region on seasonal travels.

Crystal clear streams born in the mountains feed the region's largest waterway, the Kobuk River. Nearly 350 miles (560 km) long, the Kobuk's headwaters are in the Schwatka Mountains; the river then flows south a short way before turning west, where it eventually empties into Kotzebue Sound. The Kobuk is critically important to the Inupiat, both as a transportation corridor and source of food: fish, birds, and the caribou that cross the river each year.

The cultural center of Northwest Alaska is **Kotzebue** ❼, a large, predominantly Eskimo community that is served by daily jet service out of Anchorage and Fairbanks. Kotzebue is the headquarters for NANA, one of the regional Native corporations established in 1971 with the passage of the Alaska Native Claims Settlement Act. That act granted Alaskan Natives nearly $1 billion in cash and title to some 44 million acres (18 million hectares) of land. Thirteen Native corporations, formed to manage the sudden wealth, divided up the money and the ground. NANA's share was significant and it is now one of the more successful of the corporations. In addition to its active involvement, several other business ventures of a more contemporary nature round out NANA's holdings in

Boys from Kotzebue.

BELOW: peeling birch bark from a tree, near Ambler.

industries including mining, oil and tourism. The company is providing jobs to its shareholders and is a significant economic force in northwestern Alaska.

One Kotzebue attraction that shouldn't be missed is the **NANA Museum of the Arctic**. Tours of the museum are arranged primarily for travelers on packages offered by Tour Arctic (tel: 800-468-2248; www.tour-arctic.com), but independent travelers can join the tours for a fee.

Tours include a cultural program that is among the best presented in Alaska. It includes story-telling, traditional Inupiat dancing and an award-winning slide show. Exhibits include artifacts and traditional art and examples of all the animals indigenous to the region. It is a splendid introduction to the land and its traditional Native culture. Programs are given daily from mid-May through early September. The package also includes a city tour, a visit to the National Park Service office to learn about the wildlife and wilderness areas, and a culture camp demonstration that explains Native culture from both the spiritual and the practical perspectives. Guides take visitors on a walk in the tundra to point out per-

mafrost as well as plants and their traditional uses. A "Native village excursion" to smaller communities in the region can also be arranged.

Northeast of Kotzebue, NANA also helped develop the **Red Dog Mine**, a world-class zinc mine that provides hundreds of local jobs, transforming the economy of this sparsely populated area. Cominco, a Canadian-based mining concern, has helped to develop the roads and other infrastructure necessary to support the venture. Zinc deposits are expected to last for at least 20 years and recoverable quantities of silver, lead and other minerals are also being mined.

But Kotzebue is still traditional. Fishermen tend nets in Kotzebue Sound and nearby streams. Native walrus, seal, whale and polar bear hunters still brave the elements in pursuit of their quarries. Kotzebue is a rare combination of the old and the new, and one of the few places where traditional and contemporary lifestyles are blending together in reasonable harmony.

Reaching the parks

Kotzebue is also the jumping-off point for those seeking wilderness adventure in the Noatak National Preserve and the Kobuk Valley National Park *(see page 279 for contact information)*. Also accessible by charter aircraft from Kotzebue are **Cape Krusenstern National Monument** *(see page 296)* and the **Bering Land Bridge National Preserve**. These remote lands were all set aside as part of the 1980 Alaska National Interest Lands Conservation Act.

The distances involved means that there is no easy or inexpensive way to get to these remote parks and preserves. There are no roads. Charter airplanes from Kotzebue, with prices starting at about $200 an hour, are about the only means of access. Check carefully with the National Park Service office in Kotzebue (tel: 442-3890) before you set out: activities such as reindeer herding are allowed to take place on portions of these lands, and if you are planning a wilderness trip to seek peace and solitude you won't want to land in the middle of a commercial reindeer drive.

The North Slope

Bush pilots on Alaska's north coast have little use for aerial charts, because there are few usable landmarks that can be depicted on a map to aid a pilot in this world of myriad tiny lakes and meandering rivers. Pilots usually plot their positions by counting the number of rivers crossed from a known starting point. Rivers flow from south to north on the **North Slope ❽**, a vaguely defined but huge chunk of territory that includes everything north of the Brooks Range. Once a pilot locates a particular river by flying east or west, he turns inland toward terrain with more features, the treeless northern side of the mountains about 100 miles (160 km) to the south.

There are no roads between communities and distances are great, so most people fly bush planes to get from one place to another; in winter many residents also depend on snowmobiles (and, to a lesser degree, sled dog teams). Fog is a year-round hazard: a 1,500-ft (460-meter) thick cloud of mist blankets the north coast of Alaska for many days of the year. It often stretches inland for about 20 miles (32km), thus hiding the airports of North Slope villages, which are concentrated along the coast.

Stark, trackless beauty and the undis-

The traditional parka is a good protection against the climate.

BELOW:
snow-machining through the sun fog on the North Slope.

TIP

Visiting Prudhoe Bay
Tour companies offer flights to the Prudhoe Bay oilfields, often with a return by bus over 500 miles (800km) of gravel road to Fairbanks. A fixed fee provides a bed for the two-night trip, meals at a North Slope dining facility, and the round-trip airfare. Four-hour tours of the oilfields round out the arrangement. It is also possible to take a one-day package, flying both ways.

BELOW: oil worker, Prudhoe Bay.

turbed miracles of nature surround you on the North Slope. Almost every stone or fossil is a clue to the varying layers of rock underlying the flat coastal plain, a clue that can lead – and has led – to the discovery of oil. Such clues are zealously guarded by the company that finds them, for finding and developing oil is the name of the game on the North Slope. Initial explorations by geologists are just the first move by the players.

Alaska's economy floats on an ocean of black gold, most of it pumped from beneath the tundra on the North Slope. Oil generates about 80 percent of the state government's income and provides a living for a large transient population of oil-industry workers who commute to and from the Arctic coast.

Prudhoe Bay

Prudhoe Bay ❾ is a working person's world, visited by few tourists. Several hundred people live and work at the industrial facility – there are no schools, no public roads and few entertainment facilities. The work-day is 12 hours long, seven days a week. The pace, though, is temporary. After two or three weeks on the job, workers fly to Anchorage, Fairbanks or even Dallas, Texas, for a week or sometimes two of vacation. It's not uncommon for a worker on the slope to make $75,000 a year for only 26 actual weeks on the job.

The larger oil companies house and feed their personnel, at no expense to employees. Living quarters may include a library, a gymnasium with an indoor track, weights room, game rooms and satellite television, but they tend to be quiet places where the workers settle into a routine – and there is little time for more than working, sleeping and eating.

Many Slope transient workers see nothing more than the inside of the housing building, workstation and air terminal. For them, Prudhoe Bay is the latest example of US technology transplanted into the remote wilderness. Little outside their doors interests them; it's only frozen tundra in winter and fog much of the year.

Frozen it may be for most of the year, but some people have called Alaska's Arctic coast home for centuries, and have managed to scrape out a living there. For some workers on the Slope, on the other hand, their few hours of unscheduled time are a rare opportunity for photographing summer wildlife, such as migrating caribou or birds, or winter's northern lights.

Visitors to the Prudhoe Bay oilfields are usually impressed by the neatness of the facility and how little the buildings disturb the landscape. The silver slash of the trans-Alaska oil pipeline originates here, then winds south toward the Brooks Range. Seeing all this, you realize that here beats the heart that pumps black gold, the lifeblood of Alaska's contemporary economy.

North Slope Native life

West of Prudhoe Bay and east of Barrow, **Nuiqsut** ❿ is geographically placed between oil and tradition. Unlike most northern communities, this Inupiat Eskimo village of 400 residents is several miles inland from the coast, at the apex of the Colville River delta, about

60 miles (100km) from Prudhoe. Inupiat men still hunt whales off the coast (although regulations now strictly limit the number of whales they may take each year), as well as polar bears and seals.

Although most continue to lead a traditional lifestyle of hunting and gathering, a few jobs are available, mostly in government-run organizations. But for those who still venture onto the frozen sea in search of food and skins, their safety is less in the hands of chance these days. If they are late returning to their modern frame houses in the village, one quick telephone call launches a helicopter to search the coastline near the delta's mouth.

Barrow

Located to the west and just south of Point Barrow, the northernmost tip of North America, **Barrow** ⓫ is Alaska's largest Eskimo settlement, with about 4,000 residents (most of those Inupiat). It is the headquarters of the Arctic Slope Regional Corporation, a Native corporation formed to manage the huge sums of money and vast tracts of land deeded to Alaska Native groups by the Alaska Native Claims Settlement Act of 1971. When the US Congress approved that legislation, Barrow and other key Native villages in Alaska instantly became corporate centers, modern enclaves of big business in a traditional land. Barrow today stands as the ultimate contrast between tradition and technology.

Skin whaling boats are still used for the spring hunt, while modern aluminum craft are used for the fall hunt, when sea ice is farther from shore, which means that whalers may have to travel greater distances to find whales. Whaling is now very strictly regulated, but captains teach their sons the secrets of harpooning and landing the bowhead whale, more as a means of keeping the culture alive than as a necessary tool of survival.

The opportunity to see an ancient culture and its traditions lure some visitors to Barrow; others come to see the midnight sun, which does not set here from mid-May to early August, and for a chance to stand momentarily on the continent's northern edge – for many visitors the most vivid memory of their Barrow trip.

For winter visitors, the northern lights

A Native elder in Barrow.

BELOW:
a whaling team at Barrow prepares to launch an umiaq.

Prepares salmon for drying.

RIGHT: an Inupiat blanket toss, part of a festival celebrating a successful spring whaling season.

are another attraction, but they are equally apparent in Fairbanks, which is a great deal more accessible than Barrow.

Most people come here as part of a package tour. Travel agencies offer overnight trips to Barrow from Anchorage and Fairbanks for a fee that covers a hotel room, a few local tours and the use of a parka. Contact Alaska Airlines (tel: 800-468-2248; www.alaskaair.com) for details.

The package tours and independent visitors alike stop at **Pepe's North of the Border Restaurant**, Barrow's most famous eatery, which serves typical American-Mexican food *(see listing below)*. Others may squeamishly try a bite of muktuk (whale blubber), or perhaps a piece of seal meat. But these local delicacies are available only sporadically and visitors who like to live on the culinary edge may have to search for them.

Inupiat culture

It is unfortunate that most trips to Barrow are so brief. Inupiat culture is varied and ancient, but it is difficult and time-consuming for an outsider to gain a detailed knowledge of it. And, although English is spoken by most Inupiats (except for the very old), traditional behavior may be confusing and interfere with communication.

For example, Inupiats are not being impolite when they fail to respond immediately to a question or acknowledge a statement. It is simply not their custom to do so, but outsiders may find their long pauses uncomfortable. Saying "thank you" is also not customary: traditionally, Inupiat people will simply return a favor – and expect no thanks from the recipient.

Perhaps the best advice for tourists to Barrow – or any part of the Arctic – is to assume a slower-paced style of speaking and behaving, a pace more attuned to traditional lifestyles, and to remember that the Inupiat people live not by the clock but by the change of seasons. Changing one's behavior takes a conscious effort, and may be hard at first, but a journey to the Arctic is an opportunity to live, albeit briefly, in a different way and experience an unfamiliar culture. ❏

RESTAURANTS

Barrow

Arctic Pizza
125 Upper Apayauq Street
tel; (907) 852-4222
Seafood, steaks and Mexican cuisine for lunch or dinner. Casual, family dining downstairs. Upstairs is a more formal atmosphere with a view of the Arctic Ocean. $$$

Osaka
980 Stevenson Street
tel: (907) 852-4100
Generous breakfasts and very good sushi. $$

Pepe's North of the Border Restaurant
1204 Agvik Street

tel: (907) 852-8200
Popular restaurant serving breakfast, lunch and dinner. Ample portions of Mexican and American dishes. $$$

Kotzebue

Bayside Restaurant
303 Shore Avenue
tel: (907) 442-3600
Open daily for breakfast, lunch and dinner, this restaurant located in the Bayside Inn features Chinese, American and Italian cuisine. No alcohol. $–$$$

● ● ● ● ● ● ● ● ● ● ● ● ● ● ● ● ● ●

Price is for dinner excluding tax, tip and beverages: $$$$ *$30 and up,* $$$ *$20–30,* $$ *$15–20,* $ *under $15.*

The Dalton Highway

There are no roads and few services on this remote road. Once used solely by trucks serving the pipeline, it is now being used by hunters and anglers.

The only road north of the Arctic Circle to connect with Alaska's highway system, the Dalton Highway – named after James Dalton, an Alaska-born engineer – ties Interior Alaska to the oilfields at Prudhoe Bay. Some 414 miles (666 km) long, the Dalton was built in 1974, during the state's oil-boom days, so that trucks could haul supplies to Prudhoe and pipeline construction camps in Alaska's northern reaches. Hence the Dalton's other name: the Haul Road.

Thousands of 18-wheeler rigs still drive the Dalton each year, but they now share it with hunters, anglers, and sightseers. Parts were opened to the public in 1981, but the entire route didn't officially open until 1995. That summer, nearly 6,000 people signed the Bureau of Land Management's (BLM) guest register, a large jump from previous years. Numbers have risen only slightly since then.

That doesn't mean the Dalton has suddenly become an easy drive. It's narrow as highways go, often winding, and has several steep grades where it passes through mountains. Sections may be heavily potholed or washboarded and its coarse gravel is easily kicked up into headlights and windshields by trucks that travel 65 or 70 mph (105–112 km/h) along some straight sections.

Food and fuel

Besides being tough on vehicles, the road has few visitor facilities. From its start at the Elliot Highway (84 road miles/135 km northwest of Fairbanks) to its endpoint at Deadhorse (the small construction community that serves the Prudhoe Bay oilfield workers), there are only three places to get fuel, lodging and food — and two of those are within the first 60 miles/100 km (Mile 56, at the Yukon River Crossing Visitor Contact Station and Mile 60.3, the Hot Spot Cafe); the third and last food-and-fuel stop before reaching the end of the road is at Coldfoot, Mile 175.

RIGHT: the dusty Dalton Highway, built in 1974.

Drivers are therefore urged to take four-wheel-drive cars or trucks, loaded with extra provisions for our seven-day trip: reserve gas, spare tires, several engine belts, drinking water, enough clothing to survive an alpine snowstorm (which may occur at any time of year), and food and fuel for two weeks of camping. Because of the road hazards, car-rental companies normally prohibit their vehicles from being taken up the Haul Road.

The great majority of Dalton Highway adventurers go no farther than the Arctic Circle, at Mile 115.3. A BLM wayside has picnic tables, grills, outhouses, and interpretive displays. There's also a nearby primitive campground. Other designated campgrounds are few and far between; a popular one is the BLM's Marion Creek Campground at Mile 179.7.

Beyond Coldfoot, road traffic diminishes greatly, as the road ascends gradually into the heart of the Brooks Range mountains. Though much of the highway's first 180 miles (290 km) is bordered by monotonous lowland forest, here the landscape is grandly, ruggedly beautiful.

At Mile 244.7, the Haul Road tops out at 4,800-ft (1,460-meter) Atigun Pass, along the Arctic Divide; it's the highest highway pass in Alaska and conditions may be wintry, even in mid-summer.

For road conditions at any time, telephone 511 (in Alaska) or 866-282-7577; http://511.Alaska.gov). ❑

ARCTIC NATIONAL WILDLIFE REFUGE

Alaska
Anchorage

In Alaska's far northeast corner, the refuge is home to grizzlies, packs of wolves and a thundering herd of caribou, but you can go days or weeks without seeing another person

BELOW:
a Porcupine
Caribou herd
migrates.

Drifting off to sleep his first night in the Aichilik River Valley, a back-country explorer hears, or perhaps imagines, the distant howling of *Canis lupus*. Entering the visitor's dreams, wolves celebrate a successful hunt with wolf song. Several hours later the camper is awakened by the cries of *Homo sapiens*, singing the praises of a glorious Arctic morning. He quickly leaves his tent and joins the rest of his party for breakfast beneath a cloudless cerulean sky. Stirred by breezes that keep mosquitoes away, the late-summer air is surprisingly warm. By mid-morning the group's thermometer registers 68°F (20°C) in the shade and in sunlight the air is 10–15°F (5.6–8.4°C) warmer.

The party of six – three Bostonians, two Alaskans, one Californian – have been flown into the remote and roadless **Arctic National Wildlife Refuge ⑫** (tel: 456-0250; http://arctic.fws.gov), in extreme northeastern Alaska. The refuge was established in 1960 as an 8.9-million-acre (3.6 million-hectare) "wildlife range" whose primary intent was to preserve unique wildlife, wilderness, and recreational values. The range was expanded and upgraded to refuge status in 1980. Stretching from Alaska's Interior to the Arctic's North Slope and Beaufort Sea, it protects 19 million acres (7.7 million hectares), 42 percent of which is designated wilderness.

It is home to a remarkable assemblage of birds and mammals, including some of North America's most charismatic animals: grizzly and polar bears, wolves, musk oxen, Dall sheep, moose, golden eagles, peregrine falcons. But its most famous inhabitants belong to the Porcupine Caribou Herd, which over the past decade has ranged from 130,000 to 180,000 members.

The oil issue

The Porcupine is North America's only international herd of caribou, with a range that encompasses tens of thousands of square miles in both Canada and Alaska. But that isn't the herd's only –

or chief – claim to fame. Since the early 1980s, it has been at the center of a national debate: whether to allow oil and gas development in the Arctic Refuge's 1½-million-acre (600,000-hectare) coastal plain, or preserve it as wilderness. After a few years of quiet, the debate was rekindled in 2000, following George W. Bush's election as president.

The oil industry and its supporters – including the Bush adminstration – pushed hard for oil and gas development in the refuge, while those desiring a wilderness designation for the coastal plain fought just as hard to save the wild landscape, which is seasonal home for dozens of species that use it for all sorts of activities: denning, breeding, nesting, spawning, hunting, grazing, and calving.

The caribou have become a symbol of what's at stake, largely because portions of the coastal plain serve as a traditional "core calving area" where caribou cows give birth each spring. It's also where the caribou – cows, calves, and bulls – gather in huge, densely packed crowds from mid-June to mid-July to get some relief from mosquitoes and parasitic flies. The largest single group seen by biolo-

gists numbered more than 94,000 caribou. Nearly 100,000 animals standing side by side… it's almost impossible to imagine.

While fierce debates have raged over the Arctic refuge's coastal plain, relatively little attention has been given to the refuge's other 17½ million acres (7 million hectares), though they encompass some of the world's wildest Arctic lands, including the eastern third of the Brooks Range, Alaska's northernmost mountain chain.

The northern foothills

Stretching east–west across the state, the **Brooks Range** is a gently subdued mountain kingdom, with wave after wave of ridgelines and mountain tops – mostly under 5,000 ft (1,500 meters) – that can be easily ascended in a day or less by hikers in good physical condition (this is no place for couch potatoes). Dissecting the mountains are wide, U-shaped, north-south trending river valleys that create a sense of wide-open spaces. The **Aichilik River Valley** is one of those.

Rather than backpack or float a river, as most refuge visitors do, this group of

TIP

Caribou watching
Being in the right place at the right time to witness the amazing migration of caribou is a tricky business. Your best bet may be to hire an outfitter who can guide you on a river or hiking trip across the migration route.

BELOW: a polar bear comes calling.

TIP

Weather watch
This region receives almost round-the-clock sunlight in June and July. Summer weather is generally cool and breezy, but temperatures can reach 87°F (30°C) or fall below freezing. Thunderstorms are common in August. Snowfall is possible in any season. Winter is long and severe.

BELOW:
Sierra Club hikers leave camp in the wildlife refuge.

explorers has established a "base camp" on one of the Aichilik's many gravel bars; from here they will explore the surrounding landscape on day hikes. By setting their four tents on the river's sand and gravel, the campers avoid trampling the tundra: such low-impact practices are especially important in fragile Arctic ecosystems.

It's equally important, on any Alaska backcountry trip, to bring gear that can withstand winterlike storms, which may occur at almost any time of year, and to keep a clean camp and store food away from tents and in such a way that animals – whether grizzlies or ground squirrels – aren't likely to get into it. There are no trees here, so the group has brought plastic food buckets, and build a rock cairn around them.

Tell-tale signs

This Aichilik River camp is nestled among the Brooks Range's northern foothills, within 3 miles (5km) of the coastal plain. The valley is one of many corridors used by the Porcupine Caribou Herd during seasonal migrations to and from the plain. The caribou have already moved through, but their signs are everywhere: hundreds of deep rutted trails criss-cross the landscape, thick clumps of caribou hair hang from willow bushes, and whitened, sun-bleached bones and antlers lay scattered on gravel bars, tundra wetlands, and limestone ridges.

Their first morning in the wilds, the hikers walk to a gray, nameless, cone-shaped mountain overlooking the coastal plain. Leaving the river, they cut across lowland tundra. From a distance, it appears smooth and monotonous, a green rolling carpet spread between gray and brown hills. Up close, that monotone green is transformed into a complex mix of grasses, shrubs, mosses, lichens, and wildflowers. And it's anything but smooth. They pick our way through a maze of sedge tussocks, mushroom-shaped grass mounds that are the stuff of Arctic legend.

Narrow at the base and wide on top, the tussocks are unstable to walk upon; any step slightly off center makes them lean this way or that. It's possible to walk between the tussocks, but the boggy ground between them quickly soaks boots. There's no easy solution, but at least the day hikers don't have heavy packs to balance.

As the group gradually ascends, the tussocks give way to alpine tundra; this is pleasant, like walking on a dry, spongy cushion. After a stop for lunch – the usual mix of nuts, fruit, cheese, chocolate – on a wind-swept knoll, the three men and three women jump across a clearwater creek, and leave tundra for talus. Forty minutes of strenuous rock-scrambling brings them to the hilltop, where they look upon an immense landscape of lakes, tundra plains, braided rivers, and craggy peaks. It's a wild and ancient land, one that inspires reverence.

The ridgetop reverie ends too soon, replaced by a picture-taking frenzy. Posing for group photos, the hikers are transformed from wilderness explorers into grinning tourists.

An abundance of wildlife

Returning to camp, the visitors spot two golden eagles soaring above the ridge they've just left. Later in the week they will see Dall sheep, red foxes, songbirds, ptarmigan, a couple of caribou – stragglers from the Porcupine Herd – and a grizzly bear sow with two cubs. The anglers among them will also catch grayling and Arctic char in the Aichilik's cold waters.

Continued hot weather prompts some members of the group to switch from daytime to evening walk-abouts their last few days in the refuge; temperatures here may drop 10, 20 or more degrees at night. Their final evening, a pair ascends a 2,500-ft (760-meter) limestone hill southwest of camp and are again rewarded with expansive views in all directions. To the north, beyond a series of humpbacked hills, is the undulating coastal plain stretching to the Arctic coast, where earth and sky meet in a white line: the ice-covered Beaufort Sea. To the east, across the Aichilik, are lowland plains, grading gently into tundra-covered knobs.

To the south and west are row after row of rugged ridges, culminating in the snow-capped tops of 8,000- and 9,000-ft peaks (2,400–2,700 meters), 30 miles (50km) away. The landscape invites further exploration; the hikers wonder what's over the next pass, and the pass beyond it.

The couple descends as the sun drops

Dressed to cope with the climate.

BELOW: Inupiat crafts made from marine animals including whale bone, walrus ivory, and seal intestines.

BELOW: rafters paddle down the Hulahula River.

behind the mountains. Above the darkening landscape a twilight glow paints the northern sky yellow, then orange, and crimson. Even at midnight, in mid-August, the heavens remain too bright for stars. For much of the summer, the sun never leaves the Arctic sky, though it may briefly hide behind high peaks. The pilot arrives on schedule and too quickly the backcountry visitors are headed south, back to pavement and restaurants and hot showers. In seven days they have seen no other humans. The solitude and wildness have been a blessing.

Float trips

One of the most popular ways to explore the Arctic Refuge is by float trip. Although hundreds of rivers and creeks flow out of the mountains, both north and south, only a few are large and deep enough to permit easy travel by raft, canoe, or kayak. These include the Sheenjek, Coleen, Kongakut, Canning, and Hulahula. Though experienced river-runners can organize their own trips, most refuge visitors go on guided trips that last one to two weeks.

Some trips combine river floating with overland backpacking; nearly all allow opportunities for hiking through the mountains. Contact refuge headquarters in Fairbanks (101 12th Ave., 99701; tel: 456-0250 or 800-362-4546; http://arctic. fws.gov) for a list of commercial outfitters and guides permitted to work here.

The **Hulahula** is the most challenging of the Arctic Refuge's floatable streams, with a few stretches of Class III whitewater (on a scale of VI). At high water, some rapids might even be graded higher. It therefore isn't a good stream for unguided beginners, but it's popular with guided groups.

Born near the Arctic divide, the Hulahula is one of the Arctic Refuge's largest and most heavily used north-flowing rivers. Fed by remnant glaciers as well as numerous clearwater tributaries, it passes two of the Brooks Range's three highest peaks (9,020-ft/2,749-meter Mount Chamberlain and 8,855-ft/2,699-meter Mount Michelson) while flowing 100 miles (160 km) to the sea.

The river was given its name – originally spelled Hoolahoola – by whalers and was taken from a Hawaiian word meaning "to dance." Exactly to what dance the whalers referred is unknown.

River-runners who travel the Hulahula, or other north-bound streams, are likely to see Dall sheep, grizzlies and sometimes wolves while passing through the mountains. Depending on the time of year, floaters may also cross paths with migrating members of the Porcupine Caribou Herd. Once out on the rolling and swampy coastal plain, rafters and other river travelers may see musk oxen, large prehistoric-like beasts with curved horns and long shaggy coasts. These living relics of the ice age disappeared from Alaska's North Slope in the late 1800s, probably because of human overhunting. Reintroduced to the Arctic Refuge in 1969 and 1970, the species population now numbers in the hundreds.

Most river trips into the refuge are done between early June and mid-July, when the streams are running highest. Even then, rivers don't always have enough water for easy floating. It's sometimes necessary to lift and carry rafts through shallow, riffled sections of rivers. Not only does early summer offer the best river-travel conditions, it also features prime wildlife viewing opportu-nities, especially on the coastal plain. And mosquito numbers are usually still low, particularly in June.

Entering the refuge

Because no roads lead into the refuge, nearly all visitors enter it by plane, using air-taxi services. The two most popular jumping-off spots are **Kaktovik** ⑬, an Inupiat Eskimo village along the Beaufort Sea on the refuge's northern border, and **Fort Yukon**, a small, predominantly Athabascan village 140 air miles (225km) from Fairbanks and about 450 miles (720km) from Anchorage. Both Kaktovik and Fort Yukon are served by commercial flights out of Fairbanks.

Once inside the refuge, visitors traveling on their own must be self-sufficient. There are no campgrounds or other facilities and backcountry travelers are expected to practice low-impact camping techniques. Here, as in other parts of the Arctic, it's also wise to come prepared for a wide range of weather conditions. Midsummer snowstorms are possible, particularly in the mountains, and night-time temperatures may drop below freezing at any time of the year. ❑

BELOW: first you carve your blocks of ice, then you build your igloo.

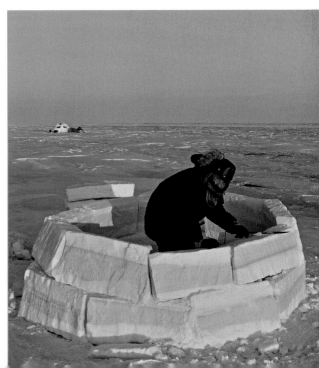

GATES OF THE ARCTIC

If you hear the call of the wilderness, the Gates of the Arctic may be the place you are looking for, but plan your trip with care, because you really are on your own

BELOW: hikers head into Anaktuvuk Pass, whose name means "the place of caribou droppings."

I n 1929, Robert Marshall, a founder of the Wilderness Society, proposed that most of Alaska north of the Yukon River be preserved as wilderness. His vision wasn't realized, but much of northern Alaska is in fact now so protected; and the place most dear to Marshall, the central Brooks Range, is preserved in **Gates of the Arctic National Park and Preserve** . In the heart of northern Alaska, the park is 200 miles (320km) northwest of Fairbanks, and 200 miles southeast of Barrow, Alaska's largest Eskimo community.

No maintained roads or trails exist within the park – no phones, TVs, radios, gas stations, restaurants, stores or hotels. No emergency services are available: no hospitals, first-aid stations, ambulances, police or fire stations. There is one permanent ranger station at **Anaktuvuk Pass**, a Native village in the middle of the park. Other park staff operate out of Bettles and the Fairbanks headquarters.

The culture of the Nunamiut Inupiat is being documented in the **Simon Paneak Memorial Museum** (Anaktuvak Pass, tel: 907-661-3413; www.co.north-slope.ak. us/nsb/55.htm). Emphasis is put on the importance of the caribou in determining the Nunamiut people's nomadic lifestyle. Local artwork and crafts are on sale.

Outdoor activities

Such wilderness provides freedom from the trappings of civilization – one that only about 2,000 experience each year. In summer, there are opportunities for mountaineering, backpacking, hiking and camping. The lakes, rivers and streams allow for rafting, canoeing, kayaking and fishing. Also popular are birding, flight-seeing and wildlife viewing.

Fall activities include blueberry and cranberry picking, and hunting for bear, Dall sheep, caribou, moose, ducks, geese, rabbits and ptarmigan (non-subsistence "sport" hunting can be done only in the preserve). In winter, the park is quiet. The sun drops below the horizon in December and doesn't appear again until January. The temperature can fall to –70°F (–57°C). In March and April, as daylight hours again exceed darkness, a few hardy adventurers use the park for cross-country skiing, dog sledding and snowshoeing.

The Gates of the Arctic area is known as "inhabited wilderness." Visitors, floating past a Native fish camp, may see orange-red salmon strips drying on birch poles or a fish net bobbing with the flow of the river. They may even encounter a trapper's secluded log home with a snow-machine outside, traps and a bearskin hanging from the cabin walls. But people are rarely seen. The area's population density is less than one person per 5,000 acres (2,000 hectares).

Gateway to Gates

Gates of the Arctic National Park and Preserve is remote, pristine wilderness. The meaning of "remote" becomes immediately evident when trying to get here. **Bettles** ⓑ is the primary gateway to Gates. You can take a scheduled flight from Fairbanks to this friendly little outpost, then hire an air taxi to fly into the park. Before going, check in at the park's ranger station and discuss your itinerary

with staff. Bettles also provides visitors to Gates with potential outfitters, guides and a lodge.

From here, any number of trips are possible into the park, but they all cost a lot. If you want to cut costs, it's sensible to travel in a group. A trip for six from Bettles can cost less than half what it costs for two. Compare services to prices and ask for references. Reputable guides will have names of people to contact who have taken their trips. The steep price of visiting Gates of the Arctic National Park can be an advantage if you like solitude, for few people make their way in. It's a place that requires time, money and the ability to face a challenge.

If you are short of money but have the time and the physical stamina you can backpack the many miles to the park, after driving along the Dalton Highway or Haul Road, built during the creation of the Trans-Alaska Pipeline *(see page 285)*. Check for road conditions on the Highway by calling 511 (within Alaska) or 866-282-7577; http://511.Alaska.gov). The road is open for more than 400 miles (640 km) to Prudhoe Bay.

Fairbanks is also a recommended stop

TIP

Be prepared
When you meet a bear in 8 million acres (3.2 million hectares) of this wilderness, you're on your own. People still freeze and starve to death in remote cabins in the Brooks Range wilderness; months may pass before their bodies are found. If you don't arrange for someone to rescue you, no one will. This is self-reliance – or, for the unprepared, suicide.

BELOW:
Anaktuvuk Pass, with 300 residents, is the only community within the national park.

*Hiding from
mosquitoes.*

BELOW: caribou
bulls cross the
Alatna River in
the Brooks Range.

for maps, information and supplies. The **Alaska Public Lands Information Center** (250 Cushman Street, tel: 456-0527; www.nps.gov/aplic) has a complete list of air services, commercial services, information books and maps. Information is also available directly from park headquarters (tel: 692-5494; www.nps.gov/gaar), the Alaska Department of Fish and Game, the Department of Transportation, the Alaska State Troopers and the State Department of Tourism.

Fairbanks is generally the last stop to shop for supplies, including stove fuel and food. Since all fuel must be flown in, many communities have erratic or non-existent supplies; camp stove fuel is not allowed on scheduled airlines. Villages are often not equipped with facilities for visitors, so travelers should have adequate food supplies and should have arranged return transportation in advance.

The Dalton Highway winds through wild and beautiful wilderness and nears Gates's eastern boundary at **Coldfoot ⑯**, approximately 250 miles (400km) north of Fairbanks. In early September, when the birch leaves are golden in the hills and the weather is sunny and dry, the drive alone is worth the trip – though early winter snowstorms may temporarily block the road in September or even August. A stop at the **Coldfoot Services Truckstop** is a must for any visitor. In the lodge-style dining hall restaurant, meals are eaten on oilcloth-covered tables with wooden benches, mining camp-style. Motel rooms are available.

The National Park Service and other federal agencies jointly operate a summer visitor center at Coldfoot. Another visitor center, the **Arctic Interagency Visitor Center**, is located just north of the Yukon River Bridge (open daily 9am–6pm in summer only; tel: 678-5209).

Trips and trails

The most easily accessed trail into the park is in **Wiseman**, 15 miles (24km) north of Coldfoot. Wiseman is a turn-of-the-20th-century mining community. Its weathered buildings are still home to a few miners. The road from Dalton Highway to Wiseman extends on to several trails that enter the park. The **Nolan-Wiseman Creek Trail** goes through the historic mining area to the Glacier River. Another approved trail follows the

Hammond River north from Wiseman.

One of the most popular areas in Gates is the North Fork of the Koyukuk River, where the peaks, **Frigid Craigs** and **Boreal Mountain**, form "The Gates" for which the park is named. The Gates can be reached either by backpacking out of Anaktuvuk or by floating the North Fork from Summit Lake. Another favored excursion involves flightseeing out of the village of Bettles.

Float trips – and combination backpacking/float trips – can be arranged throughout the park. Or seek fish-filled **Walker Lake**, a blue jewel nestled in the deep forested hills in the southern part of the park. Winter cross-country ski trips, dog-sled rides and ice fishing are available here. A few private cabins and lodges are the only places where a visitor can sleep indoors in or near the park.

If you want solitude and isolation you would be better off avoiding favored places, such as the North Fork of the Koyukuk, the Arrigetch Peaks, or Noatak River. Customized trips to unnamed valleys are available for those who want to vacation alone.

Sport hunting is allowed only in the park's preserve section, and non-Alaskans must have a guide if they want to hunt for certain big game animals. A guide familiar with local conditions is recommended even if not required. Some game can be taken only by permit. Contact the Alaska Department of Fish and Game for specifics (tel: 459-7233; www.state.ak.us/adfg).

The mosquito menace

As well as being home to grizzlies, wolves and caribou, Gates is also host to hordes of mosquitoes. During certain times of the year – July in particular – wilderness travelers can best endure the ever-present swarm of bugs by keeping their entire body, including their hands, completely covered, and wearing a head-net. Always carry a good mosquito repellent, preferably one with a high DEET concentration, and a finely screened tent.

Another wilderness creature that inhabits Gates is *Giardia lamblia*, a microscopic water organism that causes "beaver fever," an unpleasant intestinal disorder. The best prevention is to boil all drinking water or use chemical disinfectants such as iodine.

July and August are the wettest months. Thunderstorms are common. Rain has been known to start in mid-August and not stop until it turns to snow in September. Temperatures range from –70°F (–57°C) to 92°F (32°C). Snow may fall in any month. The average summer temperature ranges from freezing to 85°F (29°C), prime hypothermia (body-chilling) conditions. Wool or synthetic clothing such as fleece keeps you warm and dry, and high-quality hiking boots are needed in rocky and soggy conditions.

People have drowned sleeping on sandbars; others have found that a gentle stream can become a raging white-water river after a downpour. Three to 10 days' leeway should be allowed for water level changes if any river or creek crossings are involved. Anyone who wants to visit the Gates of the Arctic needs to do considerable research: topographical maps are vital, and every problem must be anticipated and planned for. ❑

Portrait of Wiseman
In the 1930s the mining community of Wiseman had a population of 80 men, 22 women and 25 children. Its raw life was vividly captured by Robert Marshall in his book "Arctic Village: A 1930s Portrait of Wiseman, Alaska."

BELOW: a fortified supply hut, known as a *cache*.

CAPE KRUSENSTERN

Alaska
Anchorage

The remote lands of Cape Krusenstern, whose archeological treasures reach back 4,000 years, are only for the self-sufficient and intrepid traveler, but the rewards are great

BELOW: Eskimo snow goggles dating to AD50 found on a ridge at Cape Krusenstern.

I t's hard to imagine a less likely place for buried treasure. There's nothing particularly conspicuous about **Cape Krusenstern** – no towering mountains, magnificent waterfalls, verdant forests. Only a low, ridged spit with deep furrows, dotted with countless ponds, and bordered by a relentless sea on one side and a large lagoon on the other.

Resembling a giant scythe clipping the waves of the Chukchi Sea, Cape Krusenstern stretches into polar waters in northwestern Alaska just north of Kotzebue. Hidden beneath beach ridges on the cape are archeological treasures dating back at least 4,000 years. This earthbound chronicle of early man in Alaska brought about the establishment in 1980 of the 560,000-acre (226,600-hectare) **Cape Krusenstern National Monument** ⑰ (tel: 442-3890, or 442-3760 in summer only; www. nps.gov/cakr).

Charter planes and boats headquartered in **Kotzebue** take infrequent visitors to the monument, 10 miles (16km) northwest across Kotzebue Sound at its southern border. The monument lacks visitor services – no public shelters, campgrounds or developed trails – and receives only a few thousand visitors a year.

Remote villages

The small village of **Kivalina** stretches out along the Chukchi shore north of the monument and to the east of Krusenstern, across the Mulgrave Hills, lies the village of **Noatak**. Kivalina and Noatak have airstrips but most visitors arrive via Kotzebue, which has a jet service from both Anchorage and Fairbanks.

Cape Krusenstern is a bring-your-own-shelter place, and that goes for stove, food and water. Highlands beyond the beaches have freshwater streams, but it's still best to take some – and either boil or treat any local water you do use, to prevent the risk of giardia. The Krusenstern tableau is waiting, but come prepared to be self-sustaining. Planes can land on some beaches of the monument, and floatplanes put down on nearby lagoons. Many beach areas are privately owned; visitors should check with monument headquarters staff in Kotzebue for specific locations of private property, as they are not marked. Travelers are free to explore archeological zones, but no digging for artifacts or causing other disturbances are allowed.

Winds sweep almost constantly across the lowlands of Cape Krusenstern. In winter they bring instant freezing to an already cold land. In summer, fog blankets coastal areas, although temperatures are 40–65°F (4–18°C). Inland, the skies are often clear in June and July, but visitors should always carry rain gear and be alert for hypothermia.

Formation of the cape

The cape at Krusenstern didn't always exist. About 10,000 years ago, the coastline angled straight southeast from Point Hope, skirted a small mountain, and turned east. Kotzebue Sound was mostly a giant sandy lowland, not the open waterway it is today. During the Pleistocene Era, from approximately 2 million to 10,000–15,000 years ago, great ice sheets covered much of the northern hemisphere. These ice masses absorbed water, causing the sea level to recede. As the sea shrank away from the shore, it exposed a land bridge connecting North America and Asia. When the ice sheets melted, the sea level rose once again and covered the so-called Bering Land Bridge.

Sweeping down the newly aligned coastline, prevailing winds from the northwest propelled waves, which carried bits of gravel in their churning surf, down the beach. When the waves hit the turn where the coastline swung east, they dropped the gravel offshore. Every so often, usually in the spring, the winds shifted to the southwest. Great chunks of ice were driven onshore, but not before the ice scooped up gravel from shallow offshore beds and deposited it on the beach beyond the surf. Ridge after ridge built up on the outer shore of the cape.

Slowly the cape pushed seaward. Hardy beach plants colonized the ridges, their root systems helping to stabilize the gravels. Year after year the birth and death of beach plants built up a thin layer of soil, creating suitable habitat for other plants. Over the centuries, a carpet of green followed the shoreline, advancing seaward, until 114 ridges lined an approximately 3-mile (5-km) wide spit. Lt Otto

Mineral wealth
A road to the Red Dog mine crosses the northern boundary of Cape Krusenstern National Monument. Trucks haul zinc from open pit mines to a tidewater port. Cominco Alaska operates the mine, along with the NANA Regional Corp., a Native corporation based in Kotzebue.

BELOW:
a lake at Cape Krusenstern National Monument.

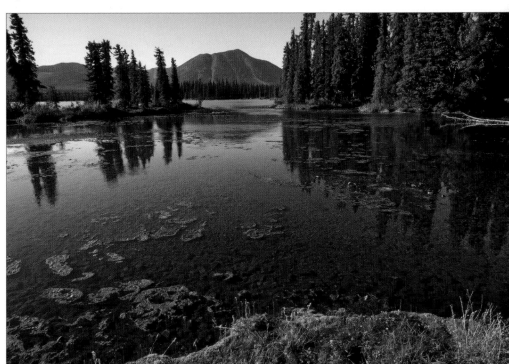

von Kotzebue, sailing with the Imperial Russian Navy, gave geographical recognition to the cape by naming it Krusenstern after the first Russian admiral to circumnavigate the globe in 1803–4.

The Old Whalers

Every once in a while the continuity of the archeological record was broken when scientists unearthed artifacts from a culture that did not fit in to the spectrum of early man in northwestern Alaska.

One such find was the record of Old Whalers on the beach ridge inland from the Choris remains. These prehistoric people, who lived for a brief time at the cape sometime between 1800 and 1500 BC, relied almost exclusively on the sea for sustenance. Their record indicates a greater use of whales than either preceding or subsequent cultures.

The cape today

Each spring, the rivers and streams of Kotzebue basin cleanse themselves when snow melt fills the channels which dump their load into Kotzebue Sound. Whitefish join this migration, leaving their inland wintering grounds and moving into summer feeding areas in coastal estuaries. This annual flooding acts as a catalyst for one of the region's major subsistence hauls.

As the floodwaters fan out into Kotzebue Sound, several species of whitefish swarm into sloughs along the Krusenstern coast, fattening throughout the summer in the brackish waters. Local residents congregate at the sloughs each fall when groundswells from the Chukchi Sea push gravel and sand across the channels by which whitefish exit the salt-water areas on their return migration. Residents harvest the fish trapped in the sloughs, to add to their winter staples.

Subsistence controls the lifestyle of Krusenstern residents today as in ancient times. Travelers should take extra care not to disturb fishing nets, boats or other gear on which local residents rely.

Also crucial is the 6-mile (10-km) flatland at the monument's southern tip, **Sheshalik**, "Place of White Whales." Several families maintain year-round homes at Sheshalik, which is a traditional gathering place for hunters of beluga, the small, white, toothed whale. Life in the community revolves around stockpiling

An Inupiat woman making parka hood ruffs from wolf skins.

BELOW:
a seal hunter
on the Cape.

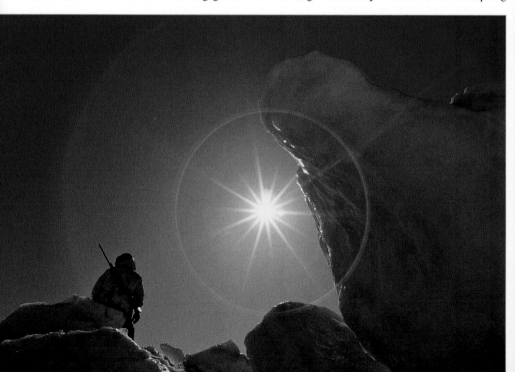

the meat, fish, berries and greenstuff that
see these families through nine months
of harsh winter.

When snow and cold blanket the
region, families keep busy ice fishing and
trapping for small fur-bearers. In spring,
marine mammal hunters take to the ice
in search of seals. When leads open in the
sea ice, belugas become the quarry.

Sealing Point

For centuries, hunters have gathered at
Sealing Point on the narrow isthmus sep-
arating the Chukchi from the inner
lagoons. Returning, their boats loaded
with sea mammal carcasses, the hunters
portage the isthmus and continue their
southerly journey over calm lagoon
waters rather than fighting the waves of
the open sea.

In May, waterfowl return from their
winter sojourn and head for Krusenstern
where snow melt has weakened the ice
and open water spreads early throughout
the lagoons. Several species of geese and
ducks nest on the ponds, joined by their
cousins on stilts, the sandhill cranes.

Later in the summer residents harvest
salmonberries, cranberries and blueberries. Women pick greens, preserving
some in seal oil for later use. Fish –
grayling, Arctic char and whitefish – are
hung to dry on wooden racks. Chum
salmon are taken for subsistence as well
as for the commercial fishery in Kotzebue Sound.

Hunting territory

After waterfowl leave in the fall, hunters
turn to caribou, ptarmigan and sometimes
walrus or – rarely nowadays – bear. Both
black and brown bears have been found
on the cape; polar bears roam offshore
ice in winter and spring and occasionally
come ashore.

Agile Arctic foxes follow behind these
northern barons, ready to inspect any tid-
bit they leave behind. Onshore, elusive
fur-bearers – wolves, wolverines, red
foxes, lynx, mink, short-tailed weasels,
snowshoe and tundra hare, and Arctic
ground squirrels – patrol the tundra.

Hunters take moose in low-lying areas

or Dall sheep in the Igichuk Hills. A
small group of musk ox, descendants of
the shaggy mammals which once roamed
all arctic North America but were wiped
out by hunters in Alaska in the mid-
1800s, thunder across the tundra of the
Mulgrave Hills.

Other species, generally not part of the
subsistence catch, share Krusenstern's
bounty. Birds such as the lesser golden-
plovers, western and semipalmated sandpipers, whimbrels, Lapland longspurs and
Savannah sparrows add their beauty and
song. Arctic and Aleutian terns float
gracefully above the tundra, ready to
defend their nests from the purposeful
forays of glaucous gulls and jaegers. An
Asian migrant, the handsome yellow
wagtail, builds its nest in tiny cavities in
the beach ridges. Overhead, rough-legged
hawks soar from their nests in the highlands to hover over the tundra, piercing
eyes searching for voles and lemmings.

The ambiance at Krusenstern is under-
stated, but for the curious and the thor-
ough, the history of early man in the
north and its modern translation in the
subsistence world of local residents are
only a step away.   ❑

*More than 10 million
ducks, swans and
geese nest in Alaska.*

BELOW: an Eskimo
examines the
remains of a whale
as they dry out.

NATIVE ART AND ARTIFACTS

Items which once had specific purposes are now highly prized as tourist souvenirs, although to the Native people their traditional cultural values are still important

In early times, all Alaska Native art served a definite purpose. The items created had either a practical or a cultural use. For instance, carvers created masks for ceremonies, totem poles to tell the histories of clans, and Chilkat blankets for special dancing, or to present as tokens of esteem.

These days, although much Native art continues to serve traditional purposes, many objects are sold into private hands. Dance fans and masks, for example, are still used in ceremonies today, but they are regularly sold as souvenirs. Often, these sales are a welcome source of income for the villages. Visitors to Alaska eagerly seek ivory scrimshaw, carvings of bone, wood, and stone, and baskets woven with colorful grasses or formed from birch bark.

Regional differences

Natives from different parts of Alaska excel in various types of art. Doll-making has been an Eskimo art form for at least 2,000 years. The detailed dolls with carved faces and fur parkas portray Eskimo ways of life, from hunters to berry-pickers and skin sewers. The Athabascans are known for colorful beadwork, usually flowers created on tanned moose hide, and incorporating porcupine quills and buttons. The Aleuts are masters at making tightly woven grass baskets, decorated with multicolored embroidery. Some baskets can take up to 15 hours an inch to complete. Southeast tribes are known for their blankets and totem poles.

ABOVE: Cultural symbol
This totemic symbol is a detail from a pole in the popular Sitka National Historic Park. It is typical of the traditional designs used by the Tlingit people when carving their ceremonial masks, rattles and everyday utensils, each with its own story to tell.

BELOW: Native dolls
These Yup'ik dolls have faces of moose skin and miniature parkas with wolverine ruffs and beaver mitts.

ABOVE: Chilkat blanket
Chilkat blankets can take over a year to make, and were once highly sought after by Native nobility. Each told a legend and was used for a special occasion: to cover a body lying in state, or as a gift to an honored guest.

TEM POLES: LEGENDS IN WOOD

Totem poles, some as high as 60 ft (18 meters) tall, are one of the most popular examples of Northwest Native woodworking. Figures, or totems, on the poles are comparable to family crests and are used to tell a story, legend or event. The totemic symbols are usually animals, such as bears, eagles or killer whales. Their significance lies in myth – stories passed down through generations about how certain animals may have affected the destiny of ancestors.

Poles could usually be found clustered along the village's shore in front of clan houses or directly on the fronts of private houses, or in cemeteries. According to early accounts of Tlingit life, deceased clan members were cremated and their ashes placed in these poles.

Missionaries and other outsiders contributed to the destruction and neglect of many totem poles. Since the 1930s, many have been restored, some of which now stand in totem parks near villages like Sawock and Saxman and at the Totem Heritage Center in Ketchikan.

LEFT: Tlingit designs

This Native house in Sitka has been covered with numerous yellow cedar plaques, all carved and painted with different Tlingit designs. The distinctive style relies heavily on the portrayal of birds, animals and fish, often in a highly stylized way. The Tlingit people's carving skills were also turned to practical use in making eating utensils and large canoes.

BELOW: Musk ox mural

This mural decorates the exterior of the Oomingmak Co-Op in Anchorage, a good place to buy articles hand-made in villages from the fine, soft musk ox wool called qiviut. Today's musk oxen – there are probably about 3,000 – are of the Greenland sub-species. The native animals were hunted to extinction by 1860. Forming defensive circles to protect their young had been effective against wolves, but not against guns as this tactic enabled hunters to kill entire herds at a time for their meat and hides.

LOW: Ceremonial headdress

Masks and headdresses such as this one, worn in Sitka, have great symbolic importance, as they portray the relationship of a particular tribe with the spirits, are worn during special ceremonies.

NOME AND THE SEWARD PENINSULA

Alaska
Nome
Anchorage

Once a Wild West gold mining boom town, Nome is
now best known as the end of the Iditarod Trail
and the Seward Peninsula's commercial hub

BELOW:
displays in Nome's
oldest saloon, the
Board of Trade.

This remote community has long been known as the city that wouldn't die, although it has had more than enough reason to disappear many times since its founding in 1899. Nome ⑱ has been burned to the ground; pounded by relentless gales; attacked by flu, diphtheria and countless other maladies; and almost starved out of existence, yet its population has always rebuilt and struggled on. Nowadays, this one-time boom town is best known for its connection to the Iditarod Trail Sled Dog Race; and it's the commercial center of the Seward

Peninsula, whose wind-whipped tundra landscape was first inhabited thousands of years ago by peoples migrating from Asia into northwest Alaska.

It was gold, discovered in 1898, that brought men, and later women, to this windswept, wave-battered beach on the Seward Peninsula, 75 miles (120km) or more from the nearest tree. Of all the Alaska gold-rush towns, Nome was the largest and the rowdiest. Best estimates put the population in excess of 20,000 people by the summer of 1900, but nobody knows for certain.

By the time gold-bearing creeks around the area were discovered, claim jumping and other less-than-ethical mining practices were well advanced in Alaska. Claim-jumping was so rampant that it took a dozen years or more before everything was straightened out. By then the boom was dying and Nome had little more than 5,000 residents. Over the years the permanent population has shrunk as low as 500. It has more or less stabilized in recent years at about 3,500 residents.

Precious beaches

Nome hosted a whole series of gold rushes, each almost blending into the next. The first gold came the traditional way – it was found in the streams flowing into Norton Sound. The thousands who rushed to Nome set their tents on the beach and explored the nearby gullies, little realizing that all they had to do was sift the sand that was their floor for the precious yellow metal.

The famed black-sand beaches of Nome count as the "second" gold rush. Since nobody could legally stake a claim on the beach, a man could work any ground he could stand on near the shoreline. The sands were turned over dozens of times and yielded millions of dollars in gold.

Then geologists pointed out that Nome had more than one beach. Over the centuries, as rivers carried silt to the ocean, the beach line had gradually extended out to sea. The geologists predicted that under the tundra a few yards back from the water, miners would find an ancient beach and, with it, more deposits of gold. And so it was that later years saw yet a third gold rush as ground behind the sea wall was dug and re-dug to extract the precious metal.

Fortune seekers still sift the sands in front of Nome. In 1984 a Nome resident walking on the beach picked up a gold nugget weighing over an ounce from under a piece of driftwood. Such are the rewards of fresh air and exercise. The beach at Nome is still open to the public. Anyone with a gold pan or a sluice box can search for gold along the waterfront,

and camping is permitted. If you're serious about finding more than a trace of gold, it's hard, back-breaking work, but then riches have never come easy for miners. Perhaps the only ones who found easy money were the gamblers and the tricksters who made their living relieving miners of their hard-earned gold.

Wyatt Earp visits

Some shifty characters who learned their crafts in the boom towns of America's Wild West converged on Nome as practiced, professional con-artists – men like Wyatt Earp, the frontier marshal, who arrived in Nome as a paunchy, 51-year-old saloon keeper (and was frequently at odds with the law).

Yet Nome's gold-rush years spawned a hero or two amid the unscrupulous. Shortly after Wyatt Earp arrived, a family named Doolittle moved to the town. One of the boys, Jimmy, delivered newspapers for the Nome Nugget, the oldest continually published newspaper in Alaska. Young Jimmy grew up to lead "Doolittle's Raiders," the daring group of army pilots who launched their over-sized, overloaded bombers from the

Pizza to go
Residents of Nome enjoy the luxury of hot, gourmet pizza delivered to their door. Those living in remote villages can also order the same pizza to be delivered via airplane. Airport Pizza, located near Nome airport, bakes and sells the pizza, and Frontier Flying Service delivers it to the local air strip – not piping hot, but free of charge. See listing, page 307.

BELOW: Unalakleet, a Native village on the Norton Sound of the Bering Sea.

decks of a Navy aircraft carrier in the darkest days of World War II.

Energetic celebrations

The ability to face all comers, whatever the odds, is what makes Nome the rollicking place it is today. Nomites bring a special energy to every project they take on. After all, in remote northwest Alaska you sometimes have to make your own fun.

The **Midnight Sun Festival** is a good example. Held on the weekend closest to the solstice (June 21), the two-day festival includes a late-night softball tournament, a street dance, a chicken barbecue, foodstalls (selling reindeer hot dogs and cotton candy) and a dart tournament. The **Nome River Raft Race** is part of the Midnight Sun Festival, and its only rule seems to be that there are no rules.

Less than two weeks later, Nome gets ready to party again with the 4th of July celebration. This event includes street games, a raffle, free ice cream (provided by the fire department) and the **Anvil Mountain Run**. Participants are required to run up the mountain on the road, but are allowed to take any path they want

Tourists pan for gold.

RIGHT:
the Bering Sea
Ice Golf Classic.

on the way down; the tundra is a shorter route, but it's not as smooth going.

As with most civic celebrations, each event has its own parade. There are hardly any spectators because most of the local residents are in the parade. And what would the 4th of July be without fireworks? In the early 1980s Nome's city council wanted to stop such devices being sold within the city limits because of the fire hazard. This particularly affected the mayor of the time, as he was one of the largest fireworks dealers in the area. He solved the problem by setting up his firework stand a few steps outside the city line and gleefully sold all manner of pyrotechnics to the people, who were more than willing to use them.

There are advantages to living in a remote frontier town. Nome is a close community, with almost anyone available to lend a hand. Consider Christmas. Christmas trees are traditional decorations in local homes just as elsewhere in the United States. The problem with this arises because the last ship of the season usually departs in October, just before Norton Sound freezes. Trees can be flown in, but that's expensive.

Seward Peninsula Road Trips

Though travel to Nome must be by air or sea, the area boasts the second-largest city road system in the state. Three unmaintained gravel roads extend for a total of 300 miles across broad regions of the southwest portion of the Seward Peninsula.

These roads allow visitors opportunities – uncommon in remote bush communities – to drive or bike past small, outlying Native villages or through prime birding or wildlife sighting areas. The visitor center (tel: 443-6624; www.nomealaska.org/vc) provides a road guide and a list of businesses offering car rentals. Check with the Alaska Department of Fish and Game (tel: 443-2271) for local information on roadside fishing or wildlife viewing opportunities.

There are no services available along any of these remote roadways, so be sure to bring along adequate fuel, food, a spare tire and bug repellent. Current weather and driving conditions for any Alaska roadway are available from the Alaska Department of Transportation and Public Facilities by dialing 511; (866) 282-7577; or online at http://511.alaska.gov.

In Alaska as a whole, only one-third of the 300 or so communities are located on the road system. Travel to the others, as well as deliveries of goods and tourists, must generally be via boat, airplane, all-terrain vehicle and/or snowmachine.

However, about 80 miles (130km) to the east is a convenient (at least by rural Alaska standards) forest, and in the weeks before Christmas residents band together and dispatch truck loads of volunteers along a bone-crunching road leading to the forest. The trucks are then filled with small spruce trees, enough to ensure that every household gets one. These aren't the magnificent Douglas firs that are favored in the Lower 48. Instead, they're straggly tundra spruces, but they are adequate for the purpose.

After the holidays, residents take their old trees out to "Nome National Forest" – a stretch of ice outside town – and "plant" them. The trees generally stay there until spring, tended by a self-appointed "ranger" who stands them up when they get blown over, and sometimes visitors to Nome are fooled into thinking there really is a forest here.

The Great Race

After Christmas, there's one more high point in the long winter, the combined **Spring Carnival** and **Iditarod Trail Sled Dog Race**, billed as "The Last Great Race on Earth" *(see pages 308–9).*

Also in March is the **Bering Sea Ice Golf Classic**. Participants, dressed in wacky outfits, play on artificial grass on top of the ice, next to the "Nome National Forest."

Today Nome is the transportation hub of western Alaska. It has a major airport with jet service to and from Anchorage, Fairbanks and Kotzebue, and provides commuter plane service to every village in the region. Almost everyone touring northwestern Alaska must at least pass through Nome.

At first glance, it may seem there is not a lot to do here; but opportunities to learn more about Nome and the surrounding region can be found. A small museum, the **Carrie McLain Museum** (in the public library at 233 Front Street, tel: 443-2566; entry free) concentrates mostly on gold rush memorabilia. There are the gold dredges just outside town. There are several shops that sell ivory carvings and other Native artwork. And of course there's the gold panning.

Ivory carvings are popular souvenirs.

BELOW: a team in the Iditarod Trail Sled Dog Race.

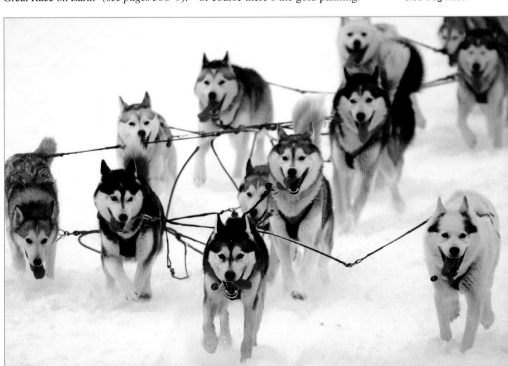

BELOW:
the waterfront
at Kotzebue.

A handful of businesses in Nome also do guided tours of the town and surrounding areas. Or, you can go for a drive: more than 300 miles (500 km) of maintained gravel roads connect Nome with other Seward Peninsula locales *(see panel, page 304)*. A couple of businesses in town rent vehicles. Information on Nome's tourist businesses and rental companies can be obtained from the Nome Convention and Visitor Bureau (tel: 443-6624; www.nomealaska.org/vc).

Adventures beyond Nome

The Seward Peninsula's road network can lead to all kinds of adventures: fishing, hiking, wildlife viewing, birding, mountain biking, to name a few. Roads connect Nome with other peninsula communities, including **Teller** (pop. 268) and the ghost town of **Council**. There's another ghost town, **Solomon**, along the Nome Council Road, and the "Last Train to Nowhere" is a rusting hulk of a goldrush era train, stranded on the tundra.

The Anvil Mountain Road goes (appropriately) to the top of **Anvil Mountain**, which presents panoramic views of Nome, the surrounding countryside, and the Bering Sea. The Nome-Taylor Highway leads to **Pilgrim Hot Springs**; about 7 miles (11 km) off the main road, this former Catholic mission and orphanage *(see margin note)* is open to the public, but visitors are asked to call ahead (tel: 443-5892) before visiting.

Bering Land Bridge Preserve

Another hot spot, the **Serpentine Hot Springs**, is located within the **Bering Land Bridge National Preserve** ⑲ (tel: 443-2522; www.nps.gov/bela) a 2.8-million-acre (1.1-million-hectare) parkland at the northern edge of the Seward Peninsula. Much closer to Siberia (55 miles/88 km away as the raven flies) than Alaska's urban center, this preserve is among the most remote and least visited units in America's National Park System.

Its landscape is dominated by volcanic features such as lava flows and maars (former volcanic craters that are now lakes). Though barren in appearance throughout much of the year, the preserve is brightened each summer by bright tundra flowers.

Surprisingly, more than 250 species of flowering plants manage to endure the region's harsh climate. And thousands of birds come here each year to breed and raise their young. More than 100 species are known to migrate to the preserve, including sandhill cranes, loons, geese, swans, and many different shorebirds and songbirds.

Other residents include grizzlies, wolves, caribou, musk oxen, and moose. Also of interest is the culture of neighboring Inuits – their villages, reindeer herds, and arts and crafts.

Thousands of years ago, during the Pleistocene Ice Age, this region was part of the Bering Land Bridge, which connected what is today North America with Asia. Up to 1,000 miles (1,600 km) wide, the bridge allowed humans to migrate from Siberia into what we now call Alaska.

The Bering Land Bridge National Preserve celebrates that past while protecting the present landscape and its wild inhabitants. As with most parklands in remote Alaska, this has no visitor facilities and is most easily reached by plane. Contact preserve headquarters or the Nome Convention and Visitor Bureau *(see above)* for up-to-date information on local air carriers.

Sepentine Hot Springs

This remote hot springs is located within the Bering Land Bridge National Preserve. You can't actually climb into the springs for a soak, because the water's too hot. There is nearby, however, a hot tub housed in a rustic bathhouse, with two pipes leading into it: one bringing hot water from the springs and the other cold water from a nearby creek. On days when the cold-water creek dries up, those hoping to enjoy a soak simply fill the tub early in the day, and let it cool.

You can also spend a few days hiking among huge granite outcroppings and sleeping in a bunkhouse.

It's not effortless to visit Serpentine Hot Springs, however. Summertime travelers must charter a fixed-wing aircraft (no helicopters) from Nome or Kotzebue to fly out to the Preserve. In winter, travel may be by snowmachine, as well. For more information, contact the Bering Land Bridge National Preserve (www.nps.gov /bela), or to find an air charter service or tour operator in the area, contact the Nome Convention and Visitors Bureau (www.nomealaska.org) or the City of Kotzebue (www.cityofkotzebue.com). ❏

Native woman in splendid furs.

RESTAURANTS

Airport Pizza Restaurant & Coffee House
406 Bering Street (near Nome Airpprt)
tel: (in Nome) 443-7992; (outlying villages) 877-749-9270
"You Buy! We Fly!' is the unique sales pitch of this one-of-a-kind restaurant featuring dine in, drive through or free delivery service, even to remote bush villages. Now open for breakfast, lunch and dinner, this is perhaps the favorite eatery in Nome. Beer and wine. $–$$$$

Fat Freddie's Restaurant
309 Front Street
tel: (907) 443-5899
Dine with the locals at the Iditarod finish line. Breakfast, lunch or dinner served daily. Gaze at the Bering Sea as you enjoy home-made soups or "burgers, steaks and shakes." Liquor may be purchased separately from hotel liquor store and consumed in the restaurant with your meal. $–$$$

Milano's Pizzeria
110 West Front Street, Suite 102
tel: (907) 443-2924
An tasty assortment of Italian and Japanese dishes. The pizzas are a local favorite. Beer, wine. $–$$

• • • • • • • • • • • • • • • • • • • •
Price is for dinner excluding tax, tip and beverages: **$$$$** *$30 and up,* **$$$** *$20–30,* **$$** *$15–20,* **$** *under $15.*

THE IDITAROD TRAIL SLED DOG RACE

They don't call it "the last great race on earth" for nothing. The Iditrod takes place over 1,150 grueling miles, taking 10 to 17 days to complete

The race begins on the first Saturday in March. The start in downtown Anchorage is strictly ceremonial, as mushers drive their teams 20 miles (32km) to Eagle River. "Iditariders" pay for the privilege to ride on the mushers' sleds for the first 11 miles (18km); contact the Iditarod headquarters in Wasilla for more information (tel: 376-5155; www.iditarod.com).

The following day, mushers and dogs begin the race for real in Wasilla (though snow conditions sometimes require the race's restart to be moved; poor snow in 2003 forced the restart to begin in Fairbanks, for the first time ever). In all, teams travel a circuitous route of more than 1,100 miles (1,770km) before reaching the finish line in Nome (the distance from Anchorage to Nome by air would be 650 miles).

A wide range of mushers compete, from professionals with large kennels to adventurers making a once-in-lifetime sled dog trip through Alaska. Four-time winner Martin Buser holds the race's speed record, finishing in less than nine days in 2002. Mushers compete with teams of up to 16 dogs against themselves, each other and the wilderness. The success a of four-time winner, the late Susan Butcher, is behind a T-shirt which reads, "Alaska, where men are men and women win the Iditarod!"

After two short races on part of the Iditarod Trail in 1967 and 1969, the frst fully-fledged race ran to Nome in 1973, recalling the 1925 "race for life," when 20 mushers relayed life-saving serum to Nome to fight a diphtheria epidemic. Many said it could not be done, yet 22 mushers got to the finishing line in 1973.

The **Knik Museum and Sled Dog Mushers Hall of Fame** is 40 miles (64km) from Anchorage is located in a former pool hall at Knik (Mile 13.9 Knik Road, south of Wasilla). Open from June to September, the museum tells the story of the Iditarod Trail and Alaskan mushers.

TOP: There are 15 dogs in the average Iditarod team,which means that more than 1,200 dogs leave Anchorage for Nome each March. Mushers must sign in at 26 checkpoints, each staffed by a veterinarian. The rules of the race insist that mushers must carry certain items – such as an arctic parka, a heavy sleeping bag, an ax, and protection for each dog's feet against ice and snow injuries – but each musher has his or her own formula for winning. Some prefer to run in daylight, others at night. Some believe in special menus for the dogs. And many struggle to hold down a full-time job while spending hundreds of hours in training for the big event. *See also box on page 69, "Is Sled Dog Racing Cruel?"*

TOP LEFT: Jeff King, a four-time iditarod winner, was born in California but moved t Alaska in 1975 to seek adventure. His kennels rear and train 100 sled dogs.

ABOVE: More than 800 people crowd a hall in Nome for the awards banquet. With prize money totaling $400,000, the race boosts the local economy.

RIGHT: The end of the race is a cause for parades and celebration in Nome. It's an annual reminder that winter will also soon come to an end.

THE MUSHERS WHO DEFIED THE ODDS

About 60 to 70 racers bring their teams to the starting line in Anchorage on the first Saturday in March. The winners reach Nome about nine days later, having traveled an actual distance of more than 1,100 miles (1,770 km) on the grueling trail. All manner of hostile terrain – and the elements – challenge the racers from start to finish.

For example, back in 1985, Susan Butcher, leading the pack a couple of days out of Anchorage, tangled with a moose. Before things were sorted out in the dark, the moose had stomped and kicked her dog team out of the race. Later the race was halted twice for bad weather. And finally, in an act of considerable courage – or foolhardiness – Libby Riddles, from Teller, a small village northwest of Nome, headed out of a checkpoint into the teeth of a howling gale only a couple of hundred miles from the finish line.

No other musher would risk traveling in the storm. But the few miles she made that night before being forced to make camp and sit out the storm gave Riddles the extra edge needed for victory, and she became the first woman to win the race since its start in 1973. Overall, she won the Iditarod four times.

Through its first 35 years, four other mushers have won at least four Iditarod titles: Alaskans Rick Swenson (the all-time leader with five championships), and Martin Buser, Jeff King, and Montana musher Doug Swingley. But for every one of those competitors, dozens of other mushers enter the Iditarod each year for the adventure and challenge of driving a sled dog team across Alaska.

TOP RIGHT: Joe Redington, Snr. (1917–99), an Oklahoma-born dog musher and kennel owner, joined with Dorothy Page to launch the first Iditarod race in 1967 to commemorate the centenary of the US purchase of Alaska from Russia.

LEFT: Lance Mackey, the 2007 Iditarod champion, hugs his lead dogs Larry and Lippy at the finishing line. It's a tradition: his father won the race in 1978.

BELOW: Four dogs wait in a truck before the race begins. A total of more than 1,200 dogs take part in each year's race, and there's usually at least one fatality.

Southwest Alaska

0 ————————— 100 miles
0 ————————— 100 km

18 Pribilof Islands

St Paul Island
Walrus Island
St Paul
Otter Island
St George
St George Island

THE SOUTHWEST

Stretching from the Alaska Peninsula to the Aleutian Chain, from the Kodiak Archipelago to the Pribilofs, Alaska's Southwest is one of the state's most remote regions

F ar from Alaska's urban centers, Southwest Alaska is a broad and diverse region that includes the Kodiak Archipelago, Alaska Peninsula, Aleutian Islands, Bering Sea Islands, and Yukon-Kuskokwim Delta. It's a place of active volcanoes, wind-swept tundra, rugged coastal shores, and storm-wracked islands. It's also home to some of the world's largest bird rookeries and marine mammal populations, and the cultural center of the Aleut, Alutiiq, and Yup'ik Eskimo peoples, who have lived off the region's lands and waters for centuries.

Though often inhospitable to humans (and perhaps because of that), the Southwest region's landscape and climate support a diverse – and in some instances, rich – population of fish, birds, and mammals. Here is North America's largest nesting area for migrating water-fowl. Here too are the world's largest – and densest populations of – brown bears. And here are the continent's largest runs of sockeye; tens of millions of these salmon return each year to the region's river-and-lake systems, but the largest runs, by far, are centered in the Bristol Bay region.

Native villages

More than 80 communities are scattered through the region, most of them small, Native villages whose residents are still largely dependent on traditional subsistence lifestyles in which they hunt, fish, trap, and gather plants, just as they have for untold generations. Most towns and villages have 200 residents or less, though a few commercial centers have between 1,000 and 6,000 people. Few roads link any of the communities and travel is primarily by air or boat year-round, plus snowmobile or dog team in winter.

In the northern Gulf of Alaska, and separated from the mainland by stormy Shelikof Strait, the **Kodiak Archipelago** consists of a couple dozen islands, most a few miles across or less. But Kodiak, itself, is the largest island in the US after Hawaii. Sometimes called Alaska's "emerald isle," **Kodiak** is 100 miles long and more than 50 miles across at its widest point

PRECEDING PAGES: brown bears beat anglers to a catch at McNeil River.
TOP: Aleut dancer. **ABOVE:** basket weaver.

(160 by 80km). Other large islands in the chain include **Afognak** and **Shuyak**, at the northernmost tip.

Approximately 14,000 people inhabit the Kodiak group; most are tied in some way to the fishing industry. The islands are ancestral homes to the Alutiiq people, close relatives of the Aleuts. Though the islands can be reached by either boat or plane, nearly all visitors arrive on commuter or air taxi flights, from Anchorage or Kenai Peninsula communities. The city of Kodiak is also visited year round by the Alaska state ferry. Portions of the archipelago's coastal forests have been cut, but much of the landscape remains wild and protected by Kodiak National Wildlife Refuge and by state parks on Shuyak and Afognak islands. Kodiak island and city are discussed in greater detail on pages 316–22.

The Alaska Peninsula

Directly west of Kodiak, sandwiched between Shelikof Strait and Bristol Bay, the **Alaska Peninsula** stretches more than 500 miles (800km) from the southern boundary of Alaska's mainland to the beginning of the Aleutian Islands. A traditional home for Yup'ik Eskimo, Aleut, and Alutiiq peoples, the area also includes prime wildlife habitat. The **Izembek National Wildlife Refuge**, an "international crossroads" for migrating shorebirds and waterfowl, is located at the southern tip of the peninsula. Following the curve of land to the northeast, you'll find ample support for Alaska's inclusion in the North Pacific's "ring of fire" at the **Aniakchak Caldera** within the seldom-visited **Aniakchak National Monument and Preserve**.

Continuing on toward the mainland will take you to an area boasting the

densest populations of brown bears in the world at **Katmai National Park and Preserve** and the **McNeil River State Game Sanctuary**. Both sites provide viewing platforms that enable visitors to observe bears congregating to grapple for salmon along remote streams.

The community of **King Salmon** (population 400) is the access point for many of the activities of the peninsula, including not only wildlife viewing, but also world-class sport fishing, hiking, backpacking and river-running.

Dillingham (population 2,300), serves as a hub for similar activities in the western Bristol Bay area. Trips can be arranged out of Dillingham to **Togiak National Wildlife Refuge** or to the nearby **Walrus Islands State Game Sanctuary**.

The Aleutian Islands

The **Aleutian Islands** extend southwest from the tip of the Alaska Peninsula in a 1000-mile (1,600-km) arc toward Asia. These islands are the traditional homeland of the Aleut people. Visitor services and information are centered at the communities of **Dutch Harbor** and nearby **Unalaska**. This area of

TOP: the Russian Orthodox Church at Karluk, Kodiak Island. **ABOVE:** camping at McNeil River. **OPPOSITE PAGE:** archeologist at work on Kodiak Island.

Alaska is of particular interest to birders and sport fishers, as well as those interested in the islands' rich history of Aleut culture, Russian influence and remnants of Alaska's World War II involvement.

The **Yukon-Kuskokwim (Y-K) Delta** region of Southwest is mostly encompassed within the 19-million-acre (7.7-million-hectare) **Yukon Delta National Wildlife Refuge**. Both the Yukon and the Kuskokwim Rivers traverse the flat, treeless plains and tundra of the Delta and empty into the Bering Sea. Among the most populated regions of rural Alaska, the Yukon Delta is home to nearly 25,000 Yup'ik Eskimo people. Visitors to the area enjoy sport fishing, hunting, photography, rafting and kayaking, and especially extraordinary birding and wildlife-viewing opportunities.

The Y-K Delta supports one of the world's largest aggregations of water birds and shorebirds. The rivers, streams, lakes, sloughs and ponds of the region provide prime spawning and rearing habitat for 44 species of fish. Land mammals include caribou, brown and black bears, moose, wolves and musk oxen. The gateway city to this roadless Refuge (as well as a transportation and services hub for the area) is Bethel (population 6,000), which has a regular airline service from Anchorage. Travel to outlying areas is by small plane or boat.

Pribilof Islands

Three hundred miles west of the Y-K Delta area, and 200 miles (320km) north of the Aleutian Islands in the Bering Sea lie the treeless **Pribilof Islands.** St Paul and St George are the only inhabited islands of the group, and fishing and tourism are their emerging economic mainstays. The islands are the summer home for a million fur seals, which may well be the largest gathering of marine mammals in the world. The nesting grounds along the rocky shores and steep cliffs of the Pribilofs draw hundreds of thousands of sea birds, and the relatively few birders who search for them. ❑

Public Lands in the Southwest

The following list includes some of the major public lands within Southwest. For more complete information on all public lands within Alaska, contact the Alaska Public Lands Information Centers at www.nps.gov/aplic.

Alaska Maritime National Wildlife Refuge (http://alaskamaritime.fws.gov)
Alaska Peninsula National Wildlife Refuge (http://alaskapeninsula.fws.gov)
Aniakchak National Monument and Preserve (www.nps.gov/ania)
Becharof National Wildlife Refuge (http://becharof.fws.gov)
Izembek National Wildlife Refuge (http://izembek.fws.gov)
Katmai National Park and Preserve (www.nps.gov/katm)
Kodiak National Wildlife Refuge (http://kodiak.fws.gov)
Kodiak District, Alaska State Parks (www.dnr.state.ak.us/parks/units/kodiak/index.htm)
Lake Clark National Park and Preserve (www.nps.gov/lacl)
McNeil River State Game Sanctuary (www.wildlife.alaska.gov/index.cfm?adfg= mcneil_river.main)
Togiak National Wildlife Refuge (http://togiak.fws.gov)
Walrus Island State Game Sanctuary (www.wildlife.alaska.gov/index.cfm?adfg= refuge.rnd_is)
Wood-Tikchik State Park (www.dnr.state.ak.us/parks/units/woodtik.htm)
Yukon Delta National Wildlife Refuge (http://yukondelta.fws.gov)

KODIAK

Two-thirds of mountainous Kodiak Island is a wildlife
reserve, famous for its brown bears, while
the city of Kodiak has a strong and
visible legacy from its Russian past

Alaska

Anchorage

A shift of the wind can change
Kodiak Island from a desolate,
windswept, rain-pounded rock isolated from the rest of the world by fog, to
a shimmering emerald of grass, spruce
trees and snow-capped mountains glow-
ing pink in the sunrise. But while the
winds may shift, they remain predominantly from the north. Both the island
itself and the city of Kodiak are places
whose characters change with the
weather, the seasons and the observer.

At first glance, the city of **Kodiak** ❶
seems to be near world's end; it is a town
of 5,900 people perched precariously on
a small ledge of land between ocean
swells and jagged mountains (another
2,700 people live in the "greater Kodiak"
area and some 14,000 people inhabit the
entire island). A look into Kodiak's economy reveals a major fishing port – one of
the top three in the United States. Kodiak
is home to a multi-million-dollar fishing
fleet which ranges from the Pacific
Northwest to Norton Sound.

Past cultures

Over 200 years of recorded history have
swept across Kodiak, each one leaving
traces of its passing. Artifacts of the
indigenous Koniag culture surface near
remnants of the Russian period or World
War II bunkers, derelict whaling stations,
collapsing herring-rendering plants or
fish-processing facilities. Just under the
top soil is a layer of volcanic ash which
covered the town in 1912 and still drifts
about, leaving a coating of fine, white

dust. White spruce tree skeletons guard
the salt marshes, monuments to the land
subsidence which occurred during the
1964 earthquake and tidal wave.

From the air Kodiak Island, beyond the
city, seems an untouched wilderness,
3,588 sq. miles (9,293 sq. km) of rugged
mountains deeply indented by bays. The
northern half is covered with spruce trees,
the southern half with grass. Foresters say
the spruce forest is advancing down the
island at the rate of a mile a century.

Landing in Kodiak (there are frequent
commuter flights from Anchorage) can

Main attractions

ALUTIIQ MUSEUM
BARANOV MUSEUM
HOLY RESURRECTION CHURCH
ABERCROMBIE STATE
   HISTORICAL PARK
PILLAR MOUNTAIN
ST PAUL HARBOR
BUSKIN RIVER STATE
   RECREATION AREA
FOSSIL BEACH
KODIAK NATIONAL WILDLIFE
   REFUGE

LEFT:
a salmon snack.
BELOW:
Kodiak's harbor.

be an adventure. As the jet approaches the airport, it drops lower and lower over the water until its landing gear seems to skim the waves. Just beyond where the runway seems to emerge from the water, the plane sets down. At the other end of the runway sits **Barometer Mountain** (2,450ft/745 meters), so called because the peak is visible only in good weather.

The airport is about 5 miles (8km) from Kodiak City and there's a connecting bus. Spruce trees cast shadows across the highway, then the road twists in sharp turns around Pillar Mountain. In the winter bald eagles, sometimes 10 to a tree, perch in cottonwoods above the highway. The road then dips down into Kodiak.

The Russian legacy

Drawn by his search for sea otter pelts, Grigor Ivanovich Shelikof arrived in Three Saints Bay on the southeast corner of Kodiak Island in 1784 with two ships, the *Three Saints* and the *St Simon*. He was not welcomed by the indigenous Alutiiq people, who proceeded to harass the Russian party *(see page 46)*.

Having established his authority with brutal force, Shelikof founded the first

Russian settlement in Alaska on **Three Saints Bay**, built a school to teach the Natives to read and write Russian, and introduced the Russian Orthodox religion.

In 1790 Alexander Andrevich Baranov arrived at Three Saints Bay to take over leadership of the Russian settlement. He moved the colony to the northeast end of the island where timber was available, and which was closer to Cook Inlet and Prince William Sound. The site chosen by Baranov is now the city of Kodiak.

Russian members of the colony took Alutiiq wives and started family lines whose names still continue – Panamaroff, Pestrikoff, Kvasnikoff. Russian heritage in the city of Kodiak is also found on its street signs: Baranov, Rezanoff, Shelikof. The island's Native culture is also apparent, and can be seen at a performance by the Kodiak Alutiiq Dancers, a troupe formed by the Kodiak Tribal Council in 1988, which includes 50 dancers who wear traditional dress and perform ethnic songs and dances. The troupe performs throughout the state, with daily summer performances in Kodiak (tel: 486-4449).

Much of the rich culture of the Alutiiqs was absorbed by the Russian culture and–

Orthodox priests play a major role in the Kodiak community.

BELOW: Kodiak fishermen empty King Crab traps.

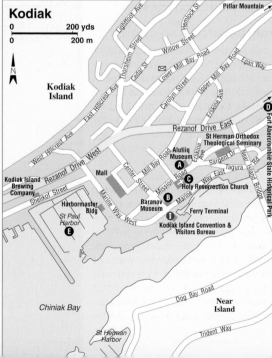

Kodiak

can only be guessed at through artifacts and the diaries of the early Russian settlers. The best window on the culture is at the **Alutiiq Museum** Ⓐ (215 Mission Road, tel: 486-7004; www.alutiiqmuseum .com; open in summer Mon–Fri 9am– 5pm, Sat 10am–5pm, Sun by appointment; in winter, Tues–Fri 9am–5pm and Sat 10:30am–4:30pm; entrance charge). This Native-owned research museum interprets artifacts from ongoing Alutiiq-directed archeological digs. Visitors can also join digs on six-day sessions at remote sites in the Dig Afognak program (tel: 800-770-6014 or 486-6357; www. afognak.org/dig.php).

The **Baranov Museum** Ⓑ (open in summer Mon–Sat 10am–4pm, Sun noon– 4pm; in winter, Tues–Sat 10am–3pm; entrance charge; tel: 486-5920; www.-baranov.us) is across from the Visitors Bureau on Marine Way and next to the ferry dock. It too contains displays of Alutiiq artifacts and clothing as well as items from the Russian and early American periods. The small museum, whose store sells Russian samovars and jewelry, is located in the **Erskine House**. Once a storehouse for furs, this was designated a National Historic Landmark in 1962, and is North America's oldest Russian building.

Holy Resurrection Church

When the United States bought Alaska from Imperial Russia, the Russian citizens left, but the Russian Orthodox church remained. The two blue onion domes of the **Holy Resurrection Church** Ⓒ on Mission Road are the town's most outstanding landmarks. Orthodoxy still plays a significant role in the Kodiak community, and is the predominant religion in the six villages in the island area.

In 1974, the **St Herman Orthodox Theological Seminary** was relocated to Kodiak: the white buildings stand near the church. Father Herman arrived in Kodiak in 1794 and settled on **Spruce Island**, where he established a school and became renowned as an ascetic and miracle worker. He was canonized in Kodiak in 1970, the first Orthodox canonization to take place on American soil.

His remains are kept in the church and the Russian Orthodox faithful make pilgrimages every August to his shrine. Other treasures of the Holy Resurrection Orthodox Church include many brilliantly colored icons. Visitors are welcome to attend services.

The Russian Orthodox Church follows the Julian calendar, making Kodiak a town of two Christmases, December 25 and January 7, and two New Years, January 1 and January 14.

During World War II, Kodiak served

The Holy Resurrection Church.

BELOW: the Baranov Museum.

Sockeye salmon.

BELOW: remnants of a World War II cannon in Fort Abercrombie State Historical Park.

as a major supply center for the Aleutian campaign. Military personnel and construction workers changed the city from a fishing village of 500 residents to a boom town of 4,000 people with another 20,000 in nearby areas. The US Navy built a major base on the site, which is now used as a US Coast Guard facility. Today all that remains of the war years years are silent, moss-covered bunkers.

Fort Abercrombie State Historical Park ⓓ, some 4 miles (6km) from the city, is dedicated to the memory of those days. A large bunker and the remains of gun emplacements overlook the sea from a cliff. Other bunkers can be found by walking through an alpine meadow and along the cliff edge. There are several guided tours a week, and some good facilities for camping within the park.

There are also bunkers on **Pillar Mountain** (1,270ft/385 meters) behind the city. Hikers working their way through the alders and spruce forests along the tops of shale cliffs often find others. Crowned with radar towers, Pillar Mountain also provides panoramic views of the surrounding area.

Kodiak's US Coast Guard facility is the largest in the United States. Among its other responsibilities, the Coast Guard uses its cutters and C-130 airplanes to keep track of foreign fishing fleets working in the Pacific Ocean and Bering Sea, to be sure they don't encroach in US waters. For locals, the Coast Guard facility is the home of "angels" who arrive in helicopters to pluck men off their sinking vessels or search the coastline for survivors of marine tragedies.

Natural events have left indelible marks on Kodiak Island. Twice in the 20th century the landscape was altered, first by a volcanic ash fall in 1912 when Mount Novarupta on the Alaska Peninsula exploded, and again by the great earthquake and tsunami in 1964.

The Good Friday earthquake in 1964, which devastated much of South Central Alaska, also set off a tidal wave that swept into the city of Kodiak and destroyed the downtown buildings, canneries and the docks. Many residents fled up Pillar Mountain and watched helplessly while the sea ran out, leaving the harbor dry, and then rolled back in across the land. Those who didn't reach high ground were swept away.

After the tidal wave, most of downtown Kodiak was redesigned and rebuilt. Fish-processing companies sent in floating processing plants to can king crab and salmon until new plants could be built. Residents who lived through the tidal wave and stayed to rebuild the town have formed a special bond. Though the tidal wave was a tragedy, it left behind a feeling of unity that still pervades the community.

A thriving fishing industry

Kodiak's economic dependence on the sea has been constant. The city of Kodiak provides temporary moorage and services for approximately 3,000 fishing boats a year. Fishermen deliver up to $100 million worth of fish and shellfish annually. Ask Kodiak residents what season it is and, if it is summer, they're likely to answer, "salmon season." Fall is king crab season; winter's marked by the Tanner crab, marketed as snow crab; spring is herring season; halibut and black cod are harvested in spring and summer, and whitefish species most of the year.

Kodiak's fishermen work year-round, switching from fishery to fishery as the seasons change. Between seasons the waterfront throbs with activity. Crane trucks and flatbeds move 500-lb (230-kg) steel crab pots from storage to the boat and back to storage. In spring, herring seines and gillnets are stretched out on the docks where crew men with shuttles can attach float and lead lines.

Visitors are welcome to wander down the ramp behind the Harbormaster Building and walk along the floats in St Paul Harbor **E**. Across the channel, on **Near Island**, is **St Herman Harbor**. In St Paul Harbor there are two loading docks where skippers load gear on board their boats.

Like its fishing industry, Kodiak's population is diverse, and you'll overhear a mixture of languages and accents as you wander around the harbor.

Touring Kodiak Island

Except for several Native villages, the populated portion of Kodiak Island is confined to the road system, and there is less than 100 miles (160 km) of it. Some stretches are only fit for 4-wheel-drive vehicles, but others can be driven in an ordinary car. The six coastal villages on the island are accessible only by plane or boat; to visit one of them, you need to make arrangements in advance.

It takes about an hour to drive to the end of the road at Fossil Beach. The road heads out of town past the **Buskin River State Recreation Area** where the headquarters and visitor center for the Kodiak National Wildlife Refuge is located. The Buskin River is a popular sport-fishing stream for salmon and steelhead.

The road continues past the airport, the Coast Guard base, the fairgrounds, the neighborhood of **Bells Flats**, and then climbs headlands, curves around bays and crosses rivers. In summer, salmon can be seen jumping in the bays and swimming up the rivers; July and August are the best months for salmon-watching or fishing. Occasionally sea lions come into the bays to feed on the fish. There

Scarce seafood

Visitors expect to come to a major fishing port and eat seafood, but most of Kodiak's fresh seafood is in refrigerated vans waiting to be loaded onto barges for shipment. The fishing industry is geared to large-volume production and sales, which has made it difficult for small, local buyers to establish a steady source of supply. The local supermarkets do offer fresh seafood in season, however, and some restaurants include it on their menus.

BELOW: a visitor greeting pinpoints one of the main local industries.

*En route to
Kodiak Island.*

are no restrictions on exploring the beaches, walking through the forests or climbing the mountains.

Eventually the road comes to a T-junction. To the left is the community of **Chiniak** (pop. 50), which contains a small winery. To the right, the road travels through cattle country where Kodiak's ranchers run about 2,000 head of beef cattle. Ahead the ocean comes into view again by **Pasagshak**, a popular river for fishing silver salmon. There is a small campsite on its banks.

The road continues past a sand-duned, surf-beaten beach and ends at **Fossil Beach**, where fossil shells lie loosely in the clay and rocks. During the fall, gray whales pass Pasagshak and Fossil Beach on their migration to California from the Bering Sea. In spring, the whales pass the island again as they migrate to their northern summer feeding grounds.

Wildlife Refuge

By traveling along the roads you will see some of the loveliest scenery on the island. But if you want real wilderness, and bears, you must visit the **Kodiak National Wildlife Refuge ❷**, which can be reached only by air or sea. This mountainous wilderness, established in 1941 and covering two-thirds of the island, belongs to bears and foxes, rabbits and birds, muskrats and otters.

Most people come here to see the brown bears – one of the world's largest carnivores. For those who aren't experienced in traveling through bear country, the best and safest way to see them is to take one of the bear-viewing tours based in Kodiak, but be warned – they are not cheap. Information on local guides and outfitters can be obtained from refuge headquarters (tel: 907-487-2600; http://kodiak.fws.gov).

Wilderness hikers should always remember to walk noisily through Kodiak's backcountry to reduce the chances of any confrontations with bears. During the salmon season, bears appear along the streams and beaches. As well as berries and salmon, the Kodiak bear enjoys a diet of calves and deer – much to the dismay of local ranchers and hunters. ❑

RESTAURANTS & BARS

Chart Room
236 West Rezanof Drive
tel: (907) 486-5712
www.kodiakinn.com/dining.htm
Gaze out on a harbor view as you enjoy breakfast, lunch or dinner in this restaurant, located in the Best Western Kodiak Inn. Specialties include Alaska king crab, prime rib and filet mignon. Bar. $$$–$$$$

El Chicano
103 Center Street
tel: (907) 486-6116
Large restaurant serving generous portions of Mexican fare. $$–$$$

Galley Gourmet
P.O. Box 1694
tel: (907) 486-5079
www.kodiak-alaska-dinner-cruise.com
For an unusual Alaska fine dining experience, take a dinner or brunch cruise aboard the 42-ft yacht, the *Sea Breeze*. Features world-class seafood (though non-seafood dishes are also available) and gourmet desserts. Dinner cruises last about 3½ hours and include sightseeing and wildlife viewing, with local information dished up as well. $$$$

Henry's Great Alaskan Restaurant
512 Marine Way
tel: (907) 486-8844
Reasonably priced seafood, steaks, gourmet burgers and sandwiches served for lunch and dinner daily. Located in the waterfront mall. Bar. $$

Mill Bay Coffee & Pastries
3833 Rezanof Drive East
tel: (907) 486-4411
A coffeehouse featuring locally roasted coffee and gourmet desserts. Also now offers breakfast and lunch featuring fresh vegetables, eggs from free-range hens and local seafood. $

Old Powerhouse Restaurant
516 East Marine Way
tel; (907) 481-1088
Fine Japanese cuisine served up in a richly renovated building that used to serve as a powerhouse for the city. Beautiful view of the sea. $$$

• • • • • • • • • • • • • • •
*Price is for dinner excluding tax,
tip and beverages:* **$$$$** *$30
and up,* **$$$** *$20–30,* **$$**
*$15–20,* **$** *under $15.*

Wildlife Refuges

Federal and state programs to protect Alaska's wildlife have been relatively successful, though the effect of global warming may put a strain on funding.

In 1980, Congress added millions of acres to America's national wildlife refuge system, by creating nine new refuges and expanding several others in Alaska. In all, Alaska has 16 national wildlife refuges, ranging in size from 300,000 to 19½ million acres (120,000–7.9 million hectares). Together they protect nearly 77 million acres (31 million hectares), including 18.6 million acres (7.5 million hectares) of designated wilderness.

The refuges encompass some of the world's most spectacular wildlands and present all sorts of opportunities for backcountry adventure: from river running and sea kayaking, to mountaineering, backpacking, fishing, hunting, and great wildlife viewing. A few can be reached by road, but most are remote, easily accessible by plane and in some instances, boat. And though several are popular with hikers, others hardly ever see people, or are used primarily by subsistence hunters and fishermen. Suggest drilling for possible oil beneath one of them, though, and political storms will rage.

A few examples of refuges, briefly noted:

● The smallest national refuge in Alaska, 303,000-acre (123,000-hectare) **Izembeck** NWR, located on the lower Alaska Peninsula, is an international crossroads for migrating waterfowl and shorebirds. Its heart is Izembeck Lagoon, where hundreds of thousands of waterfowl converge each fall. Brown bears fish salmon-rich streams, caribou migrate across the tundra. And the Aghileen Pinnacles, a group of precipitous volcanic spires, present a little-known mountaineering challenge.

● The side-by-side **Alaska Peninsula** and **Becharof** refuges in Southwest Alaska encompass towering volcanic peaks, rugged coastal fjords, rolling tundra, and glacially carved lakes. There are 14 major volcanoes, including nine that have erupted in historic times. Best known for hunting and fishing opportunities, these refuges are also prime candidates for backpackers, climbers and coastal kayakers seeking extreme challenges.

RIGHT: Alaska has five species of loon.

● The **Alaska Maritime** refuge consists of more than 2,500 islands that stretch along the Alaska coast from the northern Chukchi Sea to the Southeast Panhandle. About 80 percent of the state's 50 million nesting seabirds gather here. Marine life also includes whales, sea lions, walrus, porpoises, and sea otters. The refuge is outstanding for bird watching and for the kayak trip of a lifetime.

● The **Togiak** refuge in Southwest Alaska has more than 30 species of mammals and clearwater streams with some of the continent's finest salmon and trout fishing. Coastal areas are rich with brown bears and marine mammals. The uplands have 2.3 million acres (930,000 hectares) of designated wilderness to explore on foot or by boat.

● The **Arctic National Wildlife Refuge**, one of the world's great arctic wilderness areas, presents world-class opportunities for backpacking, mountain climbing, river running, and the chance to share a landscape with grizzlies, wolves, and thousands of caribou. *(See pages 286–91 for a more detailed description).*

Information about Alaska's national wildlife refuges can be obtained from the US Fish and Wildlife Service office in Anchorage (1011 E. Tudor Road, Anchorage, AK 99503; tel: 786-3309; www.r7.fws.gov). ❑

A SERENGETI OF THE NORTH

Wildlife-watching draws many visitors to the state. They are rarely disappointed, for the seas, parks and wilderness areas contain a remarkable variety of wildlife

Alaska is sometimes called the "Serengeti of the North." That's a bit of an exaggeration, but not much. The seas are the habitat of humpback, beluga, minke and gray whales, porpoises and dolphins, walrus, sea lions, sea otters and polar bears; while the land is inhabited by 105 species of mammals, including hoary marmots, Dall sheep, little brown bats, flying squirrels and ferocious wolverines. The state is also seasonal or permanent home for more than 400 kinds of fish, nearly 300 bird species and seven amphibians (though only one amphibian, the wood frog, lives north of the Panhandle).

The Pribilof Islands in the Bering Sea are summer home to a million fur seals and to millions of sea birds, while thousands of bull walrus haul out each year on Round Island, in Bristol Bay. The McNeil River, on the Alaska Peninsula, has the world's largest gathering of brown bears: more than 100 individuals have been observed at McNeil Falls during a single summer, feeding on the salmon runs.

Farther north, some 400,000 caribou belonging to the Western Arctic Herd roam the state's northwest region, perpetually on the move, while 130,000 or more form the Porcupine Caribou Herd, which ranges through northeastern Alaska and western Canada. And each fall between 1,000 and 4,000 bald eagles gather in Southeast Alaska's Chilkat Valley near Haines to feed on a late run of salmon.

Above: Musk oxen
These are a relic of the ice age. They live in open tundra. If predators threaten, they defend themselves by standing in a circle side-by-side, heads pointed out, in protective rings. But that didn't protect them against hunters with guns.

Above: Walrus
Two walrus bulls display their tusks as they engage in a territorial dispute along the rocky coast of Round Island, part of the Walrus Islands State Game Sanctuary in Bristol Bay. They're bulky creatures: an adult male may weigh up to 4,000 lbs (1,800 kg).

Right: Caribou
Alaska is home to some two dozen caribou herds, totaling more than 1 million animals. They are called "the nomads of the north" because they travel so extensively, and seem to be in constant movement.

Below: Moose
The largest members of the deer family, moose are the most important game animals in the state. They are herbivores and feed on a variety of plants, including aquatic weeds which they nose out from the beds of lakes and ponds.

BEAR COUNTRY

There's a good reason why Alaska is called "bear country." It's the only one of the 50 states to be inhabited by all three of North America's bears: the black bear, the polar bear, and the brown bear – also called the grizzly.

The populations of all these species are reported to be healthy, thanks in large part to the presence of vast wilderness areas. Polar bears roam the ice of the Beaufort, Chukchi and Bering seas. Both black and brown bears are found throughout most of the state, though the smaller black bears tend to be forest creatures. Browns and grizzlies prefer open areas: mountain meadows, Arctic tundra and coastal beaches.

Brown bears and grizzlies are members of the same species: the former are coastal creatures while the latter live in the interior. Grizzlies have longer claws and a bigger hump and are generally smaller and lighter than their coastal cousins. Biologists believe brown bears grow larger mainly because they have access to energy-rich foods, especially salmon, like the one being devoured in the picture above. Though classified as carnivores, brown, grizzly and black bears eat both vegetation and meat; the polar bear is a true carnivore and its favorite prey is the ringed seal.

BELOW: Gray wolves
These are symbols of the wild. They range through much of Alaska but they tend to inhabit remote wilderness and avoid humans as much as possible.

LEFT: Dall sheep
Members of the rodent family, marmots live among talus (scree) slopes or rock slides high in the mountains. Their high-pitched alarm calls sound like whistles and can carry for more than a mile.

LAKE CLARK NATIONAL PARK

Lake Clark may be the quintessential Alaska parkland, with volcanoes, rugged coastline, several major river systems, and a wide diversity of plants and animals

BELOW: dawn by the shores of Lake Clark.

t's 11pm on a late July evening. The sun has disappeared behind a gentle hill, but the northwest horizon remains brightened by an afterglow of rich pastels. A band of yellow gradually yields to orange, then rose and finally purple. Winds that swept in with an early evening rain shower have died, leaving the air utterly still yet surprisingly bug-free despite the mid-summer warmth.

With the wind and rain's departure, a shroud of silence has fallen over **Turquoise Lake**. The quiet is broken only by the soft crunching of boots on beach gravel, the occasional splash of grayling, and the intermittent screeches of two young terns calling for their parents, out busily fishing for the evening meal.

It is a magical, paradisical evening along the lake – serene, yet bursting with life. Sandpipers and plovers prowl the shoreline, skittering and dipping in their frenetic search for food. Just a few yards offshore, a family of old squaws swims past. And across the lake, an eagle circles over a small group of caribou, crossing tundra brightened by multi-colored fields of wildflowers: blue monkshood and Jacob's ladder, yellow tundra rose, pink fireweed and prickly rose.

Yet less than 10 miles (16km) to the east is an ominous and desolate world where the tundra's greens and yellows and pinks give way to the blacks and grays and whites of rock, snow and ice. Rising darkly into the sky, 8,020-ft (2,444-meter) **Telaquana Mountain** is a natural fortress of solitude, its upper reaches guarded by jagged spires and pale-blue glaciers that overhang sheer rock cliffs. It's forbidding and impenetrable. In fading light, it is a magnificent spectacle.

The essence of wild Alaska

The 4-million-acre (1.6 million-hectare) **Lake Clark National Park and Preserve ❸** may indeed be the quintessential Alaskan parkland. Within its boundaries are two active volcanoes, including one – 10,197-ft (3,108-meter) **Mount Redoubt** – that last erupted in 1990; rugged coastline whose rocky cliffs serve as rookeries for multitudes of puffins, cormorants, kittiwakes and other seabirds; two major mountain systems, the Aleutian and Alaska ranges, which join to produce the Chigmit and Neacola mountains (snow-capped and glacially carved, most of the park's high peaks remain unclimbed and unexplored); and several major river and lake systems – including three designated wild rivers – that offer world-class sport fishing opportunities for all five species of Pacific salmon and rainbow trout.

Lake Clark is also home to a remark-ably diverse mix of plant communities. Along the coast is one of the northern-most stands of Sitka spruce rain forest, while inland are lowland boreal forests typical of Interior Alaska and several varieties of tundra, including arctic tun-dra usually found in northern Alaska. Those varied ecosystems support more than 100 species of birds and nearly 40 species of mammals, including black and brown bears, wolves, Dall sheep, cari-bou and moose.

From coast to inland mountains, these varied habitats present recreational oppor-tunities for a wide spectrum of users, from hunters and anglers to river runners, sea kayakers, campers, backpackers, moun-taineers and wildlife viewers.

"Lake Clark has a fantastic diversity of resources," says Paul Haertel, who served as the park's first superintendent after it was established in 1980. "It's a place that captures the essence of wild Alaska; it has everything you could imagine." Adding to the park's appeal is its close proximity to two of Alaska's most densely populated areas, Anchor-age and the western Kenai Peninsula.

An undiscovered park

Here, then, is a national park with fan-tastic scenery, easy access by air, and diverse recreational opportunities. One would expect it to be among Alaska's most popular destinations. But it's not. In fact, Lake Clark is among the state's least known and least appreciated national parks. In a sense, it remains one of Alaska's undiscovered parks.

There are a few reasons why. For one thing, it doesn't have one or two major attractions. Denali, for example, has Mount McKinley and wildlife viewing. Katmai has its bears. Glacier Bay has its spectacular glacier-sculpted landscape

TIP

Getting There
The park can't be reached by road. Most visitors charter a flight from Anchorage, about 90 minutes from Lake Clark. Charter flights can also be taken from the Kenai Peninsula. Commercial airlines fly between Anchorage and Iliamna, a base for many charter airlines.

BELOW:
an angler lands an arctic grayling on Lake Clark.

A walk in the woods.

BELOW: a family from Port Alsworth crosses the lake.

and marine wildlife tours. An even bigger factor, perhaps, is that Lake Clark is not accessible by road (or cruise line). And it doesn't have a major destination with visitor facilities, like Denali or Katmai's Brooks Camp. Sure it's easy to reach by plane, and relatively inexpensive. But "bush plane" travel is still very foreign to most travelers. And most visitors don't like the idea of being dropped "in the middle of nowhere."

There's one other factor that likely acts as a crowd deterrent: the lack of visitor facilities. The National Park Service has intentionally kept development to a minimum. The park's main office is in Anchorage (tel: 781-2218; www.nps.gov/lacl), with a "field headquarters" at **Port Alsworth ❹**, on Lake Clark's southeast shore. There are no other public facilities within the park, although rangers may be seasonally based in the backcountry. Several privately owned wilderness lodges, most of them catering to hunters and anglers, are

located in and around the park; several are at Port Alsworth, the entry point for many visitors. In addition, dozens of guide services operate within the park. The majority specialize in sport fishing, but other guided activities include backpacking, hiking, lake-touring, mountaineering, photography and river running.

Several air-taxi operators offer flightseeing trips into the park and also transport big-game hunters. Information on commercial visitor services authorized to conduct business within Lake Clark National Park and Preserve can be obtained from the park's Anchorage office. However, with no connection to Alaska's highway system, no singular attraction to catch the public's fancy, and minimal visitor facilities, Lake Clark is likely to remain a low-profile park, at least for the near future.

Wilderness lodges

Before Congress established Lake Clark National Park and Preserve in 1980, the region's resources were utilized by two main groups: local residents (most of whom lead a subsistence lifestyle in Dena'ina Indian villages near the park's southern edge); and "sport" hunters and anglers seeking trophy wildlife and fish.

Much of the fishing pressure comes from wilderness lodges. Prime fly-in fishing grounds include the Chilikadrotna and Mulchatna rivers – also popular with river floaters – as well as the Stony, Crescent, Silver Salmon and Nondalton rivers and Telaquana, Crescent and Tazmina lakes.

And then there's Lake Clark: 42 miles long (68km), up to 860ft deep (262 meters) and covering 110 sq. miles (285 sq. km), Alaska's sixth-largest lake is a critical sockeye salmon spawning ground. Many of the park's lake and river systems contribute significantly to Bristol Bay's world-famous commercial sockeye salmon fishery. In fact, one of its primary functions is to protect watersheds that feed the salmon fishery. Rainbows and salmon get most of the angling attention, but lake trout, pike, Dolly Varden, arctic char and arctic grayling are also popular target species.

While sport fishing is permissible anywhere within the parkland, trophy hunting is restricted to Lake Clark's 1.4-million-acre (570-hectare) preserve,

where tundra-covered foothills and lowland forests support healthy populations of caribou, moose and brown bear. Prior to 1980, however, the Chigmit Mountains' Dall sheep populations were also fair game. "Back before the park was created, people would come in and take one – or two – of everything," says former Lake Clark ranger Jordan Fisher-Smith. "In some of the older cabins (within the park), people actually recorded their exploits on the walls." One such cabin overlooks upper Twin Lake.

Exploring Twin Lakes

Nearly three decades later, **Twin Lakes** ❺ remains a popular backcountry destination, but it now attracts a different sort of crowd. Some visitors use it as a starting point for float trips down the Chilikadrotna, while others are more interested in backpacking. When the weather's fine, fishermen from one or more of the region's wilderness lodges may come by. A few simply come to set up camp along the beach and relax.

Twin Lakes is a prime visitor destination for several reasons. Access is one; it's only a half-hour flight from Port

When to go
Although the park is open year-round, most people visit from mid-June to early September, when temperatures average from 60° to 75°F (16°–24°C). Coastal areas are about 10° cooler and are rainier and windier. Expect snowfall as early as September.

BELOW: a plane lands on the lake.

What the hunters claimed

Now off-limits to sport hunting, the Twin Lakes area once was popular with trophy seekers hoping to bag Dall sheep. These are a few samples of the scribblings found in one cabin:

"Shot 40-inch ram. Aug. '65. Bill Silver, Castro Valley, Calif."

"Dr. Norbert Conrad, Michigan. 1 sheep, 1 caribou, 1 black bear, 1 nice grizzly and lots of walking."

Some of the cabin's occupants got carried away with their claims. Dr. Chuck Finnell of Lapeer, Mich., for example: "Record for eating most potatoes, 8-24-67 thru 9-8-67. Record double-shovel caribou, 8-26-67. Possible record sheep, 8-27-67. Assisted capture of record kangaroo mouse and 1 large shrew. 1 gut-shot squirrel. 7½-ft grizzly, 9-2-67."

There's good fishing in the local lakes.

Alsworth. Founded in the 1940s by bush pilot Leon "Babe" Alsworth and wife Mary, Port Alsworth has become the region's "hub of activity" despite its small size (population about 100). For many visitors, this community on Lake Clark's southeast shore serves as the gateway to Lake Clark National Park and it's where the National Park Service has established its local headquarters.

The Alsworth family maintains its strong presence in the community; a structure first built by Babe and Mary Alsworth in the 1940s has been re–modeled and converted into "The Farm Lodge" (tel: 781-2208 or 888-440-2281), run by their son Glen and his wife Patty. The Alsworths also own Lake Clark Air (tel: 781-2208 or 888-440-2281; www.lakeclarkair.com) which runs daily commuter flights between Port Alsworth and Anchorage in summer.

Another factor is marketing. And word of mouth. Local entrepreneurs have publicized Twin Lakes when promoting the park to potential clients. And traditionally it's been one of the places to which air-taxi services take people.

Then there was Richard Proennicke,

who settled at Upper Twin Lake in the 1960s and became something of an Alaskan legend when he wrote the book *One Man's Wilderness: An Alaskan Odyssey*. Now deceased, Dick Proennicke lived alone in the wilderness for three decades, and people would travel to Twin Lakes just to meet him. Though hospitable to those who passed his way, Proennicke sometimes second-guessed the wisdom of writing a book that so affected his solitary lifestyle. People are still drawn to the homestead where he lived.

Diverse wildlife

The scenery around Twin Lakes is spectacular, the wildlife diverse – everything from Dall sheep, moose, and grizzlies to beavers, eagles, shorebirds, waterfowl, ground squirrels and voles. And the hiking is superb. Fed in part by glaciers born in the Neacola Mountains, the Twin Lakes are a vivid, penetrating aquamarine hue. Much of their shoreline is bordered by boreal forest that offers easy walking – at least by Alaskan standards

Above the open white-spruce forest is dry alpine tundra, which in turn gives way to lightly vegetated or bare volcanic hills, whose canyons provide endless avenues for exploration and whose ridges offer awe-inspiring vistas of the Twin Lakes valley.

Kayaks, canoes or inflatables are wonderful means of exploring Lower and Upper Twin Lakes, 5 and 7 miles (8 and 11km) long, respectively. But beware: the valley often acts as a wind funnel and what had been a mirror-smooth lake surface may, in a matter of minutes, become a white-capped chop with waves 2 ft to 3 ft (60–90cm) high.

Turquoise and **Telaquana lakes** are the park's two other "destinations" most frequently visited by backpacker-hiker-camper types, again largely because of easy access and marketing strategies. Along with Twin Lakes, they've seen a substantial increase by wilderness explorers in the past 15 to 20 years. Yet even as Lake Clark's visitor-use curve moves slowly but steadily upward, vast expanses of the park remain terra incognita.

"You talk about resources that haven't been discovered; very few people have set foot in the park's more remote mountainous areas. In fact, the park is largely unexplored north of Merrill Pass," says Paul Haertel, the park's first superintendent. "There are dozens of knife-edge ridges and steep-walled canyons where no one has ever walked, hundreds of mountains that have never been climbed. There's so much out there that remains to be discovered."

Some precautions

The weather often changes rapidly and quickly throughout Lake Clark because the park is located in a region where marine air masses from the Bering Sea and Gulf of Alaska frequently collide with drier, continental systems from Alaska's Interior. The result is extremely variable weather. The prime visitor season is June through August, when temperatures normally range from 50° to 65°F (10°–18°C). Yet even in summer temperatures may drop into the 30s, especially at higher elevations. They may also, on occasion, climb above 80°F (27°C). Windy, wet weather is the rule,

rather than the exception, especially in the park's eastern sections. The region's wettest months are August and September; winter is comparatively dry, but temperatures may plummet to –40° or colder.

Visitors exploring Lake Clark's backcountry on their own should plan to be totally self-sufficient. Quality clothing – including rain gear and wool or cold-weather synthetics – is a must, because hypothermia is a risk even in summer. Other "shoulds" include insect repellent, tents that can endure high winds and long spells of rain, and extra food. It's not uncommon for stormy weather to delay pick-up flights.

The Lake Clark region, like most of Alaska, is "bear country," and visitors should take appropriate measures to avoid close encounters with the park's ursine residents; that includes clean camping and noise-making when traveling in areas with low visibility. Bear-awareness brochures are available from the Park Service. Giardia may be a problem in some areas; when in doubt, it's best to treat drinking water. Before heading into the backcountry, it's also a good idea to leave a trip itinerary with someone reliable. ❏

A food and supplies cache at Twin Lakes.

LEFT: canoeing on Turquoise Lake.

Fishing on Lake Clark

Sport fishing is extraordinary in the lakes and streams of Lake Clark National Park, thanks largely to the abundance of rainbow trout, Dolly Varden, arctic grayling, whitefish, lake trout, northern pike, and, particularly in the Cook Inlet drainage, silver and king salmon.

The Chilikadrotna and Mulchatna Rivers offer some of the park's best prospects. Many anglers arrange to be dropped off in the upper reaches of one of these rivers and, after inflating a raft, drift and cast their way downstream for a few days. There's also good fishing in Kontrashibuna, Telaquana, and Turquoise Lakes and in the streams that flow in and out of them. Lake Clark itself has given up trout larger than 50 pounds (23kg).

It takes years for the region's trout, grayling, and char to reach trophy size, so most anglers practice catch-and-release fishing, playing a fish as briefly as possible and avoiding removing it from the water as they remove the hook and let it swim away.

For many, that means fly-fishing. Spinning gear works well, too, particularly if anglers use single, barbless hooks, rather than treble hooks on spinners and spoons. Fish taken on bait tend to swallow hooks, damaging delicate gill tissue and internal organs, which leads to bleeding and, ultimately, death.

KATMAI NATIONAL PARK

Alaska
Anchorage

Take a trip to Katmai on the Alaska Peninsula to fish and paddle, and see the strange lunar landscape created by a volcanic eruption

Main attractions
KING SALMON
BROOKS RIVER AND CAMP
VALLEY OF TEN THOUSAND
SMOKES
NOVARUPTA VOLCANO
KULIK LAKE
GROSVENOR LAKE

BELOW: river canyons were cut in the Valley of Ten Thousand Smokes after the 1912 erutpion.

Nature in **Katmai National Park and Preserve ❻** is awesome. Here in this isolated location the scenery is breathtaking, the weather is unstable, the winds can be life-threatening, and the past is reckoned in terms of before and after the volcanic eruption of 1912.

Located 290 air miles (465km) from Anchorage on the Alaska Peninsula, the park is a haven for lovers of the unspoiled wilderness. No highway system touches this area; access is primarily by small plane, or by boat out of King Salmon ❼, the park's "gateway" community. Most visitors take a one-hour commuter flight from Anchorage to King Salmon, then fly by floatplane into Katmai's backcountry. It's also possible to arrange boat rides to some destinations, most notably **Brooks River and Camp**.

The park receives nearly 60,000 visits a year by sightseers and flightseers, fishermen, hikers, climbers and canoeists. The primary attraction is Brooks Camp, on **Naknek Lake**, where a large run of sockeye salmon each summer attracts dozens of brown bears, the coastal cousins of grizzlies.

You can pick up information at the Park Service's office in King Salmon or at the Brooks Camp Visitor Center (open daily), where you're required to check in when visiting Brooks (be sure to ask about the evening ranger-led programs); or check the park's website before visiting (www.nps.gov/katm). Some people fly in for only a few hours, have a look at the bears, and then leave.

Viewing the bears

Book well in advance if you hope to stay in **Brooks Lodge** (tel: 243-0649 or 800-544-0551; email: info@ katmai-land.com; www.bearviewing.net). Besides the lodge, there's also a campground that takes reservations on a first-come, first-served basis (tel: (877) 444-6777, (877) 883-6777 (TDD), or (518) 885-3639; www.recreation.gov). There are several easy walks in the immediate vicinity, and bears can be viewed in summer from safe viewing platforms as they feed on spawning salmon in the Brooks River, particularly at Brooks Falls. The best time to see bears along the Brooks River is in July and again in September.

You can also book a place on a tour bus that provides transportation to the scene of volcanic devastation in the **Valley of Ten Thousand Smokes**. The bus takes visitors to Overlook Cabin, at the end of the road, from where you can see the valley and take a gentle, ranger-led hike, or set off on a more ambitious one on your own.

More than 90 years after the eruption, the valley remains awe-inspiring, though most of its "smokes" stopped steaming decades ago. Ash, pumice and rocks produced over 40 sq. miles (100 sq. km) of lunar landscape, sculpted by wind and water. The once-verdant valley floor, covered with shifting pumice, resists vegetation and quickly erases the imprint of hikers' boots.

Before the great eruption of 1912, a portion of the historic Katmai Trail passed through this valley. The trail was traveled by Russian fur traders and missionaries, then by a flood of gold seekers taking a shortcut to Nome. Prospectors and mail carriers used it to avoid a stormy sea passage around the Alaska Peninsula but by 1912 the gold rush had subsided and the trail was seldom traveled.

Today it is no longer visible and its ancient route is a path of obstacles. Blowing ash, rugged terrain, dense undergrowth, quicksand and narrow canyons challenge the most seasoned hiker. During severe weather, travelers are warned against the old route at Katmai Pass at the head of the valley. The interchange of air between the Gulf of Alaska and the Bering Sea streams through this pass and can cause winds over 100 miles an hour (160 km/h) – strong enough to blow hikers off their feet.

Tremors and eruptions

When the great eruption occurred, news was slow to reach the world outside Alaska because the area was so isolated, but its impact was felt hun-

For the record…
The state's highest recorded temperature was 100ºF (38ºC) in the Interior community of Fort Yukon in 1915. The lowest recorded temperature was –80ºF (–62ºC) at Prospect Creek, less than 200 air miles to the west, in 1971.

BELOW: wildlife watching in Katmai.

*Getting the
campfire going.*

BELOW:
Katmai National
Park's volcanic
landscape.

dreds of miles away. The closest account was given by a Native, American Pete, who was on the Katmai Trail only 18 miles (30 km) northeast of Mount Katmai when the violent explosions began. Earth tremors that preceded the eruption were so severe that the residents of Katmai and Savonoski, small Native villages on the Alaska Peninsula, gathered their possessions and fled to Naknek, on Bristol Bay.

Later research gave credit for the devastation not to Mount Katmai, but to **Novarupta Volcano**, a volcano formed by the eruption itself. The explosion was heard up to 750 miles (1,200km) away in in Juneau, and associated earth tremors caused immense avalanches on Denali (Mount McKinley), hundreds of miles to the north. Most heavily impacted were the Native villages of Katmai and Savonoski, later abandoned because of heavy ashfall, and the town of Kodiak on Kodiak Island, across Shelikof Strait.

The smoking valley

In the following years several expeditions were sent to the eruption site by the National Geographic Society to satisfy worldwide interest and carry out scientific research. Scientists were initially prevented from reaching the source of the eruption by seas of mud, ash slides as deep as 1,500ft (450 meters), and evidence of one of the most powerful water surges ever.

In 1916 the crater of Mount Katmai was reached and a smoking valley discovered at Katmai Pass. The valley was named by botanist Robert Griggs, who found it "one of the most amazing visions ever beheld by mortal eye. The whole valley as far as the eye could reach was full of hundreds, no, thousands – literally tens of thousands – of smokes curling up from its fissured floor." The landscape's fiery desolation prompted Griggs and his colleagues to call one stream the **River Lethe**, which in Greek mythology flows through the centre of Hades.

In 1918 the Valley of Ten Thousand Smokes was made a national monument in order to preserve an area important to the study of volcanism. In 1980 the monument was upgraded in status and greatly expanded: the new Katmai National Park and Preserve protected 4 million acres (1.6 million hectares) of coastal lands, forests, rivers, lakes, volcanic mountains, and alpine valleys.

When the Katmai monument was first created it was believed that the Valley of Ten Thousand Smokes would become a geyser-filled attraction to rival Yellowstone National Park in Wyoming, because scientists thought that the geyser field at Yellowstone was dying. But the reverse has come about. The Yellowstone geysers are still active, but the fumaroles at the Valley of Ten Thousand Smokes have subsided.

A rugged wilderness

Katmai National Park and Preserve makes available to visitors not only an area of amazing volcanic involvement but a representative and undisturbed portion of the Alaska Peninsula. Great varieties of terrain in Katmai include the rugged coastal habitat of Shelikof Strait on one side of the Alaskan range and the rivers and lakes of the Naknek River watershed on the other. Mixed spruce and birch forests, dense willow and alder thickets and moist tundra are found at lower elevations, with alpine tundra on the higher slopes.

A series of small lakes and rivers provide opportunities for canoeing, kayaking and fishing. You can paddle to a group of tiny islands on Naknek Lake's north arm, but it's about a 60-mile (100-km) round trip.

Rainbow trout, lake trout, char, pike and grayling are popular sport fish here, as well as sockeye, coho, king, pink and chum salmon. Nearly 1 million salmon return each year to the Naknek River.

Wilderness lodges at **Kulik** and **Grosvenor lakes** cater to serious fishing enthusiasts who want backcountry comfort and guided fishing, while other park visitors arrange their own fishing and float trips.

The brown bears are, of course, the main attraction, but there is a great deal of other wildlife that may be encountered elsewhere in Katmai – and you won't be quite so much part of the crowd as you would at the main bear-watching sites. Moose, caribou, land otter, wolverine, marten, weasel, mink, lynx, fox, wolf, muskrat, beaver and hare all inhabit the park.

Offshore, in coastal waters, seals, sea lions, sea otters and beluga and gray whales can be seen. Birdwatching is also a popular pastime – the park has more than 40 songbird species.

The weather

Weather in Katmai is variable, and heavy rain is characteristic of most areas in summer months. The northwestern slope of the Aleutian Range has the most comfortable weather: at Brooks Camp the average daytime temperature is 60°F (15°C).

Here, skies are only expected to be clear or partially cloudy 20 percent of the time. Warm clothing, rain gear and boots are highly recommended at any time of the year.   ❏

The 1912 eruption
As ash began to fall on Katmai in the great 1912 eruption, accompanied by nauseating gases, people believed they would suffer the fate of Pompeii and be buried alive.

BELOW: the Brooks River Falls, Katmai National Park.

McNeil River State Game Sanctuary

Each summer, dozens of brown bears come to this Alaska Peninsula stream to feed on chum salmon that have returned to spawn. People, in turn, come to watch the fishing bears

The bears have always come first at **McNeil River State Game Sanctuary** ❽. Created in 1967 by the Alaska Legislature, the sanctuary is intended, above all else, to protect the world's largest known concentration of brown bears, the coastal cousins of grizzlies. The focal point of the gathering is **McNeil Falls**, where bears come each summer to feed on chum salmon, returning to the river to spawn. Typically, the salmon begin arriving in late June or early July and remain in large numbers until mid- to late August. As many as 144 individual bears (adults and cubs) have been identified along the river in a single season. And in July 1997, biologists counted 70 bears at the falls at one time.

By nature, adult brown bears tend to be solitary creatures, with the exception of females that are raising families, or bears that temporarily pair up during mating season. For them to gather in such large numbers – and in such close quarters – is exceptional. For more than 35 years, Alaska's Division of Wildlife Conservation has enacted and enforced a series of restrictions to ensure that this unique gathering is not disrupted by conflicts with humans.

State regulations make it clear that brown bear viewing shall be the primary human activity in the sanctuary, which is located at the upper end of the Alaska Peninsula, just north of Katmai National Park and Preserve. Hunting and trapping are prohibited and all other use is allowed only as long as it does not significantly alter the bears' behavior. To limit human impacts, a permit system has been established to regulate the number of people who watch and photograph the bears.

A deadly encounter

Through the late 1960s, McNeil River was virtually unknown as a bear-viewing site. Jim Faro, a state biologist who managed the sanctuary in its early years, recalls that only a half-dozen or so people visited in 1969. Because of that, there were few rules to govern visitor behavior. By 1970, however, the media had

LEFT: bears at play.
BELOW: cooling off.

begun to bring McNeil to the public's attention. Vistation jumped. And because there were no rules to regulate public use, human activities got out of hand.

"We had people running up and down both sides of the river," Faro recalls. "There were even people fishing for salmon right at the falls, where the bears feed. If all the horror stories you heard about bears were true, we should have had lots of dead people."

Instead, the bears went into hiding. "It was like the bears were saying, 'We don't have to put up with this.' They took one look at all the people and left," Faro says. Only a handful of bears remained.

That same summer, a bear was killed by one of the sanctuary visitors. A photography guide decided to take some close-up pictures of a female with cubs, as they bears fed on the coastal mudflats. Crawling on his hands and knees, the photographer made his approach. The adult bear saw the movement and charged. It's likely she thought another bear was approaching and threatening her young. The bear came more than 300 feet across the flats. Expecting a false charge, the photographer remained on his hands and knees, rather than standing and identifying himself as human. Finally, when the bear was only 60 to 70 ft (18–21 meters) away, the man made his move: he shot the sow with a .44 pistol. On being hit, the bear turned and fled, shot fatally in the lungs.

Tighter controls were needed, both to prevent future injurious encounters between bears and humans and to bring the bears back to McNeil in large numbers. In 1973, the Alaska Board of game approved proposals to regulate visitor activities in the sanctuary during the prime-time bear-viewing period.

The permit system

Since 1973, the primary visitor control has been a permit system that limits viewing and photography opportunities. No more than 10 people a day are allowed to visit the sanctuary's bear-viewing areas; and they may do so only when accompanied by one or two state biologists. The permit period initially ran from July 1 through August 25, but it has since been expanded to include June.

That permit system *(see page 340)* has been extraordinarily successful. Since the

Catch of the day.

BELOW:
a family outing
of brown bears.

state enacted its visitor restrictions, the number of bears visiting the falls has increased nearly tenfold. Just as important, no bears have been killed within the sanctuary and no humans have been injured by bears – this despite thousands of human-bear encounters, often at close range.

Normally, bear "trespass" within the campground is not a problem. But occasionally a local resident – usually an adolescent bear – has to be taught the campground is off limits. The education proceeds in stages. Stage One is usually limited to loud, aggressive yelling. If that doesn't work, sanctuary staff "step it up a notch." That next step involves the use of a "shell cracker," which gives off a loud bang much like a firecracker. If there's still a problem, rubber pellets or even bird shot are used. But only rarely – and never in recent years – have the sanctuary staff had to go as far as Stage Three.

Mikfik Creek

Until the mid-1980s, few people visited McNeil sanctuary before July 1. That's when the chum salmon – and the bears – began to arrive at McNeil River. But in 1982, a new pattern began to emerge, because of changes at **Mikfik Creek**, a small, shallow, clearwater stream that flows through the sanctuary and enters a saltwater lagoon less than a mile from McNeil River. It hosts a run of sockeye salmon from early to mid-June, but historically the run has been so small that bears largely ignored the fish.

Then, mysteriously, Mikfik's sockeye return began to increase dramatically in size. Tens of thousands of sockeye (or red) salmon entered the creek each year. Not surprisingly, increased numbers of bears have been attracted to Mikfik's increased fishing opportunities. And following closely behind the bears were bear watchers and photographers.

As early season visitation continued to increase in the late 1980s and early '90s, state wildlife managers recognized the need to expand McNeil's permit system. The permit period now runs from early June through August 25.

The scene at the falls

While Mikfik has made the sanctuary's bear-viewing more diverse, **McNeil Falls** remains the primary focus in July and August. Located a mile above the river's

The hunting issue
Controversy erupted in 2005 when the Alaska Game Board voted to allow bear hunting on two parcels of land near the McNeil River sanctuary. Opponents said this was unethical because the bears, being used to people in the area, wouldn't flee from hunters. After a flood of protest, the board reversed its decision in 2007.

BELOW: stalking a brown bear.

How to get there

Nearly all visitors reach the sanctuary by air, using air charters based in Homer. The department can provide a list of licensed carriers; some offer individual seat fares, others charter a plane to a group of passengers.

McNeil visitors must be self-sufficient and prepared for a wilderness experience; no commercial facilities are available. Visitors must bring their own tents, camping gear, and food. Firearms are discouraged.

Even in mid-summer, equipment and clothing must be suitable for cold, wet weather. Visitors are also cautioned that bad weather can delay flights for several days. Visitors should also be in good physical shape; the 4-mile (6.4-km) round-trip hike to McNeil Falls is not especially hazardous, but it does require strenuous "slogging" across mud flats and crossing Mikfik Creek. A typical day at the falls lasts six to eight hours, on a narrow gravel pad that's about 15 ft (4.6 meters) long.

TIP

Getting Around

To obtain an application packet for McNeil River State Game Sanctuary, contact the Alaska Department of Fish and Game, Division of Wildlife Conservation, (333 Raspberry Road, Anchorage, AK 99518-1599; tel: 267-2182; www.state.ak.us/adfg).

BELOW:
viewing platform at McNeil Falls.

mouth, the falls is actually a step-like series of small waterfalls, pools, and rapids that stretch along the stream for several hundred yards. Individual bears take up their fishing positions based on their place in the ursine pecking order. The prime spots are located along the western bank, opposite the two viewing pads used by humans. Here the most dominant bears – adult males, some weighing 1,000 pounds (450 kg) or more – jockey for position.

The bears use a variety of fishing techniques. Some stand motionless in midstream. When a chum salmon swims by, the bear pins it to the river bottom with its paws, then bites into it. Others use snorkeling techniques, and a few even dive for fish. Cubs watch their mothers from the shore, closely observing mom's technique; now and then an especially bold cub will make its own attempt. But normally they'll wait until their mother brings a fish to shore. Adolescent bears – the equivalent of teenagers – that have been weaned from their mothers patrol the shorelines, hoping to find a scrap or two. Gulls and bald eagles, too, crowd the river, fighting over carcasses.

The best fishers may catch dozens of salmon in just one day. One particularly adept male once caught more than 70 fish in less than eight hours. When hungry, bears will consume the entire fish, including head and bones. But as they become satiated, bears will go for the highest calorie parts: the brain, eggs, and skin.

The chum run ends in mid- to late August, but bears begin to disperse even before then, as they go in search of another nutritious food: berries.

Applying for permits

Because only 10 people per day are allowed to visit McNeil sanctuary's bear-viewing areas, permits are required. The permits are issued through a lottery that is held each year in late March. Applications must be postmarked by March 1 and accompanied by a nonrefundable application fee of $25 per person (group applications are limited to three people).

Non-resident permit winners must pay $350 per person to visit the sanctuary for the four-day permit period (applicants get to choose the dates they wish to visit the sanctuary), while Alaskans must pay $150. ❑

Mixing bears and people

Getting close to bears allows you to recognize their individuality – some are aggressive by nature but others are mild-mannered or even timid.

I t's widely assumed that bears and people don't mix," says Larry Aumiller, the sanctuary's former long-time manager. "But here we've shown that they can mix, if you do the right things. To me, that's the most important message of McNeil: humans can peacefully coexist with bears. It's an example of what could be."

Such peaceful coexistence is possible because of a simple fact: McNeil bears are habituated to humans, but view them as neutral objects – almost a part of the landscape. People do not pose a threat; nor are they a source of food. To prevent any such association, feeding of bears is prohibited at McNeil (as it is throughout Alaska). Furthermore, a designated wood-frame building is provided for food storage, cooking, and eating. And a no-bears-allowed policy is strictly enforced within a well-defined campground area.

Aumiller's education of McNeil's bears went beyond campground discipline. Through the years he made it easier for the bears to "read" people. The close supervision of sanctuary visitors is, in part, intended to make humans more predictable to the bears. For example, visitors are permitted to watch and photograph bears from a single, defined viewing area; only 10 per day are allowed there; and viewing is done from late morning through early evening. Such routines and restrictions have made it easier for McNeil's bears to grow increasingly tolerant of people.

The truth about bears

Bears aren't the only ones to receive an education at McNeil. The sanctuary is a valuable learning ground for humans as well. Many visitors come to McNeil filled with irrational fears born of ignorance or sensationalized accounts of bear attacks. They carry the simplistic and inaccurate image of bears as menacing, dangerous creatures – unpredictable killers lurking in the shadows and waiting to attack. McNeil helps to change such misconceptions. Visitors discover first-hand that bears aren't man-eating monsters as so often portrayed in literature and news accounts.

"The first day people come here," says Aumiller, "many are fearful, usually because of things they've heard or read. But after they've seen a few bears up close and the bears go about their business, people get incredibly blasé about it. After that, they have to be cautioned about getting too careless. The transformation is almost universal."

Aumiller believes that McNeil's visitors feel safe around the bears largely because the sanctuary provides a controlled situation. The biologists act as guides. And they're armed, though they've never had to shoot a bear. The removal of irrational fears makes it easier to accept the bears on their own terms. And there's no better place to watch "bears being bears."

Watching them for hours each day, for up to four days in a row, visitors gain glimpses into the animals' lives. People start to recognize the bears as individuals, with different mannerisms and personalities. Some are aggressive, even bullies, others mild-mannered or timid around their own kind. Some are excellent fishers, others fare poorly.   ❏

RIGHT: bear-hunting photographers at Mikfik Creek.

REMOTE COMMUNITIES AND WILDLANDS

Alaska

Anchorage●

Part of the north Pacific's volcanic "ring of fire," the Alaska Peninsula has many settlements of Natives as well as some notable wildlife reserves

BELOW: Bristol Bay has large colonies of walrus.

Extending more than 500 miles (800km) from top to tip, the **Alaska Peninsula** ❾ is a rugged, storm-blasted, mostly treeless landscape inhabited by the world's densest population of brown bears: more than 1 bear per square mile. The greatest of these concentrations occur in **Katmai National Park and Preserve** and **McNeil River State Game Sanctuary** *(see pages 332 and 337 respectively)*, at the upper end of the peninsula. Dozens of brown bears gather along peninsula streams each year to feed on the spawning salmon and both

the National Park Service and Alaska Department of Fish and Game have established bear-viewing programs that give people unmatched opportunities to observe the fishing bears.

Bristol Bay

The largest salmon runs are those of the sockeye that return to **Bristol Bay** ❿ streams each summer; tens of millions of the salmon spawn here, providing nutrients for all manner of predators and scavengers, including bears, eagles, gulls, foxes, rainbow trout, and char. And humans, too. The Bristol Bay region is home to North America's largest commercial salmon fleet; and the streams that feed the bay are known around the world as a fisherman's paradise.

Though many anglers come to catch the region's salmon, rainbow trout are an even bigger draw. Dozens of fishing lodges are scattered through the Bristol Bay and Alaska Peninsula region. Other companies have fish camps or do guided day trips out of the region's communities.

Besides bears, salmon, and rainbows, Bristol Bay and the Alaska Peninsula are seasonal or year-round homes to numerous other species of mammals and birds; among the most spectacular concentrations are migrating herds of caribou, numerous colonies of sea birds and large marine mammal haulouts. Two of the world's greatest concentrations of walrus occur in Bristol Bay; one is at the **Togiak National Wildlife Refuge** ⓫; the other is at **Round Island**, within the

Walrus Islands State Game Santuary ⑫ (tel: 842-2334; www.state.ak.us/adfg). And on the lower Alaska Peninsula, the **Izembek National Wildlife Refuge** ⑬ (tel: 532-2445; www.r7.fws.gov) serves as an "international crossroads" for migrating waterfowl and shorebirds.

The refuge's heart is **Izembeck Lagoon**, where hundreds of thousands of migratory waterfowl converge each fall, including the entire world population of black brant.

Besides being home to large concentrations of wildlife, the Alaska Peninsula is also a seismically active place that is part of the North Pacific's "ring of fire." Dozens of volcanoes dot the landscape, several of them still considered active. **Pavlof Volcano**, on the lower peninsula, has erupted more than 40 times since 1790; in 1986 it sent volcanic ash more than 10 miles (16km) into the atmosphere and continued to belch smoke and ash and lava off and on for more than two years.

One of the more spectacular volcanic landscapes is **Aniakchak Caldera**, a 6-mile (10-km) wide crater formed thousands of years ago by the collapse of a huge volcano. Within the caldera are all sorts of volcanic features: lava fields, warm springs, and cinder cones. The caldera is the dominant feature of **Aniakchak National Monument and Preserve** ⑮ (tel: 246-3305; www.nps.gov/ania), one of the least visited units of the National Park System.

The Alaska Peninsula and Bristol Bay region is home to the Aleut and Yup'ik Eskimo peoples. Here, as in much of rural Alaska, most residents continue to depend on subsistence harvests of fish, mammals, birds, and plants. Dozens of small villages are scattered along the coast; the area's two hubs are **Dillingham**, in Bristol Bay, and **King Salmon**, on the upper Alaska Peninsula. Both communities are served by daily commuter flights from Anchorage and are jumping-off spots for trips into the area's parks and refuges. For information visitor services, contact the Dillingham Chamber of Commerce (tel: 842-5115; www.dillinghamak.com) or the King Salmon Visitors Center (tel: 246-4250).

The Aleutian Islands

Reaching southwest beyond the Alaska Peninsula, the **Aleutian Islands** ⑯ arc

Getting to school
Students (grades 6 and above) in the Alaska Peninsula community of South Naknek (population 74) must cross the Naknek River each day to attend school. When the river is frozen, they travel by car, ATV or snow-machine; otherwise the daily school run is via bush plane.

BELOW:
adding color to
the fishing kit.

BELOW: Mount
Cleveland is an
5,675-ft (1,730-
meter)-high active
volcano on
Chuginadak Island
in the western
Aleutian Islands.

more than 1,000 miles (1,600km) in their
bend toward Asia. More than 200 islands
make up the chain, which separates the
Pacific Ocean from the Bering Sea.

Nearly all of the islands are included
within the **Alaska Maritime National
Wildlife Refuge** (tel: 235-6546; www.
r7.fws.gov), which protects the coastal lands
and waters used by the many sea birds,
shorebirds, waterfowl, and marine mammals that inhabit the chain.

While the volcanic, tundra-covered
islands that make up the chain have a
rugged, barren appearance, the waters
surrounding the Aleutians are among the
richest in the world, supporting a billion-
dollar fishing industry. The area is also
home to some of the world's largest bird
colonies and marine mammal populations, from sea otters to seals and sea
lions and whales. Yet even here, there is
evidence of ecological stress: two once-
plentiful species, sea lions and harbor
seals, have experienced great declines in
recent decades; the populations of some
birds, too, have been greatly reduced.
Scientists have been studying the
declines, which may be tied to overfish-
ing, climate change, or other factors.

The weather in the Aleutians is generally cool and wet, and often stormy.
Annual precipitation ranges from 20 to 80
inches (50–200cm) a year. Summer temperatures rarely get much above 50°F
(10°C) and in winter don't often drop
below 20°F (−6.7°C). Winds seem to
blow constantly and fog too is common.
Visitors to the region must be prepared for
weather delays, both coming and going.

Dutch Harbor

Aleuts have inhabited the island chain
for centuries, depending on the marine
ecosystem for their survival. Small numbers of Aleuts (and even smaller numbers of non-Natives) still reside here, in
several small communities. The Aleutians' largest city and commercial hub is
Dutch Harbor, at the northern end of
the chain on **Unalaska Island** ⑰. It is
the No. 1 fishing port in the US, both in
terms of poundage and value.

With a combined population of about
4,200 people, Dutch Harbor and neighboring **Unalaska** also serve as the Aleutians' tourism center, complete with the
world-class Grand Aleutian hotel. Visitor activities here range from sport fish-

ing for salmon and halibut to bird watching, hiking, kayaking, and exploring World War II remants. Japanese troops bombed Dutch Harbor during the war and also landed on Attu and Kiska Islands; the US military later retook those islands, in the only battles fought on American soil during World War II.

Those who travel to Dutch Harbor can learn more about local history at the **Museum of the Aleutians**, which has exhibits about the Aleut culture, Russian occupation, World War II and the fishing industry. Contact the Dutch Harbor/ Unalaska Convention and Visitors Bureau (tel: 907-581-2612 or 877-581-2612; www.unalaska.info) for more information about travel to and within the area.

The Pribilof Islands

Three hundred miles (480km) off the western coast of Alaska and 200 miles north of the Aleutians lie the **Pribilof Islands** ⑱, the nesting grounds for hundreds of thousands of sea birds of almost 200 different species, and the breeding grounds and summer home of nearly a million Pacific fur seals. Five volcanic, treeless islets make up the Pribilof group, but only two of those are inhabited by humans: **St Paul** and **St George**; with a population of about 500 people, nearly all Natives, the village of St Paul is the world's largest community of Aleuts. There are small hotels on both islands, but only St Paul has a restaurant. It also is visited in summer by packaged tours, the easiest way to visit the Pribilofs (contact the Tanadgusix Village Corporation of St Paul Island for more tourism information, tel: 278-2312 or 877-424-5637; www.alaskabirding.com).

Today, the fishing and tourism industries are being developed as St Paul's main economic supports. Past revenues were generated by the fur seal harvest and government aid. With the ending of the commericial harvest in 1985, the community was forced to find other means of support. The newly completed harbor is a boon to local fishermen, who had no safe haven for their boats, and is expected to attract new industry. Tourism

also helps; the Pribilofs are known as a birders paradise. Especially attractive to serious birders are the "accidental" Asian migrants that sometimes get blown to the islands by strong western winds. These birds are rarely, if ever, seen anywhere else in North America.

Visitors to the Pribilofs should be prepared for cool and moist conditions. In June, the average daily high is 41°F (5°C) and nighttime lows fall into the 30s even in summer. And only rarely do the islands experience back-to-back sunny days.

Unalaska Island, America's top fishing port.

Yukon-Kuskokwim Delta

Encompassing 76,000 sq. miles (200,000 sq. km) in remote Southwest Alaska, the **Yukon-Kuskokwim Delta** is home to Alaska's Yup'ik Eskimos and one of the world's great waterfowl-nesting areas.

Much of the delta is within the **Yukon Delta National Wildlife Refuge** ⑲. At 19.2 million acres (7.8 million hectares), this refuge is the nation's second largest

BELOW: a fox pup in St George, Pribilof Islands.

BELOW: the First Moravian Mission building in Bethel.

(just slightly smaller than the Arctic National Wildlife Refuge). It's also the oldest refuge in Alaska; in 1909, President Theodore Roosevelt established the Yukon Delta Reservation. That reservation and some later refuges were then consolidated and expanded in 1980 to form the present Yukon Delta NWR. Within the refuge, waters from two of Alaska's four largest rivers meander through immense, tundra wetlands. The Yukon flows 1,400 miles (2,250 km) before emptying into the Bering Sea, while to the south, the Kuskokwim River winds 540 miles (870 km) through Southwest Alaska.

This is as flat as Alaska gets: nearly 70 percent of the refuge is delta lands and waters less than 100 ft (30 meters) in elevation. Innumerable streams and sloughs weave through this lowland, which is also dotted with tens of thousands of lakes, ponds, and marshes. In all, about a third of the refuge is covered in water. Higher and drier areas are covered by forests and range up to an elevation of 4,000 ft (1,200 meters), in the gently rounded **Kuskokwim** and **Kilbuck Mountains**.

The refuge's wetlands are seasonal

home to millions of birds: sea birds, shorebirds, waterfowl, songbirds, and raptors. In both diversity and numbers, the refuge is considered America's most important shorebird nesting area and is also critically important for ducks and geese. Birds come here from the Atlantic coast as well as Asia. Many nest here; others use the delta as a staging post.

Spawning ground

The Delta's waterways also serve as important spawning and rearing habitat for more than 40 species of fish, including Alaska's five species of Pacific salmon, Dolly Varden char, northern pike, grayling, and rainbow trout. Mammals range from grizzlies and black bears to caribou, moose, wolves, and musk oxen. Coastal waters are important to several types of seals, walrus, and whales.

Few people visit the refuge; those who do come here largely for the sport fishing or bird watching. As in most of Alaska's remotest parks and refuges, there are no visitor facilities here. For information on recreational opportunities, contact the refuge headquarters in Bethel (tel: 543-3151; www.r7.fws.gov).

Bethel

The Delta's Yupik residents live in scattered villages along the coast and its main rivers. Most of the 50 or so communities are small, with few or no accommodations for travelers.

The commercial and social hub of the region is **Bethel 20**, a city of about 6,000 people on the Kuskokwim River. Here you'll find a theater, banks, restaurants, radio and TV stations, a college, a hospital, and lodging options. The Moravian Church established a mission here in 1884. Information on Bethel and outlying areas can be obtained from the Bethel Chamber of Commerce (543-2911; www.bethelakchamber.org).

From the flatlands of the Y-K Delta to the volcanic peaks and bear-rich salmon streams of the Alaska Peninsula and the wind-battered islands of the Aleutian chain and Pribilof archipelago, the Southwest region presents adventurous visitors the opportunity to see parts of wild Alaska and aspects of the state's Native culture that few travelers ever encounter. ❏

Guarding the nest.

RESTAURANTS

Dutch Harbor/Unalaska

Grand Aleutian Hotel
498 Salmon Way
tel: (866) 581-3844, or (907) 581-3844
www.grandaleutian.com
This elegant hotel is by far the most luxurious of any in Alaska's bush communities. It houses three separate eateries:
Margaret Bay
Offers casual, bistro-style dining near the hotel's entrance. Open for breakfast and lunch. Good view of the harbor.
Cape Cheerful Lounge
Located next to the lobby, the comfortable lounge is a gathering spot for locals and guests. Live entertainment. Bar.
The Chart Room
Dutch Harbor's fine dining option is located on the second floor or the hotel. Panoramic view of Margaret Bay, Features steak, pasta or Alaska seafood. Bar. $–$$$$

Dillingham

Muddy Rudder
100 Main Street
tel: 842-5841

The favorite spot for locals and visitors alike is open for daily breakfast, lunch and dinner from May through November. Features steaks, seafood, burgers, sandwiches and salads. Beer and wine. $–$$$$

Twin Dragon (at the airport)
tel: (907) 842-2172
Dillingham Airport
Located within the airport, this restaurant offers delicious Chinese and American fare. Open daily for lunch and dinners. $–$$$

Bethel

Arctic Sun Café
3551 State Highway
tel: 543-3566
Located close to the Alaska Airlines terminal at the Bethel airport, this eatery is a good choice for those awaiting flights to outlying villages. Open 8am–10pm. A favorite spot for breakfast among the locals. Also serves standard burger, sandwich, soup and salad type meals with occasional specials. No alcohol. $

Brother's Pizza's and Subs
3551 State Highway
tel: (907) 543-3553
Located in the same building as Arctic Sun Café. The locals say it's the best spot in town for pizza. Also serves burgers, sandwiches and salads. Open daily 11am—11pm. No alcohol. $–$$$$

Dimitri's Restaurant
281 4th Avenue
tel: (907) 543-3434
Features Greek and Italian food, but also offers burgers, pork chops, salads and more. $–$$$

Yolanda's Restaurant
110 Osage Avenue
tel: 543-4403
Open daily for breakfast and lunch. Specializes in American or Western menu items, including omelettes, pancakes, and – the local favorite – biscuits and gravy. $

● ● ● ● ● ● ● ● ● ● ● ● ● ● ● ● ● ● ● ●
Price is for dinner excluding tax, tip and beverages: **$$$$** *$30 and up,* **$$$** *$20–30,* **$$** *$15–20,* **$** *under $15.*

INSIGHT GUIDES
TRAVEL TIPS

ALASKA

TRAVEL TIPS

TRANSPORTATION

GETTING THERE
AND GETTING AROUND

The 1½ million yearly visitors to Alaska arrive in one of three ways: by air, sea or road. The best choice for the individual traveler depends on the goals for the journey, the time available, and the costs involved. Arriving by train not an option. No train system, neither US nor Canadian, connects with Alaska's railway service.

By Air

Generally speaking, the fastest and least expensive way to travel to Alaska is to fly. Several major airlines provide regularly scheduled flights into Anchorage's Ted Stevens International Airport (and some to Fairbanks International), especially during the summer season. Alaska Airlines offers, by far, the most comprehensive coverage, with daily direct flights to Anchorage from Vancouver (British Columbia) Seattle, Portland, San Diego, Los Angeles, Denver and Chicago. Anchorage serves as the primary hub for travel to and within the state. Those wishing to travel to smaller, outlying towns and villages may do so from Anchorage by using Alaska Airlines, the smaller, regional airlines or chartered air taxi companies.

The communities of Ketchikan, Wrangell, Petersburg, Sitka, Juneau, Glacier Bay/Gustavus, Yakutat, and Cordova may be reached directly from Seattle via Alaska Airlines.

On arrival in Anchorage, or any other Alaska airport, you should expect to handle your own luggage. Ground transportation is usually available in the form of local bus service (in Anchorage, Fairbanks and

Juneau), taxis or car rentals. Most airports in Alaska are located within a few minutes' drive of the downtown area. A notable exception is Ketchikan, where the airport is located on a separate island, and a short ferry trip (fee charged) is necessary to reach the ground transportation – which you have to pre-arrange – to take you into the downtown area. The ferry runs every half-hour.

Private pilots planning to fly to Alaska should have the latest federal government flight information publication, the Alaska Chart Supplement, available from the Federal Aviation Administration, 222 W. Seventh Ave., No. 14, Anchorage, Alaska 99513-7587 or at www.alaska.faa.gov.

Useful contacts

Airport Information (Domestic or international airlines, terminal maps, ground transportation, visitor information):
Ted Stevens International Airport (Anchorage): (907) 266-2526; www.anchorageairport.com
Fairbanks International Airport: (907) 474-2500; www.dot.state.ak.us/faiiap
Juneau International Airport: (907) 789-7821; www.juneau.org/airport
Ketchikan International Airport: (907) 225-6800; www.borough. ketchikan.ak.us/airport/airport.htm

By Sea

Nearly half of all visitors to Alaska travel via **cruise ship**. There are several good reasons for this, beyond the effective marketing programs of the cruise industry. Most Alaska cruises begin – or end up – in Seattle or Vancouver, British Columbia, Canada. They offer one-way or round-

trip voyages through the protected (and therefore generally calm) waterways of the Inside Passage. Passengers may go ashore and see the sights, experience the local culture and shop in various Southeast communities without having to repeatedly pack and unpack, or sleep in a different bed every night. Cruise directors plan itineraries, work out all the details and deal with any unexpected opportunities or inconveniences.

Passengers generally have the option of adding exciting shore excursions – even extended land tours – to the basic package. The entire cost of the trip, while admittedly expensive, is known at the outset. The service is generally excellent and the journey thrilling, yet comfortable and relaxing.

But not all cruises are created equal. **Big-ship cruise lines**, such as Holland America, Princess, Celebrity, Norwegian, Regent Seven Seas, and Royal Caribbean transport thousands of passengers while offering not only luxurious travel to Alaska, but also an array of on-board entertainment for those who enjoy seemingly endless options of formal dinners (and formal dress), casinos, floor shows, spas, line dancing, art auctions, bingo and kids' programs, to name a few.

Small-ship cruise lines, like Cruise West, Clipper, Lindblad, Glacier Bay, American Safari, and American West Steamboat Company, carry 20–250 passengers, and specialize in excellent food, casual dress, close-up (sea-level) wildlife and glacier viewing and educational lectures by on-board naturalists. These smaller ships have the added advantage of being able to offer stops in less-traveled areas such as Wrangell or Petersburg.

Those who are more adventurous (and have with plenty of time) might want to consider one of the more unusual Alaska cruises to the far north, around the Pribilof Islands (these are known to be superb for bird watching) and into the Bering Sea. These are operated by the smaller, specialist expedition cruise companies.

Independent travelers may choose another excellent option: traveling to Alaska aboard one of the **Alaska Marine Highway System** ferries. The state actually operates 11 ferries providing year-round service between Bellingham, Washington (or Prince Rupert, British Columbia, Canada) and Southeast and Southcentral Alaska's coastal communities. Seasonal service is available to those in Southwest.

Twice-monthly connections (cross-gulf) between the Southeast and Southwest routes are available in summer only. Most of these communities are located far from the road system; therefore ferry travel is basic transportation. The ferries range in size from the 180-foot/149-passenger M/V *Lituya* to the 418-foot/499-passenger M/V *Columbia*. The larger ferries offer comfortable (if not luxurious) staterooms, some with private baths. During the summer, USDA Forest Service naturalists offer interpretive programs. There are large, clean public restrooms and showers (towels may be rented). Also, after 10pm, you may roll out a sleeping bag in one of the spacious lounges, kick back in a recliner, or pitch a tent (at any time) near the heated solarium, located on the upper deck. The ferries offer cafeterias or snack bars, gift shops, laundry facilities, video game rooms, occasional movies, comfortable lounges and a play area for toddlers.

It is a low-key and user-friendly way to travel, but it doesn't come cheap. Walk-on passengers from Bellingham to Skagway, for example, will pay around US$350 (one way). They may bring along their bicycle or kayak, if they wish, for $56 and $86, respectively. If they want a stateroom (for two) with a bath, it will add about $350 more. If they drive a small automobile onto the ferry, add an additional $950 (considerably more for larger vehicles, including RVs).

If you want to break up the trip and spend a few days in some of the towns along the way, the overall cost will not be greatly affected. However, you will need the luxury of time, as it may be 2 or 3 days before the next ferry comes along. There are two,

new catamaran-styled fast ferries in the system, which add considerable flexibility between certain ports. One operates between Juneau, Sitka, Haines and Skagway, and the other between the communities of Whittier, Valdez and Cordova in Prince William Sound.

Travelers planning to use the ferry system during the busy summer tourist season should make reservations at least 6 months in advance, especially if they plan to bring a vehicle aboard.

Useful contacts
Northwest CruiseShip Association: http://alaska.nwcruiseship.org
Alaska Marine Highway System: (800) 642-0066; (907) 465-3941; www.ferryalaska.com.

By Road

Traveling the Alaska Highway is a great adventure. However, because of the great distance, only well-prepared drivers with plenty of time should consider it.
By Bus: Bus service and motorcoach tours are available to Alaska by way of the Alaska Highway. From Seattle, Washington, Greyhound connects with Greyhound Canada, offering service to Whitehorse in the Yukon Territory, Canada. From Whitehorse, Alaska Direct Bus Lines and Alaska/Yukon Trails connect with several Alaska communities, including Tok, Fairbanks, and Anchorage. Several companies offer motorcoach tours between the contiguous United States and Alaska. For more information, contact a travel agent.
By Car or RV: The new improvements to the Alaska Highway have made driving enjoyable and safe, but distance may be a drawback. It is 1,488 miles (2,395 km) from Dawson Creek, BC to Fairbanks, and much of the trip will be through extremely remote, though spectacular, country. Make sure your vehicle is in dependable working order and bring along basic tools, flares, jack, spare tire, first-aid kit, and other emergency equipment. If you're traveling the road in winter, be prepared with adequate food, water, warm clothing and blankets in case of unexpected delays.

For essential information about driving Alaska's highways, refer to the latest edition of *The Milepost*, published and updated yearly by Morris Communications Company LLC. The book gives detailed descriptions of points of interest, food, gas, and lodging options, as well as road conditions for your

adventure up through Canada and along Alaska's roadways.

Useful contacts
Current driving, construction and weather conditions on Alaska highways: tel: 511 within Alaska; (866) 282-7577; http://511.Alaska.gov
Greyhound Canada Transportation Corp.: (800) 661-8747; www.greyhound.ca
Alaska Direct Bus Line: (800) 770-6652; www.alaskadirectbusline.com
Alaska/Yukon Trails: (800) 770-7275; www.alaskashuttle.com

Cruise Tours

Cruise-tours (a cruise plus a land extension) have become an increasingly popular way to see more of Alaska, particularly by those who have time and may only visit it once. This usually involves a cruise plus land stay in a hotel, or a cruise plus a train ride and hotel stay, all neatly arranged and packaged by the cruise lines, relieving passengers of all the headaches and organization.

Although the most popular cruises to Alaska are of seven days, extending your vacation by taking a cruise plus an escorted land tour can stretch to as many as 18 days, to include a cruise, plus the heart of Alaska, and the Canadian Rockies.
Alaska Cruise Trains
Specially constructed domed railcars are featured in the cruise-tour programs of the major cruise companies: Holland America Line, Princess Cruises, and Royal Caribbean International/ Celebrity Cruises. The special domed cars (some are fitted with seats that can turn to allow passengers to face forwards or backwards) are fitted aboard trains operated by the Alaska Railroad, which is owned by the State of Alaska. The railway extends northwards, from Seward through Anchorage to Fairbanks, a distance of 470 miles (760 km).
McKinley Explorer
Holland America Line has original 1950s domed railcars that have been specially converted for the company, aboard the McKinley Explorer. They were designed and built by the Budd Rail Company, and originally initially operated on the Sante Fe Railway. The railcars, each named after an Alaska river, are dubbed the Mercedez-Benz of the American rails, they are extremely smooth railcars, and run on six-wheel units (called "trucks") instead of the usual four. The train has a full service dining car.

Midnight Sun Express

Princess Cruises has had its own Midnight Sun Express train since 1984. It operates between Anchorage and Fairbanks. The upper level of the cars are completely glass-enclosed (Ultra Domes). The train has a full service dining car.

Wilderness Express

The domed railcars on the Wilderness Express were specially constructed for Royal Caribbean International and Celebrity Cruises (owned by RCI) and feature full-length vista-domes. The train has a full service dining car.

Shore Excursions

Shore excursions, too, have increased in number (and cost) over the years. They include flightseeing by floatplane or helicopter, salmon fishing, salmon bake, hiking, glacial ice treks, mountain biking, train rides, jeep safaris, whale watching. One must-do excursion (if your cruise takes you to Skagway) is a trip on the White Pass & Yukon Route Railroad.

GETTING AROUND

By Air

The secret to conquering Alaska's vastness is air travel. Commuter airlines and charter aircraft services are everywhere. More often than not, even the most remote cabins in the wilderness have some sort of airstrip nearby, or a stretch of hard-packed sand on a river bar to serve as a landing strip. Per capita, six times as many Alaskans have a pilot's license as do residents of the rest of the country.

Charter aircraft are available for those who don't wish to wait for regular, scheduled flights to remote destinations, or for those who wish to go into the middle of the wilderness.

Costs typically begin at $375 an hour (flight time) to charter a pilot and plane that can carry four passengers, depending on the amount of baggage. If you're traveling with a large group, it's even possible to charter a vintage DC-3, a twin-engine plane capable of hauling large loads for long distances. Also check local air-taxi operators for charter and commuter service to Alaskan communities.

On the facing page is a list of many of the carriers offering scheduled intrastate air service. Interline service is available to most rural Alaska points: check with carriers.

By Rail

There is no rail service directly to Alaska from either the lower 48 states or Canada. However, the Alaska Railroad provides passenger service within the state. The 470-mile (756-km) main line connects Anchorage with Fairbanks to the north and with Whittier and Seward to the south. There's daily service between Anchorage and Fairbanks in summer, but only weekly in winter. Service between Anchorage and Seward is seasonal (mid-May to mid-September).

For more information, contact: Alaska Railroad, tel: (907) 265-2494 or toll-free (800) 544-0552; www.akrr.com. The railroad offers a variety of summer packages to destinations like Denali National Park, Fairbanks, Whittier (with cruises on Prince William Sound) and Seward (with cruises into Kenai Fjords National Park). In summer, one-day trips are also available to Seward, Whittier, Talkeetna and beyond.

By Sea

Besides sailing from Seattle to southeastern Alaska, the Alaska Marine Highway operates several vehicle and passenger ferries on the Gulf Coast. Homer on the Kenai Peninsula is connected to the Prince William Sound communities of Whittier, Valdez and Cordova via the ferries. It's also possible to sail from Homer to Kodiak Island and onward to several Aleutian destinations. Check at the ferry office near the harbor if you're in any of the towns along the route, or get information in advance from the Alaska Marine Highway, PO Box 112505, Juneau, AK 99801, tel: (800) 642-0066 or (907) 465-3941; www.FerryAlaska.com.

Public Transportation

Alaska's three largest cities offer municipal bus service.

Anchorage:

Anchorage People Mover, tel: (907) 343-6543, www.muni.org/transit1/mapping.

Fairbanks:

Metropolitan Area Commuter System (MACS), tel: (907) 459-1011, www.co.fairbanks.ak.us/transportation.

Juneau:

Capital Transit System (CTS), tel: (907) 789-6901, www.juneau.org/capitaltransit.

Most communities with any road system at all will have some form of taxi service. Taxis are nice for getting around town, but can be extremely expensive for long distances.

Private Transportation

Recreational Vehicles

Renting an RV camper has become increasingly popular. There are many businesses offering this service, including these in Anchorage:
A & M RV Center
tel: (907) 279-5508 or (800) 478-4678
www.gorv.com
ABC Motorhome & RV
tel: (907) 279-2000 or (800) 421-7456
www.abcmotorhome.com

Motoring Advisories

"Highway" in Alaska generally means a two-lane roadway (one in each direction) with no turning lane and few passing lanes. The speed limit on most Alaska highways is 55 mph (88 km), although speeds of up to 65 mph (104 km) are allowed on some sections. Speed limits are lower within cities, in residential areas and especially near schools. Obey posted speed limits and you should have few problems.

Alaska law requires drivers to pull over at the first, safe opportunity whenever five or more vehicles are following behind them.

A right turn is permitted against a red light unless otherwise posted, but only after you stop long enough to confirm there is no traffic with which you will interfere. All drivers in both directions are required to stop for a school bus with its warning lights operating. Drivers may not proceed around or past a school bus until the lights have been turned off. Drivers in Alaska may see hitchhikers, but not nearly as many as in the past. Hitchhiking is most common during the milder summer season, when both residents and visitors seek rides when traveling to jobs or adventures along major routes. You pick up hitchhikers at your own risk.

Prudence dictates that you slow your speed during the winter months. Highways in Alaska are not the best in the world, and in combination with ice and snow, can be treacherous. For the latest information on road conditions, construction delays and other safety issues on Alaska roads, dial 511, or go to http://511.alaska.gov.

Airline contacts

ANCHORAGE
Consult the Anchorage Yellow Pages for an extensive listing of those airlines operating out of the state's largest city. The ones listed here are just a few of the key players.
International Carriers
Asiana Airlines
tel: (800) 227-4262
www.flyasiana.com
Cathay Pacific Airways
tel: (800) 233-2742
www.cathaypacific.com
China Airlines
tel: (800) 227-5118
www.china-airlines.com
Japan Air Lines
tel: (800) 525-3663
www.ar.jal.com
Korean Air
tel: (800) 438-5000
www.koreanair.com
Major Domestic Carriers
Air Canada
tel: (888) 247-2262
www.aircanada.com
Alaska Airlines
tel: (800) 252-7522
www.alaskaair.com
American Airlines
(800) 433-7300
www.aa.com
Continental Airlines
(800) 523-3273
www.continental.com
Delta Airlines
tel: (800) 221-1212
www.delta.com
Frontier Airlines
tel: (800) 432-1359
www.flyfrontier.com
Hawaiian Vacations
tel: (800) 770-2700
www.hawaiianvacations.com
Northwest Airlines
tel: (800) 225-2525
www.nwa.com
Sun Country Airlines
tel: (800) 359-6786
www.suncountry.com
United Airlines
tel: (800) 864-8331
www.united.com
US Airways
tel: (800) 428-4322
www.usairways.com
Local Carriers
ERA Aviation
tel: (907) 266-8394
or (800) 866-8394
www.flyera.com
Frontier Flying Service
tel: (907) 450-7200 or
(800) 478-6779
www.frontierflying.com
Grant Aviation
tel: (888) 359-4726
www.flygrant.com
Hageland Aviation Service
tel: (907) 245-0139 or
(866) 239-0119
www.hageland.com

Lake Clark Air
tel: (907) 781-2208 or
(888) 440-2281
www.lakeclarkair.com
Pen Air
tel: (907) 771-2640 or
(800) 448-4226
www.penair.com
Air Taxis
Alaska Air Taxi
tel: (907) 243-3944 or
(800) 789-5232
www.alaskaairtaxi.com
Ellis Air Taxi
tel: (907) 822-3368
www.ellisair.com
Iliamna Air Taxi
tel: (907) 571-1248
www.iliamnaair.com
Regal Air
tel: (907) 243-8535
www.regal-air.com
Rust's Flying Service
tel: (907) 243-1595 or
(800) 544-2299
www.flyrusts.com

FAIRBANKS
Major Carriers
Air North
tel: (800) 661-0407
www.flyairnorth.com
Alaska Airlines
tel: (800) 252-7522
www.alaskaair.com
Delta
tel: (800) 221-1212
www.delta.com
Northwest Airlines
tel: (800) 225-2525
www.nwa.com
Local Carriers
40-Mile Air
tel: (907) 883-5191
Arctic Circle Air Service
tel: (907) 474-0112
www.arctic-circle-air.com
Bettles Air
tel: (907) 479-7018 or
(800) 770-5111
www.bettlesair.com
Frontier Flying
tel: (907) 450-7200 or
(800) 478-6779
www.frontierflying.com
Larry's Flying Service
tel: (907) 474-9169
www.larrysflying.com
Warbelow's Air
tel: (907) 474-0518 or
(800) 478-0812
www.warbelows.com
Wright's Air Service
tel: (907) 474-0502 or
(800) 478-0502 in Alaska
www.wrightair.net

HAINES
Local Carriers
L.A.B. Flying Service
tel: (907) 789-9160
www.labflying.com

Mountain Flying Service
tel: (907) 766-3007 or
(800) 954-8747
www.flyglacierbay.com
Wings of Alaska
tel: (907) 789-0790
www.wingsofalaska.com

HOMER
ERA Aviation
tel: (907) 266-8391 or
(800) 866-8394
www.flyera.com

JUNEAU
Major Carrier
Alaska Airlines
tel: (800) 252-7522
www.alaskaair.com
Local Carriers
L.A.B. Flying Service
tel: (907) 789-9160
www.labflying.com
Wings of Alaska
tel: (907) 789-0790
www.wingsofalaska.com
Helicopter Services
Coastal Helicopters
tel: (907) 789-5600
www.coastalhelicopters.com
ERA Aviation
tel: (907) 248-4422
www.erahelicopters.com
Temsco Helicopters
tel: (907) 789-9501 or
(877) 789-9501
www.temscoair.com

KENAI
ERA Aviation
tel: (800) 866-8394
www.flyera.com

KETCHIKAN
Major Carrier
Alaska Airlines
tel: (800) 252-7522
www.alaskaair.com
Local Carriers
Promech Air
tel: (907) 225-3845 or
(800) 860-3845
www.promechair.com
Taquan Air
tel: (800) 770-8800
www.taquanair.com

KODIAK
Major Carrier
Alaska Airlines
tel: (800) 252-7522
www.alaskaair.com
Local Carrier
ERA Aviation
tel: (907) 266-8391 or
(800) 866-8394
www.flyera.com

NOME
Major Carrier
Alaska Airlines
tel: (800) 252-7522
www.alaskaair.com

Local Carriers
Bering Air
tel: (907) 443-5464 or
(800) 478-5422 in Alaska
www.beringair.com
Cape Smythe Air
tel: (907) 443-2414
Hageland Aviation
tel: (907) 443-7595
(888) 547-7595 in Alaska
www.hageland.com

PETERSBURG
Major Carrier
Alaska Airlines
tel: (800) 252-7522
www.alaskaair.com
Local Carriers
L.A.B. Flying Service
tel: (907) 789-9160
www.labflying.com
Nordic Air
tel: (907) 772-3535
Pacific Wing Air Charters
tel: (907) 772-4259
www.pacificwing.com

SITKA
Major Carrier
Alaska Airlines
tel: (800) 252-7522
www.alaskaair.com
Local Carrier
Harris Aircraft Services
tel: (907) 966-3050 or
(877) 966-3050 in Alaska
www.harrisaircraft.com

SKAGWAY
L.A.B. Flying Service
tel: (907) 789-9160
www.labflying.com
Skagway Air Service
tel: (907) 983-2218
www.skagwayair.com
Wings of Alaska
tel: (907) 983-2442
www.wingsofalaska.com

VALDEZ
Major Carrier
Alaska Airlines
tel: (800) 252-7522
www.alaskaair.com
Local Carrier
ERA Aviation
tel: (907) 266-8394 or
(800) 866-8394
www.flyera.com

WRANGELL
Major Carrier
Alaska Airlines
tel: (800) 252-7522
www.alaskaair.com
Local Carriers
Sunrise Aviation
tel: (907) 874-2319 or
(800) 874-2311
www.sunriseflights.com
Temsco Helicopter
tel: (907) 874-2010
www.temscoair.com

A CCOMMODATIONS

HOTELS, BED & BREAKFAST, CAMPGROUNDS

Choosing Accommodations

Accommodations vary greatly. Larger communities offer a range of hotels, with international standards. Bed-and-breakfasts are also very popular, with many offering outstanding service. In the very smallest communities, facilities may be mediocre or non-existent. Prices anywhere, especially in more remote areas, are high, especially during peak summer months.

Anchorage has had a boom in hotel building, with new facilities near the airport, downtown, midtown and on the east side. Many of the new hotels offer relatively lower rates but with few extras, such as full-service restaurants.

Rates given here are for standard double rooms during peak summer months. Rates during the off-season are considerably lower.

Bed-and-breakfast For information about facilities statewide, write to **Alaska Private Lodgings/ Stay With A Friend,** PO Box 1924, Homer, AK 99603 tel: (907) 235-2148; email: info@alaskaprivatelodging.com www.alaskabandb.com

Free booklet The Alaska Travel Industry Association provides an extensive list of accommodations in the Alaska Vacation Planner. To get this free booklet call them on (907) 929-2200 or visit www.travelalaska.com

Private Use Cabins

For a totally Alaskan experience, visitors can stay in remote wilderness cabins maintained by the US Forest Service (see panel on page 87). The cost of rentals is low (around $25 to $45 a night), but getting there can be expensive. For more information on public use cabins, contact the Alaska Public Lands Information Center, 605 W. Fourth Avenue, Suite 105, Anchorage, AK 99501, tel: (907) 271-2737, www.nps.gov/aplic/center. For reservations, call the National Recreation Reservation Service, tel: (877) 444-6777 and website www.reserveusa.com. You can reserve cabins on federal lands on-line up to 180 days in advance, using a Visa, MasterCard or Discover card. Information on Forest Service cabins can also be obtained at the websites for the Tongass and Chugach National Forests: www.fs.fed.us/r10/tongass and www.fs.fed.us/r10/chugach. For National Park Service cabins: www.nps.gov. For State Park Cabins write: Department of Natural Resources, 550 W. 7th Avenue, Suite 1260, Anchorage, AK 99501, or tel: (907) 269-8400; www.dnr.state.ak.us/parks/index.htm

---

BELOW: the relaxed way to tour Alaska.

Campgrounds

Federal, state, municipal and private campgrounds vary from barely organized tent sites to full hook-up recreational vehicle parking sites. There are campgrounds along all of the major highways, but it may be some distance between them. And in summer, many of them are filled by early evening or even late afternoon, especially on weekends, so it's smart to plan ahead.

Most campgrounds charge fees for overnight use. Daily rates vary from $10 at rustic sites to more than $20 for full hook-up sites in private campgrounds.

All the campgrounds are open in the summer months only.

The best sources for listings are The Milepost, available in bookstores, and the Alaska Vacation Planner, available from the Alaska Travel Industry Association, tel: (907) 929-2842; www.travelalaska.com. Also, the state publishes a list of state campgrounds. Write to the Department of Natural Resources, 550 W. 7th Ave, Suite 1260, Anchorage, AK 99501; www.dnr.state.ak.us/parks

Hostel Information

Private hostel accommodations are available throughout the state. Information is available through online listings or in The Hostel Handbook, which is available at http://hostelhandbook.com.

Many hostels are members of the Alaska Hostel Association. For inexpensive lodgings around Alaska, visit their website at www.alaskahostel association.org, or contact them at Alaska Hostel Association, PO Box 92422, Anchorage, 99509-2422.

ANCHORAGE

Alaska Budget Motel
545 E. Fourth Ave,
Anchorage, AK
tel: (907) 277-0088
fax: (907) 277-1517
email: abm@gci.net
Clean and comfy, near
downtown malls. Free
parking. $
**Anchorage Marriott
Downtown**
820 West Seventh Avenue,
Anchorage, AK 99501
tel: (907) 279-8000 or
(800) 228-9290
www.marriott.com
One of the newest
downtown hotels, with
395 rooms. Restaurant,
laundry, lounge. $$$$
Best Western Barratt Inn
4616 Spenard Road,
Anchorage, AK 99517
tel: (907) 243-3131 or
(800) 221-7550
email: info@barrattinn.com
www.barrattinn.com
Near Spenard Lake;
217 rooms, ranging from
"economy" to "luxury."
There are four buildings;
ask for the most recently
renovated. Restaurant,
lounge, laundry. $$$
Chelsea Inn Hotel
3836 Spenard Rd,
Anchorage, AK 99517
tel: (907) 276-5002 or
(800) 770-5002
fax: (907) 277-6742
Good atmosphere, free
airport shuttle bus, 34
rooms. On-site laundry. $
Comfort Inn Ship Creek
111 Ship Creek Avenue,
Anchorage, AK 99501
tel: (907) 277-6887 or toll free
(800) 424-6423
email: comfortinn@gci.net

www.choicehotels.com
Just north of downtown
near the railroad tracks;
100 rooms, some with
kitchens. $$$–$$$$
Creekwood Inn
2150 Seward Highway,
Anchorage, AK 99503
tel: (907) 258-6006 or
(800) 478-6008
email: info@creekwoodinn-alaska.com
www.creekwoodinn-alaska.com
Rooms have microwave
ovens and refrigerators;
located near midtown
shopping malls, 24-hour
restaurants and a movie
theater; 26 rooms,
plus cabin and RV park.
$$
Hilton Anchorage Hotel
500 W. 3rd Avenue,
Anchorage, AK 99501
tel: (907) 272-7411 or
(800) 445-8667
www.hilton.com
Downtown; 591 rooms with
data ports and voice mail.
Two lounges/restaurants,
gift shops. $$$$
Holiday Inn Express
4411 Spenard Road
Anchorage, AK 99517
tel: (907) 248-8848 or
(800) 465-4329
www.hieanchorage.com
Located in midtown
Anchorage with easy
access to restaurants.
128 rooms. Swimming
pool, fitness center,
laundry, breakfast room.
$$$$
Hotel Captain Cook
939 West Fifth Avenue,
Anchorage, AK 99501
tel: (907) 276-6000 or toll free
(800) 843-1950
www.captaincook.com

Among Anchorage's finest;
offers rooms with either
mountain or inlet views;
547 rooms. Restaurants,
lounges, coffee shop,
several gift shops, athletic
club with pool. $$$$
Inlet Tower Hotel & Suites
1200 L Street,
Anchorage, AK 99501
tel: (907) 276-0110 or
(800) 544-0786
www.inlettower.com
Located six blocks south
of the downtown core,
each of the 164 rooms
and suites boasts a view
of the city. Laundromat,
free shuttle. On-site
restaurant. $$$$
**Millennium Alaskan Hotel
Anchorage**
4800 Spenard Road
Anchorage, AK 99517
tel: (907) 243-2300 or
(866) 866-8086 for reservations
email: anchorage@mhrmail.com
www.millenniumhotels.com
Near airport on scenic
Lake Spenard; 248 rooms.
Has a rustic lodge motif,
with stone fireplace and
trophy heads in lobby; two
restaurants, lounge, patio,
gift shop, exercise room.
$$$$
Sheraton Anchorage Hotel
401 E. 6th Avenue,
Anchorage, AK 99501
tel: (907) 276-8700 or
(800) 478-8700 for reservations
email: info@sheratonanchoragehotel.com
www.sheratonanchoragehotel.com
Downtown luxury hotel with
acres of cream-colored
marble and winding jade
staircase; 375 rooms.
Restaurant, lounge, café.
$$$$

**Anchorage Downtown
Hotel**
826 K Street,
Anchorage, AK 99501
tel: (907) 258-7669
email: donjoyner@gci.net
www.anchoragedowntownhotel.com
Family run hotel within
walking distance of the
downtown sights; 19
rooms. All rooms have
cable TVs, phones,
refrigerators and
microwave ovens. $$$
Voyager Hotel
501 K Street,
Anchorage, AK 99501
tel: (907) 277-9501 or
(800) 247-9070
email: rsvp@alaska.com
www.voyagerhotel.com
A favorite with business
travelers as all rooms
have kitchens, queen
beds, voice mail and data
ports; 40 rooms.
Downtown. $$$
Westmark Anchorage
720 W. Fifth Avenue,
Anchorage, Alaska 99501
tel: (907) 276-7676 or
(800) 544-0970
www.westmarkhotels.com
Dark teak furniture in
rooms, done in blues and
mauve; 200 rooms. Each
has its own balcony. Bar
and grill. Japanese sushi
bar. $$$$

PRICE CATEGORIES

Price categories are for a
summer standard double
room without breakfast:
$= $90 or less
$$ = $90–130
$$$ = $130–200
$$$$ = $200 or more

FAIRBANKS

Bridgewater Hotel
723 First Avenue, Fairbanks,
AK 99701
tel: (907) 452-6661 or
(800) 528-4916
email: ftdhotels@mosquitonet.com
www.fountainheadhotels.com
Located in downtown
Fairbanks, this small 94-
room hotel overlooks the

Chena River. Free airport
and train depot shuttle.
Café open for breakfast
only. $$$
Captain Bartlett Inn
1411 Airport Way,
Fairbanks, AK 99701
tel: (907) 452-1888 or (800) 478-
7900 in Alaska and (800) 544-
7528 outside the state

email: gm@captainbartlettinn.com
www.captainbartlettinn.com
Located on a main
commercial road, the inn
tries for a rustic roadhouse
atmosphere. Restaurant
and cocktail lounge. $$$
Chena Hot Springs Resort
Chena Hot Springs Road,
PO Box 58740,

Fairbanks, AK 99711-0740
tel: (907) 451-8104 or
(800) 478-4681
email: chenahs@polarnet.com
www.chenahotsprings.com
In a wilderness setting, 59
miles (95 km) from
Fairbanks; 81 rooms, eight
rustic cabins, Mongolian-
style yurt tent, the only

"ice hotel" in the US, plus RV and tent camping. Year-round resort with swimming in mineral hot springs. $$$

Fairbanks Princess Riverside Lodge
4477 Pikes Landing Road,
Fairbanks, AK 99709
tel: (907) 455-4477 or
(800) 426-0500
email: aklodges@princesstours.com
www.princesslodges.com
In a wooded area on banks of the Chena River near the airport; 325 rooms. Two restaurants, lounge, live entertainment, laundry facilities, gift shop. $$$

Golden North Motel
4888 Old Airport Road,
Fairbanks, AK 99709

tel: (907) 479-6201 or
(800) 447-1910
email: sourdough@goldennorth motel.com
www.goldennorthmotel.com
Near shopping malls and airport; 60 budget rooms. Free van service and continental breakfast. $

Regency Fairbanks Hotel
95 Tenth Avenue,
Fairbanks, AK 99701
tel: (907) 452-3200 or
(800) 478-1230 (in Alaska)
(800) 348-1340
email: info@regencyfairbankshotel.com
www.regencyfairbankshotel.com
128 rooms, all with kitchens and digital phone with modem port and voicemail. Dining room, lounge. $$$

Sophie Station Hotel
1717 University Avenue,
Fairbanks, AK 99709
tel: (907) 479-3650 or
(800) 528-4916
email: fhdhotels@mosquitonet.com
www.fountainheadhotels.com
Elegant, all-suite hotel with 147 units. Gift shop, restaurant and lounge located on main commercial road near the airport and business district. $$$$

Wedgewood Resort
212 Wedgewood Drive,
Fairbanks, AK 99701
tel: (907) 452-1442 or
(800) 528-4916
email: fhdhotels@mosquitonet.com
www.fountainheadhotels.com
440 rooms. Some are fully

furnished condo-style one- and two-bedroom apartments, others are recently built luxury hotel rooms. $$$$

Westmark Fairbanks Hotel
813 Noble Street,
Fairbanks, AK 99701
tel: (907) 456-7722 or
(800) 544-0970
www.westmarkhotels.com
Recently remodeled with internet access, tour desk, shuttle service. Handy downtown location around a large courtyard; 400 rooms. Two restaurants, lounge, fitness center. $$$

OTHER CENTERS

Barrow

Barrow Airport Inn
1815 Momegana Street,
PO Box 933, Barrow, AK 99723
tel: (907) 852-2525 or
(800) 375-2527 in Alaska only
email: airportinn@barrow.com
A homey atmosphere across the street from the airport. 16 rooms, all but one with refrigerators and microwave ovens, 9 with kitchenettes. $$

Top of the World Hotel
1200 Agvik Street, PO Box 189,
Barrow, AK 99723
tel: (907) 852-3900 or
(800) 882-8520 (in Alaska)
(800) 882-8478
email: tow@asrc.com
The town's main accommodation and center of activities; 50 rooms with refrigerators (43 standard and 7 deluxe). Adjoining restaurant. $$$–$$$$

Copper Center

Copper Center Lodge
Mile 101 Richardson Hwy,
Loop Rd
P.O. Box Drawer J,
Copper Center, AK 99573
tel: (907) 822-3245 or
(866) 330-3245
email: info@coppercenterlodge.com
www.coppercenterlodge.com
An historic log structure with an unspoiled country

atmosphere. Includes restaurant. $$

Cordova

Reluctant Fisherman Inn
409 Railroad Avenue, PO Box 150,
Cordova, AK 99574
tel: (907) 424-3272 or
(877) 770-3272
email: reluctantfishermaninn@ak.net
40 comfortable rooms, many looking out on the mountains or the boat harbor. Common areas are lavishly decorated in a style reflecting the town's mining history. Restaurant and lounge (summer only), travel agency, car rental. Restaurant and lounge. $$

Delta Junction

Alaska 7 Motel
Mile 270.3 Richardson Highway,
PO Box 1115,
Delta Junction, AK 99737
tel: (907) 895-4848
email: manager@alaska7motel.com
www.alaska7motel.com
Has 16 budget rooms for highway travelers which have been recently renovated. $

Kelly's Alaska Country Inn
1616 Richardson Highway,
PO Box 849,
Delta Junction, AK 99737
tel: (907) 895-4667
email: motefloffice@kellysalaska

countryinn.com
www.kellysalaskacountryinn.com
A modern inn owned and operated by a "pioneer family." In the town center, 21 rooms, each with its own style. Each room has a refrigerator, TV and coffee maker. $$

Denali National Park

Camp Denali
PO Box 67,
Denali National Park, AK 99755
tel: (907) 683-2290
email: info@campdenali.com
www.campdenali.com
Offers 17 cabins in the Kantishna area, with views of Denali (Mount McKinley) and surrounded by wilderness. Shared bathrooms. Prices include all meals, lodging, transportation from park entrance, guided activities, and a unique, highly acclaimed program of naturalist-led activities deep within the national park. $$$$

Denali Backcountry Lodge
1301 West Parks Highway,
Suite 5
Wasilla, AK 99654
tel: (907) 376-1992 or
(877) 233-6254
email: info@denalilodges.com
www.denalilodge.com
Has 30 cabins plus central lodge with dining room,

library, and lounging area, beside a creek in the Kantishna area. Meals and outdoor guided activities at the edge of the park are included. $$$$

Denali Princess Lodge
Mile 238.5 George Parks Highway, PO Box 110, Denali National Park, AK 99755
tel: (800) 426-0500
www.princessalaskalodges.com
Has 280 rooms and suites, with spacious common areas, off the highway, just outside Denali National Park, with access to many park activities. Spas, gift shops, dining room, lounge, café, tour desk. $$$$

McKinley Chalet Resorts
Mile 238.5 George Parks Highway.
For reservations, contact Denali Park Resorts, 241 W. Ship Creek Avenue, Anchorage, AK 99501
tel: (907) 276-7234 or
(800) 276-7234
email: denali@aramark.com
www.denalinationalpark.com
Recently renovated resort has 345 rooms in lodges

PRICE CATEGORIES

Price categories are for a summer standard double room without breakfast:
$= $90 or less
$$ = $90–130
$$$ = $130–200
$$$$ = $200 or more

along the Nenana River plus a new central building with 34-ft high atrium ceilings. Restaurant, lounge, dinner theater and wilderness adventures available. $$$$

Dillingham

Bristol Inn
104 Main Street, PO Box 330, Dillingham, AK 99576
tel: (907) 842-2240 or (800) 764-9704 in Alaska
fax: (907) 842-3340
email: bristol@nushtel.com
www.alaskaoutdoors.com/bristolinn
The inn has 31 rooms with private baths, cable and phone, some with kitchenettes. Freezer and laundry facilities available. $$$

Dillingham Hotel
429 Second Avenue West, PO Box 550, Dillingham, AK 99576
tel: (907) 842-5316
fax: (907) 842-5666
Right in the heart of town, this was one of the first hotels built in Dillingham; 31 rooms, some with private bath. Rebuilt in the mid-1970s. $$$

Dutch Harbor

The Grand Aleutian Hotel
498 Salmon Way, PO Box 921169, Dutch Harbor, AK 99692
tel: (907) 581-3844 or (866) 581-3844
email: grand.aleutian@unisea.com
www.grandaleutian.com
This 1993 hotel has won an architechtural award for its chalet-style design; it has 112 rooms and six suites. There's a stone fireplace in the three-story lobby, two restaurants, two bars, plus meeting rooms, travel services and views of Margaret Bay. $$$

Girdwood

The Alyeska Prince Hotel/Alyeska Resort
1000 Arlberg Road, PO Box 249, Girdwood, AK 99587
tel: (907) 754-1111 or (800) 880-3880
email: info@alyeskaresort.com
www.alyeskaresort.com
Year-round luxury resort 40

miles (64 km) southeast of Anchorage in Girdwood, off the Seward Highway. Six chair lifts and tram, night skiing, convention facilities, restaurant, swimming pool, exercise room and hot tub with a view of the mountain. There's also a ski school, alpine and telemark skiing, ski rental and ice skating; dog sledding and sleigh rides can be arranged. Summer sightseeing tram lift ride. $$$$.

Glacier Bay/Gustavus

Glacier Bay Lodge
241 W. Ship Creek Anchorage, AK 99501
tel: (907) 264-4600 or (888) 229-8687
www.visitglacierbay.com
Only hotel within the park, situated above the dock where day boats begin trips to the glaciers; 55 rooms. Dining room and gift shop. $$$

Gustavus Inn
PO Box 60, Gustavus, AK 99826
tel: (907) 697-2254 or (800) 649-5220
email: dave@gustavusinn.com
www.gustavusinn.com
A luxurious country inn near Glacier Bay National Park offering all-inclusive packages for fishing, whale-watching, sea-kayaking and

other activities; 13 rooms. Prices include family-style meals. $$$$

Glennallen

Caribou Hotel
PO Box 329, Mile 187 Glenn Highway, Glennallen, AK 99588
tel: (907) 822-3302
email: info@caribouhotel.com
www.caribouhotel.com
The 25 rooms in the trailer-like annex in front of the main building are clean but spartan with shared bath; 70 nicely furnished rooms in main building cost more. Restaurant and gift shop next door. $-$$$.

Haines

Captain's Choice Motel
PO Box 392, Haines, AK 99827
tel: (907) 766-3111 or (800) 478-2345
email: capchoice@usa.net
www.capchoice.com
Centrally located overlooking Portage Cove and Chilkoot Inlet; 40 rooms. Car rental, laundromat, local tour bookings. $$-$$$

Hotel Halsingland
PO Box 1649, Haines, AK 99827
tel: (907) 766-2000 or (800) 542-6363
e-mail: reservations@

BELOW: the Alyeska Prince Hotel, Girdwood.

hotelhalsingland.com
www.hotelhalsingland.com
An historic Fort William Seward building facing the parade grounds; 50 rooms; 5 "budget" rooms share bathrooms. Cocktail lounge, restaurant featuring locally caught seafood, and activity desk. $-$$

Mountain View Inn
PO Box 62, Haines, AK 99827
tel: (907) 766-2900 or (800) 478-2902
e-mail: lodgings@mtviewinn.net
www.mtviewinn.net
Within walking distance of downtown and Fort William Seward; 9 units, some with kitchens, pet friendly, internet. $

Homer

Bay View Inn
PO Box 804, Homer, AK 99603
tel: (907) 235-8485 or (877) 235-8485
email: bayview@alaska.net
www.bayviewalaska.com
12 basic rooms, six with kitchens, plus a guest cottage, with magnificent views of the Kachemak Bay. $$

Driftwood Inn
135 W. Bunnell, Homer, AK 99603
tel: (907) 235-8019 or (800) 478-8019
email: driftwoodinn@alaska.com
www.thedriftwoodinn.com
One block from Bishop's Beach; 21 rooms (some with shared bath). Clean and cozy, with common sitting room and eating area – serve-yourself cold breakfast if desired. 22 RV hook-ups. $$

Heritage Hotel
147 E. Pioneer Avenue, Homer, AK 99603
tel: (907) 235-7787 or (800) 380-7787
email: heritagehotelandrv@alaska.net
www.alaskaheritagehotel.com
Downtown; 34 standard rooms. Large, comfortable lobby with free coffee. Within walking distance of restaurants, shopping and entertainment. The owners also have an RV park on the Homer Spit. $$

Land's End Resort
4786 Homer Spit Road, Homer, AK 99603

TRANSPORTATION

ACCOMMODATIONS

ACTIVITIES

CONTACTS

A – Z

tel: (907) 235-0400 or
(800) 478-0400
email: endofthespit@alaska.net
www.lands-end-resort.com or
www.endofthespit.com
The hotel has 108 rooms in
a variety of sizes; about
three-fourths have views of
the bay. Full-service
restaurant which specializes
in fresh seafood, gift shop/
espresso bar. $$–$$$
Ocean Shores Motel
3500 Crittenden Drive,
Homer, AK 99603
tel: (907) 235-7775 or
(800) 770-7775
email: oceanshores@acsalaska.net
www.oceanshoresalaska.com
Three blocks from downtown
in wooded residential area;
recent additions with
spacious rooms, bay view
and private beach. $$–$$$

Juneau

**Best Western Country
Lane Inn**
9300 Glacier Highway,
Juneau, AK 99801
tel: (907) 789-5005
or (888) 781-5005
www.countrylaneinn.com or
www.bestwestern.com
Near the airport and
Mendenhall Glacier; 55
rooms; all rooms have data
ports and cable TV, and
most have internet access.
Free continental breakfast
and shuttle. $$–$$$
Driftwood Lodge
435 Willoughby,
Juneau, AK 99801
tel: (907) 586-2280 or
(800) 544-2239
email: driftwood@gci.net
www.driftwoodalaska.com
Downtown; 63 rooms,
many with kitchenettes and
apartment-style floor-plans.
Laundry facilities, 24-hour
airport shuttle. $
Super 8 Motel
2295 Trout Street,
Juneau, AK 99801
tel: (907) 789-4858 or
(800) 800-8000
email:
generalmanager03050@cdhotel.com
www.super8.com
Near the airport, this motel
has 75 rooms. Freezers
available, plus 24-hour
airport and ferry shuttle.
$$$
The Breakwater Inn
1711 Glacier Avenue,

Juneau, AK 99801
tel: (907) 586-6303 or
(888) 586-6303
email: breakwaterinn@gci.net
www.breakwaterinn.com
Overlooking the small boat
harbor; 49 rooms, some
with balconies. Restaurant,
lounge. $$
**The Westmark Baranof
Hotel**
127 North Franklin Street,
Juneau, AK 99801
tel: (907) 586-2660 or
(800) 544-0970
email: westmark@westmarkhotels.com
www.westmarkhotels.com
Nine story art-deco
structure; 196 rooms.
Coffee shop, lounge,
restaurant, popular with
politicians and state
employees. $$$

Katmai

Brooks Lodge
For reservations contact:
Katmailand Inc.
4125 Aircraft Drive,
Anchorage, AK 99502
tel: (907) 243-5448 or
(800) 544-0551
email: info@katmailand.com
www.bearviewing.net
Within Katmai National
Park, on the Naknek Lake
and Brooks River and
accessible only by plane or
boat; 16 rustic cabins.
Main lodge, restaurant, bar,
sportfishing, bear-viewing,
trips to the Valley of Ten
Thousand Smokes. $$$$
Grosvenor Lodge
Katmailand Inc.
4125 Aircraft Drive,
Anchorage, AK 99502
tel: (907) 243-5448 or
(800) 544-0551
email: info@katmailand.com
www.katmailand.com
Three- to 7-night packages
available at this wilderness
fishing lodge in the heart of
Katmai National Park,
including everything from
air fare from Anchorage to
guided fishing and fishing
gear. $$$$
Katmai Wilderness Lodge
Contact PO Box 4332,
Kodiak, AK 99615
tel: (907) 486-8767 or
(800) 488-8767
email: katbears@ptialaska.net
www.katmai-wilderness.com
Located on Katmai's rugged
outer coast, accessible

only by plane or boat;
seven rooms. Stays range
from 3 nights to a week or
more. Bear-viewing, fishing,
photography, kayaking. The
cost includes air fare from
Kodiak, guided activities
and gourmet meals. $$$$

Kenai Peninsula

Gwin's Lodge
14865 (Mile 52) Sterling Highway,
Cooper Landing,
AK 99572
tel: (907) 595-1266
email: gwins@arctic.net
www.gwinslodge.com
Half a mile (1 km) from
Russian River fisheries; 13
cabins with private baths;
most have also kitchenettes
or full kitchens. $$–$$$
Kenai Merit Inn
260 South Willow,
Kenai, AK 99611
tel: (907) 283-6131
Downtown Kenai; 60
rooms. Walking distance to
shops and restaurants;
free continental breakfast.
$$$–$$$$
**Kenai Princess Wilderness
Lodge**
PO Box 676,
Cooper Landing, AK 99572
tel: (907) 595-1425 or
(800) 426-0500
email: aklodges@princesstours.com
www.princesslodges.com
An 86-room luxury resort
hotel near Cooper Landing
overlooking Kenai River.
Path from main lodge leads
to cabins; some are four-
plexes, others are
bungalow style. Restaurant,
lounge, spa and indoor and
outdoor hot tubs.
$$$–$$$$
Sunrise Inn
Mile 45 Sterling Highway,
P.O. Box 832
Cooper Landing, AK 99572
tel: (907) 595-1222
email: sunrise@arctic.net
www.alaskasunriseinn.com
On Kenai Lake, 10 units
each with TV and private
bath. Restaurant and
lounge. $$$

Ketchikan

Gilmore Hotel
326 Front Street,
Ketchikan, AK 99901
tel: (907) 225-9423 or
(800) 275-9423

email: info@gilmorehotel.com
www.gilmorehotel.com
Built in 1927, the recently
remodeled hotel is
downtown on the waterfront;
39 rooms. Restaurant and
full bar. $$
Super 8 Motel
2151 Sea Level Drive,
Ketchikan, AK 99901
tel: (907) 225-9088 or
(800) 800-8000
www.super8.com
Situated near a shopping
mall between ferry terminal
and downtown; 83 rooms.
Shuttle service and
freezers available. $$
**WestCoast Cape Fox
Lodge**
800 Venetia Way,
Ketchikan, AK 99901
tel: (907) 225-8001 or
(866) 225-8001
email: info@capefoxlodge.com
www.capefoxlodge.com
Located above downtown
Ketchikan and Tongass
Narrows, access is by
scenic tram from downtown
or a driveway; 72 rooms.
Dining room, lounge,
meeting and banquet
facilities. $$$

Kodiak

Best Western Kodiak Inn
236 W. Rezanof Drive,
Kodiak, AK 99615
tel: (907) 486-5712 or
(800) 780-7234
email: kodiakin@ptialaska.net
www.bestwestern.com
In town center above the
waterfront; 81 rooms.
Lounge, restaurant. $$$
Comfort Inn Kodiak
1395 Airport Way,
Kodiak, AK 99615
tel: (907) 487-2700 or
(877) 424-6423
email: comfortinnkodiak@gci.net
www.comfortinn.com
Located near the airport;
50 rooms with voice mail
and data ports. Salmon
fishing on nearby river,
restaurant and lounge. $$$
Kodiak Bed and Breakfast
308 Cope Street,
Kodiak, AK 99615
tel: (907) 486-5367
email: mmonroe@gci.net
www.home.gci.net/~monroe
Overlooking the boat harbor
in downtown Kodiak, within
easy walking distance of
museum, boat charters,

restaurants and bird rockeries; 2 rooms with shared bath, sitting room, deck. $$

Northland Ranch Resort
PO Box 2376,
Kodiak, AK 99615
tel: (907) 486-5578
Resort is located on a cattle and quarterhorse ranch; 14 rooms. Features horseback riding. $–$$$

Kotzebue

Nullagvik Hotel
Shore Ave. and Tundra Way,
PO Box 336, Kotzebue, AK 99752
tel: (907) 442-3331
www.nullagvik.com
Overlooking Kotzebue Sound; 74 rooms. Restaurant, gift shop and travel agency. Tours can be arranged. $$$$

Nome

Nome Nugget Inn
PO Box 1470, Nome, AK 99762
tel: (907) 443-2323 or
(877) 443-2323
Decorated in gold-rush era fashion, with frontier memorabilia in lobby and lounge. 47 rooms with private baths. Restaurant, lounge. Front Street and Bering. $$$–$$$$

Palmer Area

Hatcher Pass Lodge
Mile 17.5 Hatcher Pass Road,
PO Box 763,
Palmer, AK 99645
tel: (907) 745-5897
email: info@hatcherpasslodge.com
www.hatcherpasslodge.com
Some 60 miles (96 km) northeast of Anchorage; 9 modern cabins each with chemical toilet, plus 3 rooms in main lodge. Located near Independence Mine State Historic Park. Meals, bar, entertainment, sauna, cross-country skiing. $$–$$$

Sheep Mountain Lodge
17701 West Glenn Highway,
Sutton, AK 99674
tel: (907) 745-5121 or
(877) 645-5121
email: info@sheepmountain.com
www.sheepmountain.com
Ten cabins with bath and shower and private deck. Hiking in summer, nordic

skiing in winter on groomed trails. Restaurant, hot tub, sauna. $$$

Valley Hotel
606 S. Alaska,
Palmer, AK 99645
tel: (907) 745-3330 or
(800) 478-7666 (in Alaska)
Downtown near visitor center; hotel built in 1948 now remodeled with 43 rooms; 24-hour restaurant, cocktail lounge. $–$$

Colony Inn
325 East Elmwood (check-in handled at the neighboring Valley Hotel – see address above)
tel: (907) 745-3330 or
(800) 478-7666 in Alaska.
Lovingly restored historic building with large downstairs sitting area; 12 guest rooms decorated with quilts and antique reproductions. Restaurant. $$–$$$

Petersburg

Scandia House
110 Nordic Drive,
PO Box 689, Petersburg, AK 99833
tel: (907) 772-4281 or
(800) 722-5006
email: info@scandiahousehotel.com
www.scandiahousehotel.com
Downtown hotel rebuilt in 1995; 33 rooms. Car, bike and boat rental is available. $$

Tides Inn
307 N. First Street, PO Box 1048,
Petersburg, AK 99833
tel: (907) 772-4288 or
(800) 665-8433
email: tidesinn@alaska.net
www.tidesinnalaska.com
This inn is located downtown overlooking Petersburg's North Harbor, and has 45 rooms (some with kitchenettes). $$

Seldovia

The Seldovia Boardwalk Hotel
PO Box 72, Seldovia, AK 99663
tel: (907) 234-7816
email: seldoviaboardwalkhotel
@yahoo.com
www.alaskaone.com/
boardwalkhotel
On waterfront with a fine view of water or mountains; 14 rooms. A sun-lit parlor has wood stove. Coffee service available. $$$

Across the Bay Tent and Breakfast
PO Box 112054,
Anchorage, AK 99511 (winter),
tel: (907) 345-2571;
PO Box 81,
Seldovia, AK 99663 (summer),
tel: (907) 235-3633
email: ecotours@ptialaska.net
www.tentandbreakfastalaska.com
Sturdy wall tents with twin beds. Hearty meals served at main house, hiking, bike rentals and guided kayaking. Access is by water taxi from Homer or you can fly in. $$

Seward

Hotel Seward
221 Fifth Avenue, PO Box 670,
Seward, AK 99664
tel: (907) 224-2378 or
(800) 655-8785
email: hotelseward@seward.net
www.alaskaone.com/hotelseward
Downtown, within easy walk of many attractions; 38 rooms – some with bay views, all with cable TV, VCR and data port. $$$–$$$$

Breeze Inn Motel
1306 Seward Highway,
PO Box 2147, Seward, AK 99664
tel: (907) 224-5238 or
(888) 224-5237
email: breeze@ptialaska
www.breezeinn.com
On the main road into town right in the small boat harbor; 86 rooms (20 built in 1997). Restaurant, lounge, espresso bar and gift shops. $$$

Marina Motel
Mile 1 Seward Highway,
PO Box 1134, Seward, AK 99664
tel: (907) 224-5518
email: donnactm@alaska.com
www.sewardmotel.com
Across from the boat harbor, one mile from downtown; 26 rooms. $$–$$$

Seward Windsong Lodge
Mile .5 Exit Glacier/Herman Leirer Road, PO Box 2301, Seward, AK 99664
tel: (907) 224-7116 or
(877) 777-2805
email: info@sewardwindsong.com
www.sewardwindsong.com
Forested setting near the banks of Resurrection River; 108 rooms, most either mountain- or river-view; cafe and restaurant, TV, VCR. $$$$

Sitka

Sitka Hotel
118 Lincoln Street,
Sitka, AK 99835
tel: (907) 747-3288
email: stay@sitkahotel.com
www.sitkahotel.com
Located in the downtown area and furnished in Victorian-era decor; 60 budget rooms, some with shared bathrooms. There are also suites with kitchenettes and an attached restaurant. $–$$

Westmark Sitka
330 Seward Street,
Sitka, AK 99835
tel: (907) 747-6241 or
(800) 544-0970
www.westmarkhotels.com
Overlooking the Crescent Harbor waterfront; 101 rooms. Restaurant; lounge, high-speed internet. $$$

Skagway

Historic Skagway Inn
Seventh Ave. and Broadway,
PO Box 500, Skagway,
AK 99840
tel: (907) 983-2289 or
(888) 752-4929
email: reservations@skagwayinn.com
www.skagwayinn.com
Born as a bordello during the Klondike Gold Rush, this historic inn within Klondike National Historic Park has rooms named after the ladies who once worked there. 10 rooms, some with private baths, others shared. Remodeled in 2004. Free transportation to the famed Chilkoot Trail. $$–$$$

Sgt. Preston's Lodge
Sixth & State Street
PO Box 538, Skagway, AK 99840
tel; (907) 983-2521 or
(866) 983-2521
http://sgtprestons.eskagway.com
This clean, newly renovated establishment located in downtown Skagway offers 38 rooms and 2 suites,

PRICE CATEGORIES

Price categories are for a summer standard double room without breakfast:
$= $90 or less
$$ = $90–130
$$$ = $130–200
$$$$ = $200 or more

with TV, phones and private baths. Courtesy van service. Pet-friendly. $$

Westmark Inn Skagway
Third and Spring streets,
PO Box 515, Skagway, AK 99840
tel: (907) 983-6000 or
(800) 544-0970
www.westmarkhotels.com
Near stores and attractions, including national historic park; 151 rooms. Mostly serving package tour passengers; two restaurants and lounge. Closed in winter. $$$

Soldotna

Hooligan's Lodging and Saloon
44715 Sterling Highway,
Soldotna, AK 99669
tel: (907) 262-9951
email: hooliganslodge@myway.com
www.hooliganslodge.com
Located within walking distance of the Kenai River. Offers 34 large, clean rooms and a bar. $$–$$$

Kenai River Lodge
393 Riverside Drive,
Soldotna, AK 99669
tel: (907) 262-4292 or
(800) 977-4292
email: KenaiRiverLodge@yahoo.com
www.kenairiverlodge.com
Overlooking the famous Kenai River, yet within easy walking distance of restaurants and businesses; all 25 rooms have coffee pots, refrigerators, and TVs. Free continental breakfast. Excellent sportfishing. $$$

Soldotna Inn
35041 Kenai Spur Highway,
Soldotna, AK 99669
tel: (907) 262-9169 or
(866) 262-9169
email: soldotnainn@alaska.com
www.mykels.com
In the heart of downtown Soldotna, within walking distance of the Kenai River. 28 modern rooms with refrigerators, some with kitchenettes. Restaurant, lounge, wireless internet

PRICE CATEGORIES

Price categories are for a summer standard double room without breakfast:
$= $90 or less
$$ = $90–130
$$$ = $130–200
$$$$ = $200 or more

and continental breakfast. $$$–$$$$

Talkeetna

Mt. McKinley Princess Wilderness Lodge
Milepost 133.1 on the Parks Highway,
PO Box 13550,
Trapper Creek, AK 99683
tel: (907) 733-2900 or
(800) 426-0500
www.princesslodges.com
email: aklodges@princesstours.com
Modern lodge with large, open "Great Room" featuring a massive fireplace, evening piano music and cocktails. Deck looks out towards the Alaska Range, including Mt. McKinley; 460 bungalow-style guest rooms; bar, restaurant, cafe. About 45 minutes drive north of Talkeetna, lodge offers regular shuttle from the Talkeetna train station to the lodge. Closed in winter. $$$

Swiss-Alaska Inn
PO Box 565,
Talkeetna, AK 99676
tel: (907) 733-2424
email: vern@swissalaska.com
www.swissalaska.com
Family-run with 20 rooms all decorated in bright, floral motif, with DVD players. Restaurant and lounge, with views of Mount McKinley. East Talkeetna by the boat launch. $$$

Talkeetna Alaskan Lodge
Milepost 12.5 of the Talkeetna Spur Road, PO Box 727,
Talkeetna, AK 99676
tel: (907) 733-9500 or
(877) 777-4067
email: info@talkeetnalodge.com
www.talkeetnalodge.com
Majestic, chalet-style lodge with a large deck offering sweeping views of the Alaska Range and Mount McKinley. 201 rooms, including suites, many "mountainside" with views; restaurant, bar. $$$$

Tok

Westmark Inn-Tok
Mile 1315 Alaska Highway,
PO Box 130, Tok, AK, 99780
tel: (907) 883-5174 or
(800) 544-0970
www.westmarkhotels.com

The 92 standard rooms are in buildings connected by boardwalks. Restaurant, gift shop and laundromat. Closed in winter. $$$

Young's Motel
Mile 1313 Alaska Highway,
PO Box 482,
Tok, AK 99780
tel: (907) 883-4411
email: edyoung@aptalaska.net
Along the Alaska Highway behind the area's most popular restaurant, Fast Eddie's; 43 rooms in one-story buildings. $

Valdez

Valdez Aspen Hotel
100 Meals Avenue,
Valdez, AK 99686
tel: (907) 835-4445 or
(800) 478-4445
email: info@aspenhotelsak.com
www.aspenhotelsak.com
Conveniently located downtown; the inn has 103 rooms, views of surrounding mountains and Valdez Arm. Indoor pool and hot tub, exercise room. Cost includes continental breakfast. $$$

Valdez Harbor Inn
100 Harbor Drive
Valdez, AK 99686
tel: (907) 835-3434 or
(888) 222-3440
email: info@valdezharborinn.com
www.valdezharborinn.com
Located right on the harbor in downtown Valdez; 90 rooms. Restaurant, lounge, coffee shop, exercise room, laundry room, barber shop. $$$

BED & BREAKFAST

The following list gives the central reservations organizations in the main towns. They will help you find recommended B&B accommodation, and some will make the reservation for you.

Anchorage

Anchorage Bed & Breakfast Association Hotline
PO Box 242623
Anchorage, AK 99524

tel: (907) 272-5909 or
(888) 584-5147
www.anchorage-bnb.com

Fairbanks

Fairbanks Convention & Visitors Bureau
550 First Avenue,
Fairbanks, AK 99701
tel: (907) 465-5774 or
(800) 327-5774
email: info@explorefairbanks.com
www.explorefairbanks.com

Homer

Central Charters
4241 Homer Spit Road,
Homer, AK 99603
tel: (907) 235-7847 or
(800) 478-7847
email: central@ptialaska.net
www.centralcharter.com

Juneau

B & B Locator
c/o Juneau Convention & Visitors Bureau, One Sealaska Plaza,
Suite 305, AK 99801
tel: (907) 586-1737
or (800) 587-2201
email: info@traveljuneau.com
www.traveljuneau.com

Ketchikan

Ketchikan Reservation Service
412 D-1 Loop Road,
Ketchikan, AK 99901
tel: (907) 247-5337 or
(800) 987-5337
email: info@ketchikan-lodging.com
www.ketchikan-lodging.com

Kodiak

Visitors' Information Center
100 Marine Way, Suite 200,
Kodiak, AK 99615
tel: (907) 486-4782 or
(800) 789-4782
email: visit@kodiak.org
www.kodiak.org

Valdez

One Call Does It All
PO Box 2197,
Valdez, AK 99686
tel: (907) 835-4988 or
(800) 304-4988
email: tours@valdezalaska.com
www.valdezalaska.com

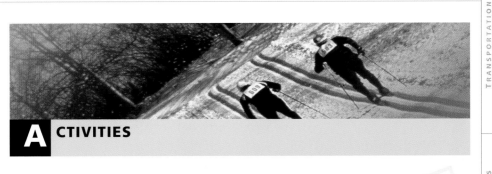

A CTIVITIES

FESTIVALS, THE ARTS, NIGHTLIFE, SHOPPING AND SPECTATOR SPORTS

HOLIDAYS & FESTIVALS

Alaska celebrates all the traditional and official US holidays. In addition, there are many unusual festivals occurring year-round within the state. Some are created purely for amusement, while others are part of the cultural heritage.

Winter festivals are popular in Alaska. The largest is the Fur Rendezvous, held each February in Anchorage. A highlight of the event is the World Championship Sprint Sled Dog Race. Homer also celebrates a winter carnival in February and the North Pole Winter Festival is held in March.

For a rare opportunity to observe the rich Native culture, visitors can attend the Savoonga Walrus Festival held on St Lawrence Island in May. This is not a tourist event, it is traditionally Eskimo. In June, Nalukataq (Whaling Feast) is celebrated in Barrow by the Eskimo community.

Other festivals are held tongue in cheek and for pure fun. Swimmers take to the icy waters of the Bering Sea in Nome for the annual Polar Bear Swim in May and locals join in the Moose Dropping Festival held in Talkeetna in July.

Dates change annually, so make sure you have a current schedule from the Alaska Travel Industry Association, tel: (907) 929-2200 or (907) 929-2842, www.travelalaska.com, or check the website of the local community's Convention and Visitors Bureau *(see listing on page 377)*.

Annual Events

(National/State holidays in bold)

January

New Year's Day (1st)
Martin Luther King's Birthday (3rd Monday)
Anchorage Folk Festival.
Klondike 300 Sled Dog Race, Big Lake.
Knik 200 Sled Dog Race, Knik.
Polar Bear Jump Off Festival, Seward.
Russian New Year and Masquerade Ball, Kodiak.
Willow Winter Carnival, Willow.

February

Presidents Day (3rd Monday)
Cordova Ice Worm Festival, Cordova.
Festival of the North, Ketchikan.
Fur Rendezvous, Anchorage.
Iron Dog Gold Rush Classic Snow-machine Race, Wasilla to Nome.
Tent City Festival, Wrangell.
Winterfest, King Salmon and Naknek.
Yukon Quest International Sled Dog Race, Fairbanks to Whitehorse.

March

Seward's Day (last Monday)
Bering Sea Ice Golf Classic, Nome.
Nenana Ice Classic Tripod Weekend, Nenana.
Iditarod Basketball Tournament, Nome.
Iditarod Trail Sled Dog Race, Anchorage to Nome.
North Pole Winter Festival, North Pole.
Pillar Mountain Golf Classic, Kodiak.
Winter Carnival, Fairbanks.
World Ice Art Championships, Fairbanks.

April

Alaska Folk Festival, Juneau.
Alyeska Spring Carnival, Girdwood.

Arctic Man Ski & Sno-go Classic, Paxson.
Piuraagiaqta (Spring Festival), Barrow.

May

Memorial Day (last Monday)
Boardwalk Boogie, Pelican.
Katchemak Bay Shorebird Festival, Homer.
Copper River Delta Shorebird Festival, Cordova.
Kodiak Crab Festival, Kodiak.
Little Norway Festival, Petersburg.
Shorebird and Wooden Boat Festival, Homer.

June

Alaska Run for Women, Anchorage.
All-Alaska Logging Championship, Sitka.
Colony Days, Palmer.
Kenai River Festival, Kenai.
Mayor's Midnight Sun Marathon, Anchorage.
Midnight Sun Festival and Softball Tournament, Nome.
Midnight Sun Run, Midnight Sun Baseball Game, Fairbanks.
Nalukataq Whaling Feast, Barrow.
Polar Bear Swim, Nome.
Sitka Summer Music Festival, Sitka.
Sitka Symposium, Sitka.
Stewart/Hyder International Rodeo, Hyder.
Summer Solstice, Statewide.

July

Independence Day (4th)
Bald Eagle Music Festival, Haines.
Bear Paw Festival, Chugiak/Eagle River.
Deltana Fair, Delta Junction.
Fairbanks Summer Arts Festival, Fairbanks.
Girdwood Forest Faire, Girdwood.
Golden Days, Fairbanks.
Moose Dropping Festival, Talkeetna.
Mount Marathon Race, Seward.

Soapy Smith's Wake, Skagway.
Southeast Alaska State Fair, Haines.
World Eskimo-Indian Olympics,
Fairbanks.

August

Alaska State Fair, Palmer.
Blueberry Arts Festival, Ketchikan.
Kenai Peninsula State Fair, Ninilchik.
Seward Silver Salmon Derby, Seward.
Talkeetna Bluegrass Festival,
Talkeetna.
Tanana Valley State Fair, Fairbanks.
Tundra Golf Classic, Unalaska.

September

Labor Day (1st Monday)
Equinox Marathon, Fairbanks.
Klondike Trail of '98 Road Relay,
Skagway and Whitehorse.
Kodiak State Fair and Rodeo, Kodiak.
Seward Art and Music Festival,
Seward.

October

Alaska Day (18th)
Alaska Day Festival, Sitka.
AlaskaFest, Anchorage.
National Wildlife Refuge Week,
Kodiak.

November

Veterans' Day (11th)
Thanksgiving (4th Thursday)
Alaska Bald Eagle Festival, Haines.
Athabascan Fiddling Festival,
Fairbanks.
Great Alaska Shootout, Anchorage.
Top of the World Classic, Fairbanks.
Whalefest, Sitka.
Winter Art Faire, Ketchikan.

December

Christmas (25th)
Bachelor Society Ball/Wilderness
Women's Contest, Talkeetna.
Colony Christmas Celebration,
Palmer.
Harbor Stars Boat Parade, Kodiak.

MUSIC, DANCE, DRAMA

Communities across Alaska have
much to offer in the way of
entertainment, although many of the
major performing groups take the
summer off to prepare for their
regular fall and winter seasons. Your
best bet is to check with local
information centers or scan local
newspapers to find out what's playing
in the communities you plan to visit.

Days of '98 Show with Soapy Smith
Good family fun for all. Spend an
evening gambling with phoney
money and see the gold-rush history
of Skagway unfold on the stage of

the 250-seat theater. Shows nightly
mid-May through mid-September.
Matinees for cruise-ships. Tickets
at the door.
PO Box 215,
Skagway, AK 99840-0215,
tel: (907) 983-2545;
email: thedaysof98show@
hotmail.com
Fairbanks Summer Arts Festival.
Two weeks of workshops, rehearsals,
performances and concerts with
studies in music, dance, theater,
opera, ice skating and visual arts in
July and/or August – an arts camp
for adults, as well as younger
dancers and ice skaters who are
experienced in those areas.
PO Box 82510,
Fairbanks, AK 99708,
tel: (907) 474-8869
email: festival@alaska.net
www.fsaf.org/
Kodiak Alutiiq Dancers
Daily summer performances of
traditional Alutiiq songs and dances;
cultural demonstrations and Native
arts and crafts.
312 West Marine Way,
Kodiak, AK 99615,
tel: (907) 486-4449;
email: tribe@ptialaska.net
New Archangel Dancers
Folk dances from various parts of
Russia. Performances in Centennial
Hall near the harbor, timed to
docking of cruise ship or by special
arrangement.
208 Smith Street,
Sitka, AK 99835,
tel: (907) 747-5516;
email: newarchangel@gci.net
www.newarchangeldancers.com
Northern Lights Theatre
A spectacular movie of the Northern
Lights accompanied by a symphony
on a wide screen with digital
surround sound.
Mile 238.9, Parks Highway,
PO Box 65,
Denali Park, AK 99755,
tel: (907) 683-4000;
email: lightstheatre@yahoo.com
Crown of Lights
Northern Lights Show
LeRoy Zimmerman's award-winning
Northern Lights show, "The Crown of
Light," at Ester Gold Camp Historic
District is a spectacular blend of
Northern Lights photography and
symphonic music.
PO Box 109, Ester, AK 99725,
tel: (907) 452-7274 or
(800) 354-7274;
http://fairbanks-alaska.com/
ester-gold-camp.htm
Pier One Theatre
Local talent lights up an intimate
stage in a "come-as-you-are"
warehouse on the Homer Spit.

Dance, drama, musicals. Seasonal
service, Memorial Day through
Labor Day.
PO Box 894,
Homer, AK 99603,
tel: (907) 235-7333.
www.pieronetheatre.org
**Anchorage Museum of History
and Art**
During the summer months the
museum regularly features visiting
Native dancing groups. The museum
has special displays and events,
many of them tied to Alaska's
Native culture, year-round.
121 W. 7th Avenue,
Anchorage, AK 99501,
tel: (907) 343-4326;
recorded info: (907) 343-6173.
email:
museum@anchoragemuseum.org
www.anchoragemuseum.org
Alaska Native Heritage Center
The center features Native dancers,
artists, cultural displays, and story
tellers.
On the Glenn Highway near Muldoon
Road in Anchorage (8800 Heritage
Center Drive).
tel: (907) 330-8000 or
(800) 315-6608;
email: info@alaskanative.net
www.alaskanative.net

Nightlife by Night Light

Baseball games at midnight.
Camping on Flattop Mountain to
honor the summer solstice.
Backyard gardening into the wee
hours. City workers leaving jobs in
the afternoon to fish prime salmon
streams all night, then driving back
to work in the morning. These are
symptoms, one and all, of a curious
relationship Alaskans have with
light in summer.
　　Alaska's far-north place on the
globe ensures that as the Earth's
axis tilts closer to the sun in June,
July, and August, the state basks in
hours and hours of rich summer
light. So significant is the annual
ebb and flow of light to Alaskans
that newspapers and radio
commentators report how many
minutes of light the state gains (or
loses) each day.
　　Anchorage sees a late-night
sunset throughout the summer. At
and above the Arctic Circle, night
disappears. In Barrow, almost 300
miles north of the Circle, the sun
rises on May 10 and does not set
again until August 1.

SHOPPING

What To Buy

Many rare crafts and products are available to buy throughout the state. Popular items include gold nuggets, jade jewelry, and Alaska Native crafts. You won't necessarily find any bargains, but the goods are generally of high quality. Gold nugget jewelry is a local speciality and makes a wonderful Alaskan souvenir or gift. Jade is found locally in Alaska, in carvings as well as jewelry. Jade stones come in various shades of green, brown, black, yellow, white and red.

Alaska also is home to many talented artists whose works can be purchased at local galleries and shops. Their works are generally inspired by the beauty of the land. In addition to works of art and jewelry, look for seal-oil candles, carved wooden totem poles, canned food products and clothing.

Native crafts are abundant and include items carved from walrus ivory, soapstone and jade. Scrimshawed ivory – scenes are etched on the ivory – is an authentic handicraft.

Visitors who wish to take ivory to a country other than the United States must obtain an export permit from the US Fish and Wildlife Service. Be sure to ask about restrictions when your purchase is made.

Alaska Native women make some of the most intricately woven baskets in the world. Materials used for the baskets include beachgrass, birch bark and whale baleen. These items have become very popular over the years and command a high price, some selling for several hundred dollars. They also make beaded slippers from seal skin and wolf hair. Unusual porcupine quill earrings are affordable and attractive.

There are two ways to ensure you're buying authentic goods. If an item was manufactured in Alaska, the tag features a polar bear and the words, "Made in Alaska." Authentic Native-made products show a silver hand with the designation "Native Handicraft."

Museums and major hotels have gift shops selling Alaskan products, ivory carvings, and the like. If you are visiting rural areas, don't buy from shops in larger communities until you've had a chance to investigate local offerings. Although opportunities to pick up bargains from the actual artisans have declined markedly in recent years, it is occasionally possible to strike a good deal in the villages. If you find nothing in the villages that appeals to you, the stores in larger cities are likely to have what you're looking for.

Alaska is still sufficiently folksy for many of the most interesting shopping places to be "Mom and Pop" operations. Your best bet for finding such establishments is to wander slowly through whatever town you're in and take time to check out the stock in even the most rundown-looking stores. Ivory, Native crafts, novelties, and just about anything is available if you look hard enough.

Shopping Areas

The suburban shopping mall has come to Alaska's larger cities to stay. Smaller communities also are beginning to establish mini-malls.

Anchorage

Fourth Avenue in downtown is still the most popular place to shop, with a variety of stores. In recent years, however, it seems that the majority have become souvenir shops, popular with tourists. Anchorage Fifth Avenue Mall, 320 W. Fifth Avenue, includes department stores, several national chain outlets, and a wide variety of specialty shops.

Dimond Center, located at the corner of Dimond Boulevard and the Old Seward Highway in south Anchorage, is the largest mall in Alaska. Besides major department and chain stores there are a variety of smaller shops. An ice rink is located at the southern end, in addition to several fast-food restaurants and a multi-screen movie theater. The area also includes many of the national chains in their own buildings, including office supply, sporting goods, book, and electronics stores.

Northway Mall, on the Glenn Highway just northeast of downtown Anchorage, has a department store, chain grocery store and lots of smaller shops. Two large discount stores are located to the east of the mall, which is easily spotted as you drive into town from the north.

Fairbanks

The main downtown shopping district runs along Cushman Avenue. Bentley Mall, on the corner of College Road and the Old Steese Highway, is Fairbanks' largest. That and other local malls were an outgrowth of the building boom of the mid-1970s.

SPORTS

Participant Sports

See pages 372–7 for operators and outfitters for the activity of your choice.

Hiking

Extensive hiking trips into Alaska's back country differ significantly from backpacking trips in most of the rest of the US and any trip should begin with a stop at one of the state's four Public Lands Information Centers (in Anchorage, Fairbanks, Tok, and Ketchikan; check the website www.nps.gov/aplic for more details). Although there are extensive hiking trails in populated regions of the state, treks in remote areas often will be more of an overland-navigation experience, which can be both extremely rewarding and challenging. You should know how to use a compass and read topographic maps when traveling across untrailed wilderness.

Hikers should take precautions to avoid surprise encounters with bears, particularly the Alaska brown/grizzly bears which thrive throughout much of the state. Make a noise as you walk, keep campsites clean, keep food away from sleeping areas, and always travel with one or more companions. Statistically, the larger the group, the lower the chances of encountering a hostile bear.

If attacked by a brown or grizzly bear, experts agree the best strategy is to curl up into a ball with hands protecting head and neck, and play dead. If the attacking bear is a black bear, it may be best to fight back, because they sometimes treat humans as prey; being smaller, less agresssive animals than grizzlies, they are easier to fight off. Trying to run from any bear may incite a predatory reflex. The best bet is to give bears as wide a berth as possible. Alaska is their domain.

Hikers and backpackers should also exercise great caution whenever crossing streams; many of Alaska's rivers are fed by glaciers and are therefore extremely cold and possibly turbulent, with loose gravel bottoms. For perspective, consider that more people die from stream crossings than bear attacks (the number of fatalities are small in both cases).

Those going on extensive hikes in the Alaskan wilderness should leave an itinerary with reliable friends or family members and the

Alaska State Troopers or, when appropriate, at the headquarters and/or trailhead of the park, refuge, or other unit being explored.

Cycling

Hundreds of cyclists make long-distance trips by pedal power along Alaska's road system every year. These trips are often as much a test of the ruggedness of the bikes and riders as they are a pleasurable journey. Cyclists should be warned that in many places bike shoulders are narrow, and it is a long way between cities, even on the road system.

Anchorage and Fairbanks have elaborate networks of bike paths/jogging trails. These often are splendid, safe paths set well off the road. In summer they are used for biking and walking, in winter for skiing.

Diving

Recreational diving in Alaska is not for the faint-hearted as the waters are quite cold. Local divers prefer dry suits to the older, more common wet suits. Currents in the salt water may be treacherous. Inquire locally before undertaking any dives.

Once underwater, the cold northern seas offer good diving. The water is clear, except near the mouths of major, silt-laden rivers. Seafood can be harvested while diving, to be enjoyed once you're on dry land.

Few recreational divers go diving in freshwater in Alaska – the major rivers are usually heavily laden with silt from headwater glaciers, and are best avoided.

There are dive shops in Craig, Sitka, Ketchikan, Juneau, Kodiak, in the Prince William Sound area, on the Kenai Peninsula, and in Anchorage. Some offer guided dives, along with opportunities to dive with Stellar sea lions and to see fresh- and salt-water fish.

Canoeing and Kayaking

For those not averse to the water, there is no better way to explore the Alaskan outdoors than in a lightweight craft you paddle yourself. Most rivers are navigable by canoe, at least to some extent, and there are enough whitewater thrills available for kayakers to last a lifetime.

Anyone setting out on an extensive canoe/kayak trip in Alaska should leave a detailed itinerary with the nearest Alaska State Trooper office or park/refuge/ forest headquarters. People who don't come out of the woods when expected are certainly a lot easier to

find if the rescue agencies have some idea of where to start looking.

A particularly good canoeing experience is the Swanson River system of canoe trails near Soldotna on the Kenai Peninsula. Weekend adventures or 2-week expeditions are possible in this region, just a 3-hour drive from Anchorage. Prince William Sound also offers endless paddling opportunities but be aware that the weather can often be overcast and rainy. For more details on the Swanson River system, contact: Kenai National Wildlife Refuge, PO Box 2139 MS 519, Soldotna, AK 99669; tel: (907) 262-7021; www.r7.fws.gov/nwr/kenai/index.htm

Fishing

The number of people who have long dreamed of fishing Alaska's pristine waters for massive king salmon, leaping trout, and wily northern pike must surely be in the millions. All those fish are there, and more. But they're not inclined to just leap in your boat. Prime fishing takes some planning; it also helps to get tips from locals.

Most roadside streams and lakes experience considerable fishing pressure and you're likely to find crowded conditions, particularly during the height of the salmon season. However, you don't always have to mount a major expedition to find good fishing.

Streams that cross Alaska's various roads will be heavily fished near the highway. But a short walk upstream, or down, may put you in all-but-unfished territory. The easiest way to calculate the necessary walking distance is to walk until there are no more footprints visible at

stream side. There are exceptions to this rule, particularly in streams with heavy runs of salmon, but if trout or grayling are your quarry, hiking up or down a clear stream rarely fails.

Those wishing to catch a monstrous salmon or halibut would do well to enlist the services of a fishing guide, located near most of the major fisheries. Rates typically are $100 or more a day per person but should provide more adventure than most anglers can imagine. Your best bet for salmon fishing with guides is on the Kenai River near Soldotna, in the Matanuska Valley, the Bristol Bay region, or on a fly-out trip from Fairbanks or Anchorage to a remote lodge or camp. Alaska's salmon and rainbow trout fisheries are famed throughout the world.

Halibut fishermen flock to Homer and Seward every year for the opportunity to latch on to these bottom fish, which can weigh 300 lbs (136 kg) or more. Several fish of 100–200 lbs (45–90 kg) are caught every year by charter boats operating from the Homer Spit and other Kenai Peninsula towns. Anglers will likely have to spend at least $150 for a day's charter-boat fishing per person, though special deals are sometimes available. Many first-class fishing resorts and wilderness lodges are scattered around Alaska, particularly in the Southwest and Southeast regions. Most are in remote areas, accessible only via floatplane. For those who have the $3,000 or more per person for a week's fishing, these offer an unforgettable experience.

If you're dreaming of fishing but sitting in a downtown Anchorage hotel, you're in luck. Head down the hill to the shores of Ship Creek,

BELOW: both fresh and saltwater fishermen need to have licenses.

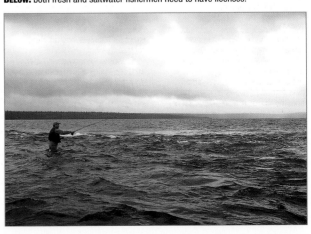

Anchorage's urban fishing hole, for an outstanding chance to reel in a salmon. Or just go to watch the fun. It's within walking distance of several hotels, many of which will rent or loan you fishing gear (check with the bell captain). Equipment for rent is also available from a fishing shack down at the water's edge. Make sure you have a fishing license.

Anyone 16 or older must have a fishing license when angling on Alaska's waters; that includes both fresh and saltwater. Fishing licenses are available at almost all sporting goods stores, most variety stores, at several grocery stores or online. For regulations and licensing information contact the Alaska Division of Sportfish at (907) 465-4180 or www.adfg.state.ak.us.

Golf

While golf in Alaska may never be as popular a draw as in destinations such as Hawaii, there are a number of courses in Anchorage and Fairbanks, as well as ones in Wasilla, Palmer, Homer and Juneau.

The three most popular public courses are in Anchorage: Moose Run, the state's oldest course, owned by the Army; Eagle Glen, considered by many to be the best in the state, on Elmendorf Air Force Base; and the Anchorage Golf Course, on Anchorage's lower Hillside. There are also two 9-hole courses: at Russian Jack Springs Park and south Anchorage's Tanglewood Lakes.

Golf tournaments in Alaska range from the serious to the hilarious, such as Nome's Bering Sea Ice Golf Classic, an annual fund-raising event played in March on a 6-hole course on the frozen Bering Sea, or Kodiak's par-70, *one-hole* spring contest which is held on the side of 1,400-ft (430-meter) Pillar Mountain.

Hunting

Citizens of countries other than the United States must enlist the services of a licensed hunting guide for hunting any big game animal in the state. Guided hunts typically cost from $2,000 for some single-species hunts to $10,000 or more for particular high-quality or multi-species hunts. A typical $2,000 hunt buys a few days of hunting caribou. The $10,000 might buy two to three weeks of hunting from several lodges or camps. A complete list of registered and master guides is available for download, or a copy may be purchased for $5 from: Department of Commerce, Community and Economic Development, Division of Occupational Licensing, Big Game Commercial Services Board, PO Box 110806, Juneau, AK 99811-0806, tel: (907) 465-2534; www.commerce. state.ak.us/occ/pgui7.htm

US residents of states other than Alaska may hunt big game without a guide, except for brown/grizzly bear, mountain goat and Dall sheep. For these animals, non-Alaska residents and US citizens must engage a guide or be accompanied by a family member – only father, mother, sister, brother, son or daughter qualify – who is a resident of Alaska.

Regulations affecting hunting areas, bag limits, and methods and means are extremely complex and vary from region to region around Alaska. To get a license and copies of the hunting regulations contact: the state Department of Fish and Game at (907) 465-4190 or www.adfg.state.ak.us.

Study the regulations carefully before hunting. If in any doubt, inquire locally with the Alaska Department of Fish and Game. License & Tag Fees: tel: (907) 465-2378 for current charges.

Skiing

Both downhill and cross-country skiing are popular in Alaska from November through May (snowfall permitting). There are trails for cross-country skiing throughout the state's populated areas and several communities have developed ski facilities, including Juneau, Anchorage, and Fairbanks.

The state's largest ski area is Alyeska, 40 miles (65 km) southeast of Anchorage in Girdwood. The resort offers 2,500 vertical feet (760 meters) of skiing, including, on occasion, night skiing. The resort has a high-speed aerial tram capable of carrying 60 passengers at a time, and the 307-room Alyeska Prince Hotel, with a pool, restaurants, exercise facilities and meeting rooms.

Closer to Anchorage is Alpenglow at Arctic Valley, which also offers downhill skiing. Hilltop Ski Area, in south Anchorage, is popular with local snowboarders and novice skiers. Several parks in the Anchorage area are popular for cross-country skiing, including Russian Jack Springs, Kincaid Park, Far North Bicentennial Park, Hillside Park and Chugach State Park. Another favorite is the Tony Knowles Coastal Trail.

In Juneau, alpine skiers head for Eaglecrest Ski Area on Douglas Island, 12 miles (19 km) from downtown Juneau. Facilities include two chair lifts and a day lodge. Fairbanks offers a few privately owned downhill areas, including Mt. Aurora/Skiland and Moose Mountain.

Popular cross-country trails in Fairbanks include the Creamers Field trail near downtown, Birch Hill Recreation area and those on the University of Alaska campus. Not far away is Chena Hot Springs Resort, with trails and after-ski relaxation.

Surfing

Most people are surprised to find that Alaska has a surfing opportunity in the northern-most Southeast community of Yakutat. Contact the Yakutat Chamber of Commerce for details: www.yakutatalaska.com.

Spectator Sports

Baseball

Alaska has one of the best semi-pro baseball leagues in the country. The Fairbanks Gold Panners, the Anchorage Glacier Pilots, the Anchorage Bucs, the Mat-Su Miners, and the Kenai Peninsula Oilers are comprised of college players lured north by the long days and opportunity to play ball. Many have gone on to Major League careers. Games are played in modest stadiums with double headers played late into the evening – sometimes without artifical light.

Prices are low. A few dollars gets you into the bleachers (the wooden seating area). Be sure to carry insect repellent, especially to games in the Fairbanks area, as well as a light jacket for cool evenings.

A good bet is the Midnight Sun Game in Fairbanks, which starts late at night on June 21, without lights, in celebration of the summer solstice.

Basketball

Probably the most-watched spectator sport in Alaska is high school basketball. Every community with seven or more students has its own school and enough players to field a team. Regional tournaments abound in late winter, with the state championship played out in March. Pick-up games and adult city league games also are popular, especially in rural areas.

The Great Alaska Shoot-Out, held the fourth weekend in November at the Sullivan Arena and hosted by the University of Alaska Anchorage, attracts top-rate college teams from across the United States. And Fairbanks has its Top of the World Classic, which also draws Division I teams north in November.

Hockey

Hockey teams from the University of Alaska Fairbanks (the Nanooks) and the University of Alaska Anchorage (the Seawolves) play between October and March against college teams from the rest of the US.

The ECHL's Anchorage Aces, a professional team, also play during the fall and winter, drawing rowdy crowds that take their hockey seriously.

Mushing

Alaska's official winter sport draws spectators to races throughout the state, from tiny villages to Alaska's urban center, Anchorage. Among the biggest events are Anchorage's Fur Rendezvous World Championship Sled Dog Race in February; Fairbanks' North American Championship in March; the 1,000-mile (1,600-km) Yukon Quest, between Fairbanks and Whitehorse in the Yukon Territory, in February; and the 1,100-mile (1,770-km) Iditarod Trail Sled Dog Race, staged each March from Anchorage to Nome.

PARKS & PRESERVES

With eight national parks (many with attached preserves), four national monuments, three separate national preserves, 16 wildlife refuges, 25 wild and scenic rivers and 12 designated federal areas – plus a state parks system of more than 3.2 million acres (1.3 million hectares) – Alaska holds more land in the public trust than any other state, by far.

National and state park rangers, US Fish and Wildlife Service personnel and US Forest Service rangers patrol these vast acreages on foot, from airplanes, in canoes, jetboats, outboard motor boats and ocean cruisers, and by car or truck.

Several of the state's wilderness areas and refuges are extremely remote, expensive and difficult to get to and provide few, if any, visitor amenities. The information listed here is, therefore, limited to those commonly visited and with specific activities or attractions.

Alaska Public Lands Information Center

605 W. Fourth Avenue, Anchorage, AK 99501, tel: (907) 271-2737; www.nps.gov/aplic
US Fish and Wildlife Service Alaska Regional Office 1011 East Tudor Road, Anchorage, AK 99503, tel: (907) 786-3309; www.r7.fws.gov

Admiralty Island National Monument

Southeast Alaska island within the Tongass National Forest, located 15 miles (25 km) west of Juneau across Stephens Passage. Primary access is by boat or floatplane from Juneau, but wheeled planes are allowed to land on beaches. Mountainous terrain in coastal rainforest. Size: about 900,000 acres (364,500 hectares).
Contact: 8461 Old Dairy Road, Juneau, AK 99801, tel: (907) 586-8800; www.fs.fed.us/r10/tongass/districts/admiralty

Alaska Chilkat Bald Eagle Preserve

Approximately 20 miles (32 km) from Haines on the Haines Highway. Winter feeding ground for thousands of bald eagles, when it holds the largest concentration of these birds in the world – the best viewing is in Nov–Dec.
Contact: Alaska State Parks, Haines Ranger Station, PO Box 430, Haines, AK 99827, tel: (907) 766-2292; www.dnr.state.ak.us/parks/units/eagleprv.htm

Alaska Maritime National Wildlife Refuge

Scattered coastal units from southeastern Alaska all the way around to the west coast, including the Aleutian Islands. More than 2,500 islands in all. Marine mammals and marine birds, including 50 million nesting seabirds: Size: approximately 4.9 million acres (1.8 million hectares). Most of that – 2.6 million acres – is wilderness.
Contact: 95 Sterling Highway, MS 505, Suite 1, Homer, AK 99603, tel: (907) 235-6546; email: akmaritime@fws.gov
www.r7.fws.gov

Alaska Peninsula and Becharof National Wildlife Refuges

Within these side-by-side refuges in Southwest Alaska are active volcanoes, towering mountains, rolling tundra, and rugged coastal fjords.The refuges are known for their fish and wildlife, particularly salmon, brown/grizzly bears, moose, caribou, wolves and wolverines. Excellent fishing and big-game hunting.
Size: 3.8 million acres combined (1.5 million hectares).
Contact: PO Box 277, MS 545, King Salmon, AK 99613, tel: (907) 246-3339; email: becharof@fws.gov
www.r7.fws.gov

Arctic National Wildlife Refuge

One of the world's great remaining Arctic wilderness areas, in extreme northeastern region of Alaska bordering Canada. Encompassing Interior lowlands, peaks and valleys of the Brooks Range, and the North Slope's coastal plain, the refuge is home to the Porcupine Caribou herd (120,000-plus animals), Dall sheep, polar bears on the coast, grizzly bears, wolves, wolverine, black bears, musk ox, 180 species of birds and spectacular plant life. Excellent hiking and river floating. Size: 19 million acres (8 million hectares).
Contact: 101 12th Avenue, Room 236, Fairbanks, AK 99701, tel: (907) 456-0250
or (800) 362-4546; email: arctic_refuge@fws.gov
www.r7.fws.gov

Chugach National Forest

Second largest national forest in the US (behind only the Tongass), the Chugach includes much of the Kenai Peninsula and Prince William Sound, as well as the Copper River Delta. Offers an abundance of recreational opportunities and is home to a great variety of land and sea mammals and birds of all kinds, from songbirds to eagles, to shorebirds, seabirds, and waterfowl. Size: 6 million acres (2.4 million hectares).
Contact: 3301 C St., Anchorage, AK 99503
tel: 743-9500
www.fs.fed.us/r10/chugach

Chugach State Park

Anchorage's "backyard wilderness," with nearly a half-million acres of land and waters within the Chugach Mountains east of town, a place of jagged spires, tundra meadows, jagged peaks and abundant wildlife. Size: 495,000 acres (200,000 hectares).
Contact: Alaska State Parks, Mile 115 Seward Highway, HC 52, Box 8999, Indian, AK 99540
tel: (907) 345-6982
www.dnr.state.ak.us/parks/index

Denali National Park and Preserve

One of Alaska's most popular tourist destinations, with an average 350,000 visitors a year, it is also home to Mount McKinley – also known by the Athabascan name Denali, The High One – at 20,320 ft (6,195 meters), the highest peak in North America. Attractions include mountain climbing, backpacking, tundra hiking, and wildlife-viewing bus tours (Dall sheep, grizzlies, moose and caribou are some of the species seen frequently). Located 121 miles (194 km) south of Fairbanks, 237 miles (382 km) north of Anchorage, on Parks Highway. Size: around 6 million acres (2.4 million hectares). You can take the cheaper, no frills shuttle bus, or the more expensive tour bus, which includes lunch and a driver who is also a natural history guide. Many shuttle bus drivers also give a narrated "tour" though they're not required to.

The four ways of obtaining advance bus or tour reservations are:
(1) online at www.reservedenali.com;
(2) download a reservation form at www.nps.gov/dena and either fax, (907) 264-4684;
(3) mail it to Doyan/ARAMAK Joint Venture, 241 West Ship Creek Avenue, Anchorage, AK 99501 (forms must be received between December 1 and August 31);
(4) by phone – from mid-February through mid-September – at (800) 622-7275 (in US) or (907) 272-7275 (international). You may also go in person to the Wilderness Access Center Desk, up to two days in advance, and make reservations or ask for assistance. Advance reservations (30 days) are strongly recommended.
Contact for general park information: Denali National Park, PO Box 9, Denali National Park, AK 99755, tel: (907) 683-2294;
www.nps.gov/dena

Denali State Park
Smaller and less celebrated neighbor of Denali National Park, "Little Denali" nonetheless offers numerous opportunities for backcountry recreation and some of the best views anywhere of Mount McKinley/Denali and other Alaska Range giants. Size: 325,460 acres (131,000 hectares).
Contact: Alaska State Parks, HC 32 Box 6706, Wasilla, AK 99654,
tel: (907) 745-3975;
www.dnr.state.ak.us/parks/index

Endicott River Wilderness
Located on the west side of Lynn Canal, about 45 miles (72 km) northwest of Juneau, its western edge bounds the eastern border of Glacier Bay National Park. Size: 94,000 acres (38,000 hectares).
Contact: US Forest Service Juneau Ranger District, 8465 Old Dairy Road, Juneau, AK 99801 tel: (907) 586-8800;
www.fs.fed.us/r10/tongass

Gates of the Arctic National Park and Preserve
The peaks and valleys of the central Brooks Range, north and south of the continental divide, lie within the 8.4 million acres (3.4 million hectares) of the park and preserve, 200 miles (320 km) northwest of Fairbanks. One of the continent's great wilderness areas, home to grizzlies, caribou, wolves, Dall sheep, and many other animals, with opportunities for backpacking, river floating, mountain climbing, and immense solitude. The most convenient access is by air with scheduled service from Fairbanks to Bettles, 40 miles (64 km) south of the park. Hire charter aircraft in Bettles for flightseeing or drop off in the park.
Contact: Visitor Information, P.O. Box 30, Bettles, AK 99726 tel: (907) 692-5494
www.nps.gov/gaar

Glacier Bay National Park
and Preserve
Located 50 miles (80 km) northwest of Juneau at the northern end of Alaska's Panhandle, Glacier Bay is an ever-changing wilderness of tidewater glaciers, towering peaks, coastal fjords, marine mammals and northern birds. Though cruise ships enter the bay, their number is limited to preserve the wilderness experience. Size: 3.3 million acres (1.3 million hectares).
Contact: PO Box 140, Gustavus, AK 99826,
tel: (907) 697-2230;
www.nps.gov/glba

Izembak National Wildlife Refuge
At the tip of Alaska Peninsula in SW Alaska, between the Pacific Ocean and Bering Sea. Outstanding birding and wildlife viewing, including caribou. Access is usually from Cold Bay, which can only be easily reached by airplane. Size: 417,533 acres (169,000 hectares).
Contact: PO Box 127 MS 515, Cold Bay, AK 99571,
tel: (907) 532-2445;
email: izembek@fws.gov
www.r7.fws.gov

Kachemak Bay State Park and Wilderness Park
Across the Bay from Homer, these side-by-side units are relatively unknown, yet they're a wilderness lover's delight, with everything from glaciers and snowfields to coastal rain forest, tidal marshes, sheltered bays, and storm-wracked outer coast. Size: 380,000 acres (154,000 hectares).
Contact: Alaska State Parks, Kenai Area Office, PO Box 1247, Soldotna, AK 99669,
tel: (907) 262-5581;
www.dnr.state.ak.us/parks/index

Katmai National Park and Preserve
Initially set aside in 1918 as a national monument to protect the Valley of 10,000 Smokes created by a massive volcanic eruption in 1912. Excellent fishing and brown bear-viewing, plus opportunities to explore mountains, valleys, and rugged coastal by boat or foot. Size: approximately 4 million acres (1.6 hectares) on the Alaska Peninsula, approximately 250 miles (400km) southwest of Anchorage.
Contact: PO Box 7, King Salmon, AK 99613,
tel: (907) 246-3305;
www.nps.gov/katm

Kenai Fjords National Park
Boat or floatplane charters from Seward, on the Kenai Peninsula, 130 road miles (210 km) south of Anchorage, are the usual means of access. Features the Harding Icefield, one of the major ice caps in the United States, plus tidewater

BELOW: the easiest way to reach many parks is by air.

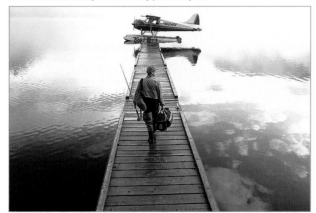

glaciers, and the steep, rugged coastal fjords for which the park is named. Abundant wildlife and marine mammal viewing. Has four public-use cabins for rent, three along the coast, one inland that's for winter-use only. Size: 567,000 acres (229,635 hectares).
Contact: PO Box 1727, Seward, AK 99664,
tel: (907) 224-7500
www.nps.gov/kefj

Kenai National Wildlife Refuge
Located on the Kenai Peninsula across Turnagain Arm south of Anchorage. Spruce and birch forests with hundreds of lakes and streams make this prime habitat for moose, bears and salmon. Size: about 2 million acres (810,000 hectares).
Contact: PO Box 2139 MS 519, Soldotna, AK 99669,
tel: (907) 262-7021;
email: kenai@fws.gov
www.r7.fws.gov

Kobuk Valley National Park
This western Brooks Range park is 350 miles (563 km) northwest of Fairbanks and 75 miles (120 km) west of Kotzebue. Great Kobuk Sand Dunes cover 25 sq miles (40 sq km). Canoe, kayak and raft trips are the primary recreational opportunities. Size: 1.7 million acres (692,550 hectares).
Contact: PO Box 1029, Kotzebue, AK 99752,
tel: (907) 442-3890;
www.nps.gov/kova/

Kodiak National Wildlife Refuge
Encompasses much of Kodiak and Afognak islands southwest of Anchorage. Excellent hunting and fishing, as well as wildlife viewing, rafting and camping amid spruce forests. Size: 1,865,000 acres

(754,325 hectares).
Contact: 1390 Buskin River Rd., MS 559, Kodiak, AK 99615,
tel: (907) 487-2600
or (888) 408-3514;
email: kodiak@fws.gov
www.r7.fws.gov

Lake Clark National Park and Preserve
Across Cook Inlet from Anchorage, Lake Clark is one of Alaska's overlooked gems, though it has a grand mix of features, from rugged coastline to pristine lakes and rivers, active volcanoes, and rugged mountains, many of them never climbed. Fishing and hiking are major recreational opportunities. Size: approximately 4 million acres (1.6 million hectares).
Contact: 1 Park Place, Port Alsworth, AK 99653,
tel: (907) 781-2218;
www.nps.gov/lacl

Misty Fjords National Monument
About 22 air miles (35 km) from Ketchikan, near the southern tip of Alaska's Panhandle. Wet, scenic region of steep mountains descending into deep fjords. Floatplane or boat access only. Size: nearly 2.3 million acres (1 million hectares).
Contact: US Forest Service, Federal Building, 648 Mission Street, Ketchikan, AK 99901;
tel: (907) 225-3101;
www.fs.fed.us/r10/tongass

Noatak National Preserve
Just north of Kotzebue, this northwestern Alaska preserve has no road access. Flights from Kotzebue are the normal means of getting to the area. Fantastic float trip opportunities within the wild Noatak

Basin. Size: 6.5 million acres (2.6 million hectares).
Contact: PO Box 1029, Kotzebue, AK 99752, tel: (907) 442-3890;
www.nps.gov/noat

Petersburg Creek-Duncan Salt Chuck Wilderness
Kupreanof Island across Wrangell Narrows from Petersburg in southeastern Alaska. Size: 50,000 acres (20,250 hectares).
Contact: Tongass National Forest, PO Box 1328, Petersburg, AK 99833;
tel: (907) 772-3871;
www.fs.fed.us/r10/tongass

Russel Fjord Wilderness
Heavily glaciated fjord about 25 miles (40 km) northeast of Yakutat. Size: 307,000 acres (124,355 hectares).
Contact: US Forest Service, PO Box 327, Yakutat, AK 99689,
tel: (907) 784-3359;
www.fs.fed.us/r10/tongass

Selawik National Wildlife Refuge
Straddles the Arctic Circle in Northwestern Alaska about 360 miles (580 km) northwest of Fairbanks. Consists mostly of lakes, estuaries, river deltas, and tundra wetlands. Home to caribou in winter and huge numbers of nesting waterfowl in spring and summer. Activities include river floating, sportfishing and hunting. Size: 2 million acres (810,000 hectares).
Contact: PO Box 270, MS 565, Kotzebue, AK 99752,
tel: (907) 442-3799
or (800) 492-8848;
email: selawik@fws.gov
www.r7.fws.gov

Shuyak Island State Park
At the northern end of the Kodiak Archipelago 250 miles (400 km) southwest of Anchorage, Shuyak can be reached only by plane or boat. With coastal rain forest and bountiful,sheltered bays, it's a kayaker's delight. Four public-use cabins come in handy, given the often stormy weather. Size: 46,000 acres (18,600 hectares).
Contact: Alaska State Parks, 1400 Abercrombie Drive, Kodiak, AK 99615,
tel: (907) 486-6339;
email: kodiakstateparks@dnr.state.ak.us
www.dnr.state.ak.us/parks/index

Sitka National Historical Park
The site of the 1804 Battle of Sitka between Tlingits and Russians. Located in a woodland setting with a collection of totem poles, a footpath through the old-growth forest, and an interpretive center for Russian and

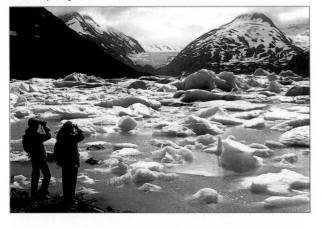
BELOW: exploring the wilderness as the ice melts.

Native history.
Contact: National Park Service, Sitka National Historical Park, 103 Monastery Street, Sitka, AK 99835, tel: (907) 747-0110; www.nps.gov/sitk

South Prince of Wales Wilderness
Approximately 40 air miles (64 km) southwest of Ketchikan on Prince of Wales Island. Size: 91,000 acres (37,000 hectares).
Contact: US Forest Service, Tongass National Forest, Craig Ranger District, PO Box 500, Craig, AK 99921, tel: (907) 826-3271, www.fs.fed.us/r10/tongass

Stikine-LeConte Wilderness
Southeastern Alaska mainland, a short distance north of Wrangell. Boats capable of navigating the Stikine River are the most common means of access. Size: 449,000 acres (181,700 hectares).
Contact: US Forest Service, Stikine Area, Tongass National Forest, PO Box 51, Wrangell, AK 99929-0051; tel: (907) 874-2323; www.fs.fed.us/r10/tongass

Tetlin National Wildlife Refuge
South side of Alaska Highway at the Canadian border. Waterfowl, moose, caribou, black bears and wolves. The area is especially critical to some 143 species of nesting birds. Two lakeshore campgrounds; duck, caribou and moose hunting. Size: 730,000 acres (295,000 hectares).
Contact: PO Box 779 MS 529, Tok, AK 99780, tel: (907) 883-5312; email: tetlin@fws.gov www.r7.fws.gov

Tracy Arm-Fords Terror Wilderness
Southeastern Alaska between Tracy Arm and Endicott Arm, bordered on the east by Canada. Access is by boat. Size: 656,000 acres (265,700 hectares).
Contact: US Forest Service, Juneau Ranger District, Tongass National Forest, 8465 Old Dairy Road, Juneau, AK 99801 tel: (907) 586-8800; www.fs.fed.us/r10/tongass

Wood-Tikchik State Park
At more than 1½ million acres, Wood-Tikchik is the nation's largest state park. Located in the Bristol Bay region, it is dominated by two river-and-lake chains that make it a critically important salmon spawning grounds. Popular with sport fishers and boaters, it draws people from around the world; some stay in plush

wilderness lodges, others camp as they explore the park. Size: 1.55 million acres (627,000 hectares).
Contact: Alaska State Parks, summer rangers: PO Box 1822, Dillingham, AK 99576; tel: 907/842-2375.
Year-round main office: 550 W 7th Ave, Suite 1380, Anchorage, AK 99501, tel: 907/269-8698; www.dnr.state.ak.us/parks/index

Wrangell-St Elias National Park and Preserve
Wrangell-St Elias occupies the eastern corner of Alaska above the Panhandle, tucked against the Canadian border. This huge park/preserve is the largest in the nation, and totals more than 13 million acres (5 million hectares); sometimes called North America's "mountain kingdom" it includes four mountain ranges, the continent's largest ice field, and a glacier larger than Rhode Island. Sections of the road system either enter the park/preserve or pass close to it, but most of its wilderness can easily reached only by plane. Access is by air is mainly from Glennallen or Yakutat, depending on the destination.
Contact: National Park Service, 106.8 Richardson Highway, PO Box 439, Copper Center, AK 99573, tel: (907) 822-5234; www.nps.gov/wrst

Yukon-Charley Rivers National Preserve
Includes a section of the Yukon River near Eagle, 325 road miles (523 km) northeast of Fairbanks by road. Also accessible by road is Circle, outside the western boundary, about 140 road miles (225 km) from Fairbanks. Home to gold-rush relics, bear, Dall

sheep, moose and a population of peregrine falcons. Size: 2.5 million acres (1.1 million hectares).
Contact: National Park Service, Eagle Visitor Center, P.O. Box 167, Eagle, AK 99738, tel: (907) 547-2233; www.nps.gov/yuch

Yukon Delta National Wildlife Refuge
Deltas of the Yukon and Kuskokwim rivers in southwestern Alaska. Plenty of waterfowl and seabirds – 170 species seen in the area and 136 species known to breed here, plus moose, caribou, brown bear and wolves. Fishing, hunting and back-country recreation are good, though access to most of the refuge is difficult and the landscape is mostly boggy – and mosquito-infested in mid-summer. Size: 19.6 million acres (7.7 million hectares).
Contact: 807 Chief Eddie Hoffman Road, PO Box 346 MS 535, Bethel, AK 99559, tel: (907) 543-3151; email: yukondelta@fws.gov www.r7.fws.gov

If You Should Meet a Bear...

"Bearanoia" is a term commonly applied to those with an unreasonable fear of bears. Others, usually inexperienced in the ways of the Alaskan wilderness, sometimes lack a healthy respect for these powerful, if generally shy, animals. Treading a middle ground, seasoned bear-country trekkers use common sense and a basic understanding of bear behavior to avoid close encounters. Here are some tips:
● Avoid surprising bears. Talk loudly or carry "bear bells," and hike in groups of three or more whenever possible. Announcing your presence

clearly allows bears to avoid you.
● Don't camp on or near bear paths. Trails along salmon streams, for example, should be avoided.
● Don't keep food in or near tents. Store food in sealed containers well away from camp. If possible, hoist containers high up in a tree.
● Avoid bear kills. Bears can remain in the area of a kill for days and can be highly protective of it.
● Give bears their space. If you happen upon a bear, turn and give it a wide berth. Walk away; never run. Running can trigger a predatory reflex in an otherwise peaceful animal.

ALL THE USEFUL ADDRESSES YOU'LL NEED

Tour Operators

Chief Shakes Clan House
Tlingit tribal House of the Bear on Shakes Island. Nine totems and community house open for cruise ships during summer and by appointment year-round.
PO Box 868, Wrangell,
AK 99929,
tel: (907) 874-4304.

El Dorado Gold Mine and Riverboat Discovery Tours
The mine has two tours daily, including a narrow-gauge train ride and gold panning, from mid-May through mid-September. The riverboat tours are 3½ hours long, on the Chena and Tanana Rivers.
1975 Discovery Drive,
Fairbanks, AK 99709,
tel: (907) 479-6673
or (866) 479 6673.
email: orders@eldoradogoldmine.com or orders@riverboatdiscovery.com
www.riverboatdiscovery.com

Frontier Excursions
Skagway's oldest independent tour company features gold-rush tours and trips to White Pass and the Yukon. Also shuttle service to Chilkoot trailhead and, in winter, sled dog tours.
PO Box 473,
Skagway, AK 99840,
tel: (907) 983-2512 or 877-983-2512;
email: info@frontierexcursions.com
www.frontierexcursions.com

**Kenai Fjords Tours
(Alaska Heritage Tours)**
Explore Resurrection Bay, Kenai Fjords National Park and the Chiswell Islands bird rookeries aboard comfortable excursion boats. Trips feature wildlife watching and tidewater glaciers. Day trips, meals, kayaking and overnight stays at an island wilderness lodge can also be arranged.

509 W. Fourth Ave.
Anchorage, AK 99501,
tel: (907) 265-4501 or
(877) 777-2805;
email: info@kenaifjords.com
www.kenaifjords.com

Klondike Tours.
Conducts historic Skagway tours and also arranges tours throughout much of Southeast Alaska, including fishing, kayaking, rafting, horseback riding, and flightseeing.
PO Box 1061, Skagway,
AK 99840,
tel: (907) 983-2075 or
(866) 983-2075;
email:klondiketours@yahoo.com
www.klondiketours.com

Kodiak Tours
Half- or full-day tours of Kodiak. Bear-viewing, flightseeing, and remote wilderness lodge stays can also be arranged.
114 Mill Bay Road, Suite 15,
Kodiak, AK 99615,
tel: (907) 486-3920;
email: deann@gci.net
www.kodiaktours.com

**New Directions Tours/
Mayflower Tours**
Escorted tours by motorcoach and air to destinations such as Anchorage, Valdez, Fairbanks and Denali, plus glacier cruises. A 30-day tour begins and ends in Chicago.
Box 490, Downers Grove,
IL 60515
tel: (630) 435-8500 in Illinois,
(800) 323-7604 outside Illinois;
email: info@mayflowertours.com
www.mayflowertours.com

Nome Discovery Tours
Offers tours of Nome and its environs, with an emphasis on the gold rush and Inupiat history of the region.
Box 2024, Nome, AK 99762,
tel: (907) 443-2814;
email: discover@gci.net

Northern Alaska Tour Company
Conducts ecotours to the Arctic Circle, Brooks Range, and Prudhoe Bay and other Arctic locales that emphasize natural and cultural history, wildlife, and geology. Some tours are completely ground-based, others combine ground and air travel.
Box 82991-W,
Fairbanks, AK 99708,
tel: (907) 474-8600 or
(800) 474-1986
email: adventure@northernalaska.com
www.northernalaska.com

Explore Tours
Ecotourism opportunities throughout the state, including cruises through the Inside Passage, fishing, wildlife viewing in Denali National Park, and viewing of the aurora borealis.
999 E. Tudor Road, Suite 200,
Anchorage,
AK 99503,
tel: (907) 786-0192 or
(800) 523-7405
e-mail: info@exploretours.com
www.exploretours.com

Sitka Tours
During ferry port stop or a day in Sitka, visit the totem park in Sitka National Historical Park, the Russian Cathedral, Russian dance performances, and the Alaska Raptor Center. Company also does shuttles to and from airport and ferrry.
PO Box 1000, Sitka,
AK 99835,
tel: (907) 747-8443 or
(866) 620-3720.
email: sitkatours@aol.com
www.sitkatours.net

Skagway Street Car Company
Take an historical tour of the city in a vintage touring car from the 1930s with guides dressed in turn-of-the-20th-century attire.
PO Box 400, Skagway,
AK 99840,

tel: (907) 983-2908;
email: info@skagwaystreetcar.com
www.skagwaystreetcar.com
Southeast Tours
Two-and-a-half-hour land tours include
the Skagway Overlook, a Gold-Rush
cemetery, White Pass, and the US-
Canadian border. Harbor cruises,
flightseeing, fishing charters, river
float trips, horseback riding and dog
sledding are also available.
PO Box 637, Skagway,
AK 99840,
tel: (907) 983-2990;
www.southeasttours.com
Tlingit Cultural Tours
Learn more about the history and
culture of Southeast Alaska's Tlingit
tribe while enjoying the songs,
language, and dance regalia of
their peoples.
c/o Sitka Tribal Enterprises
200 Katlian St,
Sitka, AK 99835,
tel: 907/747-7290
or (888) 270-8687
email: reservation@sitkatribe.org
http://sitkatours.com
Trans Arctic Circle Treks
Features custom highway treks in
Alaska, including the Dalton Highway
from Fairbanks to the Arctic Circle,
through the Brooks Range, and on to
the North Slope and Prudhoe Bay.
Coastal cruises and Alaska Railroad
trips can also be arranged.
PO Box 82720,
Fairbanks, AK 99708,
tel: (907) 479-5451 or
(800) 336-8735 (US only),
fax: (US only): (800) 479-8908;
email: ArcticTreks@Alaska.com
www.arctictreks.com
Tundra Tours
Experience Inupiat Eskimo culture,
the Arctic Ocean and the midnight
sun. Summertime at the northernmost
point in America. Cultural program
includes Eskimo arts and crafts.
PO Box 189,
Barrow, AK 99723,
tel: (907) 852-3900 or
(800) 882-8478;
www.tundratours.com
Viking Travel, Inc.
Bookings on Luxury- and Explorer-
class cruise ships, ferries and cruise
tour itineraries available. Individual
trip planning.
101 N. Nordic, PO Box 787,
Petersburg, AK 99833,
tel: (800) 327-2571 or
(907) 772-3818;
email: reservations@alaskaferry.com
www.alaskaferry.com
White Pass & Yukon Route Railroad
Built 1898–1900 during the Klondike
Gold Rush, the railroad takes
passengers on day excursions past
sheer rock cliffs and through solid

granite tunnels to White Pass Summit.
PO Box 435,
Skagway, AK 99840,
tel: (907) 983-2217 or
(800) 343-7373;
e-mail: info@whitepass.net
www.whitepassrailroad.com
World Express Tours
Tour operator and custom trip planner
organizes an array of Alaska tours
and adventure programs including
executive and private charters,
fishing packages, rafting and
sailing programs, independent
car/motorhome packages,
mountaineering and hiking trips.
PO Box 241826,
Anchorage, AK 99524,
tel: (800) 544-2235;
email: alaska@worldexpresstours.com
www.worldexpresstours.com

Cruises

Cruise West
Up-close, casual, small-ship cruises
that range from the Inside Passage
to the Bering Sea, with the option of
multi-day motorcoach tours to
Denali, Anchorage, gold-rush sites
or other destinations.
2301 Fifth Avenue, Suite 401,
Seattle, WA 98121,
tel: (888) 851-8133;
email: experience@cruisewest.com
www.cruisewest.com
Central Charters
Wildlife tour aboard classic yacht
Danny J across Kachemak Bay to
Halibut Cove's artist community and
other custom tours, including trips to
the coastal community of Seldovia.
Also specializes in halibut fishing
charters.
4241 Homer Spit Road,
Homer, AK 99603,
tel: (907) 235-7847 or
(877) 724-5425;
email: central@centralcharter.com
www.centralcharter.com
Holland America
One-day and extended air, day boat,
railroad, and motorcoach tours and
cruises covering much of the state
available for individuals and groups.
300 Elliott Avenue W.,
Seattle, WA 98119,
tel: (206) 281-3535 or
(877) 932-4259;
www.hollandamerica.com
Phillips' Cruises and Tours
4½-hour, 135-mile (217-km) cruise
within protected waters of Prince
William Sound. See whales,
seals, sea otters, porpoises,
bird rookeries and as many
as 26 glaciers in College and
Harriman fjords.
519 W. Fourth Avenue,
Anchorage, AK 99501,

tel: (907) 276-8023 or
(800) 544-0529;
email: info@26glaciers.com
www.26glaciers.com
Portage Glacier Cruises
Take a one-hour cruise to the face of
Alaska's most-visited glacier on the
Ptarmigan. Offered through Gray Line
of Alaska.
745 W. 4th Avenue, Suite 200,
Anchorage, AK 99501,
tel: (907) 277-5581 or
(888) 452-1737;
www.graylinealaska.com
Princess Cruises & Tours
Alaska vacations combine Gulf of
Alaska and Inside Passage cruises,
tours aboard the Princess Love
Boats and land tour packages.
800 5th Avenue, Suite 2600,
Seattle, WA 98104,
tel: (800) 774-6237;
www.princess.com
**Prince William Sound Cruises
and Tours**
Daily tours out of Whittier, with
opportunities to see marine wildlife
and calving tidewater glaciers.
509 W. Fourth Ave,,
Anchorage, AK 99501,
tel: (907) 277-2131 or
(877) 777-2805;
e-mail: info@princewilliamsound.com
www.princewilliamsound.com
Rainbow Tours
On the boardwalk at Homer Spit.
Boat tours include whale watching,
halibut fishing, and shuttle across
Kachemak Bay to Seldovia. Hotel
accommodation in Seldovia can be
arranged. Group rates.
PO Box 1526, Homer,
AK 99603,
tel: (907) 235-7272;
email: rainbow@rainbowtours.net
www.rainbowtours.net

MAJOR LINES visiting Alaska include:
Carnival Cruise Lines
www.carnival.com
Celebrity Cruises
www.celebrity-cruises.com
Clipper Cruise Line
www.intrav.com
Cruise West
www.cruisewest.com
Lindblad Expeditions
www.expeditions.com
Princess Cruises
www.princess.com
**Norwegian Cruise Line/
NCLAmerica**
www.ncl.com
Regent Seven Seas Cruises
www.rssc.com
Royal Caribbean Cruise Lines
www.rccl.com

TRANSPORTATION

ACCOMMODATIONS

ACTIVITIES

CONTACTS

A – Z

Adventure Tours

Adventure Alaska Tours

Wilderness and land excursions include sightseeing tours, hiking, canoeing, and biking. Specializes in small groups on trips of five to 16 days.
PO Box 64
Hope, AK 99605
tel: (907) 782-3730 or
(800) 365-7057;
email: info@adventurealaskatours.com
www.adventurealaskatours.com

Alaska Passages Adventure Cruises

Fishing, whale-watching, glacier viewing, kayaking, photography and charters for research expeditions. Features customized trips through the Inside Passage, with a maximum of six guests.
PO Box 213,
Petersburg, AK 99833,
tel: (907) 772-3967;
or (888) 434-3766
email: info@alaskapassages.com
www.alaskapassages.com

Alaska Wildland Adventures

Nationally recognized natural history and ecotourism operator offers outdoor-oriented "safaris" of varying lengths for a variety of ages to Denali, Kenai Fjords, Kenai River fishing and elsewhere. Also can arrange stays at wilderness lodges.
PO Box 389, Girdwood, AK 99587,
tel: (907) 783-2928 or
(800) 334-8730;
e-mail: reservations@alaska-wildland.com
www.alaskawildland.com

Arctic Treks

Wilderness backpacking and rafting in the Brooks Range. Two-week combination trips and seven- to ten-day base camp hiking trips in the remote Arctic National Wildlife Refuge, Gates of the Arctic National Park, and other neighboring parklands. Recognized outfitters and guides used for all programs.
PO Box 73452,
Fairbanks, AK 99707,
tel: (907) 455-6502;
email: info@arctictreksadventures.com
www.arctictreksadventures.com

Arctic Wild

Guided backpacking, hiking canoeing and rafting adventures in the Arctic National Wildlife Refuge and Gates of the Arctic National Park. Besides its scheduled trips, the company organizes custom expeditions into the wilderness.
PO Box 80562, Fairbanks,
AK 99708,
tel: (907) 479-8203 or
(888) 577-8203;
email:info@arcticwild.com
www.arcticwild.com

Great Alaska Safaris

Small-group safaris include Denali flightseeing, kayaking, bear-viewing, fishing, and tundra hiking.
33881 Sterling Highway,
Sterling, AK 99672, or
in winter PO Box 2670,
Poulsbo, WA 98570,
tel: (907) 262-4515 in summer or
(800) 544-2261 year-round;
email: greatalaska@greatalaska.com
www.greatalaska.com

Log Cabin Resort and RV Park

Log cabins, campgrounds and log house with suites. RV hookups, rustic beach cabins with modern kitchens and baths. Outboards, skiffs, canoes for fishing in rivers, lakes and saltwater for salmon or halibut. Licensed charters. Canoeing, hiking, bird- and whale-watching, and photography.
PO Box 54, Klawock,
AK 99925,
tel: (907) 755-2205 or
(800) 544-2205;
email: lcresak@aptalaska.net
www.logcabinresortandrvpark.com

Nunivak Island Guide Service

Wilderness trips include sport-fishing, musk ox sport hunting and wildlife viewing in the Yukon Delta National Wildlife Refuge.
PO Box 31,
Mekoryuk, AK 99630,
tel: (907) 827-8213
email: nunivaked@yahoo.com

Sourdough Outfitters

Guided and unguided wilderness trips in the Brooks Range. The oldest outfitting business in the Arctic offers canoe, raft and kayak trips, and backpacking throughout the Brooks Range; plus dog sled, cross-country ski and snow-machine trips; raft and canoe rentals. Does guided trips year-round.
PO Box 26066,
Bettles Field, AK 99726,
tel: (907) 692-5556;
email: info@sourdough.com
www.sourdoughoutfitters.com

TravelWild Expeditions

Natural history tours and wildlife viewing, photography and scenery in Katmai, Denali and Kenai Fjords National Parks.
PO Box 1637,
Vashon Island, WA 98070,
tel: (206) 463-5362 or
(800) 368-0077;
email: info@travelwild.com
www.travelwild.com

Wilderness Alaska

Brooks Range backpacking and river trips. Customized and scheduled trips through the Arctic National Wildlife Refuge and Gates of the Arctic National Park, with a special focus on wilderness skills and field biology unique to the high Arctic. Also guides kayak trips in Prince William Sound.
PO Box 113063,
Anchorage, AK 99511,
tel: (907) 345-3567;
email: macgill@alaska.net
www.wildernessalaska.com

Bear Viewing

Over the past decade, the demand to view bears – majestic symbols of Alaska's wild – has exploded. Prime viewing time runs from June through early September, when the salmon are running, depending on the location. Most bear-viewing areas feature brown bears (the coastal cousins of grizzlies), but a couple in Southeast Alaska also include black bears.

Most of these locales have visitor limits, so plan far ahead.

Anan Creek Bear Observatory

In Southeast Alaska's rainforest, Anan is a rarity in that both black and brown bears may be viewed here. Best viewing is in July and August, when salmon runs reach their peak. Managed by the US Forest Service, in the Tongass National Forest.
Wrangell Ranger District,
PO Box 51,
Wrangell, AK 99929,
tel: (907) 874-2323;
email: anan@fs.fed.us
www.fs.fed.us/r10/tongass

Fish Creek Wildlife Observatory Site

Fish Creek has been a local attraction for decades, but only in the last decade, as ecotourism has blossomed, has the creek become a major visitor attraction. Located near Alaska's border with Canada, at the edges of the Tongass National Forest, this salmon stream is the only one of Alaska's prime bear-watching locales to be along the road system. Mostly brown bears, but occasionally a black bear will wander through.
PO Box 126,
Hyder, AK 99923,
tel: (907) 225-2148 in Ketchikan year-round or 250/636-2367 in Hyder from April through September;
www.fs.fed.us/r10/tongass

McNeil River State Game Sanctuary

Widely regarded as the premier place to view lots of brown bears – sometimes up close – McNeil offers a wilderness adventure that requires a permit, which are awarded in a lottery fashion by the Alaska Department of Fish and Game every spring (see page 340). Staying in a designated tent camping area that includes a cooking-eating shack and a wood-fired sauna, visitors hike to either Mikfik Creek or McNeil River to watch brown bears feed. The prime gathering is at McNeil Falls, from early July through mid-August, when as many as four or five dozen bears may gather at one time.

Alaska Department of Fish and Game, Division of Wildlife Conservation,
333 Raspberry Road,
Anchorage, AK 99518-1599,
tel: (907) 267-2182;
email: mcneilinfo@fishgame.state.ak.us
www.wildlife.alaska.gov/index.cfm

Katmai National Park and Preserve
Like McNeil, Katmai is on the upper Alaska Peninsula. Prime viewing time is in July and September. Dozens of brown bears are drawn into the Brooks River by sockeye salmon, with fishing concentrated at Brooks Falls. Campground, visitor center, viewing platforms, ranger station, and a lodge with a dozen small cabins that can be rented.
Contact the national park at:
PO Box 7,
King Salmon, AK 99613,
907-246-3305;
www.nps.gov/katm

Pack Creek
Brown bears fish for salmon returning to Admiralty Island, in Southeast Alaska, a short plane ride from Juneau. Day viewing only. Prime time is July and August.
Admiralty Island National Monument
8461 Old Dairy Road,
Juneau, AK 99801,
tel: (907) 586-8800;
www.fs.fed.us/r10/tongass/districts/admiralty

Redoubt Bay Lodge
Located across Cook Inlet from Anchorage adjacent to Lake Clark National Park and Preserve, the lodge originally catered to fishermen, but is now seeing more bear viewers. Other activities include fishing, kayaking, hiking, flightseeing. For more information write to:
Within the Wild Adventure Company,
2463 Cottonwood St.,
Anchorage, AK 99508,
907-274-2710;
alaskawild@gci.net
www.withinthewild.com

Kayaking/River Trips

ABEC's Alaska Adventures
Backpacking and river-running trips in the Brooks Range, primarily the Arctic National Wildlife Refuge and Gates of the Arctic National Park. Rafting, kayaking and canoeing trips ranging from wild water to relaxing float trips. Custom trips can also be arranged elsewhere in the state.
P.O. Box 10791
Fairbanks, AK 99710,
tel: (907) 457-8907 or
(877) 424-8907;

e-mail: abec@abecalaska.com
www.abecalaska.com

Alaska Discovery Wilderness Adventures
Wilderness tours by raft, kayak, canoe, and foot. Also one-day bear-watching at Pack Creek. Completely outfitted expeditions into Glacier Bay, Admiralty Island, Icy Bay and other wilderness areas in Southeast Alaska. Also expeditions to the Noatak River in the Gates of the Arctic National Park, the Kongakut River in the Arctic National Wildlife Refuge, Denali National Park, and Kachemak Bay. Group size limited. Explorations can be lodge-based or wilderness camping.
1266 66th St., Suite 4,
Emeryville, CA 94608
tel: (907) 780-6226 or
(800) 586-1911;
email: AKDinfo@mtsobek.com
www.akdiscovery.com

Alaska Rivers Company
Scenic or whitewater raft trips and float fishing on the upper Kenai River, plus saltwater fishing in Resurrection Bay. Lodging in log cabins.
PO Box 827,
Cooper Landing, AK 99572,
tel: (907) 595-1226 or
(888) 595-1226;
email: lrg@arctic.net
www.alaskariverscompany.com

Auk Ta Shaa Discovery
Half-day and full-day guided float in large rubber rafts and half-day sea kayak trips. Mixture of rapids and calm water; for all ages.
76 Egan Drive,
Juneau, AK 99801,
tel: (907) 586-8687 or
(800) 820-2628;
tourcenter@goldbelt.com
www.goldbelttours.com

Chilkat Guides
Half-day river trips in the heart of the Chilkat Bald Eagle Preserve and upper Chilkat River and extended multi-day raft trips down the Alsek and Tatshenshini Rivers in Southeast Alaska and the Kongakut River in the Arctic National Wildlife Refuge.
PO Box 170, Haines, AK 99827,
tel: (907) 766-2491 or
(888) 292-7789;
email: raftalaska@chilkatguides.com
www.raftalaska.com

Class V White Water
Day trips and extended wilderness floats, both scenic and challenging, from the Kenai Peninsula to the Talkeetna Mountains, in Southcentral Alaska.
PO Box 641
Girdwood, AK 99587
tel: (907) 783-4354
email: info@alaskanrafting.com
www.alaskanrafting.com

Denali Raft Adventures
Two-hour, four-hour, and full-day raft trips. Mild water or whitewater, oared or paddle boats, on the Nenana River, which forms the eastern border of Denali National Park.
Drawer 190,
Denali National Park, AK 99755,
tel: (907) 683-2234 or
1-888-683-2234;
email: info@denaliraft.com
www.denaliraft.com

Kayak Adventures Worldwide
Kayak in Kenai Fjords National Park, Prince William Sound and Resurrection Bay. Year-round trips available all over the world.
PO Box 2249,
Seward, AK 99664,
tel: (907) 224-3960 seasonally;
email: fun@kayakak.com
www.kayakak.com

Keystone Raft and Kayak Adventures, Inc.
Wilderness whitewater adventures. Raft trips from two hours to two weeks. Kayak support trips and class III, IV and V kayak excursions.
PO Box 1486, Valdez, AK 99686,
tel: (907) 835-2606 or
(800) 323-8460;
email: keystone@alaska.net

McKinley Raft Tours
Float the eastern boundary of Denali National Park on the Nenana River. Great whitewater, beautiful scenery and wildlife viewing. Either scenic flatwater or whitewater trips are possible, from 21?2 to 4 hours. Available mid-May–mid-September.
PO Box 138,
Denali National Park,
AK 99755,
tel: (907) 683-2392,
fax: (907) 683-2581;

Ouzel Expeditions
Guided river float trips in western AK and Brooks Range. Fishing trips, scenic float trips on whitewater and calm rivers. Superb fishing for salmon, grayling and trout, plus birding trips with an experienced ornithologist. Custom-tailored tours.
PO Box 935, Girdwood, AK 99587,
tel: (907) 783-2216 or
(800) 825-8196;
email: paul@ouzel.com
www.ouzel.com

Southeast Exposure
Guided sea-kayaking trips through local waters of the Inside Passage, including Misty Fjords National Monument. Rental, instruction and sales.
PO Box 9143,
Ketchikan, AK 99901,
tel: (907) 225-8829;
email: seexposure@kpunet.net
www.southeastexposure.com

Tongass Kayak Adventures
Day trips, base camps and week-long sea-kayak explorations on Alaska's Inside Passage. Specializes in small-group tours.
PO Box 2169,
Petersburg, AK 99833,
tel: (907) 772-4600;
email: info@tongasskayak.com
www.tongasskayak.com

Hiking Tours

Alaska Mountaineering School
Both a climbing school and guiding company. Leads mountaineering expeditions to Denali (Mount McKinley) and Mount Foraker, plus custom expeditions to other peaks. Also guides backcountry treks in the Alaska and Brooks Ranges and Talkeetna Mountains.
PO Box 566,
Talkeetna, AK 99676,
tel: (907) 733-1016;
email: info@climbalaska.org
www.climbalaska.org

St. Elias Alpine Guides
Specializes in custom trips for individuals or small groups, while leading a full spectrum of activities in Wrangell-St Elias National Park and Preserve, from glacial walks to mountain hikes, nature tours, backpacking treks and mountaineering expeditions.
P.O. Box 92129,
Anchorage, AK 99509,
tel: (888) 933-5427 or
(907) 554-4445;
email: info@steliasguides.com
www.steliasguides.com

Skiing Tours

Alyeska Resort
Year-round resort 40 miles (64 km) southeast of Anchorage on Seward Highway. Six chair lifts and tram, night skiing, condominium accommodation and luxury hotel with convention facilities, restaurant, lounge, swimming pool, exercise room and hot tub with a view of the mountain. There's also a day lodge, ski school, alpine and telemark skiing, ski rental and repair, ski shops and ice skating; dog sledding and sleigh rides can be arranged. Summer sightseeing tram lift ride.
PO Box 249,
Girdwood, AK 99587,
tel: (907) 754-1111 or
(800) 880-3880 for reservations;
email: guestservices@alyeskaresort.com
www.alyeskaresort.com

Eaglecrest Ski Area
Twelve miles (19 km) from downtown Juneau, there's a base lodge, food service, rental shop, ski school, mountain facilities, two chairlifts, a surface lift and tube lift and mountain-top warming hut. Winter offers 640 acres (259 hectares) and 31 runs for alpine skiing and snowboarding, 40 acres (16 hectares) of snow-making (where machines produce snow during periods of low snowfall) and 5 miles (8 km) of nordic trails. Bus service weekends and holidays only.
155 S. Seward Street,
Juneau, AK 99801,
tel: (907) 790-2000;
email: ecrestak@alaska.net
www.eaglecrestskiarea.com

Fishing Tours

Alaska Adventures Unlimited
Sport-fishing charters for halibut, king salmon, coho salmon in Sitka area.
PO Box 6244,
Sitka, AK 99835,
tel: (907) 747-5576;
email: akfish@gei.net

Alaska Customized Sportfishing/Viking Travel
Itineraries feature quality lodges and guided fishing in wilderness settings.
101 N. Nordic, PO Box 787,
Petersburg, AK 99833,
tel: (800) 327-2571 or
(907) 772-3818;
email: reservations@alaskaferry.com
www.alaskaferry.com

Central Charters
This Homer-based outfit is a booking company that specializes in halibut and salmon fishing charters in Kachemak Bay and lower Cook Inlet.
4241 Homer Spit Road,
Homer, AK 99603,
tel: (907) 235-7847 or
(800) 478-7847;
email: central@centralcharter.com
www.centralcharter.com

Great Alaska Fish Camp
Deluxe adventure lodge on Kenai River. Fish the world's largest salmon, halibut and rainbow trout. Both fresh- and saltwater guided trips on Alaska's Kenai Peninsula. Retreat facilities.
33881 Sterling Highway,
Sterling, AK 99672,
tel: (907) 262-4515 in summer,
(360) 697-6454 in winter or
(800) 544-2261 year-round;
email: greatalaska@greatalaska.com
www.greatalaska.com

Juneau Sportfishing and Sightseeing
"Cruise ship style" fishing aboard fully equipped luxury boats. Half- and full-day packages include transport-ation, bait, tackle, rain gear, food. Wildlife watching is a bonus.
PO Box 20438,
Juneau, AK 99802,
tel: (907) 586-1887;
email: Sportfishing@Alaska.com
www.juneausportfishing.com

Silver Fox Charters
Sport-fishing for halibut in Kachemek Bay and Cook Inlet. High-tech navigational gear, heated cabins. Gear and bait furnished.
PO Box 402,
Homer, AK 99603,
tel: (907) 235-8792 or
(800) 478-8792;
email: info@silverfoxcharters.com
www.silverfoxcharters.com

Sportfishing Alaska
Longtime Alaskan and retired lodge owner arranges personalized fishing trips statewide.
9310 Shorecrest Drive,
Anchorage, AK 99502,
tel: (907) 344-8674 or
(888) 552-8674
email: info@alaskatripplanners.com
www.alaskatripplanners.com

BELOW: nature tours are popular with hikers in summer.

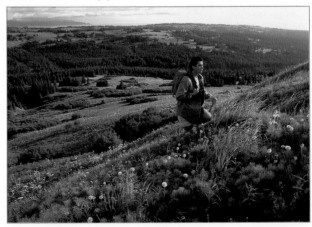

Special Interest

Alaska Hunting and Fishing Ventures
Charters for halibut and salmon. Guided hunts for big game. Overnight fishing trips include tackle, bait and fish cleaning.
PO Box 813,
Homer, AK 99603,
tel: (907) 235-7427

Alaska Outdoor Services
Guided fishing trips on the Kenai River and other Kenai Peninsula waters.
PO Box 1066,
Soldotna, AK 99669,
tel: (907) 262 4589 or
(888) 434-7425,
fax: (907) 262-4042.
email: chick@aosalaska.com
www.aosalaska.com

Redington Sled Dog Rides
Half-hour to overnight mushing trips along the historic Iditarod Trail.
PO Box 877653,
Wasilla, AK 99687
tel: (907) 376-6730;
email: redingtons@yahoo.com

Center for Alaskan Coastal Studies
Environmental education, research field trips and natural history outings studying the marine and coastal ecosystems of Kachemak Bay; beach and coastal rainforest studies.
PO Box 2225,
Homer, AK 99603,
tel: (907) 235-6667;
email: info@akcoastalstudies.org
www.akcoastalstudies.org

Crow Creek Mine
Historic gold-mining building with artifacts near Girdwood, now on National Register of Historic Places. Open to tourists to pan for gold – equipment supplied and gold guaranteed. There's also a gift shop, overnight camping, and nearby trails to explore the surrounding Chugach National Forest. Groups of up to 150.
PO Box 113
Girdwood, AK 99587
tel: (907) 278-8060;
www.crowcreekgoldmine.com

Dig Afognak
The Koniag Native village of Afognak offers professionally led archeological digs and "culture camps" at remote sites on Kodiak Island.
204 East Rezanof Drive, Suite 100,
Kodiak, AK 99615,
tel: (907) 486-6357;
www.afognak.org/dig.php

Eclipse Alaska
Personalized guiding service provided for professional photographers, videographers and film-makers from Southeast Alaska to the Arctic. Advance reservations required.
310–16 Main St. Box 689,
Haines, AK 99827-0689,
tel: (907) 766-2670
email: eclipseakweb@aol.com
www.eclipsealaska.com

Joseph Van Os Photo Safaris
Wildlife photography tours for beginners to professionals. Alaska destinations include Katmai and Denali National Parks.
PO Box 655,
Vashon Island, WA 98070,
tel: (206) 463-5383,
fax: (206) 463-5484;
email: info@photosafaris.com
www.photosafaris.com

Wilderness Birding Adventures
Bird watching expeditions throughout much of Alaska, from Prince William Sound and the Kenai Peninsula to Nome, the Bering Sea, and the Arctic National Wildlife Refuge.
5515 Wild Mountain Drive,
Eagle River, AK 99577,
tel: (907) 694-7442;
email: info@wildernessbirding.com
www.wildernessbirding.com

Tourist Information

Anchorage Convention and Visitors Bureau
524 W. 4th Avenue,
Anchorage, AK 99501,
tel: (907) 276-4118,
fax: (907) 278-5559;
email: info@anchorage.net
www.anchorage.net

Fairbanks Convention and Visitors Bureau
550 First Avenue,
Fairbanks, AK 99701,
tel: (800) 327-5774;
email: info@explorefairbanks.com
www.explorefairbanks.com

Haines Convention and Visitors Bureau
PO Box 530,
Haines, AK, 99827,
tel: (907) 766-2234 or
(800) 458-3579,
fax: (907) 766-3155;
email: hcvb@haines.ak.us
www.haines.ak.us

Juneau Convention and Visitors Bureau
One Sealaska Plaza, Suite 305,
Juneau, AK 99801,
tel: (907) 586-1737 or
(800) 587-2201;
email: info@traveljuneau.com
www.traveljuneau.com

Kodiak Island Convention and Visitors Bureau
100 Marine Way, Suite 200,
Kodiak, AK 99615,
tel: (907) 486-4782
or (800) 789-4782;
email: visit@kodiak.org
www.kodiak.org

Kenai Convention and Visitors Bureau
11471 Kenai Spur Highway,
Kenai, AK 99611,
tel: (907) 283-1991;
email: info@visitkenai.com
www.visitkenai.com

Ketchikan Visitors Bureau
131 Front Street,
Ketchikan, AK 99901,
tel: (907) 225-6166 or
(800) 770-3300,
email: info@visit-ketchikan.com
www.visit-ketchikan.com

Mat-Su Convention and Visitors Bureau
7744 E. Visitors View Court,
Palmer, AK 99645,
tel: (907) 746-5000;
email: info@alaskavisit.com
www.alaskavisit.com

Nome Convention and Visitors Bureau
PO Box 240 H-P,
Nome, AK 99762,
tel: (907) 443-6624;
email: tourinfo@ci.nome.ak.us
www.nomealaska.org

Petersburg Visitor Information Center
PO Box 649,
Petersburg, AK 99833,
tel: (907) 772-4636;
or (866) 484-4700
email: visitorinfo@petersburg.org
www.petersburg.org

Sitka Convention and Visitors Bureau
PO Box 1226,
Sitka, AK 99835,
tel: (907) 747-5940;
email: scvb@sitka.org
www.sitka.org

Skagway Convention and Visitors Bureau
PO Box 1029,
Skagway, AK 99840,
tel: (907) 983-2854;
email: info@skagway.com
www.skagway.com

Valdez Convention and Visitors Bureau
PO Box 1603,
Valdez, AK 99686,
tel: (907) 835-2984;
email: info@valdezalaska.org
www.valdezalaska.org

Wrangell Convention and Visitors Bureau
PO Box 1350,
Wrangell, AK 99929,
tel: (907) 874-3901 or
(800) 367-9745;
email: wrangell@wrangell.com
www.wrangell.com

A – Z

A HANDY SUMMARY OF PRACTICAL INFORMATION, ARRANGED ALPHABETICALLY

A ccidents

In the event of any emergency requiring police, fire or ambulance service, go to the nearest telephone and dial 911. It is a toll free call; no coins will be needed for a public telephone. For less serious accidents, call the local police department or the state troopers non-emergency lines. Dial (907) 555-1212 for directory assistance in locating the appropriate non-emergency police or trooper telephone number.

Alcohol

The legal age for purchasing and consuming alcoholic drinks is 21, and identification is often needed. Alcohol is sold or served in liquor stores, lounges and restaurants licensed by the state. Alaska state law requires a mandatory 3-day jail sentence for drivers found to be driving under the influence of alcohol – even for first-time offenders. Some small rural communities have banned the importation, sale and consumption of alcoholic drinks – and they take it seriously. You could be arrested, fined, jailed or deported for violating these local ordinances. Before traveling to a remote destination, make sure you know the local liquor laws.

Angling Tips

It takes years for the region's trout, grayling, and char to reach trophy size, so most anglers practice catch-and-release fishing. For many, that means fly-fishing. Spinning gear works well, too, particularly if anglers use single barbless hooks, rather than treble hooks on spinners and spoons. Fish that are taken on bait tend to swallow hooks, resulting in damage to their delicate gill tissue and internal organs, leading to bleeding and, ultimately, death.

When fishing catch-and-release, play a fish as briefly as possible and avoid removing it from the water. Use forceps or needle-nose pliers to grasp the hook and gently slip it from the fish's mouth. If the fish must be handled, make sure that your hands are wet. Dry hands are more likely to remove the slimy coating on the fish's body, leaving it prone to deadly fungal infections. Cradle the fish underwater for as long as necessary until it recovers and swims away under its own power.

B udgeting for a Trip

Traveling within Alaska is expensive. Unlike many locales, the further you range from urban locations, the more expensive travel, food, lodging and services may become. This is due, in part, to the transportation costs involved in shipping goods and services to far-flung regions in a vast state. Here are some examples of what you might pay in US dollars when this book went to press.
Camping. A less-expensive option, once you and your vehicle have made the trip up. Expect to pay $6–$25 per night at a state or federally managed campground.
Hotels. During the summer season, basic hotel rooms are generally over $100 per night, and can be as high

as $300 (or more) per night during periods of highest demand. Advance reservations in summer are strongly recommended.

Meals. A fast-food meal for one will typically cost less than $10. A meal in a casual restaurant will likely run between $10 and $20. Evening meals in a nice restaurant may cost $20–$30 per person, and that's just for the entrée. Add a dessert and a glass of wine, and the price is likely to be close to $40–$50 for one, not counting the tip (see Tipping, page 383).

Transportation. Most Alaska cities, of even modest size, offer **taxi** service. A trip from the Anchorage airport to the downtown area in a taxi will cost around $20 (before the expected tip). Larger cities offer municipal **bus** lines. In Anchorage, a ride on the People Mover cost $1.75 (one-way) for adults, $1 for youth and free for children aged 4 and under.

Rental cars are available in larger cities, and you can expect to pay from $50–$150 per day, depending upon the size vehicle you want. Be sure to reserve early. In peak season it can be very difficult to find a rental car at any price. Regular travel on the Alaska **Railroad** between Anchorage and Denali National Park and Preserve costs about $135 per person, one way. If you care to ride in one of the glass-dome cars, make that $220.

Attractions. Here's a sample of prices for Anchorage-area attractions: **The Imaginarium Science Discovery Center** ($5.50 adults, $5 children), **Anchorage Museum of History and Art** ($8 adults, $7 seniors, children under age 17 free, but donation suggested), **Alaska Native Heritage Center** ($23.50 adults, $21.15 for seniors and military, $15.95 for children ages 7–16), **Alaska Zoo** ($10 adults, $8 seniors, $6 ages 3–17), and **H2Oasis Indoor Water Park** ($21.95 adults, $16.95 ages 3–13).

Business Hours

Government offices (except for Post Office stations) are normally open from 8am to 4:30pm Monday through Friday, with banks and credit unions generally open from 10am to 6pm and, in some cases, during limited hours on Saturday. Except for necessary public services, most government offices and businesses are closed on public holidays (though the Post Office station at Anchorage airport is open every day from 6am to 11:59pm).

Retailers, especially in peak summer months, are the exception and often open seven days a week,

well into the evening. Some grocery stores are 24-hour.

Car Breakdown

When driving the highways in Alaska, it's always a good idea to be prepared. While excellent, dependable towing and repair services are available in the cities and even smaller towns of the state, you may find that your breakdown occurs many miles, or hundreds of miles, from their shops. It's very important that your vehicle be in reliable condition if you're planning a drive to remote areas. Check to be sure you have a working spare tire, a jack, flares, a basic tool kit, jumper cables and a first aid kit. An extra can of oil as well as transmission and brake fluids could be a godsend. If you do break down along the road, you'll likely find that other drivers in Alaska will probably stop and see if they can help.

Childcare

Bringing your children along on an Alaska vacation is a wonderful idea, because most of the things that interest you will delight them as well. Whether planning to hike, cruise, fish, kayak or journey to Denali on the train, a trip to Alaska thrills young and old alike.

Eating: Not only does Alaska have a myriad of the standard fast-food options in the larger cities, many of Alaska's restaurants offer children's menus and even crayons and paper to help them wait for their food.

Accommodations: Many hotels in Alaska allow young children to stay for free in their parents' room.

Transport: Alaska state law requires that all automobile drivers must wear safety belts. Additionally, passengers from ages 4–16 must wear a seat belt or a child restraint device, whichever is age-appropriate. Children under age 4 must be placed in a federally-approved child restraint device.

Places of Special Interest: Most any activity you might choose to do in Alaska would be fun for the children. Just getting to Alaska can be exciting, whether it's driving the highway watching for moose, or flying up and looking out the window at all those snow-covered mountains, even in summer. A trip to Alaska aboard one of the Alaska Marine Highway ferries is relaxing and fun for the whole family. Once you've arrived, the kids might enjoy camping, fishing, kayaking, or biking. Day-cruises out of any Southeast or Southcentral coastal community would likely involve watching for marine mammals and glacier viewing.

There are also many exciting options within the larger cities. Here are some fun things to do with kids in the Anchorage area: The Imaginarium Science Discovery Center (737 West Fifth Avenue, (907) 276-3179) features a planetarium, hourly science demonstrations, a Alaska marine touch tank, a life-sized dinosaur, and more. The Alaska Zoo (4731 O'Malley Road, (907) 346-3242) gives kids (and their parents) a chance to get a close-up look at some of Alaska's wildlife. The H2Oasis Indoor Waterpark's (1520 O'Malley Road, (907) 522-4420) wave pool, lazy river, pirate-ship lagoon and Master Blaster 505-foot water-coaster ride could make for an exciting day.

You could take a day trip south to Seward (by road or train) for a cruise into Kenai Fjords National Park, and while you're there visit the Alaska Sealife Center (301 Railway Avenue, (907) 224-6300) to check out the sea lions, puffins and seals. Or you could travel north to visit Denali National Park and Preserve. Spend the night in a nearby hotel (advance reservations essential) and the next day enjoy a bus tour into the park as you watch for bears, moose, sheep, wolves, and more. The problem is not so much finding something the kids would enjoy, but trying to fit all you would like to see into the limited days of a vacation.

Possible Concerns: Your children will enjoy their time in Alaska more if you remember to bring sun screen, yes, even here. The summer sun will still cause sunburn, even though the temperatures may seem mild. Another important item to have on hand is insect repellent. While Alaska has yet to have any problems with the West Nile Virus, mosquitoes are plentiful and may take much of the fun out of an otherwise splendid hike or picnic. If your plans take you onto the water, even in summer, dress your children (and yourself) warmly in layers. A tee shirt, then a light fleece jacket, topped with a wind/water-proof jacket, lightweight gloves and knit cap will allow for any changes in weather.

Climate

Alaska's vastness defies attempts to categorize its climate. For convenience, however, the state can be divided into five regions about which some climatic generalizations can be made.

Southeast: This is Alaska's Panhandle, a narrow ribbon of mountainous, mostly forested mainland and islands extending along the western edge of British Columbia. Wet and mild are the best

CLIMATE CHART

Anchorage

☐ Maximum temperature
■ Minimum temperature

terms to describe its climate. Certain communities in the region can receive more than 200 inches (5 meters) of precipitation annually. On rare, sunny days in summer, high temperatures might reach the mid-70s°F (21°C+) range. High 40s (4°C) to mid 60s (15°C) are the summer norms, under cloudy skies. Winter temperatures rarely fall much below freezing. Skagway and Haines are usually drier and cooler in winter.

Southcentral: Anchorage and most of the gulf coast comprise this part of Alaska. Some coastal communities are nearly as wet as southeastern cities, but the amount of rainfall lessens considerably just a short distance inland. Anchorage occasionally has summer highs in the 80s (26°C) but the 60s (15°C) and low 70s (21°C) are more common.

Interior: The broad expanse of inland Alaska, loosely centered on Fairbanks, gets an average of 10 inches (25 cm) of precipitation annually. Summer temperatures have reached 100°F (37°C) on occasions; 70s and 80s (21°C and 26°C) temperatures are common, with typical winter lows to –40°F (–40°C).

Northwest & Arctic Coast: This is a loosely described region encompassing most of Alaska's northern fringe and the west coast as far south as Kotzebue. High winds are common, and average temperatures are too cool to permit trees to grow. Near Nome, summer temperatures can climb into the 60s (15°C), but the high 30s (3°C) and 40s (4°C) are more common. Winter temperatures, though extreme, are never as low as some Interior temperatures. This is also an extremely dry area, receiving only minimal amounts of moisture every year. Barrow, for example, receives just 4.7 inches (11.5 cm) of precipitation annually.

Southwest & The Aleutians: The Aleutian Islands are justly known for some of the most miserable weather on earth. High winds (williwaws) can rise without warning and smash through the islands at speeds of 100 mph (165 kph). Heavy fog is common, as are rain and cool temperatures. The southwestern mainland is the meeting point for Aleutian weather and Interior weather, and often experiences unsettled conditions, frequently accompanied by high winds.

Average Daily High Temperatures
Farenheit

CITY	JANUARY	JULY
Anchorage	21.4°	65.2°
Barrow	–7.4°	45°
Cold Bay	33.1°	55.1°
Fairbanks	–1.6°	72°
Juneau	29.4°	63.9°
Kodiak	35°	60.5°
Nome	14.7°	57.7°

Centigrade

CITY	JANUARY	JULY
Anchorage	–6°	18.4°
Barrow	–22°	7.2°
Cold Bay	0.6°	12.8°
Fairbanks	–18.6°	22.2°
Juneau	–1.5°	17.7°
Kodiak	1.6°	15.8°
Nome	–9.6°	14.3°

Clothing

When packing for Alaska, remember you are traveling north. While Alaskans may describe the climate as warm in the summer, those from warmer climates find even the summer chilly. No matter what part of the state you are visiting, bring along a warm coat and a synthetic pile or fleece jacket. A wool or synthetic sweater, hat, and gloves or mittens, are also necessities.

Layering clothing is the best way to stay warm. While you may be able to run around in shirt sleeves on a warm summer day, the evenings often require a sweater or light jacket. Tour companies sometimes furnish specialty items such as parkas for overnight trips to Barrow, Kotzebue, Prudhoe Bay and other colder areas.

The key for fashion in Alaska is casual and practical. Suits and evening dresses are rarely necessary except for special occasions. Jeans or casual trousers, flannel shirts and comfortable shoes are much more common. Pants are perfectly acceptable for women year-round and in almost any social situation. Dress for comfort. Alaska is not a place where residents wear the latest haute couture. Since you will probably do a lot of walking, be sure to wear comfortable yet sturdy walking shoes. And don't buy them right before your trip. Make sure they are broken in before you leave.

No matter where you visit in Alaska, you are likely to run into periods of rain, so good-quality rainwear is needed. If your travel plans include flying to a remote area in a small plane, it is advisable to wear durable warm clothing; survival gear is required for cross-country flights in small planes. Air services and charter flight operators normally carry sufficient survival gear as required by law; it's up to passengers to dress appropriately.

Customs Regulations

Visitors entering Alaska from anywhere other than a US port of embarkation will proceed through US customs. Personal effects, such as camping gear and fishing rods, are exempt from duties. Visitors who are over the age of 21 may also bring in small amounts (for personal use) of liquor, cigarettes and cigars (not from Cuba). You may also bring personal gifts, as long as the total value is not more than $100. These exemptions may only be claimed if you plan to spend at least 72 hours in the United States, and if you have not claimed them within the preceding 6 months. A flat-rate duty of 3% applies to other goods brought into the US with you, and intended solely for personal use or personal gift up to a $1,000 value limit (fair market retail in country of acquisition). The duty amount on items beyond the first $1,000 varies.

Don't wrap any gifts you bring into the country; they will need to be available for inspection. Don't try to bring raw food or plant material into the US without a special license. Don't bring more than $10,000 in cash (US or foreign) unless you want the hassle of filling out additional documentation. Don't try to bring a firearm into the country, except for a hunting trip. Foreign hunters must obtain a permit from the Bureau of Alcohol, Tobacco and Firearms (202) 344-8320, ww.customs.ustreas.gov, before bringing along, buying or even possessing a gun. You can apply for the permit on the Bureau's website. Your application must be accompanied by a valid hunting license, and the process could take months. (For information on obtaining a hunting license and required game guides see Hunting.) Do find out the most current, correct US customs information before your trip by contacting the nearest U.S. embassy or consulate, or the U.S. Customs office, (202) 344-1770, or at www.customs.ustreas.gov.

When leaving Alaska, you will need to have a permit for any souvenir purchased that is made from protected mammals. You can get a permit from the U.S. Fish and Wildlife Service in Anchorage (907) 271-6198, a process that may take a few days. If your souvenir contains *marine* mammal parts, the permit must come from the Washington, DC office, and may take considerably longer. The simple solution is to have the store (where you purchase the item) ship it to your home, and handle all the needed documentation.

D isabled Access

Nearly all hotels, restaurants, tours and other businesses in Alaska's larger cities welcome visitors with disabilities. It is important to specify your particular special needs when making reservations. The US Coast Guard regulates tour-boat activities and therefore these vessels do not fall under the requirements of the Americans with Disabilities Act. While some smaller day-cruise boats are not structured to allow for wheelchair use, you will likely find that most tour operators make every effort to accommodate special-needs passengers.

Accessible Alaska Adventures/ Alaska Welcomes You!, Inc. offers an exciting array of adventure cruises and travel choices for visitors with special needs, including "seniors, families with young children, young at heart, fast walkers, lazy bones and disabled travelers – all age and experience levels." Contact them at PO Box 91333, Anchorage, AK 99509-1333, (907) 349-6301, (800) 349-6301 (phone/TTY), or at www.accessiblealaska.com.

Another good contact is Challenge Alaska (3350 Commercial Drive, Suite 208, Anchorage, AK 99501, (907) 344-7399, TTY (907) 344-7270, (888) 430-2738, www.challengealaska.org). Challenge Alaska is a non-profit organization that specializes in providing sports and recreational opportunities for those with disabilities. The group operates an adaptive ski school at their International Sports, Recreation and Education center, located near the base of chair 3 at Alyeska Ski resort in Girdwood, just south of Anchorage.

E lectricity

The standard for electricity throughout the US is 110 to 120 volts (60 cycle) AC. The plugs have two flat, parallel pins. Foreign visitors who don't have dual-voltage appliances will need a 110-volt transformer and an adaptor plug.

G ays and Lesbians

Identity, Inc. is a gay, lesbian, bisexual, transgender, and allied (GLBTA) organization based in Anchorage whose mission is to build the Alaska GLBTA community through programs, education and collaboration. Their new center is located at 336 East Fifth Avenue in downtown Anchorage, PO Box 200070, Anchorage 99520-0070, tel: (907) 929-4528, email: Info@identityinc.org, www.identityinc.org.

Government

Alaska elects two senators and one representative to the US Congress, in Washington, D.C., for four-year terms. From the state capital in Juneau, the governor and lieutenant governor, who run for office on the same ticket and also serve four-year terms, work along with the state legislature to conduct the business of the state. The legislature is bi-cameral, with 20 state senators elected from 20 districts for a four-year term, and 40 representatives from 27 districts for two-year terms.

An elected mayor or city manager is the top government official of local cities, municipalities and towns. Currently in Alaska there are 246 recognized tribal governments, and one community, Metlakatla, which was once a reservation, organized under federal law.

H ealth & Medical Care

Two major hospitals serve the general public in Anchorage, and there is one in Fairbanks and another in Juneau.

Additionally, there is a Native hospital in Anchorage run by a number of Native-owned corporations. Treatment there is free for anyone who is one-quarter or more Native American. There is also a hospital on Elmendorf Air Force Base, in Anchorage, which serves military personnel and their families.

If you need to visit a doctor, larger cities in Alaska have walk-in clinics open daily with no appointment necessary. Clinics typically are staffed by some combination of physicians, nurses, health aids and, occasionally, dentists. The service will be expensive, and you will need to pay first, and then apply for any re-imbursement from your personal insurance company. Alaska hospitals will render 24-hour emergency aid to anyone in critical need, but short of that standard, payment will be required before care will be given. A trip to the emergency room due to an accident or serious illness can easily cost $1,000 or more. Adequate travel insurance is highly recommended.

Alaska Regional Hospital
2801 DeBarr Road, Anchorage, tel: (907) 276-1131;
www.alaskaregional.com
Providence Alaska Medical Center
3200 Providence Drive, Anchorage, tel: (907) 562-2211;
www.providence.org
Alaska Native Medical Center
4315 Diplomacy Drive, Anchorage, tel: (907) 563-2662;
www.anmc.org
Fairbanks Memorial Hospital
1650 Cowles, Fairbanks, tel: (907) 452-8181;
www.bannerhealth.com
Bartlett Regional Hospital
3260 Hospital Drive, Juneau, tel:(907) 796-8900;
www.bartletthospital.org

BELOW: experienced campers know how big a threat hypothermia can be.

Hypothermia

One of the first signs of hypothermia is violent and uncontrollable shivering. As the core body temperature drops, shivering diminishes and muscles become rigid. The chief symptoms at this stage are what one outdoor writer calls "the umbles:" stumbling, mumbling, fumbling, bumbling. Speech is slurred, coordination poor, and comprehension dull. If not properly treated the victim quickly becomes irrational, drifts into a stupor, and loses consciousness.

If you suspect a member of your party is suffering from hypothermia, immediately try to find shelter. Put the victim into dry clothes, wrap him in blankets or sleeping bags, keep him off the ground, and provide whatever heat may be available. If the condition worsens, put the victim in a sleeping bag with another person. Alone, the victim will be unable to produce enough heat to warm the bag, much less his own body.

Sufferers of hypothermia often don't realize they're in danger and may even deny it. It only takes a few minutes to slip into the condition, and, if untreated, death can follow in less than two hours.

The best plan, of course, is prevention. Dressing properly truly can be a matter of life and death. Always bring extra clothing on outdoor adventures, and consider your options before you get into trouble.

Immigration

Visitors traveling to the United States from abroad must have a valid passport and visa, or other accepted documentation. Due to heightened security measures, the United States government's Western Hemisphere Travel Initiative requires all travelers, including those traveling to and from the Americas, the Caribbean, and Bermuda to have a valid passport to enter or re-enter the United States by air from January 2007 and by land or sea from January 2008. For the latest information on what documentation you will need to cross any U.S/Canadian border, contact:
U.S Customs and Border Protection: (202) 354-1000;
www.cbp.gov/xp/cgov/travel
Canada Border Service Agency: (800) 461-9999; www.cbsa.gc.ca

Internet Access

Internet access is available at most public libraries, hotels, intenet cafés and airports. Even smaller cities generally offer some online access.

Lost Property

Here are some numbers you may need if you lose personal belongings:
Alaska Marine Highway System: (800) 642-0066
Alaska Railroad: (907) 265-2494
Ted Steven's International Airport (Anchorage): (907) 266-2623
Fairbanks International Airport: (907) 458-2530
Juneau International Airport: (907) 789-9539

Maps

An excellent source for topographic maps of Alaska is U.S. Geological Survey, 4230 University Drive, Suite 201, Anchorage, AK 99508, (907) 786-7011. Maps may be viewed via the Alaska Travel Industry's website: www.travelalaska.com/Maps/Index.aspx

Money Matters

Travelers' checks in US dollars are advised to ease problems in dealing with the currency. National banks in Alaska's major cities – Anchorage, Fairbanks and Juneau – can convert foreign currency at the prevailing exchange rate. Outside of these metropolitan areas the opportunities to convert foreign money are dramatically reduced. Automatic Teller Machines (ATMs) can be found in just about every town on the road system.

There is no state sales tax in Alaska. However, different boroughs and municipalities across the state may impose a sales tax on all or some goods and services. If uncertain as to whether or not there is a local sales tax, ask any cashier or sales clerk.

Newspapers

The three major daily newspapers are the *Juneau Empire*, the *Anchorage Daily News* and the *Fairbanks Daily News-Miner*. Many smaller communities also put out newspapers, many of which tackle icontroversial local issues. For Native issues, the *Tundra Drums* (Bethel) is a good source.

Many bookstores and variety stores have one or more of the major Alaska dailies available for sale. In large cities, Seattle newspapers, the *New York Times*, the *Wall Street Journal*, and *USA Today* are normally available in bookstores and large grocery stores. The Loussac Library in Anchorage holds many of the country's largest newspapers.

Population Size

Population: 663,661, of which 42 percent (278,241) live in the Anchorage area. There is a population of nearly 80,000 indigenous people; more than half of those (about 41,500) are Eskimos; other Alaska Native groups include Aleut, Alutiq, Athabascan, Haida, Tlingit, and Tsimshian.
Area: 586,000 sq. miles (1,430,000 sq. km).

Postal Services

The cost for a domestic first class stamp is (as of this printing) $0.41, and a postcard stamp is $0.26.

For international mail, it will cost you $0.69 to send an airmail letter (up o 1 oz.) to Canada or Mexico, and $0.90 to send it to any other county. Mailing a postcard to Canada or Mexico will cost $0.69, and to any other country $0.90.

You can mail a letter at your hotel,

BELOW: Alaska isn't as remote as it can sometimes seem.

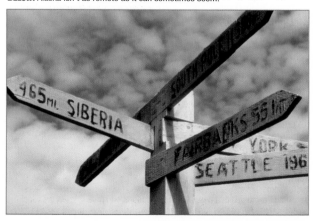

at local post office, or in any of the official US Post Office's blue collection boxes located around town.

Public Holidays

Banks, offices, post offices, and state and federal agencies will probably be closed on the following state and national holidays:
January 1: New Year's Day
Third Monday in January: Martin Luther King, Jr. Day
Third Monday in February: Presidents Day
Last Monday in March: Seward's Day
Last Monday in May: Memorial Day
July 4: Independence Day
First Monday in September: Labor Day
Second Monday in October: Columbus Day
October 18: Alaska Day
November 11: Veterans' Day
Fourth Thursday in November: Thanksgiving Day
December 25: Christmas Day

R adio Stations

Some radio stations in Alaska are still used to pass on messages to residents living in the bush. Regularly scheduled times are set aside for transmitting everything from messages of endearment to doctors' appointments.

The major radio networks have affiliates in all the larger cities, and most towns or villages will have a locally owned radio station. Quality varies from excellent to so-so. Public radio reaches communities throughout most of the state.

The vast majority of radio programs are broadcast in English, though many of the public stations also offer a limited number of programs in Spanish, Russian or the Native dialect that is spoken in a particular village or region.

S ecurity and Crime

Alaska is not crime-ridden, but occasional outbursts of violence are not unknown. Basic common sense should be followed: leave large amounts of money, jewelry and valuables in the hotel safe. Don't flaunt your money or display other valuables that could encourage a thief. Be careful where you leave handbags and luggage.

Sexual assault rates are quite high and women should not travel alone in secluded areas (such as wooded bike paths), near bars or other potentially troublesome areas. Use common sense and avoid dubious areas.

Anchorage, Fairbanks, Juneau,

Homer, and Seward are among the cities and towns to have their own police departments and most villages have public safety officers. The Alaska State Troopers, a professional police force, respond to calls in most outlying areas.

Dialing 911 will put you in touch with a dispatcher who can provide an emergency service (police, fire or ambulance). Be specific about your problem and location. Bear in mind that Alaska's vast size may mean that help is many miles away.

T elephones

Public telephones can be found almost everywhere – hotel lobbies, stores, restaurants, bars, etc. Local calls usually cost 25 cents.

Check the directory or dial 411 for local numbers. Information on telephone listings anywhere in the state can be obtained by dialing 1-907-555-1212. Information for other states and Canada can be obtained by dialing 1, followed by the appropriate three-digit area code and then 555-1212. The three-digit area code for all telephone exchanges within Alaska is 907.

To send a telegram via Western Union, call toll free: (800) 325-6000.

Cell phones can be used in most major communities and several smaller ones, such as Barrow, Fairbanks, Tok, Valdez, Anchorage, Cordova, Juneau, Kenai, Homer, and Whittier. Check with your phone provider before arriving in Alaska. Internet access is found at public libraries in most communities.

Television Stations

Only Anchorage has enough stations to affiliate actively with the four major television networks. These are CBS, Channel 11; ABC, Channel 13; NBC, Channel 2; and Fox Network, Channel 4. Other major cities will have one station or more, loosely affiliated with one of the networks, but usually offering a spread of programs from all three of the major networks along with a variety of locally produced shows. Public television (or "educational" television) is available in most of the state.

Again, most television programs are transmitted in English, although some regional shows may be broadcast in the area's Native dialect. The majority of these programs are on public television.

In the past few years, with the growing use of satellite communications equipment, even the most rural areas have gained access to

television through the Alaska Rural Communications Services (ARCS).

Time Zones

Alaska Standard Time (Pacific Standard Time minus 1 hour; Eastern Standard Time minus 4 hours; GMT minus 10 hours). The Aleutian Chain and St Lawrence Island are in the Hawaii-Aleutian Time Zone, which is 1 hour earlier.

Tipping

Airport porters usually receive $1 for the first bag and 50 cents for each additional bag. (Don't expect porters outside of Anchorage.) Similar tips are appropriate for bellhops in the larger hotels.

Waiters and waitresses normally receive about 15 percent of the bill. Tipping can be as high as 20 percent for excellent restaurant service. Tips are inappropriate in most fast-food restaurants and cafeterias. Bartenders should get 10 to 15 percent of the bill depending on the quality of service. If service is shoddy or the person performing the service is ill-mannered, no tip is necessary.

W aterproofing

Plastic Pelican boxes come with or without padding. These waterproof boxes protect a camera and other gear if dropped on rocks or handled roughly. More expensive waterproof cases are also available.

Kayakers use waterproof storage sacks known as "dry bags." A large bag is roomy enough for a sleeping bag, pad, and tent. Smaller bags are available for extra clothes, food, and personal items. Don't take the term "dry bag" literally. Always add extra protection by first wrapping everything in plastic.

Websites

State of Alaska: www.state.ak.us
Visitor Information sites:
Alaska Travel Industry Association www.travelalaska.com
Anchorage: www.anchorage.net
Bethel: www.bethelakchamber.org
Cordova: www.codovachamber.com
Denali National Park and Preserve: www.nps.gov/dena
Dillingham: www.dillinghamak.com
Fairbanks: www.explorefairbanks.com
Gustavus: www.gustavusalaska.org
Haines: www.haines.ak.us
Homer: (Seldovia): www.homeralaska.org
Juneau: www.traveljuneau.com
Kenai: www.visitkenai.com

Ketchikan: www.visit-ketchikan.com
Kodiak: www.kodiak.org
Kotzebue: www.cityofkotzebue.com
Matanuska – Susitna (Palmer,
Wasilla, Talkeetna, Sutton):
www.alaskavisit.com
Nome: www.nomealaska.org
Palmer: www.alaskavisit.com
Petersburg: www.petersburg.org
Seward: www.seward.com
Sitka: www.sitka.org
Skagway: www. skagway.org
Soldotna: www.soldotnachamber.com
Unalaska/Dutch Harbor:
www.unalaska.info
Valdez: www.valdezalaska.org
Whittier: www.ci.whittier.ak.us
Wrangell: www.wrangellchamber.org
Yakutat: www.travelalaska.com
Public Land Information Centers:
www.nps.gov/aplic

What to Read

General

*A Place Beyond: Finding Home in
Arctic Alaska*, by Nick Jans. Alaska
Northwest Books, 1996.
*Alaska's Accessible Wilderness: A
Traveler's Guide to Alaska's State
Parks*, by Bill Sherwonit. Alaska
Northwest Books, 1996.
*Alaska's Brooks Range: The Ultimate
Mountains*, by John M. Kauffmann.
The Mountaineers Books, 1992.
Alaska's Wildlife, by Tom Walker.
Graphic Arts Center Publishing Co.
1995.
Alaska: A History of the 49th State,
by Claus M. Naske and Herman E
Slotnick. University of Oklahoma
Press, 1987.
Alaskans: Life on the Last Frontier,
by Ron Strickland. Stackpole Books,
1992.
*Arctic Schoolteacher: Kulukak,
Alaska, 1931–1933*, by Abbie
Morgan Madenwald. University of
Oklahoma Press, 1992.
*As Far As You Can Go Without a
Passport: The View from the End of
the Road*, by Tom Bodett. Addison-
Wesley, 1985.
*Beluga Days:Tracking a White
Whale's Truths* by Nancy Lord.
Counterpoint Press. 2004.
*Burning the Iceberg: The Alaskan
Fisherman's Novel*, by Whit
Deschner. Eddie Tern Press, 1991.
*Degrees of Disaster: Prince William
Sound: How Nature Reels and
Rebounds*, by Jeff Wheelwright.
Simon and Schuster, 1994.
Denali: The Complete Guide, by Bill
Sherwonit. Alaska Northwest Books,
2002.
*Fast & Cold: A Guide to Alaska
Whitewater*, by Andrew Embick.
Valdez Alpine Books, 1994.

Fish Camp, by Nancy Lord.
Shearwater Books, 1997.
*How to Rent a Public Cabin in
Southcentral Alaska*, by Andromeda
Romano-Lax. Wilderness Press, 1999.
*Iditarod Classics: Tales of the Trail
Told by the Men and Women Who
Race Across Alaska*, by Lew
Freedman. Epicenter Press, 1992.
Iditarod: The Great Race to Nome, by
Bill Sherwonit and Jeff Schultz.
Sasquatch Books, 2002.
In the Shadow of Denali, by Jon
Waterman. Dell, 1994.
Into the Wild, by Jon Krakauer. Villard
Books, 1996.
*Klondike Women: True Tales of the
1897–1898 Gold Rush*, by Melanie J
Mayer. Swallow Press, 1989.
Looking for Alaska, by Peter Jenkins.
St Martin's Press, 2001.
*Midnight Wilderness: Journeys in
Alaska's Arctic National Wildlife
Refuge*, by Debbie S. Miller. Sierra
Club Books, 1990.
*Mount McKinley: The Conquest of
Denali*, by Brad Washburn and David
Roberts. Abrams, 1991.
Ordinary Wolves, by Seth Kantner.
Milkweed Editions. 2004.
*Northern Lights: Tales of Alaska's
Lighthouses and Their Keepers*, by
Shannon Lowry and Jeff Schultz.
Stackpole Books, 1992.
*Place of the Pretend People: Gifts
from a Yup'ik Eskimo Village*, by
Carolyn Kremers. Alaska Northwest
Books, 1996.
River of Bears, by Tom Walker and
Larry Aumiller. Voyageur Press, 1993.
*Shadows on the Koyukuk: An Alaskan
Native's Life Along the River*, by
Sidney Huntington. Alaska Northwest
Books, 1993.
The Alaska Almanac, Alaska

Northwest Books. Updated annually.
The Alaska Highway in World War II,
by K. S. Coates and W. R. Morrison.
University of Oklahoma Press, 1992.
*The World-Famous Alaska Highway: A
Guide to the Alcan and Other
Wilderness Roads of the North*, by
Tricia Brown, Alaska Northwest
Books, 2005.
The Alaska River Guide, by Karen
Jettmar. Alaska Northwest Books,
1993.
*The Last New Land: Stories of Alaska
Past and Present*, edited by Wayne
Mergler. Alaska Northwest Books,
1996.
*The Great Bear: Contemporary Writings
on the Grizzly*, edited by John A Murray.
Alaska Northwest Books, 1992.
*The Heart of the Sound: An Alaskan
Paradise Found and Nearly Lost*, by
Marybeth Holleman, The University of
Utah Press, 2004.
The Island Within, by Richard Nelson.
Vintage Books, 1991.
*The Whale and the Supercomputer:
On the Northern Front of Climate
Change*, by Charles Wohlforth, North
Point Press, 2004.
*To the Top of Denali: Climbing
Adventures on North America's
Highest Peak*, by Bill Sherwonit.
Alaska Northwest Books, 1990,
revised in 2000.
Travelers' Tales Alaska, edited by Bill
Sherwonit, Andromeda Romano-Lax,
and Ellen Bielawski, Travelers' Tales
Inc., 2003.
*Walking My Dog Jane: From Valdez to
Prudhoe Bay Along the Trans-Alaska
Pipeline*. Duquesne University Press,
2002.
*Way Out Here: Modern Life in Ice-Age
Alaska*, by Richard Leo. Sasquatch
Books, 1996.
*Winterdance: The Fine Madness of
Running the Iditarod*, by Gary
Paulsen. Harvest Books, 1995.

Other Insight Guides

Among other Insight titles which
cover this part of the world are:
Alaskan Wilderness, published as
part of the Discovery Travel
Adventures series, is an inspiring
guide for adventure travelers.
Insight FlexiMap: Alaska is a detailed
illustrated map, laminated for ease
of use and durability.
*Insight Guide: US National Parks
West* provides full coverage, including
striking photography and
comprehensive chapters on all the
main national parks in the western
part of the United States, including
Alaska and Hawaii.
Insight Guide: Canada gives a real
insight into this vast country, from
the Pacific-oriented west coast to
francophone Quebec.

ART & PHOTO CREDITS

4Corners 176T
AKG-images London 36BR
Alamy 9B, 96, 213, 214T, 217T&B, 218T&B, 219, 220T
Alaska Division of Tourism 6L&BR, 7TCL, CR&BR, 8TR, 9B, 10CL, 11T&CL, 19T&B, 20T&B, 64, 105T&B, 109T&B, 110T&B, 111, 125T, 131T, 135T, 146T, 154, 165T&B, 166T&B, 180T, 185, 202T, 207T, 208T, 225T&B, 226T&B, 241T, 244T, 248, 266T, 271T&B, 272T&B, 273, 276T, 281T, 283T, 284T, 289T, 299T, 304T, 313T&B, 314B, 322, 330T, 334T, 356, 366, 369, 370, 376, 381, 384
Alaska Stock 56, 57, 167, 208, 241B, 245, 276, 286
Alaska Stock/Photolibrary 4T, 6CR, 16/17, 29, 30, 39CL, 70, 75, 94, 97, 118, 119T, 120B, 122T, 124, 126, 137, 148, 160, 161, 162/163, 168, 177, 178B, 181, 182, 183, 186T&B, 187T, 188, 203T, 206, 207R, 212, 215B, 224, 228, 236, 242, 258, 259, 262, 264, 275, 278, 279, 305B, 322T, 326, 327, 328T&B, 334, 345B, 346
Brian & Cherry Alexander 59, 114T, 247
Jon Arnold Images 207L
Roy Bailet 190/191B
Bruce Bernstein Collection 263T
Bridgeman Art Library 36TL
Maxine Cass 155T
Celebrity Cruises 93
Julie Collins 281
Corbis 8BL,10B, 34/35, 37BR, 38BR, 41, 44, 47, 48, 49, 50, 51, 94/95, 117T, 124, 125B, 127T&B, 128, 129, 130, 132, 255, 265T&B, 288, 296, 297, 298B, 299B, 314T, 315, 319T, 343
Cruise West 39TR, 55L, 91, 122, 145
Alex Demyan 140B
Lee Forster 295
Getty Images 5B, 7TL, TR &BL, 9TR, 22, 38T, 39BR, 62, 65, 82, 85, 88, 112, 113, 114B, 121, 132,

139, 141, 146B, 147T&B, 184, 198T, 222/223, 227, 230T, 231T, 235T, 238, 239T, 240, 243, 283B, 284B, 323, 331B, 337, 338B
Hapag-Lloyd 89
Kim Heacox 144, 233T
Holland America 7BCL, 25, 90, 92
John Hyde/Alaska Division of Tourism 284T
Laif/Camera Press 149R, 229, 232, 302
Tom & Pat Leeson 72
Kyle Lochalsh 209B
Garry Lok 55R
James McCann 66, 68, 237T
Rick McIntyre 76R
Mary Evans Picture Library 37TL, 156
Nana Museum of the Arctic 280
Nature Picture Library 10TR, 73, 74, 150BL, 237
Mark Newman/Tom Stack & Associates 80
PA 75, 263, 266, 292, 293, 304
Photolibrary 9CL, 12/13, 21, 31, 86, 116B, 118, 119B, 120T, 136, 142T&B, 150BR, 151T, 153, 155B, 157T, 174T, 189, 190T, 193T, 197, 199, 215T, 216, 221, 250, 326, 339, 359
Robert Harding World Imagery 246B, 321, 329, 332
Allan Seiden 32
Bill Sherwonit 23, 81, 87, 98/99, 100/101, 123, 180B, 187, 194, 195, 198B, 202B, 235B, 285, 290, 294T, 330, 331T, 338T, 340, 341T&B
Jeff Schultz 14/15, 18, 26, 27, 28, 71, 84, 102/103, 234, 251T, 303, 305T, 316, 336
Science Photo Library 347
Mark Skok 83, 104
Still Pictures 287, 289B, 291L&R, 294B
SuperStock 11BR, 63, 67, 76L, 77, 116T, 117B, 133T, 138, 140T, 169, 170T, 171, 172B, 173B, 179, 200, 201, 203B, 204, 205, 209T, 220B, 233B, 239B, 246T, 260, 277, 282, 310/311, 317, 318, 320B, 333, 335, 342, 344

TopFoto 38BL, 134, 319B
Travel Lounge 175B
Unalaska 345T
University of Washington Library 6BL, 38, 42, 43, 52, 53
Vautier-de-Nanxe 1, 40, 54, 211, 279T, 306
Harry M Walker 24, 33, 60/61, 152, 172T, 173T, 175T, 176B, 180, 187B, 192B, 196, 210, 249, 251B, 252, 254T&B, 261, 267
Tom Walker 274
World Picture News 58, 178T, 268/269

PICTURE SPREADS

Pages 78–79: clockwise from bottom left-hand corner: Rick McIntyre, Bill Sherwonit, Rick McIntyre, Alex Demyan, Rick McIntyre, Bill Sherwonit, Rick McIntyre, Rick McIntyre.
Pages 148–149: clockwise from bottom left-hand corner: Corbis-Bettmann/UPI, Corbis-Bettmann, Archive Photos, Corbis-Bettmann, Archive Photos, Archive Photos, Archive Photos.
Pages 244–245: all pictures by Brian and Cherry Alexander.
Pages 280–281: clockwise from bottom left-hand corner: Harry M Walker, Harry M Walker, Harry M Walker, Harry M Walker, Bill Sherwonit, Bill Sherwonit, Harry M Walker.
Pages 322–323: all pictures by Harry M Walker, except bottom right-hand corner (totem pole) Bill Sherwonit.Roger de la Harpe/Gallo, Railfotos.

Picture Research: Hilary Genin, Jenny Kraus, Steven Lawrence and Tom Smyth

Cartographic Editor: Zoë Goodwin
Map Production: Mike Adams
© 2008 Apa Publications GmbH & Co.
Verlag KG (Singapore branch)

INDEX

Numbers in italics refer to photographs